DICTIONARY OF
CELTIC RELIGION
AND CULTURE

For Doris on the 30th August

Llyna uy attep i iti, pei caffwn dewis ar holl wraged a morynnyon y byt, y mae ti a dewisswn.

DICTIONARY OF
CELTIC RELIGION
AND CULTURE

Bernhard Maier

TRANSLATED BY
Cyril Edwards

THE BOYDELL PRESS

First published 1994 as *Lexikon der keltischen Religion und Kultur*
by Alfred Kröner Verlag, Stuttgart

English translation first published 1997
The Boydell Press, Woodbridge
Reprinted in hardback and paperback 1998, 2000

ISBN 0 85115 698 3 hardback
ISBN 0 85115 660 6 paperback

The Boydell Press is an imprint of Boydell & Brewer Ltd
PO Box 9, Woodbridge, Suffolk IP12 3DF, UK
and of Boydell & Brewer Inc.
PO Box 41026, Rochester, NY 14604–4126, USA
website: http://www.boydell.co.uk

A catalogue record for this book is available
from the British Library

Library of Congress Catalog Card Number: 96–52740

Printed in Great Britain by
Athenæum Press Ltd, Gateshead, Tyne & Wear

CONTENTS

Preface to the English Edition   vi

Translator's Note   vi

Introduction   vii

Abbreviations   xi

DICTIONARY   1

Museums   293

Select Bibliography   297
  1. Bibliographies   297
  2. Works of reference   298
  3. Editions and translations   298
  4. Archaeology, history of religion and culture until
      late antiquity   303
  5. Linguistic, literary and cultural history from the early
      Middle Ages to the beginning of the modern period   321
  6. Survival and reception, history of scholarship, Celtic
      ideology   333

PREFACE TO THE ENGLISH EDITION

The text of the present English edition of *Lexikon der keltischen Religion und Kultur* is for the most part identical to the first German edition, published in 1994. I have taken the opportunity to correct a few minor inconsistencies and mistakes, modify the contents of some articles in the light of current research, and include a small number of further articles. Most notably, the bibliography has been updated and now contains more than a hundred new items published in the years 1992–1996.

My heartfelt thanks are due to Dr Cyril Edwards for faithfully rendering a sometimes difficult German text into graceful English, inserting additional material of interest to the student of literature and art, and adapting references to secondary literature to the needs of English readers. Moreover, I wish to thank all those who by writing or word of mouth have passed on to me their comments on the original German version of this book, which have been of great value for the preparation of this revised and updated English edition. In particular, I would mention Professor Proinsias Mac Cana and Dr Patrizia de Bernardo Stempel, who published extensive reviews in *Studia Celtica* 29 (1995) and *Zeitschrift für celtische Philologie* 48 (1996) respectively.

Bernhard Maier

TRANSLATOR'S NOTE

My gratitude extends first to the author, for his amicable co-operation; to Richard Wilson, for his help with classical sources; to Thomas Charles-Edwards, for clarifying some legal points; to Paddy Considhine, for teaching me the rudiments of Old Irish; and above all to Goldsmiths' College, London, which by making me "thematically redundant" afforded me the leisure to undertake this translation. With the author's permission, I have included additional material in the articles on Myrddin and Oisín.

Die Herausgabe dieses Werkes wurde zus Mitteln von Inter Nationes, Bonn gefördert.

Published with the assistance of Inter Nationes, Bonn.

INTRODUCTION

The Celts and Ourselves

For a long time Celtic civilisation was looked upon as a marginal culture, whose achievements and character were overshadowed by the triumphs of Graeco-Roman antiquity and of Western Christendom. In recent years, however, there has been a constantly growing interest in Celtic culture, and following the political upheavals of 1989–1990 Celtic culture has increasingly commanded respect, being looked upon as the common inheritance of the majority of both Western and Eastern European states. This new interest is evinced not only by several international exhibitions, but also by the sheer bulk of scholarly and popular publications relating to the subject. Archaeological finds from pre-Roman and Roman times, medieval Irish and Welsh literature, and the reception of Celtic subject matter and motifs in modern literature have also become focal points of interest. The aim of this dictionary is to give the reader access to all these fields in a handy, self-contained and reliable work of reference.

Contents of the Dictionary

The Dictionary of Celtic Religion and Culture gives access to data previously only obtainable by consulting a variety of publications, many of them obscure. It takes into consideration both ancient and medieval Celtic culture, embracing all aspects of intellectual and material civilisation, and provides a guide to the archaeological as well as the literary heritage of the Celts. Particular attention will be paid to the reception of Celtic themes in art and literature, and to the often neglected fields of the history of scholarship, and the ideology of the Celts.

The pronunciation of Irish and Welsh names is indicated for every entry. The symbols employed are explained in full in the introduction.

The bibliography, although select, is extensive and organised thematically. Its aim is to facilitate access for students and scholars to the current state of research; it is more detailed and up-to-date than in any other work of this kind.

An appendix describing the most important museums makes the dictionary a useful guide-book for the field-worker.

Structure and Content of the Entries

Where an article relates to a Welsh or Irish name or concept the keyword is followed by a reference in round brackets to the language concerned, and a guide to pronunciation. There follows the information concerning the significance of the keyword for Celtic religion and culture. References to survivals or reception are at the end of the article, followed by details of relevant secondary literature.

Instructions for the User

All the more important subject areas are dealt with in substantial articles. Numerous cross-references (→) give ready access to shorter articles.

To readers who have no detailed knowledge of the subject or only a general interest the articles on "Celts", "History" and "Languages, Celtic" are recommended as starting-points.

An introduction to the religion of the Celts is offered in the articles on "Religion" and "Mythology", and also by those on "Druids", "Gods and Goddesses", "Otherworld, conceptions of", "Places of Worship", "Sacrifices", "Prophecy" and "Magic".

Articles relating to Celtic civilisation may be found under "Agriculture", "Food and Drink", "Commerce", "Crafts", "Hunting", "Warfare", "Art", "Medicine", "Settlements", "Death and Burial" and "Cattle-breeding".

Primary information concerning the survival, reception and study of Celtic culture may be found in the articles on "Arthurian Literature", "Irish Renaissance", "Celtic Studies" and "Celtic Ideology".

The numerous anonymous Irish and Welsh literary works of the Middle Ages are referred to by title. Cross-references may be found under the keyword "Literature", under the names of significant literary figures such as "Arthur" and in more general articles such as those on the "Finn Cycle", the "Historical Cycle", the "Mabinogion", the "Mythological Cycle" and the "Ulster Cycle".

Individual articles are devoted to the most important archaeological sites, which include references to the present location of finds. References to these locations are also found in an appendix (pp. 293–296) listing the most important museums possessing collections of Celtic and/or Gallo-Roman finds according to country or city.

Orthography of Irish and Welsh Words

Many Irish and Welsh words are affected by variations in spelling, which derive both from the manuscripts and from recent scholarly literature. These differences are based partly on the historical evolution of the different languages (or merely upon orthographic practice), partly on the translation of Celtic names and concepts into other languages. In this dictionary words are generally spelt in the oldest orthography known to us. Cross-references help the reader with regard to the English, French and German forms of Irish and Welsh names. Where the less obvious variations within the Irish and Welsh languages are concerned, there are only cross-references in those instances where it seemed necessary in order for the reader to trace a keyword.

Pronunciation

All Irish and Welsh words are accompanied by a guide to their pronunciation, which is generally based on the oldest linguistic form known to us. The phonetic symbols employed are pronounced as follows:

/a/, /e/, /i/, /o/, /u/	as in *apple, Lent, sin, cost, foot*
/a:/, /e:/, /i:/, /o:/, /u:/	as in *calm, day, seem, phone, loot*
/ə/	like *o* in *abbot*
/j/	like *y* in *year*
/w/	as in *water*
/v/	as in *venial*
/p/, /b/, /t/, /d/, /k/, /g/	as in *prat, bed, tool, death, kin, goat*
/l/, /m/, /n/	as in *lust, mood, norm*
/h/	as in *hate*
/x/	like *ch* in *loch*
/ɣ/	is the voiced variant of /x/
/ç/	as in German *ich*
/θ/	as in *thick*
/ð/	as in *then*
/ʃ/	as in *shove*
/s/	as in *mass*
/ŋ/	as in German *Ring*
/r/	an r rolled on the tongue
/r̥/	a sound peculiar to Welsh, a combination of /h/ and /r/
/ł/	a sound peculiar to Welsh, formed by positioning the speech organs for the sound /l/ but then attempting to say /h/ without moving the tongue.

/N/, /R/, /L/   sounds peculiar to Irish, resembling emphatically articulated or lengthened /n/, /r/, /l/.

indicates that the stress is on the following syllable.

after a consonant indicates that this consonant is palatalised, i.e. that the vocal mechanisms for its pronunciation move towards the position for the pronunciation of /i/. Normally palatalised /s/ is pronounced like *sh* in *dish*, and palatalised /x/ like *ch* in German *ich*; the symbol ′ does not occur in these two cases in the system employed here (/s′/ = /ʃ/ and /x′/ = /ç/). Where the other consonants are concerned, palatalisation can be reproduced by the insertion of a rapidly spoken /j/ after the consonant, or, at the end of a word, before the following consonant.

ABBREVIATIONS

I. Collections of inscriptions referred to in the dictionary

AE	*L'Année épigraphique. Revue des publications épigraphiques relatives à l'antiquité romaine*, Paris 1948–
CIL	Corpus Inscriptionum Latinarum (II Hispania, III Oriens et Illyricum, V Gallia Cisalpina, VI Urbs Roma, XII Gallia Narbonensis, XIII Tres Galliae et Germania)
Fi	H. Finke, 'Neue Inschriften' (*BRGK* 17) 1927, 1–107 and 198–231.
ILTG	P. Wuilleumier, *Inscriptions latines des trois Gaules (France)*, Paris 1963 (17. supplément à Gallia)
Ne	H. Nesselhauf, 'Neue Inschriften aus dem römischen Germanien und den angrenzenden Gebieten' (*BRGK* 27) 1937, 51–134.
NeLi	H. Nesselhauf and H. Lieb, third supplement to CIL XIII, (*BRGK* 40) 1959, 120–229.
RIB	R. G. Collingwood and R. P. Wright, *The Roman Inscriptions of Britain I. Inscriptions on Stone*, Oxford 1965.
RIG	Recueil des inscriptions gauloises I Textes gallo-grecs, Paris 1985 II,I Textes gallo-etrusques; textes gallo-latins sur pierre, Paris 1986. III Les calendriers, Paris 1986.
Schi	U. Schillinger-Häfele, fourth supplement to CIL XIII and second supplement to Fr. Vollmer, Inscriptiones Bavariae Romanae (*BRGK* 58) 1977, 447–603.
Wa	F. Wagner, 'Neue Inschriften aus Raetien' (*BRGK* 37/38) 1956/57, 215–264.

II. Journals, series and compendia referred to in the bibliographical entries.

AKorrBl	*Archäologisches Korrespondenzblatt* (Mainz 1971–)
AL	*Arthurian Literature* (Cambridge 1981–)
ANRW	*Aufstieg und Niedergang der römischen Welt* (Berlin 1971–)
ArSt	*Arthurian Studies* (Cambridge 1981–)
ASchw	*Archäologie der Schweiz* (Basle 1978–)

BBCS	*The Bulletin of the Board of Celtic Studies* (Cardiff 1921–1994; as of 1995– *Studia Celtica: The Bulletin of the Board of Celtic Studies*)
BJb	*Bonner Jahrbücher* (Bonn 1895–)
BRGK	*Bericht der Römisch-Germanischen Kommission* (Frankfurt a.M. 1904–)
Caes	*Caesarodunum* (Orléans 1967–)
Celtica	*Celtica* (Dublin 1946–)
Celticum	*Celticum* (Rennes 1961–)
CMCSt	*Cambridge Medieval Celtic Studies* (Cambridge 1981–1993; since winter 1993 *Cambrian Medieval Celtic Studies*)
CRAI	*Comptes-rendus de l'Académie des inscriptions et belles-lettres* (Paris 1857–)
EC	*Études celtiques* (Paris 1936–)
Éigse	*Éigse: A Journal of Irish Studies* (Dublin 1939–)
Ériu	*Ériu* (Dublin 1904–)
FBW	*Fundberichte aus Baden-Württemberg* (Stuttgart 1974–)
Gallia	*Gallia: fouilles et monuments archéologiques en France métropolitaine* (Paris 1943–)
Germania	*Germania: Anzeiger der Römisch-Germanischen Kommission des Deutschen Archäologischen Instituts* (Berlin 1917–)
HBA	*Hamburger Beiträge zur Archäologie* (Hamburg 1971–)
ITS	Publications of the Irish Text Society
JRGZM	*Jahrbuch des Römisch-Germanischen Zentralmuseums Mainz* (Mainz 1954–)
JRSAI	*The Journal of the Royal Society of Antiquaries of Ireland* (Dublin 1849–)
Latomus	*Latomus. Revue d'études latines* (Brussels 1937–)
Lochlann	*Lochlann. A Review of Celtic Studies* (Oslo 1958–)
MMIS	Mediaeval and Modern Irish Series
MMWS	Mediaeval and Modern Welsh Series
Ogam	*Ogam. Tradition celtique* (Rennes 1948–)
PBA	*Proceedings of the British Academy* (London 1903–)
Peritia	*Peritia. Journal of the Medieval Academy of Ireland* (Cork 1982–)
PHCC	*Proceedings of the Harvard Celtic Colloquium* (Cambridge, Mass. 1981–)
PRIA	*Proceedings of the Royal Irish Academy* (Dublin 1936–)
RAE	*Revue archéologique de l'Est et du Centre-Est* (Dijon 1950–)
RC	*Revue celtique* (Paris 1870–1934)
RHR	*Revue de l'histoire des religions* (Paris 1880–)
SGS	*Scottish Gaelic Studies* (Aberdeen 1926–)
Sp	*Speculum: A Journal of Mediaeval Studies* (Cambridge, Mass. 1926–)

StC	*Studia Celtica* (Cardiff 1966–)
StHib	*Studia Hibernica* (Dublin 1961–)
Studies	*Studies: an Irish quarterly review of letters, philosophy and science* (Dublin 1912–)
ZCP	*Zeitschrift für celtische Philologie* (Halle/Saale 1897–1943; Tübingen 1954–)

III. Places of publication

A.	Amsterdam	L.	Leipzig
B.	Berlin	Lo.	London
Bas.	Basle	Lu.	Lucerne
Be.	Berkeley, California	Ly.	Lyons
Bo.	Bonn	Ma.	Madrid
Bol.	Bologna	May.	Maynooth
Bru.	Brussels	Mi.	Milan
C.	Cambridge	Mn.	Munich
Car.	Cardiff	Mz.	Mainz
Ch.	Chicago	NY.	New York
Co.	Cologne	O.	Oxford
Du.	Dublin	P.	Paris
E.	Edinburgh	R.	Rome
F.	Frankfurt am Main	Sa.	Salzburg
Fl.	Florence	Sal.	Salamanca
Fr.	Freiburg im Breisgau	St.	Stuttgart
G.	Geneva	T.	Tübingen
Gö.	Göttingen	Up.	Uppsala
H.	Hamburg	V.	Vienna
Harm.	Harmondsworth	Wi.	Wiesbaden
He.	Helsinki	Wo.	Woodbridge, Suffolk
Hei.	Heidelberg	Wü.	Würzburg
Hl.	Halle	Z.	Zurich
I.	Innsbruck		

ab → ap/ab.

Aberffraw (Welsh /a'berfrau/). Site on the south-west coast of the island of Anglesey. In the early Middle Ages seat of the rulers of the North Welsh kingdom → Gwynedd. In the story → *Branwen ferch Lŷr* the wedding between the eponymous heroine Branwen and the Irish king Matholwch takes place there.

Abnoba. In classical → ethnography the mountainous woodland from whose heights the Danube springs, corresponding essentially to today's Black Forest. The etymology of the name is obscure. The geographical term occurs inter alia in → Pliny the Elder (Hist. Nat. 4,79) and → Tacitus (Germania I).

In Roman times a goddess of the same name was worshipped on the edge of the Black Forest. Inscriptions dedicated to her have been found near Karlsruhe-Mühlburg (CIL XIII 6326), Pforzheim (CIL XIII 6332 and 11721), Waldmössingen (CIL XIII 6356), Rötenberg (CIL XIII 6357), Stuttgart-Bad Cannstatt (CIL XIII 11746 and perhaps 11747) and Mühlenbach near Haslach (CIL XIII 6283). The interpretation of another inscription, from Badenweiler (CIL XIII 5334), was assisted by the discovery of new fragments in 1980. In the two latter dedications Abnoba is identified with Diana, on the basis of the → interpretatio romana. This identification also colours the only visual depiction of Abnoba provided with an inscription: a sandstone statuette from Karlsruhe-Mühlburg, now preserved in the Badisches Landesmuseum, Karlsruhe, which shows the goddess in standing position, dressed in a short chiton. She is accompanied by a dog which has just caught a hare. Fragments of a similar statue were found between 1970 and 1980 in a Roman temple near Friesenheim, south of Offenburg. They are now exhibited in the Museum für Ur- und Frühgeschichte in Freiburg.

As early as 1889/1890 a sculptured stone was found at the source of the Brigach near St. Georgen, high up in the Black Forest, and this has often been linked with the cult of Diana / Abnoba. This sandstone relief, 0.56 x 0.27 m., portrays a strutting stag, a leaping hare, and a bird, possibly a dove, intersected by three human heads. The original is in the Heimatmuseum in St. Georgen; a copy may be seen in the Franciscan Museum in Villingen-Schwenningen. The fact that the stone bears no inscription makes the positing of any link between the pictorial motifs and divinities known to us by name uncertain.

Lit.: F. Focke, 'Das Dreigötterrelief von der Brigachquelle' (*Bad. Fundber.* 20) 1956, 123–126; W. Heinz, 'Der Diana A.-Altar in Badenweiler' (*Antike Welt* 13,4) 1982, 37–41; R. Wiegels, 'Die Inschrift auf dem Diana A.-Altar aus Badenweiler', loc. cit. 41–43; Ph. Filtzinger et al. (eds.), *Die Römer in Baden-Württemberg*, St. [3]1986.

abstraction → ornamentation.

Acallam na Senórach

Acallam na Senórach (Ir. /'agaLav na 'ʃenoːrax/) "the Dialogue with the Elders"). The most substantial narrative of the → Finn Cycle, it survives in two fragmentary versions of c. 1200 and in a later reworking from the 13th/14th century. The chief personages in the work, which varies between verse and prose, are → Oisín, son of → Finn mac Cumaill, and his nephew → Caílte. Together with a few other survivors of Finn's band of warriors they encounter at an advanced age St. → Patrick and his followers. Wandering together through Ireland, the holy men learn of the legendary and mythic traditions which are associated with various places and significant sites in the countryside. The stories embedded in this framework derive from various cycles of sagas, and the work therefore has links with a number of genres in Irish literature. Taken in its entirety, the closest analogy is with the collections of local legends known as the → Dindsenchas.

Ed. and trans.: S. H. O'Grady, *Silva Gadelica*, Lo. 1892 (Irish-English); W. Stokes and E. Windisch, *Ir. Texte* IV.I, L. 1900 (Ir. text with trans. of the passages omitted by O'Grady); N. Ní Shéaghdha, *Agallamh na Seanórach*, 3 vols., Du. 1942–45 (Ir. text of the later version without trans.); M. Dillon, *Stories from the A.*, Du. 1970 (MMIS 23; selection with glossary).

Lit.: J. Falaky Nagy, 'Compositional Concerns in the A. na S.', in: D. Ó. Corráin et al. (eds.), *Sages, Saints, and Storytellers*, May. 1989, 149–158.

Adamnán (Ir. /'aðavnaːn/). Ninth abbot of the Scottish monastery of Iona. Born c. 624, he presided over the monastery from 679 until his death in 704. During this time he wrote in Latin the biography of the founder of the monastery, Columba (→ Colum Cille), a work of great literary and historical significance. His own life forms the subject of a predominantly legendary Irish biography, which probably originated in the 2nd half of the 10thC (*Betha Adamnáin*). This portrays Adamnán primarily as a miracle-worker and the aggressive opponent of secular rulers. The story *Fís Adamnáin* ("The Vision of A.") dates from the 9th/10thC and depicts how on the feast of John the Baptist an angel guides the soul of the abbot through the different regions of the Otherworld. This text is generally regarded as the greatest portrayal of a vision of the Beyond in the Irish language. The Old Irish legal text *Cáin Adamnáin* ("The Law of A.") was compiled, in the form in which it has come down to us, only after A.'s death. It is concerned primarily with punishments for crimes against women, children and clerics.

Lit.: M. Herbert, *Iona, Kells and Derry*, O. 1988; P. Ó Riain & M. Herbert, *Betha Adamnáin*, Lo. 1988 (ITS 54); M. O. Anderson, *Adomnán's Life of Columba*, rev. ed., O. 1991.

Aedui (Lat. Aedui, Haedui; Gk. Aiduoi). In classical → ethnography the name of a Celtic tribe in the region between the Saône and the Loire. Its most important fortified settlement was → Bibracte. According to → Caesar (Bell. Gall. 6,12), the Aedui had, by the time of his arrival in Gaul, forfeited their former significant position among the Gallic tribes, succumbing to the rule of the → Sequani. In the course of his Gallic campaigns Caesar restored the Aedui, who were well disposed towards the Romans, to a dominant position, despite the part they played in the rebellion of → Vercingetorix.

áer (Ir. /air/). Poetic diatribe or ritual curse. Cognate words in other languages suggest that the original sense of the word was that of an acerbic, insulting saying, or the employment of the word as a piercing weapon. In all probability the Celts of antiquity were familiar with such curses. This is suggested by an allusion in → Poseidonios, transmitted in Diodoros of Sicily (5,31): "Among these [sc. the Celts] there are also songmakers, who are called bards. These perform, accompanied by instruments resembling lyres, both panegyrics and diatribes." In Ireland the composition of such diatribes was one of the main tasks of the → fili. Numerous ancient sources attest that such curses were believed to be capable of causing physical deformation or even death in those against whom they were directed. In Irish law the diatribe was recognised as a means of prosecuting claims against those of a higher social status. Unjustified invective was subject to punishments, whose severity was determined by the social rank of the target. The story → Cath Maige Tuired describes how in mythical prehistoric Ireland the poet Cairbre mac Étaíne pronounced the first ritual curse.

Lit.: N. F. Robinson, 'Satirists and Enchanters in Early Ir. Lit.', in: Studies in the Hist. of Religions pres. to C. H. Toy, NY. 1912, 95–130; V. E. Orel, 'OIr. áer' (BBCS 32) 1985, 164–166; F. Kelly, A Guide to Early Ir. Law, Du. 1988.

Aeracura or Herecura. Goddess worshipped in various parts of the Roman Empire, sometimes alone, sometimes as companion of the god of the Underworld, → Dis Pater. Nothing more is known of her, in the absence of written attestation of her cult, and the etymology of her name has not yet been satisfactorily explained.

Afallach (Welsh /a'vałax/). A descendant in Welsh genealogies of the king → Beli Mawr. One tradition suggests he is the father of → Modron. The proper name is best known from the geographical designation Ynys Afallach (possibly to be translated as: the island of Afallach). In the Welsh redactions of → Geoffrey of Monmouth's Historia Regum Britanniae the word corresponds to the Latin name Insula Avallonis (the island of → Avalon). Whether Avalon derives from the name Afallach, as is suggested by the genealogies, is dubious. As Geoffrey in the Vita Merlini refers to an Insula Pomorum (island of the apple trees), it is more probable that the name Ynys Afallach is related to the Celtic word for "apple" (Welsh afall). This assumption is reinforced by Irish seafarers' stories of a Paradisiac island lined with apple trees (→ Emain Ablach).

Lit.: Th. M. Th. Chotzen, 'Emain Ablach – Ynys A. – Insula Avallonis – Ile d'Avalon' (EC 4) 1948, 255–274.

Agandecca (from Scots Gaelic aghaidh shneachda "Snow(-white) countenance"). Daughter of the cunning king → Starno of Lochlin (Scandinavia) in the "Works of Ossian", composed by James → Macpherson. In order to entice his enemy, the Scottish king → Fingal, to Scandinavia, Starno affects to promise him his daughter in marriage. When Agandecca falls in love with Fingal and warns him of her father's plan to murder him, she is slain by her father.

agriculture (arable). Together with → cattle-breeding the cultivation of arable land formed the most important economic mainstay of Celtic culture. In this respect the Celts may be sited in a continuum, traceable on the basis of archaeological finds back from the Middle Ages into the Bronze Age. The most important innovation in ancient European agriculture was the introduction of the plough in the third millennium BC. In Celtic times ploughs had iron ploughshares and coulters. Roman Gaul already possessed wheeled ploughs. In many areas dung was used to ensure that despite intensive exploitation of agricultural land the soil remained fertile. Roman authors attest the fertilisation of Celtic fields with lime and marl. Among the plants that were cultivated were various kinds of cereal such as barley, rye, oats, wheat and millet, as well as fibrous plants such as hemp and flax. The Celts also cultivated various kinds of root crops, and pulses such as beans, peas and lentils. Harvesting implements included the sickle and the long-handled scythe. Corn was ground by circular millstones which were turned by hand. Granaries were formed in many areas by digging storage pits in the ground, which were later often used as refuse pits. The layout of fields is often indeterminable now because of the intensive use of the soil in post-Celtic times. Old Irish law texts attest that the ploughed land generally belonged to kinship groups (→ fine) and not to tribal units (→ tuath).
Lit.: G. Barker, Prehist. Farming in Europe, C. 1985; K. Spindler, Die frühen Kelten, St. ²1991.

Agris. Site in the Dép. of Charente in western France, where in a cave in 1981–1986 several parts of an ornamented helmet were discovered, made of → iron, → bronze, → gold and → silver, and decorated with coral, dating from the 4thC. BC. As there were no indications of a burial site it is assumed that the helmet was buried in the cave as a votive gift to a divinity. It can now be seen in the Musée municipal in Angoulême.
Lit.: C. Eluère et al., 'Le casque d'A.' (Bull. Soc. Préhist. Franç. 84) 1987, 8–21.

aided (Ir. /'að'eð). Word meaning the violent death of men or animals, which serves in the → Lists of Sagas to classify those stories which tell of the deaths of famed heroes.
Lit.: D. F. Melia, 'Remarks on the structure and composition of the Ulster death tales' (StHib 17/18) 1978, 36–57.

Aided Cheit maic Mágach (Ir. /'að'eð çet' vik' 'vaːɣax/ "The Death of Cet mac Mágach"). Title of a story from the → Ulster Cycle, surviving in a single manuscript of the 16thC. The story begins with the warrior → Conall Cernach slaying his antagonist → Cet mac Mágach in single combat, he himself being heavily wounded. A little later a man named Bélchú arrives, and takes Conall home with him. Initially he declares to the wounded man that his intention is to fight with him after his wounds have healed. Then, however, he grows fearful and calls upon his three sons to murder Conall in his bed at night. Conall, however, forces Bélchú to lie down in the bed himself, with the result that he is pierced by the spears of his own sons. Thereupon Conall slays the three sons, taking the heads of the sons and their father back home as trophies.

Ed. and trans.: K. Meyer, *Death-Tales of the Ulster Heroes*, Du. 1906.

Aided Cheltchair maic Uthecair (Ir. /'að'eð 'çeLtxir' vik' 'uθexir'/ "The Death of Celtchar, son of Uthechar"). Title of a story from the → Ulster Cycle which survives in an incomplete version in the "Book of Leinster" (→ Lebor Laignech), and in its entirety in a manuscript of the 16thC. The story begins with the slaying of the → briugu Blaí by the warrior Celtchar. To atone he has to promise to free the population of Ulster three times from evil torment. First Celtchar is required to kill the warrior Conganchnes ("Horn-skin"), who has ravaged Ulster. Through cunning Celtchar succeeds in over-powering and slaying him. Secondly, Celtchar has to slay a fearsome hound which preys upon humans and animals in Ulster every night. In this too he succeeds. A year later shepherds find three cubs at the grave of Conganchnes. The first is given to Mac Dathó of Leinster, the second to the smith Culann, the third to Celtchar. When this last dog grows wild and attacks cattle and sheep in the pastures, the inhabitants of Ulster demand of Celtchar – as his third task – that he kill it. Celtchar pierces the dog with his spear, but a drop of its blood runs down from the spear onto him and kills him.

Ed.: K. Meyer, *Death-Tales of the Ulster Heroes*, Du. 1906 (with Engl. trans.).
Trans.: Ch.-J. Guyonvarc'h, 'La Mort violente de Celtchar fils d' Uthechar' (*Ogam* 10) 1958, 371–380.
Lit.: K. McCone, 'Hounds, Heroes and Hospitallers in Early Ir. Myth and Story' (*Ériu* 35) 1984, 1–30.

Aided Chlainne Tuirenn (Ir. /'að'eð 'xlaN'e 'tur'eN/ "The Death of the Children of Tuirenn"). Title of a story from the → Mythological Cycle, which survives in Early New Irish in several manuscripts of the 18thC. It tells how the three brothers Brian, Iuchair and Iucharba of the people of the → Tuatha Dé Danann combine to murder their blood-kinsman Cian and as penance are obliged to fulfil eight apparently impossible tasks at the behest of Cian's son → Lug mac Ethnenn. Among other things they are to procure for Lug three apples from the garden of the Hesperides, the magical pig-skin of the king of Greece, the poisonous lance of the King of Persia and the horses of the King of Sicily, which gallop with the speed of arrows. Near to completing their penance, the brothers are sorely wounded in the accomplishment of their last task. They die, because Lug refuses them his help, desiring to avenge his father's death.

Ed.: E. O'Curry, 'The Fate of the Children of Tuireann' (*Atlantis* 4 (Lo.)) 1863, 157–227; R. O'Duffy, 'Oidhe Chloinne Tuireann' (*Soc. for the Preservation of the Ir. Language*, Vol. 8), Du. 1901, 1–64.

Trans.: Ch.-J. Guyonvarc'h, 'La mort tragique des enfants de Tuireann' (*Ogam* 16) 1964, 231–256 and (17) 1965, 189–192; F. Lautenbach, *Der keltische Kessel*, St. 1991.

Aided Chonchobuir (Ir. /'að'eð 'xonxovur'/ "Conchobar's Death") Title of a story from the → Ulster Cycle, surviving in three divergent versions, in five manuscripts. The best preserved version, in the "Book of Leinster" (→ Lebor Laignech), is the continuation of the story → Cath Étair. It tells how → Cet mac Mágach of Connacht steals the brain of King Mes Gegra, which had been preserved in Ulster as a trophy. During a battle between the warriors of Connacht and those of Ulster he loads his sling with the petrified brain and deals King Conchobar of Ulster a grievous wound. The doctor tells the king that he will die immediately the petrified brain is removed from the wound in his head. For seven years Conchobar lies ill, the brain of Mes Gegra wedged in his head. Then one day he learns of the crucifixion of Christ. Incensed by this injustice – thus one manuscript concludes the narrative – Conchobar takes up his weapons in order to avenge the death of Christ. This effort, however, causes the wound in his head to open, the brain of Mes Gegra falls out, and Conchobar dies. Irish sources view Conchobar as one of the few men in Ireland to attain salvation before the spreading of the Gospel, on the basis of his willingness to fight for Christ.

Ed.: K. Meyer, *Death-Tales of the Ulster Heroes*, Du. 1906 (with Engl. trans.).

Lit.: J. Corthals, 'The Retoiric in A. C.' (*Ériu* 40) 1989, 41–59.

Aided Chon Culainn (Ir. /'að'eð xon 'kuliN'/ "The Death of Cú Chulainn"). Title of a story from the → Ulster Cycle, preserved in an incomplete version in the "Book of Leinster" (→ Lebor Laignech) and in a younger redaction, but intact, in several manuscripts of the 17th – 19thCs. In the later versions the story generally subdivides into two parts, *Brislech Mór Maige Muirtheimne* ("The Great Slaughter of Mag Muirtheimne") and *Dergruathar Chonaill Chernaig* ("The red, i.e. bloody attack of Conall Cernach"). The story tells how the hitherto unconquered Cú Chulainn loses his life, a victim of sorcery, and how he is avenged by his foster-brother Conall Cernach. The story was reworked in English by Lady Augusta → Gregory in chapters 19–20 of her book *Cuchulain of Muirtheimne*. A bronze statue of the dying Cú Chulainn inspired by the story is to be found in the hall of the main post office in Dublin. The work of the sculptor Oliver Sheppard, it is a memorial to those who died a violent death in the 1916 uprising of the Irish against British rule.

Ed.: A. G. van Hamel, *Compert Con Culainn and other Stories*, Du. 1933 (MMIS 3).

Trans.: Ch.-J. Guyonvarc'h & F. Le Roux, 'La Mort de Cúchulainn. Version A' (*Ogam* 18) 1966, 343–399.

Aided Loegairi Buadaig (Ir. /'að'eð 'loiɣar'i 'vuaðiɣ'/ "The Death of Loegaire the Victorious"). Title of a story from the → Ulster Cycle, preserved in a single manuscript of the 16thC. It tells how the warrior Loegaire dies tragically in an attempt to prevent the poet (→ fili) Aed mac Ainninne from being executed. Aed had committed adultery with the wife of King Conchobar of Ulster and was to be drowned in a lake in consequence, yet by speaking charms Aed succeeded in drying up to the last drop every lake to which he was led. His magical powers fail him only when he comes to the lake near Loegaire's house. Loegaire will however not tolerate a fili being killed at his abode and rushes forth from his house, weapon in hand. In doing so he bangs his head with such force against the lintel that he soon dies of his injuries. Aed however succeeds in escaping in the general confusion.

Ed.: K. Meyer, *Death-Tales of the Ulster Heroes*, Du. 1906 (with Engl. trans.).

Aided Muirchertaig meic Erca (Ir. /'að'eð 'vur'çeRtiɣ' vik' 'eRka/ "The Death of Muirchertach, son of Erc"). Title of a story from the → Historical Cycle. In the form in which it survives it probably dates from the 11thC; it is preserved in the → "Yellow Book of Lecan", and in one other manuscript of the 15thC. It begins with a hunting expedition of the Irish king Muirchertach mac Erca (6thC AD), in the course of which he encounters a wondrously beautiful woman called Sín, who possesses magical powers. For her sake he disowns his wife and children, and is cursed for this by the priest Cairnech. The magical wiles of Sín cause the king's mind to become increasingly confused, until finally he dies when his castle is set on fire. The story inspired the play *The Plot is Ready* (1943) by Austin → Clarke.

Ed.: L. Nic Dhonnchadha, A. M. m. E., Du. 1964 (MMIS 19).

Lit.: K. McCone, *Pagan Past and Christian Present in Early Ir. Lit.*, May. 1990.

Aided Oenfir Aífe (Ir. /'að'eð 'oinir' 'aif'e/ "The Death of Aífe's One Son"). Title of a story from the → Ulster Cycle, the oldest surviving version of which is contained in the → "Yellow Book of Lecan". → Cú Chulainn slays his son in single combat, after the latter has refused to give his name or to surrender without a battle. The motif of the father-son battle is familiar from the Old High German *Hildebrandslied* and the Persian *Shahnameh*. It has therefore been assumed that the Celtic version of this motif is a reworking of an inherited narrative. Another possibility is that it is a late borrowing from Germanic into Irish. Lady Augusta → Gregory retells the story in English in

the 18th chapter of her book *Cuchulain of Muirtheimne*. William Butler →
Yeats also reworked it in his poem *Cuchulain's Fight with the Sea* and the play
On Baile's Strand.

Ed.: A. G. van Hamel, *Compert Con Culainn and other Stories*, Du. 1933
(MMIS 3).
Trans.: J. Gantz, *Early Ir. Myths and Sagas*, Harm. 1981.
Lit.: J. de Vries, 'Le conte irl. A. o. A. et le théme du combat du père et du fils dans
quelques traditions indo-européennes' (*Ogam* 9) 1957, 122–138; R. Ó hUiginn,
'Cú Chulainn and Connla', in: H. L. C. Tristram (ed.), (*Re)Oralisierung*, T. 1996,
223–246.

Aífe (Ir. /'aif'e). Feared she-warrior in the story → *Tochmarc Emire*. Defeated
by Cú Chulainn in single combat, she later becomes the mother of his son.
The story → *Aided Oenfir Aífe* tells how Cú Chulainn slays this son in single
combat.

Ailill Áine (Ir. /'al'iL' 'a:n'e/). In the story → *Orgain Denna Ríg* a king who
purportedly ruled over the province of Leinster in the 4thC AD. The story
tells how he loses life and throne at the hands of his uncle Cobthach Coel.
His son Labraid wreaks vengeance upon his father's murderers.

Ailill Anguba (Ir. /'al'iL' 'anɣuva/). In the story → *Tochmarc Étaíne* a brother
of the king Eochaid Airem. In order to dishonour the king's wife Étaín, the
elfin prince Midir works magic to the effect that A. falls into everlasting love
with Étaín. A.'s longing for Étaín makes him severely ill. Midir's plan fails,
however, because Étaín remains faithful to her husband. When Midir revokes
his spell A. regains his health.

Ailill Aulom (Ir. /'al'iL' 'aulom/ "A. the Earless"). In the stories of the →
Historical Cycle a son of the king Eogan Mór, son-in-law of the king Conn
Cétchathach and purportedly ruler of the Southern Irish province of Munster
in the 3rdC AD (cf. → Áine, → *Cath Maige Mucrama*).

Ailill mac Mágach (Ir. /'al'iL' mak 'ma:ɣax/). In the stories of the → Ulster
Cycle the husband of Queen → Medb of Connacht and brother of the kings
of Tara (→ Temair) and Leinster. In the later version of the story of the
Cattle-Raid of Cuailnge (→ *Táin Bó Cuailnge*) a domestic quarrel between A.
and Medb leads to the great foray of the men of Connacht against the
province of Ulster. In the later stages of the story A. plays a subordinate role.

Aillén (Ir. /'aL'e:n). Fire-breathing monster in the stories of the → Finn
Cycle. In the time of king Conn Cétchathach he is supposed, every year at
the feast of → Samain, to have put to sleep by magical music the inhabitants
of Tara (→ Temair) and thereafter set the king's castle on fire. The young →

Finn mac Cumaill succeeds in staying awake despite the music, chases the monster out of the castle and finally kills him with his spear.

Áine (Ir. /'aːn'e/). The name of several fairy figures in Irish literature and folklore. The best-known of these was associated with the hill named after her in Munster, Cnoc Áine (today Knockainey Hill near Limerick). In the story of the battle of Mag Mucrama (→ *Cath Maige Mucrama*) A. and her father come upon the king Ailill Aulom, who has lain down to sleep on the hill one night. According to the legend the king then raped the fairy, who bit off his ears in her attempt to defend herself. Meanwhile Ailill's companion murders her father. On the basis of numerous parallels it may be presumed that the figure of Á. derives from an account in pre-Christian Irish mythology of the → sacred marriage of the king of the country with a tutelary goddess.

Airne Fíngein (Ir. /'ar'n'e 'fiːnɣ'in'/ "Fíngein's Night-Watch"). Title of a story from the → Historical Cycle. Originating perhaps in the ninth century, it is preserved in four manuscripts of the 14th – 15thCs. The titular hero is a man named Fíngein mac Luchta, and the story is set in the 2ndC AD. Every year on the night before the 1st of November (→ Samain) a fairy called Rothniam appears to him in order to predict the significant events of the coming year. The story tells how on one of these occasions Rothniam prophesies that a son will be born that very night to King Feidlimid, who is destined to unite the five provinces of Ireland and be the ancestor of 53 further kings. Miraculous signs such as the springing forth of rivers, the creation of new lakes and the reappearance of a tree which had been hidden since the Flood are to accompany his birth. That same night the famous king → Conn Cétchathach is indeed born. Fíngein serves him for fifty years and ultimately dies fighting for him.

Ed.: J. Vendryes, A. F., Du. 1953 (MMIS 15).

Trans.: T. P. Cross and A. C. L. Brown, 'Fingen's Night-watch' (*Romanic Review* 9) 1918, 29–47.

Aislinge Meic Chon Glinne (Ir. /'aʃl'iŋ'e vik' xon 'g'l'iN'e/ "The Dream of Mac Con Glinne"). Title of a humorous Irish narrative probably originating in the 11thC, surviving in two versions of divergent length from the 12thC. It depicts how the wandering scholar Aniar Mac Con Glinne, travelling through Ireland in the first half of the eighth century, comes into conflict with the abbot of the monastery of Cork and is condemned to death because of his alleged slighting of the Church. By dint of his presence of mind and ingenuity he succeeds in escaping execution twice and finally makes his way to the court of the king of Munster. There he employs cunning to dispel a demon of gluttony who has possessed the king, whereupon the death sentence is lifted and the wandering scholar richly rewarded. The story is told with wit and stylistic artistry; it is a malicious satire levelled at the medieval Irish monastic world, and parodies at the same time two popular literary genres: the Vision of the Otherworld (aisling, fís) and the miraculous sea-journey (→ immram). The comedy *The Son of Learning* (1926) by Austin → Clarke owes its inspiration to this story.

Ed.: K. H. Jackson, A. M. C. G., Du. 1990.

Trans.: R. Thurneysen, *Sagen aus dem alten Irland*, B. 1901.

Lit.: S. Gwara, 'Gluttony, lust and penance in the B-text of A. M. C. G.' (*Celtica* 20) 1988, 53–72.

Aislinge Oenguso (Ir. /'aʃl'iŋ'e 'oinɣuso/ "The Dream of Oengus"). One of the "prefatory tales" (→ remscéla) to the story of the Cattle-Raid of Cuailnge (→ *Táin Bó Cuailnge*), preserved in a single manuscript of the 15thC. It tells how Oengus, son of the → Dagda and → Boand, is overpowered by the love he feels for a wondrously beautiful woman whom he has seen only in dreams. With the help of the fairy prince Bodb and the royal couple → Ailill mac Mágach and → Medb of Connacht he succeeds in tracing her to Southern Ireland. There he sees the inspiration of his dream, in the form of a bird, with 150 female companions, beside a lake which she visits on a certain day of the year. In the form of swans the two lovers sleep together, circling the lake three times, and then remain together forever. In gratitude to Ailill and Medb, Oengus later proves willing to provide 300 warriors for the great foray of the men of Connacht to Cuailnge. The story is retold by Lady Augusta → Gregory in the eighth chapter of her book *Cuchulain of Muirtheimne* and by James → Stephens in his book *In the Land of Youth*.

Ed.: F. Shaw, *The Dream of Oengus*, Du. 1934.

Trans.: J. Gantz, *Early Ir. Myths and Sagas*, Harm. 1981.

aithech (Ir. /'aθ'ex/). In legal texts term designating the ignoble free peasant or serf. A. fortha referred to an ignoble free man who in the case of a legal action brought against the king (→ rí) stood in for him and if necessary was responsible for the compensation owed to the plaintiff. In this way justice was seen to be done without the king forfeiting his "honour" (→ enech).

Lit.: F. Kelly, *A Guide to Early Ir. Law*, Du. 1988.

aithed (Ir. /'aθ'eð /). Term designating the flight of a girl or woman with her lover. The word serves in the → Lists of Sagas to classify stories about such flights.

Lit.: B. K. Martin, 'Med. Ir. aitheda and Todorov's "Narratologie" ' (*StC* 10/11) 1975/76, 138–151.

Aithirne (Ir. /'aθ'ir'n'e/). The name of a poet from the province of Ulster in the stories of the → Ulster Cycle. He is universally feared because of his greed and scathing tongue and therefore bears in the stories the by-name Ailgesach, characterising him as an importunate petitioner. A. is said to be the son of the poet Ferchertne and mentor of the poet Amairgin mac Ecit Salaig. The story → *Cath Étair* tells how A. on a journey through Ireland brings upon himself and the province of Ulster by his shameless demands the enmity, in turn, of the inhabitants of Connacht, Munster, Leinster.

Alator. Celtic god identified according to the → interpretatio romana with → Mars. His cult is attested by an altar from South Shields, Tyneside (*RIB* 1055) and a small silver votive slab from Barkway in Hertfordshire (*RIB* 218, now in the British Museum), representing the god as a warrior with shield, spear and helmet and the inscription D(EO) MARTI ALATORI.

Albion. In classical → ethnography a name of the island of Britain. Probably cognate both with the name of the Celtic god → Albiorix and with Middle Welsh elfydd "world, land". Attested in → Pliny the Elder (Hist. Nat. 4,102) and elsewhere. The corresponding Celtic term is Albu or Alba, which in Irish sources in the early period denotes the whole of Britain, and, later, Scotland.

Albiorix. Celtic god whose name is probably cognate both with the geographical term → Albion and Middle Welsh elfydd "world, land". The original meaning of the name might therefore be "King of the Land" or "King of the World". The cult of A. is attested by an inscription from Sablet in the province Gallia Narbonensis (CIL XII 1300) which identifies the Celtic god with → Mars on the basis of the → interpretatio romana.

Lit.: W. Meid, *Aspekte der germanischen und keltischen Religion im Zeugnis der Sprache,* I. 1991.

Alesia. One of the most important Celtic settlements (→ oppida), near Alise-Sainte-Reine in the Dép. Côte d'Or, situated between two rivers on the steep slopes of Mont Auxois, and additionally fortified by a wall and ditch. The whole site took up an area of almost 100 hectares. In their last great rebellion against → Caesar in 52 BC the Gauls under their leader → Vercingetorix were besieged and starved in A. In contrast to many other oppida the settlement was also used by the Romans and only abandoned in the early Middle Ages. The first systematic excavations took place in 1861–1865, at the behest of Napoleon III. The name A. is attested in a Gaulish votive inscription for the Celtic god → Ucuetis, which was found on Mont Auxois in 1839.

Lit.: J. Le Gall, *A.,* P. 1985 (Guides arch. de la France 4); id., *Fouilles d'Alise-Sainte-Reine 1861–1865,* 2 vols., P. 1989; id., *A.: Arch. et Hist.,* nouv. éd., P. 1990.

Alisanus. Name of a Celtic god, of uncertain etymology. One possible derivation is from the name of the town → Alesia, but links have also been sought with the Celtic word for "rock", the name of a river *Alisos, and the Celtic word for alder or rowan. The cult of A. is attested by two votive inscriptions on bronze dishes (CIL XIII 2843 and 5468), found near Dijon and Arnay-le-Duc.

Lit.: G. Drioux, *Cultes indigènes des Lingons*, P. 1934.

Allobroges. In classical → ethnography a Celtic tribe in the area between the Western Alps, Lake Geneva and the Rhône. The name characterises its bearers as people "who live in foreign regions". It is the Gaulish equivalent of the Welsh word allfro "stranger, foreigner" (cf. → Nitiobroges). When in 218 BC Hannibal crossed the Alps, his starting-point was the area of the Allobroges. In 121 BC the tribe was conquered by the Romans and incorporated into the newly created province of Gallia Narbonensis. The chief town of the A. was Vienna (Vienne), their northernmost border town Genava (Geneva).

Altburg. Modern name of a fortified Celtic hill settlement east of the town of Bundenbach in the Hunsrück area. Intensive archaeological research in 1971–1975 demonstrated that it was inhabited from as early as the third century until at least the middle of the first century BC. While no trace remained of the buildings, which were of wood and wickerwork, their position and height could be determined, at least to some extent, on the basis of the surviving foundation pits. Several dwellings, storehouses and a palisade were reconstructed in 1985–1988 and now form an open-air museum.

Lit.: R. Schindler, *Die A. bei Bundenbach*, Mz. 1977; H. Nortmann, *Die A. bei Bundenbach: ein Führer zur keltischen Burg*, Bundenbach 1990.

Altstetten. Suburb of Zurich where in 1906, during railway works, a semi-spherical golden bowl was found, measuring 25cm in diameter and 10cm in height. Below its smooth rim it is decorated with repoussée dots and three motifs: suns, moons, stags and hinds. Its weight, 910g, is almost as heavy as that of all the gold objects from the graves of → Hochdorf and → Vix combined. It is thought that it is not of native craftsmanship, but was imported from the Iberian peninsula. Whether it served as part of a burial or whether it constituted a votive gift is not known, because of the uncertainty of the circumstances relating to the find. The bowl is now in the Schweizerisches Landesmuseum in Zurich.

Lit.: W. Kimmig, 'Die Goldschale von Zürich-A.', in: *Homenaje a Martin Almagro*, Ma. 1983, 101–118; P. Nagy, 'Technologische Aspekte der Goldschale von Zürich-Altstetten' (*Jahrbuch der Schweizerischen Gesellschaft für Ur- und Frühgeschichte* 75) 1992, 101–116.

Amaethon fab Dôn (Welsh /a'maiθon va:b do:n/). Name of a character in the story → *Culhwch ac Olwen*. The giant Ysbaddaden Bencawr presents the titular hero Culhwch with the task of making A. plough, sow and reap a newly cleared field. It is thought that a Celtic god of agriculture (Welsh amaeth) lies behind the figure of A. This remains speculative, however, as A. receives only a brief mention in the story and is not seen in action.

Amairgin Glúngel (Ir. /'avar'γ'in 'glu:nγ'el/). In the "Book of the Invasions of Ireland" (→ Lebor Gabála Érenn) the name of one of the sons of Míl, distinguished from his brothers by his magical and poetic gifts and wise powers of judgement. On his arrival in Ireland he identifies himself in mystic verses with the whole of Nature. When the sons of Míl wish to land with their ships in Ireland, the → Tuatha Dé Danann try to prevent them by bringing about a magic storm. A. however calms the wind and waves with a poem and thus makes the conquest of the island possible for his brothers.

Amairgin mac Ecit Salaig (Ir. /'avar'γ'in' mak 'eg'id' 'saliγ'/). A poet (→ fili) of the king → Conchobar mac Nesa, in the stories of the → Ulster Cycle. Son of the smith Ecet Salach ("the Dirty") and father of the warrior → Conall Cernach. His wife is Finnchaem, a sister of Conchobar. A story in the "Book of Leinster" (→ Lebor Laignech) tells how the poet → Aithirne attempts to kill the youthful A. because he is jealous of his talent, but ultimately, as a punishment, has to accept him as his foster-son and pupil. The later version of the story of the conception of Cú Chulainn (→ Compert Chon Culainn) tells how A. and his wife are entrusted by Conchobar with the education of the boy Sétanta, who later, under the name of Cú Chulainn, was to become the most celebrated hero of Ulster.

Amarcolitanus. Celtic god, identified according to the → interpretatio romana with → Apollo. His name is thought to mean "he of the distant gaze". The cult of A. is attested by a votive inscription from Branges in the Dép. Seine-et-Loire (CIL XIII 2600).

ambactus. Celtic term designating a liegeman or ministerialis, which occurs in the works of the the Roman poet Ennius and in → Caesar (Bell. Gall. 6,15). The grammarian Festus explains the etymology correctly as "he who is moved around (his lord)" (ambactus id est circumactus). Celt. *ambaktos is attested as a borrowing into Germanic by the Old High German word ambaht "servant". From the derivative ambahti "service" the New High German word "Amt" ("office") developed. Ital. ambasciata, Fr. ambassade and Engl. embassy derive from a Romance borrowing from the Celtic.

Ambarri. In classical → ethnography a Celtic tribe, whose settlement area lies between the land of the → Aedui and that of the → Allobroges. The name derives from *Ambi-arari and characterises its bearers as "those who live on both sides of the Arar (the Saône)".

amber. In ancient times amber was found predominantly on the coasts of West

Jutland and East Prussia (Samland). Trade in amber took place from the Bronze Age onwards, on routes that stretched from southern England as far afield as Greece. The Celts employed amber particularly in the late Hallstatt and early La Tène period, in the manufacture of pearls, rings, pendants and various kinds of inlay work. The evidence consists mostly in grave finds, amber rarely being found in archaeological excavations of settlements. Necklaces with several hundred amber pearls were found in grave 67 of Dürrnberg near → Hallein, in grave 6 of → Hohmichele and in grave 97 of → Magdalenenberg. In the plundered grave of → Grafenbühl lay a bone sphinx which had a small superimposed head of amber, and several small amber plates which it is thought were originally inlaid in furniture. During the archaeological excavation of the grave at → Hochdorf five amber pearls were discovered about the neck of the dead man, as well as discarded fragments resulting from the working of the amber. It is assumed therefore that the pearls were manufactured especially for the burial and served as an → amulet for the dead man rather than as → ornament. How amber came to the Celts is not known. As they had no direct contact with the inhabitants of the North Sea or Baltic coasts there must have been intermediate stages of trading.

Lit.: K. Spindler, *Die frühen Kelten*, St. ²1991; C. Beck and S. Shennan, *Amber in Prehistoric Britain*, O. 1991.

Ambiani. In classical → ethnography a Celtic tribe in the area of the mouth of the Somme. The name survives in that of the city of Amiens, originally called Samarobriva.

Ambigatus. The Roman historian → Livy (Ab urbe condita 5,34) gives this name to a Celtic king of the tribe of the → Bituriges. At the time of the Roman king Tarquinius Priscus (6thC BC) he is supposed to have sent forth his two nephews Bellovesus and Segovesus with many of his subjects in order to conquer new areas. Following the decision of the gods, Segovesus then occupied the region of the Hercynic mountains (the mountains of Central Germany), whereas Bellovesus migrated to Italy. Probably this tradition derives from a legend of the Celtic inhabitants of Italy, but the historical basis of the legend is lost to us.

Ambiorix. Gallic prince of the tribe of the → Eburones (cf. → Caesar, Bell. Gall. 5,24ff., 6,5ff., 6,29ff. and 6,43). In 54 BC, together with the prince Catuvolcus, he led a revolt of his tribe against the Roman occupying powers. After the destruction of a Roman legion near Aduatuca (Tongern) the rebellion was put down amidst much bloodshed and the land of the Eburones laid waste, whereupon Catuvolcus poisoned himself. A. however succeeded in escaping from Caesar's troops, with a few companions. A bronze statue of A. was sculptured by Jules Bertin (1826–1892) for the town of Tongern.

Amfreville. A town in the Dép. of Eure southwest of Rouen. There in an ancient riverbed of the Seine a helmet was found, ornamented with gold, belonging to a Celtic warrior of the 4thC BC; it is now in the Musée des Antiquités Nationales in Saint-Germain-en-Laye.

Lit.: V. Kruta, 'Le casque d'A.-sous-les-Monts (Eure) et quelques problèmes de l'art celtique du IVe siècle avant notre ère' (EC 15) 1978, 405–424.

Amra Choluim Chille (Ir. /'avra 'xolum' 'çiL'e/ "Panegyric of Columba"). Poem composed c. 600 in praise of Columba, the Irish missionary and founder of monasteries (Ir. → Colum Cille). According to the manuscript it was the work of a poet called Dallán (mac) Forgaill. One of the oldest survivals of Irish literature, it presents considerable linguistic and metrical difficulties.

Ed. and trans.: W. Stokes, 'The Bodleian A. C. C.' (RC 20) 1899, 30–55, 132–183, 248–289, 400–437 and (RC 21) 1900, 133–136.

Lit.: V. Hull, 'On A. C. C.', (ZCP 28) 1961, 242–252; P. L. Henry, Saoithiúlacht na Sean-Ghaeilge, Du. 1978; M. Herbert, 'The Preface to A. C. C.', in: D. Ó Corráin et al. (eds.), Sages, Saints, and Storytellers (May. 1989) 67–75; T. O. Clancy & G. Márkus, Iona: The Earliest Poetry of a Celtic Monastery, E. 1995.

Amulets. Charms worn to protect those who wear them from danger. This apotropaic ("averting") function distinguishes them from talismans, which function positively, bringing good fortune to those who wear them.

Written records relating to amulets are almost totally lacking in the field of Celtic culture, and archaeological records therefore provide the greater part of our knowledge. Most of these finds are from the graves of women and children. An accurate overall assessment of the finds is difficult because only such excavations as have been very carefully documented can be evaluated, and many finds of the previous century must therefore be disregarded. More-over, amulets made of organic materials have only rarely been preserved, whereas others made of → glass, → amber or metal are difficult to distinguish from → ornaments.

In general amulets can be identified on the basis of their unusual shape (e.g. small wheels, shoes, feet or axes), the unusual way in which they were made (e.g. incomplete rings or rings rendered useless after their manufacture) or the obvious lack of any utilitarian or decorative function (e.g. variously shaped small pieces of iron or petrified stones). It is unlikely that all of these objects were the personal property of the dead; some may have been buried with them. In such cases the amulets were perhaps destined not so much to protect the dead man as to protect the surviving against him. Thus amulets have been frequently found next to corpses buried in unusual places or skeletons with indications of unusual manipulations.

Lit.: L. Pauli, Keltischer Volksglaube: Amulette und Sonderbestattungen am Dürrnberg bei Hallein und im eisenzeitlichen Mitteleuropa, Mn. 1976.

Ancamna. Name of a Celtic goddess. In inscriptions she is coupled with the gods → Lenus and → Smertrius.

Andarta. Name of a Celtic goddess, thought to derive from the Celtic word for a bear (Ir. art, Welsh arth), and therefore perhaps meaning "big/mighty she-bear"). The cult of A. is attested by seven votive inscriptions (CIL XII 1554–1560), found in or near the town of Die in the Dép. of Drôme in Southern France.

Andecavi. In classical → ethnography a tribe from the lower Loire. The name survives today in that of the town Angers, which was previously called Iuliomagus.

Andrasta. Name of a Celtic goddess. The only record of her cult is a reference by the Roman historian Cassius Dio (Historia Romana 62,6), which records that → Boudicca, queen of the Iceni, appealed to her for help during an uprising of the British tribes in 61 AD. A few scholars have viewed Andrasta as a corruption of the name → Andarta, but there is no solid evidence for this hypothesis.

Aneirin → Neirin.

Anextlomarus. Name of a Celtic god. The first part of the name is cognate with O.Ir. anacul "protection"; hence A. means something like "great protector". On an inscription on a bronze bowl from South Shields (now in the Archaeological Museum in Newcastle) the god is equated with → Apollo. His name is thought to survive in incomplete form in an inscription from the neighbourhood of Le Mans (CIL XIII 3190). The form Anextlomara occurs in an inscription from Aventicum (Fi 94), now Avenches in Switzerland.

Anglesey → Mona.

animals. Animals played an important role in Celtic civilisation, and therefore also in Celtic → religion and → mythology. Visual representations of them are far more frequent than those of human beings (cf. → art). They were also of great importance as → sacrifices in ritual. The close association of various animals with → gods and goddesses is illustrated in Roman times by the depiction of hybrid creatures such as the god of → Bouray, and by images of gods with animals as attributes (cf. → bear, → bulls, → cock, → dogs, → hare, → horses, → pigs, → ram, → stag).
  Lit.: M. Green, *Animals in Celtic Life and Myth*, Lo. 1992.

Annales Cambriae. Name given to a collection of Welsh annals, the oldest version of which records the period from the middle of the 5thC to the middle of the 10thC. The text which has survived to our day was written down c. 1100 and is preserved in Ms. Harley 3859 in the British Museum. The annals contain the famous references to the battles of → Baddon and → Camlan.

Lit.: L. Alcock, *Arthur's Britain*, Harm. 1971.

Annwfn (Welsh /'annuvn/) denotes an → Otherworld opposed to the visible world. The word is etymologically problematic, as the second half may derive either from dwfn "deep" or from dwfn "world". Moreover it is uncertain whether An- means "very", "not" or "inner". The expression taken as a whole might therefore mean "great depth", or "non-world", or "inner or under world". In the oldest texts A. appears sometimes as an island beyond the areas inhabited by mankind, sometimes as a land beneath the earth. Later texts employ the same term to refer to the (Christian) concept of Hell. The adventures of mortal men in A. are portrayed in the poem → *Preiddeu Annwfn* and in the story → *Pwyll Pendefig Dyfed*.

Antenociticus. Name of a Celtic god worshipped in a temple near Benwell, by Hadrian's Wall. Three altars dedicated to him were found there (*RIB* 1327–1329), as well as the head and other remains of a life-size statue of the god. These are now preserved in the Archaeological Museum in Newcastle.

Anu (Ir. /'anu/) or Ana. Name in medieval sources of a pre-Christian Irish goddess. The Glossary of Bishop Cormac (→ *Sanas Chormaic*) refers to A. as "the mother of the Irish gods" (mater deorum Hibernensium). According to the etymological list → *Cóir Anmann*, A. was a fertility goddess (bandía in t*šónusa) to whom the province of Munster owed its prosperity. Íath nAnann, "Land of A.", occurs frequently in poetry as a name for Ireland, and two gently sloping hills south of Killarney in County Kerry were called Dá chích nAnann "the two breasts of A.". A variant of the name, which originally referred to a different mythological figure, is Danu or (later) Danann.

Anwyl, Edward (1866–1914), Celticist, born in Chester. After studying in Oxford he taught Welsh philology at the University College of Wales in Aberystwyth from 1892 until shortly before his death, as well as – from 1905 – comparative philology. He was the author of several studies of Welsh literature and numerous articles on Celtic religion and culture for the *Encyclopaedia of Religion and Ethics* (1908–1926). In 1906 he published a comprehensive study of *Celtic Religion in Pre-Christian Times*.

ap (before a consonant) or ab (before a vowel) means "son of . . ." (cf. Ir. → mac) and is a frequent component of Welsh names. When names are transposed into English the initial vowel is often omitted and the final consonant combined with the following patronymic (e.g. Price, derived from ap Rhŷs or Bithel from ab Ithel).

Apollo. A god imported to Rome from Greece at the beginning of the 5thC BC. His name also serves in Latin inscriptions and works of literature to denote several Celtic gods, only some of whom are in addition assigned their Celtic names (cf. → interpretatio romana). As early as → Caesar it is reported that the Gauls worshipped → Mercury, A., → Mars, → Jupiter and → Minerva. Like other peoples they held that A. dispelled diseases (Bell. Gall. 6,17). This is confirmed by the fact that in Roman Gaul A. appears to have been worshipped primarily at the site of healing springs. In inscriptions A. is equated with the Celtic gods → Amarcolitanus, → Anextlomarus, → Atepomarus, → Belenus, → Borvo, → Grannus, → Maponus, → Moritasgus, → Toutiorix and → Vindonnus. His most frequent companion in inscriptions is the goddess → Sirona.

Lit.: J. de Vries, *Keltische Religion*, St. 1961; P.-M. Duval, *Les Dieux de la Gaule*, P. 1976; J.-J. Hatt, 'Apollon Guérisseur en Gaule', in: C. Pelletier (ed.), *La Médecine en Gaule*, P. 1985, 205–238; ibid, *Mythes et dieux de la Gaule I*, P. 1989.

Aquitania. In classical → ethnography the name for southwest → Gaul, the area between the Pyrenees, the Garonne and the Atlantic (cf. Caesar, Bell. Gall. I,1). According to Pliny the Elder (Hist. Nat. 4,105) this area was in ancient times called → Aremorica (as also was Brittany).

Lit.: J. Gorrochategui Churruca, *Estudio sobre la onomástica indígena de Aquitania*, Bilbao 1982.

Arawn (Welsh /'araun/). In the story → *Pwyll Pendefig Dyfed* the name of the king of → Annwfn. He and the prince Pwyll of Dyfed change shapes, A. ruling for a year over Pwyll's kingdom, whilst Pwyll in his place defeats his enemy in Annwfn, Hafgan. During this time Pwyll leaves the wife of A. unmolested and thus wins his friendship.

Arberth (Welsh /'arberθ/). Place in South-West Wales. In the stories → *Pwyll Pendefig Dyfed* and → *Manawydan fab Llŷr* chief residence of the prince of → Dyfed.

d'Arbois de Jubainville, Henri (1827–1910). Historian and Celticist, born in Nancy. After studying law and history in Paris he worked from 1852 to 1880 as an archivist in Troyes. During this period he wrote a history of the dukes and counts of Champagne in seven volumes, as well as numerous smaller works on local history. Historical and archaeological questions drew his attention to the area of → Celtic studies. d'A. began his studies in this discipline by reading the *Grammatica Celtica* of Johann Kaspar → Zeuss and by learning Breton. In 1882 he was elected to the new chair in Celtic Language and Literature at the Collège de France in Paris. There he wrote numerous works on the history of the Celtic language, law, literature and religion, *inter alia* the twelve-volume *Cours de littérature celtique* (1883–1902). From 1885 onwards d'A. edited the journal *Revue celtique*, founded by Henri → Gaidoz, thus exerting considerable influence on the evolution of Celtic studies in France.

Arduinna. In classical → ethnography an extensive area of forestland between the Maas and the Rhine. The name is possibly cognate with Ir. ard, "high" and Welsh ardd, "high; highland". It survives in the modern name of the Ardennes.

The cult of a goddess of the same name is attested by inscriptions. It is thought that like → Abnoba she was closely associated with the mountains regarded as her home. She is recorded in a votive inscription from the region of Düren (CIL XIII 7848), and a depiction of → Diana from Rome, with the appended inscription ARDVINNE (CIL VI 46). This latter inscription was dedicated to the goddess of his homeland by the Gaul M. Quartinius Sabinus, a soldier of the imperial guard, in the third century AD. Both the depiction and the inscription are now partially obliterated and have been restored in misleading fashion.

The bronze statue of a goddess riding on a boar now in the Musée des Antiquités Nationales in Saint-Germain-en-Laye is also generally regarded as a depiction of A. Its exact place of origin is however unknown, and the pedestal bears no inscription. The identification of the rider as A. is therefore doubtful.

Lit.: P.-M. Duval, *Les Dieux de la Gaule*, P. 1976; S. Boucher, *Recherches sur les bronzes figurés de Gaule pré-romaine et romaine*, R. 1976.

Aremorica. In classical → ethnography the name of a coastal area in Gaul stretching from the mouth of the Loire to the mouth of the Seine, corresponding more or less to modern Brittany. The name Are-morici means "those (tribes) living East of the sea". It may thus be compared etymologically with the name Pomerania (from the Slavonic Po-morjane, "those living near the sea").

Arfderydd (Welsh /arv'derið/). Celtic name of a site a few miles north of Carlisle. According to the → *Annales Cambriae* a battle between rival Celtic princes took place there in c. 573 AD, in the course of which → Gwenddoleu fab Ceidiaw fell and his poet → Myrddin lost his wits. Several references to the battle in the → *Trioedd Ynys Prydein* and in medieval poets suggest that A. played a significant role in the Welsh tradition, but these allusions apart, few narrative traces survive.

Arianrhod (Welsh /ar'janɾod/). In the story → *Math fab Mathonwy* the mother of the twins Dylan Eil Ton and Lleu Llaw Gyffes, daughter of Dôn and niece of King Math. Some references to her in medieval poetry suggest that A. also played a role in other legends.

Armagh → Book of Armagh.

Armes Prydein (Welsh /ˈarmes ˈprədein/) "The Prophecy of Britain". Title of a political prophecy in verse form contained in the "Book of Taliesin" (→ Llyfr Taliesin). An unknown author prophesies that the Celts of Britain, Ireland, Scotland and Brittany will ally themselves with the Vikings of Dublin in order to expel the hated Anglo-Saxons. The poem is thought to have been composed c. 930 and to be directed primarily against the political designs of the English king Athelstan.
 Ed. and trans.: I. Williams, A. P.: The Prophecy of Britain, Du. 1972 (Engl. version by R. Bromwich, MMWS 6).
 Lit.: D. N. Dumville, 'Brittany and "Armes Prydein Vawr" ' (EC 20) 1983, 145–159.

Arnemetia. Celtic goddess (cf. → nemeton). The name occurs in the Latin place-name Aquae Arnemetiae ("the waters of A."), the ancient name of a holy spring near Buxton in Derbyshire. An inscription records the name in the form DEAE ARNOMECTE on an altar from the Roman fort of Brough-on-Noe in Derbyshire (RIB 281).

Arnold, Matthew (1822-1888), poet and critic, born in Laleham, Middlesex. After studying in Oxford he worked mostly as an inspector of schools from 1851 to 1886. The author of many literary and cultural studies, he was the first to rework the Tristan legend in the English language, with his poem Tristram and Iseult (1852).
 From 1857 to 1867 Arnold was Professor of Poetry in Oxford. There he gave in 1865–1866 four lectures on the study of Celtic literature. These appeared in 1866 in the The Cornhill Magazine, and then in 1867 in book form under the title The Study of Celtic Literature. In these lectures A. stressed the importance of → Celtic studies, as founded by Johann Kaspar → Zeuss, and pleaded for their development in Great Britain, regarding the Celtic element as one of the three components of the British national character, alongside the Anglo-Saxon and Norman elements. Taking this historical perspective as his starting-point, A. concerned himself primarily with medieval Celtic literature rather than such Celtic culture as survived in his time. As he possessed little knowledge of the Celtic languages, he relied upon English and French translations. A. was strongly influenced by his friend Ernest → Renan's Essai sur la poésie des races celtiques.
 A. regarded the Celts as being particularly gifted in their cultivation of shorter literary genres, both in terms of form and of content, in their literary depiction of the charms of nature, and their facility in representing moods of resignation and melancholy. This overall view was not without its opponents at the time, and there was much detailed criticism. Modern scholarship finds the views of A. concerning racial characteristics and the way in which they

express themselves in literature untenable. Nevertheless, as the first comparative study of Celtic literature, his lectures exerted considerable influence and led to the institution of a Chair in Celtic Studies at the University of Oxford in 1877.

Lit.: F. E. Faverty, M. A. the Ethnologist, Evanston (Ill.) 1951; R. Bromwich, M. A. and Celtic Literature: a Retrospect 1865–1965, O. 1965; L. Orr, 'The mid- nineteenth-century Irish context of A.'s Essay on Celtic Literature', in: C. Machann and F. D. Burt (eds.), M. A. in his Time and Ours, Charlottesville, Virg. 1988, 135–155.

art. From the archaeological point of view the culture of the late Western Hallstatt period (600–450 BC) is generally attributed to the Celts as they are known from classical → ethnography (cf. → Hallstatt). It was however only towards the end of this epoch, at the time of the transition to the La Tène period (cf. → La Tène), that independent Celtic art developed. To all appearances the innovations linked with this development originated in areas which were not directly dependent intellectually or materially on the ancient → princely seats of the Hallstatt period, such as the → Hohenasperg or the → Heuneburg. The areas which determined the evolution of the characteristic Celtic La Tène style are thought rather to be the Rhineland, Lothringia, Champagne and the Hunsrück-Eifel region. At the same time, Celtic art was substantially influenced by contacts with Greek and Etruscan culture initiated in the Hallstatt period, and Scythian and Thracian influences are also demonstrable.

Celtic art is characteristically lacking in a number of modes of expression which are self-evident in ancient oriental and Graeco-Roman art. There is for example no monumental stone architecture, which is why places of worship resembling temples are in pre-Roman times only to be found in southern Gaul, which was subject to Mediterranean influences (cf. → Entremont, → Roquepertuse). Moreover, there is scarcely any sculpture on a large scale depicting human figures, with the exception of the stone sculptures of the warriors of → Hirschlanden and → Glauberg, which were also influenced by Mediterranean models. Finally, the scenic depiction of sequences of action or motion is for the most part absent, the decorative plates of the famous → Gundestrup cauldron being the obvious exception. Such other sequences of scenes as are to be found are generally traceable back to eastern Alpine or upper Italian models.

For the most part Celtic works of art are the product of craftsmen; → jewellery, weapons and utensils intended for religious or magical use were created with great love of detail and technical perfection, in an unconventional manner. The artists employed polished forms of → ornamentation which are capable even today of captivating the beholder because of their intricacy and mysterious nature. This applies to the grave gifts from the → princely graves, the finds from → oppida, and also to Celtic → coins.

On the European mainland the history of Celtic art ends with the Roman conquest of Gaul. In the British Isles, however, there was in the first millennium AD a late bloom, which in combination with stylistic elements of Germanic art culminated in the Irish book decoration of the Middle Ages (cf. → Book of Durrow, → Book of Kells).

Lit.: P. Jacobsthal, *Early Celtic Art*, O. 1944; C. Fox, *Pattern and Purpose*, Car. 1958; I. Finlay, *Celtic Art*, Lo. 1973; P.-M. Duval, *Die Kelten*, Mn. 1978 (Univ. d. Kunst); I. M. Stead, *Celtic Art*, Lo. 1985; C. Eluère, *Das Gold der Kelten*, Mn. 1987; L. Zachar, *Keltische Kunst in der Slowakei*, Bratislava 1987; A. Duval, *L'art celtique de la Gaule au Musée des antiquités nationales*, P. 1989; R. & V. Megaw, *Celtic Art*, Lo. 1989; C. Nerzic, *La Sculpture en Gaule Romaine*, P. 1989; B. Raftery (ed.), *L'art celtique*, P. 1990; *Hundert Meisterwerke keltischer Kunst*, Trier 1992 (exhibition cat.).

Art (Ir. /aRt/). The name in the stories of the → Historical Cycle of a son of the king → Conn Cétchathach. His byname Oenfer ("the Only One") is explained in the story → *Echtrae Chonnlai*: he remains behind, the only surviving son of Conn, after his brother Connla, out of love for a fairy, has left the world of men. A. does not play a prominent role in the literature that has survived, but emerges as an honest, exemplary ruler. The story of the battle of Mag Mucrama (→ *Cath Maige Mucrama*) tells how A. sides with his brother-in-law Ailill Aulom in his conflict with his nephew Lugaid mac Con, and falls in battle.

Artaius. Celtic god, identified according to the → interpretatio romana with → Mercury. His name is thought to derive, like that of the god → Matunus and those of the goddesses → Andarta and → Artio from a Celtic word for "bear" (cf. Ir. art and Welsh arth "bear"). The cult of A. is attested by a votive inscription from Beaucroissant in the Dép. of Isère (CIL XII 2199).

Arthur (Welsh /'arθir/). One of the most important figures in the legends of the British Celts. His name probably derives from the Latin Artorius, and appears in Latin texts as Arturus, in French and German texts as Artus.

The earliest records of a historical A. are thought to be those preserved in the → *Annales Cambriae*. They refer to his victory in the year 72 (= presumably 518 AD) over Germanic invaders in the battle of → Baddon, and his death in the year 93 (= presumably 539 AD) in the battle of → Camlan. In the → *Historia Brittonum* of the 9thC A. appears as a victorious general (dux bellorum) in twelve battles. It is uncertain whether the reference to him in the poem Y → *Gododdin* is of roughly the same date or even earlier.

In the Welsh tradition this minimal amount of historical data takes on legendary and fairy-tale colouring. Thus in the → *Englynion Gereint* A. appears as a contemporary of king Gereint fab Erbin, who in fact must date from some generations later. In the poems → *Pa ŵr yw'r Porthor?* and → *Preiddeu Annwfn* he is portrayed as the leader of a company of bold warriors possessing all kinds of miraculous gifts. Listed among his most significant followers are the heroic figures of → Bedwyr fab Bedrawg and → Cei fab Cynyr. These also accompany A. in → *Culhwch ac Olwen*, the oldest prose narrative in the Arthurian cycle of legends. It is thought that the idea that A. was taken away before his death and will return at the end of time originated at the same time as *Culhwch ac Olwen*.

A totally new picture is drawn c. 1137 by → Geoffrey of Monmouth. In his *Historia Regum Britanniae* (History of the Kings of Britain) he portrays A. as a powerful feudal ruler who conquers the whole of Britain, and even conducts successful campaigns in Scandinavia and on the continental mainland. A. and his court are as a result of Geoffrey's influence celebrated throughout Europe as the quintessence of the courtly ideal of society (→ Arthurian literature). Many features which are for the first time attested in Geoffrey found their way into the Welsh tradition through vernacular reworkings of his *Historia*. This is evident above all in the medieval Welsh prose narratives → *Gereint fab Erbin*, → *Iarlles y Ffynnawn* and → *Peredur fab Efrawg*. Here, for the most part, Arthur retreats into the background, while individual knights from his retinue rise to prominence. He plays a central role in the satirical narrative → *Breuddwyd Rhonabwy*. Here too, though traces of an older tradition are discernible, the influence of Geoffrey and his successors is recognisable.

Lit.: Th. Jones, 'The Early Evolution of the Legend of A.' (*Nottingham Medieval Studies* 8) 1964, 3–21; L. Alcock, A.'s *Britain*, Harm. 1971; R. Bromwich, 'Concepts of A.' (*StC* 10/11) 1975/76, 163–181; A. O. H. Jarman, 'The Delineation of A. in Early Welsh Verse', in: K. Varty (ed.), *An Arthurian Tapestry*, Glasgow 1981, 1–21; D. Edel, 'The A. of "Culhwch ac Olwen" as a Figure of Epic-Heroic Tradition' (*Reading Medieval Studies* 9) 1983, 3–15; R. Barber, *King A.: Hero and Legend*, Wo. 1986; T. Charles-Edwards, 'The A. of History', in: R. Bromwich et al. (eds.), *The A. of the Welsh*, Car. 1991, 15–32; O. Padel, 'The Nature of A.' (*CMCSt* 27) 1994, 1–31.

Arthurian literature. The written versions of the originally oral tales concerning the British folk hero → Arthur (Old French and Middle High German: Artus). The beginnings of Arthurian literature are to be sought in the Welsh and Breton traditions of the 6th–11th centuries, in which the memory of historical persons of the 6thC is linked with folk-tale motifs and names from pre-Christian Celtic mythology. Most of the stories dating from this early period were transmitted orally and have therefore failed to survive. Among the few texts surviving in manuscript form are the two poems → *Pa ŵr yw'r Porthor?* and → *Preiddeu Annwfn*, and the prose narrative → *Culhwch ac Olwen*. In these texts Arthur is portrayed as the leader of a band of adventurous warriors who possess magical abilities. Allusions and references to lost legends in works such as the → *Englynion y Beddeu* or the → *Trioedd Ynys Prydein* demonstrate that originally a whole host of further tales of this kind were in circulation.

With the rise of courtly literature at the beginning of the 12thC the legends concerning Arthur and his retinue became known for the first time beyond the borders of the Celtic countries. Christened the "matière de Bretagne", they formed, along with accounts of the history of peoples and the reception of Roman classical literature, the most popular source for the authors of vernacular verse and prose romances. This extraordinary popularity is no doubt to be attributed in part to the fairy-tale character of the Celtic traditions, which gave the French, English and German poets an ideal opportunity to project the aspirations of contemporary courtly society into an indefinitely perceived past. In contrast to the oldest Celtic stories Arthur/Artus now emerges as a Christian feudal ruler in the medieval style, his band of boisterous warriors transformed into a company of model knights. The most important influences behind this reworking of the material are on the one hand the pseudo-historical works of → Geoffrey of Monmouth and of his vernacular adaptors → Wace and → Layamon, on the other the romances of the French poet → Chrétien de Troyes, closer in style to the fairy-tale. Chrétien's romances were soon followed by adaptations by the German poets → Eilhart von Oberge, → Ulrich von Zatzikhoven, → Hartmann von Aue and → Wolfram von Eschenbach. A literature of a different kind evolved around the motif of the → Grail, strongly influenced by contemporary theological movements. Among the most important Celtic works of this second phase of Arthurian literature are the Middle Welsh prose narrative → Breuddwyd Rhonabwy and the works known as the → Tair Rhamant (→ Iarlles y Ffynnawn, → Peredur fab Efrawg and → Gereint fab Erbin). The last significant late medieval reworking of the cycle of legends was the work of Sir Thomas → Malory in the late 15thC.

Since the early 19thC Arthurian literature has experienced a renaissance which persists to the present day. The Romantic revival of interest in the Middle Ages led to numerous retellings of the legends, particularly in the Anglo-Saxon linguistic area, to tone poems, paintings, and finally films. At the same time, with the rise of Germanic, Romance and Celtic philology, scholarly interest in Arthurian literature commenced. Modern scholarship holds that the English, French and German poets borrowed numerous names and motifs (rather than whole narratives) from the Celtic tradition. Their sources were primarily Welsh and Breton tales which may have become familiar to the French and Anglo-Norman authors through bilingual storytellers. The Welsh and Breton material is for the most part lost to us, only the names of the legendary figures surviving. Many characteristic narrative motifs have survived only in the richer Irish tradition. It must be emphasised that, contrary to the views of older scholarship, the Celtic names and motifs only derive in part from mythology. Many of them can be shown to derive from narratives of legendary and fairy-tale character.

Bibl.: Bulletin Bibliographique de la Société Internationale Arthurienne, P. 1949ff.; C. E. Pickford and R. Last, The Arthurian Bibliography, 2 vols., C. 1981–1983; E. Reiss et

al., *Arthurian Legend and Literature: Annotated Bibliography I The Middle Ages*, Lo. 1984.
Surveys: R. S. Loomis (ed.), *Arthurian Literature in the Middle Ages*, O. 1959; J. D. Merriman, *The Flower of Kings: A Study of the Arthurian Legend in England between 1485 and 1835*, Lawrence 1973; B. Taylor and E. Brewer, *The Return of King Arthur: British and American Arthurian Literature since 1800*, C. 1983; R. H. Thompson, *The Return from Avalon: A Study of the Arthurian Legend in Modern Fiction*, Westport (Conn.) 1985; C. L. Gottzmann, *Artus-Dichtung*, St. 1989 (Sammlung Metzler); M. Whitaker, *The Legends of King Arthur in Art*, C. 1990; N. J. Lacy (ed.), *The New Arthurian Encyclopedia*, Lo. 1991; R. Baumstark & M. Koch, *Der Gral. Artusromantik in der Kunst des 19. Jahrhunderts*, Cologne 1995.
On the Celtic background: K. H. Jackson, 'Les sources celtiques du Roman du Graal', in: *Les Romans du Graal au XIIe et XIIIe siècles*, P. 1956, 213–227; W.-D. Lange, 'Keltisch-romanische Literaturbeziehungen im MA.', in: *Grundriß der romanischen Literaturen des Mittelalters I*, Hei. 1972, 163–205; J. Frappier, 'La Matière de Bretagne', in: *Grundriß . . . IV*, Hei. 1978, 183–211; R. Bromwich, 'Celtic Elements in Arthurian Romance: A General Survey', in: *The Legend of Arthur in the Middle Ages*, C. 1983, 41–55 and 230–233; R. Bromwich et al. (eds.), *The Arthur of the Welsh: The Arthurian Legend in Medieval Welsh Literature*, Car. 1991.

Artio. Celtic goddess whose name is derived from a Celtic word for bear (*artos). Her cult is attested by an inscription found near Trier (CIL XIII 4113), and the votive inscription accompanying a pictorial representation from Muri, near Berne (CIL XIII 5160). The bronze statue, about 20cm high, shows the goddess in seated position offering a bowl of fruit to a bear. It is now in the Historisches Museum in Berne.

Artus. French and German form of the Welsh name → Arthur.

Arverni. In classical → ethnography a Celtic tribe located in the Auvergne, which was named after the tribe. Its most important fortified settlement was → Gergovia. In 121 BC the A. were defeated by the Romans and their king Bituitus taken captive, yet even at the time of the conquest of Gaul by → Caesar they still constituted an important political power (cf. Bell. Gall. 1,31). In 52 BC the Arvernus → Vercingetorix provoked the last mass uprising of the Gauls against Roman rule.

Arvernorix. Celtic god identified according to the → interpretatio romana with → Mercury. His name means "King of the → Arverni" and is perhaps a variant of the name → Arvernus. The cult of A. is attested by a single inscription from the neighbourhood of Miltenberg in Lower Franconia (CIL XIII 6603).

Arvernus. Celtic god identified according to the → interpretatio romana with → Mercury. The name is thought to be related to that of the tribe of the

→ Arverni, but all the firm evidence for the cult of the god derives from parts of Germania to the left and right of the Rhine (CIL XIII 7845, 8164, 8235, 8579, 8580 and 8709). The interpretation of an inscription from the peak of the Puy-de-Dôme in the settlement area of the Arverni (CIL XIII 1522) remains problematic.

Astérix. Titular hero of a series of French cartoon books which describe the adventures of a Gaulish village and its petty wars against the legions of the conqueror Caesar. The heroes of the stories are the diminutive but cunning A. and his enormously strong but intellectually somewhat retarded friend Obélix. Supporting characters include the chieftain of the tribe Abraracourcix (à bras raccourcis: with all one's might), the bard Assurancetourix (assurance tous risques: fully comprehensive insurance) and the druid Panoramix. In the English translations these three bear the names Vitalstatistix, Cacofonix and Getafix. The first episodes in the series appeared between 1959 and 1974 in the young people's magazine *Pilote*. The plot and texts were written by René Goscinny (1926–1977), whilst the drawings were executed by Albert Uderzo (b. 1927), who was also responsible for both plots and texts after the death of Goscinny. From 1961 onwards the stories appeared in the form of separate albums.

In their depiction of Celtic and Roman civilisation the comics are surprisingly true to life, with a wealth of realistic detail evincing meticulous and extensive study of the original sources. On the other hand the reader finds himself confronted constantly with witty anachronisms, employed by the authors to caricature the national character of the Gauls (French), the Goths (Germans), Helvetians (Swiss) and other peoples. The Gauls are shown for the most part as temperamental but basically well-meaning and childish ruffians. Here the influence of modern → Celtic ideology is evident, although the authors' parodistic intent is clear from the humorous tone of the narrative. Their increasing popularity led to the stories centring upon A. being translated into dozens of languages, with worldwide sales of over 200 million copies. No other work of the twentieth century has been so influential in determining the popular image of Celtic culture.

Lit.: A. Stoll, A.: *das Trivialepos Frankreichs*, Co. 1974.

Atepomarus. Celtic god identified according to the → interpretatio romana with → Apollo. His cult is attested by a votive inscription from the neighbourhood of Mauvières in the Dép. of Indre (CIL XIII 1318).

Atesmerius. Celtic god whose cult is attested by a votive inscription from Meaux (CIL XIII 3023), the chief town of the tribe of the → Meldi. In another inscription from Poitiers (CIL XIII 1125) the god bears the name Adsmerius and is identified according to the → interpretatio romana with →

Mercury. An inscription dedicated to a goddesss named Atesmerta was found in 1918 in the forest of Corgebin in the Dép. of Haute-Marne (ILTG 414).

Athenaios of Naukratis (Egypt). Greek writer c. 200 AD whose sole surviving work, entitled *Deipnosophistai* (The Banquet of Scholars), contains within the fictitious framework of a symposium lasting several days an abundance of information relating to various areas of scholarship, including the celebrated quotations from the lost Celtic ethnography of the Stoic philosopher → Poseidonios (Deipnosophistai 4,36; 4,37; 4,40 and 6,49). The longest of these (4,36) contains a colourful description of Celtic eating and drinking habits (→ Food and Drink).
    Lit.: B. Maier, 'Of Celts and Cyclopes: notes on Ath. IV 36 p. 152' (*StC* 30; in press).

Atrebates. In classical → ethnography a Celtic tribe in the region of Artois, which was named after the tribe. The name probably means "settlers" (from *Ad-trebates). In 57 BC the A. were conquered by → Caesar. Their name survives in that of the city of Arras, formerly called Nemetacum.

Aubrey, John (1626–1697). Classicist and naturalist, born in North Wiltshire. After studying in Oxford he lived a precarious life as a private scholar in various parts of England and Wales. He was the author of numerous works, most of which however remained unpublished. From A. derives the false assumption that the neolithic and Bronze Age stone circles of the British Isles are sacred → Druid sites. This theory was popularised especially by the writings of William → Stukeley. In fact these stone monuments originated before the Celts made their appearance in Central Europe. Moreover, there is no archaeological evidence for these sites having any function in Celtic religion.
    Lit.: M. Hunter, *J. A. and the Realm of Learning*, Lo. 1975.

Audacht Morainn (Ir. /'auðaxt 'moriN'/ "Morann's Legacy"). Title of a collection of sayings, thought to have been recorded in the 8thC. Tradition holds that they derive from the legendary judge Morann and were originally intended for his foster-son, the Irish king Feradach Find Fechtnach. At the heart of the text is the concept of the "Justice of the Ruler" (→ fír flathemon), whose beneficent influence is described in detail in numerous proverbs.
    Ed. and trans.: F. Kelly, A. M., Du. 1976; A. Ahlqvist, 'Le Testament de Morann' (EC 21) 1984, 151–170 and (EC 24) 1987, 325.
    Lit.: P. L. Henry, 'The Cruces of A. M.' (ZCP 39) 1982, 33–53; A. Ahlqvist, 'Two Notes on A. M.' (*Celtica* 21) 1990, 1–2.

Aulerci. In classical → ethnography an alliance of Celtic peoples in the region between the Loire and the Seine, consisting of the four tribes of the → Cenomani, → Diablintes, → Eburovices and → Brannovices.

Auraicept na nÉces (Ir. /'aurik'ept na 'n'e:g'es/ "a manual for learned poets"). Title of a collection of twelve dissertations on the Irish language, which survives in two divergent versions in manuscripts of the 14th-16thC. Beginning with an introduction concerning the origin of the Irish language as a consequence of the Tower of Babel, it follows with a representation of the Irish script (→ Ogam), as well as extensive discussions of grammatical and metrical problems. The collection bears witness to the efforts of the Irish monks to apply the concepts of Latin grammar to the theory and description of their mother tongue. The texts which served as their starting-point were the writings of the grammarians Donatus (4thC) and Priscianus (5th/6thC), and the *Etymologiae* of Isidore of Seville (c. 560–636).

Ed. and trans.: G. Calder, *The Scholar's Primer*, E. 1917; A. Ahlqvist, *The Early Ir. Linguist*, He. 1983.

Avalon. The customary English, French and German form of the Latin name Insula Avallonis, given by → Geoffrey of Monmouth in his *Historia Regum Britanniae* to the island to which → Arthur was taken after being wounded in the battle of → Camlan. In his poem → *Vita Merlini* Geoffrey describes this island as an Insula Pomorum (Island of Apple-Trees), on which nine women possessed of magical gifts take the king into their care. Geoffrey's descriptions conceivably reflect both classical concepts of the Islands of the Blessed and orally transmitted Celtic beliefs. The theory that there is some influence of Celtic beliefs is supported by a passage in the Middle Welsh poem → *Preiddeu Annwfn*, in which it is related that the king of → Annwfn possessed a cauldron, whose fire was kindled by the breath of nine virgins. Another parallel which has been adduced is a description of the Île de Sein off the West coast of Brittany by the Roman geographer → Pomponius Mela. This island is inhabited by nine priestesses who possess magical gifts. The Celtic derivation of the name A. is suggested by its Middle Welsh equivalent Ynys → Afallach. The Latin form Insula Avallonis was in all probability influenced by the name of the Burgundian town Avallon, which – like Afallach – is derived from a Celtic word for "apple" (Welsh afall).

Geoffrey of Monmouth, in common with most later authors, gives no details concerning the geographical location of the island of A. The identification of A. by various authors with the Benedictine abbey of Glastonbury did not occur until the late 12thC, when in 1191 monks claimed to have discovered Arthur's grave, with a Latin inscription to the effect that he was buried there. It is however probable that these finds – now lost again – were medieval forgeries.

Avienus (Rufus Festus A.). Roman poet of the 4thC AD who wrote a description of the coastlines stretching from Brittany to the Black Sea, entitled *Ora maritima*. Only the beginning has survived (c. 700 lines of verse), a description of the Spanish and Gaulish coast as far as Marseille. The evidence suggests that the poet was working from a very much older source, employing data which at least in part refer to conditions pertaining in the 6thC BC. The poem thus preserves some of the oldest geographical data concerning North-West Europe, together with the names of some Celtic peoples.

Aylesford, Kent. Site where in 1866 a Celtic cemetery was found, dating from the 1stC BC. Among the most important finds are a bucket made of wood and sheet bronze, 26.5cm in diameter, decorated with depictions of stylised animals and human heads. It had been used as an urn for one of the burials. In the 19thC the wooden parts of the bucket, which had not survived, were reconstructed, and the whole can now be seen in the British Museum.
   Lit.: J. Brailsford, *Early Celtic Masterpieces from Britain in the British Museum*, Lo. 1978.

Badb → Bodb.

Baddon (Welsh /'baðon/). Reputed site of an important victory inflicted by the British Celts upon the Germanic invaders from the East at the beginning of the 6thC. The oldest record of the battle is preserved by → Gildas, who however refers only briefly to "the siege of Mount B." (obsessio Badonici montis). In the → *Annales Cambriae* a note on the year 72 (= presumably 518 AD) names → Arthur as the leader of the Celtic warriors and reports that in the battle he bore the cross of Jesus Christ on his shoulders for three days and three nights. B. then appears in the → *Historia Brittonum* as the site of the last of Arthur's twelve victorious battles. In the Welsh tradition the battle of B. is otherwise unimportant, in sharp contrast to the battle of → Camlan.
   Lit.: L. Alcock, *Arthur's Britain*, Harm. 1971.

Bad Dürkheim. Town situated between Ludwigshafen and Kaiserslautern where in the course of railway works in 1864 a Celtic princely grave dating from the 5th/4thC BC was found. Among the grave goods were a golden torque, two golden arm-rings, a bronze Etruscan tripod and two bronze vessels. Fragments of cloth and the metal remains of a two-wheeled → cart were also found. The finds are now in the Historisches Museum of the Pfalz in Speyer and in the Hungarian National Museum in Budapest.
   Lit.: R. Echt, 'Technologische Untersuchungen an frühlatènezeitlichem Goldschmuck aus Bad D.' (*AKorrBl* 18) 1988, 183–195.

baile (Ir. /'bal'e/) or buile. (Ecstatic) vision, prophecy (in an ecstatic state) or madness. In one of the two → Lists of Sagas the word serves to classify stories in which such psychological states play a part. Aisling, "dream" and fís, "vision", are words sometimes used synonymously.

Baile Binnbérlach mac Buain (Ir. /'bal'e 'b'iN'be:rlax mak 'bu:in'/ "Baile of the Beautiful Voice, son of Buan"). Title of a story from the → Historical Cycle, thought to have originated in the 11thC and preserved in three 16thC manuscripts. The subject-matter is the unhappy love-affair between the titular hero Baile of the province of Ulster and the girl Ailinn of the province of Leinster. Both die without their relationship having been consummated. From their graves grow a yew and an apple-tree, which resemble in shape the heads of the two lovers. After seven years the trees are felled, and the poets of Ulster and Leinster write down their traditional tales on the wooden tablets made from the trees. When poets from both provinces meet in Tara (→ Temair) on the occasion of a feast at the court of the High King, both pieces of wood reunite and remain inseparable from that time forth. The story was retold by William Butler → Yeats in his poem *Baile and Ailinn*.
   Ed. and trans.: K. Meyer, 'Scél Baili Binnbérlaig' (RC 13) 1892, 220–228.

Baile in Scáil (Ir. /'bal'e in ska:l'/ "The Prophecy of the Phantom"). Title of a story from the → Historical Cycle. In its surviving form it probably originates from the 11thC; it is preserved in two manuscripts from the 15th and 16thCs. The central character is the legendary king → Conn Cétchathach, who, according to Irish tradition, lived in the 2ndC AD. The story begins with Conn walking along the rampart of the royal citadel of Tara (→ Temair). He treads upon the magical stone → Fál, which emits a loud outcry. Conn's poet (→ fili) explains to the king that the number of cries made by the stone stands for the number of kings who will in the future reign over Ireland as his heirs. All of a sudden a magical mist descends, and the king and his poet then find themselves reunited on a plain where grows a golden tree. A mysterious rider leads them into his house, where on a crystal throne, in the person of a young woman, the personification of "sovereignty" (flathius) over Ireland is seated. The rider reveals his identity: he is → Lug mac Ethnenn and predicts to the king the names of the future kings of Ireland; meanwhile the personification of "sovereignty" pours out beer in a golden pitcher (symbolising the transfer of power?). Conn's poet inscribes the names in → Ogam script on four staves of yew, whereupon the apparition suddenly disappears.
   Ed.: K. Meyer, 'B. in S.' (ZCP 3) 1901, 457–466, (ZCP 12) 1918, 232–238 and (ZCP 13) 1921, 371–382; R. Thurneysen, 'B. in S.' (ZCP 20) 1936, 213–227.
   Lit.: M. Dillon, *The Cycles of the Kings*, Lo. 1946.

Balar (Ir. /'balar/) or Balor. A leader of the → Fomoire in the story of the

Battle of Mag Tuired (→ *Cath Maige Tuired*). His most-feared weapon is his eye, the sight of which causes the death of any attacker. In the course of the battle of Mag Tuired B. slays Nuadu Argatlám, king of the → Tuatha Dé Danann. In the end, however, his own grandson → Lug mac Ethnenn, fighting on the side of the Tuatha Dé Danann, succeeds in striking out the perilous eye with a stone from his sling and decapitating B. Oral versions of the tale have been collected in various parts of Ireland from the early 19thC onwards, but in this later tradition the link with the battle between the Tuatha Dé Danann and the Fomoire has been lost.

Ballymote → Book of Ballymote.

Banba (Ir. /'banva/. In the "Book of the Invasions of Ireland" (→ *Lebor Gabála Érenn*), a queen of the → Tuatha Dé Danann. In the course of the conquest of Ireland by the sons of Míl she and her two sisters → Fótla and → Ériu obtain from the poet → Amairgin Glúngel the promise that the island will at some point bear their names. Thus in poetic language the name B. often represents Ireland. In the battle of → Tailtiu B. falls in the fight against the sons of Míl.

Bansenchas (Ir. /'banhenxas/). A medieval Irish list of historically significant women. It begins with biblical female characters and continues through heroines of Graeco-Roman mythology to the celebrated women of Ireland. The anonymous author employed as his sources for this last section the "Book of the Invasions of Ireland" (→ *Lebor Gabála Érenn*), the stories of the → Historical Cycle, → Mythological Cycle, → Ulster Cycle and various annals.
    Ed. and trans.: M. Dobbs, 'The B.' (RC 47) 1930, 283–339, (RC 48) 1931, 163–234 and (RC 49) 1932, 437–489.

banshee (Anglo-Ir. /bæn'ʃiː/). In Irish folk belief a mysterious woman who announces the imminent death of a member of the family by giving voice to loud, plaintive cries in the proximity of the family seat. These cries or wails are in most instances the only intimation of her presence. In those cases where a member of the family claims to have seen the b., she is generally described as an old woman with long white hair. B. is the anglicised form of the modern Irish term bean sí. The older form ben síde serves in medieval Irish literature to denote fairies thought to reside in the natural and artificially created (grave-)mounds of the country. Numerous medieval texts attest the belief that such fairies are particularly concerned to keep watch over the king (→ rí) of a community, and lament over his death in common with his subjects. It is thought that the concept of a fairy as a harbinger of death passed from noble families to the Irish population as a whole as a consequence of the English conquest of Ireland.
    Lit.: P. Lysaght, *The B.*, Du. 1986; É. Sorlin, *Les fées du destin dans les pays celtiques*, He. 1991 (FFC 248).

bard. Celtic word for poet. Originally it signified "he who gives voice", referring to the oral performance of poetry. In Ancient Greek texts the term occurs in its Old Celtic form bardos (Latinised: bardus). The forms bard and bardd are found in Ireland and Wales. In Ireland a distinction was made between the b. and the → fili on the basis of the former's lower social status and lack of full training in the art of poetry.

The Bard is the title of a poem published in 1757 by Thomas Gray (1716–1771). The word entered popular currency in modern times largely because of the influence of the "Works of Ossian", written by James → Macpherson, and came to be employed erroneously to refer also to Germanic poets and singers (by the German authors Klopstock and Kleist, among others).

Barrex. Name of a Celtic god. His cult is attested by a single votive inscription from Carlisle (*RIB* 947), in which he is identified according to the → interpretatio romana with → Mars.

Basse-Yutz. Site north of Metz where in 1927 during building works two bronze vessels of Etruscan origin were found, together with a pair of richly engraved Celtic bronze beaked jugs, decorated with coral and enamel. They date back to the 5th-4thCs BC and may now be seen in the British Museum.
  Lit.: J. V. S. Megaw & R. Megaw, *The Basse-Yutz find*, Lo. 1990.

Battersea, S.W. London. In 1857 the bronze mounting, c. 80 cm in length, of a Celtic shield, made of either leather or wood, was found there. It is thought to date back to the 1stC AD or earlier and is now in the British Museum.
  Lit.: I. M. Stead, *The B. Shield*, Lo. 1985.

bear. Bone finds on archaeological sites make it clear that the bear was from the beginning a beast hunted by the Celts. The role the bear played in Celtic → religion is however obscure because of the lack of relevant evidence in ancient → ethnography. The bear no doubt epitomised physical strength, which is why the Irish word for bear frequently occurs as a metaphor for "warrior". The ancient Celtic words for bear were *artos (= Ir. art, Welsh arth) and *matus (= Ir. math). From these derive the names of the gods → Andarta, → Artaius, → Artio and → Matunus. *artos and *matus also occur frequently in proper names such as Matugenus (= Ir. Mathgen), "descendant of a bear".

Beare, the Old Woman of → Caillech Bérri.

Bé Chuma (Ir. /b'e: 'xuma/). In the traditions concerning the Irish king → Conn Cétchathach the name of a woman of the → Tuatha Dé Danann. Because she commits adultery with a son of the sea-god → Manannán mac Lir she is spurned by her family. In Ireland she becomes the beloved of Conn, who at her desire sends his son Art into exile. This unjust behaviour on the king's part brings misfortune upon the land, with the result that Conn ultimately parts from his beloved.

Bedivere. English form of the Welsh name → Bedwyr.

Bedwyr fab Bedrawg (Welsh /'bedwir va:b 'bedraug/). A member of → Arthur's retinue in the poem → *Pa ŵr yw'r Porthor?* In the story → *Culhwch ac Olwen* it is recorded that he never shied away from any adventure embarked upon by his friend → Cei fab Cynyr. No-one in Britain could equal him in beauty save Arthur and Drych Eil Cibddar. Even if he only had the use of one hand, three warriors on the same battlefield could not inflict a wound upon their antagonist quicker than he. As an important member of Arthur's retinue B. also occurs in → Geoffrey of Monmouth. According to Geoffrey, B. was enfeoffed with Normandy by Arthur, and afterwards fell in battle, together with Cei, in the fight against the troops of the Roman emperor. In the verse romances of → Chrétien de Troyes and his immediate successors, B. for the most part pales into insignificance compared with other figures in the Arthurian cycle of legends. In the Middle English poem *Le Morte Arthur* (c. 1400) B. appears for the first time as the last companion of the dying King Arthur. This scene became well-known through its treatment by Sir Thomas → Malory in his work *Le Morte Darthur*: B. carries out Arthur's last request by throwing his sword into the sea in order that it shall fall into no-one else's hands. Then he lays the dying king in a boat which is to take him to → Avalon. Several modern versions of the legend have rendered the relationship between B. and Arthur problematic, making B. at the same time the loyal follower of the king and the lover of Queen → Gwenhwyfar. B. has thus taken on the role played by → Lancelot in Chrétien de Troyes.

beer → food and drink.

Bé Find (Ir. /b'e: v'ind/). In the story → *Táin Bó Froích* the name of the mother of the titular hero Froech. She is of the people of the → Tuatha Dé Danann and is a sister of → Boand.

Belatucadrus. Celtic god whose name appears in various spellings in some 25 inscriptions from the North of England. In five dedications (*RIB* 918, 948, 970, 1784 and 2044) he is identified with → Mars.

Belenus (alternative form: Belinus). Celtic god whose name is thought to derive from a Celtic word meaning "to shine, give light".
 The cult of B. is attested primarily in Northern Italy, the Eastern Alps and Southern Gaul by inscriptions and literary evidence. As early as Tertullian, B.

is referred to as a god of the Roman province of Noricum in the Eastern Alps (Apologeticum 24 and Ad Nationes 2,8). Thus far only one dedication to B. (CIL III 4774) has been found from this area. The greatest number of inscriptions have been found in or near the Roman site of Aquileia in Northern Italy. In some of these inscriptions B. is equated with → Apollo according to the → interpretatio romana. This identification is confirmed by the testimony of the historian Herodianos (Ab Excessu Divi Marci 8,3,8). He records that in 238 AD, when Aquileia was besieged by the emperor Maximinus, oracles were in circulation which promised that the town would be protected by its tutelary god Belenus / Apollo. Later, soldiers of Maximinus are said to have declared that they saw in the sky over the city an image of the god intervening in the battle. This event is also recorded in the history of the Roman emperors known as the Historia Augusta (Maximini duo 22,I). The cult of B. in Northern Italy is further attested by a total of six dedications from the ancient sites of Iulium Carnicum (CIL V 1829), Concordia (CIL V 1866) and Altinum (CIL V 2143–2146). Two further votive inscriptions to B. have been found in Rome (CIL VI 2800) and Rimini (CIL XI 353).

The late classical poet Ausonius refers to a shrine dedicated to B. in Burdigala (Bordeaux) in Gaul (Commemoratio Professorum Burdigalensium 4,7ff. and 10,22ff.), but as no inscriptions relating to this have been found it is thought that in this case the name B. is merely a scholarly paraphrase of Apollo. Several votive inscriptions to B. have however been found in the South of France. His name appears written in Greek letters on a gem (CIL XII 5693,12) and on a Latin stone inscription (CIL XII 5958). A Gaulish inscription to B., written in Greek letters, has been found in Saint-Chamas (RIG I G–28). The god's name is also thought to be present in two partially destroyed inscriptions from Marseille (RIG I *G–24) and Saint-Rémy-de-Provence (RIG I G–63).

Lit.: J. de Vries, Keltische Religion, St. 1961; P.-M. Duval, Les Dieux de la Gaule, P. 1976; J.-J. Hatt, Mythes et dieux de la Gaule I, P. 1989.

Belgians (Lat. Belgae). In classical → ethnography the partly Celtic, partly Germanic peoples in the region between the Marne, the Seine, the Rhine and the North Sea coast. For → Caesar (Bell. Gall. 2,3–4) the term embraces the tribes of the → Ambiani, → Atrebates, → Atuatuci, → Bellovaci, Caerosi, Caemani, Caleti, Condrusi, → Eburones, Menapii, Morini, Nervii, → Remi, → Suessiones, Veliocasses and Viromandui. After the B. were conquered by Caesar the area in which they had settled became, under the emperor Augustus, the Roman province of Gallia Belgica. The seat of the governor was Durocortorum, now Rheims.

Beli Mawr fab Mynogan (Welsh /'beli maur vaːb məˈnogan/). In Welsh genealogies the mythical ancestor of several important noble dynasties. The stories → Breuddwyd Macsen and → Cyfranc Lludd a Llefelys refer to him as king of Britain and father of the kings Lludd, Llefelys and Caswallawn. B. appears in the → *Historia Brittonum* as an enemy of → Caesar, his name latinised as Bellinus filius Minocanni.

Belisama. Celtic goddess, whose name means "the most shining, bright one", thought to derive from the same root as the name of the god → Belenus. The cult of B. is attested by a Gaulish inscription, written in Greek letters, from Vaison-la-Romaine, c. 15 miles north-east of Orange (RIG I G–153). This records a declaration on the part of the Gaul Segomaros from the city of Nîmes that he has dedicated a shrine (→ nemeton) to B.

A Latin inscription from Saint-Lizier in the Dép. of Ariège (CIL XIII 8) identifies B. according to the → interpretatio romana with → Minerva. The geographer Ptolemy (2, 3,2) records the name in the form Belísama eíschysis as denoting the mouth of an English river. In France the name of the goddess survives in the place-names Belesmes, Beleymas, Bellême, Blesmes and Blismes.

Lit.: Ch.-J. Guyonvarc'h, 'Le théonyme gaulois B. "la très brillante" ' (*Ogam* 14) 1962, 161–173.

Bellovaci. The name given in → Caesar (Bell. Gall. 2,4 et passim) to the most populous and influential tribe of the → Belgians. The name survives in that of the city Beauvais, which the Romans called Caesaromagus.

Beltaine (Ir. /'b'eltan'e/). In the Irish calendar the name for the beginning of summer (May 1st). The etymology of the word is obscure. According to Bishop Cormac's Glossary (→ *Sanas Chormaic*) animals were driven through the midst of two fires in the presence of → druids, to avert disease.

Lit.: K. Danaher, *The Year in Ireland*, Du. 1972.

Bendigeidfran → Brân Fendigeid.

Bergin, Osborn (1873–1950). Celticist, born in Cork. From 1897 he lectured in Celtic philology in Queen's College in the city of his birth. After periods of study in Berlin and Freiburg he taught Old and Middle Irish at University College Dublin from 1909 to 1940. He was then elected director of the newly founded → School of Celtic Studies in Dublin. A prominent figure in the development of Irish → Celtic Studies, he published linguistic aids for the study of Irish as well as philological studies and editions of medieval Irish texts.

Bergusia. Celtic goddess, whose name is recorded in a votive inscription from → Alesia (CIL XIII 11247). She is the companion of the god → Ucuetis.

Berne scholia. The name given to a collection of elucidatory glosses to the work of the Roman poet → Lucan. Originating partly in the 4thC AD, partly in the 8th-9thCs, they are preserved in a single manuscript now in the Burgerbibliothek in Berne. One passage is particularly significant for the history of religions: Lucan speaks of human sacrifices to the Gaulish gods → Teutates, → Esus and → Taranis (Pharsalia I, 444–446). Drawing upon a number of divergent sources, the anonymous author of the scholia identifies Teutates with either → Mercury or → Mars, Esus with either Mars or Mercury, and Taranis with → Dis Pater or → Jupiter. He also identifies three distinct kinds of human sacrifice: sacrifices to Teutates are made by the victim being immersed head-first in a full barrel until he drowns; the sacrificial victims of Esus are hung from a tree "until the limbs separate themselves from the body" (the exact significance of the wording is unclear); the victims sacrificed to Taranis are burned in a wooden tub. Some scholars think that such a sacrifice to Teutates is depicted on the → Gundestrup Cauldron. The sacrifices to Esus have been compared with the Germanic self-sacrifice of Odin, who was hung and wounded by a spear. It is questionable whether the equation of Gaulish and Roman gods derives from an ancient and reliable source. Inscriptions support only the identifications of Teutates with Mars and Taranis with Jupiter.

Lit.: F. Le Roux, 'Lucain et les Scholies Bernoises' (*Ogam* 7) 1955, 33–58; P.-M. Duval, 'Teutates – Esus – Taranis' (*EC* 8) 1958–59, 41–58 (= id., *Travaux sur la Gaule*, R. 1989, I 275–287); F. Graf, 'Anmerkungen zum Götterkatalog der "Commenta Bernensia" zu Lucan I, 445' (*ASchw* 14) 1991, 136–143.

Best, Richard Irvine (1872–1959), Celticist and palaeographer, born in Derry. From 1904 to 1940 librarian at and later director of the Irish National Library in Dublin; from 1940 to 1947 Professor in the → School of Celtic Studies in Dublin. He published the standard bibliographies for Irish philology, as well as numerous palaeographical studies and editions of Irish texts. His editions of the "Book of the Dun Cow" (→ Lebor na hUidre; 1929 in collaboration with Osborn → Bergin) and the "Book of Leinster" (→ Lebor Laignech; 1954–1983 in collaboration with Osborn Bergin and M. A. O'Brien) remain the standard texts.

Bibracte. Name of a fortified Celtic settlement c. 12 miles west of Autun in the Dép. of Saône-et-Loire. The site covered a surface of over 130 hectares and extended over four hills, including the 2500 ft high Mont Beuvray. In this vicinity → Caesar defeated the Celtic tribe of the → Helvetii (Bell. Gall. 1,23ff.). Towards the end of the 1stC AD the emperor Augustus had the population resettled in the new foundation Augustodunum, now Autun. The subject of archaeological investigation since 1865, B. is one of the best researched Celtic → oppida. Three votive inscriptions (CIL XIII 2651–2653) attest the cult of a goddess of the same name.

Lit.: D. Bertin & J.-P. Guillaumont, B.: *Une ville gauloise sur le Mont Beuvray*, P. 1987; O. Büschenschütz, 'Neue Ausgrabungen im Oppidum B.' (*Germania* 67) 1989, 541–550; M. Lejeune, 'Les premiers pas de la déesse B.' (*Journal des savants*) 1990, 69–96; M. Almagro-Gorbea et al., 'Les fouilles de Mont Beuvray: Rapport biennal 1988–1989' (*RAE* 42) 1991, 271–298; C. Goudineau & C. Peyre, B. *et les Eduens*, P. 1993.

Binchy, Daniel Anthony (1899–1989), Celticist and legal historian, born in Charleville (Southern Ireland). He began by studying law, politology and history in Dublin, then after medieval and Celtic studies in Munich, Paris and Bonn devoted himself entirely to the study of early Irish law. His life's work appeared in 1978: the 6-volume edition of Irish law texts, *Corpus Iuris Hibernici*, published by the → School of Celtic Studies.

birds → animals.

Bith (Ir. /b'iθ'/). The name of a son of Noah in the "Book of the Invasions of Ireland" (→ *Lebor Gabála Érenn*). He is one of the colonists who under the leadership of his daughter → Cesair are said to have taken possession of Ireland forty days before the Flood.

Bituriges. In classical → ethnography a Celtic tribe, whose name literally approximates to "kings of the world", although it is unclear what concept attached to this designation. According to the Roman historian Livy (Ab urbe condita 5,34) the B. were in the time of the king Tarquinius Priscus (6thC BC) the most powerful Celtic tribe in Gaul. On the initiative of their king → Ambigatus the Celts are thought to have migrated at this time to northern Italy. Generally classical authors distinguish between two sub-tribes of the B.: the Vivisci settled at the mouth of the Garumna (Garonne) in the area around the city of Burdigala (Bordeaux), whilst the Cubi inhabited the region surrounding the city of Bourges, called after the B.; its ancient name was Avaricum.

Black Forest → Abnoba.

Blathmac mac Con Brettan (Ir. /'blaθvak mak kon 'b'r'etan/). Religious poet of the 8thC, by whom two poems about the life of Christ have survived, in a manuscript of the 17thC. B. seeks to portray the events of the Passion in terms of the ideas and thought of the Irish society in which he lived. These poems are therefore of great value for our understanding of Irish culture in the early Middle Ages.
Ed. and trans.: J. Carney, *The Poems of B.*, Du. 1964 (ITS 47).
Lit.: B. Lambkin, 'The Structure of the B. Poems' (*StC* 20/21) 1985/86, 67–77.

Bláthnat (Ir. /'blaːθnad/). In the stories of the → Ulster Cycle the wife of the king → Cú Roí. Out of love for → Cú Chulainn she betrays her husband to his enemies and in consequence is killed by the poet → Ferchertne.

Blodeuwedd (Welsh /bloˈdeiweð/). In the story → *Math fab Mathonwy* wife of → Lleu Llaw Gyffes. She is created out of blossoms (Welsh blodeu).

Boadicea → Boudicca.

Bóand (Ir. /'boand/), or (later forms) Bóann, Bóinn. The name of the River Boyne. It appears as early as the 2ndC AD in the geographer Ptolemy in the original form Bouinda, meaning, it is thought, "white cow".

In the stories of the → Mythological Cycle B. appears as the goddess who gives the River Boyne its name. She is the spouse of → Nechtan or → Elcmar and the beloved of the → Dagda. The area around the pre-Celtic grave-mound of Newgrange in the Boyne valley bears the name → Brug na Bóinne after her.

boar → pig.

Board of Celtic Studies. Institution founded in 1919 for the furthering of Celtic studies in Wales. It embraces the fields of language and literature, history and law, art and archaeology, and, since 1969, social sciences. Its current publications include the *Bulletin of the Board of Celtic Studies* (1921–1994; since 1995 *Studia Celtica: The Bulletin of the Board of Celtic Studies*), and the periodicals *Llên Cymru* (1950ff.), *The Welsh History Review* (1960ff.) and *Studia Celtica* (1966ff.). Since 1950 the great project of the Welsh dictionary *Geiriadur Prifysgol Cymru. A Dictionary of the Welsh Language* has been appearing in fascicle form.

Bodb (1) (Ir. /boðv/). In the stories of the → Mythological Cycle the name of a son of the Dagda and king of the → Tuatha Dé Danann. His home is the fairy hill Síd ar Femin in the province of Munster. In the story → *Cath Finntrága* B. supports the band of warriors of Finn mac Cumaill in their fight against the army of the "King of the World" (rí an domhain).

Bodb (2) (Ir. /boðv/) or (later) Badb. Name of a female battle demon. She usually appears in the form of a crow, inciting warriors to do battle against one another and rejoicing over the corpses of the fallen.
Lit.: F. Le Roux & Ch.-J. Guyonvarc'h, *Mórrígan – B. – Macha: La Souveraineté guerrière de l'Irlande*, Rennes 1983.

Bodiocasses (Lat., also Baiocasses, Gk. Uadikasioi). In classical → ethnography a Celtic tribe in the region of the city of Bayeux, which takes its name from the tribe. The Celticist → Thurneysen conjectures that the name B. is a Gaulish equivalent of the Middle Irish word buidechas "blond-haired". The variants of the name listed above make this questionable.

Boii. In classical → ethnography the name of a Celtic tribe originally resident in Gaul. In the 4thC BC the B. migrated to northern Italy and settled on the Po plain. Their chief town was Bononia (Bologna), which was previously called Felsina. Conquered by the Romans in 193 BC, the B. went back over the Alps, and later settled in Bohemia, to which they gave their name (Lat. Boiohaemum). From there part of the tribe migrated westward about the middle of the 1stC BC and allied themselves with the tribe of the → Helvetii. Others migrated south-east to settle in the region of the Little Hungarian Plain.

Bolvinnus. Name of a Celtic god whose cult is attested by two votive inscriptions from Bouhy in the Dép. of Nièvre (CIL XIII 2899 and 2900), in which he is identified with → Mars on the basis of the → interpretatio romana.

Book of Armagh (Lat. Liber Ardmachanus). An Irish manuscript dating from 807, named after its place of origin. Its contents include writings concerning Saint → Patrick and the complete text of the New Testament, together with the biography of St. Martin of Tours by Sulpicius Severus. Towards the end of the 17thC the manuscript entered private hands for a time, but it is now in Trinity College, Dublin.
  Ed.: J. Gwynn, *Liber Ardmachanus: The Book of A.*, Du. 1913 (facs.)

Book of Ballymote. An Irish manuscript of miscellaneous content, compiled c. 1400 in Ballymote, near Sligo in the North-West of Ireland. It contains treatises on Irish poetry which are of great interest, as well as numerous texts of legendary, historical, genealogical and juristic nature. Since 1785 the manuscript has been in the library of the Royal Irish Academy in Dublin.
  Ed.: R. Atkinson, *The Book of Ballymote*, Du. 1887 (facs.).

Book of Deer. A gospel book, thought to have been produced in Ireland in the 9thC. It derives its name from the monastery of Deer in north-east Scotland, where it was at one time preserved. The Book of Deer is best known because of some notes in Gaelic entered in the manuscript by various scribes in the 12thC. These relate to the affairs of the monastery and are of considerable historical and cultural interest on this account alone, but they also constitute the earliest records of the Gaelic language in Scotland. Since 1715 the B. of D. has been in the Cambridge University Library.
  Lit.: K. H. Jackson, *The Gaelic Notes in the Book of Deer*, C. 1972.

Book of Durrow (Lat. Codex Durmachensis). A richly ornamented and illustrated gospel book dating from the second half of the 7thC. For a long time it was thought to originate from the Irish monastery of Durrow, founded in 553 by Saint Columba (→ Colum Cille). Some scholars however hold that it may have originated in the North of England or on the island of Iona, off the West coast of Scotland. After the dissolution of the monastery of Durrow the manuscript was for a time in private hands, but it is now in Trinity College, Dublin.

   Lit.: G. Henderson, *From Durrow to Kells: the Insular Gospel-Books 650–800*, Lo. 1987.

Book of Kells (Lat. Codex Cenannensis). A richly ornamented and illustrated gospel book dating from c. 800. The earliest reference to the manuscript dates from the year 1007, when it was stolen from the church of Kells (c. 40 miles north-west of Dublin), but found soon after in a hiding-place. The provenance of the manuscript is unknown: apart from Kells the North of England and the island of Iona off the West coast of Scotland have been considered. The latter provenance has in its favour the fact that the majority of the monks of Iona abandoned the monastery after a Viking attack in 806 and sought refuge in Kells. After the dissolution of the monastery in the 12thC the manuscript still remained in the parish church of Kells; since 1661 it has formed the most precious possession of the library of Trinity College, Dublin.

   Lit.: F. Henry, *The Book of Kells*, Lo. 1974; G. Henderson, *From Durrow to Kells: the Insular Gospel-Books 650–800*, Lo. 1987; F. O'Mahoney (ed.), *The Book of Kells. Proceedings of a conference at Trinity College Dublin 6–9 September 1992*, Du. 1994.

Book of the Dean of Lismore. A manuscript collection of ballads and bardic poems in Scottish Gaelic and Irish. It was compiled between 1512 and 1526 by the Scottish cleric James Macgregor and his brother Duncan, and preserves the oldest works of Scottish Gaelic literature known to us.

   Lit.: E. C. Quiggin, *Poems from the Book of the Dean of L.*, C. 1937; W. J. Watson, *Scottish Verse from the Book of the Dean of L.*, E. 1937; N. Ross, *Heroic Poetry from the Book of the Dean of L.*, E. 1939.

Bopp, Franz (1791–1867). Regarded as one of the founders of comparative philology. In 1838 his study *Über die celtischen Sprachen vom Gesichtspunkte der vergleichenden Sprachforschung* (Concerning the Celtic languages, from the point of view of comparative philology) succeeded in proving that the Celtic → languages formed a branch of the Indo-European linguistic family. Even before Bopp, James Cowles Prichard and Adolphe Pictet had opined this view.

   Lit.: → Celtic Studies.

Bórama (Ir. /'boːrava/). The name given by medieval sources to a tribute said to have been paid by the province of Leinster over many generations to various kings of the dynasty of the Uí Néill. A story written partly in prose, partly in verse, also called B., describes the payment of these tributes. In its surviving form it is thought to have originated in the 10th/11thC and is preserved in two versions of varying length in the "Book of Leinster" (→ Lebor Laignech) and in the manuscript known as the "Book of Lecan". According to this story the king → Tuathal Techtmar imposed the B. as weregild (éraic) in the 1stC AD, because the king of Leinster had brought about the death of his two daughters. The costly nature of the tribute led to innumerable battles, in which sometimes the kings of Leinster, sometimes the kings of the Uí Néill residing in Tara (→ Temair) proved victorious. It was not until the 7thC that the holy Mo Ling is said to have succeeded by cunning in effecting the abolition of the tribute, at the behest of the king of Leinster.

Ed. and trans.: W. Stokes, 'The B.' (RC 13) 1892, 32–124; S. H. O'Grady, *Silva Gadelica*, Lo. 1892.

Lit.: M. Dillon, *The Cycles of the Kings*, Lo. 1946.

Borvo or Bormo. Celtic god, whose name probably derives from a Celtic word meaning "to boil" and may therefore be linked with the cult of the god at sites of hot springs; it survives in the names of the bathing resorts Bourbonne-les-Bains in the Dép. of Haute-Marne and Bourbon-Lancy in the Dép. of Saône-et-Loire. Votive inscriptions to B. have been found in both these towns (CIL XIII 2805–2808 and 5911–5920), as well as in Entrains in the Dép. of Nièvre (CIL XIII 2901) and Aix-les-Bains in Savoyen (CIL XII 2443 and 2444). One of the inscriptions from Bourbon-Lancy (CIL XIII 5911) identifies B. with → Apollo on the basis of the → interpretatio romana. The goddess → Damona appears as the companion of the god in several dedications. Inscriptions in Gaul also attest divinities called Bormanus (CIL XII 494 and 1561) and Bormana (CIL XII 1561 and CIL XIII 2452). In Portugal two dedications to a god called Bormanicus (CIL II 2402 and 2403) have been discovered.

Lit.: H. Troisgros, B. et Damona, Bourbonne-les-Bains 1975; P.-M. Duval, *Les Dieux de la Gaule*, P. 1976; J.-J. Hatt, *Mythes et dieux de la Gaule I*, P. 1989.

Botorrita. Town c. 12 miles south of Saragossa, where during projected building works in the spring of 1970 an archaeological exploration of the ancient site of Contrebia Belaisca (c. 1/2m north of B.) was commenced. Among other finds made there was a bronze tablet, 40.5cm x 10cm, inscribed in a variant of Iberian script. Further investigation revealed that the inscription is written in Celtiberian and dates from towards the end of the 2nd or beginning of the 1stC BC. Despite several attempts to decipher it, the precise meaning of the text remains the subject of dispute. The first part may contain instructions relating to the ritual use of a sacred area; the second part perhaps names the persons in whose name these decrees were issued. The inscription is now in the Archaeological Museum in Saragossa.

Lit.: J.F. Eska, *Towards an Interpretation of the Hispano-Celtic Inscription of B.*, I. 1989; F. Villar Liébana, 'La linea inicial del bronze de B.', in: F. Villar (ed.), *Studia indogermanica et palaeohispanica in honorem A. Tovar et L. Michelena*, Sal. 1990, 375–392; W. Meid, *Die erste Botorrita-Inschrift*, I. 1993; P.-Y. Lambert, 'Sur la bronze celtibère de Botorrita', in: R. Bielmeier et al. (eds.), *Indogermanica et Caucasica. FS Karl Horst Schmidt*, B. 1994, 363–374.

Boudicca. In → Tacitus (Ann. 14,31–37 and Agricola 15f.) and Cassius Dio (Hist. Rom. 42) the wife of a British prince of the tribe of the → Iceni. The attacks made upon her by the Roman occupying power led to a revolt of several British tribes in 60 AD. After conquering the Roman cities of Camulodunum (Colchester), Verulamium (St. Albans) and Londinium (London), the Britons were resoundingly defeated by the Roman governor Suetonius Paulinus. Soon after this B. committed suicide by taking poison (according to Tacitus' account) or died of a disease (Cassius Dio).

An altar dedicated to a goddess named B. was found in 1921 in Bordeaux. The inscription (*ILTG* 141) reveals that it was donated by a merchant from Britain. Geological investigation of the stone has proven that the altar came from the North of England. Perhaps it served as ballast in a ship sailing to Bordeaux. The link between the historical B. and the goddess of the same name is unclear. Possibly the princess was named after the goddess, or perhaps the princess was venerated as a goddess after her death.

The historical B. is the chief personage in two plays by John Fletcher (1579–1625) and Richard Glover (1712–1785). William Cowper (1731–1800) and Alfred Lord Tennyson (1809–1892) composed ballads about her. Thomas Thornycroft (1815–1885) carved a bronze statue of the princess in her chariot, which in 1902 was erected near Westminster Bridge on the south bank of the Thames.

Lit.: G. Webster, *B.*, Lo. 1978.

Bouray. Place c. 22 miles south of Paris where in 1845 the bronze plate statue of a Celtic god, 42cm high, was found in the river Juine. The Celtic origin of the craftsmanship is confirmed by the way in which the god is depicted seated cross-legged (termed the → "Buddha-position"), as well as by the legs which end in stag's hooves and the close-fitting necklet (→ torc). On the other hand the realistic style clearly suggests Roman influence. The statue is thought to date from towards the end of the 1stC BC, perhaps somewhat later, and is now in the Musée des Antiquités Nationales in Saint-Germain-en-Laye.

Lit.: R. Lantier, 'Le dieu celtique de B.' (*Monuments et Mémoires de la Fondation Eugène Piot* 34) 1934, 35–58.

Braciaca. Name of a Celtic god whose cult is attested by a single votive inscription in Derbyshire (*RIB* 278), in which he is identified with → Mars according to the → interpretatio romana.

Brân Fendigeid (Welsh /braːn venˈdigeid/) or Bendigeidfran. King of Britain in the story → *Branwen ferch Lŷr*. His father is Llŷr, his brother and sister Manawydan and Branwen, his mother Penarddun, who in *Branwen* is referred to as the daughter of the king Beli Mawr. This is contradicted by the fact that in the story → *Manawydan fab Llŷr* Beli's son Caswallawn appears not as the uncle, but as the cousin of the three brethren B., Branwen and Manawydan. It is therefore assumed that Penarddun was originally regarded as the sister of Beli. B. himself has clear mythical characteristics in the story: because of his enormous physical proportions he cannot find a house or ship big enough for him, and in the campaign against the Irish king Matholwch he wades through the Irish sea alongside the fleet. In the battle he is wounded in the foot by a poisoned spear. Thereupon he orders the surviving warriors of his army to chop off his head and bury it in his capital, London, with the head turned towards the mainland, to protect the country. Many scholars have thought that the legend of the → Grail preserves some motifs from the B. tradition. The extent of this influence is however contentious.

Bran mac Febail (Ir. /bran mak ˈfʲevilʲ/ "Bran, son of Febal"). Titular hero of the story → *Immram Brain.*

Brannovices. In classical → ethnography a sub-tribe of the tribal grouping of the → Aulerci in the region between the Loire and the Seine. Literally the name would appear to mean "raven-fighters".

Branwen ferch Lŷr (Welsh /ˈbranwen verx liːr/ "Branwen, the daughter of Llŷr"). Title of the second of the "Four Branches of the Mabinogi" (→ Pedeir Ceinc y Mabinogi). The story begins with the wooing of Branwen, sister of the British king Brân Fendigeid, by Matholwch, king of Ireland. After Brân has already given his assent to the marriage, his half-brother Efnisyen jeopardises the happy accord between the Irish and the Britons by wilfully mutilating the horses of Matholwch. The Irish king is appeased at the last minute by the gift of new horses and a magic cauldron, which has the power of bringing the slain back to life. Branwen gives birth to one son, but at the instigation of Matholwch's Irish subjects she is obliged to carry out the most menial of tasks. When Brân finds out about this, he prepares a campaign against Matholwch. A last attempt at reconciliation is foiled by Efnisyen and in the battle that follows all the British warriors are killed, with seven exceptions. Branwen dies of a broken heart on her return to Wales. – The Welsh author Saunders Lewis (1893–1985) retells the story in his play *Branwen* (1975).

    Ed.: I. Williams, *Pedeir Keinc y Mabinogi*, Car. 1930; D. S. Thomson, *B. uerch Lyr*, Du. 1961 (MMWS 2).

Trans.: G. Jones & T. Jones, *The Mabinogion*, rev. ed. Lo. 1974; J. Gantz, *The Mabinogion*, Harm. 1976.
Lit.: P. MacCana, B. *Daughter of Llŷr*, Car. 1958; P. K. Ford, 'B.: A Study of the Celtic Affinities' (*StC* 22/23) 1987/88, 29–41.

Brehon Laws. Anglicised form of the Irish word brithemain "judges", referring to traditional Irish law as opposed to Anglo-Saxon legislation (cf. → brithem).

Breisach. Scattered finds have shown that the Münsterberg, a hill in Breisach in Baden-Württemberg (S.W. Germany) was already settled towards the end of the Neolithic Age. Excavations carried out in 1966–1975 supplied evidence that the hill was the site of an early Celtic → princely seat in the transition from the Hallstatt to the La Tène period, around the middle of the first millennium BC. In that period a hollow perhaps 50 ft. deep on the peak of the mountain was filled and additional fortifications added. Several gravemounds in the immediate vicinity of B. which were excavated in the 19thC are thought to be associated with this site.
Lit.: K. Bittel et al. (eds.), *Die Kelten in Baden-Württemberg*, St. 1981.

Brendan (Lat. Brendanus, Ir. Brénaind). 6thC Irish saint and founder of monasteries. The legend of his miraculous sea-voyage (→ immram) to the Land of Promise is thought to have originated in the 9thC, fusing narrative Celtic material with Christian concepts. The Latin version *Navigatio Sancti Brendani* was known throughout medieval Europe and from the 12thC onwards was translated into many vernacular tongues.
Lit.: K. A. Zaenker, *Sankt Brandans Meerfahrt. Ein lateinischer Text und seine drei deutschen Übertragungen aus dem 15. Jh.*, St. 1987; P. MacCana, 'The Voyage of St Brendan: Literary and historical origins', in: J. de Courcy Ireland & D. C. Sheehy (eds.), *Atlantic Visions*, Dún Laoghaire 1989, 3–16; C. Strijbosch, *De bronnen van De reis van Sint Brandaan*, Hilversum 1995.

brenin. Welsh word for "king". The term rhi (=Ir. → rí), identical in meaning, only occurs in the earliest linguistic survivals or as an element in compounds. Comparative philology traces b. back to the hypothetical form *brigantīnos. The word originally meant, it is thought, "spouse of the goddess Briganti". This assumption is supported by the concept of the → sacred marriage between the king and the goddess of that king's race, which occurs primarily in Irish sources. The worship of a goddess → Brigantia is also attested by inscriptions from the North of England and southern Scotland.
Lit.: D. A. Binchy, *Celtic and Anglo-Saxon Kingship*, O. 1970; T. M. Charles-Edwards, 'Native Political Organization in Roman Britain and the Origin of MW brenin', in: M. Mayrhofer et al. (eds.), *Anitquitates Indogermanicae: Gedenkschrift für H. Güntert*, I. 1974, 35–45.

Brennos. In Greek historiography leader of a Celtic army which in 279 BC invaded and plundered Macedonia and Thessaly. Wounded in an abortive attack of the Celts upon Delphi, he is said to have committed suicide during the retreat. In the Roman sources B. (Lat. Brennus) is the name of a Celtic prince whose army occupied Rome c. 387 BC, besieging the last defenders of the city on the Capitol. It is reported that the besieged Romans bought their liberty with a huge ransom. B. is said to have used faulty scales in weighing the sum. When the Romans complained B. threw his sword into the balance, saying "Vae victis" (Woe to the conquered). – Sebastiano Ricci (1659–1734) depicted the scene in an oil painting (Musée Fesch, Ajaccio). Friedrich August von Grevenitz (1730–1809) composed a poem on the subject entitled *Brennos*.

Bres (Ir. /b′r′es/). The name of a king of the → Tuatha Dé Danann in the story of the Battle of Mag Tuired (→ *Cath Maige Tuired*). His original name is Eochu, the appellative B., "the beautiful one", deriving, according to the story, from a prophecy made by his father Elatha that B. would be the yardstick for everything that was beautiful in Ireland.

Bretha Nemed (Ir. /'b′r′eθa 'N′ev′eð). A collection of legal treatises concerned with the laws and duties of certain privileged professional groups, particularly poets. Their origins are thought to lie in Munster, in the South of Ireland, and can be traced back at least in part to the 7thC AD.

    Lit.: L. Breatnach, 'Canon Law and Secular Law in Early Ireland: The Significance of B.N.' (*Peritia* 3) 1984, 439–459; F. Kelly, *A Guide to Early Ir. Law*, Du. 1988.

Breton. The Celtic language of Brittany. It was introduced by migrants from the south-west of Britain in the 4th-6thCs AD and thus, despite its geographical area, does not belong amongst the Celtic languages of the Continent. Breton forms, together with → Cornish, → Cumbrian and → Welsh, the British branch of the insular Celtic linguistic group. The oldest linguistic records are glosses, and personal and place names in Latin manuscripts of the 9th-12thCs. The oldest continuous texts date from the 14th-15thCs. The language is still spoken on an everyday basis in the regions of Léon, Tréguier, Cornouaille and Vannes.

    Lit.: F. Gourvil, *Langue et littérature bretonnes*, P. 1952; K. H. Jackson, *A Historical Phonology of Breton*, Du. 1967; R. Hemon, *A Historical Morphology and Syntax of Breton*, Du. 1975; H. Lewis and J. R. F. Piette, *Handbuch des Mittelbretonischen*, I. 1990; F. Broudic, *La pratique du breton de l'Ancien Régime à nos jours*, Rennes 1995.

Breuddwyd Macsen (Welsh /'breiðuid 'maksen/ "Macsen's Dream"). One of the stories known by the collective name of the → Mabinogion. It begins with the Roman emperor Macsen falling in love with a wondrously beautiful woman, a stranger to him, on the basis of what he sees in a dream. The messengers he sends out discover that the inspiration of his vision is the British princess Elen Luyddawg. Macsen thereupon conquers Britain, makes Elen his empress and enfeoffs her father with the rule of the island. During his absence from the capital the Romans elect a new emperor, but Macsen, thanks to the valorous aid of Elen's brothers, succeeds in regaining power over his empire. The name of the titular hero of the legend derives from that of the Roman emperor Maxentius (301–312), but the historical model for the character of Macsen is the Roman general Magnus Maximus, who in 383 AD was elected emperor by the troops under his authority in Britain and until his violent death reigned for five years over Britain, Gaul and Spain.

Trans.: G. Jones and T. Jones, *The Mabinogion*, rev. ed. Lo. 1974; J. Gantz, *The Mabinogion*, Harm. 1976.

Lit.: M. Rockel, 'Fiktion und Wirklichkeit im B. M.', in: H. L. C. Tristram (ed.), *Medialität u. mittelalterl. insulare Lit.*, T. 1992, 170–182.

Breuddwyd Rhonabwy (Welsh /'breiðuid ʀo'nabui/ "Rhonabwy's Dream"). Title of a satirical narrative thought to have originated in the 13thC, which survives in the "Red Book of Hergest" (→ Llyfr Coch Hergest; → Mabinogion). The story begins with King Madawg fab Maredudd of Powys (1132–1160) sending the titular hero Rhonabwy off in search of his rebellious brother. During this search Rhonabwy, together with two of his companions, is obliged to take refuge in a grubby, wretched hostelry, where at night Rhonabwy in a dream finds himself transposed to the age of → Arthur. Two splendidly clad riders escort him and his companions to the famed ruler, who has pitched camp with his court on the bank of the River Severn. In a rapid succession of scenes Rhonabwy there encounters → Caradawg Freichfras, → Cei fab Cynyr, → Owein fab Urien and other personages from Welsh legend. When Arthur's retinue finally prepares to depart for Cornwall such uproar arises in the encampment that Rhonabwy awakes from his dream.

Ed.: M. Richards, *B. R. allan o'r Llyfr Coch o Hergest*, Car. 1948.

Trans.: G. Jones and T. Jones, *The Mabinogion*, rev. ed. Lo. 1974; J. Gantz, *The Mabinogion*, Harm. 1976.

Lit.: J. A. Carson, 'The Structure and Meaning of "The Dream of Rhonabwy" ' (*Philological Quarterly* 53) 1974, 289–303; E. M. Slotkin, 'The Fabula, Story, and Text of B.Rh.' (CMCSt 18) 1989, 89–111; C. Lloyd-Morgan, 'B.Rh. and later Arthurian literature', in: R. Bromwich et al. (eds.), *The Arthur of the Welsh*, Car. 1991, 183–208.

Bricriu (Ir. /'b'r'ik'r'u/). Member of the retinue of the king Conchobar mac Nesa in the stories of the → Ulster Cycle. Because of his ubiquitously feared ability to provoke unrest by his malicious remarks he bears the appellative Nemthenga ("poison-tongue"). He plays a major role in the story → *Fled Bricrenn*.

Brigantes. In classical → ethnography a Celtic tribe in the North of England. After Britain was invaded by the Romans in 43 AD, their queen → Cartimandua at first collaborated with the occupying power. In the years 48–69 AD, however, the Romans embarked upon several campaigns against the B. By about 140 AD the building of the Antonine Wall between the estuaries of the Forth and the Clyde led to the final subjugation of the B. to Roman power.

Brigantia. Celtic goddess venerated primarily in the area of the tribe of the → Brigantes during the period of Roman rule. Her name appears in seven votive inscriptions. Two of these (*RIB* 627 and 628) equate her with the Roman goddess Victoria. Another inscription (*RIB* 1131) identifies her with the goddess Caelestis, of African origin. A relief from Birrens in southern Scotland (*RIB* 2091, now in the National Museum of Antiquities in Edinburgh) portrays the goddess as → Minerva with a mural crown and the wings of Victoria.
    Lit.: N. Jolliffe, 'Dea B.' (*Archaeological Journal* 98) 1942, 36–61.

Brigit (1) (Ir. /ˈbˈrˈiγˈ idˈ/). A pre-Christian Irish goddess, said to have been particularly revered by the poets; she is attested in the glossary of Bishop Cormac (→ *Sanas Chormaic*). According to Cormac she was a daughter of the → Dagda and had two sisters, also called B.; she was associated particularly with the art of healing and the craft of the blacksmith. The name B. derives from an older form *Brigantī, whose meaning approximates to "the sublime one". This older form occurs in Britain in the Latinised form → Brigantia as a designation of a goddess and survives in the names of the rivers Braint (Anglesey) and Brent (Middlesex). It is therefore thought that *Brigantī was a byname of several different Celtic goddesses.
    Lit.: → Brigit (2).

Brigit (2) (Ir. /ˈbˈrˈiγˈ idˈ/). The most celebrated female saint of the Irish Church, thought to have lived c. 600 and held to be the founder of the nunnery of Kildare (Ir. Cill Dara). From the 7thC onwards her cult spread through the whole island, and with the Irish mission was taken over to the European mainland.
    A hagiographer named Cogitosus wrote a Latin biography of the saint c. 650 for the nunnery of Kildare. This *Vita Brigitae* has strong legendary traits and contains little detail concerning the foundress of the monastery which is historically verifiable. It is therefore thought that by that time any precise recollection of her had already faded. The figure described in the written tradition has assumed many traits of the Celtic goddess of the same name (→ Brigit (1)). This is suggested by the fact that her feast day was celebrated on the first of February, the traditional beginning of Spring (→ Imbolc). The veneration of B. as the tutelary goddess of cattle and of agriculture, as well as the special significance attached to light and fire in her cult, have been

interpreted as survivals of pre-Christian conceptions. Even into our own century her feast day, particularly in the rural areas of Ireland, was linked with a wide variety of folk customs relating to agriculture and cattle-breeding. These include the well-known Cross of Brigit (Cros Bhríde), plaited from rushes or straw, and traditionally fixed to the roofbeam of the house in order to bring the family good fortune in the year to come.

Lit.: D. Ó hAodha, *Bethu Brigte*, Du. 1978; R. Sharpe, 'Vitae S. Brigitae: The oldest texts' (*Peritia* 1) 1982, 81–106; K. McCone, 'B. in the seventh century: a saint with three lives?' (*Peritia* 1) 1982, 107–145; S. Connolly and J.-M. Picard, 'Cogitosus, Life of Saint B.' (*JRSAI* 117) 1987, 5–27 (with Engl. trans.); S. Ó Catháin, *The Festival of Brigit. Celtic Goddess and Holy Woman*, Blackrock 1995.

Britain → Prydein.

British. The name given to the Celtic language of Scotland, England, Wales and Cornwall, before the evolution in the 5th/6thC AD of the distinct languages → Breton, → Cornish, → Cumbrian and → Welsh. B. is not attested in inscriptions and only known through the survival of individual words and names in Greek, Latin and Anglo-Saxon sources. It is thought that British bore a close resemblance to → Gaulish, hence the employment of the term "Gallo-British" for both languages in combination.

Lit.: K. H. Jackson, *Language and History in Early Britain*, E. 1953; A. Bammesberger and A. Wollmann (eds.), *Britain 400–600: Language and History*, Hei. 1990; P. Schrijver, *Studies in British Celtic Historical Phonology*, A. 1995.

brithem (Ir. /'b'riθ' ev/). The name in medieval Ireland for a judge or, more broadly speaking, a person learned in the law. The term derives from the Irish word breth, "judgment" and its literal meaning approximates to "the maker of a judgment". It is thought that every tribal community (→ tuath) had its b., appointed by the king (→ rí). These judges held a firmly established status in Irish society, which was only forfeited in the 16th and early 17thC as a consequence of the English conquest. Before this time many legal treatises for the education of the judges were compiled in the schools, the oldest of which date back to the 7th/8thC. In English, traditional Irish law is referred to as the → "Brehon Laws", the term deriving from the Anglicised from of the plural brithemain.

Lit.: F. Kelly, *A Guide to Early Ir. Law*, Du. 1988.

Britovius. Celtic god whose cult is attested by two inscriptions from Nîmes (CIL XII 3082 and 3083), in which he is identified with → Mars on the basis of the → interpretatio romana.

Brittany → Aremorica.

briugu (Ir. /'b'r'iuɣu/). The term in medieval Ireland for a man who occupies a high social station purely on the basis of his wealth and his unstinting hospitality. The customary English equivalent is "hospitaller". The annals attest that the term and the institution of the b. held sway until the 16thC. In many legends the b. is characterised by mythical traits and his house (→ bruiden) is often the scene of dire calamities.

Lit.: K. McCone, 'Hounds, Heroes and Hospitallers in Early Ir. Myth and Story' (*Ériu* 35) 1984, 1–30; F. Kelly, *A Guide to Early Ir. Law*, Du. 1988.

Broighter. Site near Londonderry (Northern Ireland) where in 1896, on the bank of Lough Foyle, several objects of → gold were discovered, among which were a tubular → torc and a model of a boat with rowing benches, a mast and moveable oars. These objects are thought to have been buried by the bank of the lake in the 1stC BC as a votive gift to a god. After their discovery they were for a short time in the possession of the British Museum, but are now in the National Museum of Ireland in Dublin.

Lit.: R. B. Warner, 'The B. Hoard', in: B. G. Scott (ed.), *Studies in Early Ireland*, Belfast 1982, 29–38.

bronze. Employed by the Celts primarily for → jewellery and items of → clothing, as well as for the manufacture of cutlery and various metal fittings. Such objects were cast and/or wrought by smiths and often decorated with engravings and coloured inlay of → amber, coral or enamel. Finds from graves and settlements include bronze shield and cart fittings, buckles, neck-, arm- and foot-rings, → fibulae and various hanging ornaments, smaller items such as nail-cutters, ear-cleaners and tweezers, sewing needles and hairpins, horse harnesses, cauldrons, beakers, bowls and pots. One masterpiece of bronze work is the 2.75m long couch, decorated with engraved images, found in the → Hochdorf grave.

Lit.: K. Spindler, *Die frühen Kelten*, St. [2]1991; D. van Endert, *Die B.funde aus dem Oppidum von Manching*, St. 1991.

Brug na Bóinne (Ir. /bruɣ na 'bo:N'e/). Name given in the stories of the → Mythological Cycle to the area surrounding the pre-Celtic hill grave of Newgrange, held to be the home of → Oengus.

bruiden (Ir. /'bruð'en/). A banqueting or feasting hall. According to the Story of the Pig of Mac Dathó (→ *Scéla mucce Meic Dathó*) there were once six such halls in Ireland, their owners (→ briugu) being → Mac Dathó, → Da Derga, → Forgall Manach, Mac Da-Reo, Da-Choca and the briugu Blaí.

Brutus. In the *Historia Regum Britanniae* of → Geoffrey of Monmouth a great-grandson of the Trojan Aeneas. On a hunting expedition he accidentally kills his father Silvius, and is therefore exiled from Italy. After an adventurous journey through the Mediterranean countries he and his followers land on the island of Britain, which receives its name from him (for the correct etymology of the name cf. → Prydein). There he becomes the first king of the Britons. The name B. survives in the titles of the Old French, Middle English and Middle Welsh adaptations of Geoffrey's work (→ Brut y Brenhinedd, → Layamon, → Wace).

> Lit.: W. G. Busse, 'Brutus in Albion: Englands Gründungssage', in: P. Wunderli (ed.), Herkunft und Ursprung, Sigmaringen 1994, 207–223.

Brut y Brenhinedd (Welsh /brit ə bren'hineð/ "Chronicle of the Kings"). The Middle and Early New Welsh adaptations of the Historia Regum Britanniae of → Geoffrey of Monmouth. Of varying length, these works originated in the 13th-15thCs and are preserved in over 60 manuscripts.

> Lit.: B. F. Roberts, 'Geoffrey of Monmouth, Historia Regum Britanniae and B. y B.', in: R. Bromwich et al. (eds.), The Arthur of the Welsh, Car. 1991, 97–116.

Brythonic → British.

Buddha position. Some 30 Celtic depictions of divinities show a god in a seated position with his legs crossed beneath him. Among the best-known examples are the bronze statue of → Bouray and the depiction of a god with a stag's antlers on the → Gundestrup cauldron. Because in Indian art Buddha is often depicted in a meditating position with crossed legs, some authors refer to the seated position of the Celtic divinities as the "Buddha position". A historical link between the Indian and Celtic pictorial motifs is however improbable. More plausible is the theory that the Celtic sculptures relate to the Celtic custom attested by → Strabo (Geogr. 4,4,3) of sitting cross-legged on the floor at meals, without tables or chairs.

> Lit.: P. Lambrechts, Contributions à l'étude des divinités celtiques, Bruges 1942; J. de Vries, Keltische Religion, St. 1961.

Budenicus. Celtic god identified on the basis of the → interpretatio romana with → Mars. His cult is attested by a single votive inscription found near Uzès in the Dép. of Grand (CIL XII 2973).

buile → baile.

Buile Suibne (Ir. /'bul'e 'huv'n'e/ "Suibne's Madness"). Title of a story from the → Historical Cycle. In its surviving form it is thought to date from the 12thC; it is preserved in three manuscripts of the 17th/18thC. The plot is closely related both in terms of time and content to the two legends → Fled Dúin na nGéd and → Cath Maige Rátha. The titular hero is Suibne mac Colmáin, king of Dál nAraide in the North-East of Ireland. After he has slain in battle a companion of St. Rónán, the saint curses him. In the tumult of the battle of Mag Rátha he loses his mind and wanders for many years through the forests of Ireland. In a monastery where the cook, at the behest of the abbot, gives him food every evening, he is ultimately slain by a jealous shepherd. The subject-matter was reworked by Austin → Clarke in his poem *The Frenzy of Suibhne*.

Ed.: J. G. O'Keefe, B. S., Du. 1932 (MMIS I).
Trans.: R. O'Mara, *König der Bäume*, Mn. 1985.
Lit.: R. P. Lehmann, 'A Study of the B.S.' (*EC* 6) 1953/54, 289–311 and (*EC* 7) 1955/56, 115–138; B. Beneš, 'Spuren von Schamanismus in der Sage B.S.' (*ZCP* 28) 1960/61, 309–334; P. Ó Riain, 'A Study of the Irish Legend of the Wild Man' (*Éigse* 14) 1971/72, 179–206; D. J. Cohen, 'S. Geilt' (*Celtica* 12) 1977, 113–124.

bull. Bulls played a major role in Celtic culture because of the central importance of → cattle-breeding. Images of them occur already in the late Hallstatt period, and they were frequently sacrificed in ritual. → Pliny's description of the role of → mistletoe in the sacrifice of two white bulls by the → druids is well-known.

Some forty depictions of three-horned bulls are known from Roman Gaul, most of them of → bronze. In all probability these figures were employed as → votive gifts. Their iconographic model is thought to be in Mediterranean art, where bulls were sometimes portrayed with a bird between their horns. Another product of Roman Gaul is a relief with the image of a deity and the inscription "the bull with the three cranes" (→ Tarvos Trigaranus). The most famous bulls in the insular Celtic tradition are → Donn Cuailnge and → Findbennach, the two protagonists in the story of the Cattle Raid of Cuailnge (→ *Táin Bó Cuailnge*).

burial → death and burial.

Buxenus. Celtic god, identified on the basis of the → interpretatio romana with → Mars. His cult is attested by a single votive inscription found near Veleron in the Dép. of Vaucluse (CIL XII 5832).

Cadbury Castle. Modern name of the site of a hill fort in Somerset. Archaeological excavation has shown that the site was occupied by man from the early Neolithic period until the Middle Ages. The Celtic fort was conquered by the Romans c. 70 AD and partially destroyed; in the 5th/6thC the site was used again for a time. Since the 16thC the hill has been identified with the castle of → Camelot in the stories relating to King → Arthur. In all probability this identification is not based upon an ancient source, but upon 16thC scholarly speculation.

Lit.: L. Alcock, 'Cadbury-Camelot: A fifteen-year perspective' (*PBA* 68) 1982, 354ff.

Cadurci. In classical → ethnography a Celtic tribe in the region between Dordogne and Aveyron. Their neighbours to the west were the → Nitiobroges, to the east the Ruteni. A major town of the C., the precise location of which is uncertain, was Uxellodunum, conquered by → Caesar in 51 BC, the last bastion of Gaulish resistance to the Romans. The name of the C. survives in the present-day town of Cahors, formerly called Divona.

Cadwaladr fab Cadwallawn (Welsh /kad'waladr va:b kad'wałaun/) and → Cynan. Two rulers in the prophetic poem → *Armes Prydein*, under whose leadership the British Celts are predicted to shake off one day the yoke of the Anglo-Saxon conquerors. According to the evidence of the → *Annales Cambriae* and the → *Historia Brittonum*, the historical C. ruled the North Welsh kingdom of → Gwynedd in the second half of the 7thC, succeeding his father → Cadwallawn fab Cadfan. He appears in the *Historia Regum Britanniae* of → Geoffrey of Monmouth as the last of the Celtic kings of Britain.

Cadwallawn fab Cadfan (Welsh /kad'wałaun va:b 'kadvan/). Ruler of the North Welsh kingdom of → Gwynedd c. 625–635 AD. In 634 he inflicted a humiliating defeat on the Angles under their king Edwin of Northumbria, but a year later fell in battle against Oswald of Mercia. Perhaps during his lifetime a poet composed a panegyric concerning his victories, *Moliant C.* ("Eulogy of C."). The manuscripts transmitting this poem can however only be traced back to the 18thC, although another poem concerning C., *Marwnad C.* ("Lament for the Death of C.") is to be found in the "Red Book of Hergest" (→ Llyfr Coch Hergest). These verses were however in all probability composed long after C.'s death. In style and content they are reminiscent of the stanzas concerning → Llywarch Hen and → Urien of Rheged.
  Lit.: R. G. Gruffydd, 'Canu Cadwallon ap Cadfan', in: R. Bromwich and R. B. Jones (eds.), *Astudiaethau ar yr Hengerdd*, Car. 1978, 25–43 (with ed. of the texts and modern Welsh trans.).

Caer Ibormeith (Ir. /kair 'ivorm'eθ'/). In the story → *Aislinge Oenguso* daughter of the elf Ethal Anbuail and beloved of the titular hero Oengus.

Caerllion-ar-Wysg (Engl. Caerleon-on-Usk). Site in South Wales of → Arthur's court according to → Geoffrey of Monmouth and the → Tair Rhamant. It is possible that the many ruins from Roman times to be found there, including an amphitheatre, gave rise to this tradition.

Caesar (Gaius Julius C.), Roman statesman, general and writer, born c. 100 BC. In the years 58–51 BC he conquered the whole of Gaul from the Pyrenees to the Rhine. He wrote his *Commentarii de Bello Gallico* (Reports of the War in Gaul) as an official account of his campaigns. In accordance with the duration of the war it is divided into seven books; chapters 11–28 of the sixth book contain an excursus concerning the customs of the Gauls and Germanic tribes which is of great interest with regard to cultural history. Caesar gives comparatively detailed descriptions of the Gaulish → Druids (6,13–14), → sacrifices (6,16) and → gods (6,17–18). Following the model of older authors he identifies the Celtic divinities with figures from Graeco-Roman mythology, thought by the Romans to correspond to them in broad terms (→ interpretatio romana). C. mentions in particular → Mercury, → Apollo, → Mars, → Jupiter, → Minerva and → Dis Pater. Much of his testimony is confirmed by the evidence of archaeology and the written traditions of the insular Celts. However, the propagandistic purport of the work and the possibility that C. is drawing upon the writings of the Stoic philosopher → Poseidonios must always be kept in mind.

Lit.: M. Rambaud, L'Art de la déformation historique dans les Commentaires de César, P. ²1966; J. Harmand, 'Le portrait de la Gaule dans le "De Bello Gallico" I–VII' (ANRW I,3) 1973, 523–595; C. F. C. Hawkes, 'Britain and Julius Caesar' (PBA 63) 1977, 125–192; G. Dobesch, 'C. als Ethnograph' (Wiener humanistische Blätter 31) 1989, 18–51; C. Goudineau, César et la Gaule, P. 1990.

Caesarius of Arles (470–542). Born in Cabillonum, now Chalon-sur-Saône. He began his career as a monk in the monastery of Lerinum. From 502 until his death he was bishop of Arelate (now Arles). The surviving works of C. comprise letters, a monastic rule, and other theological writings, including over 200 sermons. They are of particular interest because of the ways in which they reflect the bishop's encounter with the surviving traces of pre-Christian religion.

Lit.: P. Audin, 'Césaire d'Arles et le maintien de pratiques païennes dans la Provence du 6e siècle', in: La patrie gauloise d'Agrippa au 6e siècle, Ly. 1983, 327–338; W. E. Klingshirn, Caesarius of Arles. The Making of a Christian Community in Late Antique Gaul, C. 1993.

Cai → Cei.

Caillech Bérri (Ir. /'kaL'ex 'v'e:R'i/) or Sentainne Bérri, "the Old Woman of Beare". Name of a figure in Irish legend and poetry. Her original home was the peninsula of Beare in south-west Ireland, where she was held to be the ancestor of one of the principal noble families of the area. A poem of c. 900 describes her as a frail old lady who has retreated into a nunnery; full of melancholy, she looks back on her vanished youth as the beloved of kings. On the basis of numerous parallels in the Irish tradition it is thought that this poem is a Christian reworking of a pre-Christian myth, in which the C. B., as the tutelary goddess of the land, celebrated a → sacred marriage with successive kings. Austin → Clarke reworked the material in his poem The young woman of Beare (1929).

Lit.: B. K. Martin, 'The Old Woman of Beare' (Medium Ævum 38) 1969, 245–261;

G. Ó Crualaoich, 'Continuity and Adaptation in Legends of Cailleach Bhéarra' (*Béaloideas* 56) 1988, 153–178; D. Ó hAodha, 'The Lament of the Old Woman of Beare', in: D. Ó Corráin et al. (eds.), *Sages, Saints, and Storytellers*, May. 1989, 308–331 (with ed. and trans. of the Middle Ir. poem); B. Murdoch, 'In pursuit of the C. B.' (*ZCP* 44) 1991, 80–127.

Caílte mac Rónáin (Ir. /'kail't'e mak 'Ro:na:n'/). In the stories of the → Finn Cycle one of the most important heroes of the → Fianna. He is said to be the nephew of their leader → Finn mac Cumaill, and famed as a fast runner. The story → *Acallam na Senórach* tells how C. and his cousin → Oisín in their old age encounter Saint → Patrick and, wandering through Ireland, make him acquainted with the legendary and mythical traditions of the island.

cáin (Ir. /ka:n'/). Technical term in Irish law. Broadly speaking, it can refer to a law issued by a cleric or a ruler, or to the service or obligation owed to one of higher social position, yet it can also mean a financial penalty.
Lit.: F. Kelly, *A Guide to Early Ir. Law*, Du. 1988.

Cairbre Lifechar (Ir. /'kar'b'r'e 'L'if'exar/). In the stories of the → Historical Cycle a son of the king → Cormac mac Airt. In a battle against the → Fianna his spear inflicts a mortal wound upon Finn's grandson → Oscar, yet he himself is slain by the dying Oscar. Contrary to the Irish tradition, C. in the epic poem *Temora* composed by James → Macpherson, where he bears the name Cairbar, is not the son of Cormac but the the murderer of the king, who deprives him of his throne. According to Macpherson's version, the combat between Oscar and C., which proves fatal to both adversaries, takes place during a banquet to which C. has invited the grandson of his enemy, the Scottish king → Fingal.

Cairbre mac Étaíne (Ir. /'kar'b'r'e mak 'e:dain'e/). A poet (→ fili) of the → Tuatha Dé Danann in the story of the Battle of Mag Tuired (→ *Cath Maige Tuired*). Legend has it that he spoke the first ritual curse (→ áer) ever pronounced in Ireland.

Cairbre Nia-Fer (Ir. /'kar'b'r'e N'ia f'er/). King of Tara (→ Temair) in the story of the Cattle Raid of Cuailnge (→ *Táin Bó Cuailnge*). An elder brother of King → Ailill of Connacht, he is by his marriage to Fedelm Noíchride a son-in-law of King → Conchobar of Ulster. The story *Cath Ruis na Ríg* tells how C. dies in battle against → Cú Chulainn. His son Erc is therefore held to be one of the conspirators who bring about the death of Cú Chulainn by magic (→ *Aided Chon Culainn*).

Caithréim Cellaig (Ir. /'kaθ'r'e:m' 'k'eLiɣ'/ "The Noble Career of Cellach"). Title of a story from the → Historical Cycle. Two versions survive, the earlier in a manuscript of the 15thC, the later in the → "Yellow Book of Lecan" and one other manuscript of the 15thC. The story is set in the middle of the sixth century, yet both versions are thought to have originated in the period between 1200 and 1400. The titular hero, Cellach, is a son of King Eogan Bél of Connacht, and a monk in the monastery of Clonmacnoise. When his father falls in battle against warriors from the province of Ulster, Cellach is persuaded to leave the monastery without the abbot's permission, in order to succeed his father. On this account he incurs the curse of the abbot. When Cellach comes under heavy pressure from a rival called → Guaire, he gives way as king to his younger brother Muiredach and returns contritely to the monastery. His exemplary conduct there leads ultimately to his consecration as bishop, in which capacity he proves a valuable advisor to his younger brother. This irks Guaire, who has Cellach murdered by four of his most loyal companions. Muiredach avenges his brother's death on this quartet, but is then himself slain by Guaire.

Ed.: S. H. O'Grady, *Silva Gadelica*, Du. 1892 (with Engl. trans.); K. Mulchrone, C. C., Du. 1971 (MMIS 24).
Lit.: M. Dillon, *The Cycles of the Kings*, Lo. 1946.

Calatín (Ir. /'kalad':in/). Warrior in the stories of the → Ulster Cycle who is slain in single combat by → Cú Chulainn during the Cattle Raid of Cualinge (→ *Táin Bó Cuailnge*). The story → *Aided Chon Culainn* tells how his sons take vengeance, employing sorcery to kill Cú Chulainn.

Caledfwlch (Welsh /ka'ledvulx/). The name of → Arthur's sword in the story → *Culhwch ac Olwen*, corresponding to Ir. Calad-Colc or Calad-Bolg, the sword of the warrior → Fergus mac Roich in the story of the Cattle Raid of Cuailnge (→ *Táin Bo Cuailnge*). In → Geoffrey of Monmouth Arthur's sword is called Caliburnus (Gk.-Lat. chalybs, 'steel'); only in later reworkings of the Arthurian legend does it come to be called Excalibur.

Caledonia or Calidonia. The name for Scotland in classical → ethnography, deriving from the name of a presumably Celtic tribe recorded by ancient authors as Caledonii or Calidonii. It is not known which part of Scotland was inhabited by the tribe.

calendar → time.

Caliburnus → Caledfwlch.

Camelot. In the late medieval versions of the legends concerning → Arthur the site at which the Round Table assembles. Most authors offer no precise data concerning its geographical location. Sir Thomas → Malory is the only one to identify it with Winchester, the ancient capital of the Anglo-Saxon kingdom of Wessex. Since the 16thC there have been attempts to identify the site as the hill fort → Cadbury Castle.

Camlan (Welsh /'kamlan/). Supposed site of the last battle of → Arthur. The oldest reference is an entry, possibly contemporary with the event, in the → *Annales Cambriae*. There a note on the year 93 (= presumably 539 AD) records: "Gueith Camlann in qua Arthur et Medraut corruerunt" ("Battle of C., in which Arthur and Medraut perished"). Two of the → *Trioedd Ynys Prydein* name as the cause of the battle a quarrel between Arthur's queen → Gwenhwyfar and her sister → Gwenhwyfach. A more familiar tradition is attested for the first time in → Geoffrey of Monmouth, according to whom Arthur is compelled to wage war by the treachery of his nephew → Medrawd, with both of them falling in the battle. In Wales this battle became so well-known that the word C. was used proverbially to denote a rout.

Campbell, John Francis (1822–1886). One of the earliest and most prolific Scottish folklorists, born on the island of Islay. After studying in Edinburgh he held various government posts in Scotland. He was inspired by the specialist in Scandinavian studies, George Webbe Dasent (1817–1896), to collect the oral traditions of the Scottish Highlands and the Hebrides, along the lines of the Brothers Grimm. He published part of his voluminous collection both in English and in Gaelic, in his *Popular Tales of the West Highlands* (4 vols., 1860–1862) and *Leabhar na Féinne* (1872). Many further tales collected from the oral tradition were published between 1940 and 1960, edited from his manuscripts under the auspices of the Scottish Anthropological and Folklore Society.

Campbell, John Gregorson (1836–1891). Folklorist, born in Kingairloch in the Highlands of Scotland. After studying in Glasgow he served from 1860 to his death as a clergyman in the parishes of Tiree and Coll in the Inner Hebrides. A selection from his extensive records of Gaelic oral traditions appeared – in part posthumously – in *The Fians* (1891), *Clan Traditions and Popular Tales of the Western Highlands and Islands* (1895), *Superstitions of the Highlands and Islands of Scotland* (1900) and *Witchcraft and Second Sight in the West Highlands* (1901).

Camp-de-Château. Hill in the valley of the Furieuse, immediately to the west of Salins-les-Bains in the French Jura. Archaeological finds on the crest of the hill and the occurence of cart burials in the immediate vicinity suggest that the hill was the site of a Celtic → princely seat c. 500 BC.
  Lit.: M. Dayet, 'Recherches archéologiques au "Camp du Château" (1955–1959)' (*RAE* 18) 1967, 52–106.

Camulus. (Etymologically obscure) name of a Celtic god, whose cult is attested in votive inscriptions from Rome (CIL VI 32574), Rheims (*ILTG* 351), Arlon (CIL XIII 3980), Rindern (CIL XIII 8701), Mainz (CIL XIII 11818) and Bar Hill in Scotland (RIV 2166). In all except the first of these dedications C. is identified with → Mars on the basis of the → interpretatio romana.

Caoilte → Caílte.

Caradawg fab Brân (Welsh /ka'radaug va:b bra:n/). Son of the king → Brân Fendigeid in the story → *Branwen ferch Lŷr*. During Brân's Irish campaign C. remains as governor in Britain, with six other warriors. However, Brân's cousin → Caswallawn seizes the opportunity created by the absence of the king to claim the throne for himself. With the help of a hat that confers invisibility upon the wearer he slays all the governors save C., who dies broken-hearted, grieving over the death of his companions.

Caradawg Freichfras (Welsh /ka'radaug 'vreixvras/). Paramount advisor of → Arthur in the story → *Breuddwyd Rhonabwy*. His by-name signifies 'of the strong arm' (Welsh breich 'arm' and bras 'strong'). Several references in saints' lives and in the → *Trioedd Ynys Prydein* attest that C. played a major role in Welsh literature. Some traditions concerning C. also survive in the courtly literature of medieval France, where his byname was reinterpreted as 'short-arm' (Fr. bref 'short' and bras 'arm'). Thus in → Chrétien de Troyes C. appears as Karadues Briebras. He plays a major role in the anonymous 13thC *Livre de Carados*.

Caradog of Llancarfan. 12thC hagiographical author. His legendary biography of → Gildas, dating from c. 1130, records the abduction of queen → Gwenhwyfar by → Melwas, a rival of her husband → Arthur.

Carmarthen, Black Book of → Llyfr Du Caerfyrddin.

Carmichael, Alexander (1832–1912). Scottish folklorist, born in Lismore in the Highlands, worked as a tax-collector in various parts of Scotland. Between 1855 and 1899 he compiled an extensive collection of Gaelic prayers, blessings, charms and songs, part of which he published in 1900, bilingually in Gaelic and English, under the title *Carmina Gadelica*. The complete collection appeared posthumously in five volumes, with an index, between 1928 and 1971.

Lit.: F. G. Thompson, 'The Folklore Elements in Carmina Gadelica' (*Transactions of the Gaelic Society of Inverness* 44) 1966, 226–255; H. Robertson, 'Studies in Carmichael's Carmina Gadelica' (SGS 12) 1976, 220–265; J. L. Campbell, 'Notes on H. Robertson's "Studies. . ."' (SGS 13) 1978, 183–218; A. Bruford, ' "Deirdire" and A. C.'s Treatment of Oral Sources' (SGS 14) 1983, 1–24; L.

Patton, 'A.C., Carmina Gadelica, and the Nature of Ethnographical Representation' (*PHCC* 8) 1988, 58–84.

Carney, James (1914–1989). Celticist, born in Port Laoise, Ireland. After studying in University College Dublin with Osborn → Bergin and in Bonn with Rudolf → Thurneysen, he became Assistant Lecturer and later Professor in the → School of Celtic Studies in Dublin (1941–1985). A major focus of his research was the earliest Irish poetry and the traditions concerning Saint → Patrick. In the field of the sagas he was particularly interested in the influence of classical and Biblical narratives upon the composition of the native Irish material.

Carnutes. In classical → ethnography a Celtic tribe in the region between the Seine and the Loire. Its chief town was Cennabum, present-day Orléans. According to → Caesar (Bell. Gall. 6,13) the land of the C. was regarded as the centre of Gaul. There the → druids are said to have assembled at a consecrated spot to sit in judgment every year. The name of the C. survives in that of the city of Chartres, previously called Autricum after the river Autura (now the Eure).

cart → waggons.

Cartimandua. Ruler of the tribe of the → Brigantes in the North of England around the middle of the 1stC AD. According to → Tacitus (Ann. 12), in 51 AD she surrendered to the Roman troops the rebel British prince Caratacus, who had sought refuge with her. Despite the opposition of her husband Venutius she continued to collaborate with the Romans. After her rule ended the region of the Brigantes was incorporated into the Roman province of Britain.

carnyx. The Celtic war-trumpet, the bell of which ends in a metal animal head. It is mentioned by classical authors such as → Polybios (2,29) and → Diodoros of Sicily (5,30). It is also known from depictions (such as those on the → Gundestrup cauldron) and from archaeological finds.

Lit.: S. Piggott, 'The Carnyx in Early Iron Age Britain' (*The Antiquaries Journal* 39) 1959, 19–32.

Caswallawn fab Beli Mawr (Welsh /kas'waɫaun va:b 'beli maur/). A cousin of the king → Brân Fendigeid in the stories → *Branwen ferch Lŷr* and → *Manawydan fab Llŷr*. In the absence of the king he seizes power and with the assistance of a magic hat that makes him invisible kills the governors appointed by Brân. Already in the Middle Ages C. was identified with the British prince Cassivellaunus, who in 54 BC led an army formed from several different tribes against the conqueror → Caesar (cf. Bell. Gall. 5,11 and

18–22). This tradition is found in the Welsh adaptations of the *Historia Regum Britanniae* of → Geoffrey of Monmouth and in one of the → *Trioedd Ynys Prydein*. Two other mnemonics in this collection refer to a love-story which has not survived, but which apparently told how C., in pursuit of his beloved Fflur ("flower"), made his way to Rome disguised as a cobbler.

cath (Ir. /kaθ/). Term denoting combat or battle. In the → Lists of the Sagas the word serves to classify stories dealing with famous battles. Related terms which designate genres are the → orgain and the → togail.

Cathbad (Ir. /'kaθvaŏ/). A warrior and druid in the stories of the → Ulster Cycle, who acts as advisor to the king → Conchobar of Ulster and in some sources is his father. Various texts assign to him the gift of prophecy. Thus at the beginning of the story → *Longas mac nUislenn* he prophesies to the warriors of Ulster the sorrow that the as yet unborn Deirdriu will bring upon them. C. plays a similar role in the story of the Cattle Raid of Cuailnge (→ *Táin Bó Cuailnge*), in the account given by the warriors Conall Cernach and Fiachru mac Fir Febe of Cú Chulainn's boyhood deeds (→ *Macgnímrada Con Culainn*); here it is C. who gives Cú Chulainn his name and prophesies that he will die young, yet gain eternal fame.

Cath Étair (Ir. /kaθ 'e:dir'/ "The Battle of Étar"). Title of a story from the → Ulster Cycle, thought to date back to the 11thC. It survives in the "Book of Leinster" (→ Lebor Laignech) and in one other 16thC manuscript. The chief character in the story is the poet (→ fili) Aithirne, feared on account of his greed. On a journey round Ireland he succeeds in alienating by his exorbitant demands the inhabitants of Connacht, Munster and Leinster in succession. When he attempts to abduct the wives of 150 noblemen from Leinster, a battle ensues not far from the border, in which the Ulster warriors allied with Aithirne are defeated and imprisoned in the stronghold of Étar. Only after many lives are lost in battle do the besiegers retreat, and their king → Mes Gegra meets his death in combat against the warrior → Conall Cernach. At Conall's command his charioteer mixes the brain of Mes Gegra with chalk to form a ball, and with this trophy the warriors of Ulster return triumphant to their homeland.

Lit.: R. Thurneysen, *Die ir. Helden- und Königsage*, Hl. 1921.

Cath Finntrága (Ir. /kaθ 'fiNtra:ɣa/ "The Battle of Ventry"). Title of a story from the → Finn Cycle, the oldest surviving version of which dates from the 15thC and is preserved in a parchment manuscript of that date, as well as in several paper manuscripts of the 18th and 19thCs. The story concerns a great battle fought at Ventry in County Kerry, in which the warrior band of → Finn mac Cumaill, aided by the fairy prince → Bodb, rescues Ireland from the threat of conquest by a mighty army, led by a fictitious "King of the

World" (rí an domhain), which has landed on the south-west coast of the island.

Ed.: K. Meyer, The C. F., O. 1885 (with Engl. trans.); C. Ó. Rahilly, C.F., Du. 1962 (MMIS 20).

Cath Maige Mucrama (Ir. /kaθ 'maγ'e 'mukrama/ "The Battle of Mag Mucrama"). Title of a story from the → Historical Cycle which survives in the "Book of Leinster" (→ Lebor Laignech). Set in the 3rdC AD, it tells of the conflict between King Lugaid mac Con and his foster-brother Eogan, son of King → Ailill Aulom. After Eogan has defeated his opponent in open battle, Lugaid flees to Scotland. With the aid of the king of Scotland he equips a new army, with which he defeats Eogan and his ally, King → Art mac Cuinn, in the Battle of Mag Mucrama. After the death of his adversaries, Lugaid reigns unchallenged over the whole of Ireland. One day, however, he gives an unjust verdict in a legal dispute and in so doing goes against the law of the "veracity of the ruler" (→ fír flathemon). When in consequence the land becomes infertile, the people force Lugaid to abdicate, whereupon he flees to his foster-father Ailill Aulom. The latter, however, murders him in order to avenge the death of his son.

Ed. and trans.: M. O'Daly, C. M. M.: The Battle of M. Mucraime, ITS 50, Du. 1975.

Lit.: T. Ó Cathasaigh, 'The Theme of Lommrad in C. M. M.' (Éigse 18) 1980/81, 211–224.

Cath Maige Ratha (Ir. /kaθ 'maγ'e 'Raθa/ "The Battle of Mag Rath"). Title of a story from the → Historical Cycle, the oldest surviving version of which is dated on linguistic grounds to the early 10thC and is preserved in the → "Yellow Book of Lecan". The story tells of the conflict betweeen the Irish High King, Domnall mac Aeda, and his foster-son Congal Claen, king of Ulster. The two men quarrel for no good reason at a banquet, whereupon Congal forms an alliance with the king of Scotland and declares war upon his foster-father. At Mag Ráth a battle takes place which lasts three days, in the course of which the combined troops of Ulster and Scotland suffer a humiliating defeat and Congal himself loses his life.

Ed. and trans.: C. Marstrander, 'A new version of the Battle of Mag Rath' (Ériu 6) 1911, 226–247.

Lit.: M. Dillon, The Cycles of the Kings, O. 1946.

Cath Maige Tuired (Ir. /kaθ 'maγ'e 'tur'eð/ "The Battle of Mag Tuired"). Title of the most important story in the → Mythological Cycle. Allusions and references to the events portrayed therein occur in numerous works of the Middle and Early New Irish period, suggesting that several different versions of the story were in circulation. Only two have however survived. The older, Middle Irish version is thought to have been recorded in the

11thC, though it survives only in a 16thC manuscript. The later version, as it has come down to us, stems from the Early New Irish period, surviving in a manuscript of c. 1650.

The subject of the story is the battle of the → Tuatha Dé Danann, who are gifted with magical powers, against the daemonic → Fomoire. Whereas the later version concentrates entirely upon the portrayal of the decisive battle, the older version also describes the events leading up to it, beginning with the tale of how → Nuadu, king of the Tuatha Dé Danann, soon after arriving in Ireland, loses a hand in a battle against the → Fir Bolg. The doctor → Dian Cécht supplies him with a moveable hand of silver. Nuadu's crippled state means, however, that he can no longer be king, and in his stead the Tuatha Dé Danann elect → Bres mac Elathan, son of a king of the Fomoire by a woman of the Tuatha Dé Danann. Bres, however, grossly neglects his duties as ruler and imposes harsh servitude upon the leaders of the Tuatha Dé Danann. The poet Cairbre composes an invective (→ áer) against the king, which leads the people to demand his abdication. When Bres calls his kinsfolk of the Fomoire to his aid, both sides muster for battle. → Lug mac Ethnenn takes over the leadership of the Tuatha Dé Danann, and in the decisive Battle of Mag Tuired he slays → Balar, the one-eyed leader of the Fomoire, thereby ensuring the victory of the Tuatha Dé Danann over their enemies, the latter being driven out of Ireland for ever. In the older version of the story Bres does penance by teaching the Tuatha Dé Danann ploughing, sowing and harvesting, whereas in the later version he too is slain by Lug.

Ed.: B. Ó Cuív, C. M. T.: *The Second Battle of Magh Tuireadh*, Du. 1945 (later version); E. A. Gray, C. M. T.: *The Second Battle of Mag Tuired*, ITS 52, Du. 1982 (older version with Engl. trans.).

Lit.: E. A. Gray, 'C. M. T.: Myth and Structure' (*Éigse* 18–19) 1980/81; 1982/83, 183–209; 230–262; T. Ó Cathasaigh, 'C. M. T. as Exemplary Myth', in: P. de Brún et al. (eds.), *Folia Gadelica*, Cork 1983, 1–19; W. Sayers, 'Bargaining for the Life of Bres in C. M. T.' (BBCS 34) 1987, 26–40; K. McCone, 'Poet and satirist in C. M. T.', in: D. Ó Corráin et al. (eds.), *Sages, Saints and Storytellers*, May. 1989, 122–143; J. Carey, 'Myth and Mythography in C. M. T.' (*StC* 24/25) 1989/90, 53–69.

cattle-breeding. Cattle-breeding, along with → agriculture, played a decisive role in the Celtic economy. Our knowledge is based primarily on finds of animal bones made during the archaeological excavation of refuse from settlements. The most frequent domestic animals, according to this evidence, were beef cattle, which were also employed as draught animals and to work the fields, whilst cows additionally supplied milk. Second in importance were → pigs, which are also mentioned several times in the accounts of classical → ethnography. Goats and sheep, kept chiefly because of their wool, were of comparatively minor importance. Poultry consisted of hens and geese. In contrast to the Celtic → horses, their cattle and pigs were considerably smaller than their wild equivalents, which it is thought had to do with inadequate provision for the animals during the winter.

In Ireland, owning cattle was an indicator of the wealth and social status of a man and his family until late in the Middle Ages. This is also, therefore, a major factor in the sagas (cf. → táin).

Lit.: P. Meniel, Chasse et élevage chez les Gaulois, P. 1987; A. T. Lucas, Cattle in Ancient Ireland, Kilkenny 1989.

Caturiges. In classical → ethnography a Celtic tribe in the valley of the Durance in the western Alps. The literal meaning of the name is thought to be "kings of the battle", but it is unclear what concept was associated with the term. The chief town of the C. was Eburodunum, present-day Embrun. Their name survives in that of the town Chorges.

Caturix. Celtic god, identified on the basis of the → interpretatio romana with → Mars. His name means "battle king" (cf. Ir. cath "battle" and rí "king"). Votive inscriptions to C. have been found on various sites in Roman Switzerland (CIL XIII 5035, 5046, 5054, 11473; NeLi 40), and in Böckingen near Heilbronn (CIL XIII 6474).

cauldrons. Cauldrons played an important role as ritual and ceremonial utensils already in the Bronze Age. In a Celtic context they occur in association with death rites (cf. → Hochdorf) and as offerings or votive gifts (cf. → Duchcov). The most famous example, which has been the subject of much discussion, is the → Gundestrup cauldron. In the insular Celtic literatures cauldrons frequently occur, some containing inexhaustible quantities of food (cf. → Dagda), others capable of bringing the dead back to life (cf. → Brannwen ferch Lŷr).

Lit.: F. Lautenbach, Der keltische Kessel, St. 1991.

Cei fab Cynyr (Welsh /kei va:b 'kənir/). In the story → Culhwch ac Olwen foremost of Arthur's companions. He generally appears together with → Bedwyr fab Bedrawg. The narrator ascribes to him a number of magical gifts: he can hold his breath under water or survive without sleep for nine days and nine nights; a wound inflicted by his sword is beyond the powers of any doctor to heal; he can at will assume the size of the tallest tree in the forest; he exudes enough heat to warm those standing near him even in the coldest possible conditions. Another passage in the story tells how his heart and hands are always cold, and every burden he bears becomes invisible. No-one can hold out against fire and water as well as he. In the poem → Pa ŵr yw'r Porthor? it is said of Cei: when Cei drank from the horn of an ox, he drank the draught of four men; when he went to battle, the toll of those he killed was that of a hundred warriors. His attributes in the Welsh tradition are "the Fair" (gwyn) and "the Tall" (hir). Cei plays an important part in the Historia

Regum Britanniae of → Geoffrey of Monmouth, but in later → Arthurian literature he generally fades into the background. In → Chrétien de Troyes he appears as a boastful and cowardly steward at Arthur's court. He plays no major role in modern reworkings of the Arthurian legend.

Lit.: L. Gowans, *C. and the Arthurian Legend*, C. 1988; P. Noble, 'The heroic tradition of C.' (*Reading Mediaeval Studies* 14) 1988, 125–137.

Céli Dé (Ir. /'k'e:l'i d'e:/ "servants of God"). The name given to themselves by the originators of a monastic reform movement which in the 8th/9thC spread over much of Ireland. The term C. D. (anglicised: Culdees) derives from the language of Irish law, according to which the relationship between the céle ("defendant") and the flaith ("lord") is precisely determined by mutual rights and duties. The reforms of the C. D. were characterised above all by a tendency toward asceticism and their cultivation of monastic learning. In consequence the movement was of great significance for the evolution of Irish religious literature.

Lit.: P. O'Dwyer, *C. D.: Spiritual Reform in Ireland 750–900*, Du. 1981.

Celli Wig (Welsh /'keɬi wi:g/). In the story → *Culhwch ac Olwen* the place in Cornwall from which → Arthur and his warriors set off on their adventures. The text does not identify the site more precisely. Later Welsh narratives follow → Geoffrey of Monmouth in making the South Welsh city of → Caerllion-ar-Wysg the seat of Arthur's court.

Celtchar mac Uthechair (Ir. /'k'eltxar mak 'uθ'exir'/) or Celtchar mac Uthidir. In the stories of the → Ulster Cycle one of the most important heroes of Ulster. The Story of the Pig of Mac Dathó (→ *Scéla mucce Meic Datho*) calls him a "huge, grey, most terrible warrior". In the story of The Wasting Sickness of Cú Chulainn (→ *Serglige Con Culainn*) he is called "the man rich in cunning". His death is told in the tale → *Aided Cheltchair maic Uthechair.*

Celtiberi. In classical → ethnography a group of peoples who dwelt in the north-east of the Spanish tableland. They proffered fierce resistance to the advances of the Romans in wars that lasted decades, and were only finally subjugated after the fall of their chief town → Numantia in 133 BC. The language of the Celtiberi, on the basis of the few surviving inscriptions, was a particularly archaic form of Celtic (→ Celtiberian). Our knowledge of their material and intellectual culture is fragmentary, as many of the archaeological finds cannot be pinpointed with regard to their ethnic, linguistic and cultural origin.

Lit.: A. Tovar, 'The Celts in the Iberian Peninsula', in: K. H. Schmidt (ed.), *Geschichte und Kultur der Kelten*, Hei. 1986, 68–101; *Celtíberos*, Saragossa 1988 (exhibition cat.); J. de Hoz, 'The Celts of the Iberian Peninsula' (*ZCP* 45) 1990,

1–37; M. Lenerz-de Wilde, *Iberia Celtica: Archäologische Zeugnisse keltischer Kultur auf der Pyrenäenhalbinsel*, 2 vols., Wi. 1991; M. Almagro-Gorbea & G. Ruiz Zapatero (eds.), *Los Celtas: Hispania y Europa*, Ma. 1993.

Celtiberian. The now extinct language of the Celts of the Iberian peninsula. We know it through inscriptions in Iberian script of the 3rd-1stC BC and through some inscriptions in the Roman alphabet. Among the most important linguistic records are the bronze tablet of → Botorrita and the rock inscription of → Peñalba de Villastar.

Lit.: M. Almagro-Gorbea & G. Ruiz Zapatero (eds.), *Los Celtas: Hispania y Europa*, Madrid 1993; J. de Hoz, 'La epigrafia celtibérica', in: *Reunión sobre epigrafia hispánica de época romana-republicana*, Saragossa 1986, 43–102; ibid., 'Hispano-Celtic and Celtiberian', in: G. W. MacLennan (ed.), *Procs. of the First North American Congress of Celtic Studies*, Ottawa 1988, 191–207; D. E. Evans, 'The identification of Continental Celtic with special reference to Hispano-Celtic', in: J. Untermann & F. Villar (eds.), *Lengua y cultura en la Hispania prerromana*, Salamanca 1993, 563–608; W. Meid, *Celtiberian Inscriptions*, Budapest 1994; id, *Kleinere keltiberische Sprachdenkmäler*, I. 1996.

Celtic-Germanic cultural links. A problem frequently discussed by scholars, encroaching upon archaeology, comparative linguistics and comparative religion.

The Celts and the Germani share a stratum of common linguistic, religious and cultural characteristics, dating back to the 2nd millennium BC, with other peoples who spoke Indo-European languages such as Italic, Greek and Indo-Iranian. This stratum includes, for example, the Celtic word for "god" (*dēvos; cf. → gods and goddesses), which, together with Latin deus, Old Indian deva, the name of the Germanic god Týr and that of the Greek god Zeus, goes back to a common Indo-European root.

A later layer of correspondences consists of common characteristics which the Celts and the Germanic tribes share only with other peoples of ancient Europe.

There are still later parallels which developed through the direct contact between the Celts and the Germani in the pre-Roman Iron Age. Archaeology points to a strong influence upon Germanic culture by the Celtic Late Hallstatt and La Tène cultures. The close contact between both cultures is reflected linguistically by common terms such as the words for "iron" (O.Irish iarn; German Eisen) or "oath" (O.Irish oeth; German Eid). Words such as Gothic reiks "king" and andbahts "servant", by contrast, are borrowings from Celtic (cf. → rí, → ambactus), whereas words such as German "Hose" (hose, breeches, Gaulish brāca) or "Hemd" (shirt, Gallo-Lat. camisia) were Celtic borrowings from Germanic.

A broad zone of contact between the Germani and the Romanised Celts evolved in the first centuries AD along the border of the Roman Empire, particularly in the Rhineland, where there is also much evidence of corresponding religious beliefs (cf. → Matronae/Matres).

From the 5thC onwards there evolved a lively cultural intercourse in the British Isles between Celts on the one hand and Anglo-Saxons, North Germanic tribes (from c. 800) and Anglo-Normans (from c. 1100) on the other. These contacts were echoed in insular Celtic → literature and → art.

Lit.: H. Birkhan, *Germanen und Kelten bis zum Ausgang der Römerzeit*, Vienna 1970; D. E. Evans, 'Celts and Germans' (*BBCS* 29) 1980/82, 230–255; O. H. Frey, 'Einige Überlegungen zu den Beziehungen zwischen Kelten und Germanen in der Spätlatènezeit', in: *Gedenkschrift für G. v. Merhart*, Marburg 1986, 45–79; K. H. Schmidt, 'Keltisch-germanische Isoglossen und ihre sprachgeschichtlichen Implikationen', in: H. Beck (ed.), *Germanenprobleme in heutiger Sicht*, B. 1986, 231–247; H. E. Davidson, *Myths and Symbols in Pagan Europe*, Manchester 1988; G. Sigurðsson, *Gaelic Influence in Iceland*, Reykjavik 1988; K. H. Schmidt, 'The Celts and the ethnogenesis of the Germanic people' (*Historische Sprachforschung* 104) 1991, 129–152.

Celtic ideology. Term referring to the misappropriation of Celtic culture for philosophical or political ends. The origins of modern Celtic ideology lie in the accounts of classical → ethnography, in which the Celts are to some extent idealised for moralising purposes, but are also portrayed, for political or war-oriented reasons, in a negative light or even caricatured. Similarly, in medieval historiography Ireland may appear, according to the theological affiliation or political motivation of the author, as either a morally exemplary "island of saints" or as a retrograde region much in need of colonisation and civilisation. Celtic culture is in each case "different" (judged by the standards of the home culture of the writer) and from the time of the consolidation of the English and French monarchies onwards comes increasingly to be regarded as a marginal culture.

From the 16thC onwards the concept of the Gauls as forefathers of the French occurs in France, wishful thinking projecting various political, philosophical and religious ideals backwards into the pre-Roman past, of which only limited knowledge was available. At this time too, however, the scholarly investigation of the Celtic → languages and of prehistoric stone monuments begins. Of considerable influence in this context was the erroneous attribution of Stone and Bronze Age grave and ritual sites (→ dolmen, → menhir, → Stonehenge) to the Celtic → druids, particularly as practised in the 17th/18thC by John → Aubrey, Henry → Rowlands, and William → Stukeley. The popular image of Celtic → literature and mentality was determined to a great extent in the second half of the 18thC by the "Works of Ossian", written by James → Macpherson, which have little in common with authentic Celtic poetry.

It was only with the emergence of archaeological research and modern → Celtic studies in the second half of the 19thC that a more informed knowledge of Celtic culture was facilitated. At the same time, however, Celtic ideology, in the wake of the Napoleonic wars, the Franco-Prussian war of 1870/1871 and the rise of the Irish independence movement, bore plentiful nationalistic fruit. Thus the authors of the → Irish Renaissance, drawing on the writings of Ernest → Renan and Matthew → Arnold, idealised the Celtic past in biased fashion, whereas the Germans and the French sought to locate the underlying causes of contemporary political conditions in what were assumed to be Germanic or Celtic racial origins.

Among the most recent developments in Celtic ideology are the reception of a hypothetically reconstructed Celtic religion by the New Age and the appropriation of the Celts for the ideal of European unity. The cartoon series → Astérix has since 1959 provided a brilliant parody of nationalistic Celtic ideology.

Lit.: C.-G. Dubois, *Celtes et Gaulois au XVIe siècle*, P. 1972; M. Chapman, *The Gaelic Vision in Scottish Culture*, Lo. 1978; P. Viallaneix & J. Ehrard (eds.), *Nos ancêtres les Gaulois*, Clermont-Ferrand 1982; P. Sims-Williams, 'The Visionary Celt: The Construction of an Ethnic Preconception' (CMCSt 11) 1986, 71–96; S. Piggott, *Ancient Britons and the Antiquarian Imagination*, Lo. 1989; M. Chapman, *The Celts: The Construction of a Myth*, Lo. 1992; A. D. Hadfield & J. McVeagh, '*Strangers to that Land*': *British Perceptions of Ireland from the Reformation to the Famine*, Gerrards Cross 1993; M. Dietler, 'Our Ancestors the Gauls' (*American Anthropologist* 94) 1994, 584–605; T. Brown (ed.), *Celticism*, A. 1996.

Celtic Renaissance → Irish Renaissance.

Celtic Studies. The study of Celtic culture employing the methods of linguistics and philology. Its object of study is thus all linguistic utterances of the Celtic peoples from ancient times to the present day.

The origins of modern C.s. go back to the 16thC. The Scottish humanist George Buchanan (1506–1582) was one of the first to recognise that insular and continental Celtic were related (→ languages, Celtic). The first comprehensive comparison of the surviving insular Celtic languages was undertaken c. 1700 by the Welsh scholar Edward → Lhuyd. It was in the last third of the 18thC, with the publication of the Ossian poetry of the Scot James → Macpherson, that a wider public outside the Celtic countries first became aware of the existence of Celtic languages and literatures. This newly awakened interest was nourished in the first half of the 19thC by the post-Romantic rise of historical philology. The basis for a historical study of the Celtic languages was created by the Indo-European scholar Franz Bopp (1791–1867). He was the first to prove that Celtic belonged to the Indo-European family of languages and is thus related to Germanic, Sanskrit and the languages of classical antiquity.

The true founder of C.s. was Johann Kaspar → Zeuss, whose *Grammatica Celtica* (1851) formed the foundation for all further research. The first scholarly periodicals in the field were the *Revue celtique* in France (1870–1934; since 1936 *Études celtiques*), and the *Zeitschrift für celtische Philologie* in Germany (since 1897). The first chairs in C.s. were held by John → Rhŷs in England, Henri → d'Arbois de Jubainville in France, and Heinrich → Zimmer in Germany.

Celtic studies on the European mainland was and still is characterised by its close relationship with comparative Indo-European linguistics. Important scholars in this direction were Georges → Dottin and Joseph → Vendryes in France, and among those writing in German Ernst → Windisch, Rudolf → Thurneysen, Leo → Weisgerber, Julius → Pokorny and Heinrich → Wagner. In Great Britain and Ireland, on the other hand, research has tended to concentrate on Irish and Welsh philology. Many editions, translations and studies of Old and Middle Irish texts were produced by the Irishmen Whitley → Stokes, Richard I. → Best, Osborn → Bergin, Daniel A. → Binchy, Gerard → Murphy, Myles → Dillon, and James → Carney, not to mention the prolific German scholar Kuno → Meyer. The leading experts in the field of Welsh language and literature were the Welshmen John → Morris-Jones, Ifor → Williams, and Henry → Lewis. The Englishman Kenneth H. → Jackson is among the most important scholars who have worked on both insular Celtic traditions.

As early as 1903 the → School of Irish Learning had been created in Dublin, one of the first centres for research and education in Irish Celtic studies. Other research institutes were founded, including The → Board of Celtic Studies in Wales (1921) and The → School of Celtic Studies in Ireland (1940). Apart from the countries already mentioned Celtic studies are today also well represented in the United States.

Lit.: V. Tourneur, *Esquisse d'une histoire des études celtiques*, Liège 1905; J. Pokorny, 'Keltologie', in: K. Hönn (ed.), *Wissenschaftliche Forschungsberichte*, Geisteswissenschaftliche Reihe Bd. 2, Bern 1953, 95–186; G. Bonfante, 'Some Renaissance Texts on the Celtic Languages and their Kinship' (EC 7) 1955/56, 414–427; ibid., 'A Contribution to the History of Celtology' (*Celtica* 3) 1956, 17–34; G. J. Williams, 'The History of Welsh Scholarship (*StC* 8/9) 1973/74, 195–219; K. H. Schmidt, 'Stand und Aufgaben der deutschsprachigen Keltologie', in: M. Rockel & S. Zimmer (eds.), *Akten des ersten Symposiums deutschsprachiger Keltologen*, T. 1993, 1–35.

Celtomania → Celtic ideology.

Celts (Gk. Keltoi or Galatai, Lat. Celtae or Galli). In classical → ethnography a succession of peoples in western central Europe. In Roman times central → Gaul was regarded as their main settlement area. According to → Caesar (Bell. Gall. 1,1) the C. were separated from the Germani by the Rhine, from the Aquitanians by the Garonne and from the Belgae by the Seine and the Marne.

In today's usage the term Celts refers to all the speakers of an Indo-

European language related to Germanic and Latin, defined by precise linguistic criteria (cf. → languages, Celtic). Thus the inhabitants of Great Britain and Ireland before the English conquest are now also regarded as Celts, although they are never given this name by classical authors. From an archaeological point of view, the peoples of the late West Hallstatt and La Tène cultures are regarded as Celts (cf. → history, → Hallstatt, → La Tène).

The term → Galatians is now used only to refer to the Celts of Asia Minor, whereas in antiquity it was frequently synonymous with Keltoi and not restricted to any specific region.

Lit.: → Galatians, → Gaul, → history, → Celtiberians.

Celts, depictions of. Depictions of the Celts from antiquity occur predominantly in Etruscan, Greek and Roman art. The subjects depicted are for the most part warriors, identified as Celts by their hair, combed back from the forehead in strands, their long moustaches and twisted neck-rings (→ torcs). Among the best-known examples are those depictions of the Celts by means of which the rulers of the Hellenistic kingdom of Pergamon celebrated their victories in the 3rd and 2ndC BC over the → Galatians of Asia Minor. Some of these images, among them that known as the Dying Gaul, have survived in Roman marble copies. By contrast, depictions made by the Celts of themselves, such as the warrior of → Hirschlanden, are exceedingly rare.

Modern depictions of the Celts occur as early as the 16thC. They were based initially on the descriptions found in classical authors, but since the 18th/19thC have increasingly taken archaeological finds into account. The nationalistically oriented depictions of the 19thC in particular tended to portray the Celts in an heroic and romantic light (→ Celtic ideology). The most recent depictions of the Celts – for example in museums or in archaeological books intended for popular consumption – profit by our enhanced knowledge of Celtic culture, but it is frequently the case that they are heavily dependant upon the descriptions in classical → ethnography, which have formed the standard image.

Lit.: P. Bieńkowski, *Die Darstellung der Gallier in der hellenistischen Kunst*, V. 1908; id., *Les Celtes dans les art mineurs gréco-romains*, Krakau 1928; E. Künzl, *Die Kelten des Epigonos von Pergamon*, Wü. 1971; P. Viallaneix & J. Ehrard (eds.), *Nos ancêtres les Gaulois*, Clermont-Ferrand 1982; S. Piggott, *Ancient Britons and the Antiquarian Imagination*, Lo. 1989; U. Höckmann, 'Gallierdarstellungen in der etruskischen Grabkunst des 2. Jhs. v. Chr.' (*Jahrbuch des Deutschen Archäologischen Instituts* 106) 1991, 199–230.

Cenomani. In classical → ethnography a sub-tribe forming part of the tribal alliance of the → Aulerci in the region between the Loire and the Seine. There the name survives in that of the region of Maine and its capital Le Mans. Some of the C. participated in the migration of the Celts to northern

Italy and settled in the region between the Oglio, the Po and the Etsch. The chief town of this group of the C. was Brixia, present-day Brescia.

Ceramics. Celtic ceramics have survived in great quantity and variety. Celtic pottery forms part of a tradition in central Europe, which reaches back as far as the 5th millennium BC. What is known as the slow-turning wheel was employed to make vessels as early as the Hallstatt period. The fast-turning wheel which is customary today arrived from the Mediterranean area towards the end of the Hallstatt period and only established itself gradually, in the course of the La Tène period. Following this technological innovation came the serial manufacture of vessels in specialised workshops, which continued to take place after the Roman conquest of Gaul (cf. → La Graufesenque). The form of the vessels was subject to drastic change in the course of time and there was also considerable regional variation. Typical of the eastern early La Tène period, for example, is what is known as the *Linsenflasche*, a flask with a flat, lentiform body and a long, narrow neck (cf. → Matzhausen). The pots were often decorated with carved or stamped ornamentation, or painted.

Lit.: I. Kappel, *Die Graphittonkeramik von Manching*, Wiesbaden 1969; F. Maier, *Die bemalte Spätlatène-Keramik von Manching*, St. 1970; V. Pingel, *Die glatte Drehscheiben-Keramik von Manching*, St. 1971; W. Stöckli, *Die Grob- und Importkeramik von Manching*, St. 1979; M. Tuffreau-Libre, *La ceramique en Gaule romaine*, P. 1992.

Ceridwen (Welsh /ke'ridwen/). Sorceress who prepares drinks in a magic cauldron which give the gift of poetic powers to the drinker. Allusions to this tradition are to be found in poets of the 12th-14thCs; it is then reworked as a fairy-tale in the story → Hanes Taliesin. In a novel by Friedrich Theodor Vischer (1807–1887), *Auch Einer*, the material appears in the "Pfahldorf Story", in the "Märchenlied von Coridwen" ("Song of Coridwen").

Cernunnos. Celtic god, the etymology of whose name is unclear. It seems unlikely that (as some have maintained) the name is connected with a Celtic word for "horn"; one would expect, on linguistic grounds, the first vowel to be a rather than e. Both the name and a depiction of C. are preserved on the monument of the → Nautae Parisiaci, dating from the time of the emperor Tiberius (14–37 AD). This fragmentarily preserved relief shows the head and shoulders of a bearded man with the ears and antlers of a stag. Both antlers have → torcs hanging from them. The lower half of the relief is lost, yet the dimensions suggest that the god was depicted sitting in the so-called → Buddha position. The name C. is not attested in inscriptions or literature elsewhere, but in Celtological works it occurs frequently to designate divinities depicted in similar fashion. Among the best-known examples are the rock-carving of an upright figure with stag's antlers and torcs in the → Val

Camonica, and the depiction of a god with stag's antlers on the → Gun-destrop Cauldron. Sculptures depicting gods which have two openings in the head for the insertion or removing of antlers have also been discovered.

Lit.: Ph. P. Bober, 'C.' (*American Journal of Archaeology* 55) 1951, 13–51; H. Vertet, 'Observations sur le dieu C. de l'autel de Paris' (*Bulletin des Antiquaires de France*) 1985, 163–175.

Cesair (Ir. /'k'esir'/). A granddaughter of Noah in the "Book of the Invasions of Ireland" (→ *Lebor Gabála Érenn*). Together with three men and fifty women she is said to have taken possession of Ireland forty days before the Flood. Tradition has it that all these immigrants, with the exception of → Fintan mac Bóchra, died in the Flood.

Lit.: J. Carey, 'Origin and Development of the C. Legend' (*Éigse* 22) 1987, 37–48.

Ces Ulad → Noínden Ulad.

Cet mac Mágach (Ir. /k'et mak 'ma:γax/). In the stories of the → Ulster Cycle one of the most important warriors of the province of Connacht. In the story → *Scéla mucce Meic Dathó* he puts the assembled warriors of Ulster to shame by his challenging speeches, and is only put in his place by the newly arrived → Conall Cernach, who proves superior to him. In one version of the story of the Birth of → Cú Chulainn (→ *Compert Chon Culainn*) it is he who gives Cú Chulainn his original name Sétanta. The story → *Aided Cheit maic Mágach* tells of the death of the hero.

Chamalières. Site west of Clermont-Ferrand in the Dép. of Puy-de-Dôme, where in 1968–1971 a Gallo-Roman sanctuary at the source of two natural springs was the subject of archaeological excavation. Several thousand wooden → votive gifts were found there, and in January 1971 a lead tablet inscribed with an incantation in Gaulish, dating from the first half of the first century AD. Its 336 letters make it the second longest Gaulish text (after the tablet of → Larzac, which is inscribed with curses), and one of the longest ancient Celtic texts. The detail of the meaning is disputed, but it is clearly an appeal to the god → Maponus for protection against → magic. The tablet is now in the Musée Bargoin in Clermont-Ferrand.

Lit.: M. Lejeune and R. Marichal, 'Textes gaulois et gallo-romains en cursive latine II. Ch.' (EC 15) 1976/77, 156–168; L. Fleuriot, 'Le vocabulaire de l'inscrip-tion gauloise de Ch.' (EC 15) 1976/77, 173–190; P.-Y. Lambert, 'La tablette gauloise de Ch.' (EC 16) 1979, 141–169; K. H. Schmidt, 'The Gaulish Inscription of Ch.' (BBCS 29) 1980/82, 256–268; P. L. Henry, 'Interpreting the Gaulish Inscription of Ch.' (EC 21) 1984, 141–150; P.-Y. Lambert, 'A restatement on the Gaulish tablet from Ch.' (BBCS 34) 1987, 10–17.

chariot → waggons.

Châtillon-sur-Glâne. Modern name of an early Celtic settlement on the mouth of the Glâne, where it enters the Saane south of Fribourg. In the 6th-5thCs BC a fortified site existed there, which has been the subject of archaeological excavations since 1974. Already in 1865–1903 large quantities of grave goods of iron, bronze and gold were found in a radius of 10 miles. It is therefore thought that Ch. was the site of an early Celtic → princely seat.

Lit.: D. Ramseyer, 'Ch. (FR): un habitat de hauteur du Hallstatt final' (*Jahrb. d. Schweiz. Ges. f. Ur-und Frühgesch.* 66) 1983, 161–188.

children. The children of the Celts were generally subject to the supervision of their fathers. This is already clear from a remark of → Caesar (Bell. Gall. 6,19) and is confirmed by the decrees of Irish → law. In another passage Caesar records that the Germanic king Ariovist took as hostages the children of the nobles of the → Sequani (Bell. Gall. 1,31). This recalls the widespread custom in Ireland of parents having their children brought up in noble families with whom they were on more or less friendly terms (cf. → foster children).

It is striking that archaeology has revealed only a small number of children's graves, out of proportion to the doubtless high infant mortality. It may therefore be assumed that many dead children and babies were for religious reasons buried outside the customary burial places, without any special formalities. The children's graves known to us are for the most part characterised by grave goods in the form of → amulets. Evidently it was thought that the dead children were in need of special protection.

A Celtic god → Iovantucarus ("he who loves youth") is known from Roman times; he may have been worshipped as a protector of children.

Lit.: G. Coulon, *L'enfant en Gaule romaine*, P. 1994.

Chrétien de Troyes. Old French poet of the 12thC. What we know of him derives exclusively from what he says in his works and yields little concerning the precise dates and circumstances of his life. He undoubtedly enjoyed a thorough literary and philosophical education, and was conversant with the most varied strata of society. There is much that suggests that he was acquainted with southern England as well as northern France.

His lasting fame as a poet derives from his five great verse romances, which make him effectively the founder of → Arthurian literature. The personages surrounding king → Arthur had already been introduced from Celtic tradition into medieval Latin and Old French literature by → Geoffrey of Monmouth and his translator → Wace. In contrast to his predecessors, C. rendered the characters of the legend to a large extent independent of their historical and geographical framework of reference. Moreover, it is not Arthur himself who forms the focal point of the plots of his romances, but in each case a knight of the king's retinue. The poet's essential concern is with the fictional representation of the way in which these knights are tested and prove themselves worthy, whereas the Arthurian court merely serves as the backdrop, albeit a brilliant one. C. confers contemporary relevance upon his Celtic source material by his skilful integration of 12thC political, social and philosophical ideas.

Between 1160 and 1190 he wrote the romances *Erec et Enide*, *Cligès*, *Lancelot ou Le chevalier de la charette*, *Yvain ou Le chevalier au lion* and the incomplete *Perceval ou Le conte del graal*. On the evidence of the dedications the first four works originated at the court of Marie de Champagne, while the last is dedicated to Philip, Count of Flanders. Celtic names, subject matter and motifs are to be found in all of these romances; moreover, there is an exact correspondence between *Erec*, *Yvain*, and *Perceval* and the Middle Welsh prose narratives → *Gereint fab Erbin*, → *Iarlles y Ffynnawn* and → *Peredur fab Efrawg*. It is thought that the Welsh and French works derive independently from French reworkings of Celtic narrative material.

Lit.: N. J. Lacy, *The Craft of C.*, Lei. 1980; L. J. Topsfield, *C.: A Study of the Arthurian Romances*, C. 1981; D. Kelly (ed.), *The Romances of C.*, Lexington (Kentucky) 1985; D. Maddox, *The Arthurian Romances of C.*, C. 1991.

Christianisation. The oldest accounts of the Christianisation of the Celts derive from Roman Gaul, where there were Christian communities of a significant size in existence as early as the 2ndC AD. The new religion won ground most rapidly in the southern towns; by the end of the 4thC, however, Christianity had also gained ground in the rural areas of the north and was organised throughout Gaul in dioceses, on the pattern of Roman civil administration.

Christian communities in Britain are referred to by the ecclesiastical writer Tertullian as early as c. 200. There is documentary evidence of the presence of three British bishops at the synod of Arles in 314. Even after the departure of the Roman troops from Britain at the beginning of the 5thC Christianity continued to play an important role among the Romanised Celts of the country and spread from there to beyond the boundaries of the Roman Empire. The most important contemporary written source for the "Dark Ages" of the Anglo-Saxon conquest of Britain is → Gildas' *De Excidio Britanniae*.

The conversion of Ireland took place in the course of the 5thC, although there are thought to have been earlier isolated Christian communities, especially in the south of the island. Later Irish sources attribute the conversion from paganism to the missionary activity of St. → Patrick. From the 7th to the 12thCs a flourishing monastic culture evolved in Ireland, with Irish missionaries bringing decisive influences to bear upon spiritual life in Britain and on the European mainland.

The detail of the conversion of the Celtic countries remains for the most part obscure because of the paucity of contemporary written sources. Irish hagiography, in contrast to the Germanic north, identifies no Christian martyrs, yet there were certainly conflicts between the old and the new religion, for the Celtic priests (→ druids) are described consistently in early Irish literature as indefatigable opponents of Christianity. Recent research assumes that it was not because of their literary or historical interests that the medieval monks recorded pre-Christian traditions, but that their motives were for the most part quite specifically didactic, moral or political (cf. → Origin Legends).

Lit.: N. Gauthier, L'évangelisation des pays de la Moselle, P. 1980; C. Thomas, Christianity in Roman Britain to AD 500, Lo. 1981; R. Chevalier, 'Recherches sur la christianisation des cultes de la Gaule', in: La patrie gauloise d'Agrippa au 6e siècle, Ly. 1983, 283–326; P. Ní Chatháin & M. Richter (eds.), Irland und die Christenheit, St. 1987; E. R. Henken, Traditions of the Welsh Saints, C. 1987; J. P. Mackey (ed.), An Introduction to Celtic Christianity, E. 1989; K. McCone, Pagan Past and Christian Present in Early Irish Lit., May. 1990; R. Sharpe, Medieval Irish Saints' Lives, O. 1991; H. Mytum, The Origins of Early Christian Ireland, Lo. 1992; T. O. Clancy & G. Márkus, Iona: The Earliest Poetry of a Celtic Monastery, E. 1995; M. Low, Celtic Christianity and Nature. The Early Irish and Hebridean Traditions, E. 1995.

Cian (Ir. /kʹianʹ/). A son of the doctor → Dian Cécht, of the → Tuatha Dé Danann, in the stories of the → Mythological Cycle. According to the story of the Battle of Mag Tuired (→ Cath Maige Tuired), he was married to Ethne, a daughter of the one-eyed → Balar, of the → Fomoire. Their son was → Lug mac Ethnenn, who with a stone from his sling blinded his grandfather in the Battle of Mag Tuired and then struck off his head. The story of the Death of the Children of Tuirenn (→ Aided Chlainne Tuirenn) tells how C. is murdered by the three brothers Brian, Iuchar and Iucharba, because of a private grudge.

Cicollus. Celtic god identified on the basis of the → interpretatio romana with → Mars. His name may mean 'great protector' (cf. Ir. cích 'breast; protection' and oll 'great', and the Gaulish name of the god → An extlomarus). The worship of the god is attested by altar inscriptions from Dijon (CIL XIII 5479), Aignay-le-Duc (CIL XIII 2887) and Mâlain (CIL XIII 5597–5599, 5601), and an inscription on a metal circlet from Windisch in the Swiss canton of Aargau (NeLi 54). In several inscriptions the goddess → Litavis appears as his companion.

Cín Dromma Snechta (Ir. /kʹiːnʹ ˈdroma ˈʃnʹexta/ "The Booklet of Druim Snechta"). Lost Irish manuscript thought to have originated in the first half of the 8thC. Later manuscripts which refer to it as a source suggest that it contained many saga texts.

Lit.: T. Ó Concheanainn, 'Texts Derived from C. D. S. through Leabhar na hUidhre' (CMCSt 16) 1988, 1–40.

Cissonius. Celtic god identified with → Mercury, to judge from the ten surviving inscriptions (CIL XIII 3659, 4500, 5373, 6085, 6119, 6345, 7359, 8237, 11476 and 11607).

Ciumeşti. Site in north-western Roumania, not far from the Hungarian border. When a sand-dune south of C. was levelled in August 1961, the grave of a Celtic warrior of the 3rdC BC was discovered. An iron lance was found, together with a shirt of iron mail that had been folded together, two bronze leggings and a bell-shaped iron helmet decorated with spread wings of bronze. The latter is now in the Historical Museum of Bucharest.

Lit.: M. Rusu, 'Das keltische Fürstengrab von C. in Rumänien' (BRGK 50) 1969, 267–300.

clan. English form of the Irish word *clann* (older form: *cland*), corresponding to the Welsh plural *plant* (sing.: *plentyn*). Both words derive from Latin *planta*, originally signifying "seedling", but also presumably having the meaning "offshoot" or "offspring". In the oldest Irish legal texts *clann* denotes those members of a family group who can lay claim to the inheritance of clerical offices. In Middle Irish literature *clann*, and the term *cenél*, refer in general terms to a group of people who can trace their line back to a common ancestor. This is also the significance of the term in the Highlands of Scotland. In contemporary Irish, Scottish Gaelic and Welsh *clann* or *plant* signifies the children of a family.

Lit.: T. M. Charles-Edwards, *Early Irish and Welsh Kinship*, O. 1993.

Clarke, Austin (1896–1974). Anglo-Irish author, born in Dublin. After studying there at University College, he was temporarily employed as a lecturer in English, and worked as a literary critic, before devoting himself full-time to writing. Among those works in which he drew upon material from Old and Middle Irish literature are the poems *The Vengeance of Fionn* (→ *Tóruigheacht Dhiarmada agus Ghráinne*), *The Wooing of Becfola* (→ *Tochmarc Becfola*), *The Sword of the West* and *The Cattle Drive in Connaught* (→ Ulster Cycle), the two plays *The Plot is Ready* (→ *Aided Muirchertaig meic Erca*) and *The Plot Succeeds* (→ *Compert Mongáin*), and the comedy *The Son of Learning* (→ *Aislinge meic Chon Glinne*).

Lit.: M. Harmon, *Austin Clarke*, Du. 1989.

clothing → dress.

Clothru (Ir. /'kloθru/). In the stories of the → Ulster Cycle a daughter of the king → Eochaid Fedlech and sister of Queen → Medb. Her castle is thought to have been on Inis Clothrann ("Island of C.") in Loch Rí (today's Lough Ree, north of Athlone).

Cnabetius. Celtic god, identified on the basis of the → interpretatio romana with → Mars. Etymologically, his name has been interpreted as "the Crippled One". While this must needs remain hypothetical, such a designation would suggest a link with the one-armed Irish king → Nuadu Argatlám, or possibly also with the Germanic war-god Týr. Votive dedications to C. have been found in Tholey in the Saarland (CIL XIII 4258), Wahlscheid (Nordhrein-Westfalen) and Hüttigweiler, near Saarbrücken (CIL XIII 4507 and 4508), Erbstetten in the Backnang district (CIL XIII 6455) and Osterburken, Baden-Württemberg (CIL XIII 6572).

Lit.: S. Gutenbrunner, 'Mars Cnabetius' (ZCP 20) 1936, 278–283.

Cobthach Coel (Ir. /'kofθax koil/). In the story → *Orgain Denna Ríg* a king said to have ruled over Ireland in the 4thC BC. According to tradition he murdered his brother Loegaire Lorc and the latter's son Ailill Áine, which led to his death and that of all his retinue at the hands of Ailill's son, Labraid.

Cocidius. Celtic god worshipped in the North of England, primarily by members of the Roman army. Of some twenty inscriptions dedicated to him five (*RIB* 602, 933, 1017, 2015 and 2024) identify him with → Mars, one (*RIB* 1578) with the Roman god of the woods Silvanus, and one (*RIB* 1102) with a Celtic god named Vernostonus. On the relief of an altar (*RIB* 1207) C. is depicted as a huntsman with a dog and a stag. Two votive plaques of repoussé silver (*RIB* 986 and 987, now in the Carlisle museum) depict the god as a warrior with shield and spear.

cock. Finds of bones and visual depictions attest that domestic fowl were introduced to the regions north of the Alps from the Mediterranean area in the late Hallstatt period. That a special significance attached to the cock in Celtic religion is suggested above all by the observation of → Caesar (Bell. Gall. 5,12) that the British accounted it wrong to eat poultry. The bronze → fibula in the shape of a cock which was found in the grave of the princess of → Reinheim was perhaps a talisman or an → amulet to ward evil fortune away from the wearer. The employment of the cock as a symbol of the French nation is a modern phenomenon deriving from the double meaning of the Latin word gallus ("cock" and "Gaul").

Lit.: P. Meniel, *Chasse et élevage chez les Gaulois*, P. 1987.

Cogitosus → Brigit (2)

cóiced (Ir. /'koːgʹeð/). Term denoting the distinct areas of sovereignty or "provinces" of Ireland. The original meaning of the word is "fifth". All the sources distinguish between the provinces of Ulster, Leinster, Munster and Connacht. In some texts the last "fifth" is named as Meath, whereas others arrive at five by halving the province of Munster. According to the "Book of the Invasions of Ireland" (→ *Lebor Gabála Érenn*) this division of the country derives from the → Fir Bolg.

Lit.: A. and B. Rees, *Celtic Heritage*, Lo. 1961; P. MacCana, 'Early Irish Ideology and the Concept of Unity', in: R. Kearney (ed.), *The Irish Mind*, Du. 1985, 56–78.

coins. Coins were first used by the Celts at the beginning of the 3rdC BC. The evidence of archaeological finds reveals a wide variety of different types, whose area of circulation was however always regionally restricted. In all probability the coins in the fortified town-like settlements (→ oppida) were circulated at the instigation of individual tribal chieftains. However, attributing specific types of coin to Celtic tribes whose names we know proves difficult, particularly outside Gaul.

Coins were minted by first casting the metal (generally → gold, → silver or → bronze) in moulds of burnt clay (known as *Tüpfelplatten*, "dot-plates") that had been prepared beforehand, resulting in pieces of exactly equal weight. These pieces (*Schrötlinge*) were then worked manually, hammered between two stamps.

It is not known what terms the Celts used for their coins. The names customary today, such as tetradrachme or stater, are borrowed from the Greek, it being evident that Celtic minting was indebted above all to Greek models. This is apparent also in the images on the coins, although the Greek and Roman models were for the most part treated in an arbitrary manner. It is probable that many images on the coins also had a religious significance, but given the lack of legends or other literary sources relating to coins this significance is scarcely accessible to us. In post-Celtic times coins therefore frequently gave rise to imaginative speculation (cf. → *Regenbogenschüsselchen*).

In Ireland coins were not introduced until the Viking invasions.

Lit.: R. Forrer, *Keltische Numismatik der Rhein-und Donaulande*, rev. ed. in 2 vols., Graz 1968; K. Pink, *Einführung in die keltische Münzkunde*, V. 1974; D. F. Allen, *The Coins of the Ancient Celts*, E. 1980; B. Overbeck, *Die Welt der Kelten im Spiegel der Münzen*, Mn. 1980; B. Cunliffe (ed.), *Coinage and Society in Britain and Gaul*, Lo. 1981; P.-M. Duval, *Monnaies gauloises et mythes celtiques*, P. 1987; D. Nash, *Coinage in the Celtic World*, Lo. 1987; R. D. van Arsdell, *Celtic Coinage of Britain*, Lo. 1989; K. Gruel, *La Monnaie chez les Gaulois*, P. 1989; *Celtic Coinage: Britain and beyond*, O. 1992.

Cóir Anmann (Ir. /koːr' 'anmaN/ "The Fitness of Names"). Etymological list of Irish personal and tribal names which survives in two versions of divergent length. The older, short version is preserved in alphabetical order in four manuscripts of the 14th-15thCs. The later, extended version is arranged on a chronological basis in a single manuscript of c. 1500. The collection comprises a total of some 300 names. The authors attempt to explain the origin and meaning of these with reference to legends, only some of which are known to us.

Ed. and trans.: W. Stokes and E. Windisch, *Ir. Texte*, Lo. 1880–1905, vol. 3.2.

Coirbre → Cairbre.

Coligny. Site in the Dép. of Ain in south-east France, where in November 1897 the remains of a bronze Gallo-Roman statue of the god → Mars were found, together with c. 150 fragments of a bronze tablet bearing a Gaulish inscription written in Roman letters. Further investigation revealed that the bronze tablet is a Gaulish calendar covering a period of five solar years.

The basis of the time division was formed by a lunar year of 12 months consisting of 355 days (7 x 30 + 5 x 29). The deviation from the solar year was compensated for by the insertion of a 30-day intercalendary month every two and a half years, i.e. after every 30 months. The five-year cycle depicted on the calendar thus embraces 62 months, each of which was divided into two halves comprising 15 + 15 or 15 + 14 days. The individual months are assigned names and demarcated, depending upon their length (30 or 29 days), by the abbreviations M(AT) and ANMAT. These terms may have the same meaning as the linguistically cognate Middle Welsh words *mad* "lucky" and *anfad* "unlucky". It is however conceivable that they denote merely the "completeness" or "incompleteness" of the months to which they refer.

It is thought that the calendar, like the statue of the god, was originally erected in a sanctuary and had *inter alia* a ritual function. For a long time the calendar was dated to the 1stC AD, but it is now placed not before the end of the 2ndC AD. Until the discovery of the inscriptions of → Chamalières and → Larzac it constituted the most substantial document in the Gaulish language. It is now in the Musée de la civilisation gallo-romaine in Lyons.

Lit.: *Recueil des inscriptions gauloises III: Les calendriers*, P. 1986; G. Olmsted, *The Gaulish Calendar*, Bo. 1992.

Coll fab Collfrewi (Welsh /koːɫ vaːb koɫˈvrewi/). Custodian of the sow → Henwen, one of the "three mighty swineherds of Britain" in the → *Trioedd Ynys Prydein*. (The other two are → Pryderi fab Pwyll Pen Annwfn and → Drystan fab Tallwch.)

Colum Cille (Ir. /ˈkolum ˈkʼiLʼe/). One of the most important saints, founders of monasteries and missionaries of the Irish church. His name means "Dove of the Church", corresponding to the customary term in the Latin sources, Columba. His life and work are recorded in the → *Vita Columbae* of → Adamnán, Bede's History of the English Church, and a verse eulogy which was written shortly after Columba's death (→ *Amra Choluim Chille*). A Middle Irish biography with a heavy admixture of legend has also survived. The historical sources record that Columba was born c. 520, a scion of the noble family of the Uí Néill in the north of Ireland. His father Fedlimid was a greatgrandson of the founder of the dynasty, Niall Noigiallach, and on his birth the boy was given the name Crimthann. In 546 Columba founded the monastery of Derry, and thereafter the monasteries of Durrow and Kells. He made his way with a small band of followers to Scotland c. 565 and went on missions to the → Picts in the north. One of his most important foundations was the monastery of Iona, on a Hebridean island, where C. was buried on his death in 597 and was worshipped as the patron saint of Scotland.

Lit.: M. Herbert, Iona, Kells, and Derry, O. 1988.

Commenta Bernensia → Berne Scholia.

Commius. A Gaul of the tribe of the → Atrebates, appointed king by → Caesar after the subjugation of his people in 57 BC. Two years later, acting on behalf of Caesar, he sought to establish the recognition of Roman authority by the Celtic tribes of Britain. He and his tribe were accorded preferential treatment in return; nevertheless, in 52 BC Commius joined the rebellion of → Vercingetorix. At the siege of → Alesia he led the army which sought in vain to relieve the besieged Gaulish forces. After the suppression of the rebellion C. at first joined forces with the Germani, then returned to Britain. The ancient sources supplied the inspiration for the story Komm l'Atrébate (1897) by Anatole France (1844–1924).

compert (Ir. /'komb'eRt/). Term denoting conception which serves in one of the two → Lists of Sagas to classify those stories concerned with the begetting and birth of celebrated heroes.

Compert Chonchobuir (Ir. /'komb'eRt 'xonxovur'/ "The Begetting of Conchobar"). Title of a story from the → Ulster Cycle, the oldest version of which is preserved in the → "Yellow Book of Lecan" and in the → "Book of Ballymote". It begins with the druid and warrior → Cathbad slaying in a raid the twelve foster-fathers of the girl Asa, a daughter of the king Eochu Sálbuide of Ulster. Set on vengeance, Asa ("the Gentle One") becomes the leader of a band of warriors, acquiring the byname Ni-Asa ("Ungentle") or Nesa. One day Cathbad succeeds in capturing Nesa, who saves her life at the price of becoming Cathbad's wife. Later she presents her husband with a son, → Conchobar mac Nesa, who after the death of his grandfather reigns over the province of Ulster.

Ed.: K. Meyer, 'C. C.' (RC 6) 1884, 173–182 (with Engl. trans.)

Trans.: R. Thurneysen, Sagen aus dem alten Irland, B. 1901; Ch.-J. Guyonvarc'h, 'La Naissance de Conchobar' (Ogam 11) 1959, 56–65 and 335–336; (Ogam 12) 1960, 235–240.

Compert Chon Culainn (Ir. /'komb'eRt xon 'kuliN'/ "The Begetting of Cú Chulainn"). One of the prefatory tales (→ remscéla) to the story of the Cattle Raid of Cuailnge (→ Táin Bó Cuailnge). It is preserved in two divergent versions in the "Book of the Dun Cow" (→ Lebor na hUidre), and in several later manuscripts. The story tells how the sister (in some MSS:

daughter) of the king → Conchobar mac Nesa mysteriously becomes pregnant and gives birth to the boy Sétanta, who later under the name of → Cú Chulainn becomes the most celebrated hero of Ulster. The name of Cú Chulainn's mother is rendered variously in the manuscripts as Deichtir(e) or Deichtine. His father in the older version of the saga is the deity → Lug mac Ethnenn. Elsewhere Cú Chulainn takes his name from his mother's human spouse: mac Sualtaim ("son of S."). The story is reworked by Lady Augusta → Gregory in the first chapter of her book *Cuchulain of Muirthemne*.

Ed. A. G. van Hamel, C. C. C. and Other Stories, Du. 1933 (MMIS 3).

Trans.: R. Thurneysen, *Sagen aus dem alten Irland*, B. 1901; Ch.-J. Guyonvarc'h and F. Le Roux, 'La Conception de Cúchulainn' *(Ogam* 17) 1965, 363–410; J. Gantz, *Early Irish Myths and Sagas*, Harm. 1981.

Lit.: T. Ó Concheanainn, 'The textual tradition of C. C. C.' *(Celtica* 21) 1990, 441–455.

Compert Mongáin ocus serc Duibe Lacha do Mongán (Ir. /ˈkombˈeRt ˈvoŋgaːnˈ ogus ʃerg ˈduvˈe ˈLaxa do ˈvoŋgaːn/ "The Birth of Mongán and Mongán's Love for Dub Lacha"). Title of a tale from the → Historical Cycle, preserved in Early New Irish in a single manuscript of the 15thC. It tells how → Manannán mac Lir aids the Irish king Fiachna in battle, in return for which he claims the right to spend a night with Fiachna's wife in the guise of Fiachna. From this union springs Mongán, who grows up with his father and learns his magic arts. Later he marries Dub Lacha, who was born in the same night as he. The remainder of the story tells how Mongán forfeits his wife to the king of Leinster as the consequence of a rashly worded promise. Mongán falls into a wasting sickness because of the loss of his love, but ultimately succeeds in winning her back by dint of his magical powers.

The story is retold by James → Stephens in his *Irish Fairy Tales* (1920) and by Austin → Clarke in his play *The Plot Succeeds* (1950).

Ed. and trans.: K. Meyer, *The Voyage of Bran*, Lo. 1895–1897.

Lit.: M. Dillon, *The Cycles of the Kings*. Lo., 1946; J. Falaky Nagy, 'In Defence of Rómánsaíocht' *(Ériu* 38) 1987, 9–26.

Conaire mac Moga Láma (Ir. /ˈkonarˈe mak ˈmoɣa ˈLaːva/). Son and heir of the king → Conn Cétchathach in the tales of the → Historical Cycle. After he is murdered by a rival called Nemed, Conn's son → Art becomes king of Ireland.

Conaire Mór (Ir. /ˈkonarˈe moːr/ "C. the Great"). Chief personage in the tale → *Togail Bruidne Da Derga*.

Conall Cernach (Ir. /ˈkonaL ˈkˈernax/). A foster-brother of the hero → Cú Chulainn in the tales of the → Ulster Cycle; son of the poet → Amairgin mac Ecit Salaig and his wife → Finnchaem. In the tale → *Táin Bó Froích* C. helps the titular hero Froech mac Idaith in the search for his wife, his sons and his cattle, who have been stolen by enemy warriors. In the Story of the Pig of Mac Dathó (→ *Scéla mucce Meic Dathó*) his indisputed reputation is such that he is the only one of the warriors of Ulster present who is able to put in his place the Connacht warrior → Cet mac Mágach. A further confrontation with Cet which ends in the death of the latter is told in the tale → *Aided Cheit maic Mágach*. In the tale of the Death of Cú Chulainn (→ *Aided Chon Chulainn*) C. wreaks his vengeance on the murderers of his foster-brother. How C. kills in single combat the king of Leinster to avenge the death of his two brothers is told in the tale → *Cath Étair*.

Conchobar mac Nesa (Ir. /ˈkonxovar mak ˈNˈesa/). King of the province of Ulster in the tales of the → Ulster Cycle; son of the druid Cathbad and his wife Nesa, a daughter of King Eochu Sálbuide of Ulster (→ *Compert Chonchobuir*). His sister is Deichtine, mother of the hero → Cú Chulainn. It is only in the tale of the Exile of the Sons of Uisliu (→ *Longas mac nUislenn*) that C. is portrayed in pronouncedly negative fashion. Otherwise the tales describe him consistently as a capable and just ruler. In the story of the Cattle-Raid of Cuailnge (→ *Táin Bó Cuailnge*) he leads his army to victory over the troops of the royal couple Ailill and Medb, thus proving himself to be a successful war-leader. The tragic end of the king is told by the tale → *Aided Chonchobuir*.

Condatis. Celtic god whose name is probably related to the place-name Condate, "confluence (of two rivers)", which was frequently employed, particularly in Gaul, to denote settlements located at such places. The cult of C. is attested by three votive inscriptions from Bowes in Yorkshire (*RIB* 731), Piercebridge near Darlington (*RIB* 1024) and Chester-le-Street near Durham (*RIB* 1045). In all three instances C. is identified with → Mars on the basis of the → interpretatio romana.

Conn Cétchacath (Ir. /koN ˈkˈeːdxaθax/ "Conn of the Hundred Battles"). In the tales of the → Ulster Cycle a king said to have lived in the 2ndC AD. According to tradition his birth was accompanied by miraculous signs (→ *Airne Fíngein*). After he becomes king the personification of sovereignty (flathius) appears to him, and the elf → Lug mac Ethnenn prophesies to him the length of his rule and that of the future kings of Ireland (→ *Baile in Scáil*). It is said that at first C. ruled in Tara over the northern half of Ireland, whilst Eogan Mór was king over the southern half of the island. Only after Eogan dies in the Battle of Mag Léna does C. come to rule over both parts of the land. The story → *Echtrae Chonnlai* tells how Connla, one of the king's two sons, falls in love with a fairy (→ síd) and leaves the world of men forever. Conn's other son, Art, is said to be the father of the celebrated hero → Cormac mac Airt.

Connla (Ir. /'koNla/). In the tales of the → Historical Cycle a son of the king → Conn Cétchatach, whose fate is the subject of the tale → *Echtrae Chonnlai*.

continental Celtic → languages, Celtic.

Cormac Conn Longas (Ir. /'kormak koN 'Loŋgas/). In the tales of the → Ulster Cycle a son of the king → Conchobar mac Nesa. His mother is Clothru, a daughter of King Eochaid Fedlech and sister of the queen → Medb. According to the tale → *Longas mac nUislenn* Cormac, together with → Fergus mac Roich and → Dubthach Dael Ulad, had acted as guarantors of the safety of the sons of Uisliu. After the latter are assassinated by Conchobar, Cormac, together with the two other guarantors and many other warriors, goes over to King → Ailill of Connacht. His by-name is interpreted as "head (conn) of the exiles (longas)". The tale of the Cattle-Raid of Cuailnge (→ Táin Bó Cuailnge) describes how C. and his companions take part in the great campaign of the men of Connacht against the inhabitants of Ulster, without being able to conceal their sympathy for their former compatriots and friends.

Cormac mac Airt (Ir. /'kormak mak aR't'/). In the tales of the → Historical Cycle a king said to have lived in the 3rdC AD. The medieval tradition celebrates him as an ideal ruler, whose reign was characterised by justice, prosperity and peace. A fictitious biography of the king dating from the 5th-8thC combines international fairy-tale motifs with specifically Irish views concerning the nature of kingship and the political tendencies of the early Middle Ages. Of the tales that have survived which draw upon this biography, the *Scéla Eogain agus Cormaic* tells the story of C. from his birth to the time when he becomes king, whereas the later narrative *Geneamuin Cormaic* tells his whole life-story, ending with his death and burial. A single episode, the wooing of his bride, forms the subject of *Esnada Tige Buchet*. The king's visit to the land of elves and fairies (→ síd) is the subject of the tale *Echtra Chormaic*.
  Lit.: T. Ó Cathasaigh, *The Heroic Biography of C. m. A.*, Du. 1977.

Cormac mac Cuilennái (Ir. /'kormak mak 'kul'eNa:n'/). Bishop of Cashel, and from 902 to 908 king of the southern Irish province of Munster. Author of the etymological glossary → *Sanas Chormaic*.

Cornish. The Celtic language of Cornwall, which evolved from → British in the 5th/6thC, together with → Breton, → Cumbrian and → Welsh. Already in the Middle Ages its distribution seems to have been limited to the western part of the peninsula, and subsequently because of the immigration of English speakers and the increasing commercial importance of English it declined more and more. When Edward → Lhuyd travelled through Cornwall around 1700, the population was already entirely bilingual, and in the second half of the 18thC the language died out. Scarcely any Cornish literature survives apart from a little religious poetry.

Lit.: M. F. Wakelin, *Language and History in Cornwall*, Leicester 1975; G. Price, *The Languages of Britain*, Lo. 1984; H. Lewis, *Llawlyfr Cernyweg Canol*, Car. ²1945 (= *Handbuch des Mittelkornischen*, trans. S. Zimmer, I. 1990); B. Murdoch, *Cornish Literature*, C. 1993.

Corotiacus. Celtic god, identified with → Mars on the basis of the → interpretatio romana. His cult is attested by a single votive inscription from Martlesham in Suffolk (*RIB* 213).

cosmogony. Term given in comparative religion to beliefs concerning the origins of the world. That the Celts were acquainted with creation myths is concluded from an allusion in → Caesar, according to which the → Druids were interested, among other things, in the movement of the stars, and the size of the universe and of the earth (Bell. Gall. 6,14). After they were converted to Christianity, however, the Celts – in complete contrast to the Germani – kept no written record of these beliefs, with the consequence that this part of their mythology is now entirely lost to us.

Cososus. Celtic god, whose cult is attested by a votive inscription from the neighbourhood of Bourges (CIL XIII 1353), in which he is identified with → Mars on the basis of the → interpretatio romana.

costume → dress.

Coventina. Celtic goddess, worshipped in the period of Roman rule. A sanctuary devoted to her, excavated in 1876, is situated near what is now Carrawburgh, on Hadrian's Wall. In the sanctuary well numerous → votive and sacrificial gifts were found, including bronze animal statuettes, vessels and over 13,000 coins. 14 inscriptions with the name C. (*RIB* 1522–1535) were found, as well as pictorial representations of the goddess as a water-nymph.

Lit.: L. Allason-Jones & B. McKay, *C.'s Well*, Chesters 1985.

craft. Our knowledge of Celtic craftsmanship in the pre-Christian era is based upon archaeological finds, accounts in classical → ethnography and visual representations from the field of Gallo-Roman culture. Although these sources do to some extent complement one another, what they have to say is on the whole limited, and our knowledge is therefore fragmentary. For example, luxury products of craftsmanship have been found in the → princely graves of the 6th/5thC BC, yet the tools and workshops of this time are for the most part unknown to us. On the other hand, many tools originating from specialised workshops have been found in the settlements resembling towns (→ oppida) of the 2nd/1stC BC, but no grave goods of corresponding value. Inevitably, metal artefacts have on the whole survived far better than products made of organic materials such as wood, leather or → textiles. Our knowledge of the Celtic names of individual crafts, basic materials, tools and products in the pre-Roman and Roman era is for the most part inadequate. These names only surface for the most part in medieval literary sources from Ireland and Wales, and – with a few exceptions – it is only through comparative philology that we can surmise their earlier form.

Despite these qualifications the sources yield insights into a variety of methods of manufacture. Woodwork was highly advanced, needed as it was from the outset for building houses and forts (→ Murus Gallicus), to make barrels, vats and buckets, and to build ships and boats. The ability to work with wood was also necessary for making light and manoeuverable → waggons with two or four wheels, which also found use as grave goods.

There is evidence of pottery in Central Europe dating back to the 5th millennium BC. Even before the advent of the Celts the mass production of specific types of vessels had established itself (cf. → ceramics). From the last third of the first millennium onwards the Celts worked → glass in workshops specially equipped for the purpose. Also highly developed and specialised was the working of → iron, → bronze and → gold, whereas → silver was rarely used, and then predominantly on the fringes of the Celtic world. Bronze was both cast and wrought into sheet metal. Iron was always worked by smiths and was of great importance particularly for → agriculture and → warfare, and in consequence → smiths were doubtless much sought-after specialists. Little is known concerning the social position of craftsmen apart from smiths. They play no dominant role in insular Celtic literature prior to the beginning of the modern period, which is not surprising in view of the fact that those who passed down the traditions addressed themselves primarily to an aristocratic audience.

Lit.: M. Reddé, 'Les scènes de métier dans la sculpture funéraire gallo-romaine' (Gallia 36) 1978, 43–63; D. Timpe, 'Das keltische Handwerk im Lichte der antiken Literatur', in: Das Handwerk in vor- und frühgeschichtlicher Zeit I–II, Gö. 1981–1983, I, 36–62; W. Kimmig, 'Zum Handwerk der späten Hallstattzeit', ibidem, II, 13–33; F. Fischer, 'Das Handwerk bei den Kelten zur Zeit der Oppida', ibidem, II, 34–49; K. H. Schmidt, 'Handwerk und Handwerker in altkeltischen Sprachdenkmälern', ibidem, II, 751–763; W. Gillies, 'The craftsman in early Celtic literature' (Scottish Archaeological Forum 11) 1981, 70–85.

crannóg (Ir. /'kraNoːg/). Term denoting a building erected on piles in a lake. Most of these edifices date back to early Christian times; some however are traceable to the Neolithic period.

Crédne (Ir. /'krʹeːðʹnʹe/). Name of the metalworker or artificer of the →

Tuatha Dé Danann in the tale of the Battle of Mag Tuired (→ *Cath Maige Tuired*). In the course of the battle against the → Fomoire he supplies the warriors with rivets for their spears, swords, shields and bosses.

Creiddylad (Welsh /krei'ðəlad/). In the tale *Culhwch ac Olwen* daughter of → Lludd Llawereint. She is promised to a warrior called Gwythyr fab Greidiawl, but shortly before her wedding she is abducted by → Gwyn fab Nudd. The ensuing dispute between Gwythyr and Gwyn is settled by the verdict of → Arthur, who proclaims that henceforth, until Judgement Day, the two are to fight in single combat on the first of May every year, the prize being C. He who is victor at the end of time will keep C. as his wife.

Cridenbél (Ir. /'k'r'ið 'env'e:l/). A poet of the → Tuatha Dé Danann in the tale of the Battle of Mag Tuired (→ *Cath Maige Tuired*). By the threat of a poetic diatribe (→ áer) he compels the → Dagda to reserve the three best morsels of his supper for him every day. On the advice of his son → Oengus, the Dagda conceals three gold pieces in his food, and C. dies by eating these. The Dagda is pronounced innocent of murder, on the grounds that he did indeed only keep back for C. "the best" he had at his disposal.

Críth Gablach (Ir. /k'r'i:θ 'gavlax/ "branched purchase"). Title of an Old Irish legal text of the early 8thC. In question and answer form it gives information concerning the various ranks of Irish society and the rights and duties associated with them. The title is explained at the beginning of the treatise: the individual purchases with his property the right to belong to a certain rank; the different ranks are "branched", divided into many subdivisions.
  Ed.: D. A. Binchy, C. G., Du. 1941 (MMIS 11).
  Trans.: E. MacNeill, 'The Law of Status or Franchise' (PRIA 36) 1923, 265–316.
  Lit.: P. L. Henry, 'Interpreting C. G.' (ZCP 36) 1978, 54–62; T. Charles-Edwards, 'C. G. and the Law of Status' (Peritia 5) 1986, 53–73.

Croker, Thomas Crofton (1798–1854). Irish folklorist, born in Cork. After an apprenticeship in trade he worked for the Admiralty in London from 1818 to 1850. He occupied his leisure time with the study of the history and oral traditions of his Irish homeland. These formed the subject of his first book, *Researches in the South of Ireland* (1824). His subsequent collection of southern Irish fairy-tales, *Fairy Legends and Traditions of the South of Ireland*, published anonymously in 1825, proved a commercial success; within a year of its publication it was translated into German by the Brothers Grimm and provided with a scholarly introduction concerning beliefs in elves and fairies, appearing under the title *Irische Elfenmärchen*. Further translations of stories from the second volume of *Fairy Legends*, which appeared in 1828, were not published in translation until 1986, after they were found among the papers of Wilhelm Grimm. C. has at times been the subject of severe criticism, on the grounds that his adaptations of the traditions he collected were excessively tailored to meet public taste, yet his work remains of enduring importance as a pioneering achievement in the field of Irish folklore.

Lit.: B. G. MacCarthy, 'Th. C. C. 1798–1854' (*Studies* 32) 1943, 539–556; J. Hennig, 'The Brothers Grimm and Th. C. C.' (*Modern Language Review* 41) 1946, 44–54; W. Moritz et al. (eds.), *Ir. Land- und Seemärchen*, Marburg 1986.

cromlech (Welsh /'kromlex/). Term denoting a pre-historic chamber grave (→ dolmen).

Cruachain (Ir. /'kruaxin'/) or (later) Cruachu. Seat of the kings of Connacht in the tales of the → Ulster Cycle, identical with the archaeological site of Rathcroghan in County Roscommon.

Cruithin → Picts, → Prydein.

Crunnchu (Ir. /'kruNxu/). Husband of → Macha in the story → Noínden Ulad.

Cuailnge (Ir. /'kual'n'g'e/). In the tales of the → Ulster Cycle a hilly area in the north-east of what is now County Louth, on the east coast of Ireland. It forms part of the dominion of the king → Conchobar mac Nesa and is the home of the famed bull called Donn C. ("The Brown Bull of C."). The story of the Cattle Raid of C. (→ *Táin Bó Cuailnge*) tells how the inhabitants of the province of Connacht, headed by the royal couple Ailill and Medb, lead a mighty force into battle in order to capture the bull.

Cú Chulainn (Ir. /ku: 'xuliN'/). Chief hero of the tales of the → Ulster Cycle. His mother is Deichtine, a sister (or, in a variant tradition, daughter) of the king of Ulster → Conchobar mac Nesa; his father is the elf → Lug mac Ethnenn. C. is sometimes given the name mac Sualtaim ("son of Sualtaim"), after his foster-father Sualtaim mac Roich, his mother's husband. His home is said to be the Plain of → Mag Muirthemne.

The oldest branch of traditions concerning C. is preserved in the tale of the Cattle Raid of Cuailnge (→ *Táin Bó Cuailnge*), in which C., still in his early youth, accompanied by his charioteer Loeg mac Riangabra, fights without foreign aid against the host of the royal couple → Ailill and → Medb of Connacht. Several tales concerning the youthful deeds of C. are intertwined in the description of these battles, including one explaining his name, "Hound of Culann" (→ *Macgnímrada Con Culainn*). Other tales have survived concerning his birth (→ *Compert Chon Culainn*), his bridal quest (→ *Tochmarc Emire*), his journey to the land of elves and fairies (→ *Serglige Con Culainn*), his combat with his own son (→ *Aided Oenfir Aífe*) and, finally, his death (→ *Aided Chon Culainn*). In the "Works of Ossian", composed by James → Macpherson, C. appears under the name → Cuthullin. The tales concerning him were an important source for the → Irish Renaissance and in particular inspired the dramatist William Butler → Yeats.

Lit.: A. Bruford, 'Cú Chulainn – An Ill-Made Hero?', in: H. L. C. Tristram (ed.), *Text und Zeittiefe*, T. 1994, 185–215.

Culann (Ir. /'kulaN/). In the tales of the → Ulster Cycle the smith whose hound gives → Cú Chulainn his name ("Hound of C.") (cf. → *Macgnímrada Con Culainn*).

Culdees → Céli Dé.

Culhwch ac Olwen (Welsh /'kilhux ak 'olwen/). The oldest Welsh tale belonging to the legends concerning → Arthur. It tells of how the titular hero Culhwch woos Olwen, daughter of the giant → Ysbaddaden Bencawr. Because his stepmother has determined that he is fated to marry none save Olwen, Culhwch, advised by his father, seeks help from his cousin Arthur. In the company of Arthur and his retinue he then makes his way to the stronghold of Ysbaddaden in order to advance his suit. Ysbaddaden assents to the union, but demands that Culhwch fulfil in return forty arduous tasks. Only a few of the adventures that ensue are described in detail; these include the quest for → Mabon fab Modron and the hunt for the wild boar → Twrch Trwyth. The story ends with the death of Ysbaddaden and the marriage of Culhwch and Olwen.

Ed.: R. Bromwich and D. S. Evans, *C. ac O.*, Car. 1992.

Trans.: G. Jones & T. Jones, *The Mabinogion*, rev. ed., Lo. 1974; J. Gantz, *The Mabinogion*, Harm. 1976; H. Birkhan, *Kelt. Erzählungen vom Kaiser Arthur*, Kettwig 1989.

Lit.: D. Edel, *Helden auf Freiersfüßen: "Tochmarc Emire" und "Mal y Kavas Kulhwch Olwen"*, A. 1980; P. Sims-Williams, 'The Significance of the Irish Personal Names in C. ac O.' (BBCS 29) 1980–82, 600–620; J. N. Radner, 'Interpreting Irony in Medieval Celtic Narrative: The Case of C. ac O.' (CMCSt 16) 1988, 41–59.

cumal (Ir. /'kuval/). Term denoting a "female slave", which appears frequently in legal texts as a unit of value, and, in an extended sense, occasionally denotes the price of purchase or a monetary punishment of variable value. The legal text → *Críth Gablach* renders the "price of honour" (cf. → enech) of the king highest in rank (cf. → rí) as 14 c., or 42 milch-cows.

Lit.: F. Kelly, *A Guide to Early Ir. Law*, Du. 1988.

Cumbrian. The language of the Celtic population of Northern England and Southern Scotland. It evolved out of → British in the 5th/6thC, together with → Breton, → Cornish and → Welsh. Owing to the advance of the

Germanic tribes it rapidly lost ground and to all appearances was extinct as early as the 12thC. Our knowledge of Cumbrian is limited for the most part to place-names and a few words and names in Latin sources. Many scholars believe that a few works composed in Cumbrian by the poets → Neirin and → Taliesin (both c. 550–600) were originally transmitted orally and later recorded in Wales. This is perfectly feasible, as Cumbrian and Welsh are thought to have been virtually indistinguishable in the early period, and there were close cultural links between the two linguistic communities. It is however also conceivable that the verses in question – like many others – were only attributed to the named poets, but in reality originated after their lifetimes.

Lit.: G. Price, The Languages of Britain, Lo. 1984.

Cunedda (Welsh /ki'neða/). A prince of the tribe of the Gododdin in southern Scotland in the → Historia Brittonum, who settles with his eight sons in North Wales and there succeeds in repelling the invading Irish. If this account is based upon a historical source, then it is probably concerned with events which occurred towards the end of the 4th or in the middle of the 5thC. In the medieval tradition C. is regarded as the ancestor of prominent noble families and many saints.

Lit.: R. G. Gruffydd, 'Reflections on the story of C.' (StC 24/25) 1989/90, 1–14.

Cunobellinus. British king who ruled over the tribe of the Catuvellauni in South-East England in the first half of the 1stC AD. His name survives in the title of Shakespeare's play Cymbeline, although the plot derives not from Celtic tradition but from material supplied by the English chronicler Holinshed.

curad-mír (Ir. /'kurað m'i:r'/ "hero's morsel"). The choice part of the meat of a slaughtered animal, so named because legend had it that it fell to the part of the bravest warrior. Quarrels deriving from the claim to the hero's morsel are related in the tales → Fled Bricrenn and → Scéla mucce Meic Dathó.

Cú Roí mac Dáiri (Ir. /ku: Roi mak 'da:r'i/ "Cú Roí, son of Dáire"). A king of the province of Munster in the tales of the → Ulster Cycle. His royal residence is said to be Cathair Con Roí, now Caherconree in the hills of Slemish west of Tralee. He plays a major role in the stories → Fled Bricrenn, → Mesca Ulad, Aided Con Roí, and in the text known as Amra Con Roí. In Welsh tradition he figures in the elegy Marwnat Corroi mab Dayry, preserved in the Book of Taliesin (→ Llyfr Taliesin). Tradition holds that his wife Bláthnat betrayed him to his mortal enemy → Cú Chulainn, who slew him.

Curtin, Jeremiah (c. 1840–1906). American folklorist, born in Greenfield (Wisconsin). After studying in Harvard, he was employed in various posts by the American and Russian governments. His extensive travels in Europe, Asia and North America yielded a comprehensive collection of the oral traditions of the most diverse peoples and cultures. The traditional material he collected in Ireland was published in his *Myths and Folklore of Ireland* (1890), *Hero-Tales of Ireland* (1894) and *Tales of the Fairies and of the Ghost World* (1895). Other fairy-tales which C. had not published in book form were edited in 1942 by the Irish folklorist Séamus Ó Duilearga (James Delargy) under the title *Irish Folktales*.

Lit.: U. Clemen (ed.), *Ir. Märchen*, Mn. 1971 (Ger. trans. with commentary); J. & G. Dunleavy, 'J. C.'s Working Methods' (*Éigse* 18) 1981/82, 67–86.

Cúscraid Menn Macha (Ir. /'kuːskriðˈmˈeN 'maxa/). In the tales of the → Ulster Cycle a son of the king → Conchobar mac Nesa and foster-son of the warrior → Conall Cernach. His byname Menn Macha ("the Stammerer of Macha") is explained in the tale → *Scéla mucce Meic Dathó*: the Connacht warrior → Cet mac Mágach, in single combat with C., pierced his neck and damaged his vocal chords.

Cuthullin. Guardian and general of the young king Cormac of Ireland in the "Works of Ossian" composed by James → Macpherson. The epic *Fingal* tells of his vain attempt to prevent an invasion by King Swaran of Lochlin (Scandinavia). Only Cormac's ally, the Scottish king Fingal, succeeds in defeating Swaran in single combat, thus compelling him to accept a truce and return to his homeland. In the tale *The Death of C.* C. dies in battle against a rebel called Torlath. The model for Macpherson's character C. is the legendary Irish hero → Cú Chulainn. Tradition however holds that Cú Chulainn did not live at the court of King Cormac in the 3rdC AD, but at the court of King → Conchobar mac Nesa of Ulster, about the time of Christ's birth.

Cyfranc Lludd a Llefelys (Welsh /'kəvraŋk ɬiːð a ɬeˈvelis/ "The Tale of Ll. and Ll."). The shortest of the tales known by the collective title → Mabinogion, it tells of how the British king Lludd, with the aid of his brother Llefelys, frees his country of three plagues: the people of the Coranieid, from whose ears no spoken word can be hidden; a dragon, whose annual, spine-chilling call renders man and beast sterile; and a magician who steals all the provisions of the king's court every night. Georges → Dumézil, in the first volume of his work *Mythe et Epopée* (1968), proffers an interpretation of the story as a reflex of Indo-Germanic mythology.

Ed.: B. F. Roberts, *C. LL. a LL.*, Du. 1976 (MMWS 7).

Trans.: G. Jones & T. Jones, *The Mabinogion*, rev. ed., Lo. 1974; J. Gantz, *The Mabinogion*, Harm. 1976; P. K. Ford, *The Mabinogi and other Medieval Welsh Tales*, Be. 1977.

Cymric → Welsh.

Cynan (Welsh /'kənan/). In the tale → *Breuddwyd Macsen* a brother of the British princess Elen Luyddawg. The story tells how he helps his brother-in-law, Macsen, to regain the Roman imperial throne, using Britain as his base. Thereafter he and his retinue, instead of returning home, took possession of Brittany. There he and his men, it is told, cut out the tongues of the local women in order to preserve the purity of their native language. (The Welsh name for Brittany is Llydaw, here interpreted according to folk-etymology as lled-taw, "half-dumb". For the correct etymology cf. → Litavis.) In the prophetic poem → *Armes Prydein* C. appears as one of the two rulers under whom the Celts of Britain are to shake off the yoke of Anglo-Saxon domination.

Cynddylan (Welsh /kən'ðəlan/). A king said to have ruled over the Welsh kingdom of → Powys in the 7thC AD. The tragic fate of his family is the subject of a cycle of poems dating from the 9th / 10thC, the central figure of which is his sister → Heledd.

Cynfeirdd (Welsh /'kənveirð/ "early poets"). Term referring to the first poets of the British Celts who are known by name. The → *Historia Brittonum* identifies these as → Neirin, → Taliesin, Talhaearn, Blwchfardd and Cian; they are all said to have lived in Northern England and Southern Scotland in the second half of the 6thC. Their language was therefore → Cumbrian, of which few traces have survived. Of the three latter poets only the names are preserved, all their works having been lost. Neirin and Taliesin, however, were recognised in the Middle Ages as authors of poems which have been preserved in Middle Welsh (→ Welsh). Today it is held that many of these poems are clearly later in origin and were only attributed to the named poets after their deaths. Whether some of the poems do in fact go back to the 6thC is disputed. As there are scarcely any contemporary literary sources for this period, the historical context of the poets and their work is for the most part obscure. The date of the poems in question therefore has to be determined predominantly by internal criteria such as style, language and metre. These aspects however, like the transmission of the poems, have been the subject of much contention.

Lit.: R. Bromwich & R. B. Jones (eds.), *Astudiaethau ar yr Hengerdd: Studies in Old Welsh Poetry*, Car. 1978; A. O. H. Jarman, *The C.*, Car. 1981; B. F. Roberts, *Early Welsh Poetry*, Aberystwyth 1988.

Cynon fab Clydno (Welsh /'kənon va:b 'klədno/). In the poem Y → *Gododdin* one of the participants in the attack on Catraeth. After his death C., like other princes of Northern England and Southern Scotland, became a figure in Welsh legend. In the tale → *Iarlles y Ffynnawn* he appears as a knight at the court of King → Arthur, where his telling of the story of the miraculous spring triggers off the action. One of the → *Trioedd Ynys Prydein* refers to his love for Morfudd, a daughter of King → Urien of Rheged, but no saga telling this story has survived.

Lit.: R. Bromwich, 'C. fab C.', in: R. Bromwich and R. B. Jones (eds.), *Astudiaethau ar yr Hengerdd*, Car. 1978, 150–164 (in Welsh).

Da Derga (Ir. /da 'd'erga/). In the story → *Togail Bruidne Da Derga* a friend of the king Conaire Mór. He is the owner (→ briugu) of the hostel (→ bruiden) in which Conaire is slain by his foster-brothers.

Dagda, the (Ir. /'daɣða/). In the tales of the → Mythological Cycle a leader of the → Tuatha Dé Danann. Etymologically his name means "the good god" (*Dago-dēvos), suggesting that his origins lie in pre-Christian Celtic mythology. Other names of the Dagda are Eochaid Ollathair ("E., the Great Father") and Ruad Rofesa ("the Mighty One of Great Knowledge"). D.'s attributes are a cauldron which contains inexhaustible quantities of food, and a club which can not only slay the living but bring the dead back to life. It is this latter characteristic in particular which has led to his being compared with the Celtic god → Sucellus, attested in inscriptions. D. plays a major role in the tale of the Battle of Mag Tuired (→ *Cath Maige Tuired*).

dál (Ir. /da:l/). Term denoting tribe or family at an early stage in the evolution of Irish tribal names. The word is attested over a hundred times, generally followed by the name of a mythical or legendary ancestor. In historical times, however, this form of nomenclature no longer seems to have been current. Many of the tribes thus designated were only known by name.

Dallán (mac) Forgaill (Ir. /'daLa:n mak 'forgiL'/). Irish poet of the late 6thC AD. Tradition holds that he was the author of the poem → *Amra Choluim Chille*.

Damona. Celtic goddess whose name probably derives from a Celtic word for "cow" (cf. O.Ir. dam "ox; cow"). D. appears as companion of the god → Borvo/Bormo on several dedications from Bourbon-Lancy in the Dép. of Saône-et-Loire (CIL XIII 2805–2808) and Bourbonne-les-Bains in the Dép. of Haute-Marne (CIL XIII 5914–5920). Two further dedications from Bourbonnne-les-Bains (CIL XIII 5921) and Rivières in the Dép. of Charente (*ILTG* 155) refer only to D. She also occurs as the companion of a god named Albius on an inscription on a vessel from Chasseray in the Dép. of Côte-d'Or (CIL XIII 2840–11233). Remains of a statue of the goddess have been found in → Alesia, with an inscription (AE 1965, 181) identifying her as companion of the god → Moritasgus.

dance → music.

Danu → Anu.

death and burial. The evidence of archaeological finds and the accounts of classical → ethnography suggest that death and burial were accompanied by special and in some cases decidedly expensive religious rites. The belief in an after-life was common (cf. → Otherworld, concepts of), but where the customs associated with death were concerned, there was considerable regional, chronological and social variation. Appearances suggest a distinction in pre-Roman times between older mound burials and later flat graves, although the transition took place at different times in different areas. Grave-mounds were constructed sometimes for individual burials, sometimes for one central grave which was followed by several subsequent burials (cf. → Totenfolge). In the late Hallstatt and early La Tène cultures a burial custom was prevalent whereby the male or female corpse was laid to rest in the natural position of repose. At the beginning of the middle La Tène culture the custom of the burning of the corpse gradually imposed itself, also described by → Caesar (Bell. Gall. 6,19). There was a widespread custom of providing the dead with grave gifts, which in the case of the early Celtic → princely graves could involve massive expenditure. The evaluation of grave goods therefore yields valuable insights into the material and intellectual culture of the period (cf. → amulets).

De chophur in da muccida (Ir. /d'e 'xofur in da 'vuk'iða/ "Of the . . . of the Two Swineherds"). One of the prefatory tales (→ remscéla) to the story of the Cattle Raid of Cuailnge (→ *Táin Bó Cuailnge*), preserved in two divergent versions in the "Book of Leinster" (→ Lebor Laignech) and in a manuscript of the 16thC. The compilatory character of one of the two surviving redactions, and allusions to the story in the tale → *Togail Bruidne Da Derga* suggest that originally there were still other versions in circulation.

The titular heroes of the story are the two swineherds of the elf-kings of Connacht and Munster, possessed of magical gifts. To prove their magical powers they take on the shape of, successively, two birds, fishes, stags, warriors, spirits, dragons and water-snakes. When two cows at water swallow the water-snakes, they become pregnant and give birth to two bull calves. These grow to be the two steers whose fate is told in the story of the Cattle Raid of Cuailnge.

Various interpretations have adduced the story as evidence of Celtic belief in → reincarnation. On this basis the most recent editor of the text has sought to explain the word *cophur*, which is not attested elsewhere, on an etymological basis as the Irish equivalent of the Sanskrit word *saṃsāra*. Indian philosophy employs this concept to explain the woeful cycle of rebirths to which man is subject. It is however questionable whether one may in fact deduce from the tale of the two swine-herds that the Celts believed in the migration of souls or reincarnation.

Ed.: U. Roider, *Wie die beiden Schweinehirten den Kreislauf der Existenzen durchwanderten*, I. 1979 (with Ger. trans.).

Trans.: Ch.-J. Guyonvarc'h, 'La conception des deux porchers' (*Ogam* 12) 1960, 73–90; F. Lautenbach, *Der keltische Kessel*, St. 1991.

Lit.: C. Dröge, 'Betrachtungen zur Frage der "keltischen Seelenwanderungslehre" ' (*ZCP* 39) 1982, 261–268.

De duodecim abusivis saeculi ("Concerning the Twelve Abuses of the World"). Title of a Latin treatise on social morality which was well-known in the Middle Ages. Its authorship was then variously attributed to Saint → Patrick, Augustine of Hippo and Cyprian of Carthage, but in fact the work originated in southern Ireland in the 7thC. The unknown author drew primarily upon the seventh chapter of the Benedictine Rule, the *Etymologiae* of Isidore of Seville and Jerome's Commentary on the Gospel according to Matthew. Conceivably concepts derived from traditional Irish law also found their way into the work. In particular the section concerning the unjust king (rex iniquus) has been seen as evidence that the author drew upon the concept of the "Justness of the Ruler" (→ fír flathemon), which dates back to pre-Christian times.

Lit.: H. H. Anton, 'Pseudo Cyprian D.d.a.s. und sein Einfluß auf den Kontinent' in: H. Löwe (ed.), *Die Iren und Europa im früheren MA*, St. 1982, 568–617; A. Breen, 'The Evidence of Antique Ir. Exegesis in Pseudo-Cyprian's D.d.a.s.' (*PRIA* 87) 1987, 71–101.

Deer → Book of Deer.

Defixio (Lat. "enchantment"). Term given in the ancient world to a widespread kind of → magic whereby one sought to subject one's enemies to persecution by divine or daemonic powers. The d. took the form of an oral or written curse, occasionally accompanied by actions of magical import. Written curses were frequently etched on lead tablets, a large number of which have survived. On a few of these tablets the name of a Celtic divinity has also been preserved (cf. → Moltinus, → Ogmios, → Sulis).

Lit.: J. G. Gager, *Curse tablets and binding spells from the ancient world*, NY 1992.

Deichtine (Ir. /'d'eçt'in'e/) or Deichtir(e). In the tales of the → Ulster Cycle the mother of → Cú Chulainn, she is generally held to be the sister (or, in some texts, the daughter) of the king → Conchobar mac Nesa.

Deirdre (Ir. /'d'er'd'r'e/) or (an earlier form) Deirdriu. Female protagonist in one of the most celebrated Irish love-stories. The oldest surviving version is the tale → Longas mac nUislenn. The story was extant until the recent past in

Scotland and Ireland in numerous folk versions. Modern English reworkings include those by James → Macpherson in his poem *Darthula*, Lady Augusta → Gregory in the seventh chapter of her book *Cuchulain of Muirthemne*, William Butler → Yeats in his play *D.* and James → Stephens in his novel of the same name.

Lit.: H. V. Fackler, *The D. Legend in Anglo-Irish Lit.*, Sa. 1978; M. Herbert, 'Celtic Heroine? The archaeology of the Deirdre story', in: T. O'Brien Johnson & D. Cairnes (eds.), *Gender in Irish Writing*, Philadelphia 1991, 13–29.

deisel (Ir. 'd'eʃel/). Term denoting the direction of the circumambulation of the sun, or the clockwise direction. Movement in this direction was regarded as lucky, whereas that in the opposite direction (Ir. tuaithbel) was regarded as ominous.

Delargy, James Hamilton (1899–1980). Folklorist, born in Cushendall, Co. Antrim. After graduating in Celtic studies, he became a lecturer in Irish language and literature and later professor of folklore at University College Dublin. He was among the founders of the Folklore of Ireland Society in 1925 and for forty-six years edited its journal *Béaloideas* (1927ff). From 1925 onwards, the Irish Folklore Commission under his direction recorded and transcribed a vast corpus of stories and folklore from Ireland's dying oral tradition.

derbfine → fine.

Diablintes. In classical → ethnography the name of a sub-tribe forming part of the tribal alliance of the → Aulerci in the area between the Loire and the Seine. It survives in the name of the town Jublains, which the Ancients called Noviodunum.

Diana. In Roman religion a goddess originally regarded primarily as a moon deity and protectress of women. She soon came to be identified with the Greek Artemis and was regarded as the goddess of the hunt and protector of game.

In the provinces of the Roman Empire the name D. was accorded to a large number of native deities. Inscriptions and pictorial representations identify D. with the Celtic goddesses → Abnoba and → Arduinna.

Dian Cécht (Ir. /d'ian k'e:xt/). A doctor of the → Tuatha Dé Danann in the stories of the → Mythological Cycle. In the tale of the Battle of Mag Tuired (→ *Cath Maige Tuired*) he supplies the former king → Nuadu, who has lost his hand in battle, with an artificial hand of silver. In the course of the battle against the → Fomoire he throws the fallen and sorely wounded warriors of the Tuatha Dé Danann into a "spring of health" (Tipra Sláine), in which the wounded are cured and the dead awakened to new life.

Diarmait mac Aeda Sláine (Ir. /'d'iarmid' mak 'aiða 'sla:n'e/). Irish king who reigned from 642–664 AD, together with his brother Bláthmac. He plays a major role in the tale → *Tochmarc Becfola*.

Diarmait mac Cerbaill (Ir. /'d'iarmid' mak 'k'erviL'/). 6thC king. The annals attest that in the year 560 he was the last ruler to celebrate the pre-Christian rite of the "Feast of Tara" (feis Temro). In the *Vita Columbae* of → Adamnán, however, D. is described as "by God's counsel the appointed king of all Ireland". A tradition of the monastery of Clonmacnoise holds him to be the patron of the founder Ciarán.

Diarmait ua Duibne (Ir. /'d'iarmid' ua 'duv'n'e/). Titular hero of the story → *Tóruigheacht Dhiarmada agus Ghráinne*, foster-son of the elf-prince → Oengus, famed on account of his beauty.

díchetal di chennaib (Ir. /'d'i:çedal d'i 'çeNiv/). A particular kind of prophecy attributed to the poets (→ fili). According to the Glossary of Bishop Cormac (→ *Sanas Chormaic*) such prophecies were, in contrast to similar practices, not forbidden by Saint → Patrick, because no idolatry was involved.

diet → food and drink.

Dillon, Myles (1900–1972). Celticist, born in Dublin. He studied with Osborn → Bergin, Julius → Pokorny, Rudolf → Thurneysen and Joseph → Vendryes. Subsequently he taught Celtic philology and comparative linguistics in Dublin, Madison (Wisconsin), Chicago and Edinburgh. He published many editions and studies in Irish philology and literature, as well as works in a more popular vein: *The Cycle of the Kings* (1946) and *Early Irish Literature* (1948). Together with Nora Chadwick (1891–1972) he wrote *The Celtic Realms* (1967). A recapitulation of his many years of research into the common features of Indo-Celtic cultures was published in 1975 under the title: *Celts and Aryans: Survivals of Indo-European Speech and Society*.

Dindsenchas (Ir. /'d'indhenxas/). Title of a collection of sagas which served to explain place-names. The term is formed from *dind* "hill, slope" and *senchas* "knowledge that has been handed down"; it refers not merely to the hills designated by *dind*, but also to every place with reference to which a story is handed down. The sagas of the D. were recorded in their surviving form in the 9th-12thCs, although some features may be based on older tradition. Three different versions have been identified, which survive in more or less complete form in over 40 manuscripts.

The oldest version (A) is to be found in the "Book of Leinster" (→ Lebor Laignech). It consists of over 100 poems with a few interspersed sections of prose. Some of these poems are attributed to named authors of the 9th-11thCs, but most of them are anonymous. On the basis of this first collection a second version (B) evolved, consisting of short prose sections with a few lines of verse at the end of every section. Both collections formed the basis for the third and most widespread version (C), which contains one or more explanations in prose for every place-name, followed by poems. The individual sections are ordered according to geographical criteria in such fashion that the reader is led clockwise (→ deisel) from Tara (→ Temair) through the provinces of Meath, Leinster, Munster, Connacht and Ulster.

It is characteristic of all three versions of D. that the etymology of many place-names appears highly improbable, whether for linguistic or factual reasons. Moreover it is probable that the sagas which are adduced derive only in part from local oral traditon and are in many cases the product of medieval scholarly speculation.

Ed. & trans.: W. Stokes, 'The Bodleian D.' (Folk-Lore 3) 1892, 467–516; id., 'The Edinburgh D.' (Folk-Lore 4) 1893, 471–497; id., 'The Prose Tales of the Rennes D.' (RC 15) 1894, 272–336 & 418–484, (RC 16) 1895, 31–83, 135–167 & 269–313; E. Gwynn, The Metrical D., 5 vols., Du. 1903–1935.

Lit.: C. Bowen, 'A Historical Inventory of the D.' (StC 10/11), 1975/76, 113–137; B. Ó Cuív, 'D.: the literary exploitation of Irish placenames' (Ainm 4) 1989/90, 90–106.

Dinomogetimarus. Celtic god whose cult is attested by a single votive inscription from Saint-Pons in the Dép. of Hérault (CIL XII 4218), in which he is identified with → Mars on the basis of the → interpretatio romana.

Diodoros of Sicily (Lat. Diodorus Siculus). Greek historian of the 1stC BC, author of a world history in 40 volumes, spanning the time from the origin of the world to Caesar's expedition to Britain in 54 BC. Books 1–5 and 11–20 of this history have survived intact, the rest in excerpts and fragments. The fifth book contains in chapters 25–32 a detailed description of Gaul and its inhabitants, derived by D. from the work of the Stoic philosopher → Poseidonios. The first part of this section consists of a few introductory remarks on the geography, climate and economy of Gaul; it is followed by a description of the appearance of the Celts, their diet (→ food and drink) and their → dress. Then comes a description of their methods of → warfare, including their weapons and the function of the chariot (→ waggons). D. goes into some detail on the Celtic custom of collecting the heads of fallen opponents as trophies. The few remaining observations concern → bards and → druids, → prophecy and → sacrifices.

Lit.: → ethnography, classical.

Dioscures ("Sons of Zeus"). In Graeco-Roman mythology the name of the twin brothers Castor and Pollux. They were venerated in particular as helpers in battle and against the perils of the sea. Pictorial representations generally show them as two mounted youths. According to → Diodoros of Sicily (4,56,4), the Celtic inhabitants of the Atlantic coastlands worshipped the D. above all other gods because an ancient tradition had it that they had once come to them out of the ocean. Conceivably Diodoros is referring to two native Celtic gods, as the worship of divine twin brothers also occurs among other peoples of the Indo-Germanic linguistic family, such as the Germani (the Alci) or the Indians (the Aśvins). This hypothesis is supported by the frequent pictorial depictions of the D. in Roman Gaul. However, their Celtic names are not known to us. The conjecture that the Celtic D. might be the Gaulish gods → Divanno and → Dinomogetimarus has no firm support.

Lit: E. Krüger, 'Die gallischen und die germanischen Dioskuren' (*Trierer Zeitschrift*) 1940, 8–27 and 1941/42, 1–66.

Dis Pater. In Roman religion the god of wealth and of the underworld. According to → Caesar (Bell. Gall. 6,18) all the Gauls believed that they were descendants of D. P., having been so taught by the Druids. Which Celtic god Caesar means is not known. Among those gods attested in inscriptions, → Sucellus comes closest to the characterisation outlined above. It is possible that the god → Smertrius was also identified with D. P. A comparable figure in Irish tradition is → Donn.

Divanno. Celtic god whose cult is attested by a single votive inscription from Saint-Pons in the Dép. of Hérault (CIL XII 4218), in which he is identified with → Mars on the basis of the → interpretatio romana.

Divico. In → Caesar's Bell. Gall. (1,13–14) a prince of the tribe of the → Helvetii. Under his leadership the Helvetian tribe of the Tigurini conquered a Roman army in 107 BC and as a humiliating gesture put the captured soldiers under the yoke. In 58 BC D. was the self-assured leader of a Helvetian embassy to Caesar. The triumph of D. over the Romans formed the subject of a painting by Charles Gleyre (1806–1874), *The Helvetians put the conquered Romans under the yoke* (1858, now in the Musée cantonal des beaux-arts, Lausanne). Gleyre's painting inspired the poem *Das Joch am Léman* ("The Yoke by Lake Léman") by Conrad Ferdinand Meyer (1825–1898).

divination → prophecy.

divine kingship → sacred marriage.

dog. Archaeological finds attest that dogs were common domestic pets of the Celts. Accounts in classical → ethnography state that they were also employed in → hunting and in war. In depictions of the gods they appear frequently as attributes of gods with powers of healing, mother goddesses (→ matronae/matres) and divinities associated with hunting, such as → Abnoba. A sanctuary near Nettleton Shrub in Wiltshire is dedicated to a god with the byname Cunomaglus ("Lord of the Dogs"), who is equated with → Apollo on the basis of the → interpretatio romana. In Irish sagas cú ("dog") is frequently employed as a synonym for "warrior" (cf. → Cú Chulainn).
    Lit.: K. McCone, 'Hounds, Heroes and Hospitallers in Early Ir. Myth and Story' (*Ériu* 35) 1984, 1–30.

dolmen. Prehistoric burial grave, typically consisting of several vertically placed load-bearing stones, and one or two stone slabs placed horizontally on top of them. Originally they were covered over by a mound of piled-up earth. The name is of Celtic derivation (Breton *taol* "table" and *maen* "stone"); however, these stone constructions are older in date than the emergence of the Celts.

Domnall mac Aeda (Ir. /'dovnaL mak 'aiða/). Irish King of the 7thC, mentioned as early as the *Vita Columbae* of → Adamnán. The tales → *Fled Dúin na nGéd*, → *Cath Maige Rátha* and → *Buile Suibne* are set in the time of his reign (628–642).

Dôn (Welsh /do:n/). Sister of the titular hero Math in the tale → *Math fab Mathonwy*; mother of the children → Gwydion, → Gilfaethwy, → Arianrhod and → Gofannon. The story → *Culhwch ac Olwen* names a further son → Amaethon. The hypothesis of a link with the Celtic name for the Danube (Lat. Danuvius) and the pre-Christian Irish goddess Danu (→ Anu) is problematic on linguistic grounds.

Donn (Ir. /doN/ "the Brown One" or "the Dark One"). One of the sons of → Míl in the "Book of the Invasions of Ireland" (→ *Lebor Gabála Érenn*). He is said to have drowned in the bay Inber Scene (today's Kenmare Bay in Kerry), before his brothers even landed in Ireland. His grave is said to be the little rock island Tech Duinn, "the House of D." (now Bull Rock off the island of Dursey). According to a poem of the second half of the 9thC D.'s dying wish was that all his descendants should assemble after their death in his house. Correspondingly, the story → *Airne Fíngein* calls Tech Duinn the place "where the Dead hold a rendezvous". These allusions have led to the hypothesis that D. in pre-Christian times was regarded as the ancestral father of the Irish, to whom all are called upon their death. A comparable figure in continental Celtic mythology is → Dis Pater, the underworld god referred to by → Caesar.

Donn Cuailnge

Lit.: K. Meyer, 'D. ir. Totengott und die Toteninsel' (*Sitzungsber. d. Kgl. Preuss. Ak. d. Wiss., Phil.-hist. Kl.*) 1919, 537–546; K. Müller-Lisowski, 'Traditions about D.' (*Béaloideas* (Dublin) 18) 1948, 142–199.

Donn Cuailnge (Ir. /doN 'kual'n'g'e/ "the Brown One of C."). The most famous bull in the province of Ulster (→ *De chophur in da muccida*) in the story of the Cattle Raid of Cuailnge (→ *Táin Bó Cuailnge*).

Dottin, Georges (1863–1928). Celticist, born in Liancourt in the Dép. of Oise. After studying in Rennes and Paris he became professor of Greek language and literature in Rennes. From 1910 until his death he taught Celtic literature and philology there as successor to the Celticist Joseph Loth. He was the author of several works on cultural and literary history, but the focal point of his researches was the field of the older Celtic → languages. Of primary importance in this area is his work on → Gaulish in his book *La langue gauloise* (1920). His two-volume handbook of Middle Irish (*Manuel d'irlandais moyen*, 1913) has not been superseded.

dress. Like → jewellery, dress was one of the outward signs by which the Celts expressed their membership of a certain group and their social status. It was therefore not only subject to constant change in the course of time but also to considerable regional and social differentiation.

The sources of our knowledge of Celtic dress are for a number of reasons very thin on the ground. It is only in exceptional cases that organic materials such as leather or → textiles have survived; there are very few indigenous depictions, and the descriptions in classical → ethnography are for the most part expressed in very general terms. The most detailed description of Celtic dress is that of → Diodoros of Sicily (5,30), according to whom the Celts preferred conspicuous, colourful materials and wore trousers, which in their tongue they called "braca" (cf. → Celtic-Germanic cultural links). Above these they wore striped or brightly coloured check cloaks fastened with brooches (→ fibulae). According to the geographer → Strabo members of the nobility also wore clothes embroidered with gold.

There is a remarkable depiction of Celtic dress (shirt-like underclothing, wide hose and a narrow-fitting cloak resembling a jacket with tails) on a bronze fibula of the 5thC BC from Dürrnberg near → Hallein (now in the Celtic museum there; compare the reconstruction of the Celtic grave-chamber in the open-air museum on the Dürrnberg).

drinking horns → food and drink.

druids (Lat. pl. *druidae* and *druides*; Gk. pl. *druidai*). In classical → ethnography the name given to the priests of the Celts. The term derives from the

Celtic *dru-vid-es, thought to mean "those knowledgeable about the oak" (cf. → oak).

Archaeology can only attest the function of the druids in ritual; it can yield no evidence of their physical presence. Thus the situation of Celtic → places of worship is known, and the remains of the → sacrifices made there can be identified, but not the specific ritual actions or prayers which accompanied them. Unambiguous pictorial representations or graves of druids have thus far not been found. References to d. in medieval Irish → literature can only have limited value as sources, because in this area in particular we have to reckon with the possibility of the distortion of pre-Christian traditions for propagandistic reasons, as a consequence of Christianisation; moreover, knowledge of pre-Christian ritual practice must have been constantly declining. The most important source for our knowledge of the Druids consists therefore in the accounts of Greek and Roman authors, dating from the 2ndC BC to the 4thC AD. These refer exclusively to Gaul and Britain.

The most detailed account of the d. is that of → Caesar. He portrays them as the only respected and privileged class in Gaul apart from the nobility. The Roman general has it that they supervised divine worship, the performance of sacrifices, public and private (including human sacrifices), the interpretation of ritual prescriptions and the proclamation of the law. The d. were organised hierarchically throughout the land; every year they assembled at a consecrated spot in the country of the → Carnutes. In some cases their education lasted twenty years; it was conducted on a purely oral basis. It was part of the teaching of the d. that the human soul is immortal and enters another body after death (cf. → reincarnation). In addition they passed on to young men astronomical, scientific and theological knowledge (Bell. Gall. 6,13–14). Some features of this description which may have been borrowed from the lost historical work of → Poseidonios are also found in the descriptions of → Diodoros of Sicily (5,31), → Strabo (4,4) and → Pomponius Mela (3,2,18). → Pliny the Elder gives an account of the use of → mistletoe in the ritual of the druids, in a passage of his natural history which has become famous (Hist. Nat. 16, 249–251).

In the course of the Roman conquest of Gaul and Britain the significance of the druids progressively declined. In 54 AD the office of druid was finally prohibited by the emperor Claudius. The paucity of written sources led in the 18thC to much speculation concerning the d., which has influenced the popular image of the Celtic priests unto the present day (cf. → Celtic ideology).

Lit.: A. L. Owen, *The Famous Druids*, O. 1962; N. K. Chadwick, *The Druids*, Car. 1966; G. Zecchini, *I Druidi e l'opposizione dei Celti a Roma*, Mi. 1984; S. Piggott, *The Druids*, rev. ed. 1985; F. Le Roux & Ch.-J. Guyonvarc'h, *Les Druides*, 4ème éd., Rennes 1986.

Drystan fab Tallwch (Welsh /ˈdrəstan vaːb ˈtaɬux/). Personage in the cycle of

legends concerning → Arthur. The → *Trioedd Ynys Prydein* allude to his fame
as a warrior, as well as to his love of → Essyllt. His name, like that of his
father Tallwch, is thought to have been borrowed into Celtic from the language of the → Picts. It is possible that some of the stories concerning D.
stem from Pictish tradition, but later these were linked with localities and
characters from Wales, Cornwall and Brittany. The only Celtic survivals are
an obscure poem in the "Black Book of Carmarthen" (→ *Llyfr Du Caerfyrddin*) and the fragmentary *Ystorya Trystan*. The sources flow more freely in the
courtly literature of medieval France and Germany. Between 1150 and 1210
the poets Thomas and Béroul wrote their versions of the legend, which have
survived, albeit incomplete. → Eilhart von Oberge's *Tristrant* survives in its
entirety, while the romance of → Gottfried von Straßburg remains a fragment. The relationship between these works and older sources unknown to
us is highly problematic, both in terms of stages of transmission and individual motifs. The culture that is portrayed and the psychological motivation of
the characters are to be seen in the light of the background of the courtly
environment that spawned the individual texts, yet international fairy-tale
motifs and the models proffered by Classical literature have also influenced
the evolution of the legend. Influence by oriental works such as the Persian
epic poem of *Wis and Ramin* is also conceivable. Within Celtic culture there
are clear parallels in the Irish tradition.

> Lit.: S. Eisner, *The Tristan Legend: A Study in Sources*, Evanston (Ill.), 1969; J. Hill
> (ed.), *The Tristan Legend*, Leeds 1977; R. Bromwich, 'The "Tristan" Poem in the
> Black Book of Carmarthen' (*StC* 14/15) 1979/80, 54–65 (with text & Engl.
> trans.): O. J. Padel, 'The Cornish Background of the Tristan Stories' (*CMCSt* 1)
> 1981, 53–81; W. A. Trindade, 'The Celtic Connections of the Tristan Story'
> (*Reading Mediaeval Studies* 12 and 13) 1986, 93–107; 1987, 71–80; R. Bromwich,
> 'The Tristan of the Welsh', in: R. Bromwich et al. (eds.), *The Arthur of the Welsh*
> (Car. 1991), 209–228.

Duanaire Finn (Ir. /'duanir'e f'iN'/ "Finn's Songbook"). Title of a collection
of 69 poems and ballads from the cycle of legends concerning → Finn mac
Cumaill. The individual texts were composed between the 12th and the early
17thCs, and survive in a single manuscript dating from c. 1627. The ballads
have as their subject for the most part hunting and warring expeditions,
together with other adventures of the → Fianna; they are frequently attributed to one of the survivors of this band of warriors.

> Ed. & trans.: E. MacNeill & G. Murphy, *Duanaire Finn*, Lo. & Du. 1908–1953
> (ITS 7, 28 & 43).

Dub Lacha (Ir. /duv 'Laxa/). Wife of the titular hero Mongán in the story →
Compert Mongáin.

Dub Sainglenn (Ir. /duv 'san'γ'l'eN/). In the stories of the → Ulster Cycle
one of the two horses, fleet as the wind, of the hero → Cú Chulainn.

According to the older version of the Birth of Cú Chulainn (→ *Compert Chon Culainn*) it was born in the same night as its master.

Dubthach (Ir. /'dufθax/). In the tales of the → Ulster Cycle a feared warrior of Ulster. On account of his malicious speeches he bears the byname Dael Ulad, "Dungbeetle of Ulster" or Daeltenga "Dungbeetle-Tongue". From the hero → Celtchar mac Uthechair he has acquired the lance Lúin for his weapon. This lance never misses its target, yet before battle its point must be dipped in poison, lest it burn the shaft together with its bearer. The story → *Longas mac nUislenn* describes how D., after the assassination of Noisiu and his two brothers by King → Conchobar mac Nesa, goes into exile in Connacht. In the tale of the Cattle Raid of Cuailnge (→ *Táin Bó Cuailnge*) D. participates in the campaign of the men of Connacht against Ulster, on the side of the royal couple → Ailill and → Medb.

Duchcov. Town in Bohemia on the southern edge of the Erzgebirge. Regulation works carried out there in 1882 led to the discovery at a natural spring of a bronze cauldron and c. 2,000 fibulae, rings and other metal objects of the early La Tène period.

Dürrnberg → Hallein.

Dumézil, Georges (1898–1986). Linguist and comparative religionist, born in Paris. He first taught at the École pratique des hautes études; from 1949 to 1968 he was professor of Indo-European linguistics at the Collège de France. His main scholarly interest was the mythology of the Indo-European peoples, the structure of which he sought to reconstruct primarily with the aid of Roman and Indo-Iranian sources. In a long series of writings D. developed the theory of an Indo-European "ideology of three functions". According to this theory both the Indo-European conception of the world and their social structure were based upon a hierarchical tripartite division, which distinguished between the basic functions of sovereignty (*souveraineté*), war (*force*) and fertility (*fécondité*). D's works found widespread agreement among scholars in the fields of linguistics and comparative religion, but also provoked strong dissent. The question of how far Celtic sources bear out his theories is controversial.

Lit.: C. S. Littleton, *The New Comparative Mythology: An Anthropological Assessment of the Theories of G.D.*, Be. 1982; W. Belier, *Decayed Gods: Origin and Development of G.D.'s 'Idéologie tripartite'*, Lei. 1991.

Dumiatis. Celtic god identified with → Mercury on the basis of the → interpretatio romana. His cult is attested by a bronze tablet (CIL XIII 1523), found in 1874 in a Gallo-Roman temple area on the peak of the Puy-de-Dôme near Clermont-Ferrand.

Dumnonii. In ancient → ethnography a Celtic tribe in Cornwall and the West of England. Its chief town in Roman times was Isca Dumnoniorum, today's Exeter. After the departure of the Romans in the 5thC AD, the Celtic kingdom of Dumnonia came into being in the settlement area of the D., from which base some parts of Brittany were also settled. The name of the D. survives in that of the English county of Devon and the geological formation named after it.

Durrow → Book of Durrow.

Dyfed (Welsh /'dəved/). Region in southern Wales, whose name derives from the tribe of the Demetae, mentioned as early as the second century AD by the Greek geographer Ptolemy. In the early Middle Ages D. constituted an independent kingdom, whose rulers claimed to be of Irish origin. After the death of the last king of D. at the beginning of the 10thC the region was incorporated into the newly-created kingdom of Deheubarth. The modern county of Dyfed was created in 1974, combining the counties of Pemrokeshire, Carmarthenshire and Cardiganshire, and thus stretches considerably further to the north and east than the ancient kingdom of Dyfed.

Dylan Eil Ton (Welsh /'dəlan eil ton/). Character in Welsh legend concerning whom little is known. The tale → Math fab Mathonwy tells of the birth of D. and his twin brother → Lleu Llaw Gyffes. Immediately after his baptism he heads for the sea and in no time at all can swim like the most nimble of fishes, which is why he is called Eil Ton ("Son of the Wave"). He is slain by a single blow at the hands of his uncle → Gofannon. Apart from this short narrative D. is also mentioned in a few poems in the "Book of Taliesin" (→ Llyfr Taliesin). A reference in the → Englynion y Beddeu records that his grave is to be found not far from the church of St. Beuno near Clynnog Fawr in north-west Wales.

Lit.: S. L. Keefer, 'The Lost Tale of D. in the Fourth Branch of the Mabinogi' (StC 24/25) 1989/90, 26–37.

Eadaoin → Étaín.

Éber (Ir. /'e:v'er/). One of the Sons of Míl in the "Book of the Invasions of Ireland" (→ Lebor Gabála Érenn). He is said to have ruled over the southern half of the island after its conquest, but died a year later in battle against his brother Éremón.

Eburones. In classical → ethnography a Celtic tribe in the area between the Rhine and the Meuse. During the conquest of Gaul by → Caesar they offered fierce resistance under their leaders → Ambiorix and Catuvolcus and were in consequence virtually annihilated. The land of the E. was later settled by the Germanic Tungri, from whom the town of Tongern takes its name.

Eburovices. In classical → ethnography a sub-tribe of the tribal grouping of the → Aulerci in the area between the Loire and the Seine. The name would appear to mean "yew-fighters", yet the underlying concept is obscure. It survives in the name of the city of Évreux, known in ancient times as Mediolanium.

éces (Ir. /'e:g'es/). Term denoting the learned poet, possibly deriving from a word meaning "to see" and therefore originally denoting – much like → fili – the inspired seer. → *Auraceipt na n-éces* is a primer for would-be learned poets.

echtrae (Ir. /'extre/). Term signifying an (adventurous) journey or an adventure, which serves in the → lists of sagas to denote tales which treat of experiences in wondrous regions beyond the world inhabited by man. These regions are generally located beyond the sea, or at the centre of the earth, or shrouded in a magical mist. A similar generic term is → immram.
> *Lit.*: D. N. Dumville, 'E. and Immram: Some problems of definition' (*Ériu* 27) 1976, 73–94.

Echtrae Chonnlai (Ir. /'extre 'xoNli/ "The Adventure of Connla"). Title of a tale from the → Historical Cycle which tells how Connla, a son of the Irish king → Conn Cétchathach, is consumed with love for a fairy (cf. → síd) and is ultimately, against his father's will, abducted by her in a glass ship which sails out of the world of men.
> *Ed.*: J. Pokorny, 'Conle's abenteuerliche Fahrt' (*ZCP* 17) 1927, 193–205; H. P. A. Oskamp, 'E.C.' (*EC* 14) 1974, 207–228 (with Engl. trans.)
> *Lit.*: K. McCone, *Pagan Past and Christian Present in Early Ir. Lit.*, May. 1990.

Echtrae Nerai (Ir. /'extre 'n'eri/ "The Adventure of Nera"). Title of one of the "prefatory tales" (→ remscéla) to the story of the Cattle Raid of Cuailnge (→ *Táin Bó Cuailnge*). It is thought to date back to the 10th/11thC and is preserved in the → "Yellow Book of Lecan" as well as in a manuscript of the 15thC. The story is set in Cruachain, the seat of the royal couple → Ailill and → Medb. It begins on the eve of the feast of → Samain, on which according to Irish belief the elf-mounds (→ síd) are opened and man can make contact with supernatural creatures. During this night the titular hero Nera, returning from a test of his courage, finds to his astonishment that the castle of Cruachain is on fire and its inhabitants slain. In secret he follows the enemy army, which is in the process of departing from the scene of destruction, and is led into a nearby elf-mound. There a fairy explains to him that he has been the victim of an optical illusion: what he has seen will only take place in reality at the next feast of Samain. Thereupon Nera returns to the castle of Cruachain to warn the inhabitants, and thus Ailill and Medb succeed in forestalling the dwellers of the síd when the feast next comes round. They destroy and plunder the elf-mound, but spare Nera and the fairy, who are left to reside there alone.

The story is retold by Lady Augusta → Gregory in the ninth chapter of her *Cuchulain of Muirthemne* and by James → Stephens in *In the Land of Youth*.

Ed. & trans.: K. Meyer, 'The Adventures of Nera' (*RC* 10) 1889, 212–228.

Lit.: A. Watson, 'A structural analysis of E.N.' (*EC* 23) 1986, 129–142; J. Carey, 'Sequence and Causation in E.N.' (*Ériu* 39) 1988, 67–74; S. Ó Coileáin, 'E.N. and its analogues' (*Celtica* 21) 1990, 427–440; M. Ó Flaithearta, 'E.N., Táin Bó Regamna und ihr Verhältnis zu Táin Bó Cuailnge', in: H. L. C. Tristram (ed.), *Deutsche, Kelten und Iren*, H. 1990, 155–176.

economy → agriculture, → cattle-breeding.

Efnisyen → Nisyen and Efnisyen.

Eigr (Welsh /eigr/). Daughter of the prince Anlawdd Wledig and wife of the duke Gwrlais of Cornwall in the Welsh adaptations of the *Historia Regum Britanniae* of → Geoffrey of Monmouth. In the course of a banquet King → Uthyr Bendragon falls in love with her. With the help of → Myrddin's magic powers he lies with her in the guise of her husband whilst the latter is absent on a war campaign. In the first night that they spend together E. conceives → Arthur, who on the death of his father becomes king of Britain at the age of 15.

Eilhart von Oberge. Middle High German poet of the 12thC. Between 1170 and 1190 he composed his verse romance *Tristrant*, the oldest version of the Tristan (→ Drystan) legend to have survived intact.

Éire → Ériu.

Eisteddfod (Welsh /ei'steðvod/). Term denoting a meeting or assembly of poets. These meetings are first attested in the 15th/16thC, at a time when the poets (Welsh Beirdd) still constituted a distinct class with orally transmitted rules and norms. With the decline of the status of poet in the 17th/18thC the tradition of the E. lost a great deal of its original significance; it was however revived in the 19thC. The "Assembly of the Bards of the Island of Britain", founded by Edward → Williams (Iolo Morganwg), exerted a decisive influence on the form taken by these assemblies. In the second half of the 19thC the tradition of the National E. (E. Genedlaethol) evolved. These literature and music festivals are still celebrated on an annual basis today, taking place in the first week of August at varying locations in Wales.

Elatha (Ir. /'elaθa/). A king of the → Fomoire in the story of the Battle of Mag Tuired (→ *Cath Maige Tuired*). His son → Bres is elected king of the → Tuatha Dé Danann after the abdication of → Nuadu Argatlám. In the battle of Mag Tuired E. is wounded in combat with Nuadu, and ultimately slain by → Lug mac Ethnenn.

Elcmar (Ir. /'elkvar/). In the tales of the → Mythological Cycle the husband of → Bóand and original owner of the elf-mound → Brug na Bóinne. The story of the wooing of Étaín (→ *Tochmarc Étaíne*) tells of how the → Dagda slept with Elcmar's wife and she bore by him the elf → Oengus, and of how the latter by cunning wins possession of Brug na Bóinne.

Elen Luyddawg (Welsh /'elen 'lijðaug/). In the tale → *Breuddwyd Macsen* the British princess with whom the Roman emperor Macsen falls in love after seeing her in a dream, and whom he marries after conquering Britain.

elves → síd.

Emain Ablach (Ir. /'evin' 'avlax/). In the tales of the → Mythological Cycle the residence of the sea-god → Manannán mac Lir. The story of the Voyage of Bran (→ *Immran Brain*) tells of a sea-voyage made by mortals to E.
Lit.: Th. M. Th. Chotzen, 'E. A. – Ynys Avallach – Insula Avallonis – Ile d'Avalon' (EC 4) 1948, 255–274; P. MacCana, 'The Sinless Otherworld of Immram Brain' (*Ériu* 27) 1976, 95–115.

Emain Macha (Ir. /'evin' 'vaxa/). In the tales of the → Ulster Cycle the seat of the kings of Ulster, identical with the archaeological site of Navan Fort about 3 miles west of the city of Armagh. Archaeological excavations have shown that the oldest traces of human presence in E. reach back into the neolithic period. It is however not clear whether or to what extent the site was still in use in the first millennium AD.
Lit.: B. Wailes, 'The Irish Royal Sites in History and Archaeology' (CMCSt 3) 1982, 1–29.

Emer (Ir. /'ev'er/). Wife of → Cú Chulainn in the tales of the → Ulster Cycle. She plays a major role in the stories → *Tochmarc Emire* and → *Serglige Con Culainn*.

Emrys Wledig (Welsh /'emris 'wledig/). In Welsh tradition a warleader of the British Celts in their fight against the Saxon invaders. He appears in → Gildas under the name of Ambrosius (= Emrys) Aurelianus, as a member of the country's Romanised aristocracy. A good 300 years later, in the → *Historia Brittonum*, he has clearly acquired legendary traits. There it is told how the British king → Gwrtheyrn in North Wales is preparing to build a fortress, but the foundations keep falling down. The king's wise men advise that he should make a sacrifice to the building in the form of an orphan boy. The choice falls upon E., who claims he is the son of a Roman consul. By dint of his superior wisdom he puts the counsellors of the king to shame and names the true reason for the collapse of the foundations: in the bowels of the earth below the foundations a red and a white dragon lie hidden; the red dragon symbolises the British Celts, the white the Germanic invaders. When the dragons are discovered they fight one another, the red dragon winning the victory. The story is reshaped by → Geoffrey of Monmouth; in his *Historia Regum Britanniae* it is however not E. but the magician Merlin (→ Myrddin) who plays the central role in this episode. In Geoffrey's work E. appears under the name Aurelius Ambrosius as an important warleader in the fight against the Saxons. He is said to be the son of the British king Constantine and elder brother of → Uthyr Bendragon.

Endlicher's Glossary (Endlichers Glossar). Name given after its first editor to a late antique list of 17 Gaulish words with their Latin equivalents. As well as authentic Celtic linguistic material it contains several words of doubtful origin.
Lit.: P.-Y. Lambert, *La Langue gauloise*, P. 1994.

enech (Ir. /'en'ex/). Term denoting the face and – by extension – the honour of a man. E. possesses this secondary meaning in the legal term lóg n-enech "honour-price". This designated the social and legal position held by a person, determining for example the value of his oath or – in the case of his rights being injured – the degree of compensation owed to him. It was only free men who had such an honour-price; where offences against women were concerned, compensation was paid to the husband and in the case of offences against serfs, to their lord. A free man lost his honour if he were convicted of perjury or if a poet (→ fili) denounced his misconduct publicly in an invective poem (→ áer). The corresponding term to lóg n-enech in Welsh law was wynebwerth (from wyneb "face" and gwerth "value").
Lit.: F. Kelly, *A Guide to Early Ir. Law*, Du. 1988.

englyn (Welsh 'eŋlin/). The oldest known strophic form in Welsh literature. Its origins are obscure, but it is thought to have been fully developed by the 8th/9thC and is still widespread today. Each e. consists of three or four lines linked by end-rhyme and alliteration according to rigidly prescribed rules. A poem frequently consists of a single strophe.

Englynion Gereint (Welsh /eŋ'lɔnjon 'gereint/ "The Stanzas of Gereint"). A group of 27 strophes devoted to the legendary hero → Gereint fab Erbin, who is said to have ruled over the Celtic kingdom of Devon c. 600 AD. The strophes are thought to have originated in the 9th-11thCs; they are preserved in the "Red Book of Hergest" (→ Llyfr Coch Hergest) and in the "Black Book of Carmarthen" (→ Llyfr Du Caerfyrddin). Conceivably they constituted the dramatic highlights of a saga whose plot would be narrated in prose, or perhaps audience familiarity with the plot was taken for granted. Much of the poem is taken up by the description of a battle in which not only Gereint but also → Arthur is said to have taken part. It is a characteristic tendency of the Welsh tradition to incorporate historical and mythical figures of diverse origin into the Arthurian cycle of legends.

Lit.: J. Rowland, *Early Welsh Saga Poetry*, C. 1990.

Englynion y Beddeu (Welsh /eŋ'lənjon ə 'beðei/ "The Stanzas of the Graves"). A group of poems which tell of the burial-places of celebrated heroes. On the basis of internal and linguistic criteria they are thought to have originated in the 9th/10thC, whereas the manuscript transmission does not begin until the 13thC, with a collection of 73 such e. in the "Black Book of Carmarthen" (→ Llyfr Du Caerfyrddin). Only a small number of the places named in the stanzas can be identified with any certainty. The collection is however of particular importance because of the many allusions to lost narratives of the British Celts.

Lit.: Th. Jones, 'The Black Book of Carmarthen "Stanzas of the Graves"' (PBA 53) 1967, 97–137 (with ed. and trans.).

Enid (Welsh 'enid/). Female protagonist in the Middle Welsh prose narrative → Gereint fab Erbin. In → Chrétien de Troyes' verse romance *Erec* the corresponding name is Enide. The name may derive from the Celtic word for the kingdom of Vannes (Breton: Gwened), which in the 6thC was ruled by a king named Weroc (= Erec). If this theory is valid, then it is conceivable that the story of Erec and Enide has its origins in a legend concerning the union of the ruler Weroc and the female personification of his country. Comparable stories are particularly widespread in Ireland and are probably based on pre-Christian conceptions of royal succession which linked it to a → sacred marriage between the king and a goddess.

Lit.: R. Bromwich, 'Celtic Dynastic Themes and the Breton Lays' (EC 9) 1961, 439–474.

Entremont. Modern name of a Celtic settlement situated on a plateau on the highest point of a hill about a mile north of Aix-en-Provence. In 122 BC it was destroyed by the Romans and in its stead the new foundation Aquae Sextiae, now Aix, was built. At its peak, in the 3rd/2ndC BC, Entremont stretched over an area of c. 4 hectares and was fortified by walls on all sides. On the north side these walls were protected additionally by towers, parts of which have survived, some 12 feet in height. In the ruins of a sanctuary in the north-western part of the settlement several stone pillars have been found with chiselled carvings of heads, and many fragments of life-size figures, among them five heads with closed eyes; a hand grasps the heads by a plait. 15 human skulls were also discovered which were originally attached to parts of the buildings by iron nails, some of which have survived. The finds are now to be seen in the Musée Granet in Aix-en-Provence.

> Lit.: F. Benoit, *Entremont*, P. 1969; F. Salviat, *E. antique*, Aix-en-Prov. 1973; *Archéologie d'E. au Musée Granet*, Aix-en-Prov. 1987 (exhibition cat.).

Eochaid Airem (Ir. /'eoxið' 'ar'ev/). In the tales of the → Ulster Cycle the brother of and successor to the king → Eochaid Fedlech; he plays a major role in the story of the wooing of Étaín (→ *Tochmarc Étaíne*).

Eochaid Fedlech (Ir. /'eoxið' 'f'eð'l'ex/). In the tales of the → Ulster Cycle a king said to have ruled over Ireland about the time of Christ's birth; brother of the king → Eochaid Airem and father of the queen → Medb.

Eochaid mac Eirc (Ir. /'eoxið' mak er'k'/). Last king of the → Fir Bolg in the "Book of the Invasions of Ireland" (→ *Lebor Gabála Érenn*), said to have fallen in battle against the → Tuatha Dé Danann.

Eochaid Ollathair (Ir. /'eoxið' 'oLaθir'/). A byname of the → Dagda, signifying "great / mighty father".

Eogan mac Durthacht (Ir. /'eoɣan mak 'durθaxt/). In the tales of the → Ulster Cycle the king of Fernmag (now Farney in County Monaghan), vassal of the king → Conchobar mac Nesa of Ulster. In the story → *Longas mac nUislenn* E., with the assent of Conchobar, kills the sons of Uisliu.

Eogan Már (Ir. /'eoɣan ma:r/). In the tales of the → Historical Cycle a king said to have ruled over the South of Ireland in the 2ndC AD. Legend tells how he was given the byname Mug Nuadat ("Servant of Nuadu") because as a young man he helped a master builder called Nuadu to build a stronghold. As a result the southern half of Ireland came to be called in later times Leth Moga, "Mug's Half".

Epona. Goddess of Celtic origin venerated in many parts of the Roman Empire. Her name derives from the Celtic word for "horse" (Old Celtic *epos, Ir. ech), characterising her as a protectress of horses. The earliest reference to her cult is in one of the Satires (8,155–157) of the Roman poet Juvenal (1st/2ndC AD), in which he pours scorn on a member of the Roman aristocracy for swearing by E., like a stableboy. In the 2ndC AD the poet Apuleius refers in his *Metamorphoses* (3,27,2) to an image of the goddess erected inside a stable and adorned with roses. Other allusions to the veneration of E. in the context of riding and draught animals occur in the Christian authors Tertullian (Apologeticum 16,5 and Ad Nationes 1,11) and Minucius

Felix (Octavius 28,7). The name E. is attested in c. 60 inscriptions whose distribution area ranges from the Iberian peninsula across Britain, Gaul and Italy to the Balkans. In addition, over 250 pictorial representations of E. have survived, most of which show the goddess as a rider or sitting on a throne between two or more horses. In her hands she frequently bears a bowl of fruit or a horn of plenty. E. has been compared with figures in the insular Celtic tradition, in particular → Macha and → Rhiannon.

Lit.: R. Magnen & E. Thevenot, E., Bordeaux 1953; K. M. Linduff, 'E.: A Celt among the Romans' (*Latomus* 38) 1979, 817–837; M. T. Hanoteau, 'E., déesse des chevaux: Figurations découvertes en Suisse' (*Helvetica archaeologica* 11) 1980, 2–20; G. Fellendorf-Boerner, 'Die bildlichen Darstellungen der E. auf den Denkmälern Baden-Württembergs' (*FBW* 10) 1985, 77–141; C. Sterckx, *Elements de cosmogonie celtique*, Bru. 1986; M. Euskirchen; 'Epona' (*BRGK* 74) 1993, 607–850.

Erc mac Cairbri Niad-Fer (Ir. /eRk mak 'kar'b'r'i n'iað f'er/). Son of the king Cairbre Nia-Fer of Tara and his wife Fedelm Noíchride in the story of the Cattle Raid of Cuailnge (→ *Táin Bó Cuailnge*). His maternal grandfather is the king → Conchobar mac Nesa of Ulster, whom E. aids in the battle against the army of the men of Connacht, without the knowledge and against the wishes of his father. When however Cairbre falls in battle against Conchobar's nephew → Cú Chulainn, E. avenges the death of his father upon his killer (cf. → *Aided Chon Culainn*).

Erec. Titular hero of an Old French verse romance by → Chrétien de Troyes and its Middle High German adaptation by → Hartmann von Aue. The corresponding Celtic text is the Middle Welsh prose narrative → *Gereint fab Erbin*.

Érémon (Ir. /'e:r'evo:n/). One of the Sons of → Míl in the "Book of the Invasions of Ireland" (→ *Lebor Gabála Érenn*). After the conquest of Ireland, he is said to have ruled over the northern half of the island initially, but only a year later became king of all Ireland by virtue of a victory over his brother Éber.

Ériu (Ir. /'e:r'u/). A queen of the → Tuatha Dé Danann in the "Book of the Invasions of Ireland" (→ *Lebor Gabála Érenn*). During the conquest of Ireland by the Sons of → Míl she and her two sisters, → Banba and → Fótla, are each said to have won from the poet → Amairgin Glúngel the promise that the island will one day bear her name. The name in its New Irish form Éire (originally a dative) is indeed still today the name by which Ireland and the Irish state refer to themselves. In English the form Erin (originally a genitive) serves as a poetic name for Ireland. É. is said to have fallen in the Battle of → Tailtiu fighting against the Sons of Míl.

Ernmas (Ir. /'ernvas/). Mother of the war goddesses → Bodb, → Macha and → Morrígain in the tales of the → Mythological Cycle. Her name is identical with the Irish word ernbas, denoting death by the power of weapons (from íarn "iron" and bás "death").

Erstfeld. Site north of the St. Gotthard Pass in the Swiss canton of Uri. In 1962 in the process of earthworks intended to avert avalanches four golden arm-rings and three neck-rings dating from c. 300 BC were found there, concealed under a huge boulder on an impassable slope. It is uncertain whether they were hidden there or placed as an offering to a divinity.

Lit.: R. Wyss, Der Schatzfund von E., Z. 1975; F. Müller, 'Zur Datierung des Goldschatzes von E.' (Jahrb. d. Schweizer Ges. für Ur- und Frühgesch. 73) 1990, 83–94; Gold der Helvetier, Z. 1991 (exhibition cat.).

eschatology ("doctrine of the last things"). We possess only limited knowledge concerning Celtic conceptions of the end of the world. According to → Strabo the → druids taught that the soul and the universe were indestructible, yet one day fire and water would triumph (Geogr. 4,4,4). Apart from this, there is only one further observation, by the Greek historian Arrian, according to which Celtic warriors are said to have told Alexander the Great that they feared nothing in the world – save that the sky might fall on their heads (Anabasis 1,4,7). The idea that the heavens might collapse is also attested in the Irish tradition. Conceivably the Celts believed that the firmament was supported by a pillar which might one day collapse. A "Pillar of the Sun" (Solis columna) at the sources of the Rhône is mentioned by the Roman poet → Avienus.

Lit.: W. Sayers, ' "Mani maidi an nem . . ." ' (Ériu 37) 1986, 99–116.

Essyllt (Welsh /'essilt/). The name in Welsh tradition of the wife of the king → March and beloved of his nephew → Drystan; it is thought to derive from an older form *Adsiltia and characterises its bearer as "she who is gazed upon" (cf. Welsh syllu "to observe"). The corresponding spellings in Old French and Middle High German literature are Iseut and Iso(l)t. These however are thought to derive in all probability from a Germanic name of a similar sound rather than direct from the Celtic word.

Esus. Celtic god whose name appears in several compound personal names such as Esunertus (meaning perhaps "powerful by virtue of E.") and Esugenus (meaning perhaps "descended from E."). The etymology of the name has yet to be satisfactorily explained. If one assumes that the initial vowel is long, then a link with Venetic aisu "god" would be conceivable. If however the word originally had a short e, then a link with Lat. erus "lord, master" is feasible.

Literary references: E. appears in the works of the Roman authors Lucan

(Pharsalia 1, 444–446) and Lactantius (Divinae Institutiones 1,21,3). According to Lucan the Gauls offered human sacrifices to E. The → Berne Scholia, commenting on Lucan, yield the additional information that the victims were killed by being hung "until their limbs separated from their bodies" (the precise meaning of the wording is unclear).

Where inscriptions are concerned, the name E. has so far only been found on the Paris monument, the → Nautae Parisiaci. (One other inscription which survives in fragmentary fashion, on a statue of the god → Mercury from Lezoux, is now interpreted differently.) Beneath the Paris inscription is a depiction of the god as a bearded man in the clothing of an artisan, next to a tree. With his left hand he holds the trunk of the tree, while his right hand prepares to chop off the branches with a blow of his scythe. Immediately next to the figure of E. is a bull with three cranes and the inscription → Tarvos Trigaranus.

The precise significance of both images is unknown, but they are commonly compared with a depiction from Trier, a relief on a stele dedicated to the god → Mercury (CIL XIII 3656; now in the Rheinisches Landesmuseum in Trier). This shows a beardless man in the clothes of an artisan who is about to fell a tree with an axe. In the thick foliage of the treetop three birds and the head of a bull can be discerned. Conceivably both the Trier relief and the two Paris depictions derive from a myth concerning E. which has not survived.

Lit.: A. Ross, 'E. et les trois "grues" ' (EC 9) 1960, 405–438; P.-M. Duval, 'E. und seine Werkzeuge auf Denkmälern in Trier und Paris' (Trierer Zeitschrift 36) 1973, 81–88 (=ibid., Travaux sur la Gaule, P. 1989, I 463–470).

Étaín (Ir. /'e:dain'/). Titular heroine of the tale → Tochmarc Étaíne.

Etarscél (Ir. /'edarʃk'e:l/) or Eterscél(e). In the tales of the → Ulster Cycle a son-in-law of the king → Eochaid Airem. According to the story → Togail Bruidne Da Derga, E. fathered by the magically gifted → Mes Buachalla the king → Conaire Mór, who succeeded E. on his death.

Ethal Anbuail (Ir. /'eθal 'anvu:il'/). In the tale → Aislinge Oenguso an elf-prince from the province of Connacht. His daughter is Caer Ibormeith, the beloved of the titular hero → Oengus.

ethnography, classical. The data concerning the Celts to be found in Greek and Roman authors constitute the main source, other than archaeological finds, of our knowledge of Celtic history and literature. Here ethnology, geography and history frequently overlap; the Ancients did not of course distinguish between the disciplines.

The oldest reports concerning the Celts derive from the 6th / 5thC BC. The text of the account of the historian → Herodotus has survived, whereas that of the geographer → Hekataios is only known through allusions on the part of later authors. The source of the late Roman poet → Avienus is also thought to date back to the 6thC BC. Apart from isolated observations on the part of authors such as Xenophon, Plato and Aristotle we possess valuable data from the Hellenistic period in the historical work of → Polybios. Among the most impressive pieces of evidence in ancient ethnography are the descriptions of → Poseidonios, which survive in extract form in the works of → Athenaios, → Diodorus of Sicily and → Strabo. In → Caesar there occurs for the first time the distinction between the terms Celts and the Germani, which, however, only becomes generally accepted in Latin literature. In the Augustan and post-Augustan period the authors → Livy, → Pomponius Mela, → Lucan, → Pliny and → Tacitus are of particular significance.

There are three potential sources of error in particular which need to be borne in mind with regard to the interpretation of this evidence. Firstly, there is the possibility of errors, oversights or faulty information on the part of the authors themselves. A second source of error is the tendency to neglect the world-view of classical ethnography, which may express itself in an idealised, or in a totally dismissive attitude to its subject matter. Because the Greeks and Romans were frequently involved in military conflict with the Celts, particular emphasis is, moreover, placed upon Celtic warfare. The third source of error, finally, lies in the failure to recognise classical literary conventions. These include, for example, the employment of what are known as migratory motifs; in this context, this involves the arbitrary transfer of ethnographic observations from one foreign people to another. In consequence, all the evidence deriving from classical ethnography must be subjected to careful scrutiny with regard to its source, and wherever possible be collated with the evidence from archaeological finds.

Sources: J. Zwicker, Fontes historiae religionis Celticae, B. 1934–1936; P.-M. Duval, Les sources de l'histoire de France, T. 1, P. 1971; J. Herrmann (ed.), Griech. und lat. Quellen zur Frühgeschichte Mitteleuropas, 4 vols., B. 1988–1992.

Lit.: K. E. Müller, Geschichte der antiken E. und ethnologischen Theoriebildung, 2 vols., Wi. 1972–80; T. C. Champion, 'Written sources and the study of the European Iron Age', in: T. C. Champion & J. V. S. Megaw (eds.), Settlement and Society, Leicester 1985, 9–22; G. Dobesch, 'Ancient Literary Sources', in: The Celts, Mi. 1991, 35–41; B. Kremer, Das Bild der Kelten bis in augusteische Zeit: Studien zur Instrumentalisierung eines antiken Feindbildes bei griechischen und römischen Autoren, S. 1994; P. Freeman, 'Elements of the Ulster Cycle in Pre-Posidonian Literature', in: J. Mallory & G. Stockman (eds.), Ulidia, Belfast 1994, 207–216; G. Dobesch, Das europäische "Barbaricum" und die Zone der Mediterrankultur, V. 1995.

Euffigneix. Site in the Dép. of Haute-Marne, about 35 miles east of Troyes, where was found the fragmentary sandstone statue of a Celtic divinity of the time between 100 BC and 100 AD. Beneath the neck-ring (→ torc) the deity's body has been shaped in the form of a roughly square stele, without any attempt at anatomical detail. The torso is decorated on the front with a bas-relief of a wild boar standing in a vertical position, and on the left-hand side with a huge eye, also in a vertical position. The statue stands about a foot high. Nothing further is known of the circumstances in which it was originally found; it is now in the Musée des antiquités nationales in Saint-Germain-en-Laye.

euhemerism. The theory that the belief in gods derives from the worship of human beings who came to be regarded as divine. The concept derives from the Hellenistic author Euhemeros of Messina (Sicily), who was the first to explain belief in the Greek gods in this way, in c. 300 BC. Through the writings of the Church fathers this interpretation of the gods of the ancient world held sway throughout the Middle Ages. Taking this as their model, medieval scholars, particularly in Scandinavia and Ireland, treated the figures of Germanic and Celtic mythology as people in the distant past who were possessed of magic powers. A typical Irish example of this process is the "Book of the Invasions of Ireland" (→ *Lebor Gabála Érenn*).

Lit.: J. D. Cooke, 'Euhemerism: A Mediaeval Interpretation of Classical Paganism' (*Speculum* 2) 1927, 396–410; P. Alphandéry, 'L'Evhémerisme et les débuts de l'histoire des religions au moyen âge' (*RHR* 109) 1934, 5–27; K. W. Bolle, 'In Defense of Euhemerism', in: J. Puhvel (ed.), *Myth and Law among the Indo-Europeans*, Be. 1970, 19–38.

Evans, John Gwenogvryn (1852–1930). Born in South Wales; after studying theology he served from 1876 to 1880 as a priest of the Unitarian Church in England and Wales. He had already abandoned this office for health reasons when in 1882 he attended the lectures of the Celticist Sir John → Rhŷs in Oxford. Under Rhŷs' influence he devoted himself thenceforth entirely to palaeography. From 1887 to 1911 he published a series of diplomatic editions of Welsh manuscripts which surpassed all earlier editions in their accuracy and reliability. Then, from 1898 to 1920, he compiled a comprehensive catalogue of surviving Welsh manuscripts, describing the content of nearly nine hundred MSS. For his editions, some of which remain the basis of scholarship today, he was awarded honorary doctorates by the universities of Oxford (1903) and Wales (1905).

Excalibur → Caledfwlch.

fairies → síd.

fairy-tale → folktale.

Fál (Ir. /faːl/) or Lia Fáil. A stone said to have been in the royal castle of Tara (→ Temair). The "Book of the Invasions of Ireland" (→ Lebor Gabála Érenn) records that it was brought to Ireland by the → Tuatha Dé Danann. Ancient belief held that it determined who was to be chosen as king by emitting a loud cry when the rightful king stepped upon it. According to some later sources the stone was phallic in shape. The majority of ancient sources, however, depict it as a flat stepping-stone. In poetic language F., or Inis Fáil, "Island of F.", denotes Ireland, a connotation appropriated by the Irish party Fianna Fáil (→ Fianna), founded in 1926.

Lit.: T. O' Broin, 'Lia Fáil: fact and fiction in the tradition' (Celtica 21) 1990, 393–401.

family → children, → clan, → fine, → foster-children, → incest, → matri-linearity, → woman.

Fann (Ir. /faN/). In the story of the Wasting Sickness of Cú Chulainn (→ Serglige Con Culainn) the wife of the sea-god → Manannán mac Lir, for a time the beloved of Cú Chulainn.

feasts. Scarcely anything is known about the seasonally determined feasts of the pre-Christian Celts. Even the calendar known as the Calendar of → Coligny yields no information concerning them. Only the note TRINOX SAMONI SINDIU "Today (is) Trinox Samoni" relating to the second day of the second half of the first month in the year suggests that this date was of particular significance to the Gauls. Where medieval Ireland is concerned, four important feasts are known, which were in each case celebrated at the beginning of a season. The two most important were → Samain at the beginning of winter, on the first of November, and → Beltaine at the begin-ning of summer, on the first of May. The two feasts of → Imbolc on the first of February and → Lugnasad on the first of August marked the beginning of spring and autumn. All these feasts began on the evening of the previous day, as the Celts divided → time on the basis of nights rather than days. It is noteworthy that none of the great feasts coincided with the solstice or equi-nox. They were therefore not determined by astronomical observations but on the basis of the rhythms of nature.

Lit.: F. Le Roux, 'Études sur le festiaire celtique' (Ogam 13) 1961, 481–506 and (14) 1962, 174–184 and 343–372; K. Danaher, The Year in Ireland, Du. 1972.

Fedelm (Ir. /ˈfʲeðʲelm/). A female seer in the story of The Cattle Raid of Cuailnge (→ Táin Bó Cuailnge). She goes up to the army of the royal couple → Ailill and → Medb as they set off from Connacht and prophesies to them their downfall. In a poem of ten strophes she describes the appearance of the hero → Cú Chulainn and the deeds he will perform.

Fedelm Noíchride (Ir. /'feð'elm 'noiçr'ið'e/). In the story of The Cattle Raid of Cuailnge (→ *Táin Bó Cuailnge*) a daughter of the king → Conchobar mac Nesa of Ulster. She is married to the king Cairbre Nia-Fer and has a son by him called Erc. In the tale → *Fled Bricrenn*, however, F. appears as the wife of the warrior → Loegaire Buadach.

Fellbach-Schmieden. Site near Stuttgart where in 1977–1980 a newly discovered Celtic → Viereckschanze of the 2ndC BC was the subject of archaeological excavation. In a 20-yard deep shaft, which was originally lined with wood, the remains of a wooden bucket were discovered, together with the bones of horses and cattle. A further find was of three animal figures carved from oak (two goats and a stag), outstanding examples of Celtic carving. These are now preserved in the Württembergisches Landesmuseum in Stuttgart.

> *Lit.*: D. Planck et al., 'Eine neuentdeckte kelt. Viereckschanze in F.' (*Germania* 60) 1982, 105–172; D. Planck, 'Die Viereckschanze von F.', in: *Der Keltenfürst von Hochdorf*, St. 1985, 341–354.

Ferchertne (Ir. /'f'er'çer't'n'e/). A celebrated poet (→ fili) in early Irish literature. He appears in the tale → *Orgain Denna Ríg* as a companion of the king → Labraid Loingsech. In the stories of the → Ulster Cycle, however, he appears as a poet either of the king → Conchobar mac Nesa of Ulster or of the king → Cú Roí of Munster. He plays a major role in the tale → *Immacallam in dá thuarad.*

Fer Diad (Ir. f'er 'd'iað/). In the story of The Cattle Raid of Cuailnge (→ *Táin Bó Cuailnge*) a warrior regarded as invulnerable because of his horny skin. Because, like → Cú Chulainn, he learned the use of weapons from the she-warrior → Scáthach, the royal couple → Ailill and → Medb regard him as an opponent equal in worth to the Ulster hero. By cunning the two of them succeed in persuading F., who is at first reluctant, to fight in single combat against his former brother-in-arms. At the ford later named after him, Áth Fir Diad (now Ardee in County Louth), F. is finally killed by Cú Chulainn's spear → gae bolga.

Fergus mac Roich (Ir. /'f'eryus mak Roiç/) or F. mac Rosa Ruaid. One of the main characters of the → Ulster Cycle. The story of The Exile of the Sons of Uisliu (→ *Longas mac nUislenn*) tells how in anger at a breach of faith on the part of the king → Conchobar mac Nesa of Ulster F. leaves his homeland and goes into exile, to the royal couple → Ailill and → Medb in Connacht. In the story of The Cattle Raid of Cuailnge (→ *Táin Bó Cuailnge*) F. takes part in the great campaign of the men of Connacht against Ulster, siding with Ailill and Medb. Even though he is an exile he still feels tied to his earlier homeland, and therefore tries repeatedly to protect his former compatriots and in particular his brother-in-arms, → Cú Chulainn, from misfortune. According to tradition F. was the lover of Medb and was therefore murdered at the instigation of Ailill.

Lit.: R. Ó hUiginn, 'Fergus, Russ and Rudraige: A brief biography of Fergus mac Róich' (Emania 11) 1993, 31–40.

Ferguson, Samuel (1810–1886). Anglo-Irish poet and antiquarian, born in Belfast. He composed many imitations of Irish bardic poems and metrical reworkings of Irish sagas (1865 *Lays of the Western Gael,* 1872 *Congal,* 1880 *Deirdre* and *Poems*). His collection of such → ogam inscriptions as were then known (*Ogham Inscriptions in Ireland, Wales, and Scotland*) was published by his widow a year after his death.

Lit.: M. Brown, Sir S. F., Lewisburg (Penn.) 1973; T. Brown & B. Hayley, S. F.: a centenary tribute, Du. 1987; P. Denman, S. F.: the literary achievement, Gerrards Cross 1990.

féth fíada (Ir. f'e:θ 'f'iaða/). The magic mist that hides the → Tuatha Dé Danann from the eyes of mortal man, said to be one of the three magic gifts that → Manannán mac Lir conferred upon the princes of the Tuatha Dé Danann.

Fianna (Ir. /'f'iaNa/). The retinue of → Finn mac Cumaill in the tales of the → Finn Cycle. The name is the plural of the Irish word fian, a general term for a band of warriors. It survives in the name of the Irish party F. Fáil (→ Fál), founded in 1926.

fibulae. Brooches constructed on the same principle as the modern safety-pin, used in great quantities by the Celts (in lieu of the buttons and zips of nowadays). Celtic f. are generally made of → iron or → bronze and are frequently decorated with ornaments, figurative representations or inlaid enamel. They are classified on the basis of many different types, such as snake, bow, boat, drum, foot ornament, mask and animal head fibulae. Their form and size were constantly changing, with the result that f. form an important basis for the dating of archaeological finds.

Lit.: G. Mansfeld, Die F. der Heuneburg 1950–1970, B. 1973; V. Kruta, 'Remarques sur les fibules de la trouvaille de Duchcov (Dux), Bohème', in: P.-M. Duval et al. (eds.), Recherches d'archéologie celtique et gallo-romaine, P. 1973, 1–33; S. Kurz, 'Figürliche F. der Frühlatènezeit in Mitteleuropa' (FBW 9) 1984, 249–278; R. Gebhard, Die F. aus dem Oppidum von Manching, St. 1991.

fidchell → gwyddbwyll.

fili (Ir. /'f'il'i/) or (later) file. Term denoting the learned poet, who occupied a high position in medieval Irish society. Among his duties was the composition of eulogies and invectives (→ áer) and the handing down of traditional lore. Various allusions indicate that he was also involved in the maintenance and codification of the law. Some texts ascribe additionally the gift of prophecy to the f. His office was hereditary and he was much respected, his rights being recognised even outside his own tribal group (→ tuath). Seven ranks of f. were distinguished, depending upon their degree of knowledge and education. The highest of these was the → ollam. There is much to suggest that the filid occupied the same position in medieval Ireland which the → druids possessed before the christianisation of the country. The question of continuity between the office of druid and that of f. has however been the subject of much controversy in recent research.

Lit.: J. E. C. Williams, 'The Court Poet in Medieval Ireland' (PBA 57) 1971, 1–51; K. McCone, *Pagan Past and Christian Present in Early Ir. Lit.*, May. 1990.

Findabair (Ir. /'f'indavir'/). Daughter of the royal couple → Ailill and → Medb of Connacht in the tales of the → Ulster Cycle. Her name is a compound of find "white" and siabair "ghost, apparition" and corresponds etymologically to the Welsh name → Gwenhwyfar. In the story of The Cattle Raid of Cuailnge (→ *Táin Bó Cuailnge*) Ailill and Medb use F. as a lure to persuade as many warriors as possible to fight against → Cú Chulainn.

Findbennach. (Ir. /'f'indveNax/) "the White-Horned One". In the story of The Cattle Raid of Cuailnge (→ *Táin Bó Cuailnge*) the most famous bull in the province of Connacht (→ *De chophur in da muccida*).

fine (Ir. /'f'in'e/). Term denoting kin, in legal texts further sub-classified. Gel-fine denoted a group of relations descending in the male line from the same grandfather. The íar-fine, on the other hand, included all relations descending in the male line from the same great-great-grandfather. Most important was the derb-fine, referring to members of a family who traced their descent back along the male line to the same great-grandfather. Such a kin group possessed land in common (fintiu) and was responsible under certain circumstances for the crimes or debts of its individual members. The supreme head of the f. was called agae f. or cenn/conn f. He was elected on the basis of his means, his social position and his character, and represented the interests of the f. in public.

Lit.: F. Kelly, *A Guide to Early Ir. Law*, Du. 1988; T. M. Charles-Edwards, *Early Irish and Welsh Kinship*, O. 1993.

Fingal. In the "Works of Ossian" by James → Macpherson the ruler of the (fictitious) Scottish kingdom of Morven. In the Gaelic version of the poems his name is Fionnghal or Fionn, derived from the name of the originally Irish legendary hero → Finn mac Cumaill, about whom many ballads and stories were also in circulation in Scotland. In memory of a visit to Fingal's Cave, a rock formation named after Fingal on the Hebridean island of Staffa, Felix

Mendelssohn-Bartholdy (1809–1847) gave his overture op. 26 the title "Fingalshöhle" ("Fingal's Cave"). William Turner (1775–1851) gave the same title to his painting of Staffa, begun in 1831 and exhibited for the first time in 1832.

Fingal Rónáin (Ir. /'f'inɣal 'Ro:na:n'/ "Rónán's Killing of his Kin"). Title of a tale from the → Historical Cycle, surviving in the "Book of Leinster" (→ Lebor Laignech) and in a manuscript of c. 1500. The story tells of how the second wife of the king Rónán of Leinster falls in love with her step-son, and when her love is not returned, denounces him to his father. In a rage, Rónán has one of his warriors run his spear through his son, but before the latter's death finds out the truth of the matter. When a foster-brother of the dead man then avenges him by slaying the father of the queen and his family, Rónán's wife takes her own life. Rónán dies of grief concerning the guilt which he has heedlessly brought upon himself.
   Ed.: D. Greene, *F. R. and other stories*, Du. 1955 (MMIS 16).
   Trans.: R. Thurneysen, *Sagen aus dem alten Irland*, B. 1901.
   Lit.: T. Ó Cathasaigh, 'The Rhetoric of F. R.' (*Celtica* 17) 1985, 123–144.

Finnchaem (Ir. /'f'iNxaiv/). In the stories of the → Ulster Cycle the wife of the poet → Amairgin mac Ecit Salaig and mother of the warrior → Conall Cernach. She is said to be the sister of the king → Conchobar mac Nesa.

Finn Cycle or Ossianic Cycle. The prose narratives and ballads centred upon the legendary hero → Finn mac Cumaill and his retinue, the → Fianna. They are set in the time of the king → Cormac mac Airt at the beginning of the 3rdC AD. The heroes, apart from Finn, the leader of the Fianna, are his son → Oisín, his grandson → Oscar, and the warriors → Caílte mac Rónáin, → Goll mac Morna and → Lugaid Lága. Most of the stories concerning F. are about hunting adventures, love-affairs (cf. → *Tóraigheacht Dhiarmada agus Ghráinne*) and military disputes (cf. → *Cath Finntrága*). The most substantial work of this kind, combining various episodes within a narrative framework, is → *Acallam na Senórach*. The ballads concerning F. gained in popularity from the later Middle Ages onwards and were the most important source of James → Macpherson's "Works of Ossian".
   Lit.: G. Murphy, *The Ossianic Lore and Romantic Tales of Medieval Ireland*, Du. 1955; J. Falaky Nagy, *The Wisdom of the Outlaw: The Boyhood Deeds of Finn in Gaelic Narrative Tradition*, Be. 1985; J. MacKillop, *Fionn mac Cumhaill: Celtic Myth in English Literature*, Syracuse, NY 1986; A. Bruford, 'Oral and Literary Fenian Tales', in: B. Almqvist et al. (eds.), *The Heroic Process*, Dun Laoghaire 1987, 25–56; D. Ó hÓgáin, *Fionn mac Cumhaill: Images of the Gaelic Hero*, Du. 1988.

Finn mac Cumaill (Ir. /f'iN mak 'kuviL'/). The central character in the tales of the → Finn Cycle. He is the leader of a community of outstanding warriors, conjoined by oath (→ Fianna), who in peace-time devote themselves primarily to hunting and in the time of war fight on the side of their sover-

eign lord, the king → Cormac mac Airt. F. himself in the olde.
characterised not only as a warrior, but also as a seer and poet. He i.
have acquired the gift of prophecy by sucking his thumb – a motif
developed with variations in a number of stories and occurs in similar fo
relation to the Welsh poet → Taliesin and the North Germanic legen
hero Sigurd. Ever since the Middle Ages F. has been among the most popu
folk heroes in the legends of Ireland and Scotland, and is the model for th
Scottish king Fingal in James → Macpherson's "Works of Ossian".
   Lit.: → Finn Cycle.

Fintan mac Bóchra (Ir. /'f'intan mak 'bo:xra/). In the "Book of the Invasions
of Ireland" (→ Lebor Gabála Érenn) the only survivor of the Flood in Ireland.
He is said to have landed on the island together with Noah's granddaughter
→ Cesair forty days before the Flood, and to have witnessed the whole course
of Irish history in the form of a salmon, an eagle and a hawk.

Fir Bolg (/f'ir' volg/). In the "Book of the Invasions of Ireland" (→ Lebor
Gabála Érenn) the third group of settlers to occupy Ireland after the Flood.
The division of Ireland into five "provinces" (→ cóiced) and the estab-
lishment of the kingship (→ rí) is traced back to the F. B. According to
tradition they were descendants of the followers of → Nemed, who left
Ireland for a time under the dictatorial rule of the → Fomoire. The F. B. are
said to have been conquered in battle by the → Tuatha Dé Danann.
   Lit.: J. Carey, 'F. B.: A Native Etymology Revisited' (CMCSt 16) 1988, 77–83.

fír flathemon (Ir. /f'i:r 'flaθ'evon/). In legal texts and in the sagas term
denoting the "justice (fír) of the ruler (flathem)". The giving of judgement
was one of the chief duties of the king (→ rí), who thus guaranteed that both
he and his subjects prospered. The "injustice of the ruler" (gáu flathemon)
was correspondingly regarded as the cause of all the misfortunes with which
the king or his people might meet. The concept of the f.f. plays an important
role in the sayings which survive under the title → Audacht Morainn. It is
thought that the f.f. was already a characteristic of the Celtic concept of
sovereignty in pre-Christian times. Similar concepts and ideas are known in
India (ṛta, dharma) Greece (dikē) and Egypt (maat).
   Lit.: H. Wagner, 'Old Ir. fír "truth, oath" ' (ZCP 31) 1970, 1–45, 57–58 & 146; C.
Watkins, 'Is tre f.f.: Marginalia to Audacht Morainn' (Ériu 30) 1979, 181–198; B.
Ó Cuiv, 'Is tre f.f.: an addendum' (Celtica 13) 1980, 146–149.

Fís Adamnáin → Adamnán.

Fled Bricrenn (Ir. /f'l'eð 'v'r'ik'r'eN/ "Bricriu's Feast"). Title of a story of the
→ Ulster Cycle, preserved with various omissions, additions and gaps in the
"Book of the Dun Cow" (→ Lebor na hUidre) and later manuscripts of the

Fled Dúin na nGéd

15th/16thC. The story begins with the preparations for a banquet to which Bricriu, feared as a troublemaker, has invited the heroes of Ulster. Because Bricriu has promised not only → Loegaire Buadach but also → Conall Cernach and → Cú Chulainn the place of honour at table (→ curad-mír), the feast immediately leads to fighting. On the advice of the wise → Sencha the heroes agree to yield the decision concerning precedence to an independent arbitrator. The three warriors, however, accept neither the judgement of the king → Ailill of Connacht, nor that of the king → Cú Roí of Munster, and thus the quarrel remains unsettled. One day a gigantic stranger enters the royal hall of Ulster. He asks the heroes there present if any of them dares to strike off his head with an axe, under the condition that on the following day he may do the same to him in return. On two successive days first Loegaire and then Conall Cernach declare themselves ready for the challenge. Yet both are seized by fear when the stranger, contrary to their expectation, survives their blows and demands that they carry out their promise. Only Cú Chulainn, the third to strike the bargain, keeps his word and puts in an appearance the following morning to have his head struck off. Thereupon the stranger, who in reality is Cú Roí, only touches the nape of his neck lightly with his axe, and then pronounces him to be the foremost warrior of Ireland. The story is retold by Lady Augusta → Gregory in the fourth and fifth chapters of her book *Cuchulain of Muirthemne*. The motif of trial by beheading is best known through its occurrence in the Middle English verse narrative *Sir Gawain and the Green Knight* (late 14thC).

Ed.: G. Henderson, F. B., Lo. 1899 (with Engl. trans., ITS 2); L. C. Stern, 'F. F. nach dem Codex Vossianus' (ZCP 4) 1903, 143–177.

Trans.: J. Gantz, *Early Irish Myths and Sagas*, Harm. 1981; K. Hollo, 'The Feast of Bricriu and the Exile of the Sons of Dóel Dermait' (*Emania* 10) 1992, 18–24.

Lit.: E. M. Slotkin, 'The Structure of F. B. before and after the Lebor na hUidre Interpolations' (*Ériu* 29) 1978, 64–77.

Fled Dúin na nGéd (Ir. /fʼlʼeð duːnʼna ŋʼeːð/ "The Feast of Dún na nGéd"). Title of a story from the → Historical Cycle. The version that has survived is thought to go back to the 11thC; it is preserved in the → "Yellow Book of Lecan" and a few other manuscripts. The story tells of the conflict between the Irish High King Domnall mac Aeda and his foster-son Congal Claen, the king of Ulster. Congal had helped his foster-father Domnall to attain the rank of High King, but the rich reward for which he had hoped did not materialise. On the occasion of Domnall's inaugural banquet in his residence Dún na nGéd the two men quarrel. Congal succeeds in gaining allies among foreign kings, yet he falls in the decisive Battle of Mag Ráth (→ *Cath Maige Rátha*).

Ed.: R. Lehmann, F. D., Du. 1964 (MMIS 21).

Trans.: R. Lehmann, 'The Banquet of the Fort of the Geese' (*Lochlann* 4) 1969, 131–159.

Lit.: M. Herbert, 'F. D.: A Reappraisal' (CMCSt 18) 1989, 75–87.

Flidais (Ir. /'f'l'iðiʃ/). Wife of the warrior → Fergus mac Roich in the tales of the → Ulster Cycle. In the "Book of the Invasions of Ireland" (→ *Lebor Gabála Érenn*), however, she is numbered amongst the → Tuatha Dé Danann. In the family tree of the southern Irish noble family of Eoganacht Caisil F. bears the byname Foltchain ("Beautiful Hair") and is said to be the mother of a king called Nia Segamain. Buar F., "F.'s Cattle", occurs in several texts as a poetic term for "deer" or "stags". It is therefore thought that the figure of F. derives from a pre-Christian goddesss of the forest and protectress of deer.

folktale. In all probability the Celts of ancient times regaled themselves with stories of marvellous events, which had no claim to be credible but were intended primarily to entertain. We possess no detailed knowledge of these, as the Celts transmitted such tales purely through the oral tradition, and classical → ethnography took no account of this matter.

We are better informed with regard to the Celtic literatures of the Middle Ages, which reveal in many instances the influence of motifs circulating internationally in folktales and fairy-tales. This influence reveals itself directly even in the earliest Irish and Welsh tales, and indirectly in → Arthurian literature, which is coloured by the Celtic tradition. In many cases, however, it is difficult to differentiate between folktale elements in the tradition and those which are mythical or legendary. Moreover the texts available to us have all to a greater or lesser extent been influenced by literary conventions and are thus no true reflection of the narratives of oral tradition.

The earliest recordings of folktales are as late as the 19thC. Among the best-known collectors in Ireland are Th. C. → Croker, D. → Hyde, and J. → Curtin, in Scotland J. F. → Campbell, in Wales J. → Rhŷs and W. J. → Thomas, in Brittany F.-M. Luzel. The most extensive collections come from Ireland, where the practice of narration from the oral tradition has survived into the 20thC, particularly in rural areas.

Lit.: T. P. Cross, *Motif Index of Early Irish Literature*, Bloomington (Ind.) 1952; K. H. Jackson, *The International Popular Tale and Early Welsh Tradition*, Car. 1961; S. Ó Súilleabháin & R. Th. Christiansen, *The Types of the Irish Folktale*, He. 1963; J. H. Delargy, 'The Gaelic Story-Teller' (PBA 31) 1967, 177–221; A. Welsh, 'The Traditional Narrative Motifs of the Four Branches of the Mabinogi' (CMCSt 15) 1988, 51–62.

Fomoire (Ir. /'fovor'e/). In the tales of the → Mythological Cycle a group of prehistoric demons. Their original nature and the meaning of their name are both obscure. Of the etymological explanations that have hitherto been advanced, a derivation from the Celtic word for "sea" or, on the other hand, a Celtic root corresponding to English "mare" (as in "nightmare"; German "Mahr", ghost) seem most probable. According to the "Book of the Invasions of Ireland" (→ *Lebor Gabála Érenn*), the F. were already in Ireland when, three hundred years after the Flood, → Partholón and his followers landed on the island. The latter fought against the F. in the first battle on Irish soil. The adherents of → Nemed, a later wave of immigrants, were suppressed by the Fomoire and forced to pay tribute. It was only the → Tuatha Dé Dannan who succeeded in defeating the F. in battle and expelling them from Ireland.

food and drink. Particular attention is paid to diet in the earliest reports of classical authors concerning the Celts. The description of → Poseidonios, which is preserved in → Athenaios (4,36), is well-known. According to this the Celts held their meals seated on a bed of hay at low tables. The chief source of nourishment was meat, which was either boiled in a cauldron or roasted and served on a spit. In the manner of lions, the Greek author tells us, they seized huge pieces and separated the meat from the bone either with their teeth or with a small knife. During communal meals they sat in a circle, with the most important person seated in the middle. They ate from plates of bronze, wood or wickerwork, and drank from vessels of clay or silver. The prosperous drank wine imported from Italy or the South of France, while the less well-off contented themselves with a kind of mead or with beer.

Celtic eating, drinking, cooking and storing utensils are known primarily through excavations in → settlements. Particularly frequent finds are fragments of clay vessels of various shapes, metal cauldrons, carving forks, spits and fire-dogs. The presence of vessels or spoons made of wood is generally attested only by the survival of their metal handles. The sites known as → princely seats have yielded drinking horns (or their metal fittings), pottery and metal utensils (such as bronze beak-shaped cans) imported from the Mediterranean area. Zoological and botanical studies, particularly of refuse from settlements, have provided information concerning the preferred diet. The chief forms of nourishment were cereals, beef and pork, whereas game and poultry played a subordinate role.

In the insular Celtic literature of the Middle Ages, which was intended for an aristocratic public, splendid banquets play an important role, not infrequently marking a climax in the plots of the sagas (cf. → Fled Bricrenn or → Scéla mucce Meic Dathó).

Lit.: K. Simms, 'Guesting and Feasting in Gaelic Ireland' (JRSAI 108) 1978, 67–100; P. O'Leary, 'Contention at Feasts in Early Ir. Lit.' (Éigse 20) 1984, 115–127; H. L. C. Tristram, 'Feis und fled', in: H. L. C. Tristram (ed.), Medialität und mittelalt. insulare Lit., T. 1992, 183–220; P. Reynolds, 'The Food of the Prehistoric Celts', in: J. Wilkins et al. (eds.), Food in Antiquity, Exeter 1995, 303–315.

Forgall Manach (Ir. /ˈforgaL ˈmanax/). Father of the titular heroine Emer in the tale of Cú Chulainn's Wooing of Emer (→ Tochmarc Emire). His maternal uncle is → Tethra, a king of the → Fomoire. The Story of the Pig of Mac

Dathó (→ *Scéla mucce Meic Dathó*) records that F. owned one of the six great feasting-halls (→ bruiden) of Ireland.

foster children. Foster children are frequently mentioned both in Irish → law and in the saga texts. The Old Irish terms for foster-parents correspond to the names of affectionate address which in related languages are employed by children towards their parents (compare. O.Ir. muimme "foster mother" with Engl. Mummy; O.Ir. aite "foster father" and Gothic atta "dear father"). This usage points both to the frequency of fostering as well as to the close tie existing between foster parents and foster children. The relationship between two foster children was also intimate (cf. in the tales of the → Ulster Cycle the relationships between → Cú Chulainn, his foster father → Fergus mac Roich and his foster brother → Fer Diad). The aim of this system was to strengthen amicable relations between two families or to preclude hostility. There was also the possibility of taking on fostering as a contractual, remunerative agreement.

Lit.: F. Kelly, *A Guide to Early Ir. Law*, Du. 1988.

Fótla (Ir. /'fo:dla/). A queen of the Tuatha Dé Danann in the "Book of the Invasions of Ireland" (→ *Lebor Gabála Érenn*). In the course of the conquest of Ireland by the sons of → Míl she and her two sisters → Ériu and Banba are all three said to have won from the poet → Amairgin Glúngel the promise that the island shall bear their name. Thus the name F. frequently stands for Ireland in poetic language. F. is said to have fallen in the Battle of → Tailtiu, fighting against the Sons of Míl.

Four Ancient Books of Wales. Title of an edition in two volumes of Middle Welsh poetry with English translations, published in 1868 by the Scottish lawyer William Forbes → Skene. The contents are taken from four medieval manuscripts: the "Book of Taliesin" (→ Llyfr Taliesin), the "Book of Aneirin" (→ Gododdin), the "Black Book of Carmarthen" (→ Llyfr Du Caerfyrddin) and the "Red Book of Hergest" (→ Llyfr Coch Hergest). Although the editions and in particular the translations of the texts have become dated, they amount to a significant pioneer achievement in the field of Welsh philology.

Froech mac Idaith (Ir. /froiç mak 'iðiθ '/). Titular hero of the story → *Táin Bó Froích*. He is said to be the son of the fairy Bé Find and the most handsome man in all Ireland and Scotland. In the older version of the story of The Cattle-Raid of Cuailnge (→ *Táin Bó Cuailnge*) F. is the first to fall in single combat against → Cú Chulainn.

Fuamnach (Ir. /'fuamnax/). The magically gifted wife of the elf-prince Midir in the story → *Tochmarc Étaíne*.

gae bolga (Ir. /gai 'bolga/). The name of the spear of the hero Cú Chulainn in the tales of the → Ulster Cycle. In the story of The Cattle-raid of Cuailnge (→ *Táin Bó Cuailnge*) he kills his opponent Fer Diad with this spear, and in the story → *Aided Oenfir Aífe* his own son. Both stories have it that the spear could only be used in water and inflicted particularly deep and dangerous wounds because of its many barbs.

Gaelic. The name given to the Celtic languages of Ireland, Scotland and the Isle of Man. To avoid confusion, the terms → Irish (Gaeilge), → Scots or Scottish Gaelic (Gàidhlig) and → Manx (Gaelg) are employed by linguists. All three languages are closely related and up until the 10thC there was apparently little distinction between them. This early phase of their history is therefore referred to as Common Gaelic. An older form of the word G. is Goidelic, now used to refer to the language from which Gaelic developed in historical times. Goidelic is – like Indo-European – not attested in documents, but can only be reconstructed on a comparative basis.

Lit.: K. H. Jackson, ' "Common Gaelic": The Evolution of the Goedelic Languages' (PBA 37) 1951, 71–97; J. T. Koch, 'Ériu, Alba and Letha: when was a language ancestral to Gaelic first spoken in Ireland?' (Emania 9) 1991, 17–27.

Gaidoz, Henri (1842–1932). French anthropologist and Celticist. In 1870 he founded the first scholarly journal in the Celtic field, the *Revue celtique* (since 1936: *Études celtiques*), which enjoyed a high international reputation. G.'s two works *Esquisse de la religion des Gaulois* (1879–1881) and *Études de mythologie gauloise* (1886) are concerned with Celtic religion and mythology.

Galatian. Term denoting the language of the Celts in Asia Minor (→ Galatians). It is known primarily from names and individual words occurring in the works of classical writers. As far as one can tell, it bore a great resemblance to → Gaulish. When Galatian died out is unclear, but all appearances suggest that it was still alive in the 3rd/4thC AD. This is intimated by the famous remark by the church historian Jerome that the Galatians spoke practically the same language as the inhabitants of Trier (Galatas . . . propriam linguam eandem habere quam Treviros). However it is most probable that this was not based upon personal observation but upon a note of the ecclesiastical author Lactantius.

Lit.: L. Weisgerber, 'Galatische Sprachreste' in: *Natalicium. Johannes Geffcken zum 70. Geburtstag*, Hei. 1931, 151–175; F. Müller, 'Der zwanzigste Brief des Gregor von Nyasa' (Hermes 74) 1939, 66–91; W. Dressler, 'Galatisches', in: W. Meid (ed.), *Beiträge zur Indogermanistik und Keltologie, J. Pokorny zum 80. Geburtstag gewidmet*, I. 1967, 147–154; K. H. Schmidt, 'Galatische Sprachreste', in: E. Schwertheim (ed.), *Forschungen in Galatien*, Bo. 1994, 15–28.

Galatians. The name given to those Celts who in 278 BC migrated across the Balkans to Asia Minor. Classical → ethnography distinguishes between three tribes, the Tolisto(b)agii, the Trocmi and the Tectosages, which were in turn subdivided into four divisions (tetrarchies) in each case. All twelve tetrarchies held a communal council of 300, whose assemblies met in a sacred grove (→ nemeton). Originally the G. had been summoned as auxiliaries by the Bithynian king Nicomedes I. After the end of their service as mercenaries they undertook pillage on their own initiative, finally settling as residents. The G. fought long wars with the kings of Pergamon, who celebrated their victories in a series of works of art. Several sculptures which date from the time of Attalos I. and Eumenes II. have survived in Roman marble copies; the most famous example is the "Dying Gaul" (now in the Museo Capitolino in Rome). Despite a decisive defeat inflicted by the Romans in 189 BC, the G. succeeded in preserving their independence until 25 BC, when Augustus made their settlement area into a Roman province. The letter of the apostle Paul to the G. is thought to be addressed to Christian communities in a rural area of this province. There the population probably still spoke their hereditary Celtic language (→ Galatian) as late as the 3rd/4thC AD.

Lit.: F. Stähelin, *Geschichte der kleinasiatischen G.*, Bas. 1907; K. Strobel, 'Die G. im hellenistischen Kleinasien', in: *Hellenistische Studien*, Mn. 1991, 101–134; S. Mitchell, *Anatolia: Land, Men and Gods in Asia Minor. I. The Celts in Anatolia and the Impact of Roman Rule*, O. 1993.

Gaul (Lat. Gallia). In classical → ethnography the area settled by the Gauls (→ Celts). Gallia Cisalpina or Gallia Citerior ("Gaul this side of the Alps") was the term for the area settled by the Celtic tribes in Upper Italy. Gallia Transalpina or Gallia Ulterior ("Gaul beyond the Alps") was the contrasting term for the area between the Rhine, the Pyrenees, the Alps, the Mediterranean and the Atlantic.

The Celts of Upper Italy were already conquered by the Romans in the 3rd/2ndC BC. In 89 and 49 BC they acquired Roman citizenship. In 125–118 BC the Romans conquered part of southern France and there founded the Roman province of Gallia Narbonensis. In 58–51 BC → Caesar conquered the rest of Gaul, which in 27 BC was divided by Augustus into the three provinces of Aquitania (in the south-west), Gallia Lugdunensis (central Gaul) and Gallia Belgica (in the north-east). The mid-point of these "three Gauls" (Tres Galliae) was the colony of Lugdunum (now Lyons), founded in 43 BC. There the assembly of the Gauls also met (Concilium Galliarum).

From the middle of the 1stC BC an independent Gallo-Roman culture evolved in Gaul, amalgamating native and foreign elements into a new whole. The second century saw the beginnings of the spread of Christianity in Gaul. Repeated invasions by Germanic tribes took place in the 3rdC, and G. was, after the departure of the Roman troops in the 5thC, conquered in its entirety by the Germani and divided amongst the tribes of the Franks, the Alemanni, the Burgundians and the Visigoths.

Lit.: C. Ebel, *Transalpine Gaul: the emergence of a Roman province*, Lei. 1976; R. Chevallier, *La romanisation de la Celtique du Pô*, R. 1983; J. F. Drinkwater, *Roman Gaul*, Ithaca (NY) 1983; E. M. Wightman, *Gallia Belgica*, Lo. 1985; P.-M. Duval, *La vie quotidienne en Gaule pendant la paix romaine*, P. [3]1988; A. L. F. Rivet, *Gallia Narbonensis: Southern Gaul in Roman Times*, Lo. 1988; A. King, *Roman Gaul and Germany*, Lo. 1990; G. Coulon, *Les Gallo-Romains: Au carrefour de deux civilisations*, 2 vols., P. 1990.

Gaulish. The language of the Celtic inhabitants of Central Europe. It is thought to have borne a great resemblance to → British and → Galatian. We know of G. primarily through names and words in the works of classical authors, and through many inscriptions, recorded in three distinct alphabets. In Upper Italy a few inscriptions have survived in the Etruscan alphabet of the 2ndC BC. Southern France has yielded some 60 stone inscriptions in Ionic-Greek script, mostly dating from the 1stC AD. Thirdly, in various parts of Gaul more than 100 texts have been found in the Latin alphabet, dating from the 1st-4thC AD. Among the most important of these inscriptions are the calendar of → Coligny, the graffiti from the potteries of → La Graufesenque, and the lead tablets from → Chamalières and → Larzac.

Lit.: G. Dottin, *La langue gauloise*, P. 1920; L. Weisgerber, 'Die Sprache der Festlandkelten' (BRGK 20) 1930, 147–226; J. Whatmough, *The Dialects of Ancient Gaul*, Cambridge (Mass.) 1970; W. Meid, *Zur Lesung und Deutung gallischer Inschriften*, I. 1989; W. Meid, *Gaulish Inscriptions*, Budapest 1992; P.-H. Billy, *Thesaurus Linguae Gallicae*, Hildesheim 1993; P.-Y. Lambert, *La langue gauloise*, P. 1994; P.-H. Billy, *Atlas Linguae Gallicae*, Hildesheim 1995.

Gauvain. French equivalent of the Welsh name → Gwalchmei.

Gawain. English and German equivalent of the Welsh name → Gwalchmei.

Gebrinius. God identified on the basis of the → interpretatio romana with → Mercury. He is attested in several inscriptions discovered during excavations in the 1920s beneath the cathedral in Bonn. Uncertainty regarding the etymology makes it unclear whether the god is of Germanic or Celtic origin.

Lit.: S. Gutenbrunner, 'Mercurius G.' (ZCP 20) 1936, 391–394.

geis (Ir. /g'eʃ/). Term denoting an absolute prohibition or tabu, the breach of which led, people feared, to devastating consequences. In medieval literature some such tabus are linked with specific offices such as that of the king, whereas others apply only to individuals. In early texts a g. generally appears to be predetermined by fate and irrevocable. Frequently a hero incurs death because extraordinary circumstances oblige him to transgress against his g. Thus → Cú Chulainn, for example, shortly before his death, goes against the prohibition that he should under no circumstances eat of the flesh of a dog (cú). In modern texts (e.g. → folktales), by contrast, a tabu is frequently a kind of magical command or prohibition which people possessed of magic powers may at will impose upon others.

Lit.: D. Greene, 'Tabu in early Irish narrative', in: H. Bekker-Nielsen et al., *Medieval Narrative: A Symposium*, Odense 1979, 9–19; R. Power, 'Geasa and Álög: Magic Formulae and Perilous Quests in Gaelic and Norse' (*Scottish Studies* 28) 1987, 69–89; P. O'Leary, 'Honour-bound: the Social Context of Early Irish Heroic G.' (*Celtica* 20) 1988, 85–107.

genii cucullati (Lat. pl.). Anonymous Celtic divinities which were depicted in a hooded cloak (cucullus). They occur both singly and in groups of three, and are sometimes also depicted in the company of a seated goddess. They frequently hold in their hands an egg or a scroll. The lack of relevant literary sources means that one can only speculate concerning the significance of the g.

Lit.: R. Egger, 'Genius cucullatus' (*Wiener Praehistorische Zeitschrift* 19) 1932, 311–323; F. M. Heichelheim, 'G.c.' (*Archaeologica Aeliana* (4) 12) 1935, 187–194; J. M. C. Toynbee, 'G. c. in Roman Britain', in: *Hommages à Waldemar Deonna*, Bru. 1957, 456–469; W. Deonna, 'Télesphore et le "genius cucullatus" celtique' (*Latomus* 14) 1959, 43–74; H. Kenner, 'Genius cucullatus' (*Röm. Österreich* 4) 1976, 147–161.

Geoffrey of Monmouth (Lat. Galfridus Monemutensis). Author writing in Latin in the first half of the 12thC. His fame is entirely dependent upon his literary output; we know scarcely anything of his life otherwise. He is thought to have been born in South Wales c. 1100, possibly into a family of Breton origin. There is documentary evidence of his presence in Oxford between 1129 and 1151. In 1152 G. was consecrated bishop of St. Asaph in north-east Wales. Welsh chronicles attest that he died in 1155.

In the 1130s G. wrote his main work, the *Historia Regum Britanniae*, in which he relates the history of the kings of Britain from their beginnings to the conquest of the island by the Anglo-Saxons. For G. the mythical ancestor of the kings of Britain is → Brutus, a great-grandson of the Trojan Aeneas. The real hero of his work, however, is → Arthur, whom G. portrays as a glorious ruler, an opponent on equal terms of the Roman Empire. G.'s sources were the work of → Gildas, the Ecclesiastical History of Bede, the → *Historia Brittonum*, and oral traditions of Wales and Brittany. The purpose of G.'s work is thought to have been not least to provide a quasi-historical base for the claims to rightful kingship of the Anglo-Norman kings of the 12thC. Although G. was deprecated by the historians of immediately succeeding generations for his imaginative treatment of traditional sources, his work was widely transmitted and exerted a lasting influence on the courtly literature of the 12th/13thCs (→ Arthurian literature).

G. concerned himself in his verse epic *Vita Merlini* (c. 1150) with the life of the prophet Merlin (→ Myrddin), who already figured in his *Historia*. This poem was however accorded only limited popularity and survives complete in only one manuscript.

Ed.: B. Clarke, *G. of M.: Vita Merlini*, Car. 1973 (with Engl. trans.); N. Wright, *The Historia Regum Britanniae of G. of M. I Bern, Burgerbibliothek Ms. 568*, C. 1985; id., *The Historia Regum Britanniae of G. of M. II The First Variant Version*, C. 1988; W. & J. MacQueen, 'Vita Merlini Silvestris' (*Scottish Studies* 29) 1989, 77–93 (with Engl. trans.).

Trans.: L. Thorpe, *G. of M.: The History of the Kings of Britain*, Harm. 1966.

Lit.: W. F. Schirmer, *Die frühen Darstellungen des Arthurstoffs*, Co. 1958; N. Wright, 'G. of M. and Gildas' (*AL* 2) 1982, 1–40; O. Padel, 'G. of M. and Cornwall' (*CMCSt* 8) 1984, 1–27; J. C. Crick, *The Historia Regum Britanniae of G. of M. III A Summary Catalogue of the Manuscripts*, C. 1989; id., *The Historia Regum Britanniae of G. of M. IV Dissemination and reception in the later Middle Ages*, C. 1991.

Gereint fab Erbin (Welsh /'gereint vaːb 'erbin/). Title of one of the "three romances" (→ Tair Rhamant). The hero of the story is the young knight G., who in the course of an adventure which takes him a long distance from Arthur's court wins a bride; on his return he celebrates with a magnificent wedding. When the other knights later reproach him with neglecting chivalric life for the sake of his wife, the married couple undergo a crisis, which is only resolved after a series of adventures. The titular hero G. was possibly a historical figure of the late 6thC, who also plays a role in a number of poems in the "Black Book of Carmarthen" (→ Llyfr Du Caerfyrddin) and the "Red Book of Hergest" (→ Llyfr Coch Hergest). Cf. → *Englynion Gereint*.

Ed.: B. Jones, *Y Tair Rhamant*, Aberystwyth 1960.

Trans: G. Jones & T. Jones, *The Mabinogion*, rev. ed., Lo. 1974; J. Gantz, *The Mabinogion*, Harm. 1976.

Lit.: N. Thomas, ' "Geraint" and "Erec" ' (*Trivium* 22) 1987, 37–48; J. Rowland, *Early Welsh Saga Poetry*, C. 1990; R. Middleton, 'Chwedl G.', in: R. Bromwich et al. (eds.), *The Arthur of the Welsh*, Car. 1991, 147–157.

Gergovia. Fortified chief town of the Gaulish tribe of the → Arverni, situated on a remote high plateau south-east of present-day Clermont-Ferrand. It covered a surface of c. 75 hectares. G. was the home town of → Vercingetorix and during the revolt of the Gaulish tribes which he led in 52 BC it was unsuccessfully besieged by → Caesar.

Germani. The name given in classical → ethnography, following → Poseidonios and → Caesar, to the Eastern neighbours of the Celts. According to → Tacitus (Germania 2), the name initially denoted the tribe which first crossed the Rhine, but came to be applied to all the peoples right of the Rhine. In the course of their history the G. developed many cultural features in common with the Celts (→ Celtic-Germanic cultural links).

Gildas. British monk writing in Latin in the 6thC. His political and theological diatribe *De excidio Britanniae* ("Concerning the Fall of Britain") attacks the moral failings of the Celtic nobility of his time and interprets the Anglo-Saxon conquests as divine retribution. In the absence of comparable literary evidence his work is a major source of our knowledge of the British history of the period.

Ed. and trans.: M. Winterbottom, G.: *The Ruin of Britain and Other Works*, Lo. 1978.

Lit.: P. Sims-Williams, 'G. and the Anglo-Saxons' (CMCSt 6) 1983, 1–30; M. Lapidge & D. Dumville (eds.), G.: *New Approaches*, Wo. 1984; F. Kerlouégan, *Le De Excidio Britanniae de G.: Les destinées de la culture latine dans l'île de Bretagne au VIe siècle*, P. 1987; N. Wright, 'G.'s Reading: A Survey' (*Sacris Erudiri* 32) 1991, 121–162; N. J. Higham, *The English Conquest. Gildas and Britain in the fifth century*, Manchester 1994.

Gilfaethwy (Welsh /gil'vaiθui/). One of the two nephews of King Math of Gwynedd in the story → *Math fab Mathonwy*.

Ginevra. German form of the Welsh name → Gwenhwyfar.

Giraldus Cambrensis (Gerald de Barri; Welsh Gerallt Gymro). Cleric writing in Latin in the 12th/13thC. Born c. 1146 in south-west Wales, the youngest son of an Anglo-Norman noble and a mother of Welsh descent, he studied theology in Gloucester and Paris. From 1176 to 1179 he taught at the university of Paris, and from 1184 to 1194 was chaplain at the court of Henry II. of England. During this time he accompanied Prince John on his expedition to Ireland (1185–1186) and Archbishop Baldwin of Canterbury on his journey to Wales (1188). After twice failing to be elected bishop of St. David's, G. withdrew from all offices in 1203, devoting himself entirely to literary activities until his death in 1223. His most significant contributions to the history of Celtic culture include his description of Ireland (*Topographia Hiberniae*), an acccount of the Norman conquest of Ireland (*Expugnatio Hibernica*), and two books concerning his travels in Wales (*Itinerarium Kambriae* and *Descriptio Kambriae*).

Lit.: R. Bartlett, *Gerald of Wales*, O. 1982; B. F. Roberts, *Gerald of Wales*, Car. 1982; J. G. Griffiths, 'G. C.: Descriptio Kambriae' (BBCS 31) 1984, 1–16; J. Stewart, 'Topographia Hiberniae' (*Celtica* 21) 1990, 642–657; J.-M. Boivin, *L'Irlande au moyen âge. Giraud de Barri et la Topographia Hibernica (1188)*, P. 1993.

glám dícenn (Ir. /glaːv 'ð'iːg'eN/). Term denoting a ritual curse, which was thought to cause boils to appear on the face of the accursed person (cf. → áer).

Glanum. Roman name of an ancient site not far from the modern town of St.-Rémy-de-Provence near Marseilles. As early as the 6th/5thC BC a settlement arose there near a sacred spring; its inhabitants had contacts with the Greek colony of Massalia (Marseilles). Towards the end of the 3rdC BC the Greek settlement of Glanón originated near the sacred spring; towards the end of the 2ndC BC this was conquered by the Romans and only abandoned c. 270 AD. The ruins of this settlement are still to be seen on the site, whilst many archaeological finds from pre-Roman and Roman times are preserved in the Hôtel de Sade in St.-Rémy-de-Provence.

Lit.: F. Salviat, G., P. 1979.

glass. The Celts of the 6th/5thC BC knew glass almost exclusively in the form of (imported) coloured beads. Most finds derive from the graves of women and children, whereas archaeological exploration of settlements of this period has only rarely yielded glass. In the 4thC BC the first Celtic glass-making workshops originated, for the exclusive manufacture of → jewellery (beads and rings). The use of glass to make crockery, mirrors or windows was however not known to the Celts.

Lit.: M. Feugère (ed.), *Le verre préromain en Europe occidentale*, Montagnac 1989; R. Gebhard, *Der Glasschmuck aus dem Oppidum von Manching*, St. 1989; K. Spindler, *Die frühen Kelten*, St. ²1991.

Glastonbury → Avalon.

Glauberg. Village and nearby hill-crest c. 5 miles west of Büdingen (Hessen). The earliest traces of settlement date from the Stone Age, the oldest fortifications from the → Urnfield Culture. In 1988 a Celtic → princely grave of the 5thC BC was discovered on the southern slope, and methodical excavations took place in 1994. The grave contained among other things a Celtic → bronze beaker manufactured on an Etruscan pattern and a richly ornamented neck-ring of → gold. In June 1996, a sandstone sculpture (possibly representing the deceased prince) was found in the immediate vicinity of the grave. The finds are to be described by the regional archaeologist of Hessen in Wiesbaden.

Lit.: F.-R. Herrmann and O. H. Frey, *Die Keltenfürsten von. G.*, Wi. 1996.

Glewlwyd Gafaelwar (Welsh /'gleuluid ga'vailvaur/). The name of the watchman or porter at the court of → Arthur in the stories → *Iarlles y Ffynnawn*, → *Gereint fab Erbin*, and → *Culhwch ac Olwen*. The two latter stories record that he only held this office on special feastdays, whereas otherwise he was represented by various subordinates. The fragmentary poem → *Pa ŵr yw'r porthor?* would seem to derive from a different tradition; there G. is the gatekeeper of a stronghold which Arthur and his retinue desire to enter.

glosses. Name given since the Middle Ages to the explanatory additions in manuscripts which occur between the lines or in the margins of texts. For the Celticist particular importance attaches to the Breton, Welsh and Irish glosses in medieval Latin manuscripts. The Old Irish glosses are the most important, being in the oldest Celtic language capable of virtually complete reconstruction. The most important Old Irish glosses are the Würzburg glosses on the Epistles of St. Paul (for the most part 8thC), the Milan glosses on a Latin commentary on the Psalms (9thC) and the St. Gall glosses on the work of the Latin grammarian Priscian (9thC).

Ed. and trans.: W. Stokes & J. Strachan, *Thesaurus palaeohibernicus*, 2 vols., C. 1901–1903.

Lit.: K. H. Schmidt, 'Die Würzburger G.' (ZCP 39) 1982, 54–77; E. G. Quin, 'The Irish glosses', in: P. Ní Chatháin & M. Richter (eds.), *Irland und Europa*, St. 1984, 210–217; K. McCone, 'The Würzburg and Milan Glosses: Our Earliest Sources of "Middle Irish" ' (*Ériu* 36) 1985, 85–106.

Gododdin, Y (Welsh /ə go'doðin/ "The Gododdin"). Title of a poem which tradition holds to be the work of the poet → Neirin. Its theme is the defeat of a select band of Celtic warriors of the tribe of the Gododdin in southern Scotland. In their campaign to conquer Catraeth (Catterick in Yorkshire), they are said to have fallen in battle against Germanic invaders. The work survives in the "Book of Aneirin" (Llyfr Aneirin), a parchment manuscript of c. 1250 which survives in incomplete form, now preserved in South Glamorgan County Library in Cardiff. It contains strophes from two different versions of the poem, together with four other poems also attributed to Neirin. It is thought that all these poems were written down after having been transmitted orally for a long time. The circumstances of their origin and the history of their transmission are however bones of scholarly contention.

Ed.: I. Williams, *Canu Aneirin*, Car. 1938; A. O. H. Jarman, *Aneirin: Y. G.*, Llandysul 1988 (with Engl. trans.).

Trans.: K. H. Jackson, *The G.: The Oldest Scottish Poem*, E. 1970.

Lit.: T. M. Charles-Edwards, 'The Authenticity of the G.: An Historian's View', in: R. Bromwich & R. B. Jones (eds.), *Astudiaethau ar yr Hengerdd*, Car. 1978, 44–71; K. Klar et al., 'Welsh poetics in the Indo-European tradition: the case of the Book of Aneirin' (StC 18/19) 1983/84, 30–51; B. F. Roberts, *Early Welsh Poetry: Studies in the Book of Aneirin*, Aberystwyth 1988; G. R. Isaac, *The verb in the Book of Aneirin*, T. 1996.

gods and goddesses. Divinities played an important role in Celtic religion right from the beginning. This is clear from the fact that the Indo-European word for "god / goddess" (*deivos / *deivā, hence Lat. deus, dea) is well attested in all Celtic languages. In Gaulish and British the root *devo- or its variant *divo- occurs in many → place-names and → personal names. The frequent form Deva "goddess" survives in the name Dee, today the name of several British rivers. In Irish día (pl. dé) "god" serves to denote the one

Christian God as well the many pre-Christian gods. The corresponding Welsh form of the word is duw (older form: dwyw).

We remain in considerable ignorance as to the Celts' conceptualisation of their gods and what myths they told concerning them. Where the oldest period is concerned, there is a lack of literary sources and clear visual depictions. The French comparative religionist Georges → Dumézil attempted an approximate reconstruction of the world of Celtic gods by adducing extensive comparative material from other Indo-European cultures. Working on the basis of Dumézil's theories the French archaeologist Jean-Jacques Hatt (*1913) has attempted to identify symbolic depictions of divinities in the art of the Hallstatt and La Tène periods with the names known only from later sources. Both these approaches are however heavily dependent upon speculation and have not found general assent among scholars. The names of Celtic divinities and details concerning their cults are only transmitted in greater detail in Roman times. The major sources from this period are the accounts in classical → ethnography, and votive inscriptions written in Gaulish and Latin.

Works of classical literature yield knowledge of → Andrasta, → Belenus, → Epona, → Esus, → Grannus, → Ogmios, → Taranis and → Teutates. A much greater number of names is known only from inscriptions, in which the Celtic gods and goddesses are frequently identified with Roman divinities (what is known as the → interpretatio romana). Indeed many divinities are only known to us through the equation of their names with the Roman gods → Apollo, → Mars and → Mercury. Other names attested in inscriptions which rarely or never occur in conjunction with a Roman divinity are → Abnoba, → Andarta, → Antenociticus, → Arduinna, → Artio, → Atesmerius, → Belatucadrus, → Belisama, → Bergusia, → Borvo, → Brigantia, → Cernunnos, → Cocidius, → Coventina, → Damona, → Icauna, → Intarabus, → Iovantucarus, → Latobius, → Litavis, → Matrona, → Matunus, → Moltinus, → Nantosuelta, → Nemetona, → Noreia, → Rosmerta, → Rudianus, → Rudiobus, → Sequana, → Sirona, → Smertrius, → Souconna, → Sucellus, → Tarvos Trigaranus, → Ucuetis, → Veteris, → Visucius and → Vosegus.

After the christianisation of the Celts some gods were recast as mortals (the process known as → euhemerism) and appear in the medieval literatures of Ireland and Wales generally as legendary heroes from the distant past, whose origin in pre-Christian mythology can only be discerned by the interpretation of attributes accorded to the warriors in the traditions.

Lit.: → religion.

gods, pairs of. Pairs of gods are known to us through many inscriptions and pictorial representations from Gallo-Roman times. In a few cases both partners bear a Roman name in accordance with the → interpretatio romana, although the connection between the two is at odds with Roman mythology, for example → Mars and → Diana. In other cases the god bears an entirely or partially Roman name, whereas the goddess has an exclusively Celtic name, e.g. → Mercurius and → Rosmerta, Apollo → Grannus and → Sirona, or Mars → Leucetius and → Nemetona. Other inscriptions, however, give a Celtic name to both partners, e.g. → Sucellus and → Nantosuelta, → Borvo and → Damona, or → Ucuetis and → Bergusia. Many of these alliances are only attested by a single inscription. In other cases it happens that the same divinity is assigned different partners in different inscriptions. Thus the goddess Damona appears alongside the gods Apollo → Moritasgus, Borvo and Albius.

Such evidence as has survived leaves the religious significance of these pairs of gods very much in the dark. We do not know, for example, whether both partners were of equal significance, and it is also unclear as to whether the believer held the god and goddess to be spouses in every case. Conceivably two divinities were linked with one another because of similar functions or areas of competence.

Lit.: C. Bémont, 'A propos des couples mixtes gallo-romains', in: L. Kahil et al. (eds.), Iconographie classique et identité regionale, P. 1986, 131–153; M. Green, Symbol and Image in Celtic Religious Art, Lo. 1989.

Gofannon fab Dôn (Welsh /go'vannon va:b do:n/). Personage mentioned in the story → Culhwch ac Olwen. The giant Ysbaddaden Bencawr gives the titular hero Culhwch the task of ploughing a field newly cleared of trees. He reveals to him at the same time that this can only be done with the aid of G. The name G. derives from a Celtic word meaning "smith", and it is therefore thought that the figure of G. goes back to a Celtic god of ironwork (cf. → Goibniu, → Vulcan).

Goibniu (Ir. /'gov'n'u/). Smith of the → Tuatha Dé Danann in the stories of the → Mythological Cycle. In the story of the Battle of Mag Tuired (→ Cath Maige Tuired) he forges spear-points and swords for the warriors.

Goidelic → Gaelic.

Golasecca Culture. A regional culture of the early Iron Age (7th-4thCs. BC) whose home was in western Lombardy. It is named after a site not far from the southern end of Lago Maggiore. It is thought that the people of this culture were in part of Celtic origin.

Lit.: R. C. de Marinis, 'Golasecca Culture and its Links with Celts beyond the Alps', in: The Celts, Mi. 1991, 93–102.

gold. In prehistoric times gold was obtained both from rivers and from open-cast and subterranean mines. Classical authors such as → Diodoros of Sicily, → Pliny the Elder and → Strabo lavish particular praise on the wealth in gold of the Iberian peninsula, southern Gaul and the Alpine area. The Celts employed gold predominantly for → jewellery and → coins. What we know concerning manufacturing processes is based, in the absence of literary sources, on finds. These generally derive from graves (→ princely graves) or from hoards and sacrificial offerings, and suggest that gold was for the most part hammered and worked. The techniques of casting, welding, soldering and granulating were also known to some extent, but did not play a major role.

Lit.: C. Eluère, *Das Gold der Kelten*, Mn. 1987; *G. der Helvetier*, Z. 1991 (exhibition cat.); *Hundert Meisterwerke keltischer Kunst*, Trier 1992 (exhibition cat.).

Goll mac Morna (Ir. /goL mak 'morna/). The most important antagonist of → Finn mac Cumail in the stories of the → Finn Cycle. Sometimes his true name is rendered as Aed ("fire"), and Goll ("the one-eyed one") serves only as his byname. Tradition has it that the name G. derives from his losing one eye in the Battle of Cnucha, in which he slew Finn's father.

Goloring. Modern name of an early Celtic → place of worship near Koblenz, consisting of a circular fortification, c. 200m in diameter, with a wooden post at its centre which had ritual significance. It is thought to have been constructed in the 6thC BC.

Goreu fab Custennin (Welsh /'gorei va:b ki'stennin/). Son of the shepherd Custennin in the story → *Culhwch ac Olwen*. Until the arrival of Arthur and his companions his mother keeps him hidden in a chest, because the giant → Ysbaddaden has previously slain no less than 23 of her sons. G. becomes a member of Arthur's retinue and in the end avenges his brothers by decapitating Ysbaddaden.

Gorsedd Beirdd Ynys Prydein → Williams, Edward.

Gottfried von Straßburg. → Hartmann von Aue, → Wolfram von Eschenbach and Gottfried were the most important writers of courtly romances in medieval German. In the first decade of the 13thC G. composed the most famous Middle High German version of the Tristan legend (→ Drystan).

Gournay-sur-Aronde. Site in the northern French Dép. of Oise of a Celtic sanctuary in the period from the 3rd-1stC BC, the subject of archaeological excavation since 1975. In a rectangular area c. 40 metres in lateral length the remains of countless → sacrifices have been found. Apart from fragments of swords, sword-sheaths, shield buckles, spear-points and many other iron implements and utensils, the bones of at least 200 animals (for the most part sheep, cows and pigs) and at least 12 human beings were found. The finds may now be seen in the Musée Vivenel in Compiègne.

Lit.: J.-L. Brunaux & P. Meniel, 'Das Oppidum von G.' (*Antike Welt* 14,1) 1983,

41–45; J. L. Brunaux et al., *G. I. Les fouilles sur le sanctuaire et l'oppidum (1975–1984)*, Amiens 1985; J.-L. Brunaux & A. Rapin, *G. II. Boucliers et lances; dépôts et trophées*, P. 1988; Th. Lejars, *Gournay III. Les fourreaux d'épées*, P. 1994.

Grafenbühl. Modern name of the site of a Celtic → princely grave in the eastern part of the town of Asperg in the Ludwigsburg area (Baden-Württemberg). It is thought that it is linked, like some other grave-mounds in the vicinity, with an early Celtic → princely seat on the → Hohenasperg. During the archaeological excavation of the mound in 1964–1965 the skeleton of a man of about thirty was found in the central grave-chamber, together with the remains of a chariot, a drinking vessel and several pieces of furniture imported from the Mediterranean. These are now preserved in the Württembergisches Landesmuseum in Stuttgart. The grave had clearly already been plundered in ancient times and is now totally destroyed as a result of other buildings being erected above it.

Lit.: K. Bittel et al. (eds.), *Die Kelten in Baden-Württemberg*, St. 1981.

Grail. In a body of → Arthurian literature a mysterious object which confers upon its owner earthly and heavenly bliss, to which however only he who is chosen can attain. The word grail (O.Fr. graal/greal, Provençal grazal, Middle High German grâl) is thought to derive from medieval Latin and to have denoted originally a kind of vessel. The legend of the Grail in the form in which it is known to us is a creation of the Christian Middle Ages and not derived from Celtic tradition.

Lit.: K. H. Jackson, 'Les sources celtiques du Roman du Graal', in: *Les Romans du Graal au XIIe et XIIIe siècles*, P. 1956, 213–227; F. Karlinger, *Der Graal im Spiegel romanischer Volkserzählungen*, V. 1996.

Gráinne (Ir. /ˈgraːNˈeˌ/). Titular heroine of the story → *Tóraigheacht Dhiarmada agus Ghráinne*, daughter of the king → Cormac mac Airt, wife of the ageing → Finn mac Cumaill and beloved of the young warrior → Diarmait ua Duibne. The narrator praises her unusual beauty, yet her name actually means "the Ugly One". In consequence the theory has been put forward that the character of G. retains features of the personification of "sovereignty" (flathius), who in other Irish tales is portrayed before her marriage with the rightful ruler as an ugly old hag, but thereafter as a miraculously beautiful young woman (→ sacred marriage).

Grannus. A Celtic god equated in Roman times with → Apollo, whose aid was sought in times of sickness in many parts of the Roman empire. According to the historian Cassius Dio (77,15,5ff), in the year 213 the emperor Carcalla called on his aid. In a verse inscription from Bonn (CIL XIII 8007) the god is given the name G., whereas elsewhere he is always called Apollo G. Votive inscriptions have been found in or near Arnheim in Holland (CIL

XIII 8712), Erp near Euskirchen, Nordrhein-Westfalen (CIL XIII 7975), Trier (CIL XIII 3635), Alzey, Rheinhessen (Ne 88), Speyer (Ne 71), Horbourg in the Alsace (CIL XIII 5315), Neuenstadt on the Linde (CIL XIII 6462), Ennetach in the Saalgau, Swabia (CIL III 5861), Faimingen on the Upper Danube (CIL III 5870, 5871, 5873, 5874, 5876, 5881), Branges near Chalon-sur-Saône (CIL XIII 2600), Musselburgh in Scotland (RIB 2132), the Roman site of Brigetio in Hungary (CIL III 10972), Grand in the Dép. of Vosges (CIL XIII 5942 and ILTG 416) and Astorga in Spain. A Roman bronze bucket with a dedication to Apollo G. was found in 1818 in a grave-mound in Sweden. In 1905 a Greek inscription dating from 217/218 AD was found in a wall east of the library of Ephesus in Turkey; it records that a distinguished citizen of the town had travelled through the whole of the Roman empire "as far as Apollo G.". This is possibly a reference to the sanctuary dedicated to the god in Faimingen, or that in Grand. That there was also a sanctuary of G. in Aachen is deduced from the Latin name of the city, Aquae Granni (the waters of G.). This name, however, is not attested until 765 AD and thus far no votive inscriptions to G. have been found in Aachen. In many inscriptions the goddess → Sirona appears as the companion of the god. Dedications to the gods as a couple have been found in or near the monastery of Baumburg in Bavaria (CIL III 5588, Rome (CIL VI 36) and Bretea Romîna in Roumania (CIL III 74*); the authenticity of this inscription has been contested). It is thought that several inscriptions in which Apollo alone, or Apollo and Sirona are mentioned, also relate to Apollo Grannus.

Lit.: → Apollo, → religion.

grave → death and burial.

Gregory, Lady Augusta (1852–1932). Anglo-Irish authoress, born Isabella Augusta Persse in the West of Ireland. In 1880 she married the former Governor of Ceylon, Sir William Gregory. After the death of her husband in 1892 she became an adherent of the Irish independence movement, and with William Butler → Yeats campaigned for the creation of an Irish theatre. In 1902 her book *Cuchulain of Muirthemne* appeared, in which she attempted to mould various Old and Middle Irish legends into an artistic whole and retell them for an English-speaking public. As she herself possessed no philological training, she relied upon earlier translations by Celticists such as → Arbois de Jubainville, → Meyer, → O'Curry, → Stokes, → Windisch and → Zimmer. The language of the tales is an approximation to the idiom of the rural population of her home in the West of Ireland. The main sources of her work were the stories of the → Ulster Cycle. She retold stories from the → Mythological and → Finn Cycles in her book *Gods and Fighting Men*, which appeared in 1904. For this work she used translations of Middle Irish texts, but also drew to a greater extent upon the collections of folklore made by J. F.

→ Campbell, Jeremiah → Curtin and Douglas → Hyde. Under Hyde's influence she herself also published several volumes of oral Irish traditions: *A Book of Saints and Wonders* (1906), *The Kiltartan History Book* (1909), *The Kiltartan Wonder Book* (1910) and *Visions and Beliefs in the West of Ireland* (1920).

Lit.: M. L. Kohlfeldt, *Lady G.*, NY 1985; A. Saddlemyer & C. Smythe (eds.), *Lady G.: Fifty Years After*, Gerrards Cross 1987.

Gronwy Pybyr (Welsh /ˈgronui ˈpəbir/ "G. the Strong"). The beloved of Blodeuwedd in the story → *Math fab Mathonwy*.

groves, sacred → nemeton.

Gruffydd, William John (1881–1954). Celticist, born in South Wales. After studying philology with, among others, Sir John → Rhŷs, he taught Celtic and Welsh philology in Cardiff from 1906 to 1946. He published poems and a volume of childhood reminiscences (*Hen Atgofion*, 1936), as well as many studies in the area of Welsh literary history. He published his researches into the mythological background of the "Four Branches of the Mabinogi" (→ *Pedeir Ceinc y Mabinogi*), which were in part extremely speculative, in the three volumes *Math Uab Mathonwy* (1928), *Rhiannon* (1953) and *Folklore and Myth in the Mabinogion* (1958).

Guaire Aidne (Ir. /ˈguarˈe ˈaðˈnˈe/). Historically attested 7thC king who reigned over the province of Connacht from 655 to 666. He plays a major role in the stories → *Scéla Cano meic Gartnáin* and → *Caithréim Cellaig*.

Gúbretha Caratniad (Ir. /ˈguːvˈrˈeθa ˈkaradnˈiað/ "The false judgements of Caratnia"). Title of a collection of verdicts deviating from the customary principles of Irish law. The text is thought to date from c. 800 and survives in a compendium manuscript of the 12thC. In its surviving form the collection contains 51 judgements relating to all areas of Irish law. Tradition has it that they were pronounced in the 2ndC AD by Caratnia, a judge of the king → Conn Cétchathach.

Lit.: F. Kelly, *A Guide to Early Ir. Law*, Du. 1988.

Guenièvre. French form of the Welsh name → Gwenhwyfar.

Guest, Lady Charlotte Elizabeth (1812–1895). Born in Uffington, Lincolnshire, daughter of the Earl of Lindsey. In 1835 she married the Welsh industrialist Sir Josiah John Guest (1785–1852). Between 1838 and 1849 she published, with the aid of many helpers versed in Welsh, an English translation of twelve medieval Welsh prose tales. These achieved widespread fame under the collective title she had chosen, the → *Mabinogion*, and had considerable influence on the reception of the Celtic literatures in the 19thC.

Lit.: D. Rh. Philips, *Lady C. G. and the Mabinogion*, Swansea 1921; R. Bromwich, 'The Mabinogion and Lady C. G.' (*Transactions of the Honourable Society of Cymmrodorion*) 1986, 127–141.

Guinevere. English form of the Welsh name → Gwenhwyfar.

Gundestrup. Town in North Jutland near which a silver cauldron bearing figurative depictions in a high relief technique was found in a peat bog in May 1891. It had been carefully dismantled into its component parts. Further investigation led to the conclusion that the component parts were not originally buried in the bog, but had been secreted in a dry place or deposited as a sacrifice. In a plain round silver dish, the original base of the cauldron, two tubular fragments were found, which came from the edge of the cauldron, and twelve arched, rectangular plates, which had formed the inner and outer sides of the cauldron. The place of origin and date of the cauldron are not known, but it is thought that it dates from the last third of the first millennium BC and was manufactured by Celts or under Celtic influence. This is suggested in particular by the depiction of the decorated helmets, shields and war-trumpets (→ carnyx) of a band of warriors, as well as the image of a divinity with a neck-ring (→ torcs) and antlers (cf. → Cernunnos). Many of the stylistic details and the depiction of a sequence of animals (lions, gryphons and elephants among others) are however indubitably influenced by the Orient and recall Thracian works of art that bear a Hellenistic hallmark. All this points to the view prevalent today that the cauldron was manufactured in the Balkans in the 2nd/1stC BC and was taken to Denmark as spoils of war. It may now be seen in the National Museum of Copenhagen.

Lit.: G. S. Olmsted, *The G. Cauldron*, Bru. 1979; A. Bergquist & T. Taylor, 'The Origin of the G. Cauldron' (*Antiquity* 61) 1987, 10–24; R. Hachmann, 'G.-Studien' (*BRGK 71*) 1990, 565–904; F. Kaul et al., *Thracian Tales on the Gundestrup Cauldron*, Amsterdam 1991.

Gutuater. The name of a Gaul of the tribe of the → Carnutes, who, according to the Roman historian Aulus Hirtius, was executed on the orders of → Caesar in 51 BC for inciting others to war (concitator belli) (cf. Bell. Gall. 8,38.) By contrast, the word G. appears in four inscriptions from Roman Gaul, designating a priest or religious dignitary (cf. CIL XIII 1577, 2585, 11225 and 11226). It is therefore probable that the use of the word G. as a proper name is based upon a misunderstanding and that it was in reality a title. The exact meaning of this title is however unknown, as is the religious function of the G. The Irish word guth "voice" suggests however that G. denoted the priest in his function as "appellant" (to the divinity).

Lit.: D. E. Evans, *Gaulish Personal Names*, O. 1967.

Gwalchmei fab Gwyar (Welsh /'gwalxmei va:b 'guiar/). A nephew of →
Arthur in the story → *Culhwch ac Olwen*. The narrator praises him as an
exceedingly fast runner and rider who always succeeds in whatever he under-
takes. In the story → *Breuddwyd Rhonabwy* he is mentioned along with many
other heroes of Welsh legend as one of Arthur's counsellors. In the → Tair
Rhamant G. plays the role which falls to the knight Gauvain in the corresponding Old French romances. He reunites the long-lost knight → Owein
with his companions, wins the friendship of the new arrival → Peredur and is
generally regarded as the foremost knight in Arthur's retinue.
Lit.: → Arthurian literature.

Gwenddoleu fab Ceidiaw (Welsh /gwen'ðolei va:b 'keidjau/). Royal patron
of the poet → Myrddin, said to have fallen in the battle of → Arfderydd, c.
573 AD.

Gwenhwyfach (Welsh /gwen'huivax/). A sister of → Gwenhwyfar in the tale
→ *Culhwch ac Olwen*. Two of the → *Trioedd Ynys Prydein* name a quarrel
between her and Gwenhwyfar as the cause of the Battle of → Camlan. These
are the only three references to G. in Welsh tradition; she is otherwise
unknown.

Gwenhwyfar (Welsh /gwen'huivar/). Wife of → Arthur in Welsh tradition.
She is mentioned in the story → *Culhwch ac Olwen*, but it is not until the
"three romances" (→ Tair Rhamant) that she plays a role in the action.
According to the *Vita Gildae* of → Caradog of Llancarfan, G. was abducted by
a rival of Arthur called Melwas and kept captive for one year. In → Chrétien
de Troyes this motif of abduction is linked with the figure of → Lancelot, a
name foreign to the Welsh tradition. According to → Geoffrey of Monmouth, G. committed adultery with Arthur's nephew → Medrawd and after
the death of her lover ended her days in a nunnery.
Lit.: K. G. T. Webster, *Guinevere: A Study of her Abductions*, Milton, Mass. 1951; P.
Korrel, *An Arthurian Triangle*, Lei. 1984.

Gwerthefyr (Welsh /gwer'θevir/). Son of the British king → Gwrtheyrn
(Vortigern). The → *Historia Brittonum* reports that he led many victorious
onslaughts on the Saxon invaders. Before his death he is said to have ordered
his dependants to bury him on the sea-shore in order to frighten the Saxons
away. His family, however, ignored this order and buried him elsewhere. →
Geoffrey of Monmouth tells a similar story in his *Historia Regum Britanniae*.
He has it that Vortimer (= G.) was appointed by the British to replace his
father as king; after his victories over the Saxons he was poisoned by his
stepmother. In contrast to this tradition one of the → *Trioedd Ynys Prydein*
records that the bones of the dead king were indeed buried in the most

important harbours of the country, and that as long as they lay there no Saxons dared invade.

Lit.: R. Bromwich, *Trioedd Ynys Prydein*, Car. ²1978.

Gwion Bach (Welsh /gwion ba:x/ "little Gwion"). In the story → *Hanes Taliesin* the original name of the poet Taliesin.

Gwrtheyrn Gwrtheneu (Welsh /'gurθeirn gur'θenei/). British king said to have been the first to form an alliance with the pagan Saxons, around the middle of the 5thC. In the → *Trioedd Ynys Prydein* he is therefore regarded as one of the "three shameful men of the island of Britain". The oldest records concerning him are preserved in Bede's *History of the English Church* (c. 730) and the → *Historia Brittonum* (c. 830). The most detailed account is that of → Geoffrey of Monmouth in his *Historia Regum Britanniae*, according to whom Vortigern (= G.) becomes king of Britain after the murder of the rightful king Constantine. He allies himself with the Saxons against the → Picts and marries a Saxon princess. Because he favours the Saxons, G. is however deposed by the Britons in favour of his son Vortimer (→ Gwerthefyr), but after the latter's death seizes power again. After many British nobles have been murdered by the Saxons, G. flees to North Wales where he meets the wise Merlin (→ Myrddin), who prophesies to him that his end is nigh. Soon afterwards G. is killed when his stronghold is besieged by Ambrosius Aurelianus (→ Emrys Wledyg).

Lit.: R. Bromwich, *Trioedd Ynys Prydein*, Car. ²1978.

gwyddbwyll (Welsh /'gwiðbuił/). Board game mentioned in several Middle Welsh stories. In → *Breuddwyd Macsen* the Roman emperor Macsen sees in a dream two young men playing the game with golden pieces on a silver board. Near them sits a white-haired old man on a throne of ivory, carving pieces. In → *Peredur fab Efrawg* the titular hero Peredur sees in an apparently uninhabited castle two sets of pieces playing against one another, as if they were alive. In → *Breuddwyd Rhonabwy* Rhonabwy sees in a dream the heroes → Arthur and → Owein playing against one another. All these descriptions suggest that g. was played by two players, each with a set of pieces. Consequently g. is occasionally translated as "chess", to facilitate the modern reader's understanding. In Irish narratives the game is given the (etymologically identical) name fidchell (from gwydd or fid "wood" and pwyll or cíall "intelligence").

Gwyddno Garanhir (Welsh /'gwiðno ga'ranhir). In the story → *Culhwch ac Olwen* the name of the possessor of a basket containing inexhaustible supplies of food. The theft of this basket is one of the tasks imposed upon the titular hero Culhwch by the giant Ysbaddaden. In later tradition G. occurs as the ruler of a now submerged stretch of land off the coast of north-west Wales. In the story → *Hanes Taliesin* G.'s son Elffin finds the boy Taliesin in a weir by the coast.

Gwydion (welsh /'gwidjon/). In the story → *Math fab Mathonwy* one of the two nephews of King Math of Gwynedd.

Gwynedd (Welsh /'gwineð/). Region in north-west Wales, where after the departure of the Roman troops at the beginning of the fifth century AD one of the first independent kingdoms originated. While its extent varied, it survived until the English conquest towards the end of the thirteenth century. In 1974 County G. was recreated, consisting of the old counties of Anglesey, Caernarfon and Merioneth.

Gwyn fab Nudd (Welsh /gwin va:b ni:ð/). Character in Welsh tradition of whom relatively little is known. His name first appears in the story → *Culhwch ac Olwen*, where he is listed as a member of → Arthur's retinue. Another passage in the tale has it that G., as a consequence of a judgment pronounced by Arthur, must fight on the first of May every year against a rival for the hand of the maiden → Creiddylad. In a third passage the giant Ysbaddaden explains to the titular hero Culhwch that G. must at all costs participate in the hunt for the boar → Twrch Trwyth, as God has conferred upon him the power of the demons inhabiting → Annwfn. G. appears as ruler over Annwfn in the legend of St. Collen (6thC); the manuscript transmission of this legend goes no further back than the 16thC, however. Apart from this, we possess from the Middle Ages a few strophes in the "Black Book of Carmarthen" (→ Llyfr Du Caerfyrddin), which contain a dialogue between G. and → Gwyddno Garanhir, in the course of which G. is characterised as a feared warrior. There are later folk traditions concerning G., but the possibility exists that these do not derive from ancient oral tradition, but instead from scholarly speculation of the 19thC.

Lit.: J. Rowland, *Early Welsh Saga Poetry*, C. 1990.

Haedui → Aedui.

Hafgan (Welsh /'havgan/). Antagonist of Arawn, king of → Annwfn, in the story → *Pwyll Pendefig Dyfed*. He is slain in single combat by the titular hero Pwyll.

Hallein. Austrian regional capital on the west bank of the Salzach, c. 9 miles south of Salzburg.
 On the Dürrnberg, a high plateau interspersed with pits south-west of H., traces of human habitation have been found dating back to the beginning of

the Neolithic period, c. 4000 BC. At the beginning of the later Hallstatt period, c. 600 BC, the Dürrnberg developed into one of the most important centres of salt-mining in Central Europe. As early as c. 500 BC a hill-fort settlement was erected on the Ramsauerkopf, a long, steeply descending mountain ridge. About the same time many artisans' workshops originated in the Ramsau valley, whilst less advantageous terrain was employed for burial fields. The majority of the graves date from the period between 470 and 250 BC, at which time the Dürrnberg settlement reached its fullest extent. Because of the wealth of grave goods these graves are an important source of our knowledge of the material and intellectual culture of that period. Particularly significant is a bronze beaker of the early 4thC BC (now in the Museum Carolino Augusteum in Salzburg), one of the most important examples of Celtic artisanship. The mining of salt from the Dürrnberg seems to have lost a great deal of its importance c. 100 BC, probably because of the growth of the salt industry in nearby Reichenhall. After the Roman conquest of 15 BC it is thought that salt-mining on the Dürrnberg either ceased altogether or from then on only supplied local needs.

Since 1980 a Celtic Museum in H. has informed visitors about the history of the Dürrnberg. On the site an open-air exhibition displays a reconstruction, based on archaeological finds and contemporary depictions, of the interior of a princely grave, and a farm with domestic quarters, a sty and a barn.

Lit.: F. Moosleitner, L. Pauli & E. Penninger, *Der Dürrnberg bei H.*, 3 vols., Mn. 1972–1978; *Die Kelten in Mitteleuropa*, Hallein 1980; F. Moosleitner, *Die Schnabelkanne vom Dürrnberg*, Sa. 1985; T. Stöllner, 'Neue Grabungen in der latènezeitlichen Gewerbesiedlung im Ramsautal am Dürrnberg bei H.' (*AKorrBl* 21) 1991, 255–269; W. Irlinger, *Der Dürrnberg bei Hallein IV: Die Siedlung auf dem Ramsaukopf*, Mn. 1994.

Hallstatt. Site on the west bank of Lake Hallstatt in the Upper Austrian Salzkammergut, which formed between the 9th and the 5thC BC one of the first and most significant centres of salt-mining in Europe. The earlier phase of the pre-Roman Iron Age in Central Europe is named the H. period after the finds discovered in a prehistoric grave-field near H. in 1846. The older H. period (known to archaeologists by the abbreviation HaC) lasted from 750–600 BC, the later period (HaD) from 650–450/400 BC. A geographic distinction is drawn between a western area (eastern France, Switzerland, southern Germany and western Austria) and an eastern area (eastern Austria and the Balkans), with H. itself in the border area of the two cultural regions. From an archaeological point of view it is only the representatives of the later H. civilisation of the western region whom it is possible to identify with the Celts as known in classical → ethnography. The most important archaeological evidence of this period derives from the fortified residences of the upper social stratum (cf. → princely seats) and the graves belonging to these (cf. → princely graves). Some of the archaeological finds from H. itself may be seen on site in the Prehistoric Museum, others are in the prehistoric section of the Natural History Museum in Vienna.

Lit.: R. Kromer, *Das Gräberfeld von H.*, Fl. 1959; L. Pauli, *Die Gräber vom Salzberg zu H.*, Mz. 1975; E. Lessing, *H.: Bilder aus der Frühzeit Europas*, V. 1980; *Die H.kultur. Bericht über das Symposium in Steyr 1980*, Linz 1981; P. Brun, *Princes et princesses de la Celtique. Le premier âge du fer en Europe*, P. 1987; K. Peschel, 'Kelten u. nordwestalpine H.kultur' (*Ethnogr.-archäolog. Zeitschrift* 29) 1988, 259–300; *La civilisation de H.: Bilan d'une rencontre*, Liège 1989; K. Spindler, *Die frühen Kelten*, St. ²1991.

Hanes Taliesin (Welsh /'hanes tal'jesin/ "The Story of Taliesin"). Title of a story concerning the poet Taliesin, the oldest version of which is to be found in the world chronicle of the Welsh writer Elis Gruffydd (c. 1490–1552). It tells how Gwion Bach, a servant of the sorceress Ceridwen, contrary to her command drinks of her magic potion and thus acquires the gift of poetry and prophecy. Fleeing from Ceridwen, Gwion shifts shape many times and is finally, in the form of a small child, exposed to the sea by the enraged sorceress. On the coast of North Wales he is found by Elffin, son of the king → Gwyddno Garanhir, who adopts the boy and gives him the name Taliesin. At the court of King → Maelgwn of Gwynedd, Taliesin puts the ruler's poets to shame by virtue of his superior wisdom and comes to the aid of Elffin when the latter is in danger of losing the favour of the king because of his vainglorious talk.

Ed.: P. K. Ford, *Ystoria Taliesin*, Car. 1992.

Trans.: P. K. Ford, *The Mabinogi and other Medieval Welsh Tales*, Be. 1977.

Lit.: J. Wood, 'The Folklore Background of the Gwion Bach Section of H.T.' (BBCS 29) 1980–82, 621–634; ead., 'The Elphin Section of H.T.' (EC 18) 1981, 229–244.

hare. According to → Caesar (Bell. Gall. 5,12) the British accounted it wrong to eat hares, but kept them for pastime or pleasure. The reason for this prohibition is however not known to us. Remains found during excavations on various pre-Roman and Roman holy sites attest that the hare was a sacrificial animal. According to the historian Dio Cassius (Hist. Rom. 62,6) the British queen → Boudicca let a hare run free when she appealed to the goddess → Andrasta for help in battle against the Romans. In depictions of the gods the hare sometimes appears as an attribute of Celtic divinities associated with hunting, such as → Abnoba.

Hartmann von Aue. Middle High German poet of the 12th/13thC. Between 1180 and 1205 he wrote the first Middle High German Arthurian romances, adaptations of two of the verse romances of → Chrétien de Troyes, *Erec et Enide* and *Yvain*. While the German poet's *Iwein* adheres closely to its Old French source, *Erec* is considerably longer than Chrétien's romance of the same name and diverges from the source in many points of detail. In the

Celtic field the Middle Welsh prose tales → *Gereint fab Erbin* and → *Iarlles y Ffynnawn* correspond to the verse romances concerning Erec and Yvain/Iwein.

head. Both archaeological and literary sources attest that the human head played a prominent role in the → mythology, ritual and therefore also in the → art of the Celts. According to the evidence of classical → ethnography it was a common custom to cut the head off a fallen enemy and preserve it as a trophy. The historian → Diodoros of Sicily (5,29) attests that the Celts hung the heads of their enemies from the necks of their horses, embalmed the heads of their most noble antagonists, and preserved them with great care in a chest. According to → Strabo (4,4,5) such heads were also nailed to doorposts. In Ireland head-hunting is thought to have survived into the period after → christianisation, and is described in the Irish heroic sagas (cf. → Ulster Cycle). From an archaeological point of view the ritual significance of the head is confirmed by finds of whole skulls and fragments during the exploration of → settlements and → places of worship (cf. → Entremont, → Roquepertuse). The representation of human heads or faces is very frequent in Celtic art (cf. → tête coupée); sculptures of heads with two or three faces also occur, but the symbolism of these is obscure.

Lit.: P. Lambrechts, *L'Exaltation de la tête dans la pensée et dans l'art des Celtes*, Bruges 1954.

Heidelberg. Site of the finding of one of the most important early Celtic sculptures. The fragment of a head, 31 cm. high, of red sandstone, was discovered in the Bergheimer Straße in 1893 and is now dated to the 5th/4thC BC. It is thought to have originally formed the top of a grave stele. It may now be seen in the Badisches Landesmuseum in Karlsruhe.

Lit.: K. Bittel et al. (eds.), *Die Kelten in Baden-Württemberg*, St. 1981.

Heidengraben. Modern name of a fortified Celtic settlement on the Swabian Alb north-east of Urach. The site as a whole occupied an area of some 1660 hectares and was defended by walls and gates. An area of 153 hectares in the southern part of the walled-in site was additionally protected by a rampart and pits and is thought to have been the home of the settlement proper. Various finds of pottery, coins and other metal objects suggest that this area was settled in the 2nd/1stC BC, but full-scale archaeological excavation has yet to be undertaken.

Lit.: F. Fischer, *Der H. bei Grabenstetten*, St. [3]1982; F. Fischer et al., 'Neue Beobachtungen am H. bei Grabenstetten' (*FBW* 6) 1981, 333–349.

Hekataios of Miletos (Asia Minor). Greek geographer of the 6th/5thC BC. After travelling widely he wrote a description of the earth, the text of which has not survived; it is only known from references in later authors. It is thought that H. described the Celts as neighbours of the Ligurians and inhabitants of the hinterland of Massalia (Marseilles). It is not clear, however, how well he really knew these regions.

Lit.: → ethnography.

Heledd (Welsh /'heleð/). A sister of King Cynddylan, who is said to have reigned over the Welsh kingdom of → Powys in the 7thC AD. Her fate is the subject of a cycle of poems thought to have originated in the 9th/10thC, preserved in the "Red Book of Hergest" (→ Llyfr Coch Hergest) and a few other manuscripts. Possibly these poems constituted the dramatic highlights of a saga, the plot of which was told in prose or assumed to be common knowledge. In the central poem *Stafell Gynddylan* ("The Hall of Cynddylan"), H. portrays the disconsolate state of the royal castle, which was destroyed by enemies after the death of the king. Where once fires and candles burned, now darkness reigns, where song resounded, silence prevails. In other strophes H. laments the death of her brothers, the devastation of her country and the fate which exposed her defenceless to her enemies. At three points in the poems she accuses herself of being to blame for the downfall of the royal house. The meaning behind these lines is not however clear from the surviving strophes.

Lit.: J. Rowland, *Early Welsh Saga Poetry*, C. 1990.

Helico. In → Pliny the Elder (Hist. Nat. 12,2) the name of a Celtic craftsman of the people of the → Helvetii. After a sojourn in Rome he is said to have been the first to acquaint the Celts with figs, grapes, oil and wine and thus instigated the Celtic migration to northern Italy. As other classical authors are unfamiliar with this account it is conceivable that Pliny took it from native Celtic tradition, but we can only speculate concerning the sources.

Lit.: T. Köves-Zulauf, 'H., Führer der gallischen Wanderung' (*Latomus* 36) 1977, 40–92.

Helvetii. In classical → ethnography the name of the Celtic inhabitants of what is now Switzerland. According to → Tacitus (Germania 28) the H. originally settled in the area between the Rhine, the Main and the Mittelgebirge, i.e. what is now south-west Germany. In the course of the 1stC AD they migrated from there to central Switzerland. → Caesar (Bell. Gall. 1,2) has it that they were separated by the Rhine from the Germani, by the Jura from the Celtic Sequani, and by Lake Geneva and the Rhône from the Roman Province of Gallia Narbonensis, created in 121 BC. Some of the H. joined the migrating Germanic Cimbri and in 107 BC defeated a Roman army near Agen in the South of France. In 58 BC the whole tribal group, following a design of the prince → Orgetorix, left their territory in order to settle in south-west France. They were however defeated by Caesar at →

Bibracte and forced to retreat. Under the emperor Augustus the settlement area of the H. was incorporated into the Roman Empire. After the retreat of the Roman troops at the beginning of the 5thC their lands were settled by the Germanic Burgundians and Alemanni.

Lit.: D. van Berchem, *Études sur les Hélvètes et leurs voisins*, G. 1982; A. Furger-Gunti, *Die H.*, Z. 1984; F. Fischer, 'Caesar und die H.' (*BJb* 185) 1985, 1–26; *Gold der H.*, Z. 1991 (exhibition cat.).

Henwen (Welsh /'henwen/). A sow gifted with magic powers in the → *Trioedd Ynys Prydein*. Her keeper is the swineherd → Coll fab Collfrewi, who follows her from Cornwall through Gwent and Dyfed as far as Gwynedd. In the course of this journey H. gives birth to wheat, barley and bees in the south of Wales. In the north, however, she gives birth to a wolf, an eagle and a cat-like monster.

Hercules. Latin name of the Greek hero Herakles. Held to be the son of Zeus and Alkmene, hero of countless adventures, he was one of the most popular personages of myth and legend. Over 100 inscriptions consecrated to H. are known from Roman Gaul, most of them from the north-east of the Province. Some 350 visual depictions have also been found, showing H. with a club and a lionskin, following the Classical model. Only occasionally is H. given indigenous Celtic bynames in the inscriptions, such as Andossus (CIL XII 4316 and CIL XIII 226), Graius (CIL XII 5710) or Ilunnus (CIL XII 4316). The identification of H. with → Ogmios is only attested in literature.

Lit.: P. Lambrechts, *Contributions à l'étude des divinités celtiques*, Bruges 1942; J. de Vries, *Keltische Religion*, St. 1961.

Herecura → Aeracura.

Hergest, Red Book of → Llyfr Coch Hergest.

Herodotus. One of the first Greek historians. He was born c. 484 BC in Halikarnassos (Asia Minor), and after travelling widely wrote a history of the conflicts between the Greeks and the barbarians, which is also of anthropological interest. The first classical author to do so, he refers to the Celts at two points (2,33 and 4,49). He has it that they settled near the source of the Istros (the Danube) and beyond the Pillars of Hercules (i.e. in the Iberian peninsula). It is thought that his source for this information was reports of Greek mariners of the 6thC BC.

Lit.: F. Fischer, 'Die Kelten bei H.' (*Madrider Mitteilungen* 13) 1972, 109–124.

Heuneburg. Modern name of a fortified site on the west bank of the Danube in the Sigmaringen district, which was occupied from the Bronze Age until the early Middle Ages. One of the best researched early Celtic → princely seats was situated there in the 6th-5thC BC. It occupied an area of three hectares and was fortified by walls on all sides. According to archaeological evidence these walls were renewed at various stages, almost always employing a combination of wood, stones and earth. In one case however, a wall 3–4 metres high made of air-dried clay bricks was erected on top of a base made of limestone blocks, following a Mediterranean model. Several thousand cubic metres of blocks were procured for the purpose from a limestone quarry four miles away. Within the ancient fort remains were found of living rooms, granaries and workshops, built of wood and clay and separated from one another by little alleyways. During excavations large quantities of broken pottery were found, whereas relatively few objects of bronze, iron or precious metal emerged. This suggests either that H. towards the end of its period of occupation was totally ransacked, or that its inhabitants abandoned it, taking with them all their chattels.

Several grave-mounds in the proximity of H., one of which being the → Hohmichele, still attest today the imposing position of this early Celtic settlement. In the nearby village of Herbertingen-Hundersingen the H.-Museum, in the former tithe barn of the monastery of Heiligkreuztal, has since 1985 hosted an exhibition describing the history and study of H., including written documentation, an audio-visual display, original finds and a diorama. A circular walk of some five miles leads from the museum to the nearby grave-mounds and to a late Celtic → Viereckschanze.

Lit.: H.-Studien, B. 1962ff.; K. Bittel et al. (eds.), Die Kelten in Baden-Württemberg, St. 1981; W. Kimmig, Die H. an der oberen Donau, St. ²1983.

hieros gamos → sacred marriage.

high crosses. A group of monumental stone sculptures with figurative and/or ornamental decoration, which are to be found in the vicinity of monastic buildings, particularly in central and northern Ireland. Typically a high cross takes the form of a dice-shaped or pyramid-shaped base with a cross placed upon it, the vertical and horizontal arms of the cross being linked with one another by a ring; on top of the cross is a stone which takes the form of a cone or a small square house. Some crosses are carved from a single block of stone, whereas others are made of several parts dowelled together. The employment of stone of various colours (limestone, sandstone, granite) suggests that the natural colour of the surface as we see it today was originally painted over. Most high crosses date from the 8th-10thC; their function was apparently to adorn the monasteries and to educate the beholder, which is why the iconography of the crosses is inspired primarily by biblical and apocryphal Christian writings.

Lit.: F. Henry, Irish High Crosses, Du. 1964; P. Harbison, The High Crosses of Ireland, 3 vols., Bo. 1992.

Hirschlanden. Village near Ludwigsburg (Swabia), in the proximity of which in 1963–1964 two Celtic → princely graves of the late Hallstatt period were the subject of archaeological excavation. These are thought to be linked with an early Celtic princely seat on the → Hohenasperg. The most significant find is the life-size stele of a warrior of the Hallstatt period, now to be seen in the Württembergisches Landesmuseum in Stuttgart. The sculpture is carved in the round from fluviatile sandstone, and probably originally stood on top of one of the two hills. The warrior is depicted naked, ithyphallic, wearing only a neck-ring and a girdle with a slender dagger tucked into it. His headgear is probably intended to represent a hat of birch-bark, such as have been found in the grave of → Hochdorf. The face seems to have slipped slightly in a downward direction, and it is therefore thought that the statue may represent a dead man with a death-mask. Nothing of the graves is to be seen in the vicinity today.

Lit.: H. Zürn, 'Eine hallstattzeitliche Stele von H., Kr. Leonberg' (*Germania* 42) 1964, 27–36; J. Beeser, 'Der Kouro-Keltos von H.' (*FBW* 8) 1983, 21–46; W. Kimmig, 'Eisenzeitliche Grabstelen in Mitteleuropa' (*FBW* 12) 1987, 251–297.

Historia Brittonum. Title of a history of Britain and its inhabitants from the first settlement of the island until the 7thC AD. Written in Latin, the work is thought to have been compiled c. 830 on the basis of written and oral sources of various origins. It survives in six different versions, transmitted in over 40 manuscripts. One branch of the transmission names the author as a Welsh cleric called Nennius, but this attribution was only appended later to the work, which was transmitted anonymously. The H. B. is one of the most important sources of our knowledge of early medieval Welsh history, well-known because of its remarks upon five British poets of the late 6thC (→ Cynfeirdd) and the mention of the twelve victorious battles of the military leader → Arthur against Saxon invaders.

Lit.: D. N. Dumville, 'The Historical Value of the H.B.' (*AL* 6) 1986, 1–26; id., 'H. B.: an Insular History from the Carolingian Age', in: A. Scharer & G. Scheibelreiter (eds.), *Historiographie im frühen Mittelalter*, V. 1994, 406–434.

Historical Cycle. Term introduced by Eugene → O'Curry to designate a sequence of Irish narratives whose plot dates from the 3rdC BC to the 11thC AD. The surviving versions were written down for the most part from the 8th to the 14thC and combine authentic historical sources with mythical, legendary and fairy-tale traditions. Frequently a celebrated king is at the centre of one or several stories, which is why the Historical Cycle is also known as the Cycle of the Kings. Among the most important rulers who play a role in these tales are → Labraid Loingsech, → Conn Cétchathach, → Lugaid mac Con, → Cormac mac Airt, Rónán mac Colmáin (cf. → *Fingal Rónáin*), → Mongán mac Fiachna, → Domnall mac Aeda, → Diarmait mac Aeda Sláine and →

Guaire Aidne. The story known as → *Bórama* has a time-span of several centuries.

Lit.: M. Dillon, *The Cycles of the Kings*, Lo. 1946.

history. The history of the Celtic peoples spans a period of more than a thousand years. Geographically it embraces extensive regions of central and western Europe, the British Isles and Ireland, and parts of south-east Europe and Asia Minor.

The beginnings of Celtic history are to be found in the period named after the archaeological site → Hallstatt, c. 600–450/400 BC. From this period stem both the earliest archaeological evidence (→ princely graves, → princely seats) and the oldest reports of classical → ethnography. There follows the period named after the site → La Tène, ranging from the middle of the 5thC BC to the conquest by the Romans of the areas settled by the Celts in the 2nd/1stC BC. This period may be subdivided into a time of expansion (4th-3rdC BC), in which Celtic peoples took possession of parts of Upper Italy, the Balkans and Asia Minor, and the phase of the → oppida (2nd-1stC BC), ending about the middle of the 1stC BC with the Roman conquest of Gaul by → Caesar. In the course of the 1stC AD most of Britain was conquered by the Romans, whilst Ireland remained outside the borders of the Roman Empire.

The → christianisation of the Celts began as early as the 2ndC AD, starting in southern Gaul; it embraced Roman Britain in the 3rd-4thC, whence it spread to parts of the regions settled by the Celts which lay outside the borders of the Roman Empire. The attacks of the Germani led to the withdrawal of the last of the Roman troops from Britain at the beginning of the 5thC. Germanic peoples crossed the border of the Rhine, conquered Rome and established their kingdoms in the settlement area of the Romanised Celts. In the 5th/6thC the Anglo-Saxons conquered large parts of Britain. Irish Celts settled in parts of Scotland and the outlying islands, while at the same time Celts from the South-West of Britain, under pressure from the advancing Anglo-Saxons, emigrated to Brittany.

From the 6thC onwards monastic culture flourished in Ireland, influencing spiritual life in the Anglo-Saxon kingdoms and in the Frankish Empire. In the course of the 7thC the inhabitants of the Celtic kingdoms in the north of Britain were, as a consequence of the Anglo-Saxon conquests, separated from their kinsmen in Wales, and underwent a gradual process of assimilation. From this point onwards Celtic → languages were only spoken in Ireland, Scotland, Wales, Cornwall and Brittany. All these areas in the course of the Middle Ages succumbed to the power of the English and French kings, gradually losing their political and territorial independence. The descendants of the Celts, who were regarded as the most important race north of the Alps in the ancient world, are today only to be found on the westernmost edge of Europe.

General surveys: J. Moreau, *Die Welt der Kelten*, St. 1958; T. G. E. Powell, *The Celts*, Lo. 1958; M. Dillon & N. K. Chadwick, *The Celtic Realms*, Lo. 1967; E. Lessing, *Die Kelten*, Fr. 1979; B. Cunliffe, *The Celtic World*, Lo. 1979; *Die Kelten in Mitteleuropa*, Hallein 1980 (exhibition cat.); V. Kruta, *Die Kelten*, Lz. 1986; A. Ross, *The Pagan Celts*, Lo. 1986; K. H. Schmidt (ed.), *Geschichte und Kultur der Kelten*, Hei. 1986; H. D. Rankin, *Celts and the Classical World*, Lo. 1987; *The Celts / I Celti*, Mi. 1991 (exhibition cat.); H. Dannheimer & R. Gebhard (eds.), *Das keltische Jahrtausend*, Mz. 1993 (exhibition cat.); K. H. Schmidt, 'Celtic Movements in the First Millenium B.C.' (*Journal of Indo-European Studies* 20) 1992, 145–178; K. H. Schmidt, 'The Celtic Problem: Ethnogenesis (Location, Date?)' (*ZCP* 45) 1992, 38–65; S. James, *Exploring the World of the Celts*, L. 1993; B. Cunliffe (ed.), *The Oxford Illustrated Prehistory of Europe*, O. 1994; M. Green (ed.), *The Celtic World*, Lo. 1995.

Regional surveys: M. Szabó, *Auf den Spuren der Kelten in Ungarn*, Budapest [2]1979; G. Dobesch, *Die Kelten in Österreich nach den ältesten Berichten der Antike*, V. 1980; E. Campanile (ed.), *I Celti d'Italia*, Pisa 1981; K. Bittel et. al. (eds.), *Die Kelten in Baden-Württemberg*, St. 1981; S. de Laet, *La Belgique d'avant les Romains*, Wetteren 1982; A. Cahen-Delhaye et al. (eds.), *Les Celtes en Belgique et dans le Nord de la France*, Lille 1984; C. Thomas, *Celtic Britain*, Lo. 1986; D. Vitali (ed.), *Celti ed Etruschi nell'Italia centro-settentrionale*, Bol. 1987; J. G. Rozoy et al., *Les Celtes en Champagne*, Charleville-Mézières 1987; M. Szabó et al., *Les Celtes en Pannonie*, P. 1988; Ll. & J. Laing, *Celtic Britain and Ireland*, Du. 1990; I. Wernicke, *Die Kelten in Italien*, St. 1991; *Les Celtes en Champagne*, Epernay 1991 (exhibition cat.); *Les Celtes dans le Jura*, Yverdon 1991; M. Szabó, *Les celtes de l'est. Le second âge du fer dans la cuvette des Karpates*, P. 1992; M. Py, *Les Gaulois du Midi. De la fin de l'Age de Bronze à la conquête romaine*, P. 1993; P. Jud (ed.), *Die spätkeltische Zeit am Oberrhein – Le Rhin supérieur à la fin de l'époque celtique*, Basle 1993; P. Drda & A. Rybová, *Les Celtes de Bohême*, P. 1994; S. Fichtl, *Les Gaulois du Nord de la Gaule (150–20 av. J.-C.)*, P. 1994; B. Raftery, *Pagan Celtic Ireland*, Lo. 1994.

See also → Gaul, → Galatians, → Celtiberians.

Hochdorf. Place in the Ludwigsburg area (Swabia), near which in 1968 one of the most important Celtic → princely graves was found, dating from the second half of the 6thC BC. The grave-mound, situated in a field, had been almost completely levelled; it formed the subject of archaeological investigations in 1978/79, during which an intact, richly endowed grave-chamber was discovered. It contained the well-preserved skeleton of a man of about forty, lying on a couch (Gk. kline) of punched bronze sheet-metal. Many personal objects were buried with the dead man, including a hat of birch-bark, three fishing hooks and a quiver with some arrows. Moreover his clothing for the burial had been adorned with specially prepared gold jewellery. Other grave gifts were a four-wheeled → waggon with harness, and a large set of eating and drinking vessels which included a bronze cauldron with a capacity of 500 litres, imported from the Mediterranean area.

Because of favourable environmental conditions the organic materials were unusually well preserved and enable some conclusions to be drawn concerning the living conditions and the environment of the period. For example, examination of the quiver and arrows yielded information concerning the types of wood, which had been selected with considerable expertise. The cauldron still contained the residue of some mead, the analysis of which yielded indications as to the way in which the drink had been made and the nature of the plant life in the surrounding area. Study of remnants of → textiles led to valuable insights into the materials, their manufacture and the dyeing of the cloths.

In 1985 the grave-mound was raised to its original proportions (6m high and 60m in diameter), employing 7,000 cubic metres of soil and 280 tons of stone. The finds from the grave, after extensive conservation and restoration work, are now to be seen in the Württembergisches Landesmuseum in Stuttgart. On the site the Hochdorf/Enz Celtic Museum, opened in 1991, instructs visitors about the grave finds by means of faithful reconstructions. There are plans to reconstruct several Celtic houses in the vicinity in the next few years and to make these accessible in the form of an open-air museum.

Lit.: J. Biel, *Der Keltenfürst von H.*, St. 1985; *Der Keltenfürst von H.: Methoden und Ergebnisse der Landesarchäologie*, St. 1985 (exhibition cat.).

Hochscheid. Site in the district of Bernkastel-Wittlich in the Hunsrück (Moselle basin). In 1939 during waterworks a Gallo-Roman spring sanctuary was found in a moor about a mile south-east of H. An archaeological excavation carried out in the same year unearthed a Gallo-Roman ambulatory temple, several stone sculptures, coins and pottery. Many fragments of beakers attest that the water of the spring was drunk for medical purposes. During further excavations in 1962–1966 and 1972 a nearby hostel, a bath-house and one other building were the subject of archaeological investigation. According to an inscription found in 1940 the temple was dedicated to a pair of Celtic gods. The name of the goddess is recorded as → Sirona, whereas her male companion was equated with → Apollo on the basis of the → interpretatio romana. Archaeological study of the finds revealed that the site was erected between 50 and 150 AD. Towards the end of the 3rdC it was abandoned, and the temple destroyed – perhaps by Christians.

Lit.: G. Weisgerber, *Das Pilgerheiligtum des Apollo und der Sirona von H. im Hunsrück*, Bo. 1975.

Hohenasperg. Hill west of Ludwigsburg (Swabia). Although no archaeological excavation has taken place on the hill itself in view of its being so extensively built over, the H. is generally regarded as the site of one of the most important early Celtic → princely seats. This is deduced on the one hand from the commanding position of the hill, on the other because of the geographical proximity of many → princely graves of the late Hallstatt and early La Tène periods. As with the → Heuneburg, the later graves lay nearer the settlement than the earlier ones. Among the most important of these monuments are the → Grafenbühl and the → Kleinaspergle, as well as the graves of → Hochdorf and → Hirschlanden.

Lit.: K. Bittel et al. (eds.), *Die Kelten in Baden-Württemberg*, St. 1981.

Hohmichele. Celtic → princely grave situated about a mile west of the → Heuneburg. Almost 80m in diameter and 14m high, it is one of the biggest grave-mounds in central Europe. In 1937–1938 part of the hill was explored by archaeologists, who found, in the middle of the site, the central grave-chamber, lined with wooden boards; the contents had however almost all been plundered. On the edge of the hill the excavators found several subsidiary graves, among which was the intact grave of a man and a woman (subsidiary chamber 6), which contained a four-wheeled → waggon and harness, as well as many utensils and items of jewellery.

Lit.: G. Riek & H.-J. Hundt, *Der H.*, B. 1962.

Holder, Alfred (1840–1916). Palaeographer and philologist, born in Vienna. After studying in Heidelberg and Bonn he worked from 1870 until his death as librarian in the Großherzoglich Badische Hof- und Landesbibliothek in Karlsruhe. During this period he published many descriptions of manuscripts, as well as studies and editions, primarily of Latin texts. From 1891 to 1913 his major work appeared in three volumes, the *Alt-celtischer Sprachschatz*, an alphabetically arranged compilation, intended to be complete, of the Celtic linguistic material contained in ancient inscriptions and literary works. No similarly comprehensive work has yet replaced this, although the progress made in Celtic philology, and numerous new archaeological finds mean that much of its detail is sorely in need of supplementation and correction.

Holzgerlingen. Site in the Böblingen district (Baden-Württemberg) where around the middle of the last century an image of a double-faced god was found, 2.3m high, made of fluviatile sandstone. It is thought to date back to the 5thC BC and may now be seen in the Württembergisches Landesmuseum in Stuttgart.

Lit.: K. Bittel et al. (eds.), *Die Kelten in Baden-Württemberg*, St. 1981.

Holzhausen. Suburb of Munich where in 1957–1963 one of the best-known Celtic → Viereckschanzen was the subject of archaeological excavation. It proved possible to distinguish between five different phases in which the ritual site was extended. Remains of a wooden building were found in one corner of the enclosure, and three shafts, 35, 12 and 6.5 metres deep, which were presumably intended for the disposal of sacrificial remains.

horses. Horses played a major role in Celtic culture and religion. They were used both as riding and as draught animals; in the latter case they were always harnessed to the waggons in pairs. This is attested by indigenous visual depictions, as well as by finds of bridles and harness, and references in classical → ethnography. Finds of bones have shown that the Celtic h. were conspicuously bigger than those of the Bronze Age, which points to specialised breeding and careful grooming. Celtic horses were in consequence held in high regard in Roman times.

The importance of horses in ritual is confirmed by the very frequent employment of h. as sacrificial animals. There is also occasional evidence of the custom of burying h. or placing them in the same grave as a nobleman. H. are particularly frequently portrayed on Celtic → coins. The originally Celtic goddess → Epona was worshipped as a patroness of horses in many parts of the Roman Empire.

Lit.: F. Le Roux, 'Le cheval divin et le zoomorphisme chez les Celtes' (Ogam 7) 1955, 101–122; J. Marek, 'Das helvetisch-gallische Pferd' (Abhandlungen der Schweizerischen Paläontologischen Gesellschaft 25) 1988, 1–62; U. A. Müller, 'Das Pferd in der griechisch-keltischen Frühgeschichte' (Helvetia Archaeologica 21) 1990, 153–166.

human sacrifice → sacrifice.

hunting. Hunting and fishing played a subordinate role in the Celtic economy, compared with → agriculture and → cattle-breeding. The amount of time needed and the relatively small practical benefit of these activities suggest that it was primarily members of the aristocracy who indulged in them.

Archaeological and literary sources suggest that hunting was carried out on foot or on horseback, and that spears and slings were employed as well as bows and arrows. According to → Pliny (25,5,25) poisoned arrows were also used. Dogs were employed to hound game. The beasts that were hunted included big game such as aurochses, elks, bears, stags and wild boar, smaller game such as deer, badgers, beavers and hares, beasts of prey such as wolves, foxes and martens, as well as birds such as geese, ducks, cranes and various fowl of the forest.

As the Greek author Arrian (2ndC AD) records, the hunt was for the Celts always associated with religious rites (Kynegetika 34). Those divinities attested in inscriptions and/or in visual depictions who are thought to have had a particular link with hunting include → Abnoba, → Arduinna, → Artio, → Cocidius, → Nodons and → Vosegus.

In the insular Celtic literature of the Middle Ages hunting is of great importance, especially in the tales of the → Finn Cycle. Frequently a story begins with a huntsman being separated from his companions whilst pursuing game and then being enticed into a realm in which the laws of the known world cease to function.

Lit.: P. Meniel, Chasse et élevage chez les Gaulois, P. 1987.

Hyde, Douglas (1860–1949). Linguist and folklorist. He grew up in the West of Ireland, the son of a Protestant clergyman. He learned the Irish language as a child and became acquainted with the oral traditions of the native inhabitants of his homeland. In order to ensure the preservation and spread of Irish, in 1893 H. founded with a few like-minded people the Gaelic League (Conradh na Gaeilge), which became a nucleus of the nationalist movement. He published collections of Irish oral traditions which have since become classics: *Leabhar Sgeulaigheachta* (1889), *Beside the Fire* (1890) and *Love Songs of Connacht* (1893). In 1899 he wrote the one-volume *Literary History of Ireland*, one of the first general surveys of Irish literature. After studying at Trinity College Dublin, in 1909 he was appointed to the first chair in Modern Irish at University College Dublin. In 1937 he was elected the first president of the Republic of Ireland.

Lit.: S. Ó Tuama (ed.), *The Gaelic League Idea*, Cork 1972; D. Daly, *The Young D. H.*, Du. 1974; J. E. & G. W. Dunleavy, *D. H.: A Maker of Modern Ireland*, Be. 1991; R. Ó Glaisne, *Dúbhglas de h-Íde (1860–1949)*, Du. 1991.

hygiene. Great importance was attached to hygiene by the Celts according to the late antique historian Ammianus Marcellinus (15,12,2). This is confirmed by the many objects that have been found which relate to the care of the body. Apart from scissors for cutting hair, they also had razors, tweezers, scrapers, nail-cutters, little spoons for cleaning the ears, combs and mirrors. Sets of toilette articles are attested as early as the graves of the Hallstatt period. Where the related area of cosmetics is concerned we have the testimony of → Pliny (Hist. Nat. 28,51) that "soap" was an invention of the Celts, made of tallow and ashes, and served to dye the hair red. Pliny further reports of the Celts that they sought to preserve the freshness of their complexion by washing with beer-foam (Hist. Nat. 22,25). The custom of cleaning one's teeth with urine is only recorded of the → Celtiberians (cf. → Diodoros of Sicily 5,33 and Catullus 37 and 39).

Iarlles y Ffynnawn (Welsh /ˈjarɬes ə ˈfənnaun/ "The Lady of the Fountain"). Title of one of the "three romances" (→ Tair Rhamant). It tells how the knight Owein fab Urien leaves Arthur's court in search of adventure, and in single combat slays a mysterious Black Knight, the guardian of an equally mysterious fountain. Later Owein marries the widow of the slain knight and guards the fountain for three years in his stead. One day, however, Arthur and his retinue seek him out and take him back with them. Owein promises to his wife that he will return to her after a certain time has elapsed. When he fails to do so their relationship undergoes a crisis, and only after many adventures are they reconciled with one another.

Ed.: B. Jones, Y *Tair Rhamant*, Aberystwyth 1960; R. L. Thomson, *Owein*, Du. 1968 (MMWS 4).

Trans.: G. Jones & T. Jones, *The Mabinogion*, rev. ed. Lo. 1974; J. Gantz, *The Mabinogion*, Harm. 1976.

Lit.: T. Hunt, 'The Art of I. y Ff. and the European Volksmärchen' (*StC* 8/9) 1973/74, 107–120; id., 'Some Observations on the Textual Relationship of Li Chevaliers au Lion and I. y Ff.' (*ZCP* 33) 1974, 93–113; A. H. Diverres, 'I. y Ff. and Le Chevalier au lion: Adaptation or Common Source?' (*StC* 16/17) 1981/1982, 144–162; B. F. Roberts, 'The Welsh Romance of the Lady of the Fountain (Owein)', in: P. B. Grout et al. (eds.), *The Legend of Arthur in the Middle Ages*, C. 1983, 170–182; R. L. Thomson, 'Owain: Chwedl I. y Ff.', in: R. Bromwich et al. (eds.), *The Arthur of the Welsh*, Car. 1991, 159–169 (in English).

Icauna. Celtic name for the Yonne, a left tributary of the Seine (→ Sequana). The cult of a goddess of the same name is attested by a votive inscription from Roman times (CIL XIII 2921), found in Auxerre at the beginning of the 18thC, but now lost.

Iceni. In classical → ethnography the name of a Celtic tribe resident in the area of the present-day county of Norfolk. The tribe's amicable relations with Rome led to its being able to preserve a considerable degree of independence even after the invasion of Britain by the Romans in 43 AD, but the rebellion of the I. under their queen → Boudicca in 61 AD ended with the subjugation of the tribe.

imbas forosna (Ir. /'imbas for'osna/). A kind of prophecy said to be the province of the poet (→ fili). According to the Glossary of Bishop Cormac (→ *Sanas Chormaic*), it consisted in the poet chewing the raw flesh of a pig, a dog or a cat, speaking a charm over it and offering it to the gods with a prayer. Thereafter he had to lie down, placing the palms of both hands upon his cheeks. In a dream he then saw whatever he wished to have revealed. Cormac explains the word imbas on the basis that the poet during this procedure placed both palms (*bas*) on (*im*) his cheeks. In fact, however, the word i. would seem to be derived from *fis* 'knowledge', with an intensive prefix *imb*. The i.f. is said to have been forbidden by Saint → Patrick, and it is therefore questionable whether in Cormac's times it was still possible to give an accurate description of this kind of prophecy.

Lit.: R. Thurneysen, 'I.f.' (*ZCP* 19) 1933, 163f.; N. K. Chadwick, 'I. f.' (*SGS* 4) 1935, 97–135.

Imbolc (Ir. /'imbolg/). The beginning of spring in the Irish calendar (February 1st). The day is still celebrated today, particularly in rural areas of Ireland, as the Feast of St. → Brigit.

Lit.: K. Danaher, *The Year in Ireland*, Du. 1972; E. Hamp, 'imbolc, óimelc' (*StC* 14/15) 1979/80, 106–113.

Immacallam in dá Thuarad (Ir. /'imagaLav in da: 'θuaraδ/ "The Colloquy of the two Sages"). Title of a story from the → Ulster Cycle, thought to date back to c. 800. It is preserved in complete form, as well as in some fragments, in eleven manuscripts of the 12th-16thC. The subject of the tale is a competition between the two poets Néde and Ferchertne, both of whom after the death of the highest poet (→ ollam) contest the succession. In obscure, barely comprehensible language the two poets reply to various questions they set themselves regarding their identity and origin. Asked about the future, Néde portrays a Golden Age in which general prosperity will prevail. When he in turn is asked, Ferchertne portrays a time of terror which will only end with Judgment Day. Thereupon Néde kneels down before Ferchertne and admits his superiority.

Ed. and trans.: W. Stokes, 'The Colloquy of the Two Sages' (RC 26) 1905, 4–64.

Lit.: R. Thurneysen, *Die irische Helden- und Königsage*, Hl. 1921.

immram (Ir. /'imrav/). The word means "rowing", and by extension refers to a sea-voyage. It serves in one of the two → Lists of Sagas to classify those stories which report of journeys to fantastic islands beyond the world populated by human beings. The → echtrae is a related category. The Latin text *Navigatio Sancti Brendani* (→ Brendan) also belongs to the genre of the i.

Lit.: S. MacMathúna, 'The Structure and Transmission of Early Irish Voyage Literature', in: H. L. C. Tristram (ed.), *Text und Zeittiefe*, Tübingen 1994, 313–357; id., 'Motif and Episodic Clustering in Early Irish Voyage Literature', in: H. L. C. Tristram (ed.), *(Re)Oralisierung*, T. 1996, 247–262.

Immram Brain (Ir. /'imrav bran'/ "The Voyage of Bran"). Title of a narrative of a sea-voyage (→ immram) dating from the early 8thC, written partly in prose, partly in verse. It is the oldest surviving example of this literary genre and combines Christian doctrine with concepts deriving from pre-Christian Irish religion. The plot begins with the appearance of a mysterious woman in the castle of the titular hero Bran mac Febail. She has about her a silver twig which emits marvellous music and comes, she maintains, from an apple-tree in the Paradisian land → Emain Ablach. When this visitor and her twig disappear, Bran embarks in a boat with thrice nine (→ numbers) companions in search of this island. After two days at sea they encounter → Manannán mac Lir, who shows them the way to an island full of laughing people. Thereafter they make their way to another island, inhabited exclusively by females. There Bran and his companions spend many years in splendour and happiness, the time seeming to them but one year. When however Bran's comrade Nechtan becomes homesick for Ireland, the voyagers finally commence their return journey. The queen of the island warns them against returning, and impresses upon Bran that he should by no means set foot upon Irish soil. When Nechtan transgresses this prohibition on arrival in Ireland, he immediately turns to dust, as if he had been dead for some time. Bran however sets off again, after telling the story of his adventures from on board his ship to some Irishmen assembled on the shore.

Ed. and trans.: S. MacMathúna, *I. B.: Bran's Journey to the Land of the Women*, T. 1985.

Lit.: K. McCone, *Pagan Past and Christian Present in Early Ir. Lit.*, May. 1990.

Immram Curaig Maíle Dúin (Ir. /'imrav 'kuriɣ' 'vail'e ðu:n'/ "The Voyage of the Boat of Máel Dúin"). Title of a narrative of a sea-voyage (→ immram) of the 10thC, written partly in prose, partly in verse. It is preserved complete in the → Yellow Book of Lecan and in fragmentary form in the "Book of the Dun Cow" (→ Lebor na hUidre), and in two other manuscripts. The titular hero of the story is Máel Dúin, the son of a warrior and a nun from the nunnery of Kildare. After his father has been killed he grows up at the royal court; only as a young man does he learn of his true descent. When he is told of the death of his father, he, with some companions, equips a boat and sets off to avenge his father. In the course of their journey across the open sea the occupants of the boat experience a series of fantastic adventures. On one island, for example, they encounter man-eating giant ants, and on another birds who live on huge golden apples. On a third island they receive hospitality at the hands of a nobly dressed woman and are entertained for three days, but when one of the men asks their hostess if she would like to share her bed with Máel Dúin, the voyagers find themselves, the following morning, back in their boat on the open sea. After many further adventures they return safe and sound to Ireland.

Ed. and trans.: H. P. A. Oskamp, *The Voyage of Máel Dúin*, Groningen 1970.

Lit.: M. Aguirre, 'The Hero's Voyage in I. C. M. D.' (EC 27) 1990, 203–220.

incest. Motif that occurs occasionally in sagas to emphasise the mythical nature of the hero's birth. Thus Eochaid Airem fathers by his own daughter the famed ruler Conaire Mór (cf. → *Tochmarc Étaíne*). It is not however possible to deduce from the texts whether incest played a significant role in real life.

Indech mac Dé Domnann (Ir. /'ind'ex mak d'e: 'dovnaN/). A king of the → Fomoire in the story of the Battle of Mag Tuired (→ *Cath Maige Tuired*). He slays → Ogma of the → Tuatha Dé Danann, but then falls in battle against → Lug.

Insular Celtic → languages, Celtic.

Insubres. In classical → ethnography a Celtic tribe in upper Italy which settled west of the area of the → Cenomani. Their chief town was Mediolanum, present-day Milan. In 231 BC the I. formed an alliance with the → Boii against Rome, but in 225 BC they suffered a crushing defeat at the hands of the Romans in the Battle of Telamon. In the Second Punic War (218–201 BC) they joined forces with Hannibal, and after the defeat of the Carthaginians in 197 and 196 BC they were finally subjugated by the Romans.

Intarabus. The (etymologically obscure) name of a Celtic god whose cult is attested by votive inscriptions from Foy in Belgium (CIL XIII 3632) and from the tribal area of the Treveri near present-day Trier (CIL XIII 3653, 4128, 11313; Fi 11; Schi 21). The inscription CIL XIII 3653 identifies Intarabus with Mars on the basis of the → interpretatio romana.

interpretatio romana. A practice widespread in the ancient world whereby barbarian divinities were designated by the name of a Roman god or goddess. The term derives from a passage in the 43rd chapter of → Tacitus' Germania. There the Roman historian identifies two Germanic gods, worshipped as brothers and youths, "according to the Roman interpretation" (interpretatione Romana) with the Roman twin gods Castor and Pollux. It was not only in literature, however, that the i.r. was general practice, but also in religion. Thus in votive inscriptions the native name of the divinity was frequently juxtaposed with the Roman name. In cases where only the Roman designation was employed, the added word DEO or DEAE ("to the god. . . / to the goddess . . ."), which is unusual where Roman divinities are concerned, points to the fact that the donor was thinking of a native god. The basis for the equation of two divinities was a quite specific link, the nature of which is not always clear to us now. Consequently, only a vague view of the nature of an indigenous divinity can be obtained on the basis of the i. r. Many Celtic divinities of whom we know nothing but the name are referred to in inscriptions and literary works by a relatively small number of Roman names, predominant among which are → Apollo, → Mars and → Mercury. Celtic gods whose name is attested several times are generally identified consistently with the same Roman divinity; it is rare for a single Celtic god to be equated with two distinct Roman divinities.

Lit.: G. Wissowa, 'I.R.' (Archiv für Religionswissenschaft 19) 1918, 1–49; J. de Vries, 'Die I.R. der gallischen Götter', in: Indogermanica. Festschrift W. Krause, Hei. 1960, 204–213; P.-M. Duval, 'Problèmes des rapports entre la religion gauloise et la rel. romaine', in: P. MacCana & M. Meslin (eds.), Rencontres de religions, Paris 1986, 39–56; J. Webster, 'Translation and Subjection: Interpretatio and the Celtic Gods', in: J. D. Hill & C. G. Cumberpatch (eds.), Different Iron Ages, O. 1995, 175–181.

Iovantucarus. Celtic god whose name is thought to derive from an older form *Iovantutokaros, the approximate meaning being "he who loves youth (= children)". This may mean that he was a patron god of adolescents. An inscription from the vicinity of Tholey (CIL XIII 4525, now lost) identified I. with → Mercury on the basis of the → interpretatio romana, whereas five inscriptions from Trier (Fi 15–19) identify him with → Mars. His name occurs, without any further addition, on a silver ring from Heidenburg near Kreinbach (CIL XIII 10024,6).

Ipswich, Suffolk. In 1968 and 1970 a total of six Celtic → torcs made from gold and dating from the 1stC BC were found near the town in the course of building and gardening work. They are now on display in the British Museum.

> Lit.: J. W. Brailsford & J. E. Stapley, 'The I. Torcs' (Procs. of the Prehistoric Soc. 38) 1972, 219–234.

Irish. Term denoting the Celtic language of Ireland. Together with → Manx and → Scottish Gaelic it forms the Gaelic branch of the insular Celtic group of languages. The earliest known phase in its development is attested by the evidence of the inscriptions known as → Ogam. Thereafter comes Old Irish, known predominantly from → glosses in Latin manuscripts of the 8th-9thC. The language of the 10th-13thC is termed Middle Irish, known from a large number of literary works, the transmission of which begins c. 1100. Subsequent periods of the language are termed Early New Irish (14th-16thC) and New Irish (since the 17thC). In the course of its history Irish has lost ground increasingly at the expense of English and today only survives as an everyday language in a few areas of the West of Ireland.

> Lit.: B. Ó Cuív (ed.), A View of the Irish Language, Du. 1969; R. Thurneysen, A Grammar of Old Irish, rev. ed., Du. 1975.

Irish Renaissance. Literary movement in Ireland in the late 19th and early 20thC. The struggle for political independence from Great Britain combined with a pronounced nationalism to create a new interest in the Irish language and medieval Irish literature. Among the founders of the I. R. were Standish James → O'Grady, Sir Samuel → Ferguson and Douglas → Hyde. Their most important literary advocates were William Butler → Yeats and Lady → Gregory. Austin → Clarke and James → Stephens were among the chief authors who reworked Irish literary material.

> Lit.: R. Fallis, The Irish Renaissance, Syracuse, NY 1977; J. Sheehy, The Rediscovery of Ireland's Past, Lo. 1980; J. W. Foster, Fictions of the Irish Literary Revival, Du. 1987; B. Freitag, Keltische Identität als Fiktion, Hei. 1989; H. Kosok, Geschichte der anglo-irischen Literatur, B. 1990; P. O'Leary, The prose literature of the Gaelic revival, 1881–1921: ideology and innovation, Univ. Park /Penna 1994; G. Grote, Torn between politics and culture: the Gaelic League 1893–1993, New York 1994.

iron. In the Europe of the first millennium BC iron was of such paramount importance that this period of history is today known as the "Iron Age". The knowledge of how to work iron stems from the Orient and is thought to have reached central and western Europe via the Balkans, the eastern Alpine region and Upper Italy. Isolated objects made of iron are traceable back to the urnfield culture of the 10th/9thC BC, but it was not until the transition to the Hallstatt period that the new metal established itself in general use. The Celts employed iron for weapons (spear and lance points, swords, shield fittings), tools (axes, saws, hammers, drills, tongs), household utensils (knives, scissors, carving forks, spits, fire-dogs), agricultural implements (shovels, hoes, sickles, scythes, ploughshares), as well as for individual items of → clothing and → jewellery (needles, → fibulae, belt buckles and hooks).

In contrast to → bronze, iron was not cast, but only worked. The craft of the → smith was so highly developed that smiths came to be held in high regard as specialists. This is confirmed by the role that they play in the insular Celtic literatures. The smelting and working of iron was an important branch of the economy. In some cases the discovery of rich ore deposits was clearly decisive in the siting of large-scale settlements (→ oppida). Iron was traded in the form of bars shaped like double pyramids or rods, and weighing from 4 to 20 lbs. Over 700 of these have been found, the majority in Lorraine, South-West Germany and Switzerland.

Isolde. German equivalent of the Welsh name → Essyllt.

Iupiter → Jupiter.

Iwein. German equivalent of the Welsh name → Owein. The verse romance of → Hartmann von Aue which has been given this title has a Celtic equivalent in the Middle Welsh prose narrative → *Iarlles y Ffynnawn.*

Jackson, Kenneth Hurlstone (1909–1991). One of the most versatile Celticists of the recent past. After studying in Cambridge, Bangor (Wales) and Dublin, he lectured in Celtic languages and literatures at Cambridge. From 1940 to 1950 he taught at Harvard and from 1950 to 1979 was professor of Celtic Studies at the University of Edinburgh. His great work, *Language and History in Early Britain* (1953), is still the standard work today, a study of → British and the early history of its daughter languages → Breton, → Cornish, → Cumbrian and → Welsh. It was supplemented by the philological study, *A Historical Phonology of Breton* (1967). In 1951 Jackson published the anthology *A Celtic Miscellany*, a thematically arranged anthology of passages selected from all the Celtic languages, in English translation. In his study *The International Popular Tale and Early Welsh Tradition* (1961) he explored the influence of widely circulating folk-tale motifs on some of the oldest Welsh prose tales. His book *The Oldest Irish Tradition: A Window on the Iron Age* (1964) proved extremely influential: J. put forward the hypothesis that the Irish heroic saga reflects characteristic traits of Celtic culture prior to christianisation. This theory was taken up in many popular treatments of the subject, but more recently it has been increasingly called into question (cf. → Ulster Cycle).

Jacobsthal, Paul (1880–1957). Archaeologist, born in Berlin. After studying in Berlin, Göttingen and Bonn he taught from 1912 in Marburg as professor of archaeology. One of his chief areas of research concerned the contacts between Graeco-Roman antiquity and the contemporary cultures of central Europe. He was responsible for the inauguration of the first chair in prehistory and early history in Germany, in Marburg. In 1935, because of his Jewish descent, J. was suspended from teaching and emigrated to England. From 1937 he taught in Oxford, where he passed his declining years. His major work in the area of Celtic archaeology was published as *Early Celtic Art* (1944), still a standard work today.

jewellery. Jewellery was worn by both men and women among the Celts. This is attested both by allusions in classical → ethnography (cf. → Strabo 4,4,5 and → Diodoros of Sicily 5,27), and even more so by finds from graves. Celtic jewellery was made, to judge from these finds, primarily of → bronze, more rarely of → gold or → iron, and only in a few cases of → silver. Other substances used in its manufacture were → glass, coral and the fossile materials → amber, jet and sapropel. In the graves of pre-Roman times, foot and neck rings are exclusively for female use, whereas arm and finger rings are found worn by both men and women. The twisted neck-ring (→ torc) of the Celtic warrior is familiar from buried treasure, and from pictorial representations and the descriptions of classical authors. The frequency with which jewellery has been found in children's graves suggests that many objects now interpreted as jewellery also served as → amulets.
   Lit.: → art.

judge → brithem.

Jullian, Camille (1859–1933). Born in Marseilles, he studied in Paris, Rome, Vienna and Berlin, before teaching ancient and local history in Bordeaux. From 1905 he held the chair in Histoire et antiquités nationales at the Collège de France in Paris. His major work is the eight-volume *Histoire de la Gaule* (1907–1926), which treats the history of Gaul from the settlement of the country by the Celts to the end of the classical period. J. regarded Gaul as a part of both Celtic and Roman civilisation and sought to do justice to all aspects of the material and intellectual culture of the country. His study had recourse to an abundance of literary, epigraphic and archaeological sources which was unsurpassed at the time, and his work is of lasting importance, a milestone in French historiography.

Lit.: O. Motte, C. J.: *Les années de formation*, R. 1990; C. J., *L'histoire de la Gaule et le nationalisme français: Colloque Lyon 1988*, Ly. 1991.

Jupiter. Supreme god of the Roman religion, possessing the characteristics of a prehistoric god of light and the heavens. The name J. occurs as a term referring to a Celtic divinity in → Caesar, according to whom the Gauls regarded J. as the ruler of the heavenly realm (Bell. Gall. 6,17). We have however no knowledge of which Celtic god Caesar had in mind. Among those divinities known to us by name, → Taranis comes closest to the characterisation suggested above; his name derives from the Celtic word for "thunder". In the → Berne scholia on the work of the Roman poet → Lucan, Taranis is identified with J. A dedication to Iupiter Taranucus (CIL III 2804) survives from Scardona in Dalmatia. J. is given the byname Tanarus in an inscription from Chester (*RIB* 452); this is possibly a corruption of Taranus. In pictorial representations dating from the Gallo-Roman period J. is shown as a bearded man with a sceptre, lightning and an eagle, following classical models. Occasionally, however, J. is accorded a wheel as an attribute, either in addition to or instead of these motifs.

Lit.: P. Lambrechts, *Contributions à l'étude des divinités celtiques*, Bruges 1942; J. de Vries, *Keltische Religion*, St. 1961.

Jupiter-Giant columns. A type of cultic monument widespread in the northern parts of Upper Germania and in the east of the Roman Province of Gallia Belgica in the 2nd/3rdC AD. These were pillars, several metres in height, generally decorated with scales. At the top of the monuments there was a figurative representation of the god → Jupiter, trampling upon a giant whose feet are in the form of serpents. The plinths are generally four-sided, forming what are termed *Viergöttersteine*, decorated with reliefs of various Roman divinities (usually Juno, Minerva, Mercury and Hercules). Above the *Viergötterstein* there is often an additional, intermediary plinth which most frequently bears images of the gods relating to the days of the week, although other divinities are also depicted. The distribution and the evidence of the votive inscriptions suggests that the donors of the J. were for the most part Romanised Celts. It is therefore thought that the Jupiter figure is a representation of the Celtic Sky-god (cf. → Taranis), and the form of the pillars is regarded as a continuation of the veneration of sacred trees (cf. → oak).

Lit.: G. Bauchhenss, *Jupitergigantensäulen*, St. 1976; Bauchhenss & P. Noelke, *Die Iupitersäulen in den germanischen Provinzen*, Co. 1981.

Keating, Geoffrey (Ir. Seathrún Céitinn, c. 1570–1650). Born in Tipperary; after studying theology in Bordeaux and Salamanca he served as a clergyman in his southern Irish homeland. According to his own testimony, he was prompted by some excessively negative accounts of Irish history on the part of English writers to write his own history of Ireland, in which he wanted to do justice both to the indigenous Irish people and to the Anglo-Norman conquerers of the 12thC. Completed c. 1633/64, his *Foras Feasa ar Éirinn* ('Elements of the History of Ireland') deals with the period from the first settlement of the country, shrouded in legend, until the Norman invasion towards the end of the 12thC. The work takes into consideration many sources which are lost today and contains an abundance of mythological, legendary and popular traditions. As a model of classical New Irish prose it was available in numerous manuscripts right into the 19thC, but it was only at the beginning of this century that a complete edition was printed.

Ed. and trans.: D. S. Comyn & P. S. Dinneen, *Foras Feasa ar Éirinn: Elements of the Hist. of Ireland*, 4 vols., Lo. 1902–1914 (ITS 4, 8, 9, 15).

Lit.: A. Cronin, 'Sources of K's Forus Feasa ar Éirinn' (*Celtica 4*) 1943/44, 235–279 & (*Celtica 5*) 1945–1947, 122–135; B. Cunningham, '17th cent. interpretations of the past: the case of G. K.' (*Ir. Historical Studies 25*) 1986, 116–128; B. Bradshaw, 'Geoffrey Keating: Apologist of Irish Ireland', in: B. Bradshaw et al. (eds.), *Representing Ireland. Literature and the origins of conflict, 1534–1660*, C. 1993, 166–190.

Kells → Book of Kells.

Kilchberg. Site near Tübingen (Swabia) where in 1968 during the archaeological exploration of a grave-mound of the late Hallstatt period three stelai of fluviatile sandstone were found. One of these was intact, the other two fragmentary. Because of the significance of the finds the grave-mound, which was in an area of new buildings, was not flattened after excavation, but piled up again and surrounded by a small green area. Casts of the three stelai are to be seen there, the originals being now in the Württembergisches Landesmuseum in Stuttgart.

Lit.: A. Beck, 'Der hallstattzeitliche Grabhügel von Tübingen-Kilchberg' (*FBW* 1) 1974, 251–281; W. Kimmig, 'Eisenzeitliche Grabstelen in Mitteleuropa' (*FBW* 12) 1987, 251–297.

kings. Kings are frequently mentioned in the reports concerning the Celts in classical → ethnography. Greek authors generally refer to them by the words basileus "king" or basiliskos "minor king", whereas authors writing in Latin generally designate the kings of the Celts as reges (sing. rex). The Celtic word for king was *rīg-s (cf. → rix, → rí and → brenin). Various references in Caesar (Bell. Gall. 2,4; 5,24; 5,26 and 5,54) suggest that some tribes of the → Belgae were familiar with a kind of double monarchy. Among the peoples of southern and central Gaul kingship had by the time of Caesar fallen very much out of fashion and had been replaced by other forms of rule (cf. Bell.

Gall. 1,16 and 7,33). References to divine kingship are found particularly in the Irish tradition (cf. → sacred marriage).

Kings, Cycle of → Historical Cycle.

Kleinaspergle. Site of a Celtic → princely grave south of the town of Asperg in the Ludwigsburg area (Swabia). Like some other grave-mounds in the vicinity is is thought to be connected with an early Celtic → princely seat on the → Hohenasperg. When the mound was excavated in 1879 all the contents of the central grave-chamber proved to have been plundered. In a neighbouring chamber, however, a richly endowed grave of the early La Tène period was found, containing several pieces of jewellery and a large collection of drinking vessels. Two Attic dishes were found, imported pottery dating from c. 450 BC; these had been decorated with a subsequent layer of ornamental gold foil. All the finds are now preserved in the Württembergisches Landesmuseum in Stuttgart. Even today, Kleinaspergle, with a height of 6m and a diameter of 60m, conveys a good impression of what the grave must originally have looked like.

Lit.: W. Kimmig et al., *Das Kleinaspergle*. St. 1988.

Labraid (Ir. /'Lavrið/). A king in the tales of the → Historical Cycle said to have reigned over the province of Leinster in the 4th or 3rdC BC. His standing epithets are Loingsech "the Exile", Moen "the Dumb" and Lorc "the Fierce". The reasons for these bynames emerge from the story → *Orgain Denna Ríg*, the surviving version of which is thought to have been written down in the 9thC. A folk-tale of a slightly later date tells of how L. had horse's ears. To keep this secret he has every barber who cuts his hair executed. When he spares the son of a widow in response to his mother's pleas, the barber cannot keep the secret; he is advised by a druid to whom he turns in his extremity to tell it to a willow-tree. When the willow is felled and a harp made of the wood, everyone hears in the sound of the music: "L. has horse's ears".

In all probability this story evolved under the influence of the classical legend of the ass's ears of King Midas (cf. Ovid, *Metamorphoses* 11,146–193). In the 17thC it found its way into the historical work of Geoffrey → Keating, and from Keating, it is thought, into the orally transmitted repertoire of many Irish story-tellers.

Lit.: M. Ó Briain, 'Cluasa Capaill ar an Rí: AT 782 i dTraidisiún na hÉireann' (*Béaloideas* 53) 1985, 11–74.

Ladra (Ir. /'Laðra/). In the "Book of the Invasions of Ireland" (→ *Lebor*

Gabála Érenn) the helmsman who brings → Cesair and her retinue to Ireland forty days before the Flood.

Laegaire → Loegaire.

La Graufesenque. Site on the left bank of the Tarn not far from the village of Millau in the Dép. of Aveyron in the South of France. In the 1st-2ndC AD one of the most important centres of Gaulish pottery was situated there. The graffiti which have been found there since excavations began in 1901 are important for our knowledge of the Gaulish language. These consist for the most part of the names of individual potters, as well as the various types, size and quantity of the pottery produced there. These data were carved into fragments of burnt clay in a cursive Latin script.
Lit.: R. Marichal, *Les graffites de La Graufesenque*, P. 1988.

Lancelot. The lover of Queen Guenevere (= Guenièvre/Ginevra/ → Gwenhwyfar) in some works of French and German → Arthurian literature. The oldest surviving treatments of this motif are by → Chrétien de Troyes and → Ulrich von Zatzikhoven in the 12thC. The name L. does not occur in → Geoffrey of Monmouth, nor in the Middle Welsh sources. It is probably of French rather than Celtic origin.

languages, Celtic. The Celtic languages form an independent branch of the Indo-European linguistic family, as do the Germanic and Slavonic languages. Their defining characteristics include the disappearance of p initially and before a vowel (compare Ir. athair and Lat. pater "father"), and the change from ē to ī (compare Gaulish rīx and Lat. rēx "king"). It is customary to distinguish between a continental Celtic and an insular Celtic group of languages, although this distinction is based less upon linguistic than on geographical and chronological criteria, and the way in which the material has been transmitted historically.

The continental Celtic group of languages is known to us from inscriptions, names occurring in classical authors, and words surviving in substrate form, primarily in Romance languages. The group may be subdivided into → Gaulish (predominantly in France and Belgium), → Celtiberian (in Spain and Portugal), → Lepontic (in upper Italy) and → Galatian (in Asia Minor). All these languages had died out by the early Middle Ages.

The insular Celtic group, by contrast, is attested by literary works from the Middle Ages onwards, and to some extent survives today. It comprises → Breton (in Brittany), → Cornish, → Cumbrian (in the North of England), → Irish, → Manx, → Scottish Gaelic (in the Scottish Highlands and the Hebrides) and → Welsh. Sometimes Irish, Scottish Gaelic and Manx are referred to as → Gaelic languages or q-Celtic. Breton, Cornish, Cumbrian and Welsh, on the other hand, are known as → British languages, or p-

Celtic. Supplanted to an ever increasing extent by English and French, Celtic languages are today only spoken in the West of Ireland, in the Hebrides and in some areas of Wales and Brittany.

Lit.: H. Lewis & H. Pedersen, A Concise Comparative Celtic Grammar, Gö. ²1961; K. H. Schmidt, 'The Celtic Languages in their European Context' (Procs. of the 7th. Int. Congress of Celtic Studies, O. 1986, 199–121; D. MacAulay (ed.), The Celtic Languages, C. 1992; G. Price (ed.), The Celtic Connection, Gerrards Cross 1992; M. J. Ball with James Fife (eds.), Celtic Languages, Lo. 1993; W. Meid & P. Anreiter (eds.), Die größeren altkeltischen Sprachdenkmäler. Akten des Kolloquiums Innsbruck 1993, I. 1995.

Larzac (l'Hospitalet-du-Larzac). Site c. 9 miles south of → La Graufesenque in the Dép. of Aveyron. In August 1983 during the archaeological excavation of a Gallo-Roman grave-field a lead tablet inscribed with curses written in the Gaulish language was found, dating to c. 100 AD. About a thousand letters, amounting to over 160 words, make it the longest continuous text in Gaulish yet found. The tablet had been used as the cover of an urn containing ashes and was presumably intended to work black magic. Because of our inadequate knowledge of Gaulish many points in the text are contentious.

Lit.: M. Lejeune et al., 'Textes gaulois et gallo-romains en cursive latine III Le plomb du L.' (EC 22) 1985, 95–177; K. H. Schmidt, 'Zum plomb du L.', in: A. T. E. Matonis & F. Melia (eds.), Celtic Languages, Celtic Culture, Van Nuys, Calif. 1990, 16–25.

La Tène. Present-day name of a shallow near Marin off the north shore of Lake Neuchâtel in Switzerland. In pre-Roman times it was the site of a Celtic → place of worship, where countless spears, swords, shields, → fibulae and other votive gifts were cast into the lake. On the basis of these archaeological finds the later period of the pre-Roman Iron Age is designated the La Tène Period. This era embraces the five hundred years from the 5th to the 1stC BC. Generally a distinction is drawn between an early, a middle and a late stage, with the chronological demarcation subject to regional variation. At the beginning of the La Tène period came the development of new economic and cultural centres on the edge of those areas belonging to the older Hallstatt culture (cf. → Hallstatt), and the evolution of a distinct Celtic → art, which is thought to relate to considerable religious and philosophical changes. These were followed by intensive contacts and wars between the Celts and the peoples of the Mediterranean area. At the end of this period comes the time of the Celtic → oppida, which ends with the conquest of Gaul by → Caesar.

Lit.: → history.

Latobius. Etymologically obscure name of a Celtic god, attested in four votive inscriptions from the area of the Roman province of Noricum. Two of these (CIL III 5320 and 5321) were found in Seggau in Styria, two others (CIL III 5097 and 5098) in St. Paul in Carinthia. In the first of these inscriptions L. is identified with → Mars on the basis of the → interpretatio romana. The remains of a colossal statue of the god are now to be seen in the Stiftmuseum in St. Paul (Carinthia).

law. Like Celtic → mythology, the law of the Celts was in the oldest period handed down exclusively by word of mouth. The earliest records are there-fore to be found in classical → ethnography; these are however limited to a few scattered and for the most part unsystematic observations. Among these are the remarks of → Caesar on the function of the → druids as judges and their annual law-giving assembly at a consecrated spot in the land of the → Carnutes (Bell. Gall. 6,13), and his notes concerning the legal position of → women and → children (Bell. Gall. 6,19). Legal texts and decrees, on the other hand, are not written down until the time after → christianisation. The oldest such texts are from Ireland (7th/8thC), whereas the legislature in the Welsh laws owes its origin to the Law of Hywel (the 10thC king Hywel Dda), though the laws are in part of later date.

It is only in the past few decades that Irish law has become the subject of extensive study, with scholarly attention initially concentrating itself on the archaic features. More recently, in contrast, the influence of Christianity and of medieval social conditions has been increasingly taken into account (cf. also → Brehon Laws, → brithem).

Lit.: D. A. Binchy (ed.), *Corpus iuris Hibernici*, 6 vols., Du. 1978; F. Kelly, *A Guide to Early Irish Law*, Du. 1988; W. D. H. Sellar, 'Celtic law and Scots law' (*Scottish Studies* 29) 1989, 1–27; T. M. Charles-Edwards, *The Welsh Laws*, Car. 1989; N. McLeod, *Early Irish contract law*, Sydney 1992; H. Pryce, *Native Law and the Church in Early Medieval Wales*, O. 1993; R. C. Stacey, *The Road to Judgment: From custom to court in medieval Ireland and Wales*, Philadelphia 1994.

Layamon. English cleric who translated the *Roman de Brut* of the Anglo-Nor-man poet → Wace into English, c. 1200. On the model of Anglo-Saxon poetry, his work is written in alliterating long lines; its 32,241 lines make it about twice as long as its source.

Lit.: H. Pilch, *L.s 'Brut'*, Hei. 1960; F. H. M. Le Saux, *L.'s 'Brut': The Poem and its Sources*, C. 1989.

Leborcham (Ir. /'L'evorxam/). An old woman at the court of the king → Conchobar mac Nesa in the stories of the → Ulster Cycle. Possessed of a repulsive ugliness, she is universally feared because of her biting invective poetry. She frequently carries messages for the king or for other members of the court.

Lebor Dromma Snechta → Cín Dromma Snechta.

Lebor Gabála Érenn (Ir. /'L'evor 'gava:la 'e:r'eN/ "The Book of the Taking (or Invasions) of Ireland"). Title of a fictitious history of Ireland compiled in the 11thC, preserved in two divergent versions from c. 1100. The narrative begins with the events of the Creation and treats of the changing fate of Ireland and its inhabitants from the time of its first settlement by → Cesair, said to be one of the granddaughters of Noah, through to the time when the work was composed. Much of the work is devoted to the description of six successive waves of invasions: after Cesair and her companions follow → Partholón and → Nemed with their retinue, then the → Fir Bolg and the → Tuatha Dé Danann, and finally the sons of → Míl. The latter is regarded as the father of all the Irish, being descended in his turn from Noah's son Japhet.

The work attests the endeavours of the medieval clerics to reconcile or harmonise the history of Ireland prior to → christianisation with Biblical tradition. It reworks both Christian literature and indigenous myths and sagas, with the personages of pre-Christian mythology being portrayed as historical figures of a distant past in accordance with the method of → euhemerism.

Ed. and trans.: R. A. Macalister, L. G. É. *The Book of the Taking of Ireland*, Du. 1938–1941 (ITS 34, 35, 39, 41).

Lit.: R. M. Scowcroft, 'L. G. É.' (*Ériu* 38) 1987, 80–142 & (39) 1988, 1–66.

Lebor Laignech (Ir. /'L'evor 'Laɣ'n'ex/ "The Book of Leinster"). Title given by the palaeographer Eugene → O'Curry to the most compendious of the older Irish miscellaneous manuscripts. It originated c. 1160 and has today some 187 parchment leaves. Among the texts it contains are the "Book of the Invasions of Ireland" (→ *Lebor Gabála Érenn*), versions of the → *Dindsenchas* and of the → *Táin Bó Cuailnge*, as well as several stories from the → Ulster Cycle. Since 1782 the manuscript has been in the library of Trinity College Dublin.

Ed.: R. Atkinson, *The Book of Leinster*, Du. 1880 (facs.); R. I. Best, O. Bergin et al., *The Book of Leinster, formerly Lebor na Núachongbála*, 6 vols., Du. 1954–1983 (diplomatic ed.).

Lebor na hUidre (Ir. /'L'evor na 'hið'r'e/ "The Book of the Dun Cow"). The oldest of the surviving great Irish compendium manuscripts, it originated c. 1100 in the monastery of Clonmacnoise; today only 67 parchment leaves survive, some of them damaged. The content comprises for the most part stories from the → Historical, → Mythological and → Ulster Cycles. Since 1844 the manuscript has been in the library of the Royal Irish Academy in Dublin.

Ed.: R. I. Best & O. Bergin, *L. na hUidre: The Book of the Dun Cow*, Du. 1929 (diplomatic ed.).

Lecan → Yellow Book of Lecan.

Leherennus. Name of a god who, to judge from votive inscriptions (CIL XIII 96–117), was worshipped in the area surrounding the present-day town of Ardiège in the Dép. of Hautes-Pyrénées. He is thought to be of pre-Celtic origin, and on the basis of the → interpretatio romana was equated with → Mars after the Roman conquest of Gaul.

Lit.: E. Thevenot, *Sur les traces des Mars celtiques*, Bruges 1955; J.-J. Hatt, *Mythes et dieux de la Gaule I*, P. 1989.

Leinster, Book of → Lebor Laignech.

Lemovices. In classical → ethnography a Celtic tribe in the region surrounding the city of Limoges, named after the tribe. Its Roman name was Augustoritum.

Lenus. Celtic god equated with → Mars on the basis of the → interpretatio romana. His cult is attested by eight votive inscriptions from the western settlement area of the → Treveri (CIL XIII 3654, 3970, 4030, 4137, 7661; Fi 20 and 21; Ne 9). The name of the god also appears on the plinth of a statue (the rest of which has not survived) from Caerwent in south-east Wales (*RIB* 309), and on an altar from Chedworth in Gloucestershire (*RIB* 126). A relief beneath the latter inscription (now in the Chedworth museum) shows L. with a spear in his right hand and an axe in his left. Other survivals are a bronze statue of L. (now in the Rheinisches Landesmuseum in Bonn) and fragments of a stone votive image, greater than life-size (now in the Rheinisches Landesmuseum in Trier).

Lit.: E. Gose, *Der Tempelbezirk des L. Mars in Trier*, B. 1955.

Lepontii. In classical → ethnography a Celtic tribe in the central Alps. The name survives in that of the Livinental (Ital. Valle Leventina) in Tessin.

Lepontic. The extinct language of the Celts in upper Italy. It is known from some 40 short inscriptions from the area around Lugano; they were recorded in two distinct variants of Etruscan script and date from the 6th/5thC BC or later.

Lit.: M. Lejeune, 'Lepontica' (*EC 12*) 1968–71, 337–500; M. G. Tibiletti Bruno, 'Ligure, leponzio e gallico', in: A. L. Prosdocimi (ed.), *Lingue e dialetti dell'Italia antica*, R. 1978, 129–208; A. L. Prosdocimi, 'Note sul celtico in Italia' (*Studi etruschi 57*) 1991, 139–177.

leprechaun. In Irish folk-belief a nimble dwarf or goblin. He generally appears as the guardian of hidden treasure, but also occurs in some stories as a helpful domestic spirit. The English term l. corresponds in Modern Irish dialects to the variants luprachán, loimreachán, lúracan (Leinster), luchramán (Ulster), lúracán (Connacht), luchragán, lurgadán and clúracán

(Munster). The Middle Irish form of the word is luchorpán (literally "little body").

Lit.: D. Ó Giolláin, 'The Leipreachán and Fairies, Dwarfs and the Household Familiar: A Comparative Study' (*Béaloideas* 52) 1984, 75–150.

Leucetius or (a later form) Loucetius. Celtic god whose name is derived from a Celtic word meaning "to beam, shine". The cult of L. is attested by votive inscriptions from Worms (CIL XIII 6221), Marienborn near Mainz (CIL XIII 7241 and 7242), Ober-Olm (CIL XIII 7249a), Klein-Winternheim near Mainz (CIL XIII 7252), Großkrotzenburg am Limes, Hessen (CIL XIII 7412), Wiesbaden-Frauenstein (CIL XIII 7608), Strasbourg (CIL XIII 11605), and in England Bath (*RIB* 140). The god would accordingly seem to have been worshipped primarily in the region of the Treveri, particularly as the donors of the last two inscriptions identify themselves as members of this tribe in the dedications. L. was equated with → Mars on the basis of the → interpretatio romana.

Lewis, Henry (1889–1968). Born in Ynystawe in South Wales, he studied in Cardiff, and in 1921 was elected to the first chair in Welsh Language and Literature at University College Swansea, which he held until 1954. In 1937 L. published together with the Danish linguist Holger Pedersen (1867–1953) *A Concise Comparative Celtic Grammar*, a revised version in summarising form of Pedersen's two-volume *Vergleichende Grammatik der keltischen Sprachen* (1909–1913). L. was also the author of two standard handbooks written in Welsh, guides to the study of Middle Cornish (*Llawlyfr Cernyweg Canol* ²1946) and Middle Breton (*Llawlyfr Llydaweg Canol* ²1966). His book *Datblygiad yr Iaith Gymraeg* (1931), aimed at a wide audience, appeared in a German revision in 1989 under the title *Die kymrische Sprache. Grundzüge ihrer Entwicklung.*

Lexovii. In classical → ethnography a Celtic tribe on the lower Seine. Its name survives in that of the city of Lisieux, whose Roman name was Noviomagus.

Lhuyd, Edward (c.1660–1709). Welsh naturalist and linguist, born in South Wales. After studying at Jesus College, Oxford, he worked in the Ashmolean Museum in Oxford from 1684 until his death. There he conducted research into natural history, philology, archaeology and history. From 1697 to 1701 he made extensive field trips to Wales, Scotland, Ireland, Cornwall and Brittany. The huge amount of linguistic material he collected on these journeys was published in 1707 in the first volume of his never completed great work *Archaeologia Britannica*, which made him the most important forerunner of modern → Celtic studies.

Lit.: A. Sommerfelt, 'E. Lh. and the comparative method in linguistics' (*Norsk tidsskrift for Sprogvidenskap* 16) 1952, 370–374; F. Emery, *Edward Lhuyd F.R.S. (1660–1709)*, Car. 1971; B. F. Roberts, *Edward Lhuyd: The Making of a Scientist*, Car. 1980; id., 'E. Lh. and Celtic Linguistics', in: *Procs. of the 7th International Congress of Celtic Studies*, O. 1986, 1–9.

Lia Fáil → Fál.

Liath Macha (Ir. /L'iaθ 'maxa/). One of the two steeds, fleet as the wind, of the hero → Cú Chulainn in the stories of the → Ulster Cycle. According to the older version of the tale of "How Cú Chulainn was Begotten" (→ *Compert Chon Culainn*) it was born in the same night as its master.

Lí Ban (Ir. /L'i: ban/). Wife of the elf Labraid Luath-lám-ar-chlaideb and sister of the fairy Fann in the story of "The Wasting Sickness of Cú Chulainn" (→ *Serglige Con Culainn*).

Libenice. Place near Kolín in central Bohemia near which a Celtic → place of worship of the 4th/3rdC BC was the subject of archaeological excavation in 1959. The site consisted of an enclosure of more than 80 x 20m (300 x 75ft), surrounded by a rampart and ditch. Near the centre the grave of a woman was discovered, and at the eastern end several pales of ritual significance, arranged in pairs, pits for offerings of food and drink, and a stone stele. Two bronze neck-rings (→ torcs) are thought to have originally served to adorn wooden images of deities. Bone finds suggest that animals were also sacrificed there.

Lindow Moss. Peat bog near Wilmslow (Cheshire) where in August 1984 the corpse of a young man was found, probably deposited as a → sacrifice in the bog in the 4thC BC. The dead man was naked apart from an armlet of fox-hair, but his manicured fingernails suggest he was a member of a high social caste. Further investigation revealed that death occurred as a result of his being simultaneously beaten, strangled and having his throat cut. Conceivably this threefold method of execution is connected with the motif of a triple death which is particularly frequent in Irish sagas (cf. → numbers). Traces of → mistletoe pollen in the dead man's stomach led to the inference that he may have been the victim of a druidic sacrifice (→ druids). The bog corpse is now to be seen in the British Museum.
   Lit.: I. M. Stead et al., *Lindow Man*, Lo. 1986; R. C. Turner & R. G. Scaife, *Bog Bodies. New Discoveries and New Perspectives*, Lo. 1995.

Lingones. In classical → ethnography a Celtic tribe on the upper Marne. The name survives in that of the town of Langres, whose Roman name was Andemantunnum.

Lir → Manannán mac Lir.

lists of sagas → sagas, lists of.

Litavis. Celtic goddess, whose name (with Celtic disappearance of initial p-) corresponds to Old Indian pṛth(i)vī, O. Engl. folde "earth". The original meaning of the word is thought to have been "the wide/broad". In insular Celtic the name survives in the form Llydaw, the Celtic term for Brittany. Dedications to L. have been found in the Dép. of Côte-d'Or in Aignay-le-Duc (CIL XIII 2887) and Mâlain (CIL XIII 5599, 5601 and 5602). The partner of the goddess in the inscriptions is the god Mars → Cicollus.

literature. The beginnings of Celtic l. reach back into pre-Christian times, as is clear from a comparison of the formulaic language of the oldest Celtic poetry with comparable literary survivals from other cultures in Indo-European languages. In the oldest period this l. was transmitted exclusively in the oral tradition, as is confirmed by a remark of → Caesar (Bell. Gall. 6,14). While the Celts were familiar with various writing systems which had evolved in the Mediterranean area, they made very restricted use of these. Classical → ethnography records that it was primarily the → bards and the → druids who were the bearers of tradition.

The first writing down of the oral traditions of the Celtic peoples took place after → christianisation in medieval Ireland and Wales. As → glosses and short poems in the margins of Latin manuscripts show, this process of committing things to writing began in the early Middle Ages, yet the oldest surviving manuscripts which contain Irish or Welsh texts of any great length are much later, of the 12th/13thC (cf. → Lebor na hUidre, → Lebor Laignech, → Book of Ballymote, → Llyfr Coch Hergest, → Llyfr Du Caerfyddin, → Llyfr Gwyn Rhydderch, → Llyfr Taliesin).

Among the earliest Irish literary texts are alliterating rhymeless poems, texts concerning Irish → law, hagiographical writings (cf. → Brigit, → Patrick, → Oengus mac Oengobann), as well as a large number of prose narratives, which incorporate both material and motifs from sagas and → fairy-tales, and historical events and traditions of pre-Christian → mythology.

It has become customary since the 19thC to divide this narrative literature into cycles. Generally a distinction is drawn between the → Finn, the → Historical, the → Ulster and the → Mythological Cycles. This classification is only makeshift, however, as many tales are common to several cycles, and important works such as, for example, the → Dindsenchas or the → Lebor Gabála Érenn are independent of this system. The way forward for the evolution of the modern Irish literary language was Geoffrey → Keating's reworking of the indigenous saga material in the 17thC.

Medieval Welsh literature is much smaller in extent, as much has been lost in transmission. The survivals include the early poetry of the → Cynfeirdd, prophetic poems such as → *Armes Prydein*, mnemonics such as the → *Trioedd Ynys Prydein*, cycles of strophes concerning saga heroes such as → Gereint fab Erbin, → Heledd, → Rhydderch Hael and → Urien Rheged, and the prose tales known today by the name of the → Mabinogion. For the evolution of European literature the adaptation of Celtic material and motifs in Latin and Old French literature, following the Norman Conquest, was of great significance (→ Arthurian literature).

Apart from Ireland and Wales, indigenous Celtic literature has only survived from the later Middle Ages and the early modern period (cf. → Breton, → Cornish, → Manx and → Scottish Gaelic).

Lit.: M. Dillon, *Early Ir. Lit.*, Ch. 1948; T. Parry, *A History of Welsh Lit.*, O. 1955; A. O. H. Jarman & G. R. Hughes, *A Guide to Welsh Lit.*, 2 vols., Swansea 1976–1979; M. McKenna, 'The Breton Literary Tradition' (*Celtica* 16) 1984, 35–51; D. Thomson, *An Introduction to Gaelic Poetry*, E. ²1989; G. Williams, *An Introduction to Welsh Lit.*, Car. 1992; J. E. C. Williams, *The Irish Literary Tradition*, Car. 1992; P. MacCana, 'On the early development of written narrative prose in Irish and Welsh' (*EC* 29) 1992, 51–67; B. F. Roberts, *Studies on Middle Welsh Literature*, Lewiston/NY 1992; D. Johnston, *The Literature of Wales*, Car. 1994; M. Richter, *The Formation of the Medieval West. Studies in the Oral Culture of the Barbarians*, Blackrock 1994; C. Davies, *Welsh Literature and the Classical Tradition*, Car. 1995; S. Davies, *Crefft y Cyfarwydd*, Car. 1995.

Livy (Titus Livius). Roman historian writing around the time of Christ's birth. His major work is a large-scale history of the Roman people from the beginnings to the reign of the Emperor Augustus. In the manuscripts it bears the title *Ab urbe condita* "From the founding of the City (Rome) onwards". It originally consisted of some 142 books, of which however only books 1–10 (753–293 BC), 21–45 (219–167 BC) and a few shorter fragments have survived. Livy's descriptions of the migration of the Celts to upper Italy (cf. → Ambigatus) and of their plundering of Rome (cf. → Brennos) are well-known.

Lit.: H. Homeyer, 'Zum Keltenexkurs in Livius' 5. Buch (33,4–35,3)' (*Historia* 9) 1960, 345–361; A. Grilli, 'La migrazione dei Galli in Livio', in: *Studi in onore di F. R. Vonwiller II*, Como 1980, 183–192; S. Fasce, 'Le guerre galliche di Livio e l'epopea mitologica celtica' (*Maia* 37) 1985, 27–43.

Llacheu (Welsh /ˈɬaxei/). A son of → Arthur in the story → *Breuddwyd Rhonabwy*. He appears in the → *Trioedd Ynys Prydein* as one of the "Three Well-Endowed Men" and "Three Fearless Men" of the island of Britain. His name also occurs in the poem → *Pa ŵr yw'r porthor?* and in a few poets of the 12th–14thCs. Nothing further is known about him, as he plays scarcely any role in the surviving stories of the Arthurian cycle of legends.

Llefelys (Welsh /ɬeˈvelis/). A son of the king → Beli Mawr in the story → *Cyfranc Lludd a Llefelys*. Through his marriage to the daughter of the king of France he succeeds to the French throne.

Lleu Llaw Gyffes (Welsh /ɬei ɬau ˈgəfes/ "Lleu of the Deft Hand"). Son of Arianrhod and nephew of the magician Gwydion in the story → *Math fab Mathonwy*.

Lludd (Welsh /ɬiːð/). Oldest son of and successor to the king → Beli Mawr. The story → *Cyfranc Lludd a Llefelys* describes how together with his brother Llefelys he frees Britain of three plagues.

Lludd Llawereint (Welsh /ɬiːð ɬauˈereint/). Father of → Creiddylad in the story → *Culhwch ac Olwen*. His byname Llawereint means "of the Silver Hand", thus corresponding to the byname of the Irish → Nuadu Argatlám. This correspondence suggests that the name Lludd also originated from Nudd (= Nuadu), by a process of assimilation caused by the beginning of the word Llawereint. An older form of the names Nudd and Nuadu is the name of the god → Nodons, attested in inscriptions. Probably both Welsh and Irish traditions here preserve, independently of one another, the memory of a figure from pre-Christian Celtic mythology. Apart from the allusion in → *Culhwch ac Olwen* nothing has survived of the legends concerning Ll. There have been various suggestions of a link between Ll. and the legendary figure of → Llŷr, who is almost equally obscure. There are however no sound reasons for this link apart from the occasional confusion of both names in the manuscripts.

Llyfr Coch Hergest (Welsh /ɬivr koːx ˈhergest/ "The Red Book of Hergest"). One of the most important Welsh compendium manuscripts, named after the place where it was once preserved. It is thought to have originated c. 1400 and contains examples of almost all genres of Middle Welsh poetry and prose. Only religious and legal texts are conspicuous by their absence. Indigenous material is reworked in the eleven stories which are today known by the collective term → Mabinogion. The manuscript also contains Welsh reworkings of foreign literary works, medical and grammatical treatises, proverbs and eulogies of princes of the 12th-14thCs. Today it is preserved in the Bodleian Library in Oxford.

    Ed.: J. G. Evans & J. Rhŷs, *The Text of the Mabinogion from the Red Book of H.*, O. 1887 (diplomatic ed.); J. G. Evans & J. Rhŷs, *The Text of the Bruts from the Red Book of H.*, O. 1890 (diplomatic ed.); J. G. Evans, *The Poetry in the Red Book of H.*, Llanbedrog 1911 (diplomatic ed.).
    Lit.: G. Charles-Edwards, 'The Scribes of the Red Book of H.' (*Journal of the Nat. Library of Wales* 21) 1980, 246–256.

Llyfr Du Caerfyrddin (Welsh /ɬivr diː kairˈvərðin/ "The Black Book of Carmarthen"). A compendium manuscript of 108 pages named after its presumed place of origin. For a long time it was thought that part of it was written in the 12thC and that it was thus the oldest Welsh manuscript. On a palaeographic basis it is now dated to the second half of the 13thC. The poems it contains are almost all anonymous, ranging from religious poetry to eulogies of Welsh princes of the 11th/12thC, and many poems of legendary content. The latter include the → *Englynion Gereint* and → *Englynion Beddeu*, the poem → *Pa ŵr yw'r porthor?*, and strophes concerning the legendary figures of → Myrddin and → Llywarch Hen. The manuscript is today preserved in the National Library of Wales in Aberystwyth.

Ed.: J. G. Evans, *Facsimile of the Black Book of Carmarthen*, O. 1908; id., *The Black Book of Carmarthen*, Pwllheli 1906 (diplomatic ed.); A. O. H. Jarman & E. O. Jones, *Ll. Du C. gyda rhagymadrodd, nodiadau testunol a geirfa*, Car. 1982 (ed. with intro., notes and glossary).

Lit.: A. O. H. Jarman, 'The Black Book of Carmarthen' (PBA 71) 1985, 333–356.

Llyfr Gwyn Rhydderch (Welsh /ɬivr gwin 'r̩əðerx/ "The White Book of Rhydderch"). A compendium manuscript named after its previous owner, which is thought to have originated in South Wales in the first half of the 14thC. It contains numerous Welsh translations of foreign literary works, many of them religious texts. Its sources include the Latin world chronicle *Imago Mundi* of Honorius of Autun (12thC), the apocryphal gospels of Nicodemus and Pseudo-Matthew, and hagiographical writings. The manuscript also contains the stories known by the collective term of the → Mabinogion, (with the exception of → *Breuddwyd Rhonabwy*). It is now preserved in the National Library of Wales in Aberystwyth.

Ed.: J. G. Evans, *The White Book Mabinogion*, Pwllheli 1907 (diplomatic ed.).

Lit.: D. Huws, 'Ll. G. Rh.' (CMCSt 21) 1991, 1–37.

Llyfr Taliesin (Welsh /ɬivr tal'jesin/ "The Book of Taliesin"). The name of a parchment manuscript of the early 14thC, surviving in incomplete form, which contains many poems. According to Ifor → Williams some twelve of these poems are the work of the historically attested poet → Taliesin. Eight of these are eulogies in praise of King → Urien of Rheged, one is a lament for the death of Urien's son → Owein, and the other three are eulogies addressed to other rulers of the late 6thC. More recently the attribution of these verses to Taliesin has been questioned. 15 other poems are based on the later legendary tradition concerning Taliesin. The manuscript also contains ten prophetic poems (including → *Armes Prydein*), verses of religious and biblical content, poems concerning Alexander the Great and Hercules, some laments over the death of personages in Welsh legend, and the poem → *Preiddeu Annwn*. The manuscript is now preserved in the National Library of Wales in Aberystwyth.

Ed.: J. G. Evans, *Facsimile and Text of the Book of T.*, Llanbedrog 1910.

Llyn Cerrig Bach (Welsh /ɬin 'kerrig baːx/). Lake on the west coast of the island of Anglesey. In 1942/43 during the building of a military airport large quantities of animal bones and many metal objects of the La Tène period were found there, including swords, spear-points and shield buckles, as well as parts of war-chariots and harness. It is thought that all these objects were cast into the lake as votive gifts in the time between the 2ndC BC and the Roman conquest in the first century AD.

Lit.: C. Fox, *A Find of the Early Iron Age from Ll. C. B. Anglesey*, Car. 1947.

Llŷr (Welsh /łi:r/). Father of Branwen, Brân and Manawydan in the tales → *Branwen ferch Lŷr* and → *Manawydan fab Llŷr*. Elsewhere in Welsh poetry Ll. frequently signifies the sea, corresponding to the Irish word ler (genitive: lir). Mac Lir, "Son of the Sea", occurs in Irish sources as the fixed epithet of the legendary ruler → Manannán. A theory of the Celticist Joseph → Vendryes holds that this expression has a figurative meaning approximating to "seafarer", but that after the byname was borrowed into Welsh this was no longer understood. Instead Lir was interpreted as being a proper name, and in consequence a personage named Ll. was invented. Ll. does not in fact play an active role in *Branwen* and *Manawydan*. He plays a significant part only in the Welsh reworkings of → Geoffrey of Monmouth's *Historia Regum Britanniae*. The story these tell of a ruler called Leir, which was later used by Shakespeare for his tragedy *King Lear*, does not however derive from the Celtic tradition. Moreover, the names Ll. and Leir/Lear are not identical in origin, as Leir is in all probability derived from the place-name Leicester (O.E. Laegreceaster).

Lit.: J. Vendryes, 'Manannán mac Lir' (*EC* 6) 1952, 239–254.

Llywarch Hen (Welsh /'łəwarx he:n/). A cousin of the king → Urien of Rheged in Welsh legend. He is said to have lived in the north of Celtic Britain in the late 6thC. Later tradition, however, linked his memory with places and features in the landscape of North Wales. His fate and that of his sons forms the subject of a cycle of poems thought to have originated in the 9th/10thC, which is preserved in the "Red Book of Hergest" (→ Llyfr Coch Hergest) and in a small number of other manuscripts. In the poem known as *Cân yr Henwr* ("Song of the Old Man") the poet has Ll. describe himself as an embittered, lonely and ailing old man. In other strophes Ll. bemoans the death of his 24 sons, who, following his wishes, went to war and were killed. In all probability the poems, which are in parts difficult to comprehend, formed the dramatic highlights of a saga, the plot of which was told in prose or was presumed to be common knowledge.

Lit.: J. Rowland, *Early Welsh Saga Poetry*, C. 1990.

Loda. A spirit worshipped by the Germanic warriors from Lochlin (Scandinavia) in the "Works of Ossian", written by James → Macpherson. According to the poem *Cath-Loda* the firmament is the dwelling-place of the spirit, and a tree the place where he expresses his will through oracles. In the poem

Carric-Thura a stone circle is the place where he is worshipped. There the Scottish king → Fingal meets the spirit and proves victorious in battle against him. – This episode inspired the painting *Fingals Kampf mit dem Geist von L.* (*Fingal's Battle with the Spirit of L.*, 1796, Statens Museum for Kunst Copenhagen) by Asmus Jacob Carstens (1754–1798), and the Lied *Lodas Gespenst* (1815) by Franz Schubert (1797–1828).

Loegaire Buadach (Ir. /ˈLoiɣarˈe ˈbuaðax/ "L. the Victorious"). One of the most important warriors of Ulster in the tales of the → Ulster Cycle. He is also called mac Connaid or Connaich after his father Connad or Connach. His death is related in the story → *Aided Loegairi Buadaig*.

Loeg mac Riangabra (Ir. /Loiɣ mak ˈRˈianɣavra/). Charioteer and faithful companion of the hero → Cú Chulainn in the tales of the → Ulster Cycle.

Longas mac nUislenn (Ir. /ˈLoŋgas vak ˈnuʃlˈeN/ "The Exile of the Sons of Uisliu"). One of the prefatory tales (→ remscéla) to the story of the Cattle-Raid of Cuailnge (→ *Táin Bó Cuailnge*). Its oldest version is thought to have originated in the 9thC; it survives in the "Book of Leinster" (→ Lebor Laignech), in the → "Yellow Book of Lecan" and in a manuscript of the early 16thC.

The story tells how the ageing king Conchobar of Ulster has the girl Deirdriu brought up on a remote farmstead with the intention of marrying her at some future time. Deirdriu however falls in love with the young warrior Noísiu, Uisliu's son. Fleeing Conchobar's wrath, the two go into exile together with two other sons of Uisliu. Pressed by his subjects, Conchobar offers the fugitives the possibility of returning to Ulster. As security he sends them his son Cormac and the two warriors Fergus and Dubthach as guarantors. On the way to Conchobar's castle, however, the sons of Uisliu are killed by King Eogan, an ally of Conchobar. Thereupon the three guarantors, angered at the treachery of the king, go over to King Ailill of Connacht, an enemy of Ulster. Deirdriu however is brought back in chains to Conchobar. After a year of captivity in which she neither eats nor sleeps and never smiles, she finally takes her own life. – Through the reworking of this material in the literature of the → Irish Renaissance the female protagonist of the story became known far beyond the borders of the Celtic countries (cf. → Deirdre).

Ed.: V. Hull, *L. m. nU.: The Exile of the Sons of Uisliu*, Lo. 1949 (with Engl. trans.).
Trans.: R. Thurneysen, *Sagen aus dem alten Irland*, B. 1901; J. Gantz, *Early Irish Myths and Sagas*, Harm. 1981.
Lit.: R. J. Cormier, 'Remarks on "The Tale of Deirdriu and Noisiu" and the Tristan Legend' (EC 15) 1976/77, 303–315; M. Tymoczko, 'Animal Imagery in L. m. nU.' (StC 20/21) 1985/86, 145–166.

Lucan (Marcus Annaeus Lucanus). Roman poet of the 1stC AD. Of his many works only one survives, an incomplete epic in 10 books concerning the civil war between Pompey and Caesar. In the manuscripts it bears the title *Bellum civile*, but today is also known as the *Pharsalia*, following a remark made by Lucan. The first book of the work contains in lines 396–465 a wealth of ethnographic detail concerning the tribes of Gaul, including a description of the Celtic → bards and → druids, as well as the well-known mention of the Celtic gods → Teutates, → Esus and → Taranis. In the third book L. describes a Gaulish sacred grove (→ nemeton), whose trees are felled by Caesar during a siege. This episode inspired the poem *Das Heiligtum* ("The Sanctuary") by Conrad Ferdinand Meyer (1825–1898).

Lit.: R. Nierhaus, 'Zu den geogr. Angaben in L.s Gallien-Exkurs' (*BJb* 153) 1953, 46–62.

Luchta (Ir. /'Luxta/). The carpenter of the → Tuatha Dé Danann in the story of the Battle of Mag Tuired (→ *Cath Maige Tuired*). In the course of the battle against the → Fomoire he provides the warriors with shields and shafts for their spears.

Lugaid Lága (Ir. /'Luɣið′ 'La:ɣa/). A brother of the king → Ailill Aulom in the tales of the → Historical Cycle. In the story of the Battle of Mag Mucrama (→ *Cath Maige Mucrama*) he accompanies → Lugaid mac Con into exile and fights at his side in the battle for supremacy. In single combat he slays the Irish king → Art mac Cuinn, but later serves his son and successor → Cormac mac Airt. He is therefore regarded as one of the most important warriors of the → Fianna in the stories of the → Finn Cycle.

Lugaid mac Con (Ir. /'Luɣið′ mak kon/). A king in the tales of the → Historical Cycle, said to have ruled over Ireland in the 3rdC AD. The story → *Cath Maige Mucrama* tells of how he proves victorious in the disputes with his foster-brother Eogan and the latter's brother-in-law Art, yet loses the throne and his life after an unhappy period of rule.

Lug mac Ethnenn (Ir. /Luɣ mak 'eθn′eN/). A figure in the → Mythological Cycle. His father is → Cian, a son of the doctor → Dian Cécht of the → Tuatha Dé Danann; his mother is Ethne, a daughter of the giant → Balar of the people of the → Fomoire. L. plays a major role in the story of the Battle of Mag Tuired (→ *Cath Maige Tuired*), leading the Tuatha Dé Danann to victory over the Fomoire. His customary appellatives are Samildánach "skilled in all crafts" and Lámfada "of the Long Arm". In the story → *Baile in Scáil* L. appears to the king → Conn Cétchathach, and in the tales of the → Ulster Cycle he is the father of the hero → Cú Chulainn. It is possible that L. retains features of the Celtic god → Lugus, whose cult may be attested by →

place-names such as Luguvalium (Carlisle) and Lug(u)dunum (Lyon, Laon, Leiden).

Lugnasad (Ir. /'Luɣnasað/). The beginning of autumn (August 1st) in the Irish calendar. The day, which marked the beginning of the harvest season, was celebrated with communal feasts. The customs linked with the feast were, according to the Glossary of Bishop Cormac (→ *Sanas Chormaic*), initiated in prehistoric times by → Lug mac Ethnenn, and the name of the festival is also thought to derive from him.

Lit.: K. Danaher, *The Year in Ireland*, Du. 1972; M. MacNéill, *The Festival of Lughnasa*, Du. ²1982.

Lugus. Celtic god possibly mentioned in the inscription from → Peñalba de Villastar. Several other inscriptions record the forms Lugoues (nom.) and Lugoibus (dat.), which denote a number of male or female divinities. The place-name Lug(u)dunum, which is common primarily in the area corresponding to present-day France, is often adduced as evidence for a widespread cult of the divinity, but most of the data stems from the Middle Ages. Since Henri → d'Arbois de Jubainville, Caesar's observation concerning the supreme Gaulish god (Bell. Gall. 6,17,1) has been taken to refer to L., but there is much that speaks against such an identification.

Lit.: A. Tovar, 'The god Lugus in Spain' (*BBCS* 29) 1982, 591–599; B. Maier, 'Is Lug to be identified with Mercury (Bell. Gall. VI 17,1)? New suggestions on an old problem' (*Ériu* 47; in press).

lunulae (Lat. "small moons"). A type of flat ornament shaped like a crescent moon. They were hammered of gold plate, and decorated particularly at the edges and ends with engraved geometrical patterns. Over 100 l. have been found in Western Europe, about 80 of them in Ireland. In 18th and 19thC depictions of the Celts l. sometimes occur as part of the ornamental dress of the → druids, but in fact they go back to the early Bronze Age and are thus of pre-Celtic origin.

Lit.: J. J. Taylor, 'L. reconsidered' (*Procs. of the Prehistoric Soc.* 36) 1970, 38–81; id., *Bronze Age Goldwork of the British Isles*, C. 1980.

Luzel, François-Marie (1821–1895). Folklorist, born in Keramborgne in Brittany. He worked in various places in his native land as a grammar school teacher, journalist and archivist. He published editions of Breton mystery plays, and also many volumes of indigenous tales and songs, including the bilingual collections of Breton folksongs *Gwerziou Breiz-Izel* (1868–1874) and *Soniou Breiz-Izel* (1890), as well as the collection of Breton fairy-tales in French translation entitled *Contes populaires de Basse-Bretagne* (1887).

Lit.: P. Batany, *L., poète et folkloriste breton*, Rennes 1941.

mabinogi (Welsh /mabi 'nogi/). Word translating Latin infantia "childhood" in a manuscript of the 14thC. It is therefore thought that m. originally denoted a person's childhood, and later by extension the story of a person's childhood. The meaning of the term as it occurs in → Pedeir Ceinc y M. ("The Four Branches of the M.") is contentious. In the manuscript tradition this is the title given to a group of four stories which report the wondrous adventures of a large number of mythical and legendary figures. It is widely held that the story of the birth and childhood of → Pryderi in the first Branch formed the original core of these tales. It is however unclear why the term m. was retained for the present form which these tales take. The explanation supported by Sir John → Rhŷs, Alfred → Nutt and Joseph → Loth, whereby m. denotes the narrative repertoire of a mabinog, i.e. of a poet in his formative years, is no longer tenable. The word mabinog is in fact an invention of Edward → Williams.

Mabinogion (Welsh /mabi'nogjon/). Title under which Lady Charlotte → Guest published in 1838–1849 a three-volume translation of twelve Welsh prose texts. It comprises the tales: → Pwyll Pendefig Dyfed, → Branwen ferch Lŷr, → Manawydan fab Llŷr, → Math fab Mathonwy, → Breuddwyd Macsen, → Cyfranc Lludd a Llefelys, → Culhwch ac Olwen, → Breuddwyd Rhonabwy, → Iarlles y Ffynnawn, → Peredur fab Efrawg, → Gereint fab Erbin and → Hanes Taliesin.

M. is a plural form of the Middle Welsh word → mabinogi, but this plural only occurs once in the manuscripts and is in all probability based upon a scribal error. Moreover, the singular only refers to the first four of the tales listed above. Nevertheless, the term coined by Lady Guest found widespread currency and was retained in the title of the classic translations by Joseph → Loth (Les M., ²1913) and Gwyn Jones and Thomas Jones (The M., 1948). Contrary to Lady Guest's practice, the term M. is today restricted to the first eleven of the tales listed above. They are transmitted in two versions among with other texts in the "Red Book of Hergest" (→ Llyfr Coch Hergest) and in the "White Book of Rydderch" (→ Llyfr Gwyn Rhydderch). The last of the Guest tales, Hanes Taliesin, is not preserved in either of these manuscripts and is therefore not now counted among the M.

All the texts are written recordings of stories that originally circulated orally. Various allusions in medieval Welsh poetry indicate that versions divergent from those that have survived were in circulation. It is clear from comparative study that the content of the stories derives in part from myth, in part from saga, in part from fairy-tale.

Lit.: S. Davies, Crefft y Cyfarwydd. Astudiaeth o dechnegau naratif yn y M., Car. 1995; see also under the individual tales.

Mabon fab Modron (Welsh /'mabon va:b 'modron/). A member of the retinue of → Uthyr Bendragon in the poem → Pa ŵr yw'r porthor? The tale →

Culhwch ac Olwen records that M. as a new-born child was taken away from his mother → Modron and held captive in Caer Loyw (Gloucester). Ultimately → Arthur and his retinue succeed in freeing him. An allusion to this tradition is found in one of the → *Trioedd Ynys Prydein*. There M. is designated "one of the Three Exalted Prisoners of the Island of Britain".

It would appear that the motif of captivity in association with the name of M. was also adopted in courtly → Arthurian literature. In his verse romance *Erec* → Chrétien de Troyes describes an enchanted garden watched over by a knight named Mabonagrain. A comparable figure bearing the name Mabuz appears in the verse romance *Lanzelet* by → Ulrich von Zatzikhoven. The surviving sources give no clear indication of the meaning of the motif of imprisonment in the Celtic tradition. W. J. → Gruffydd has suggested that it may be of mythological origin and is linked with the abduction of the boy → Pryderi in the story → *Pwyll Pendefig Dyfed*. An allusion to mythological contexts is seen in the fact that an older form of the name M. designates a Celtic god in inscriptions from ancient times (cf. → Maponus).

Lit.: R. Bromwich, *Trioedd Ynys Prydein*, Car. ²1978.

mac (Ir. /mak/). Word meaning "son of . . .", a frequent component of Irish and Scottish names (cf. → ó). Etymologically, the word corresponds to the Welsh name component → ap/ab and has the same meaning as Anglo-Norman Fitz (Fitzgerald = MacGearailt). The female form is ní "daughter of . . ." or nic (< ní mhic "daughter of the son of . . ."), corresponding to Welsh merch/ferch.

Mac Cuill, Mac Cécht and **Mac Gréine** (Ir. /mak kuL', mak k'e:xt, mak 'g'r'e:n'e/). The three kings of the → Tuatha Dé Danann in the "Book of the Invasions of Ireland" (→ *Lebor Gabála Érenn*) who are said to have ruled over Ireland together, when the sons of → Míl arrived. Their spouses are said to be → Banba, → Fótla and → Ériu.

Mac Dathó (Ir. /mak 'daθo:/). Titular hero of the story → *Scéla mucce Meic Dathó*. His real name is Mes Roeda "acorn harvest of the great forest".

Macgnímrada Con Culainn (Ir. /'makγ'n'i:vraða kon 'kuliN'/ "Cú Chulainn's Boyhood Deeds"). Title of a chapter in the story of the Cattle Raid of Cuailnge (→ *Táin Bó Cuailnge*). It tells the story of the youth of → Cú Chulainn, in the words of some of the warriors exiled from Ulster.

As the army of the men of Connacht advances upon Ulster, → Fergus mac Roich first tells how Cú Chulainn was once victorious in playing ball against three times fifty boys. Then → Conall Cernach tells how Cú Chulainn came by his name. Still bearing his old name Sétanta, he killed in self-defence the feared dog of the smith Culann, which had to be kept on three chains by nine warriors. Because the boy promised the smith to guard his cattle for him himself in future, he was called from that point on Cú Chulainn, i.e. "Cu-lann's Dog". (In the later version of this work it is → Cormac Conn Longas who tells this story.) Finally a warrior called Fiachu mac Fir Febe tells how Cú Chulainn once returned to Ulster after an adventure with the heads of three enemies he had slain, a live stag and a flock of wild swans which he had bound to his chariot with string. In order to calm his belligerence, at the king's command naked women are sent to meet him, and then warriors place the raging youth in three successive vats of cold water to cool his ardour.

Macha (Ir. /ˈmaxa/). Character in the tales of the → Ulster Cycle. The story → *Noínden Ulad* describes her as the wife of a rich farmer named Crunnchu, but other sources portray her as a king's daughter or a mythical figure resembling the → Morrígain. It is possible that M. was originally seen as a goddess of sovereignty, with whom the king of Ulster was thought to have allied himself by a → sacred marriage.

Lit.: F. Le Roux & Ch.-J. Guyonvarc'h, *Mórrigan-Bodb-Macha*, Rennes 1983; J. Carey, 'Notes on the Irish War-Goddess' (*Éigse* 19) 1982/83, 263–275.

MacNeill, Eoin (1867–1945). Historian and politician, born in Glenarm, Co. Antrim. After studying law, he joined with Douglas → Hyde and others in the founding of the Gaelic League (1893) and edited its official organ, the *Gaelic Journal*. In 1908 he was appointed Professor of Early Irish History at University College Dublin. His most important works in this field are *Phases of Irish History* (1919) and *Celtic Ireland* (1921).

Macpherson, James (1736–1796). Born in Ruthven in the Highlands of Scotland. After studying in Aberdeen and Edinburgh he at first taught in his local village school, and then as a tutor in Edinburgh. In 1759 he made the acquaintance of the dramatist John Home (1722–1808) and the theologian Alexander Carlyle (1722–1805). When they both revealed their interest in the Gaelic poetry of the Scottish Highlands, M. showed them 16 short texts which he claimed to have translated from the Gaelic. Home's influence led to these texts finding their way into the hands of Hugh Blair (1718–1800), Professor of Rhetoric and Belles Lettres at Edinburgh University, and on his initiative they were published in July 1760 under the title *Fragments of Ancient Poetry, Collected in the Highlands of Scotland*. The encouraging reception accorded to this book prompted M., after journeys in the Highlands, to publish two further volumes of epic poetry. *Fingal* appeared in 1762 and *Temora* in 1763. An addition to the title of these two books named the author as the Gaelic poet → Ossian, who according to the editor M. lived in the 3rdC AD. All three books appeared in 1765 together with a "critical dissertation" by Hugh Blair, in a two-volume collected edition entitled *The Works of Ossian, the Son of Fingal*. By this time an embittered dispute concerning the authenticity of the poems had already arisen in Great Britain.

As we know today, M. had to a large extent composed the "Works of Ossian" himself, having recourse to names, episodes and motifs from various Celtic saga cycles. The Scots Gaelic version of the poems, published for the first time in 1807, is therefore not the original version, as M. claimed, but on the contrary a retrospective translation from the English. In his sentimental treatment of the material M. followed the popular taste of his time, but the "Works of Ossian" were held by many of his contemporaries to be translations, however inferior, of authentic Celtic poetry. They achieved widespread circulation throughout Europe in numerous translations and had a far-reaching influence upon the German Storm and Stress movement (*Sturm und Drang*) and upon the Romantics. Among the most celebrated admirers of Ossianic poetry in Germany were Herder (*Auszug aus einem Briefwechsel über Ossian und die Lieder alter Völker*, "Extract from a correspondence concerning Ossian and the songs of ancient peoples", 1773) and the young Goethe, who translated part of the "Works of Ossian" into German and used them in his novel *Die Leiden des jungen Werthers* ("The Sorrows of young Werther", 1774).

Bibl.: G. F. Black, 'M.'s Ossian and the Ossianic Controversy: a contribution towards a bibliography' (*Bull. of the N.Y. Public Library* 30) 1926, 424–439 & 508–524; J. J. Dunn, 'Supplem. Bibliography' (*Bull. of the N.Y. Public Library* 75) 1971, 465–473.

Author and works: F. Stafford, *J. M. and the Poems of Ossian*, E. 1988; P. J. de Gategno, *J.M.*, Boston, 1989; H. Gaskill (ed.), *Ossian revisited*, E. 1991; *J. M., The Poems of Ossian and Related Works*, ed. H. Gaskill with an introduction by F. Stafford, E. 1995.

Celtic background: L. C. Stern, 'Die ossianischen Heldenlieder' (*Zeitschrift für vergleichende Literaturgeschichte* 8), 1895, 51–86 & 143–174; D. S. Thomson, *The Gaelic Sources of M.'s 'Ossian'*, E. 1952; J. Weisweiler, 'Hintergrund und Herkunft der ossianischen Dichtung' (*Literaturwissenschaftliches Jahrbuch der Görres-Gesellschaft* 4) 1963, 21–42; J. Bysveen, *Epic Tradition and Innovation in J.M.'s 'Fingal'*, Up. 1982; H. Gaskill, ' "Ossian" M.: towards a rehabilitation' (*Comparative Literature* 8) 1986, 113–146; D. S. Thomson, 'M.'s Ossian: ballads to epics' (*Béaloideas* 54/55) 1986/87, 243–264; H. Gaskill, 'What did J.M. really leave on display at his publisher's shop in 1762?' (*SGS* 16) 1990, 67–89.

Reception: R. Tombo, *Ossian in Germany*, NY 1901; P. van Tieghem, *Ossian en France*, 2 vols., P. 1917; id., *Ossian et l'Ossianisme dans la littérature européenne du XVIIIe siècle*, Groningen 1920; H. Okun, 'Ossian in Painting' (*Journal of the Warburg and Courtauld Institutes* 30) 1967, 327–356; *Ossian und die Kunst um 1800*, H. 1974 (exhibition cat.); I. D. Levin, *Ossian v russkoj literature*, Leningrad 1980; A. Grewe, 'Ossian und seine europäische Wirkung', in: K. Heitmann (ed.), *Europäische Romantik II*, Wi. 1982, 171–188; S. M. Gilardino, *La tradizione ossianica nella poesia dell'Alfieri, del Foscolo e del Leopardi*, Ravenna 1982; S. Manning, 'Ossian, Scott and 19thC Scottish Literary Nationalism' (*Studies in Scottish Lit.* 17) 1982, 39–54; M. Jahrmärker, *Ossian: eine Figur und eine Idee des europäischen Musiktheaters um 1800*, Co. 1993.

Mac Roth (Ir. /mak Roθ/). Scout and messenger of King → Ailill of Connacht in the story of The Cattle Raid of Cuailnge (→ *Táin Bó Cuailnge*). It is said that he could walk through the whole of Ireland in a single day.

Mael Dúin (Ir. /mail du:n′/). Titular hero of the the story → *Immram Curaig Maíle Dúin*.

Maelgwn (Welsh /'mailgun/). Ruler over the North Welsh kingdom of → Gwynedd in the first half of the 6thC AD. The oldest account of him is by his contemporary → Gildas, who strongly criticises M.'s way of life in his work *De excidio Britanniae*. He appears in legend in the story → *Hanes Taliesin*.

Lit.: J. Wood, 'M. Gwynedd: A Forgotten Welsh Hero' (*Trivium* 19) 1984, 103–117.

Mael-Muire mac Célechair (Ir. /mail 'mur′e mak 'ke:l′exir′/). One of the two scribes who wrote the "Book of the Dun Cow" (→ Lebor na hUidre). According to an entry in the work known as the Annals of the Four Masters he was murdered in 1106 by men who were pillaging the stone church of the monastery of Clonmacnoise, for which reason the oldest parts of the manuscript can be dated to c. 1100.

Märchen → folktale.

Maeve. English form of the Irish name → Medb.

Magdalenenberg. Present-day name of the site of a Celtic → princely grave near Villingen-Schwenningen (Baden-Württemberg). One of the biggest grave-mounds of central Europe, with an original diameter of 104m and height of 8–10m, it is also – apart from the → Hohmichele – the oldest of these monuments. The central part of the hill with its central grave-chamber, plundered in ancient times, was excavated as early as 1890. In 1970–1974 an exhaustive study of M. was conducted, opening up the central grave-chamber and a total of 126 other graves. The small objects found in these graves and the central grave-chamber, constructed of oak boards, are now to be seen in the Franziskaner-Museum in Villingen-Schwenningen. After the excavation was completed the mound was piled up again; its height of 6.5m conveys a good impression of its original appearance.

Lit.: K. Spindler, M. *I–VI*, Villingen-Schwenningen 1971–1980; ibid., *Der M. bei Villingen*, St. 1976; H. Parzinger, 'Zur Belegungsabfolge auf dem M. bei Villingen' (*Germania* 64) 1986, 391–407.

magic (→ defixio, → amulet, → religion). Magic may be defined as the ability to control superhuman powers at will for one's own benefit or to harm others. It is characteristic of magic – as opposed to → religion – that these effects are not sought through prayer on a communal basis or with the approval of the community, but are brought about by the individual through certain actions or words.

In → Welsh the word for magic is hud, which corresponds etymologically and in meaning to the Old Norse word seiðr (cf. → Celtic-Germanic cultural links). In → Irish the word bricht "charm" occurs, which has a very similar earlier equivalent in → Gaulish (in the inscription of → Larzac).

One form of magic which occurs very early, among the Celts of the Hallstatt and La Tène cultures, is the use of → amulets intended to ward off harm. A form of malevolent magic, on the other hand, is the use of curse-tablets (→ defixio), which is attested among the Romanised Celts of Gaul and Britain, influenced by the practice of classical antiquity. In medieval Irish texts there are many references to the magic power of curses (cf. → áer), the power of magic commands or prohibitions (cf. → geis), and of various forms of → prophecy or divination. It is however frequently not clear which descriptions derive from the imagination of the narrator (cf. the sorceress → Ceridwen in the story → Hanes Taliesin), and which are actually based in a recollection of pre-Christian magic. Interpretation is further encumbered by the fact that Christian authors frequently viewed acts inspired by religion (for example those of the → druids) as magic.

Lit.: → geis, → religion.

Mag Mell (Ir. /maɣ m'eL/ "Plain of Joys"). A Paradisian region beyond the world of human habitation, whose whereabouts are not defined more precisely.

Mag Muirthemne (Ir. /maɣ 'mur'θ'ev'n'e/). Home of the hero → Cú Chulainn in the tales of the → Ulster Cycle. His residence is said, particularly in late texts, to be the castle Dún Delga or (later) Dún Delgá(i)n (Engl. Dundalk). The name M. M. refers to the plain south of Dundalk.

Mag Tuired (Ir. /maɣ 'tur'eð/). Plain in the north-west of the province of Connacht. Tradition has it that in prehistoric times it was the scene of two important battles between the → Fir Bolg and the → Tuatha Dé Danann, and between the Tuatha Dé Danann and the → Fomoire. The course of the second battle and the events leading up to it are described in the tale → Cath Maige Tuired.

Malory, Sir Thomas. English author, born in Warwickshire at the beginning of the 15thC, died in London in 1471. Between 1450 and 1470 he was the author of a huge compilation of retellings of the courtly romances concerning King → Arthur. The stories, which are only loosely connected with one another, were after the death of the author combined in a book by the printer William Caxton, and published in 1485 under the title *Le Morte Darthur*. The work marks the end of medieval → Arthurian literature and exerted great influence on the modern reception of the genre, particularly in the Anglo-Saxon world.

Lit.: T. Takayima & D. Brewer (eds.), *Aspects of M.*, C. 1981; J. W. Spisak (ed.), *Studies in M.*, Kalamazoo (Mich.) 1985; F. Riddy, *Sir Th. M.*, Lei. 1987.

Malvina. (Scots Gaelic mala mhín "beautiful forehead"). Daughter of a noble warrior called Toscar in the "Works of Ossian" by James → Macpherson. The poems tell how she was betrothed to → Oscar, the only son of the poet → Ossian, and after the early death of her betrothed took care of his aged father. Both name and character are inventions of Macpherson and have no equivalent in the Celtic tradition.

Manannán mac Lir (Ir. /'manaNa:n mak L'ir'/). In Irish literature the ruler of a mysterious kingdom beyond the sea, designated in the texts variously as → Emain Ablach, → Mag Mell or → Tír Tairngiri. The name mac Lir ("Son of the Sea") indicates that M. lives in the ocean. High and late medieval scholarship explained the word "Lir" as the name of M.'s father, but it is only in the tale *Oidheadh Chlainne Lir*, an Irish version of the folktale about the swan knight dating from the 15thC, that Lir appears in action.

Among the earliest stories in which M. plays a role are → Compert Mongáin, → Immram Brain and → Serglige Con Culainn. In later texts M. is frequently counted among the numbers of the → Tuatha Dé Danann and is described as the giver of gifts with magical qualities such as the magic mist → féth fiada.

Lit.: J. Vendryes, 'M.' (*EC* 6) 1952, 239–254; D. B. Spaan, 'The Place of M. in Irish Mythology' (*Folklore* 76) 1965, 176–195.

Manawydan fab Llŷr (Welsh /mana'wədan va:b ɬi:r/). Title of the third of the "Four Branches of the Mabinogi" (→ Pedeir Ceinc y Mabinogi).

The chief figure in the story is M., brother of the British king Brân. After returning from Brân's campaign in Ireland he marries Rhiannon, widow of the prince Pwyll of Dyfed and mother of his comrade-in-arms Pryderi. One day a mysterious spell causes all the human beings and domesticated animals in Dyfed to disappear, leaving behind only M., Rhiannon, Pryderi and his wife, Cigfa. The four spend two years in complete solitude, but then they leave the country. In England M. and Pryderi endeavour to earn their living as saddlers, shield-makers and cobblers successively, but on each occasion the hostile attitude of the local craftsmen forces them to move from one place to the next. Finally they leave England and return to Dyfed, which is still devoid of other human habitation. There a spell causes Rhiannon and Pryderi to become captive in a castle, which then vanishes without trace, together with the captives. At the end of the story, however, M. succeeds in finding out who is the cause of all these machinations; he frees Rhiannon and Pryderi, and releases Dyfed from the spell which has been cast upon it.

Ed.: I. Williams, *Pedeir Keinc y Mabinogi*, Car. 1930.

Trans.: G. Jones & T. Jones, *The Mabinogion*, rev. ed., Lo. 1974; J. Gantz, *The Mabinogion*, Harm. 1976.

Lit.: P. K. Ford, 'Prolegomena to a Reading of the Mabinogi: "Pwyll" and "Manawydan" ' (*StC* 16/17) 1981/82, 110–125.

Manching. Place c. 5 miles south of Ingolstadt (Bavaria), directly east of which one of the biggest Celtic → oppida was situated in the 2nd/1stC BC. It occupied an area of 380 hectares and was surrounded by a wall some five miles long and five yards in height. After the first digs in the 19thC and an archaeological excavation carried out in 1938, M. has since 1955 been the subject of a concerted series of excavation campaigns, and is in consequence one of the best-known oppida. The archaeological finds are partly in the Prähistorische Staatssammlung in Munich, partly in the Stadtmuseum of Ingolstadt. Since 1988 a small museum on the site, with an archaeological trail, has kept visitors informed of the results of the study of M.

Lit.: H. Dannheimer & R. Gebhardt (eds.), *Das keltische Jahrtausend*, Mz. 1993 (exhibition cat.).

Manx. The Celtic language of the Isle of Man. Together with → Irish and → Scots Gaelic it forms the Gaelic branch of the Insular Celtic group of languages. M. was introduced by Irish settlers on the island in the 4th/5thC; the first thousand years of its development are however only attested in the form of place names and personal names. The first linguistic documents of any length survive in manuscripts and books of the 18th/19thC. These take the form of translations of religious writings, dictionaries and grammars, as well as songs and ballads of the island whose origin reaches in some cases back into the 16thC. Already in the early 19thC the language began to decline as a consequence of the spread and increasing influence of English. The last speaker of Manx died in 1974, aged 97.

Lit.: R. L. Thomson, 'The M. traditional ballad' (*EC* 9) 1960/61, 521–548 & (*EC* 10) 1962/63, 60–87; id., 'The Study of M. Gaelic' (*PBA* 55) 1969, 177–210; G. Price, *The Languages of Britain*, Lo. 1984; G. Broderick, *A Handbook of Late Spoken M.*, 3 vols., T. 1984–1986.

Maponus. Celtic god whose name is derived from a Celtic word meaning "child" or "son" (cf. Ir. mac and Welsh mab "son, boy"). The cult of M. is attested by several inscriptions from the North of England (*RIB* 583, 1120–1122, 2063; AE 1975, 568), and by the lead tablet of → Chamalières discovered in 1971. The first four of these dedications identify M. with → Apollo on the basis of the → interpretatio romana. Accordingly the only two unambiguous pictorial representations portray him in comformity with the classical model as a standing naked figure with a lyre. In Welsh tradition the name M. survives in the figure of legend → Mabon fab Modron.

Lit.: J. MacQueen, 'M. in Mediaeval Tradition' (*Transactions of the Dumfriesshire and Galloway Nat. History and Antiquarian Soc. 31*) 1954, 43–57.

March fab Meirchiawn (Welsh /marx va:b 'meirxjaun/). In the → *Trioedd Ynys Prydein* one of the "Three Seafarers of the Island of Britain". In the story → *Breuddwyd Rhonabwy* he arrives with a band of warriors from Scandinavia, and is depicted as a cousin and advisor of → Arthur. Another Welsh triad mentions M. as the husband of → Essyllt and uncle of her lover → Drystan. He thus corresponds to King Mark(e) in the courtly versions of the Tristan material.

Marcellus of Bordeaux (M. Empiricus). Medical writer c. 400 AD. His work *De medicamentis* is strongly influenced by the folk medicine of his time and preserves Gaulish elements in a small number of formulaic expressions. These are, however, difficult to interpret.

Lit.: P.-Y. Lambert, *La langue gauloise*, P. 1994.

Marne → Matrona.

Mars. In Roman religion the god of war. His name also serves to designate many Celtic deities in Latin inscriptions and literary works; sometimes, but not always, these are also given their Celtic names (what is known as the → interpretatio romana). → Caesar is the first to record that the Gauls viewed M. as the god who determined the outcome of wars: "when they have determined on a decisive battle, they dedicate as a rule whatever spoil they may take to him. After a victory they sacrifice such living things as they have taken, and all the other effects they gather into one place. In the regions of many tribes mounds may be seen in hallowed spots, consisting of such objects piled up." (Bell. Gall. 6,17). As the great number of votive inscriptions shows, the cult of M. was widespread in the Celtic provinces of the Roman Empire. As bynames the following are attested in inscriptions: → Alator, → Albiorix, → Barrex, → Belatucadrus, → Bolvinnus, → Braciaca, → Britovius, → Budenicus, → Buxenus, → Camulus, → Caturix, → Cicollus, → Cnabetius, → Cocidius, → Condatis, → Corotiacus, → Cososus, → Dinomogetimarus, → Divanno, → Iovantucarus, → Latobius, → Lenus, → Leucetius, → Medocius, → Mogetius, → Mullo, → Nabelcus, → Nodons, → Ocelus, → Randosatis, → Rigisamus, → Rudianus, → Segomo, → Smertrius and → Teutates. The equation of M. with Teutates is also attested in literature, in the → Berne Scholia on the work of the Roman poet → Lucan. Many of the bynames listed above, however, only occur once or twice. It is therefore thought that these are local tribal deities.

Lit.: E. Thevenot, *Sur les traces des M. celtiques*, Bruges 1955; P.-M. Duval, *Les dieux de la Gaule*, P. 1976; H. Merten, 'Der Kult des M. im Trevereraum' (*Trierer Zeitschrift* 48) 1985, 7–113; J.-J. Hatt, *Mythes et dieux de la Gaule I*, P. 1989.

Math fab Mathonwy (Welsh /maːθ vaːb maˈθonwi/). Title of the fourth of the "Four Branches of the Mabinogi" (→ *Pedeir Ceinc y Mabinogi*). It tells the complicated story of the magically gifted king Math of Gwynedd, his two nephews Gwydion and Gilfaethwy, and their nephew Lleu Llaw Gyffes.

The story begins with Gilfaethwy falling in love with the maiden Goewin, a serving-maid of his uncle, Math. As Math in time of peace can only live as long as his feet rest in a maiden's lap, Gilfaethwy's brother Gwydion insti-gates a war between Math and Prince Pryderi of Dyfed, in order to separate the king from Goewin. While Math is campaigning, Gilfaethwy forces his way in to Goewin and rapes her. When the king finds out about this, he imposes upon his nephews the punishment that they must spend successive years in the guise of a pair of stags, of wild boars and of wolves, and sire progeny by one another. Thereafter he takes them back into his favour at the court. In what follows, Arianrhod, the niece of the king and sister of Gwy-dion and Gilfaethwy gives birth in mysterious fashion to the two boys Dylan Eil Ton and Lleu Llaw Gyffes. Because Arianrhod decrees that Lleu may never take a human being to wife, Math and Gwydion make him a wife out of flowers, called Blodeuwedd (Welsh blodeu "flowers, blossom" and gwedd "appearance, aspect"). The story ends with Blodeuwedd deceiving Lleu and, with her lover Gronwy, attempting to murder him, but with Gwydion's help Lleu succeeds in killing his rival.

Ed.: I. Williams, *Pedeir Keinc y Mabinogi*, Car. 1930.

Trans.: G. Jones & T. Jones, *The Mabinogion*, rev. ed., Lo. 1974; J. Gantz, *The Mabionogion*, Harm. 1976.

Lit.: W. J. Gruffydd, *M. fab M.: An Enquiry into the Origins and Development of the Fourth Branch of the Mabinogi*, Car. 1928; J. Loth, 'Le Mabinogi de M. vab M. d'après W. J. Gruffydd' (RC 46) 1929, 272–300; G. Dumézil, 'La quatrième branche du Mabinogi et la théologie des trois fonctions', in: P. MacCana & M. Meslin (eds.), *Rencontres de religions*, P. 1986, 25–38.

matière de Bretagne. Term denoting those medieval narratives which rework predominantly Celtic material (→ Arthurian literature). It derives from the Old French poet Jean Bodel, who in the introduction to his "Song of the Saxons" (Chanson de Saisnes, c. 1200) differentiated between the Celtic material, the classically based "matière de Rome", and the historicising "ma-tière de France". In accordance with the taste of his time the poet charac-terised the adaptations of classical material as "wise and instructive", the national heroic epics as "true", and the reworking of Celtic material, in a manner that often resembles the fairy-tale, as "futile, but pleasing" (vain et plaisant).

matriarchy → woman, → Celtic ideology, → matrilinearity.

matrilinearity. Term denoting kinship transmitted exclusively through the maternal line. In societies with a matrilinear structure, children are accordingly regarded as related to the family of their mother, but not to the family of their father. Thus royal succession among the (non-Celtic) → Picts was in fact handed down according to the principle of matrilinearity, as early sources attest. In Ireland however kinship (→ fine) was always based on the patrilinear system, with the relatives of the mother only retaining certain rights and duties with regard to her children.

M. has nothing to do with a matriarchy in which women exert social and political power in their own right.

Matrona. Celtic name of the Marne. According to → Caesar (Bell. Gall. 1,1) it formed together with the lower reaches of the Seine (→ Sequana) the border between Gaul proper and the settlement area of the → Belgae. The cult of a goddess of the same name is attested by a votive inscription (CIL XIII 5674) found in 1831 near the source of the Marne, not far from the town of Langres.

Matronae/Matres/Matrae. A type of mother-goddess. Their cult is attested by over 1100 votive inscriptions and stone statues, dating primarily from the 2nd to the 4thC AD, and found in many regions of the Roman Empire settled by the Celts and the Germani. Most of these monuments were not found in isolation but occur in large numbers in the neighbourhood of cult centres such as, for example, Bonn or Pesch and Nettersheim in the Eifel (bordering on Belgium).

Depictions generally show the M. as a group of three (→ numbers) seated, richly clothed women, holding in their hands flowers, fruit, ears of corn or the like. Both married and unmarried women (the latter identifiable by their lack of bonnets and their long flowing hair) are depicted as M. In the inscriptions the M. are as a rule assigned bynames, which are sometimes Latin in origin, but in most cases Celtic or Germanic. Frequently these bynames are derived from terms denoting peoples, tribes or places.

To judge by the inscriptions and depictions the M. were regarded as providers of abundant harvests and fertility. Families, or larger groupings of people, or a place's whole population would place themselves under their protection. Nothing in detail is known about their cult, although it is thought that Germanic and Celtic beliefs intermingled.

Lit.: G. Bauchhenss & G. Neumann (eds.), *Matronen und verwandte Gottheiten*, Bo. 1987.

Matunus. Celtic god whose cult is attested by a single votive inscription (*RIB* 1265) found near High Rochester (Northumberland) c. 1715. The name of

M. is presumably, like those of the god → Artaius and the goddesses → Andarta and → Artio, derived from a Celtic word for bear (cf. O. Ir. math "bear").

Matzhausen. Site near Neumarkt in the Upper Palatinate where one of the most beautiful *Linsenflaschen* (lentiform flasks) was found (→ ceramics). It comes from the grave of a man, a woman and a child and on the basis of the → fibulae found in the same grave is dated to the early 4thC BC. The upper side of the lens-shaped body of the flask is – uniquely in Celtic → art – decorated with an animal frieze enframed by a stamped pattern. Four pairs of animals are carved on it (hart and hind, roebuck and doe, boar and sow, gander and goose), as well as a dog or wolf in pursuit of a hare. The flask may now be seen in the Museum für Vor- und Frühgeschichte in Berlin.

Mavilly. Site in the Dép. of Côte-d'Or where in Gallo-Roman times there was an important spring sanctuary. A stone pillar was found there, decorated with depictions of Gaulish divinities on all four sides. Best-known is the depiction of a bare-headed standing god, who wears a neck-ring (→ torc) and chain-mail, and is armed with a spear and shield. To his left stands a goddess whose hand rests on his shoulder, while on his right a ram-headed snake writhes upwards (→ snake, ram-horned). On a stylistic basis the pillar is dated to the early 1stC AD. In the absence of any inscription any attempt to identify the deities on the pillar can only be conjectural.

Lit.: E. Thevenot, 'Le monument de M.' (*Latomus* 14) 1955, 75–99; J.-J. Hatt, *Mythes et Dieux de la Gaule I*, P. 1989.

Medb (Ir. /m'eðv/). Wife of the king → Ailill of Connacht in the stories of the → Ulster Cycle. She is said to be the daughter of the High King Eochaid Feidlech, and to have had three husbands prior to her marriage with Ailill. She plays a major role in the story of the Cattle Raid of Cuailnge (→ *Táin Bó Cuailnge*); through her unremitting hostility towards the inhabitants of Ulster she is largely responsible for the course of action. It is possible that the figure of M. derives from a goddess of sovereignty, with whom the king was thought to be allied by a → sacred marriage.

medicine. An area of Celtic culture concerning which little is known. This stems above all from the fact that medical knowledge was transmitted exclusively orally, with the result that none has survived from pre-Roman times. It is sometimes the case that the anthropological study of skeletons permits conclusions concerning illnesses or injuries, but these finds leave us completely in the dark with regard to methods of treatment. In many graves of the 3rd–1stC BC the dead were buried together with medical instruments of → bronze and → iron; saws for cutting through skulls have also been found. What success treatment with these might have met is not clear.

We owe important insights into m. in Roman Gaul to the archaeological investigation of healing spring sanctuaries such as those in → Chamalières, → Glanum, → Hochscheid, or by the springs of the Seine (→ Sequana). Apart from the dedicatory inscriptions, the → votive gifts which were offered to the deity are particularly interesting. They can inform us of the frequency of certain illnesses and afflictions, as they often portrayed the organs or limbs concerned.

Lit.: J. M. de Navarro, 'A Doctor's Grave of the Middle La Tène Period from Bavaria' (Procs. of the Prehistoric Soc. 21) 1955, 231–248; W. Meid, 'Dichtkunst, Rechtspflege und Medizin im alten Irland', in: M. Mayrhofer et al. (eds.), Antiquitates Indogermanicae, I. 1974, 21–34; B. Rémy, 'Les inscriptions de médecins en Gaule' (Gallia 42) 1984, 115–152; C. Pelletier (ed.), La médecine en Gaule, P. 1985; W. Davies, 'The place of healing in early Irish society', in: D. Ó. Corráin et al. (eds.), Sages, Saints, and Storytellers, May. 1989, 43–55; C. Bourgeois, Divona, 2 vols., P. 1991–1992.

Mediomatrici. In classical → ethnography a Celtic tribe living in the region of present-day Lorraine. The name perhaps survives in that of the city of Metz, whose Roman name was Divodurum.

Medocius. Celtic god equated with → Mars on the basis of the → interpretatio romana. His cult is attested by a votive inscription found in Colchester in 1891 (RIB 191).

Medrawd. (Welsh /'medraud/; English Mo(r)dred). Warrior in the cycle of legends concerning → Arthur. According to an entry in the → Annales Cambriae he died in the battle of → Camlan in c. 539 AD. He was still regarded as the epitome of valour by the Welsh poets of the 12thC. It is → Geoffrey of Monmouth who first describes Mordred as Arthur's treacherous nephew, who in the absence of the king usurps the throne and commits adultery with Queen → Gwenhwyfar. M. is therefore one of the "Three Dishonoured Men of the Island of Britain" in the → Trioedd Ynys Prydein.

Lit.: P. Korrel, An Arthurian Triangle: A Study of the Origin, Development and Characterization of Arthur, Guinevere and Modred, Lei. 1984.

Meldi. In classical → ethnography a Celtic tribe on the lower Marne. It was in their territory that the ships were built with which → Caesar undertook the second expedition to Britain in 54 BC. The name of the M. survives in that of the city of Meaux.

menhir. A kind of prehistoric stone monument, taking the form of a single, upright stone up to 20m in height. The term derives from the Celtic (Breton maen "stone" and hir "long"), although the monuments were erected long before the first emergence of the Celts.

Mercury. The god of commerce in Roman religion. His name also serves to denote many Celtic gods in Latin inscriptions and literary works; these are not always given in addition their Celtic names (→ interpretatio romana). → Caesar reports that the Gauls worshipped Mercury most amongst the gods and that he is the most frequent subject of images; they regard him as the inventor of all arts, and a guide on all roads and journeys. They regard him as the god with most influence on money-making and commercial dealings (Bell. Gall. 6,17). The → Berne Scholia, glossing the work of the Roman poet → Lucan, drawing upon divergent sources, equate the Gaulish gods → Teutates and → Esus with M. Human sacrifices to M. are recorded by the patristic writers Tertullian (Apologeticum 9,5) and Minucius Felix (Octavius 30,4). Celtic bynames of M. recorded in the inscriptions are: → Adsmerius, → Artaius, → Arvernorix, → Arvernus, → Cissonius, → Dumiatis, → Iovantucarus, → Moccus and → Visucius.

Lit.: F. Benoit, *Mars et Mercure*, Aix-en-Provence 1959; S. Boucher, 'L'image de Mercure en Gaule', in: *La patrie gauloise d'Agrippa au 6e siècle*, Ly. 1983, 57–69; J.-J. Hatt, *Mythes et dieux de la Gaule I*, P. 1989.

Merlin. English, French and German form of the Welsh name → Myrddin.

Mes Buachalla (Ir. /m′es 'buaxaLa/). Mother of the king Conaire Mór in the story → Togail Bruidne Da Derga.

Mesca Ulad (Ir. /'m′eska 'ulað/) "The Intoxication of the Ulaid"). Title of a story from the → Ulster Cycle. The ending survives in an Old Irish version in the "Book of the Dun Cow" (→ Lebor na hUidre), the beginning in a later Middle Irish reworking in the "Book of Leinster" (→ Lebor Laignech). A Scottish manuscript of the 16thC preserves a combination of both versions.

The story begins with King → Conchobar mac Nesa persuading his two foster-sons Fintan and → Cú Chulainn to make over to him for a year their respective thirds of the province of Ulster, of which he had appointed them rulers one year before. After this year has elapsed both Fintan and Cú Chulainn hold banquets for Conchobar. In order to offend neither of his foster-sons Conchobar intends to spend the first half of the night with Fintan, but the second with Cú Chulainn. Around midnight the topers set off in their war-chariots on a wild journey to the castle of Cú Chulainn. In their drunkenness they lose their way, however, and early in the morning arrive at Temair Luachra, the castle of their enemy, King → Cú Roí. The latter affects to give the unexpected guests hospitality in an iron house, disguised with wood, which when darkness descends he has bound in chains and set on fire. With the aid of Cú Chulainn the warriors succeed in escaping from the house and destroying Temair Luachra.

Ed.: J. C. Watson, *M. U.*, Du. 1941 (MMIS 13); U. MacGearailt, 'The Edinburgh Text of M. U.' (*Ériu* 37) 1986, 133–180.

Trans.: J. C. Watson, 'M. U.' (*SGS* 5) 1942, 1–34; Ch.-J. Guyonvarc'h, 'L'ivresse des Ulates' (*Ogam* 12) 1960, 487–506 & (*Ogam* 13) 1961, 343–360; J. Gantz, *Early Ir. Myths and Sagas*, Harm. 1981.
Lit.: T. Ó Concheanainn, 'The Manuscript Tradition of M. U.' (*Celtica* 19) 1987, 13–30.

Mes Gegra (Ir. /m'es 'g'eɣra/). A king of Leinster in the tales of the → Ulster Cycle. The story → *Cath Étair* tells of how the warrior → Conall Cernach slays him in single combat and takes his brain to Ulster as a trophy. In the story → *Aided Chonchobuir* → Cet mac Mágach of Connacht uses the dead king's brain, mixed with lime, as ammunition for his sling, dealing the king → Conchobar mac Nesa of Ulster a mortal blow.

Meyer, Kuno (1858–1919). Celticist, younger brother of the ancient historian Eduard Meyer (1855–1930). Born in Hamburg, after studying philology with Ernst → Windisch and others, he taught German language and literature at the University of Liverpool from 1884 to 1911. His main scholarly interest was Irish language and literature, which he sought to make accessible to a wider public through editions and translations (into English). In 1903, on his initiative, the → School of Irish Learning in Dublin was founded. He was responsible for founding two specialist journals for Celtic studies: in Germany, together with Ludwig Christian → Stern, the *Zeitschrift für celtische Philologie*; in Ireland, together with John → Strachan, the journal *Ériu*. In 1911 M. succeeded Heinrich → Zimmer to the Chair in Celtic Philology in Berlin, which he held until his death. The cities of Dublin and Cork granted him honorary citizenship in 1912 for his contributions to Irish language and culture.
Lit.: S. Ó Lúing, *K. M. 1858–1919*, Du. 1991.

Miach (Ir. /m'iax/). A son of the physician → Dian Cécht in the story of the Battle of Mag Tuired (→ *Cath Maige Tuired*). When his father replaces the deposed king → Nuadu's hand, which has been chopped off, with a hand of silver, M. speaks a magic charm which causes the artificial limb to grow a covering of skin. Incensed at this intervention, Dian Cécht slays his own son. Over his grave there grow 365 herbs, corresponding to the number of his joints and sinews; these are picked by the dead man's sister and arranged according to their healing qualities. Dian Cécht however, out of jealousy, muddles the herbs up, with the effect that the knowledge of their healing powers is lost.

Midir (Ir. /'m'ið'ir'/). In the tales of the → Mythological Cycle a prince of the → Tuatha Dé Danann. He plays a major role in the story → *Tochmarc Étaíne*, as the foster-father of the elf → Oengus and husband of the titular heroine Étaín.

migration of souls → reincarnation.

migrations → history.

Míl (Ir. /m'i:l'/). Mythical ancestor of the Irish in the "Book of the Invasions of Ireland" (→ *Lebor Gabála Érenn*). His forefathers are said to be descendants of Japheth, one of the sons of Noah. According to the *Lebor Gabála* they first lived in the land of the Scythians and later in Egypt, where they were persecuted. After diverse adventures they are said to have made their way by ship to Spain, where M. was born. Both among the Scythians and in Egypt he distinguishes himself as a general. He is said to have had a total of eight sons by the daughters of the king of the Scythians and of the Pharaoh of Egypt; after the death of their father these sons took possession of Ireland and divided the island among themselves.

It would appear that the tradition concerning M. and his sons originated in the early Middle Ages under the influence of writings from the Old Testament and works of Latin literature. The legend of the Scythian and Spanish origins of the Irish is based in all probability on etymological speculations concerning links between the Latin terms Scythae "Scythians" and Scoti "Irish" on the one hand, and (H)iberia "Spain" and Hibernia "Ireland" on the other.

Minerva. Goddess of arts and crafts in the Roman religion. From the end of the 3rdC BC she was equated with the Greek goddess Athene. The name M. occurs in → Caesar to denote a Celtic deity. According to his account the Gauls believed that M. taught the first principles of arts and crafts (Bell. Gall. 6, 17). A Gaulish M. also occurs in the Roman author Justinus, who in the 3rdC AD compiled a selection from the now lost historical work of Pompeius Trogus. He describes how during the siege of the city of Marseille a goddess appears to the leader of the besieging army in a dream. This apparition terrifies him so much that he abandons the siege. Later he recognises the model for the apparition in a statue of M. in Marseille (Epitome 43,4f). The cult of M. in Gaul is also attested in literature by the Christian writers Salvianus of Marseille (De Gubernatione Dei 6,60) and Gregory of Tours (De miraculis Sancti Martini 17,5). As late as the 7thC Bishop Eligius of Noyon urges women engaged in weaving, dyeing or other work not to appeal to M. (Vita Sancti Eligii 2,16). Which Celtic goddess is concealed behind the name M. in these instances, is far from clear.

In inscriptions M. is identified with the goddesses → Belisama and → Sulis. Among the visual depictions of the Gaulish M. the head of a bronze statue deserves mention; it dates from early in the 1stC AD and was found in 1913 near Kerguilly in the Dép. of Finistère. It is now in the Musée de Bretagne in Rennes.

In the insular Celtic tradition it is the figure of → Brigit in particular who retains some characteristics of M.

Lit.: R. Sanquer, 'La grande statuette de bronze de Kerguilly en Dinéault (Finistère)' (*Gallia* 31) 1973, 61–80; J.-J. Hatt, 'La divinité féminine souveraine chez les Celtes continentaux d'après l'épigraphie gallo-romaine et l'art celtique' (*CRAI*) 1981, 12–30.

mistletoe. An evergreen plant with a short stem that lives as a parasite on various deciduous trees and conifers. Its fruit is eaten by birds and the seed thus propagated. According to → Pliny the Elder (Hist. Nat. 16, 249–251) nothing was more sacred to the → druids than mistletoe, and the tree on which it grew, provided it was an → oak. His account has it that such mistletoe was very rarely found and was approached with great reverence. The most favourable time for this was regarded as the sixth day after the new moon, when the moon was rising in strength, but not yet full. "They call the mistletoe by a native word that means 'all-healer'. After preparing a ritual sacrifice and a banquet under the tree according to their custom, they lead up two white bulls, whose horns are bound for the first time on this occasion. A priest in white vestments climbs the tree and cuts the mistletoe down with a golden sickle. It is caught in a white cloak. Then they slaughter the sacrificial animals, praying to God to render his gift propitious to those on whom he has bestowed it. They believe that mistletoe given in drink will impart fertility on any animal that is barren and regard it as an antidote to all poisons."

Moccus. Celtic god equated with → Mercury on the basis of the → interpretatio romana in a votive inscription from Langres (CIL XIII 5676). The name is thought to be cognate with Ir. mucc and Welsh mochyn "pig".

Modron ferch Afallach (Welsh /'modron verx a 'vaɫax/). The mother of the boy → Mabon in the story → *Culhwch ac Olwen*. He is abducted at birth and later rescued by → Arthur and his retinue. One of the → *Trioedd Ynys Prydein* describes M. as the mother also of the brother and sister → Owein fab Urien and → Morfudd ferch Urien. The older form of the name, attested in inscriptions, is → Matrona (Lat. pl. → Matronae).

Mogetius. Celtic god identified with → Mars on the basis of the → interpretatio romana. His name appears in two votive inscriptions from Bourges (CIL XIII 1193) and Seggau in Styria (CIL III 5320).

Mog Ruith (Ir. /moɣ Ruθ'/. A druid versed in magic said to have lived in the first or third century AD. According to a story preserved in the → "Yellow Book of Lecan" and in the → "Book of Ballymote", he was the son of an Irish sage (éces) and a British slave-girl taken in war. His tutors in the magic arts are said to be not only the druids of Ireland, but also the magician Simon

Magus mentioned in the New Testament (Acts of the Apostles 8). The name M. was explained with reference to a king named Roth mac Riguill as meaning "servant of Roth". Other authors interpreted it as meaning Magus Rotarum, i.e. "the Wheel Magician", and attributed to M. the ability to predict the future with the aid of wheels. It is said that M. was the only man prepared to cut the head off John the Baptist, and that this crime brought cold, famine and sickness upon all the Irish.

Lit.: K. Müller-Lisowski, 'Texte zur M. R. Sage' (ZCP 14) 1923, 145–163.

Moltinus. Celtic god whose name is found on an inscription from Mâcon in the settlement region of the → Aedui (CIL XIII 2585), and on a curse-tablet (cf. → defixio) from Wilten-Veldidena near Innsbruck. Etymologically the name is cognate with Ir. molt and Welsh mollt, "ram". The corresponding Gaulish word has survived in French mouton, English mutton.

Mona (Welsh Môn). In classical → ethnography the name of the island of Anglesey, off the north-west coast of Wales. According to → Tacitus (Ann. 14, 29–30) the Roman troops under their commander-in-chief Suetonius Paulinus met with fierce resistance during the conquest of the island in 60 AD. The Celtic warriors lined the shore, supported by torch-bearing women in black robes and with dishevelled hair, while → druids, lifting their hands to heaven, called down the curse of the gods on the invaders. After a few moments the legionaries overcame their stupefaction at the sight of this scene, cut down the island's defenders and destroyed the sacred groves of the island. Taking this description of the Roman historian as his starting-point, the Welsh antiquarian Henry → Rowlands, at the beginning of the 18thC, popularised the idea that M. was one of the main strongholds of the British druids. An authentic Celtic place of worship dating back to pre-Roman times was discovered there in 1942/43, on the bank of the lake → Llyn Cerrig Bach on the west coast of the island.

Lit.: F. Lynch, *Prehistoric Anglesey*, Llangefni 1970.

Mongán (Ir. /'moŋgaːn/). Historically attested king of the 7thC AD, focal point of many later legends. He came to be regarded as a son of the sea-god → Manannán mac Lir, possessing close contacts with the world of the fairies (→ síd) and was thought to have the ability to take on the shape of various animals at will. A late reworking of this tradition is the story → *Compert Mongáin ocus serc Duibe Lacha do Mongán*.

Mont Lassois. Hill not far from Châtillon-sur-Seine in the Dép. of Côte-d'Or, site in the 6th/5thC BC of one of the biggest early Celtic → princely seats. Less than three miles south of the hill a total of five → princely graves were found, among them the famous grave of → Vix.

Lit.: R. Joffroy, *L'oppidum de Vix et la civilisation hallstattienne finale*, P. 1969; id., *Vix et ses trésors*, P. 1979.

moon → time.

Morann (Ir. /'moraN). Wise judge of legendary fame, said to have lived in the 1stC AD. He was thought to have been the author of the mirror for princes entitled → *Audacht Morainn*, and one of the few people to merit salvation before the christianisation of Ireland. Tradition holds that M. wore a collar (id, sín) which always contracted about his neck when he was in danger of pronouncing an unjust verdict. Another source holds that the collar indicated the guilt or innocence of the accused by contracting about the neck of the guilty man.

Mo(r)dred (and similar forms). English, French and German forms of the Welsh name → Medrawd.

Morfran fab Tegid (Welsh /'morvran va:b 'tegid/). A son of the sorceress → Ceridwen in the story → *Hanes Taliesin*. His mother prepares for him a drink whereby he is to acquire the gift of prophecy and poetry, but Ceridwen's servant → Gwion Bach anticipates him. M. is referred to as one of the advisors of → Arthur in the story → *Breuddwyd Rhonabwy*. In the tale → *Culhwch ac Olwen* M. is said to have escaped unscathed in the Battle of → Camlan because everyone thought he was a demon on account of his ugliness.

Morfudd ferch Urien (Welsh /'morvið verx 'irjen/). The daughter of the king → Urien of Rheged in the story → *Culhwch ac Olwen*. According to one of the → *Trioedd Ynys Prydein* her mother was → Modron ferch Afallach. Another triad makes her the beloved of → Cynon fab Clydno. A poet of the 14thC also alludes to this tradition, although no legend dealing with the subject has survived.

Morganwg, Iolo → Williams, Edward.

Moritasgus. Celtic god identified with → Apollo in two inscriptions from → Alesia (CIL XIII 11240 and 11241). In another inscription from Alesia (AE 1965, 181) Apollo M. appears as the partner of the goddess → Damona.

Morrígain (Ir. /'moRi:yin'/) or (later forms) Morrígu/Mórrígu). War-goddess, the original meaning of whose name was presumably "mare-queen" (cf. Engl. nightmare and O. Ir. rígain "queen"). Later the word was reinterpreted as "great (Ir. mór) queen". M. is held to be the sister of the war-goddesses → Bodb and → Macha, with whom she is indeed sometimes identified. In the story of the Battle of Mag Tuired (→ *Cath Maige Tuired*) M. mates with the → Dagda before the decisive battle, and promises him and his people her aid in the fight against the → Fomoire. In the tale of the Cattle Raid of Cuailnge

(→ *Táin Bó Cuailnge*) M. approaches the hero → Cú Chulainn in the form of a beautiful young woman, an eel, a wolf and a heifer, seeking to hinder him in his fight against the army of the royal couple → Ailill and → Medb.

Lit.: J. Carey, 'Notes on the Irish War-Goddess' (*Éigse* 19) 1982/83, 263–275; F. Le Roux & C. Guyonvarc'h, M. – *Bodb – Macha: La Souveraineté guerrière de l'Irlande*, Rennes 1983; R. Clark, 'Aspects of the M. in Early Irish Poetry' (*Irish Univ. Review* 17) 1987, 223–236.

Morris-Jones, John (1864–1929). Celticist, born on the island of Anglesey. After studying mathematics and Celtic philology in Oxford, he taught Welsh language and literature in Bangor from 1889. Among his chief works are *A Welsh Grammar, Historical and Comparative* (1913) and *Cerdd Dafod*, a description and analysis of the classical Welsh poetic metres, written in Welsh. To the book *The Welsh People* (1900) by John → Rhŷs and David Brynmore-Jones M. contributed a section on "Pre-Aryan Syntax in Insular Celtic", in which he examined the influence of pre-Celtic → substrata on Irish and Welsh; he was one of the first to point to correspondences in the syntax of the insular Celtic languages and the Hamitic languages of North Africa. For his services to Welsh culture M. was ennobled in 1918.

Lit.: A. James, J. M., Car. 1987.

Morte Arthure. Title of a Middle English alliterative poem dating from c. 1400. The anonymous author tells in some 4346 lines of the conflict between → Arthur and the Roman emperor, his victorious march on Rome and his death in battle against the traitor Mordrede (→ Medrawd). The plot of the poem follows for the most part the works of → Geoffrey of Monmouth and his adaptors → Wace and → Layamon. It in turn influenced in particular Sir Thomas → Malory. M. A. is not to be confused with *Le Morte Arthur*, a Middle English strophic poem which was also written c. 1400.

Lit.: K. H. Göller (ed.), *The Alliterative M. A.*, C. 1981.

Morven (Scots Gaelic mór-bheinn, "great mountain"). In James → Macpherson's "Works of Ossian" the realm of King → Fingal in the west of the Scottish Highlands. It is an invention of Macpherson, not known in the older Celtic tradition.

mother-goddesses → Anu, → Matronae/Matres.

Moytura → Mag Tuired.

Mšecké Žehrovice. Place about 17 miles west of Prague near which a Celtic settlement of the La Tène period and a → *Viereckschanze* have been excavated. In 1943 a sandstone head was found there, one of the most expressive creations of Celtic → art. Apparently it was broken into several parts in the late 2ndC BC and then buried together with some fragments of pottery and animal bones. It may now be seen in the National Museum of Prague.

Lit.: R. & V. Megaw, 'The Stone Head from M. Ž.' (*Antiquity* 62) 1988, 630–641.

Mugain (Ir. /'muɣin'/). Wife of the king → Conchobar mac Nesa of Ulster in the stories of the → Ulster Cycle. She is said to be the daughter of the king → Eochaid Fedlech and the sister of Queen → Medb of Connacht.

Muirchertach mac Erca (Ir. /'mur'çertax mak 'erka/). Historically attested king of the 6thC AD, concerning whom many sagas evolved in later times, the best known of which is → *Aided Muirchertaig meic Erca*.

Muirchú (Ir. /'mur'xu:/). Irish cleric of the 7thC who composed a Latin life of St. → Patrick c. 670.

Mullo. Celtic god equated with → Mars on the basis of the → interpretatio romana. There is no consensus regarding the etymology of the name, Lat. mulus, "mule", and Ir. mul "hill, heap" both having been adduced. With regard to the latter possibility, the custom to which → Caesar refers (Bell. Gall. 6,17), whereby the Gauls brought all their booty to one site and piled it up into a hill (cumulus), has been brought into the argument. Inscriptions dedicated to M. have been found in Craon (CIL XIII 3096), Nantes (CIL XIII 3101 and 3102), Rennes (CIL XIII 3148 and 3149; AE 1969/70 405) and Allonnes (*ILTG* 343–345).

Lit.: Ch.-J. Guyonvarc'h, 'Le théonyme gaulois (Mars) M.' (*Ogam* 12) 1960, 452–458.

Murphy, Gerard (1901–1959). Celticist, born in Northern Ireland. After studying classical and Irish philolgy he worked at first under R. I. → Best in the Irish National Library in Dublin. From 1930 he taught Celtic philology at University College (Dublin). Apart from being founding editor of the journal *Éigse* (1939ff), he published groundbreaking studies of the Finn Cycle (*Duanaire Finn* II–III, 1933–1954), a bilingual selected edition and commentary on Old and Middle Irish poetry (*Early Irish Lyrics*, 1956) and two descriptions of early Irish literature aimed at a wider audience: *Saga and Myth in Ancient Ireland* and *The Ossianic Lore and Romantic Tales of Medieval Ireland* (both 1955).

Murus Gallicus (Lat. "Gaulish Wall"). A characteristic mode of fortifying late Celtic towns (→ oppida). It consisted of a box-shaped arrangement of balks, all placed horizontally at right angles to one another, and nailed together. The inner part of the box arrangement was filled with earth and gravel, and the facade stopped up with blocks of stone. According to → Caesar (Bell. Gall. 7,23) this construction was equally resistant to fire and battering rams during a siege. The distribution of the M. was restricted for the most part to the area left of the Rhine and a few sites in southern Germany. The eastern Celtic oppida in Bohemia and Moravia are, by contrast, characterised by what is known as the *Pfostenschlitzmauer* (post slit wall); vertical posts were erected at regular intervals, linked by horizontal beams with earth and stone piled up behind them. The gaps at the front between the vertical posts were lined with blocks of stone.

Two typical modes of fortifying Celtic oppida: Murus Gallicus and *Pfostenschlitzmauer*.

music. Little is known of the music of the ancient Celts. The primary reason for this is the fact that there is no surviving documentation of music made by the Celts themselves, and Greek and Roman authors paid no great heed to this subject. Moreover, archaeological finds and visual depictions of musical instruments are similarly rare. The Celtic war-trumpet ($\rightarrow$ carnyx) is mentioned by several authors, as is a stringed instrument resembling the lyre, with which the bards accompanied their songs (cf. $\rightarrow$ Diodoros of Sicily 5,31,2). Depictions of such string instruments, to a certain extent stylised, are to be seen on many Celtic $\rightarrow$ coins.

As for the songs of the bards, a distinction between eulogies and invectives was made as early as Diodoros. Classical authors also mention songs concerning heroic deeds of the past and battle-songs which were accompanied by the rhythmical beating of weapons (cf. $\rightarrow$ Athenaios 4,37 and 46,49; $\rightarrow$ Lucan 1,447ff; $\rightarrow$ Livy 10,26; 21,28; 23,24; 38,17; $\rightarrow$ Polybios 3,44 and $\rightarrow$ Diodoros 5,29,4). In all probability some prayers and incantations were also accompanied by song.

Depictions of dancers on the bronze couch of $\rightarrow$ Hochdorf and the bronze statuettes of $\rightarrow$ Neuvy-en-Sullias show that dances also played a role in worship.

In the Celtic literatures of the Middle Ages songs and other forms of musical performance are frequently mentioned. Particularly in Ireland, they are markedly characteristic of the world of the fairies ($\rightarrow$ síd) and the Islands of the Blessed. Our understanding of musical practice, however, is rendered difficult by the fact that such descriptions are often fantastic in nature and we do not know the exact meaning of some of the vocabulary. Illustrations in manuscripts and on stone sculptures can only be adduced to a limited extent, as visual representations even in early times are frequently dependant on foreign models. It is only on rare occasions that outsiders such as → Giraldus Cambrensis have committed their experiences of the music of the Celtic countries to writing.

There are scarcely any medieval survivals of those musical instruments which have been regarded as typically Celtic since modern times began. The oldest harp is that known as the harp of Brian Boru (now in Trinity College, Dublin), dating from the 15th/16thC. The bagpipes are not attested in Ireland and Scotland before the 16thC. Presumably they came to Central Europe from the eastern Mediterranean or the Balkans, where they are attested as early as the 12thC.

It was only in the 17thC that the music of the Celtic lands began to be recorded in notation. In many cases it is no longer possible to establish whether this notation is a true mirror of musical practice or whether it has been adapted to the taste of a certain time or a certain public. Recently, records and tapes have attempted to preserve the musical traditions of the Celtic lands for posterity.

Lit.: O. Seewald, 'Die Lyrendarstellung der ostalpinen Hallstattkultur', in: Festschrift A. Orel, V. & Wi. 1960, 159–171; J.-M. Guilcher, La tradition de la danse populaire en Basse-Bretagne, P. 1963; F. Collinson, The Trad. and Nat. Music of Scotland, Lo. 1966; F. L. Harrison, Music in Medieval Britain, Lo. 1968; B. Breathnach, Folk Music and Dances of Ireland, Du. 1971; O. Ellis, The Story of the Harp in Wales, Car. 1980; F. Harrison, 'Celtic musics', in: K. H. Schmidt (ed.), Geschichte und Kultur der Kelten, Hei. 1986, 252–263; A. Bruford, 'Song and recitation in early Ireland' (Celtica 21) 1990, 61–74; J. V. S. Megaw, 'Music Archaeology and the Ancient Celts', in: The Celts, Mi. 1991, 643–648; K. Sanger & A. Kinnaird, Tree of Strings – A history of the harp in Scotland, Shillinghill Temple 1992; Le Carnyx et la Lyre. Archéologie musicale en Gaule celtique et romaine, Besançon 1993; B. Ó Madagáin, 'Echoes of Magic in the Gaelic Song Tradition', in: C. J. Byrne et al. (eds.), Celtic Languages and Celtic Peoples, Halifax 1992, 125–140.

Myrddin (Welsh /'mərðin/; Engl. Merlin/). Famed poet and seer in the Welsh sources. He is said to have belonged to the retinue of the king → Gwenddoleu fab Ceidiaw and to have lost his reason in the battle of → Arfderydd. Fearing Gwenddoleu's enemy, → Rhydderch Hael, he sought refuge in the woods of Scotland; there, in solitude, he acquired the gift of prophecy.

M. became widely known by the name Merlin(us) because of the influence of the Historia Regum Britanniae of → Geoffrey of Monmouth. From the Welsh tradition Geoffrey borrowed little more than the name and the characterisation of Merlin as a famous seer. However, in his later verse epic Vita Merlini Geoffrey adapted the legend of Merlin as a wild man of the woods, reminiscent of the Irish story → Buile Suibne. In contrast to Geoffrey's History of the Kings of Britain this work found little resonance.

The Arthurian Revival of the mid-19thC, and in particular the rediscovery of → Malory's *Morte dArthur*, reawakened interest in Merlin in Britain. In particular, Alfred Lord Tennyson's emphasis on Merlin in his treatment of the Arthurian material (*Enid and Nimuë*, 1857; *Vivien* 1859; *Idylls of the King*, 1869) led to Merlin becoming a frequent subject of portraiture and photography. Two of the Pre-Raphaelites' murals for the Oxford Union (1857) have Merlin as their subject. One of these, *Merlin being Imprisoned Beneath a Stone by the Damsel of the Lake*, is by Edward Burne-Jones, who was to paint two further major Merlin pictures, the gouache *Merlin and Nimuë* (1861) and *The Beguiling of Merlin* (begun 1869–1873; finished 1874–1877). Julia Margaret Cameron had her husband Henry Hay Cameron pose for her photographic treatment of Merlin's enchantment to illustrate a new edition of Tennyson's *Idylls* (1874). In 1898 Mark Twain's *A Connecticut Yankee at the Court of King Arthur* cast Merlin as an impostor and villain; the novel has inspired more films than any other Arthurian or neo-Arthurian work, among them the Bing Crosby musical (1949). Merlin is a central character in John Boorman's film *Excalibur* (1981), a loose treatment of Malory. Merlin has continued to be a central character in British and American fiction, notably in the novels of T. H. White (*The Once and Future King; The Sword in the Stone*, 1939–1941, the latter filmed by Walt Disney in 1963; *The Book of Merlyn*, 1977); C. S. Lewis (*That Hideous Strength*, 1945); no doubt he also influenced J. R. R. Tolkien's figure of Gandalf in *The Hobbit* (1937) and *The Lord of the Rings* (1954–1955). Postwar Merlin novels include Mary Stewart's trilogy (*The Crystal Cave, The Hollow Hills, The Last Enchantment*, 1970–1979), and Marion Zimmer Bradley's *The Mists of Avalon* (1988). Most recently, M. has become a central figure in New Age pseudo-mythology (R. J. Stewart, *The Way of Merlin*, 1991; Ean Begg and Deike Rich, *On the Trail of Merlin*, 1991).

In Germany, the figure of Merlin was especially popular among the Romantics. Worthy of note are the *Geschichte des Zauberers Merlin* ("The Story of the Magician Merlin", 1804) by Dorothea Schlegel (1763–1839), the poem *Merlin der Wilde* ("Merlin the Wild", 1831) by Ludwig Uhland (1787–1862) and the important role played by the Celtic poet in the *Waldlieder* ("Songs of the Forest", 1843–1844) of Nikolaus Lenau (1802–1850). More recently, the material has been reworked by Tankred Dorst (b. 1925) in the play *Merlin oder das Wüste Land* ("Merlin or the Waste Land", 1981).

Lit.: A. O. H. Jarman, 'Early stages in the development of the M. Legend', in: R. Bromwich & R. B. Jones (eds.), *Astudiaethau ar yr Hengerdd*, Car. 1978, 326–349; J. Watson and M. Fries (eds.), *The Figure of Merlin in the 19th and 20th Centuries*, Lampeter 1988; P. Goodrich (ed.), *The Romance of Merlin*, Lo. 1990; A. A. Macdonald, *The Figure of Merlin in Thirteenth Century French Romance*, NY 1990; A. O. H. Jarman, 'The Merlin legend and the Welsh tradition of prophecy', in: R. Bromwich et al. (eds.), *The Arthur of the Welsh*, Car. 1991, 117–145; S. Brugger-Hackett, *Merlin in der europäischen Literatur des Mittelalters*, St. 1991.

Mythological Cycle. Modern term referring to a series of Old and Middle Irish stories whose narrative focus is on elves and fairies, rather than mortals. In Irish the protagonists of these stories are generally termed fir/mná/áes síde "men/women/people of the → síd", because the hills and mountains naturally occurring in the country and the artificially created, piled up gravemounds of the pre-Celtic population of Ireland are regarded as their dwellings. Many texts identify the áes síde with the → Tuatha Dé Danann, regarded by modern scholarship as euhemerised figures of pre-Christian Irish → mythology (cf. → euhemerism).

The most important narrative in the Cycle is the story of the Battle of Mag Tuired (→ *Cath Maige Tuired*), which treats of the fight of the Tuatha Dé Danann against the daemonic → Fomoire. A similar tale is → *Tochmarc Étaíne*, whereas → *Aided Chlainne Tuirenn* is of a later period, and the two tales → *Aislinge Oenguso* and → *Serglige Con Culainn*, although they incorporate mythic elements, are customarily included in the → Ulster Cycle. Motifs and material from pre-Christian mythology are also reworked in the → *Dindsenchas*, the → *Lebor Gabála Érenn*, and the stories termed → echtrae and → immram.

Lit. → literature, → mythology.

mythology. In the terminology of comparative religion m. refers to the sum total of the religious narratives of a culture, which are thought to interpret and at the same time affirm human experience as well as religious and social institutions in a wider sense. As the Celtic peoples formed neither a cultural nor a political unity, they did not possess a uniform mythology, but rather a host of different myths which would appear to have been compatible only to a limited extent. Our knowledge of the subject is highly fragmentary in view of the fact that in the oldest period Celtic m. was handed down exclusively in the oral tradition.

Details concerning → gods and goddesses, concepts of the → next world, the creation (→ cosmogony) and the end of the world (→ eschatology) first occur in the form of sparse and unsystematic allusions in classical → ethnography. Moreover, our understanding of these is impeded by the employment of Greek and Roman terms in all these sources, as well as the dominant principle of the → interpretatio romana (or graeca).

The narratives of Irish and Welsh → literature give fuller accounts, but these were recorded after → christianisation. In consequence they are no true reflection of pre-Christian mythology, but rather a creative interpretation from the point of view of medieval Christendom. Evaluating these sources from the point of view of comparative religion therefore requires detailed knowledge of the medieval Irish or Welsh sources, and the results of such study need to be constantly reviewed in the light of as wide-ranging comparative material as possible.

Lit.: P. MacCana, Celtic Mythology, Lo. 1983; D. Bellingham, An Introduction to Celtic Mythology, Lo. 1990; M. Green, Celtic Myths, Lo. 1993.

Nabelcus. Celtic god identified with → Mars on the basis of the → interpretatio romana. His cult is attested in three votive inscriptions from Saint-Didier in the Dép. of Vaucluse (CIL XII 1169–1171).

Lit.: G. Barruol, 'Mars N. et Mars Albiorix' (Ogam 15) 1963, 345–368.

names → place names, → personal names, → tribal names.

Namnetae. In classical → ethnography a Celtic tribe in the area north of the lower Loire. The name survives in that of the city of Nantes, whose Roman name was Condevincum.

Nantosuelta. Celtic goddess who appears on inscriptions and in visual depictions from Roman Gaul; she occurs sometimes alone, sometimes as the companion of the god → Sucellus (cf. → gods, pairs of). Her characteristic attribute is a sceptre, which has at the top a little house or hut and perhaps designates N. as a patroness of home and hearth.

Nautae Parisiaci ("Seamen of the City of Paris"). The name given to themselves in a Latin votive inscription (CIL XIII 3026 = ILTG 331) by the donors of a monument to the god → Jupiter. The remains were found in March 1711 beneath the cathedral of Notre-Dame in Paris. It is thought that the monument consisted originally of eight stone blocks with a square base, placed on top of one another. Two of these belonged together in each case, with the effect that 4 x 4 surfaces for images became available. As three of these eight blocks are missing, only four of these surfaces are preserved complete, with only the upper part of the other twelve surviving. One of these incomplete surfaces bears the votive inscription rather than an image. According to the inscription the monument was erected during the rule of the emperor Tiberius (14–37 AD). On the other fifteen areas it has proved possible to identify several Graeco-Roman divinities. On the basis of inscriptions or characteristic attributes the following have been identified: the → Dioscures, Fortuna, → Jupiter, → Mars, → Mercury, → Venus, and → Vulcan. There are also depictions of the Celtic gods → Cernunnos, → Esus, → Tarvos Trigaranus and → Smertrius, all of whom are named (cf. RIG II,1 *L-14). The monument is therefore of great importance for the study of Celtic religion and of Gallo-Roman art. It may now be seen in the Musée de Cluny in Paris.

Lit.: P.-M. Duval, 'Le groupe de bas-reliefs des "N. P." ' (Monuments et mémoires de la Fondation Eugène Piot 48,2) 1956, 64–90 (= id., Travaux sur la Gaule, R. 1989, I 433–462).

Navan Fort

Navan Fort → Emain Macha.

Navigatio Sancti Brendani → Brendan.

Nechtan (Ir. /'N'extan/). Husband of the → Bóand in the stories of the → Mythological Cycle. His residence is said to be Síd Nechtain, the "Elf-hill (→ síd) of N." by the source of the River Boyne.

Neirin (Welsh /'neirin/). One of the first poets of the British Celts (→ Cynfeirdd) known to us by name. In later literature his name is usually given as Aneirin, but the original form N. occurs in the → Historia Brittonum, compiled c. 830. According to the *Historia*, N. was a contemporary of the poet → Taliesin in the late 6thC, living in northern England or southern Scotland. His native language was therefore presumably → Cumbrian, of which we know little. Tradition has it that he was the author of the poem Y → *Gododdin*.
> Lit.: M. E. Owen, 'Hwn yw e Gododin. Aneirin ae Cant', in: R. Bromwich & R. B. Jones (eds.), *Astudiaethau ar yr Hengerdd*, Car. 1978, 123–150 (in Engl.); P. K. Ford, 'The Death of Aneirin' (*BBCS* 34) 1987, 41–50.

Néit (Ir. /N'e:d'/). Name of an Irish god of war according to an entry in the Glossary of Bishop Cormac (→ *Sanas Chormaic*). His wife is named as → Nemain.

Nemain (Ir. /'N'evin'/). Wife of the war-god → Néit. She was credited with the ability to confuse the senses of warriors in battle. Comparable war-goddesses are → Bodb, → Morrígain and → Macha.

Nemed (Ir. /'N'ev'eð/). In the "Book of the Invasions of Ireland" (→ *Lebor Gabála Érenn*) the leader of a group of settlers who are said to have taken possession of Ireland after the death of the heirs of → Partholón. The "Book of the Invasions" tells of how N. and many of his followers are killed off by a plague. The survivors are forced by the → Fomoire to pay a yearly tribute of two thirds of their corn, their milk and their children. In consequence a large proportion of the tribe deserts the island. The survivors of these emigrants are said to be the ancestors of the → Fir Bolg and the → Tuatha Dé Danann.

nemeton. Celtic word related to Gk. némos "glade" and Lat. nemus "(sacred) grove". Its original meaning was probably "sacred grove", as has been concluded from etymology and from a reference in the Indiculus superstitionum et paganiarum, an 8thC Frankish source. There the word nimidae (pl.) occurs as a synonym of sacra silvarum "wood shrines". Moreover → Strabo (Geogr. 12,5,1) mentions a drunémeton "oak grove" as the place of assembly of the

→ Galatians of Asia Minor. That the Celts had such sacred groves is also mentioned by authors such as → Lucan (Pharsalia 1,454), → Pliny the Elder (Hist. Nat. 16,249) and → Tacitus (Ann. 14,30). The original meaning shifted in that n. later came to signify in addition a shrine or temple built of stone. This is attested already in Gaulish, in an inscription written in the Greek alphabet dedicated to the goddess → Belisama (RIG I G153). In Old Irish too, the word nemed, derived from n., could designate a building, as is attested by by the use of the word as a gloss on Lat. sacellum "little chapel" in a St. Gall manuscript. N. occurs in derivative words and compounds in many names of → gods, → place-names and → personal names. In all probability the word was borrowed into Etruscan at an early stage, given the occurrence of the genitive of a personal name *Nemetios.

> Lit.: K. H. Schmidt, 'Gallisch n. und Verwandtes' (Münchener Studien zur Sprachwissenschaft 12) 1958, 49–60; Ch.-J. Guyonvarc'h, '*nemos, nemetos, n.: les noms celtiques du "ciel" et du "sanctuaire"' (Ogam 12) 1960, 185–197; C. de Simone, 'Gallisch *Nemetios – etruskisch Nemetie' (Zeitschrift für vergleichende Sprachforschung 94) 1980, 198–202; ibid., 'Celtico nemeto "bosco sacro" ed i suoi derivati onomastici', in: Navicula Tübingensis: studia in honorem A. Tovar, T. 1984, 349–351; Les Bois sacrés, Naples 1993.

Nemetona. Celtic goddess whose name derives from the Celtic word → nemeton and characterises her as "she who belongs to the shrine". The worship of N. is attested by a dedication from Bath (RIB 140), and three votive inscriptions from Germany: Altrip, near Speyer (CIL XIII 6131), Klein-Winternheim near Mainz (CIL XIII 7253) and Trier (Fi 324). In three of the four inscriptions N. is the companion of the god → Mars, together with whom she was worshipped in temples in Klein-Winternheim and Trier.

Nera (Ir. /'N'era/). Titular hero of the story → Echtrae Nerai.

Nes (Ir. /N'es/) or Nesa. Mother of the king → Conchobar of Ulster in the tales of the → Ulster Cycle. The way she came by her name is recounted in the tale "How Conchobor was Begotten" (→ Compert Chonchobuir).

Neuvy-en-Sullias. Site near Orléans, on the left bank of the Loire, where during quarrying works in 1861 a cache of bronze statuettes of Gallo-Roman origin were found. These included a horse, a stag, three wild boars, and nine human figures, each of them different. The posture of the head, arms and legs suggests that they are male and female dancers. The significance or function of this group of figurines remains however unclear, in the absence of comparable finds. It is noticeable that the proportions of the five male and four female figures clearly differ from those of Greek, Roman and Etruscan bronzes. The base of the horse statuette bears a votive inscription to a Celtic god called Rudiobus (CIL XIII 3071). It is thought that all the figures derive from a shrine of this god, and that they were only intended to be hidden for a short time at the site where they were found. The statuettes may now be seen in the Musée historique et archéologique in Orléans.

Lit.: S. Boucher, *Recherches sur les Bronzes figurés de Gaule préromaine et romaine*, R. 1976.

Newgrange → Brug na Bóinne.

next world, concepts of. Our knowledge of Celtic concepts of the next world prior to → christianisation is far from adequate. One indirect indication of their existence lies in the customs associated with death which are archaeologically attested. These point to the concept of a continuation of earthly life in the next world (cf. → death and burial). Accounts in classical → ethnography mention several times the belief in → reincarnation, although the terminology is influenced by Graeco-Roman philosophy and is therefore difficult to interpret. Isolated references to the concept of a realm of the dead beyond the sea have to be seen in the context of classical folk tales and may not necessarily possess any value as sources for the understanding of Celtic religion. The same applies to medieval Irish and Welsh stories which also rework fairy-tale motifs and are moreover always coloured by a Christian view of the world.

The next world proper is to be distinguished from insular Celtic beliefs in a land of the elves and fairies (Ir. → síd, Welsh → Annwfn), which is not thought of in terms of a realm of the dead (cf. → otherworld).

Lit.: → religion.

Niederzier. Site near Düren in the Rhineland where between 1977 and 1982 a Celtic settlement of the La Tène culture, dating from the 2nd/1stC BC, was the subject of archaeological excavation. Next to a ritual stake in the western part of the site two golden neck-rings, a golden arm-ring and 46 gold coins of c. 100 BC were found. The objects were presumably hidden at the site as a sacrifice or votive gift to a god. They are now in the Rheinisches Landesmuseum in Bonn.

Lit.: J. Göbel, et al., 'Der spätkeltische Goldschatz von N.' (*BJb* 191) 1991, 27–84.

Nisyen and **Efnisyen** (Welsh /'nisjen/ and /ev'nisjen/). Two halfbrothers on the maternal side of the king → Brân Fendigeid in the story → *Branwen ferch Lŷr*. In the narrator's words, it was N.'s habit to settle matters peacefully, no matter how hostile two parties were towards one another, whereas E. could incite to conflict even brothers who were devoted to one another. In the story of Branwen E. often appears as a troublemaker and by the murder of the king's son, Gwern, provokes the decisive battle between the kings Brân and Matholwch.

Nitiobroges. In classical → ethnography a Celtic tribe in the region of Agen in south-west France. The name characterises its bearers as people "who live in their own settlement areas" (cf. → Allobroges). The land of the N. was conquered by → Caesar in 58–51 BC, and in 27 BC became part of the Roman province of Aquitania.

Nodons or Nodens. Celtic god whose name has been compared with Gothic niutan "to achieve, attain" and nuta "catcher, fisherman". It may therefore have meant "fisher, hunter, catcher". In Roman times N. was identified with Mars on the basis of the → interpretatio romana. His cult is attested by two votive inscriptions, now lost, from Cockersand Moss in Lancashire (*RIB* 616 and 617), and three further inscriptions from a sanctuary dedicated to N. at Lydney Park in Gloucestershire (*RIB* 305–307). Among the figures of the insular Celtic tradition it is possible that → Lludd Llawereint and → Nuadu Argatlám retain characteristics of N.

> *Lit.:* F. Le Roux, 'Le dieu-roi N./Nuada' (*Celticum* 6) 1963, 425–454; J. Carey, 'N. in Britain and Ireland' (*ZCP* 40) 1984, 1–22; H. Wagner, 'Zur Etymologie von keltisch N., Ir. Nuadu, Kymr. Nudd/Lludd' (*ZCP* 41) 1986, 180–188.

Noínden Ulad (Ir. /ˈNoinˈdˈen ˈulað/) or *Ces Ulad* "The Debility of the Ulidians". Title of a story from the → Ulster Cycle, which purports to explain the weak state (ces, noínden) of the inhabitants of Ulster at the time of the beginning of the story of the Cattle Raid of Cuailnge (→ *Táin Bó Cuailnge*). The story survives in three versions, consistent for the most part, preserved in manuscripts which include the → "Yellow Book of Lecan" and the "Book of Leinster" (→ Lebor Laignech). The beginning tells of how the rich farmer Crunnchú boasts before the king of Ulster that his wife, Macha, is quicker than the swiftest horses of the king. The king has him arrested and threatens Macha, who is in an advanced state of pregnancy, that he will execute her husband if she does not immediately race against the royal horses. Macha is compelled to acquiesce, wins the race and in the end gives birth to twins amidst great pain, which is why from that point on the residence of the kings of Ulster is called → Emain Macha ("Macha's Twins"). Macha prophesies to the inhabitants of Ulster that as a punishment for this disgrace, whenever they are in peril they will be overcome by a state of weakness like that of a woman in labour.

> *Ed.:* V. Hull, 'N.U.: The Debility of the Ulidians' (*Celtica* 8) 1968, 1–42 (with trans.).
>
> *Trans.:* J. Gantz, *Early Ir. Myths and Sagas*, Harm. 1981.
>
> *Lit.:* B. K. Martin, ' "Truth" and "modesty": a reading of the Irish N.U.' (*Leeds Studies in English* 20) 1989, 99–117; E. M. Slotkin, 'Noínden: Its Semantic Range', in: A. T. E. Matonis & F. Melia (eds.), *Celtic Languages, Celtic Culture*, Van Nuys, Calif. 1990, 137–150.

Noísiu, Ardán and **Ainnle** (Ir. /'Noiʃu, 'arda:n, 'aN'l'e/). Eponymous heroes of the story → *Longas mac nUislenn.*

Noreia. Goddess worshipped under Roman rule in Carinthia, Styria and the bordering areas of Slovenia (cf. CIL III 4806, 4809, 4810, 5123, 5188, 5193 and 5300). The etymology of the name is obscure. It is therefore open to question whether N. was originally a goddess of the Celtic inhabitants or of the indigenous Illyrian population of these regions.

Nuadu Argatlám (Ir. /'nuaðu 'argadla:v/ "Nuadu of the Silver Hand"). King of the → Tuatha Dé Danann in the story of the Battle of Mag Tuired (→ *Cath Maige Tuired*). He lost his right arm in battle against the → Fir Bolg, and then obtained an artificial replacement, made of silver, from the doctor → Dian Cécht. Because of his injury he relinquished the kingship temporarily, but was reappointed before the decisive battle against the → Fomoire. He fell in battle against the daemonic → Balar. It is thought that N., like the Welsh saga character → Lludd Llawereint, preserves a recollection of the Celtic god → Nodons, who is attested in inscriptions.

Numantia. Presumably Celtic name of a fortified settlement on the Castilian plateau a few miles north-east of Soria. The resistance of the → Celtiberians against the Romans was concentrated there in the years from 153 to 133 BC. In 133 BC N. was conquered after being besieged for several months, and destroyed. Under Augustus a small Roman town arose on the site of the Celtiberian settlement.

numbers. Numbers certainly played a role in Celtic → religion, → art and presumably also in → magic, but our speculations concerning this are limited to conjecture. Appearances suggest that particular significance was attached to the numbers three (cf. → *Trioedd Ynys Prydein*), (3 x 3 =) nine, and thirty (cf. → time).

numismatics → coins.

Nutt, Alfred (1856–1910). Folklorist, born in London. Son of a bookseller and publisher, he devoted himself to the study of the pre-Christian religions of Europe, editing and publishing anthropological studies. Among his most important works in the Celtic area are his *Studies on the Legend of the Holy Grail* (1888), and the annotated edition and translation of the Irish sea-voyage narrative → *Immram Brain* (*The Voyage of Bran*, 2 vols., 1895–1897, in collaboration with Kuno → Meyer).

ó (Ir. /oː/, older forms: úa, óa). Meaning "grandson/ granddaughter/descendant of", it is a frequent component of Irish names (cf. → mac). The plural is Uí.

oak. According to the testimony of classical → ethnography the oak tree played a role of great importance in Celtic religion. → Strabo (Geogr. 12,5,1) refers to a drynémeton ("oak grove") as the place where the → Galatians of Asia Minor assembled. According to → Pliny the Elder (Hist. Nat. 16,249) nothing was more sacred to the → druids than → mistletoe and the tree on which it grew; the druids favoured oak groves for their rituals and conducted no sacrifices without oak leaves. Pliny therefore presumes that the druids may have received their name from the Greek word for oak (cf. Gk. drŷs "oak" and dryídēs "druid"). The → Berne Scholia, commenting on the work of the Roman poet → Lucan, hold that the druids derived their name from the oak because they inhabited remote groves, or because it was their custom to speak prophecies after eating acorns. The Greek philosopher Maximos of Tyre (2ndC AD) maintains that the Celts worshipped the god Zeus and that the Celtic symbol for Z. was a tall oak. A special meaning attaches to the oak in legal proceedings in the Loire area, according to the Latin comedy *Aulularia* (4thC AD). In the insular Celtic tradition, contrastingly, the oak is no more important than any other tree, nor is there any specific link between the druids and the oak in Irish and Welsh literature.

O'Brien, Michael Alphonsus (1892–1962). Celticist, born in Clonmel, Co. Tipperary. After studying at University College Dublin with Osborn → Bergin and in Berlin with Julius → Pokorny he was appointed Lecturer in Celtic at Queen's College, Belfast in 1926, and in 1947 became Senior Professor in the → School of Celtic Studies in Dublin. His most important work on Irish genealogies was published shortly before his death (*Corpus genealogiarum Hiberniae* 1962, repr. with an introduction by J. V. Kelleher 1976).

Ocelus. Celtic god, identified with → Mars on the basis of the → interpretatio romana. His cult is attested by three votive inscriptions from Carlisle (*RIB* 949) and Caerwent in South Wales (*RIB* 309 and 310).

O'Curry, Eugene (1796–1862). Palaeographer and historian, born in Southern Ireland. From 1834 to 1837 he worked with John → O'Donovan in the topographical and historical section of the Ordnance Survey of Ireland. Thereafter he earned a living translating, copying and cataloguing Irish manuscripts in Dublin, Oxford and London. In 1855 he was appointed to the chair in Irish History at the newly founded Catholic University in Dublin. His first lectures there were published in 1860 under the title *Lectures on the Manuscript Materials of Ancient Irish History*. A further series of lectures from the years 1857 to 1862 appeared posthumously under the title *Lectures on the manners and customs of the Ancient Irish* (3 vols., 1873).

Lit.: M. Tierney, 'E. O'C. and the Irish tradition' (*Studies* 51) 1962, 449–462.

O'Donovan, John (1809–1861). Palaeographer and philologist, born in Southern Ireland. For a time he worked together with Eugene → O'Curry in the topographical and historical section of the Ordnance Survey of Ireland. From 1840 onwards he produced many editions and translations of Irish manuscripts. His main work is the bilingual edition of an extensive collection of Irish annals dating from the 17thC known as the Annals of the Kingdom of Ireland or the Annals of the Four Masters, which appeared in seven volumes in 1848–1851 under the title *The Annals of the Kingdom of Ireland by the Four Masters*.

Lit.: P. Boyne, J. O'D. (1809–1861): a biography, Kilkenny 1987.

Oengus (Ir. /ˈoinɣus/). The son of the → Dagda and the → Bóand in the stories of the → Mythological Cycle. His second name is Mac ind Óc or (later) in Mac Óc "the young boy". The story → *Tochmarc Étaíne* tells of his birth and boyhood. It also describes how O. by cunning obtains possession of the elf-mound → Brug na Bóinne and in the cause of his foster-father → Midir seeks the hand of Étaín, the most beautiful woman in Ireland. The story → *Aislinge Oenguso* tells how O. himself, with the aid of the royal couple → Ailill and → Medb, wins a bride. O. appears as the protector of the pair of lovers, Diarmait and Gráinne, in the story → *Tóraigheacht Dhiarmada agus Ghráinne*.

Oengus mac Oengobann (Ir. /ˈoinɣus mak ˈoinɣovaN/; byname: "the Culdee" (→ Céli Dé)). Irish monk and hagiographer, a pupil of abbot Máel-Ruain of Tallaght, he lived as a hermit near the church he founded, Dísert Oengusa, in County Leix. He was the author, c. 830, of the Old Irish versified calendar of the saints, *Félire Oenguso*, which provides a short sketch of the Roman and Irish saints for every day of the year. Because of the paucity of dated Old Irish literary survivals the work is of great importance not only in terms of hagiography and the history of the Church, but also for the study of the Irish language.

offerings → sacrifices and offerings.

Ogam (Ir. /ˈoɣam/). The earliest Irish writing system. In its oldest known form it distinguishes between 20 different sounds by means of points and strokes placed on a continuous straight line. In all probability Ogam originated in the South of the Ireland in the 3rd or 4thC AD, under the influence of the Latin alphabet. The oldest evidence of its use consists in some 300 short inscriptions on stone which have been found in various parts of

Ireland, as well as in Wales, Devon, Cornwall and on the Isle of Man. Linguistic evidence suggests that the majority of these inscriptions date from the 5th/6thC. They include the oldest records of the Irish language, but for the most part this is limited to personal and tribal names. Knowledge of O. survived into modern times in Ireland, but its origins were a mystery by the Middle Ages. Sometimes the invention of O. is attributed to → Ogma mac Elathan. Many Irish sagas report that O. was used not merely for inscriptions on stone, but also for recording written communications on wood. It is however possible that this is merely a backward projection of medieval conceptions concerning the original use of Ogam into the distant past. Whether O. was also employed for magical purposes, like the Germanic runes, is doubted by modern scholars.

Lit.: D. McManus, A Guide to O., May. 1991.

Ogma (Ir. /'oɣma/). A warrior of the → Tuatha Dé Dannan in the story of the Battle of Mag Tuired (→ Cath Maige Tuired). On the paternal side he is a half-brother of the tyrannical king → Bres, on his mother's side a half-brother of Bres' antagonist, → Lug. While Bres ruled, O., like the → Dagda, was compelled to carry out menial tasks. After the tyrant was deposed, O. fought on the side of the Tuatha Dé Danann against Bres and his kinsmen of the people of the → Fomoire in the Battle of Mag Tuired. In some medieval texts O. is also regarded as the inventor of → Ogam, the earliest Irish script. This tradition may, however, only have originated in the Middle Ages, on the basis of the coincidence of names; the etymology of both Ogam and Ogma is obscure. Matters are further complicated by classical accounts of a Gaulish god of eloquence called → Ogmios.

Ogmios. Celtic god whose name, though not attested in inscriptions, occurs on two lead curse tablets (→ defixio), written in Latin, found in Bregenz in the Vorarlberg (Wa 8 and 9). As one of these tablets invokes O. together with → Dis Pater and → Aeracura, it is thought that he too is a god of the Underworld.

The description of O. in Greek by the travelling lecturer and satirist Lukian of Samosata (2ndC AD) is well-known. In a prolalia (prologue or introduction to a longish treatise on the arts) entitled Herakles, he writes that O. is the Celtic name for Hercules. He himself has seen an image in Gaul, depicting O. as a dark-skinned, bald old man in a lion's skin, with a club and a bow. The most curious aspect of the image was, however, that this aged Hercules was dragging behind him a large number of people by fine chains made of gold and amber. These chains were attached to Hercules' pierced tongue, and to the ears of the people following in his wake. A Gaul explained to Lukian that the Celts imagined the power of eloquence as personified not by Hermes, like the Greeks, but by Hercules, in view of his superior strength. Hercules was depicted as an old man because it is only in old age that eloquence becomes fully developed.

There are a number of difficulties regarding the interpretation of this account by Lukian. It is of course not certain whether the Greek author did in fact see an image in Gaul corresponding to every detail of his description. Above all, however, we cannot know whether the interpretation of the image as an allegorical figure representing eloquence is in fact that of a Gaul, or whether it is the invention of Lukian himself. If O. was in reality a god of the Underworld, the image might be a portrayal of him as a leader of those consecrated to death, or of the dead. The interpretation of O. as a god of eloquence is however possibly supported by the fact that in Irish tradition a character in the sagas named → Ogma (older form: Ogmae) is held to be the inventor of writing. For linguistic reasons one would then have to assume that the name O. was borrowed comparatively late from Gaulish into Irish, as otherwise the name would be Óme rather than Ogmae. Given the lack of comparable Gaulish loan-words in Irish this seems doubtful. The character and function of the god thus remain a mystery in spite of all the efforts of scholarship.

Lit.: F. Benoit, 'L'O. de Lucien et Hercule Psychopompe', in: FS für R. Egger, Klagenfurt 1952, 144–158; G. Hafner, 'Herakles – Geras – O.' (JRGZM 5) 1958, 139–153; F. Le Roux, 'Le dieu celtique aux liens' (Ogam 12) 1960, 209–234; J. Loicq, 'O.-Varuna et l'organisation de la fonction de souveraineté dans le panthéon celtique', in: Orientalia J. Duchesne-Guillemin emerito oblata, Lei. 1984, 341–382.

O'Grady, Standish James (1846–1928). Anglo-Irish author born in Castletown Berehaven (Southern Ireland). After studying at Trinity College Dublin he initially practised as a lawyer. In 1878–1880 he published his first great work, History of Ireland, a two-volume account of early Irish history. In the years that followed he wrote many English-language recapitulations of Irish sagas, among them Finn and his Contemporaries (1892), The Coming of Cuculain (1894), In the Gates of the North (1901) and The Triumph and Passing of Cuculain (1920). These works made him one of the most important pioneers of the → Irish Renaissance.

Lit.: P. L. Marcus, S. J. O'G., Lewisburg (Penn.) 1971.

Oisín (Ir. /'oʃiːn'/). Son of → Finn mac Cumaill in the stories of the → Finn Cycle. His mother is said to be a fairy, who for a time took on the shape of a fawn. The 12thC story → Acallam na Senórach tells how O. and his nephew → Caílte in old age encounter St. → Patrick. This episode enjoyed such popularity in later times that it was constantly reworked in ballad form, right into the recent past. In the course of these reworkings, O. changed character from a warrior and hunter to a wise poet. The popular tradition of the Scottish Highlands knows O. by the name Oisean (later: Oisein). In the English form → Ossian, he became widely known through the "Works of Ossian", by James → Macpherson. A Scottish Gaelic folktale concerning Ossian was collected from the oral tradition in the 1970s.

Lit.: 'Stoiridh Oisein' (*Tocher* 4) 1977–1978, 292–301; M. Ó Briain, 'Oisín's Biography: Conception and Birth', in: H. L. C. Tristram (ed.), *Text und Zeittiefe*, T. 1994, 455–486.

ollam (Ir. /ˈoLav/). The highest of the seven degrees in rank attainable by a learned poet (→ fili). The official poet of a ruler, who enjoyed the especial confidence of his master, was termed an o. flatha. In New Irish o. (ollamh) denotes a (university) professor.
Lit.: P. A. Breatnach, 'The Chief's Poet' (*PRIA* 83) 1983, 37–79.

Olloudius. Celtic god identified with → Mars on the basis of the → interpretatio romana. His cult is attested by two votive inscriptions from Custom Scrubs in Gloucestershire (*RIB* 131) and Antibes in the South of France (CIL XII 166).

Olwen (Welsh /ˈolwen/). Female protagonist in the story → *Culhwch ac Olwen*.

oppida (Lat.; sing. oppidum). In archaeology term employed to denote the town-like settlements of the late La Tène period (2nd-1stC BC). The study of these is a major source of our knowledge of the material culture of the Celts of the period.
Like the → princely seats of the 6th-5thC BC, oppida were for the most part built on hills or mountains, in bends of rivers or in similarly protected positions. They differed from the sites of earlier and later centuries, however, in their extent, ranging over several hundred hectares in some cases. Fortified by walls and gates, o. served in times of war as places of refuge for the surrounding population, and in times of peace as centres for → trade and → crafts. In choosing a site, apart from a strategically favourable position, the presence of mineral wealth seems also to have played a role in many cases. It is possible that the town-like settlements of the Mediterranean area, with which the Celts became familiar during their migrations in the 4th–3rdC BC, served as models for the building of the o.
Among the biggest and most important o. were → Alesia, → Bibracte and → Gergovia in France, the → Heidengraben and → Manching in Germany, and → Staré Hradisko and → Závist in the eastern Celtic area.
Lit.: J. Collis, *Oppida: Earliest Towns North of the Alps*, Sheffield 1984.

oracle → prophecy.

O'Rahilly, Cecile (1894–1980). Younger sister of the Celticist T. F. → O'Rahilly, born in Listowel (Southern Ireland). She studied Celtic and Romance languages in Dublin and Bangor, her teachers including Osborn → Bergin and Ifor → Williams. From 1956 she was a professor at the → School of

Celtic Studies in Dublin. Her bilingual editions of the 'Tale of the Cattle-Raid of Cuailnge' (→ *Táin Bó Cuailnge*) remain the standard works.

O'Rahilly, Thomas Francis (1883–1953). Celticist, born in Listowel (Southern Ireland). After studying at Trinity College Dublin, he taught Irish philology in Dublin and Cork from 1919 to 1940. From 1941 to 1947 he was the successor of Osborn → Bergin as Director of the School of Celtic Studies in Dublin. In his early works O'R. was concerned primarily with the New Irish dialects and New Irish literature. Later he turned his attention to the Middle Irish depictions of Irish prehistory and early history. He published a comprehensive synthesis of his views in this area in 1946 under the title *Early Irish History and Mythology*. Although the work treats an impressive range of sources, its speculative character is such that it may only be used with caution.

orality, oral tradition → literature.

Ordovices. In classical → ethnography a Celtic tribe in North Wales. The name would appear to mean "hammer warriors", but its precise significance is unclear. The O. met the advance of the Romans with fierce resistance and in consequence were almost completely wiped out towards the end of the 1stC AD.

orgain (Ir. /'orgin'/). Term denoting the killing of people or the devastation of a place. In the → Lists of Sagas it serves to classify stories dealing with such events.

Orgain Denna Ríg (Ir. /'orgin' 'd'eNa R'iːɣ'/ "The Destruction of Dinn Ríg"). Title of a story from the → Historical Cycle. In its present form the text is thought to date from the 9thC and survives in three manuscripts: the "Book of Leinster" (→ Lebor Laignech), the → "Yellow Book of Lecan" and MS Rawlinson B 502 of the 12thC.

The hero of the tale is a son of the king Ailill Áine of Leinster. Because he did not speak for a long time as a child, he was called Moen ("the Dumb One"). When one day he is hurt in the course of a game, he calls out suddenly: "I have hurt myself!" Then the other children said: "The Dumb One speaks (Labraid Moen)", and this became his name. After Labraid's father Ailill was poisoned by his uncle Cobthach Coel, Labraid had to go into exile together with the harper Craiftine and the poet Ferchertne. From then on he also bore the byname Loingsech ("the Exile"). Labraid found a hospitable welcome in Munster, where he won the hand of the king's daughter Moriath. With the help of her father he finally succeeded in reconquering Dinn Ríg, the royal fortress of Leinster. He enticed the usurper Cobthach and his retinue into an iron house and then set fire to the walls, bringing it to a red heat, so that all who were within perished.

Ed.: D. Greene, *Fingal Rónáin and other stories*, Du. 1955 (MMIS 16).
Trans.: J. Vendryes, 'La destruction de Dind Rig' (EC 8) 1958/59, 7–40.

Orgetorix. A nobleman of the tribe of the → Helvetii in → Caesar (Bell. Gall. 1,2–5). In 61 BC he organised the migration of the Helvetian tribes from their homes in the centre of Switzerland to the South of France. According to Caesar's account he was imprisoned by the Helvetians because of his ambitions to seize the kingship for himself, but with the aid of his dependants escaped trial. He is said to have committed suicide soon afterwards. Plays concerning O. were written by Karl von Müller-Friedberg (1755–1836), Josef Viktor Widmann (1842–1911) and Edith Countess Salburg (1868–1942).

origin legends. It is probable that the Celts of antiquity cherished such legends, but as they did not record them in written form, early sources are limited to a few allusions in classical authors. According to → Caesar (Bell. Gall. 6,18) all the Gauls, following the doctrine of the → Druids, referred to themselves as descendants of the underworld god → Dis Pater. Other classical sources tend to link the origins and early history of the Celts with Graeco-Roman mythology. On the basis of → euhemerism the personages of myth were seen as famed mortals who were elevated to divine status after their death. The historian Appian (2ndC AD) attempts to explain the names of the Celts and Galatians by assuming the existence of two kings "Keltos" and "Galas", whom he regards as the sons of the Cyclops Polyphemus and his wife Galatea (Hist. Romana 10,1). Dionysius of Halikarnassos (1stC BC / 1stC AD) is familiar with a tradition whereby Keltos was a son of Hercules and Asterope, a daughter of Atlas (Archaeologia Romana 14,1). According to the historian → Diodoros of Sicily (5,24) the Celts or Galatians derived their name from "Galates", whose parents were Hercules and the daughter of a local ruler.

Tracing back individual dynasties or whole races to a hero, however obscure, who was thought to have given them their name, remained customary in Europe until the later Middle Ages. Motifs and material from the indigenous tradition merged with Graeco-Roman and Christian traditions, and mythological figures were interpreted euhemeristically as historical personages. Many Irish and Welsh rulers derived their legitimacy from kings in mythical or legendary pre-history. This was of great significance for the evolution of the Celtic literatures, because a number of legends owed their initial recording to the need to substantiate such claims by reference to (pseudo-)historical narratives.

Lit.: D. Ó Corráin, 'Ir. Origin Legends and Genealogy', in: *History and Heroic Tale*, Odense 1985, 51–96; P. Sims-Williams, 'Some Functions of Origin Stories in Early

Med. Wales', op. cit., 97–131; K. McCone, *Pagan Past and Christian Present in Early Ir. Lit.*, May. 1990.

ornamentation. O. plays a dominant role in Celtic → art, to which realistic depiction or the representation of sequences of action or movement are fundamentally alien. First of all there is the strictly geometric o. of the late Hallstatt period (6th/5thC BC). This is followed by the o. of the early La Tène period (5th/4thC BC), which is influenced by Greek and Etruscan stylistic elements, and works with gentle, flowing forms. It is characterised by the abstraction, ambiguity and mysteriousness that is typical of Celtic art as a whole. In this period for the first time the representation of animals, fabulous creatures, human faces and plant motifs becomes part of o. The o. of the Tendril or Waldalgesheim style (4th/3rdC BC; cf. → Waldalgesheim) prefers by contrast intertwined tendrils and spirals, whereas the Late or Plastic style (3rd-1stC BC) is distinguished by strongly abstract, three-dimensional o.

There is no doubt that Celtic o. – like Celtic art in general – was influenced by magical and religious concepts. This is attested, for example, by the frequently recurring number three (cf. → numbers), which plays an important role later in the → literature of the insular Celts. Thus far, however, there has been no success in establishing convincing links between the archaeological and the literary traditions and thus unravelling the symbolism underlying Celtic o.

Oscar (Ir. /'oskar/). One of the most important warriors of the → Fianna in the stories of the → Finn Cycle. His father is → Oisín, his grandfather → Finn mac Cumaill. In James → Macpherson's "Works of Ossian", O. is accordingly the son of the aged poet → Ossian and grandson of the Scottish king → Fingal. He is betrothed to Malvina, who after he is killed by the usurper Cairbar (→ Cairbre Lifechar) takes care of his aged father. Because of the popularity of the "Works of Ossian", O. became a popular Christian name in the 19thC within and beyond the Celtic countries.

Ossian. The (fictitious) author of the "Works of Ossian", published by James → Macpherson in 1760–1765. According to Macpherson he was the son of the Scottish king → Fingal, and lived in the western part of the Scottish Highlands in the 3rdC AD. Accompanied by Malvina, the betrothed of his murdered son → Oscar, Ossian composed – so Macpherson has it – as an aged, blind singer his songs concerning the heroic deeds of Fingal and his warriors. The model for the figure of O. was the – originally Irish – hero of legend, → Oisín. – Paintings inspired by Macpherson's descriptions include *O. singing at the harp* (Statens Museum for Kunst Kopenhagen) by Nicolai Abraham Abildgaard (1743–1809), *The Dream of O.* (Musée Ingres Montauban) by Jean Auguste Dominique Ingres (1780–1867), *O. conjures the spirits by the sound of his harp, on the banks of the Lora* (Kunsthalle Hamburg) by Baron François Gérard (1770–1837), O., *alone and blind, sings of times past* (Bibliothèque Nationale Paris) by Jean-Baptiste Isabey (1767–1855) and *The Death of O.* (Musée Girodet Montargis) by Anne-Louis Girodet de Roussy Trioson (1767–1824). Another painting by Girodet (now in the Musée National du Château Malmaison) was commissioned by Napoleon I. It shows the ghosts of fallen French soldiers who are led by the goddess of victory into a celestial elysium, where they are welcomed by the spirits of O. and his warriors. Where music is concerned, Macpherson's works inspired the Danish composer Niels Wilhelm Gade (1817–1890) to write his overture *Efterklang af O.* (1840), not to mention Felix Mendelssohn's *Fingal's Cave* or *The Hebrides*, inspired by a visit to the islands in 1829.

Lit.: → Macpherson, James.

Ossianic Cycle → Finn Cycle.

Otherworld. Especially in books about the Celts aimed at the popular market the 'Otherworld' serves to describe Celtic conceptions of a world of elves and fairies. Underlying the term is the Christian conception of a distinction between "this", visible world and an "other" world beyond it. This is reflected in Celtic culture in contrasting pairs of terms such as Ir. cenntar = the here and now / alltar = the beyond or Ir. í-siu = here below / í-thall = yonder. These are however only employed in a Christian context, whereas the world of the spirits is called in Irish → síd, in Welsh → Annwfn. According to the testimony of the Roman poet → Lucan the → druids believed that the spirits of the dead lived on in "orbe alio" (Pharsalia I,457). In this context the Latin term orbis alius does not however connote an "other world", but rather a "different area" (of the world known to us).

Lit.: P. Sims-Williams, 'Some Celtic Otherworld Terms', in: A. T. E. Matonis and F. Melia (eds.), *Celtic Languages, Celtic Culture*, Van Nuys, Calif. 1990, 57–81.

Owein fab Urien (Welsh /'owein va:b 'irjen/). A son of the king → Urien of Rheged. The oldest surviving elegy in Welsh is devoted to him; it is preserved under the name of the poet → Taliesin. O. appears as a figure in the legends concerning → Arthur in the Middle Welsh tales → *Breuddwyd Rhonabwy* and → *Iarlles y Ffynnawn*.

pairs of gods → gods, pairs of.

Parisii. In classical → ethnography a Celtic tribe dwelling on the middle Seine. The name survives in that of the city of Paris, formerly called Lutetia. One of the most important pieces of evidence concerning Celtic religion comes from there, the monument of the → Nautae Parisiaci.

219

Partholón (Ir. /ˈparθoloːn/). Leader of a group of settlers in the "Book of the Invasions of Ireland" (→ *Lebor Gabála Érenn*). They are said to have taken possession of Ireland 300 years after the Flood, and to have fought the first battle on Irish soil, against the daemonic → Fomoire. Tradition has it that all the descendants of P. and his followers died of a plague, with the exception of → Tuan mac Cairill.

Parzival. German equivalent of the Welsh name → Peredur. Hero of the verse romance of → Wolfram von Eschenbach, the Celtic equivalent of which is the Middle Welsh prose tale → *Peredur fab Efrawg*.

Patrick (Lat. Patricius). The most important saint and patron of Ireland. The New Irish form of the name is Pádraig (older orthography: Pátraic), whereas in the oldest sources the form Cothr(a)ige occurs.

The earliest accounts of the saint's life are contained in two works of which he himself is the author, which survive under the Latin titles *Confessio* and *Epistula ad Coroticum* (Letter to Coroticus). The *Confessio* is an autobiographical work with an apologetic tendency, which Patrick is thought to have composed in old age. The *Epistula* is an open letter in which P., in his capacity of bishop of the Irish, takes the British prince Coroticus to task for enslaving Irish Christians. These apart, we also possess two Latin writings concerning P. dating from c. 670, which are the work of the Irish clerics Muirchú and Tírechán. The biography *Bethu Phátraic* (The Life of Patrick), written for the most part in Irish, dates from c. 900. Because of its tripartite structure it is also known as the *Vita Tripartita*.

According to the *Confessio*, P. came from a family of Romanised British Celts, and was abducted by Irish pirates at the age of 16. He spent six years as a slave in Ireland before he succeeded in escaping, leaving the coast on a ship bound for the European mainland. However, inspired by a vision, he returned to Ireland to spread Christianity there. This scant information apart, we know little concerning P. It is commonly agreed that he lived in the 5thC, but we know neither the year of his birth nor of his death. Also unknown quantities are the place in which he was imprisoned in Ireland, the length of time he spent on the continent and the scope of his activities as missionary.

The year of his arrival in Ireland was regarded by the Irish in the early Middle Ages as a turning-point in their history. In this context, the motif of P.'s encounter with the great personages of Irish saga (cf. → *Acallam na Senórach*) occurs in Middle Irish literature. A large number of legends preserve the memory of the saint, whose feast-day on the 17th March has been celebrated by ceremonial processions in many towns since the 19thC.

Lit.: D. A. Binchy, 'Patrick and His Biographers Ancient and Modern' (*StHib* 2) 1962, 7–173; R. P. C. Hanson, *The Life and Writings of the Historical St. P.*, NY 1983; P. K. Ford, 'Aspects of the Patrician Legend', in: P. K. Ford (ed.), *Celtic Folklore and Christianity*, Los Angeles 1983, 29–49; *Saint Patrick, AD 493–1993*, C.

1993; F. J. Byrne & P. Francis, 'Two Lives of Saint Patrick: Vita Secunda and Vita Quarta' (JRSAI 124) 1994, 5–117.

Pa ŵr yw'r porthor? (Welsh /pa uːr iur 'porθor/ "Who is the gatekeeper?"). Name given on the basis of its first line to the fragment of a poem preserved in the "Black Book of Carmarthen" (→ Llyfr Du Caerfyrddin). It consists of a dialogue between → Arthur and the gatekeeper → Glewlwyd Gafaelfawr, who desires to know of Arthur the names of his retinue. Arthur names → Bedwyr, → Cei and → Manawydan among others and descibes the heroic deeds of each of them in a few words. The poem is thought to have originated before 1100 and is therefore amongst the earliest documents of → Arthurian literature.

    Ed.: B. F. Roberts, 'Rhai o Gerddi Ymddiddan Llyfr Du Caerfyrddin', in: R. Bromwich & R. B. Jones (eds.), *Astudiaethau ar yr Hengerdd*, Car. 1978, 281–325.

    Lit.: P. Sims-Williams, 'The Early Welsh Arthurian Poems', in: R. Bromwich et al. (eds.), *The Arthur of the Welsh*, Car. 1991, 33–71.

p-Celtic → q-Celtic

Pedeir Ceinc y Mabinogi (Welsh /'pedeir keiŋk ə mabi'nogi/ "The Four Branches of the Mabinogi"). The name given in the manuscripts to the four Middle Welsh prose tales → *Pwyll Pendefig Dyfed,* → *Branwen ferch Lŷr,* → *Manawydan fab Llŷr* and → *Math fab Mathonwy.* They are transmitted in their entirety in the "White Book of Rhydderch" (→ Llyfr Gwyn Rhydderch) and in the "Red Book of Hergest" (→ Llyfr Coch Hergest). Two fragments are contained in an older manuscript of the first half of the 13thC. All four tales are the work of a single author, thought to be of the 11thC, but they rework material and motifs from fairy-tales, sagas and pre-Christian myths, which had previously been transmitted in oral form. In the form in which they have survived the tales are intended to entertain a medieval aristocratic public. They are set in a past age that is not precisely defined, and describe the adventures and marvellous experiences of a large number of people whose destinies are only loosely linked (cf. → mabinogi).

    Lit.: P. MacCana, *The Mabinogi,* Car. 1977; J. K. Bollard, 'The Role of Myth and Tradition in the Four Branches of the Mabinogi' (CMCSt 6) 1983, 67–86; A. Welsh, 'The Traditional Narrative Motifs of the Four Branches of the Mabinogi' (CMCSt 15) 1988, 51–62.

Peñalba de Villastar. Place in the Spanish province of Teruel, near which in 1908 several rock inscriptions were discovered. The longest and most important of these inscriptions was carved in Latin letters in the Celtiberian language in the 1st/2ndC AD. Although interpretations diverge in detail, it would appear that the text is a votive inscription to the Celtic god → Lugus.

    Lit.: H. Schwerteck, 'Zur Deutung der großen Felsinschrift von P.', in: *Actas del II coloquio sobre lenguas y culturas prerromanas de la Península Ibérica*, Sal. 1979, 185–196; R. Ködderitzsch, 'Die große Felsinschrift von P.', in: H. M. Ölberg & G. Schmidt (eds.), *Sprachwissenschaftliche Forschungen*, I. 1985, 211–222; F. Marco Simón, 'El dios céltico Lug y el santuario de P.', in: *Estudios en homenaje a A. Beltrán Martínez*, Saragossa 1986, 731–753; J. F. Eska, 'Syntactic notes on the great inscription of P.' (*BBCS* 37) 1990, 104–107; W. Meid, 'Die "große" Felsinschrift von Peñalba de Villastar', in: R. Bielmeier et al. (eds.), *Indogermanica et Caucasica*. *FS Karl Horst Schmidt*, B. 1994, 385–394.

Penarddun (Welsh /pe'narðin/). Mother of the eponymous heroine Branwen in the tale → *Branwen ferch Lŷr*. She is said to be the daughter or – according to another tradition – sister of the king → Beli Mawr.

Perceval. French equivalent of the Welsh name Peredur. The Celtic equivalent of the verse romance of Chrétien de Troyes concerning P. is the Middle Welsh prose tale → *Peredur fab Efrawg*.

Peredur fab Efrawg (Welsh /pe'redir va:b 'evraug/). Title of one of the "Three Romances" (→ Tair Rhamant). The story tells of the transformation of the knight P. from an ignorant youth to a respected member of the Arthurian court; many of the episodes are only loosely connected. The work has many features in common with the verse romance *Perceval* of → Chrétien de Troyes and the verse epic *Parzival* of → Wolfram von Eschenbach. The question of the sources of the three works and their mutual dependance remains a matter of scholarly debate.

Ed.: B. Jones, *Y Tair Rhamant*, Aberystwyth 1960.

Trans.: G. Jones & T. Jones, *The Mabinogion*, rev. ed., Lo. 1974; J. Gantz, *The Mabinogion*, Harm. 1976.

Lit.: G. Goetinck, *P.*, Car. 1975; C. Lloyd-Morgan, 'Narrative structure in "P." ' (*ZCP* 38) 1981, 187–231; G. Goetinck, 'P. . . . upon reflection' (*EC* 25) 1988, 221–232; I. Lovecy, 'Historia P.', in: R. Bromwich et al. (eds.), *The Arthur of the Welsh*, Car. 1991, 171–182.

personal names. Personal names from early Celtic times survive in the works of Greek and Roman authors, and in inscriptions. Their interpretation causes the Celticist considerable difficulties, as often the etymology of a name may not be determined with any certainty, or despite etymological clarity the reason behind the assignation of the name cannot be understood. In many cases the interpretation is therefore purely conjectural.

Personal names such as Cintugenus and Cintugena "firstborn" (cf. Welsh cyntaf "first" and geni "to give birth") would seem to contain a reference to the position of a child in the family. Physical and intellectual qualities presumably form the basis for personal names such as Nertomaros "Strong One" (cf. Welsh nerthfawr "powerful") and Exobnus "Bold One" (cf. Welsh eofn "fearless"). Celtic personal names ending in -rix "king" (cf. Ir. → rí "king") such as → Ambiorix, → Orgetorix and → Vercingetorix are well-known. Some names such as Camulogenus, Esugenus and Totatigenus are perhaps to be interpreted mythologically, as meaning that their bearers were regarded as the descendants of the gods → Camulus, → Esus and → Teutates.

Lit.: K. H. Schmidt, 'Die Komposition in gallischen Personennamen' (ZCP 26) 1957, 33–301; D. E. Evans, Gaulish Personal Names, O. 1967; D. Ó Corráin & F. Maguire, Gaelic Personal Names, Du. 1981; T. J. Morgan & P. Morgan, Welsh Surnames, Car. 1985; J. Uhlich, Die komponierten Personennamen des Altirischen, T., forthcoming.

Petrucorii. In classical → ethnography a Celtic tribe in the Dordogne. Etymologically, the name would appear to mean "Four Tribes"; it survives in the name of the town Périgueux, which was formerly called Vesunna.

Pfalzfeld. Site c. 20 miles south of Koblenz. In the 17th/18thC, not far from the church, a Celtic stele of c. 400 BC stood there. The original position of this monument of quartz sandstone is not known, but it is thought that it adorned a grave-mound not far from P. In 1938, after many changes of location, the stele arrived in the Rheinisches Landesmuseum in Bonn, where it may be seen today. Only the lower part of the obelisk-shaped shaft is preserved. It rests upon a semi-globular base, and has on all four sides spiral ornamentation and depictions of mask-like heads. The height of the stele today is 1.48m, but an illustration dating from the beginning of the 17thC suggests that its then height was c. 2.20m and that it had a circular pedestal beneath its present base. Eye-witness accounts of 1690 maintain that the shaft was originally surmounted by the stone sculpture of a human head.

Lit.: H.-E. Joachim, 'Eine Rekonstruktion der keltischen "Säule" von P.' (BJb 189) 1989, 1–14.

Picts (Lat. Picti). In classical → ethnography the name given to a succession of tribes in northern Scotland. It is not clear whether the name is of Latin origin, referring to the custom of tattooing (Picti = the Painted Ones), or whether this is a linguistic connection with the Gaulish → tribal names Pictavi and Pictones (in the neighbourhood of Poitiers). In Irish texts the P. are called Cruithin, in Welsh texts Prydyn (cf. → Prydein). The P. are first mentioned towards the end of the 3rdC AD, when together with Celtic tribes they attempted to penetrate Hadrian's Wall. The P. were probably of pre-Celtic origin and originally spoke a non-Indo-European language. They created a kingdom north of the Firth of Forth, to which in the second half of the 6thC Saint Columba led a mission, with their ruler's permission. The realm of the Picts and Scots was united as a single Scottish kingdom c. 850 by King Kenneth mac Alpin. The language of the P. seems to have died out soon afterwards.

Lit.: F. T. Wainwright (ed.), The Problem of the Picts, E. 1956; I. Henderson, The Picts, Lo. 1967; J. G. P. Friell & W. G. Watson, Pictish Studies, O. 1984; A. Small (ed.), The Picts: a new look at old problems, Dundee 1987; Ll. & J. Laing, Celtic

Britain and Ireland, Du. 1990; Ll. & J. Laing, *The Picts and the Scots*, Lo. 1993; E. Sutherland, *In Search of the Picts*, Lo. 1994; E. H. Nicoll (ed.), *A Pictish Panorama*, Forfar 1995.

Pictones / Pictavi. In classical → ethnography names given to a Celtic tribe in the area south of the lower Loire. The name survives in that of the city of Poitiers, formerly called Lemonum or Limonum.

pigs. After cows the most common domestic animals of the early Celts (cf. → cattle breeding). The pigs of the Celts were notably smaller than their wild equivalents or today's breeds, and according to the geographer → Strabo (4,4,3) were noted for their strength and agility. In autumn they were driven to the woods to feed on acorns and beechnuts.

The religious significance of pigs is suggested by the early Celtic custom of assigning whole pigs or parts of them to members of the nobility as grave goods. The period immediately before the Roman age, and the Roman age itself yield many depictions, some of which clearly relate to cults; among these are some small bronze figures, the depiction of a warrior with a wild boar adorning his helmet on the → Gundestrup cauldron, the carving of a wild boar on the sandstone sculpture of a god from → Euffigneix, and the almost lifesize bronze figure of a wild boar from → Neuvy-en-Sullias.

In the insular Celtic literatures pigs also play a major role. In the tale → *Math fab Mathonwy*, the prince → Pryderi possesses a herd of pigs, which his father acquired from → Arawn, king of the Otherworld → Annwfn. In the collection of mnemonics → *Trioedd Ynys Prydein*, → Drystan (Tristan) is one of the "Three Famed Swineherds of Britain". The dissection of a gigantic pig plays an important role as the climax of a banquet (cf. → curad-mír) in the story → *Scéla mucce Meic Dathó*.

The hunting of wild boar is attested among the early Celts, yet this was not, as readers of → Asterix comics might assume, a major constituent part of the Celtic diet. Various insular Celtic tales emphasise the dangerous nature of such hunts, which might sometimes lead to the death of the huntsman (cf. → *Culhwch ac Olwen*, → *Tóraigheacht Dhiarmada agus Ghráinne*).

Lit.: P. Meniel, *Chasse et élevage chez les Gaulois*, P. 1987.

place-names. As the results of place-name research show, many geographical terms, particularly in central and western Europe, are of Celtic origin. A large number of these names, however, only reveal their Celtic origins to the linguist through characteristically Celtic sound changes or word-formation syllables. Some compound place-names are recognisably Celtic even to the layman because of the characteristic way in which the words begin or end.

Among the oldest of these Celtic names are those ending in -briga, which is thought to mean "hill". These names range from as far south as Portugal (Setúbal < Cetobriga) to France (Avrolles < Eburobriga). Much more common are place-names ending in -dunum "stronghold, town" (cf. Ir. dún "stronghold" and the linguistically related English "town"). The great number and broad spread of such names is to be explained by the fact that -dunum, in contrast to -briga, was still in use in Roman times. Typical examples are Autun (< Augustodunum), Isoudun (< Uxellodunum), Kempten (< Cambodunum), Lyon (< Lugdunum), Verdun (< Virodunum) and Yverdon (< Eburodunum). Place-names ending in -magos "field, plain" (= Ir. mag) were also still customary in Roman times. Typical examples are Remagen (< Rigomagus), and Neumagen, Nijmegen, Noyon and Nyons (all < Noviomagus). Some of the names of this type which originated in Roman times have not survived, such as Iuliomagus (now Angers) and Caesaromagus (now Beauvais). At river-crossings names ending in -briva "bridge" and -ritum "ford" (= Ir. rith and Welsh rhyd) are particularly frequent. The names Samarobriva (now Amiens), Augustoritum (now Limoges) and Darioritum (now Vannes) survived until the end of the Ancient World. The suffix -ritum is preserved today in Chambord (Camboritum).

The religious concept of the sacred centre of an area is thought to lie behind the very frequent place-name Mediolanum (cf. Ir. mide "midpoint"). In classical times Évreux and Saintes, among other places, bore this name, and it is preserved today in Milan (It. Milano). Another place-name element of religious significance is → nemeton "sacred grove; sanctuary", which is found in the classical place-names Augustonemetum (now Clermont-Ferrand), Nemetacum (now Arras), and in the modern name Nanterre (< Nemetodurum).

The most frequent formative component in place-names is -(i)acum, indicating derivation from a personal name. Well-known examples are Andernach (Antunnacum), Jülich (Iuliacum), Nancy (Nanciacum), Orly (Aureliacum) and Tournai (Turniacum).

Towards the end of antiquity many Celtic and Roman place-names fell into disuse, particularly in Gaul, and were replaced by the names of the peoples settled there. Some thirty French cities thus derive their names from Celtic → tribal names.

Lit.: W. F. H. Nicolaisen, *Scottish Place-Names*, Lo. 1976; A. Dauzat & C. Rostaing, *Dict. étymologique des noms de lieux en France*, P. ²1979; A. L. F. Rivet & C. Smith, *The Place-Names of Roman Britain*, Lo. 1979; O. J. Padel, *Cornish Place-Name Elements*, C. 1985; ibid, *A Popular Dictionary of Cornish Place-Names*, Newmill, Penzance 1988; J.-M. Plonëis, *La toponymie celtique: L'origine des noms de lieux en Bretagne*, P. 1989; G. Broderick, *Placenames of the Isle of Man*, 2 vols, T. 1994–1995.

places of worship. Before the Roman conquest of the regions settled by the Celts their cult foci were scarcely ever provided with stone buildings. Among the few exceptions are the well-known sanctuaries of → Entremont, → Roquepertuse and → Glanum in southern Gaul, which reflect Mediterranean influence (cf. → temples). This marginal area apart, places of worship are not indicated by any building structures (cf. → nemeton), or these were limited simply to the enclosure of the sacred site by means of ramparts, ditches and/or wooden pallisades. Such sites could be both of circular, rectangular or approximately square shape (cf. → Goloring, → Libenice). As these enclosures are not in principle to be distinguished from those of profane sites, places of worship can, from an archaeological point of view, frequently only be identified on the basis of traces of ritual acts. Remnants of sacrifices and finds of dedicatory and votive gifts are of paramount importance in this respect. Among the most important places of worship in pre-Roman Gaul is the sanctuary of → Gournay-sur-Aronde, which continued to exist after the region was conquered by → Caesar, and has been the subject of archaeological exploration since 1975. It has not yet been possible to establish any such continuity with regard to the sites known as *Viereckschanzen*.

Lit.: J. Filip, 'Keltische Kultplätze und Heiligtümer in Böhmen', in: H. Jankuhn (ed.), *Vorgeschichtliche Heiligtümer und Opferplätze in Mittel- und Nordeuropa*, Gö. 1970, 55–77; S. Piggott, 'Nemeton, Temenos, Bothros', in: *I Celti e la loro cultura*, R. 1978 (in English); A. Reichenberger, 'Temenos – Templum – Nemeton – Viereckschanze' (*JRGZM 35*) 1988, 285–298; L. Pauli, 'Heilige Plätze und Opferbräuche bei den Helvetiern und ihren Nachbarn' (*ASchw 14*) 1991, 124–135; *Les sanctuaires celtiques et leurs rapports avec le monde méditerranéen*, P. 1991; I. Fauduet, *Les temples de tradition celtique en Gaule romaine*, P. 1993; I. Fauduet, *Atlas des sanctuaires romano-celtiques de Gaule romaine*, P. 1993; *Les sanctuaires de tradition indigène en Gaule romaine*, P. 1994.

Pliny (Gaius Plinius Secundus / P. the Elder). Roman officer, naturalist and author of the 1stC AD. Of his many works only the *Historia Naturalis* (Natural History), amounting to some 102 books, has survived. In this P. gives an encyclopaedic survey of what was known of natural history in his time, based upon a large number of specialised sources. The rich detail of the work renders it invaluable for many aspects of our knowledge of ancient times. P.'s account of the → druids and the esteem in which they held → mistletoe is well-known.

Pokorny, Julius (1887–1970), linguist and Celticist, born in Prague. After studying law and philology he was appointed to the chair in Celtic Studies at the university of Berlin, previously held by Kuno → Meyer. Suspended from his duties and persecuted because of his Jewish origins, O. fled to Switzerland in 1943, and lived as a private scholar in Zurich for the rest of his life. P. is most famous for his *Indogermanisches etymologisches Wörterbuch* (2 vols., 1959–1970). He was also the author of many editions and translations of Irish texts, linguistic aids for the study of Irish, and works relating to European pre-history. His research on the influence of pre-Celtic → substrata on the insular Celtic languages was continued by his pupil Heinrich → Wagner, among others. – As a researcher into Celtic mythology "Professor P. of

Vienna" appears in the tenth chapter of *Ulysses*, the novel by James Joyce (1882–1941).

Polybios. Greek historian of the 2ndC BC. Born in Megalopolis (Greece), he came to Rome as a hostage in 168 BC, and undertook several journeys in the western Mediterranean area. His major work, only part of which survives, is a universal history in 40 books of the time between 264 and 144 BC, in which his intention was to depict and analyse the rise of Rome as a world power. In chapters 27–31 of the second book P., in the course of his description of the battle of Telamon (255 BC), records valuable information concerning Celtic → warfare.   ? ?5

Lit.: R. Urban, 'Die Kelten in Italien und in Gallien bei P.', in: *Hellenistische Studien*, Mn. 1991, 135–157.

Pomponius Mela. Author of the earliest surviving geographical work in Latin, entitled *De Chorographia*, written in 43/44 AD. P.'s accounts of the → druids (3,2,18ff) and of the sanctuary of a Gaulish deity on the island of Sena (now Sein) off the west coast of Brittany (3,6,8) are well-known. According to the Roman geographer, this sanctuary was guarded by nine virgins. They were credited with the ability to cause storms by singing magic chants, to transform themselves into animals of all kinds, to heal incurable diseases and to predict the future. It is thought that this tradition corresponds to the insular Celtic legend of the isle of → Avalon, found in → Geoffrey of Monmouth.

Poseidonios. Greek philosopher, geographer and historian of the 2nd/1stC BC, born in Apameia (Syria). After extensive travelling in the whole of the Mediterranena area, he taught Stoic philosophy on Rhodos. He was the author of numerous works, over twenty of which we know by title and content. His major historical work is a continuation of the universal history of → Polybios, amounting to 52 volumes; only fragments have survived. In the 23rd book there was a detailed description of Gaul and its inhabitants, which it is possible to reconstruct in part from quotations and borrowings in → Athenaios, → Diodoros of Sicily and → Strabo. P.'s descriptions, because of their precision and vivid nature, occupy a prominent place amongst the accounts of the Celts in Greek and Roman → ethnography. They determined the classical view of Celtic culture over a long period and also had considerable influence on the modern image of the Celts (cf. → Celtic ideology).

Lit.: M. Truscelli, 'I "Keltika" di Posidonio e loro influsso sulla posteriore etnografia' (*Rendiconti della Reale Accademia Nazionale dei Lincei* 11) 1935, 609–730; J. J. Tierney, 'The Celtic Ethnography of P.' (*PRIA* 60) 1960, 189–275; D. Nash, 'Reconstructing P.'s Celtic Ethnography: some considerations' (*Britannia* 7) 1976, 111–126; J. E. C. Williams, 'P.'s Celtic Parasites' (*StC* 14/15) 1979/80, 313–342; J. Malitz, *Die Historien des P.*, Mn. 1983; W. Meid, 'Remarks on the Celtic Ethnography of P. in the Light of Insular Celtic Traditions' (*Anzeiger der Österreichischen Akademie der Wissenschaften* 123,4) 1986, 60–74.

pottery → ceramics.

Powys (Welsh /'powis/). Region in mid-Wales in which an independent Celtic kingdom developed after the departure of the Roman troops at the beginning of the 5thC AD. Its extent varied but it survived until its dissolution in the second half of the 12thC. The modern county of P. was formed in 1974, from the old counties of Brecon, Radnor and Montgomery, thus reaching much further to the south than the medieval Powys.

Preiddeu Annwfn (Welsh /'preiðei 'annuvn/). Title of a poem in the "Book of Taliesin" (→ Llyfr Taliesin), which tells of how → Arthur sailed with his retinue to → Annwfn, in the ship → Prydwen. His purpose was to gain possession of a magic cauldron, decorated with precious stones, which belonged to the ruler of Annwfn and was kept in a square stronghold made of glass. The fire beneath the cauldron was kept alight by the breath of nine virgins. The story holds that only a courageous warrior could cook his food in this cauldron. The expedition apparently failed, however, as in the refrain of each strophe the poet laments that only seven warriors returned from this campaign.

Ed.: M. Haycock, 'P. A. and the figure of Taliesin' (*StC* 18/19) 1983/84, 52–78 (with Engl. trans.).

Lit.: P. Sims-Williams, 'The early Welsh Arthurian poems', in: R. Bromwich et al. (eds.), *The Arthur of the Welsh*, Car. 1991, 33–71; A. Budgey, ' "Preiddeu Annwn" and the Welsh Tradition of Arthur', in: C. J. Byrne et al. (eds.), *Celtic Languages and Celtic Peoples*, Halifax 1992, 391–404; H. Pilch, 'The Earliest Arthurian Tradition: the P. A. of the Book of Taliesin', in: id. (ed.), *Orality and Literacy in Early Middle English*, T. 1996, 147–166.

priests → druids.

princely graves. Term denoting burial sites of prehistoric and early historical times whose architecture and grave goods are indicative of considerable expense.

The Celtic princely graves of the pre-Roman Iron Age are regarded as the earliest archaeological evidence of Celtic culture in Central Europe – together with the sites known as → princely seats. In all probability the people buried in these graves belonged to politically and economically dominant tribal aristocracies. An eminent social and political role is indicated in the first instance by the expenditure that must have been incurred by the building of the graves. This required a high degree of collaborative work and organisation. The economic power of this stratum of society is indicated most obviously by the grave goods. Frequently to be found among these are goods and objects imported from the Mediterranean, made of precious metals, above all of → gold. The religious and legal basis of the social eminence of the people buried in this way is however for the most part obscure, in view of the lack of written sources.

The oldest princely graves (up to c. 400 BC) are to some extent still visible today in the countryside, in the form of monumental grave-mounds. It was only later that burial in the form of flat graves was established. There are clear differences between the older graves of the Hallstatt period and the later ones of the La Tène period. The Hallstatt graves, for example, have usually been found to contain, apart from the bones of the dead, a four-wheeled cart or chariot (→ waggon), but by way of weapons nothing more than a dagger. In the graves of the La Tène period, on the other hand, it is customary to find a two-wheeled cart, and not infrequently a sword, helmet and other weapons. The geographical site of the graves also marks a difference between one civilisation and the next. Princely graves of the Hallstatt period occur predominantly in close proximity to princely sites in Burgundy, Switzerland and Baden-Württemberg (→ Grafenbühl, → Hirschlanden, → Hochdorf, → Hohmichele, → Magdalenenberg, → Vix). La Tène period graves, on the other hand, are to be found predominantly in Champagne, in the Rhineland and Saarland, in Bohemia and in Austria (→ Bad Dürkheim, → Rodenbach, → Schwarzenbach, → Waldalgesheim, → Weiskirchen). Only in a few isolated cases is there any continuity evident between the Hallstatt and the La Tène sites. The best-known example is the La Tène period grave-mound → Kleinaspergle, which is linked with the Hallstatt period princely seat on → Hohenasperg.

Lit.: F. Fischer & J. Biel, 'Frühkeltische Fürstengräber im Mitteleuropa' (*Antike Welt* 13) 1982, special number; *Trésors des princes celtes*, P. 1987 (exhibition cat.); K. Spindler, *Die frühen Kelten*, St. ²1991; *Hundert Meisterwerke keltischer Kunst*, Trier 1992 (exhibition cat.); S. Verger, 'De Vix à Weiskirchen. La transformation des rites funéraires aristocratiques en Gaule du Nord et de l'Est au Ve siècle avant J.-C.' (*Mélanges de l'École Française de Rome* 107) 1995, 335–458.

princely seats. Term given in modern archaeology to a type of settlement belonging to the late → Halstatt period (6th-5thC BC). Its characteristics include a markedly high situation, elaborate fortifications, the occurrence of goods imported from the Mediterranean area, and the immediate proximity of richly endowed → princely graves. In all probability these sites were the residences of opulent tribal aristocracies which had extensive trade contacts. Among the most important examples are → Mont Lassois near Châtillon-sur-Seine, → Camp-de-Château near Salins-les-Bains in the French Jura, Châtillon-sur-Glâne near Fribourg in Switzerland, the → Üetliberg near Zurich, the Münsterberg of → Breisach, → Hohenasperg near Ludwigsburg and the → Heuneburg on the Upper Danube. These sites, taken together with

prophecy

the graves that belong with them, constitute the earliest archaeological evidence of the presence of the Celts in Central Europe. Research into them is far from concluded, the archaeologists' work being hampered by the sheer size of the settled areas, and in part by the problems posed by later building on the sites.

Lit.: M. K. H. Eggert, 'Die "Fürstensitze" der Späthallstattzeit' (*Hammaburg N. F.* 9) 1989, 53–66; K. Spindler, *Die frühen Kelten*, St. ²1991; C. F. E. Pare, 'Fürsten-sitze: Celts and the Mediterranean World. Developments in the West Hallstatt Culture in the 6th and 5th Centuries BC' (*Proceedings of the Prehistoric Society* 57) 1991, 183–202.

prophecy. Prophecy or divination is often referred to in ancient accounts of the Celts. According to → Diodoros of Sicily (5,31) and → Strabo (4,4) one method consisted in sticking a dagger into a person's body and foretelling the future on the basis of the direction in which he fell and the twitching of his limbs. Other prognostications depended upon interpreting the flight of birds or inspecting sacrificial animals (→ sacrifices). Among the various kinds of prophecy mentioned in medieval → literature are → imbas forosna, teinm láeda and → tarbfeis.

Lit.: F. Le Roux, 'La divination chez les Celtes', in: A. Caquot & M. Leibovici (eds.), *La Divination*, P. 1968, 233–256.

Prydein (Welsh /'prədein/; later form Prydain). Celtic form of the name Britain (Lat. Britannia). The word is cognate with Welsh Prydyn and its Irish equivalent Cruithin. The Celts of Britain and Ireland used the name to refer to the people known as the → Picts. Comparative philology traces both Prydyn and Cruithin back to an older form *Qritenī, which probably derives from a word meaning "to cut, carve". The original meaning of the word may therefore be "the Tattooed Ones" (=Lat. Picti "the Painted Ones"?). The oldest Greek authors borrow the word, retaining the initial P-. Only later, for reasons obscure to us, does the form with initial B- establish itself.

Pryderi (Welsh /prə'deri/). Son of the prince → Pwyll of Dyfed and his wife → Rhiannon in the "Four Branches of the Mabinogi" (→ Pedeir Ceinc y Mabinogi). The first of the four tales narrates the mysterious circumstances surrounding his birth, and tells of his youth up to the point of marriage. The second story refers to P. as one of the seven survivors of the campaign led by the British king Brân against the Irish king Matholwch. P. plays a major role in the third tale which describes the misfortunes which P. and his family have to suffer because of the enchantments perpetrated by an enemy of his father. The fourth tale, finally, relates how P. dies – again as a result of magic. The Celticist Edward → Anwyl propounded the theory that the life of P. was originally the unifying bond and central theme of the Pedeir Ceinc. In the form these traditions survive in today P. gives way to other characters and retreats into the background for long stretches of the narrative.

Prydwen (Welsh /'prədwen/). In the Welsh tradition the name of → Arthur's ship. The story → *Culhwch ac Olwen* describes how Arthur and his companions sail in this boat to Ireland in order to steal the cauldron of a man called Diwrnach. A similar motif occurs in the poem → *Preiddeu Annwfn*. There, however, the goal of the expedition is → Annwfn rather than Ireland, and the cauldron belongs to the ruler of Annwfn. In → Geoffrey of Monmouth, by contrast, P. is the name of Arthur's shield, adorned with an image of the Madonna.

Pwyll Pendefig Dyfed (Welsh /puɫ pen'devig 'dəved/ "Pwyll, prince of Dyfed"). Title of the first story of the "Four Branches of the Mabinogi" (→ Pedeir Ceinc y Mabinogi). It begins with Pwyll meeting Arawn, king of → Annwfn, whilst hunting. At Arawn's suggestion the two change form and semblance for a year. During this period Pwyll defeats in single combat Arawn's enemy Hafgan in Annwfn, while Arawn rules in exemplary fashion in Dyfed. The service that Pwyll and Arawn thus show one another renders them staunch friends. Back again in Dyfed, Pwyll encounters the magically gifted → Rhiannon and marries her. Three years later their son → Pryderi is abducted shortly after his birth, whereupon Rhiannon's serving-maids accuse their mistress of infanticide. The new-born child has in fact been mysteriously transported to the household of the nobleman Teyrnon Twrf Liant. When the latter finds out who the proper parents of the child are, he returns it to them, whereupon Rhiannon is rehabilitated. When Pwyll dies many years later, Pryderi succeeds him as ruler over Dyfed, and reigns successfully for a long time.

Ed.: I. Williams, *Pedeir Keinc y Mabinogi*, Car. 1930; R. L. Thomson, *P. P. D.*, Du. 1957 (MMWS 1).

Trans.: G. Jones & T. Jones, *The Mabinogion*, rev. ed., Lo. 1974; J. Gantz, *The Mabinogion*, Harm. 1976.

Lit.: C. M. McKenna, 'The Theme of Sovereignty in P.' (*BBCS* 29) 1980–82, 35–52; E. Hanson-Smith, 'P. P. D.: The Narrative Structure' (*StC* 16/17) 1981/82, 126–134; A. Welsh, 'Traditional Tales and the Harmonizing of Story in P. P. D.' (*CMCSt* 17) 1989, 15–41; J. Fife, 'Legal aspects of the hunting scene in "Pwyll" ' (*BBCS* 39) 1992, 71–79.

q-Celtic. Term given to those Celtic → languages in which the sound k^w, inherited from pre-Celtic times, is either preserved or has developed into k. What is known as p-Celtic, by contrast, has the sound p instead. Of the continental Celtic languages of the Ancient World → Celtiberian has k^w, but → Lepontic has p. In → Gaulish p is predominant, although there are also some words with k^w (written qu). Of the insular Celtic languages, concerning which we have fuller knowledge, → Irish, → Scottish Gaelic and →

ram-headed (or ram-horned) snake

Manx evince the development from k^w to k (written as c), whereas → Welsh, → Cornish and → Breton have replaced the older sound k^w with p.

ram-headed (or ram-horned) snake. Term denoting a fabulous Celtic creature possessing the body of a snake, but the head and horns of a ram, and – sometimes – the tail of a fish. The ram-headed snake occurs in Celtic and Gallo-Roman art, sometimes alone (e.g. on the cheek-plates of the helm of → Agris or on → coins), sometimes as an attribute of various deities (e.g. on the. → Gundestrup cauldron or on the altar of → Mavilly). The lack of literary sources means that the interpretation of the religious significance of the r. is limited to conjecture.

Lit.: P. Lambrechts, *Contributions á l'étude des divinités celtiques*, Bruges 1942; J. de Vries, *Keltische Religion*, St. 1961.

ráth (Ir. /Ra:θ/). Term denoting a circular enclosure separated from the outside world by one or more earth ramparts with pits placed before them. Most sites of this kind date from the first millennium AD and were originally agricultural settlements.

Rathcroghan → Cruachain.

rebirth → reincarnation.

Redones. In classical → ethnography a Celtic tribe in eastern Brittany. The name survives in that of the city of Rennes, whose ancient name was Condate.

Regenbogenschüsselchen. A type of dish-shaped Celtic → coin common predominantly in south Germany and Bohemia. The name refers to the popular superstition that the rainbow, at the point where it touches the ground, leaves behind a trace of gold in the the form of these coins. Rainbow dishes are generally minted from → gold, more rarely from → silver or a silver alloy, and have on their front and back sides pictorial motifs such as birds' heads, → torcs, globes or abstract ornamentation. The coins were popularly held to have healing qualities and to bring good luck.

reincarnation, rebirth or transmigration of souls (Gk. metempsychosis). In comparative religion a term denoting various conceptions of life after death. According to → Caesar (Bell. Gall. 6,14), the → druids believed in the immortality of the soul and that after death the soul passes from one body to another. → Diodoros of Sicily (5,28) expresses himself in very similar vein, linking the Celtic conceptions with Pythagoras' doctrine of the transmigration of souls. It is however possible that the Celts did not believe in r. in the sense of Pythagorean or Indian philosophy. The classical accounts might be interpreted as referring to Celtic belief in the kingdom of the dead as a continuation of earthly life (cf. → Beyond, conceptions of). The insular Celtic narratives concerning a reincorporation of specific personages in animal form (cf. → *De chophur in da muccida* and → *Scél Tuain meic Chairill*) clearly bear the character of folktales and are of no value as evidence of Celtic belief in r.

Lit.: C. Dröge, 'Betrachtungen zur Frage der "keltischen Seelenwanderungslehre"' (ZCP 39) 1982, 261–268.

Reinheim. Site on the Franco-German border c. 12 miles south-east of Saarbrücken, where in February 1954 a Celtic → princely grave dating from c. 400 BC was found in a sand and gravel pit. Nothing remains of the skeleton of the person buried there, as the terrain is corrosive. The nature of the grave gifts suggests however that it was a woman of high social rank. She wore a neck-ring, several golden arm-rings and finger-rings, and two bracelets of glass or oil-shale. To her right there lay a hand mirror of bronze, which had originally been inside a bag of finely woven material. To her left a cluster of pieces of jewellery was found, of amber, glass and metal. Probably they were originally in a container of organic material, of which nothing has survived. The grave also contained an eating and drinking service, consisting of a gilded bronze jug, two bronze plates and fragments of two drinking vessels. The finds may now be seen in the Landesmuseum für Vor- und Frühgeschichte in Saarbrücken.

Lit.: F. J. Keller, *Das keltische Fürstengrab von R.*, Mz. 1965.

religion. By Celtic religion are meant the myths, cults and rites of the Celtic-speaking inhabitants of ancient Europe before → christianisation. Our knowledge of the subject is based upon archaeological finds of pre-Roman and Roman times, accounts in classical → ethnography, allusions in the Irish and Welsh → literature of the Middle Ages, and recordings of folklore in modern times. Thus research into Celtic religion is dependant upon the findings of prehistory and ancient history, archaeology, comparative philology and → Celtic studies.

One of the peculiarities of Celtic religion is that primary sources such as prayers, hymns or sacred writings are for the most part lacking, whilst the indirect evidence can tell us very little. In consequence very few definite statements can be made concerning many aspects to which a great deal of space is devoted in descriptions of better documented religions. Moreover, it is often virtually impossible to distinguish between religion and magic.

Celtic religion was – like almost all religions – polytheistic. However, we know nothing but the names of most of the → gods and goddesses, and only a sketchy reconstruction of a mythology is possible. The myths of the Celts concerning the Creation (→ cosmogony), and the end of the world (→ eschatology), as well as their concepts of the → Beyond are thus for the most part obscure. Archaeological finds have led to knowledge of many → places of worship, and yield, if nothing more, an insight into the → sacrifices performed there. Our knowledge of other aspects of religion such as, for example, → prophecy, or the ritual of the → sacred marriage, is limited almost exclusively to the statements of classical authors or allusions in medieval sources. Similarly, the → druids are only known to be the priests of the Celts from literary sources. Celtic → art did not originally create images of the gods; it was only as a result of Mediterranean, above all Graeco-Roman influences, that these became customary. In art as in worship the principle of the → interpretatio romana was prevalent.

It is particularly important to take into account the circumstance that the links between the sources, deriving as they do from widely disparate periods and areas, are not founded in any ethnic or cultural unity (cf. → history). The justification for referring to "the" Celtic religion derives primarily from the demonstrable links between the Celtic → languages which give expression to religious concepts, hand down myths and denote or describe ritual acts.

Overall surveys: J. Vendryes, 'La R. des Celtes', in: A. Grenier (ed.), *Mana III,* P. 1948, 239–320; J. de Vries, *Keltische Religion,* St. 1961; F. Le Roux, 'La R. des Celtes', in: H. C. Puech (ed.), *Histoire des Religions,* P. 1970, I 781–840; M. Green, *The Gods of the Celts,* Gloucester 1986.

Gaul and Roman Germania: G. Drioux, *Cultes indigènes des Lingons,* P. 1934; P. Lambrechts, *Contributions à l'étude des divinités celtiques,* Bruges 1942; C. B. Pascal, *The Cults of Cisalpine Gaul,* Bru. 1964; S. Deyts, *Divinités indigènes en Bourgogne à l'époque gallo-romaine,* Dijon 1967; E. Thevenot, *Divinités et sanctuaires de la Gaule,* P. 1968; F. Benoit, *Art et dieux de la Gaule,* P. 1969; id., *Le Symbolisme dans les sanctuaires de la Gaule,* Bru. 1970; J.-J. Hatt, 'Les dieux gaulois en Alsace' (*RAE* 22) 1971, 187–276; P.-M. Duval, *Les Dieux de la Gaule,* P. 1976; H. Lavagne, 'Les Dieux de la Gaule Narbonnaise' (*Journal des savants*) 1979, 155–197; P. M. M. Leunissen, 'Römische Götternamen und einheimische Religion in der Provinz Germania Superior' (*FBW* 10) 1985, 155–195; E. M. Wightman, 'Pagan Cults in the Province of Belgica' (*ANRW II* 18.1) 1986, 542–589; L. Brunaux, *Les Gaulois: sanctuaires et rites,* P. 1986; M. Green, *Symbol and Image in Celtic Religious Art,* Lo. 1989; *Aspects de la religion celtique et gallo-romaine dans le nord-est de la Gaule à la lumière des découvertes récentes,* Saint-Dié-des-Vosges 1989; S. Deyts, *Images des dieux de la Gaule,* P. 1992; C. Landes (ed.), *Dieux Guérisseurs en Gaule romaine,* Lattes 1992.

Austria, Switzerland and the Alpine region: R. Frei-Stolba, 'Götterkulte in der Schweiz zur römischen Zeit' (*Bull. des antiquités luxembourgoises* 15) 1984, 75–126; H. Kenner, 'Die Götterwelt der Austria Romana' (*ANRW II* 18.2) 1989, 875–974 & 1652–1655.

Britain: A. Ross, *Pagan Celtic Britain,* Lo. 1967; M. Henig, *Religion in Roman Britain,* Lo. 1984; G. A. Wait, *Ritual and R. in Iron Age Britain,* Lo. 1985; G. Webster, *The British Celts and their Gods under Rome,* Lo. 1986; E. Birley, 'The

Deities of Roman Britain' (*ANRW II* 18.2) 1989, 875–974 & 1652–1655; M. Green, 'The Iconography and Archaeology of Romano-British R.' (*ANRW II* 18.2) 1989, 875–974 & 1652–1655; Hutton, R., *The Pagan Religions of the Ancient British Isles. Their Nature and Legacy*, Lo. 1991.

Remi. In classical → ethnography a Celtic tribe in the area between the Marne and the Aisne. As early as 57 BC they formed an alliance with the Romans, thereby winning influence and importance. According to → Caesar (Bell. Gall. 6,12), the R. were in his times the most respected tribe in Gaul, after the → Aedui. Their name survives in that of the city of Rheims, the Roman name for which was Durocortorum.

remscéla (Ir. /'R'ev'ʃk'e:la/ "prefatory tales"). The name given in the "Book of Leinster" (→ Lebor Laignech), the → "Yellow Book of Lechan" and in one other manuscript to a number of tales from the → Ulster Cycle. The only thing they have in common is that all the stories precede, directly or indirectly, the plot of the → *Táin Bó Cuailnge*. Among the most important remscéla are → *Aislinge Oenguso*, → *Compert Chon Culainn*, → *Compert Chonchobuir*, → *De chophur in da muccida*, → *Echtrae Nerai*, → *Longas mac nUislenn*, → *Táin Bó Froích* and → *Tochmarc Emire*.
   Lit.: R. Thurneysen, *Die irische Helden- und Königsage*, Hl. 1921; N. Backhaus, 'The Structure of the List of Remscéla Tána Bó Cualngi in the Book of Leinster' (CMCSt 19) 1990, 19–26.

Renan, Ernest (1823–1892). Theologian and orientalist, born in Tréguier in Brittany. He nade his name by his book *La Vie de Jésus* (1863), a novellistic treamtent of the life of Jesus. Before that, in 1854, R. had written an essay published in the journal *La Revue des Deux Mondes* entitled "Essai sur la poésie des races celtiques", which appeared in revised, book form in 1859. R. characterised the Celtic peoples and their literatures as spontaneous, unspoilt by education, and sentimental. He also emphasised the (supposed) disinclination of the Celts towards discipline, political organisation and healthy pragmatism. In his view, the inhabitants of the Celtic lands were characterised by a love of the past and a passive, introverted attitude to life. This judgment was however only to a limited extent based upon first-hand knowledge of the Celtic peoples, languages and literatures. It was coloured to a great extent by the ideas of the Romantics and the author's own recollections of his childhood. R.'s acquaintance with Celtic literature was limited to a very small number of works in English and French translations. Many of his thoughts were taken up by his friend, Mattthew → Arnold, which led to their having extensive influence on the popular image of the Celts (cf. → Celtic ideology).
   Lit.: R. M. Galand, *L'Ame celtique de R.*, P. 1959.

research, history of → Celtic studies.

retoiric → roscada.

Rhenus. The name of the Rhine in classical → ethnography. Comparative philology has reconstructed as the original form *reinos, which would appear to mean "river". This developed to Celtic *rēnos, which was the form adopted by the Romans. In Germanic, however, *reinos became *rīnaz, resulting in Old High German Rīn, modern German Rhein.

Several classical authors record that the Celts sought to test the legitimacy of their new-born children by trial by water, in the Rhine. The Roman poet Propertius (Elegiae 4,10,41) notes, moreover, that the Celtic prince Vir(i)domarus (3rdC BC) regarded himself as a descendant of the Rhine. In Gallo-Roman times the concept of "Father Rhine" occurs on a votive altar bearing the inscription RHENO PATRI (AE 1969/70, 434), which was found in Strasbourg in 1970, and may now be seen in the city's Archaeological Museum.

Lit.: R. Vollkommer, 'Vater Rhein und seine römischen Darstellungen' (BJB 194) 1994, 1–42.

Rhiannon (Welsh /ɹiˈannon/). Protagonist in the first and third stories of the "Four Branches of the Mabinogi" (→ Pedeir Ceinc y Mabinogi). In the first branch the story is told of how Rh. encounters the prince → Pwyll of Dyfed, marries him and bears a son by him (cf. → Pwyll Pendefig Dyfed). The action of the third branch (→ Manawydan fab Llŷr) takes place many years after these events. After the death of her first husband, Rh. has married Manawydan, a comrade in arms of her son → Pryderi. The magical machinations of an enemy of the family lead to all three suffering great calamities, until Manawydan succeeds in establishing who is responsible for the spell and punishing him. Particularly in the first of these two tales Rh. clearly reveals mythical traits of character: when she encounters Pwyll she is riding a magical horse, and the birth of her son is inexplicably linked with the birth of a foal. Many authors therefore assume a link between Rh. and the Celtic goddess → Epona.

Rhydderch Hael (Welsh /ˈɹəðerx hail/). Ruler of a kingdom in the north of Celtic Britain c. 600 AD. The earliest mention of him is in the 7thC, by → Adamnán in his biography of Saint Columba (→ Colum Cille). According to this source his territory was the area around present-day Strathclyde in southern Scotland. The → Historia Brittonum refers to Rh. as one of four kings who fought against the Angles towards the end of the 6thC. Allusions to Rh. also occur in several poems concerned with the fortunes of the poet → Myrddin. From these it may be gleaned that Myrddin's royal patron Gwenddoleu fell in battle against Rh., and that Myrddin himself then sought refuge in the forests of Scotland, fearing the vengeance of his enemy. In the → Trioedd Ynys Prydein Rh. appears as one of the "Three Generous Men (hael) of the Island of Britain". According to the → *Englynion y Beddeu* his grave is in Abererch on the peninsula of Llŷn in north-west Wales.

Rhydderch, White Book of → Llyfr Gwyn Rhydderch.

Rhŷs, John (1840–1915). Celticist, born near Ponterwyd in South Wales. After studying philology in Bangor, Oxford, Paris and Leipzig, he at first worked as an inspector of schools in Wales. In 1877 he was appointed to the newly founded Chair in Celtic Studies at the University of Oxford. His primary interests were, from that point on, questions relating to the history of the Celtic languages and philology. He also published *The Welsh People* (1900, together with D. Brynmor-Jones), aimed at a wider public, and *Celtic Folklore, Welsh and Manx* (2 vols., 1901). He concerned himself with problems of Celtic religion and mythology in the works *Studies in the Arthurian Legend* (1881) and *On the Origin and Growth of Religion as Illustrated by Celtic Heathendom* (1888). Rh. was awarded honorary doctorates by the universities of Edinburgh and Wales, and was knighted in 1907. Among his most prominent pupils were John → Morris-Jones and John Gwenogvryn → Evans.
  Lit.: J. Parry-Williams, *J. Rh. 1840–1915*, Car. 1954.

rí (Ir. /R'iː/). Term denoting a king. The law texts distinguish between the king of a tribal group (rí tuaithe; cf. → tuath), the king occupying a higher position who rules over several tribal groups (rí tuath or ruiri), and, still more powerful, the king of one of the Irish "provinces" (rí cóicid; cf. → cóiced). The title of High King (ard-rí) or King of Ireland (rí Érenn), on the other hand, had no practical significance until the high Middle Ages, and played a major role only in literature. The chief tasks of the king included the raising of an army (slógad) in time of war, and the preservation of law and order in time of peace. Here the concept of the "justice of the ruler" (→ fír flathemon) was of central importance; the good or ill fortune of the king and of his subjects was held to be dependant on this being put into practice. Many sagas and poetic eulogies describe the accession to the office of king as a marriage of the ruler with his country or with the personification of "Sovereignty" (flathius). In all probability these texts preserve pre-Christian concepts of a → sacred marriage between the king and a goddess of kingship.
  Lit.: D. A. Binchy, *Celtic and Anglo-Saxon Kingship*, O. 1970; F. J. Byrne, *Irish Kings and High-Kings*, Lo. 1973; D. Ó Corráin, 'Nationality and Kingship in pre-Norman Ireland', in: T. W. Moody (ed.), *Nationality and the Pursuit of National Independence*, Belfast 1978, 1–35; P. Wormald, 'Celtic and Anglo-Saxon Kingship: some further thoughts', in: P. E. Szarmach (ed.), *Sources of Anglo-Saxon Culture*, Kalamazoo, Mich. 1986, 151–183; M. Gerriets, 'Kingship and exchange in pre-Viking Ireland' (CMCSt 13) 1987, 39–72; ead., 'The King as Judge in Early Ireland' (*Celtica* 20) 1988, 1–24.

Rigani. Gaulish word for "queen", etymologically equivalent to the Irish word rígain (cf. → Morrígain), which has the same meaning. It is possible that R. is the name of a goddess in a votive dedication written in Gaulish, which was found during excavations in Lezoux in the Dép. of Puy-de-Dôme. The inscription dates from the first half of the 1stC AD and reads "e . . . ieuririgani rosmertiac". This may be translated as "This I dedicated to R. and Rosmerta". It is however also conceivable that the dedication was to one single divinity, in which case R. would be the byname or honorary title of the goddess → Rosmerta. The attempts of the archaeologist Jean-Jacques Hatt (b. 1913) to identify a goddess R. in visual depictions of pre-Roman times should be viewed with caution.

Lit.: M. Lejeune & R. Marichal, 'Textes gaulois et gallo-romains en cursive latine I Lezoux' (EC 15) 1976/77, 151–156; J.-J. Hatt, 'La divinité féminine souveraine chez les Celtes continentaux, d'après l'épigraphie gallo-romaine et l'art celtique' (CRAI) 1981, 12–20.

right → deisel.

rix (rīgs). Gaulish word for "king", attested in numerous personal names such as → Ambiorix, → Orgetorix and → Vercingetorix. The Irish form of the word is → rí. In Welsh the word was supplanted at an early stage by → brenin. Celtic *rīg-s corresponds etymologically to Latin rēx and Old Indian rājā. In English it appears in the third syllable of the name Frederick.

Rodenbach. Site c. 6 miles north of Kaiserslautern (Pfalz), where in 1874 a Celtic → princely grave of the 5thC BC was found. The excavation unearthed, among other things, a sword, a knife, three big lance-heads and several bronze dishes. The corpse had been given golden rings to adorn both arms and fingers. The finds may now be seen in the Historisches Museum der Pfalz in Speyer.

Lit.: H.-J. Engels, 'Der Fürstengrabhügel von R.' (Bonner Hefte zur Vorgeschichte 3) 1972, 25–52.

Roquepertuse. Present-day name of a prehistoric settlement situated on a rocky summit in the valley of the Arc, c. 9 miles west of Aix-en-Provence. Archaeological finds attest the presence of mankind from late Neolithic times until the end of the 2ndC AD, when the settlement was destroyed by a fire and abandoned. In 1860 two fragments of stone sculptures were found in R., depicting warriors, presumably Celts, in the so-called → Buddha position. Further excavations in 1919–1927 found fragments of one or more similar statues, as well as a frieze decorated with horses' heads, a stone sculpture of a two-headed divinity, a statue of a bird of prey, and three stone pillars with recesses in which human skulls had originally been embedded. Until recently these finds were exhibited in Marseille in a reconstruction which left something to be desired. After detailed archaeological research they are in the future to be displayed in the newly established Musée de la Vieille Charité in Marseille.

Lit.: *Voyage en Massalie: 100 ans d'archéologie en Gaule du Sud*, Marseille 1990; R. *et les Celto-Ligures*, Marseille 1992.

roscada (Ir. /'Roskaða). Name given in medieval Ireland to texts which stand in an intermediary position between the literary genres of prose and rhyming, syllabic and strophic poetry. They are composed in language which is deliberately obscure, characterised by a concise, allusive mode of expression, unusual word-order, alliteration and a preference for rare or archaic words. The same characteristics occur in texts which are presented as monologues in the prose tales and referred to as retoiric. Many of these texts have yet to be exhaustively researched, owing to the difficulties they pose. It is improbable that r. in every case derive from pre-Christian oral poetry.

Lit.: P. MacCana, 'On the use of the term retoiric' (*Celtica* 7) 1966, 65–90; D. A. Binchy, 'The so-called "rhetorics" of Irish Saga', in: H. Pilch & J. Thurow (eds.), *Indo-Celtica*, Mn. 1972, 29–38; L. Breatnach, 'Zur Frage der r. im Irischen', in: H. L. C. Tristram (ed.), *Metrik und Medienwechsel*, T. 1991, 197–205.

Rosmerta. Celtic goddess worshipped predominantly in north-eastern Gaul, sometimes alone, sometimes as a companion of the god → Mercury. Her attributes include the patera (sacrificial bowl) and the horn of plenty, but she is also, because of her close association with Mercury, sometimes depicted with his caduceus (herald's staff). Her name contains the same root as that of the god → Smertrios, and is thought to refer to the protective function attributed to her.

Rowlands, Henry (1655–1723). Antiquarian, born on the island of Anglesey (cf. → Mona), where he spent the whole of his life. His office as a clergyman of the Anglican church gave him sufficient leisure to devote himself to historical research. In his book *Mona Antiqua Restaurata* (1723) he concerns himself with the monuments of Anglesey dating from prehistoric and early historical times; he quite arbitrarily attributes their erection to the Celtic → druids. In consequence he, together with John → Aubrey and William → Stukeley, exerted a lasting influence upon the popular image of Celtic religion and its priests (cf. → Celtic ideology).

Ruad Ro-fesa (Ir. /'Ruað 'Roesa/). A byname of the → Dagda, meaning "the Mighty One possessed of Great Knowledge".

Rudianus. Celtic god whose cult is attested by four votive inscriptions. Two of these come from St. Etienne and St. Génis in the Dép. of Drôme (CIL XII 1566 and 2204), the other two from St. Michel de Valbonne in the Dép. of

239

Rudiobus

Var (CIL XII 381 and 382). In the latter two R. is identified with → Mars on the basis of the → interpretatio romana.

Rudiobus. Celtic god. The sole evidence of his cult is the votive inscription (CIL XIII 3071) on the plinth of a statuette of a horse from → Neuvy-en-Sullias, Loiret, France.

Ruteni. In classical → ethnography a Celtic tribe in the region of the French Dép. of Aveyron. The name survives in that of the town of Rodez, whose Roman name was Segodunum.

sacral kingship → sacred marriage, → kings.

sacred marriage (Gk. Hieròs Gámos). In comparative religion the name given to a sequence of rites and myths at the heart of which is always the union of two human beings, or of a god and a goddess, or of a divinity and a human partner. In the field of Celtic religion the term s. m. generally refers to the idea that the king (Ir. → rí) is the spouse of a goddess or of the female personification of the country. This motif is particularly prevalent in the Irish literature of the Middle Ages and the early modern period, but the role it played in the nexus of pre-Christian cultic practice remains obscure. The idea that the king enters a s.m. with a goddess on becoming sovereign occurs as early as the Sumerians; historical links with corresponding concepts in later cultures have not however been established.

Lit.: J. Weisweiler, *Heimat und Herrschaft*, Hl. 1943; R. A. Breatnach, 'The Lady and the King' (*Studies* 42) 1953, 321–336; P. MacCana, 'Aspects of the Theme of the King and Goddess in Ir. lit.' (*EC* 7) 1955, 76–114, 356–413 & (*EC* 8) 1959, 59–65; R. Bromwich, 'Celtic Dynastic Themes and the Breton Lays' (*EC* 9) 1961, 439–474; J. K. Bollard, 'Sovereignty and the Loathly Lady in English, Welsh and Irish' (*Leeds Studies in English* 17) 1986, 41–59; B. Maier, 'Die keltische Auffassung des Königtums und ihre orientalischen Parallelen', Diss. Bonn 1991; M. Herbert, 'Goddess and king: the sacred marriage in early Ireland', in: L. O. Fradenburg (ed.), *Women and Sovereignty*, E. 1992, 264–295.

sacrifices and offerings. Sacrifices played a central role in Celtic religion, as in all ancient religions. The evidence of archaeological finds and the accounts in classical → ethnography show that the Celts made offerings of objects, as well as animals and human beings. Before being sacrificed, objects were frequently rendered useless by being broken or bent. Animals were quite commonly burned or buried whole, but there is also archaeological evidence of ritual meals.

The classical literature concerned with the Celts frequently alludes to human sacrifices and there are some detailed accounts. According to →

Caesar (Bell. Gall. 6,16) the → druids performed such sacrifices particularly in time of war or dire need, as they were of the opinion that the gods could only be induced to save lives if a man's life were offered in return. The poet → Lucan's account of human sacrifices to the gods → Esus, → Teutates and → Taranis (Pharsalia I, 444–446) is well-known. → Diodoros of Sicily (5,31) and → Strabo (4,4) mention human sacrifices for the purpose of → prophecy. Perhaps the most striking archaeological evidence of Celtic sacrificial customs is the bog corpse of → Lindow Moss.

In medieval Irish and Welsh literature sacrifices are scarcely ever mentioned, presumably a consequence of → christianisation.

Lit.: T. Capelle, 'Eisenzeitliche Bauopfer' (*Frühmittelalt. Studien* 21) 1987, 185–205; P. Meniel, *Les sacrifices d'animaux chez les Gaulois*, P. 1992; G. Kurz, *Keltische Hort- und Gewässerfunde in Mitteleuropa*, St. 1995.

sagas, lists of. Modern scholarship generally divides the narrative literature of medieval Ireland into "cycles" on the basis of its content. Customarily a distinction is drawn between the → Finn, → Ulster, → Historical and → Mythological Cycles. The medieval story-tellers themselves, however, seem to have organised the traditional saga material according to types, rather like modern researchers into folktales. A major source for our knowledge of this classification is provided by two medieval lists of sagas. One of these (A) is preserved in the "Book of Leinster" (→ Lebor Laignech), as well as in a manuscript of the 16thC. The other (B) is embedded in the Middle Irish narrative *Airec menman Uraird maic Coise*, the manuscript transmission of which can be dated back to the 14thC. The most important terms employed in these lists to distinguish between types are → aided, → aithed, → baile, → cath, → compert, → echtrae, → immram, → orgain, → táin, → tochmarc and → togail.

Lit.: P. MacCana, *The Learned Tales of Medieval Ireland*, Du. 1980; N. Ní Chonghaile & H. L. C. Tristram, 'Die mittelirischen Sagenlisten zwischen Mündlichkeit und Schriftlichkeit', in: H. L. C. Tristram (ed.), *Deutsche, Kelten und Iren*, H. 1990, 249–268.

Salluvii (Gk. Salyes or Sallyes, Lat. Sallui or Salluvii). In classical → ethnography a people composed of Celts and Liguri dwelling in the area between the Rhône and the maritime Alps. In c. 600 BC the Greek Phokaians founded the colony of Massalia there (today's Marseille). In 122 BC the S. were conquered by the Romans, their chief town of → Entremont destroyed and their country incorporated into the newly-created Province of Gallia Narbonensis.

salt. In prehistoric times salt was used primarily to preserve meat. An increasing demand is noticeable from the beginning of the first millennium BC, which may relate to changes in climatic conditions. → Hallstatt and the Dürrnberg near → Hallein were salt-mining centres, with prosperous settlements evolving out of the places where salt was worked into a commodity.

Samain (Ir. /'savin'/). The day marking the beginning of winter in the Irish calendar (1st Nov.), it was celebrated as the beginning of the New Year, with the evening of the 31st October being included in the festivities. The night between the 31st October and 1st November (Hallowe'en) plays a major role in legends and customs, as it was believed that in these hours human beings could make contact with the world of spirits.

Lit.: K. Danaher, *The Year in Ireland*, Du. 1972.

Samildánach (Ir. /'sav'ilda:nax/ "skilled in all arts"). Byname given to → Lug mac Ethnenn in the story of the Battle of Mag Tuired (→ *Cath Maige Tuired*), on account of the fact that he incorporates the gifts and capacities of all imaginable craftsmen and artists.

Sanas Chormaic (Ir. /'sanas 'xormik'/ "Cormac's Whispering"). Title of an etymological glossary of c. 900, which attempts to explain archaic or unusual words in Irish legal and poetic language, as well as a series of place-names and personal names. It is named after its author, the Southern Irish bishop and king of Munster, Cormac mac Cuilennáin. The etymological observations of Cormac derive from the *Etymologiae* of Isidore of Seville and are therefore from the point of view of modern linguistics erroneous for the most part, but the glossary is valuable in Irish literary history, as the literary quotations which are adduced show which works were available in writing to Cormac; the manuscripts preserving these works are of later date. Moreover, some entries yield interesting information concerning what ideas a clerical author of the 9th/10thC, educated in a Latin culture, entertained concerning pre-Christian Irish religion and mythology.

Ed. and trans.: J. Ó Donovan & W. Stokes, *Cormac's Glossary (S. Ch.)*, Calcutta 1868.

Lit.: R. Thurneysen, 'Zu Cormacs Glossar', in: *FS Ernst Windisch*, L. 1914, 8–37; P. Russell, 'The Sounds of a Silence: The Growth of Cormac's Glossary' (CMCSt 15) 1988, 1–30.

sanctuaries → places of worship.

Santones. In classical → ethnography a Celtic tribe living near the lower Charente. The name survives in that of the town Saintes, whose Roman name was Mediolanum.

Saône → Souconna.

Scáthach (Ir. /'ska:θax/). A feared she-warrior in the tales of the → Ulster

Cycle. → Cú Chulainn is said to have received his training in arms at her hands, as is recounted in detail in the story → *Tochmarc Emire*. The tale also contains a poem entitled *Verba Scáthaige* ("Words of S."), in which S. prophesies to her pupil in obscure formulation the course and outcome of the Cattle Raid of Cuailnge (→ *Táin Bó Cuailnge*). This poem is thought to have been contained in the lost manuscript → Cín Dromma Snechta, which is dated to the first half of the 8thC. On this basis it is assumed that an early version of the story of the Cattle-Raid of Cuailnge was already in circulation at that time.

Lit.: P. L. Henry, 'Verba Scáthaige' (*Celtica* 21) 1990, 191–207 (with ed. and Engl. trans.).

Scéla Cano meic Gartnáin (Ir. /'ʃk'eːla 'kano vikʲ 'ɣaRtnaːnʲ/ "The Story of Cano, Son of Gartnán"). Title of a tale from the → Historical Cycle. The surviving version is thought to date from the early 11thC and is preserved in the → "Yellow Book of Lecan".

The story tells of how the titular hero Cano mac Gartnáin is persecuted by his grandfather Aedán mac Gabráin and forced to flee from Scotland to Ireland in consequence. He is hospitably received by the kings Diarmait and Bláthmac of Ulster, and with the aid of a daughter of Diarmait successfully evades, by the skin of his teeth, a further attack from his grandfather. From Ulster Cano makes his way to Connacht, where he falls in love with Créd, a daughter of the king Guaire, and wife of the warrior Marcán. During a feast Créd puts a sleep-charm on all save herself and Cano. Cano, however, does not wish to become her lover until he has gained the royal throne of Scotland. He leaves Connacht, but gives to Créd as a token of his love a magic stone; his life depends upon this stone remaining intact. After Cano has indeed become king of Scotland he attempts to meet with Créd again, but Marcán's son, Colcu, prevents this and deals Cano a serious wound. When Créd sees this, believing her lover to be slain, she smashes her head against a rock. The magic stone breaks, and Cano dies a few days later.

Ed.: D. A. Binchy, S. C. m. G., Du. 1963 (MMIS 18).

Trans.: R. Thurneysen, 'Eine irische Parallele zur Tristan-Sage' (*Zeitschrift für Romanische Philologie* 43) 1924, 385–402.

Lit.: T. Ó Cathasaigh, 'The Theme of Ainmne in S. C. m. G.' (*Celtica* 15) 1983, 78–87; id., 'The Rhetoric of S. C. m. G.', in: D. Ó. Corráin et al. (eds.), *Sages, Saints, and Storytellers*, May. 1989, 233–250.

Scéla mucce Meic Dathó (Ir. /'ʃk'eːla 'mukʲe mikʲ 'daθoː/ "The Tale of Mac Dathó's Pig"). Title of a tale from the → Ulster Cycle, the oldest version of which is preserved in the "Book of Leinster" (→ Lebor Laignech). The story begins with the kings → Conchobar of Ulster and → Ailill of Connacht both at the same time sending messengers to Mac Dathó to ask for his hound

Ailbe. As Mac Dathó does not dare refuse either of the groups of messengers, he promises the hound to both Conchobar and Ailill, and invites both parties to a banquet, at which an enormous pig is served. A fierce dispute ensues in which the warriors of Ulster and Connacht contest the right to divide the pig (cf. → curad-mír). When → Conall Cernach proves victorious and intends to concede only the pig's foretrotters to the men of Connacht, a fight develops, in the course of which the heroes of Ulster put their opponents to flight. During the pursuit of the men of Connacht the dog Ailbe is killed by Ailill's charioteer.

Ed.: R. Thurneysen, S. M. M. D., Du. 1935 (MMIS 6).

Trans.: J. Gantz, Early Ir. Myths and Sagas, Harm. 1981.

Lit.: N. K. Chadwick, 'The Story of Mac Dathó's Pig' (SGS 8), 1958, 130–145; C. G. Buttimer, 'S. M. M. D.: a reappraisal' (PHCC 2) 1982, 61–73.

Scél Tuain meic Chairill (Ir. /ʃk′eːl 'tuːin′ vik′ 'xar′iL′/ "The Story of Tuan, son of Cairell"). Title of a tale from the → Mythological Cycle, preserved in the "Book of the Dun Cow" (→ Lebor na hUidre) and three manuscripts of the 14th-16thC. The story tells of the settlement of Ireland from the Flood to the early Middle Ages, in a historical sketch placed in the mouth of the eponymous hero Tuan. He is said to have arrived on the island together with the first settlers after the Flood (cf. → Lebor Gabála Érenn), and to have witnessed the subsequent history of the country, assuming the form of a stag, a boar, an eagle and a salmon. In the 5thC AD he was reborn as the son of the king Cairell, and in advanced age told his story to Saint Finnian of Mag Bile. – The story is reworked by James → Stephens in his Irish Fairy Tales.

Ed.: J. Carey, 'S. T. m. C.' (Ériu 35) 1984, 93–111 (with Engl. trans.)

Lit.: J. Carey, 'Suibne Geilt and Túan mac Cairill' (Éigse 20) 1984, 93–105.

School of Celtic Studies (Ir. Scoil an Léinn Cheiltigh). Institution founded in 1940 for the furtherment of Celtic studies in Ireland. Its primary function is the education of advanced students and the organisation of seminars, courses and conferences. Other focal points of the institution are the publication of research in the Celtic field and of editions of Irish, Welsh, and Hiberno-Latin texts. Its bulletin is the journal Celtica (1946ff.).

Lit.: S. of C. S.: Fiftieth Anniversary Report 1940–1990, Du. 1990.

School of Irish Learning. Research and educational institute for Irish Celticists founded in 1903 by Kuno → Meyer. It survived until 1926, when for financial reasons it merged with the Royal Irish Academy. Its bulletin, the journal Ériu (1904ff), is also now published by the Royal Irish Academy.

Schwarzenbach. Place near Idar-Oberstein (Rhineland/Pfalz), near which in 1849 two Celtic → princely graves of the 5th/4thC BC were found. Grave gifts included → jewellery, the broken golden mounting of a dish, and some small masks that had been worked from gold plate. A few other objects from the graves, including a bronze beaker and several iron weapons, disappeared in mysterious circumstances soon after they were discovered. Other finds have been missing since 1945, when they were last seen in Berlin.

Lit.: O.-H. Frey, 'Die Goldschale von S.' (HBA 1) 1971, 85–100; A. Haffner, Die westliche Hunsrück-Eifel-Kultur, B. 1976.

Scottish (or Scots) Gaelic. The Celtic language of Scotland, forming, together with → Irish and → Manx, the Gaelic branch of the insular Celtic → languages. Introduced by Irish settlers in the 5thC AD, it appears to have diverged only to a small extent from its sister languages until the 12th/13thC. This is attested by the earliest records of Gaelic in Scotland, the notes in the → Book of Deer. As early as the 11th-13thC English acquired increasing importance as the language of the court, of administration, and of the towns as commercial centres. From the 17thC at the latest Scottish Gaelic was only widespread in the Highlands and the Hebrides. There too, a series of restrictive measures sought to limit its use. After the suppression of the Jacobite rebellion, originating in the Highlands, the English government began in 1782 to deport large parts of the Gaelic-speaking population overseas. Thereafter Scottish Gaelic was spoken almost exclusively on the northern and western coasts, and on the offshore islands. Despite increasing state support in recent decades, its use has declined more and more even in these areas. As an everyday language S. G. today is limited almost exclusively to the Hebrides.

Lit.: G. Price, The Languages of Britain, Lo. 1984; Ch. W. J. Withers, Gaelic in Scotland 1698–1981, E. 1984; W. Gillies (ed.), Gaelic and Scotland, E. 1989; D. S. Thomson (ed.), Gaelic and Scots in Harmony, Glasgow 1990; K. MacKinnon, Gaelic: a past and future prospect, E. 1991.

Segomo. Celtic god identified with → Mars on the basis of the → interpretatio romana. His cult is attested by five votive inscriptions from the settlement area of the → Sequani and their neighbours in south-east France (CIL XIII 1675, 2532, 2846 and 5340; CIL V 7868).

Seine → Sequana.

Selma (Scots Gaelic sealladh math "good sight", i.e. "Belvedere"). The name of the castle of the Scottish king Fingal in James → Macpherson's "Works of Ossian". The name is Macpherson's own creation, and does not occur in Celtic tradition proper. The Songs of S. are among the most celebrated of Macpherson's poems, because of their lyrical and elegiac character. Goethe translated them into German prose for Friederike Brion in 1771, and used this translation three years later in his novel Die Leiden des jungen Werthers ("The Sorrows of Young Werther").

Sencha mac Ailella (Ir. /'ʃenxa mak 'al'eLa/). A poet (→ fili) of the king → Conchobar mac Nesa in the tales of the → Ulster Cycle. Always concerned to effect a peaceful settlement, he forms a counterpoint to figures such as → Bricriu Nemthenga or → Dubthach Dael Ulad.

Senchas Már (Ir. /'ʃenxas maːr/ "Great Tradition"). The most important collection of Old Irish law texts, thought to have originated in the first half of the 8thC in the northern half of the island. It comprises some 30 treatises on the most divergent areas of Irish law.

Lit.: F. Kelly, A Guide to Early Ir. Law, Du. 1988; N. W. Patterson, 'Gaelic Law and the Tudor Conquest of Ireland' (Ir. Hist. Studies 27) 1991, 1–23.

Senones. In classical → ethnography a Celtic tribe which settled in upper Italy and central Gaul. In upper Italy the region of the S. was on the east coast, north of the river Esino. In Gaul the S. resided between the central Loire and the Seine. In 57 BC they formed an alliance with → Caesar in his war against the → Belgae (cf. Bell. Gall. 2,2). Three years later, however, they seceded from the Romans and in 52 BC joined the rebellion of → Vercingetorix. The name of the S. survives in that of the town of Sens, formerly called Agedincum.

Sequana. Celtic name for the Seine. The geographical term occurs in → Caesar (Bell. Gall. 1,1 et passim) and elsewhere.

The cult of a goddess of the same name is attested by numerous archaeological finds of Roman and pre-Roman date, as well as a number of inscriptions (CIL XIII 2858–2865). An important sanctuary dedicated to S. was excavated as early as 1836–1842 near the source of the Seine, about 20 miles north-west of Dijon. → Votive gifts of wood and bronze were found, together with a vase containing 836 coins; all these had been dedicated to the goddess. During further excavations in 1933 the bronze statue of a female figure, c. 60cm in height, was found, standing upright in a boat, her arms outstretched. This is thought to be an image of the goddess. During archaeological excavations in 1963–1967 c. 200 unusually well-preserved votive gifts of wood came to light. They are now to be seen in the Archaeological Museum in Dijon, as is the bronze statue of the goddess.

Lit.: S. Deyts, Les Bois Sculptés des Sources de la Seine, P. 1983; ead., Le Sanctuaire des Sources de la Seine, Dijon 1985.

Sequani. In classical → ethnography a Celtic tribe in the region between the Jura, the Rhône and the Saône. Its most important town was Vesontio, present-day Besançon. According to → Caesar (Bell. Gall. 6,12), when he arrived in Gaul the S. had, with the aid of the Germani, won dominance over their rivals, the → Aedui, thus becoming one of the most powerful tribes in Gaul. Because of Caesar's intervention, however, the S. lost much of their importance in the time that followed, in contrast to the Aedui and the → Remi.

Serglige Con Culainn ocus oenét Emire (Ir. /'ʃergl'iɣ'e kon 'kuliN' ogus 'oine:d 'ev'ir'e/ "The Wasting Sickness of Cú Chulainn and The Only Jealousy of Emer"). Title of a tale from the → Ulster Cycle, preserved in the "Book of the Dun Cow" (→ Lebor na hUidre), and in a 15th/16thC manuscript.

The story tells of the love of the fairy Fann for the mortal hero → Cú Chulainn. Its title refers to an inexplicable sickness which one day befalls Cú Chulainn; he is only cured of this by the news of Fann's love for him. On the invitation of the fairy Lí Ban, a sister of Fann, Cú Chulainn and his charioteer Loeg mac Riangabra make their way to the "Plain of Delights", the home of the fairies and elves. There Cú Chulainn fights successfully against the enemies of the elf Labraid Luath-lám-ar-chlaideb, who is married to Lí Ban. As a reward he is permitted to share the bed of Fann for one month. When after this he arranges to meet his beloved in Ireland, his wife Emer finds out about it and comes to the rendezvous with fifty serving women, seeking to kill Fann. Fann, however, is surprisingly taken back by her husband → Manannán mac Lir to her home. Druids bring Cú Chulainn and Emer a magic potion, whereupon he forgets his pain at the loss of his beloved and she forgets her jealousy. – The story was reworked by Lady Augusta → Gregory in the 14th chapter of her book *Cuchulain of Muirthemne*. It also inspired the symphonic poem *The Garden of Fand* (1916) by Arnold Bax (1883–1953).

Ed.: M. Dillon, 'The Trinity College Text of S. C. C.' (SGS 6) 1949, 139–175; id., S. C. C., Du. 1953 (text after the LU; MMIS 14).

Trans.: M. Dillon, 'The Wasting Sickness of Cú Chulainn' (SGS 7) 1953, 47–88; J. Gantz, *Early Ir. Myths and Sagas*, Harm. 1981.

Sétanta (Ir. /'ʃe:daNta/). The real name of the hero → Cú Chulainn. According to the story of his conception and birth (→ *Compert Chon Culainn*) he received this name from his father → Lug mac Ethnenn. How S. came by his later name, "Hound of Culann", is the subject of the story of "The Boyhood Deeds of Cú Chulainn" (→ *Macgnímrada Con Culainn*).

settlements. Settlements in the Celtic regions have hitherto been the subjects of relatively infrequent and often less than exhaustive archaeological research. Such efforts as have been made have concentrated upon the early Celtic → princely graves of the late Hallstatt period, and on the late Celtic → oppida of the middle and late La Tène culture. The majority of Celts, however, undoubtedly lived in small, open villages, which frequently reveal a marked continuity of habitation. These settlements are for the most part in the middle of cultivated fields (cf. → agriculture), near streams or rivers. The houses were generally constructed of wood and wattle and daub, with roofs of straw or reeds.

Lit.: H. Härke, *Settlement Types and Settlement Patterns in the West Hallstatt Prov-*

ince, O. 1979; O. H. Frey & H. Roth (eds.), *Studien zu Siedlungsfragen der Latènezeit*, Marburg 1984; F. Audouze & O. Buchsenschutz, *Villes, villages et campagnes de l'Europe celtique*, P. 1989.

Sgilti Ysgafndroed (Welsh /'sgilti əs'gavndroid/ "S. the Light-Footed"). One of → Arthur's retinue in the story → *Culhwch ac Olwen*. He is renowned for his peculiar ability to carry out messages for his lord without using the roads. He is attributed with the capacity to make his way through wooded regions by leaping from treetop to treetop, and over the hills on the tips of the sedge grass, being so light-footed that not a single blade of grass bent beneath him. It is thought that both the name and the figure of S. derive from the Irish tradition, where there is a corresponding figure in the tales of the → Finn Cycle, the warrior → Caílte mac Rónáin, famed for his fleetness of foot.

síd (Ir. /ʃiːð/). The name in the tales of the → Mythological Cycle of the underground residences of the beings thought to have inhabited Ireland in mythical pre-history. They were imagined to live both in the natural mountains and hills of the country, and in the man-made burial mounds of the pre-Celtic population of Ireland. The inhabitants of a s. were called síde (pl.) or fir/mná/áes s. "men/women/people of the s.". In English the terms "fairies" or "elves" are rough equivalents. The síde are often equated with the → Tuatha Dé Danann, who are said to have fled to these subterranean homes in order to escape invading Celtic tribes.

    Lit.: Ch.-J. Guyonvarc'h, 'Irlandais s., gaulois *sedos "siège, demeure des dieux"' (*Ogam* 14) 1962, 329–340; T. Ó. Cathasaigh, 'The Semantics of S.' (*Eigse* 17) 1978, 137–155.

silver. Compared with → gold, silver played only a minor role in Celtic culture. The metal was known, but it was only rarely worked by craftsmen and to all appearances it was not accorded any extraordinary value. The two most important pieces of evidence of the silversmith's craft, the ring of → Trichtingen and the pictorial plates of the → Gundestrup cauldron, probably originated in an area on the edge of the Celtic world. Silver only acquired conspicuous economic significance with the development of Celtic → coins in the 4th/3rdC BC.

singer → bard.

Sirona. Celtic goddess. Her name appears in inscriptions as Sirona/Ðirona; it is thought to derive from a Celtic word meaning 'star'. Inscriptions dedicated to S. have been found in the neighbourhood of Trier (CIL XIII 3662), Wiesbaden (CIL XIII 7570), Mainz (CIL XIII 6753), Merlenbach in Lorraine (CIL XIII 4498), Corseul near Dinan (CIL XIII 3143) and Bordeaux (CIL XIII 582 and possibly 586). S. appears as the companion of the god Apollo → Grannus in inscriptions from → Hochscheid (Hunsrück, NeLi 9), Bitburg

(CIL XIII 6272), Alzey (Ne 85 & 86), Nierstein near Mainz (CIL XIII 6272), Großbotwar near Ludwigsburg (CIL XIII 6458), Hausen near Dillingen (CIL III 11903), Kloster Baumburg in Bavaria (CIL III 5588), Vienna, Augst near Basle (NeLi 97), Luxeuil-les-Bains (Haute-Saône; CIL XIII 5424), Graux in the Dép. of Vosges (CIL XIII 4661), Flavigny in the Dép. of Cher (*ILTG* 169), Rome (CIL VI 36), Roman Aquincum in Hungary and Bretea Romîna in Roumania (CIL III 74*; the authenticity of this inscription is contested). S. is depicted as a female figure without specific attributes, as a woman in a long dress with grapes and ears of corn, or, following the Greek model of Hygieia (health), with a snake. Her cult is attested primarily in association with healing springs.

Lit.: G. Weisgerber, *Das Pilgerheiligtum des Apollo und der S. von Hochscheid im Hunsrück*, Bo. 1975.

Sjoestedt, Marie-Louise (1900–1940). Celticist, pupil of Joseph → Vendryes. Her first works were linguistic studies concerned with the Irish verb system and Irish dialect geography. Her book *Dieux et Héros des Celtes*, published in Paris a few weeks after her death, is better known. The author sought through a synthesis of the Irish literary and the continental archaeological evidence to define the essential characteristics of Celtic religion and mythology. The book appeared in a translation by Myles → Dillon in 1949, entitled *Gods and Heroes of the Celts*, and has had a lasting influence on subsequent research into Celtic religion. It is however speculative in many parts and somewhat problematic in its linking of sources which are geographically and chronologically greatly disparate.

Skene, William Forbes (1809–1892). Scottish lawyer and historian. After studying in Edinburgh and Hanau/Hessen he worked as a notary. The close friendship his father bore the author Sir Walter Scott (1771–1832) prompted an early interest on Skene's part in the history of his homeland. In 1867 he edited the oldest sources of Scottish history under the title *Chronicles of the Picts and Scots*. In the following year he published some of the earliest Welsh literary texts in his → *Four Ancient Books of Wales*. His chief work appeared in 1876–1880, the three-volume *Celtic Scotland: A History of Ancient Alban*, in which S. was one of the first to apply historical criticism to the early phases of Scottish history.

slaves. Male and female slaves formed the lowest social class in all parts of the Celtic world. Some of these were prisoners taken in war, others bankrupt debtors, others the victims of slave-traders (the most prominent example being Saint → Patrick). The frequency with which slaves are mentioned in legal texts and the use of the word → cumal ("female slave") to denote a unit of currency suggest that slaves still performed the bulk of the work in early medieval Ireland.

Smertrius. Celtic god whose name is thought to derive from a root *smer-, linked with the concept of protection and providence. The root is not attested in Celtic place-names, but it does occur in several personal names and in the names of gods such as → Rosmerta. The name and image of S. appear on the monument of the → Nautae Parisiaci, dating from the time of the emperor Tiberius (14–37 AD). Part of the name has been obliterated, but the surviving fragments of letters permit it to be reconstructed as SMERTRIOS. The surviving part of the relief shows the head, chest and shoulders of a bearded man, and the coiled tail of a snake. In his raised right hand the man holds a club with which he is about to strike the snake. The depiction is thought to refer to a myth telling of a fight between S. and a snake. The god is not attested in literature, but inscriptions from the neighbourhood of Trier name a → Mars S. (CIL XIII 4119 and 11975). A further inscription from Großbuch in Carinthia is perhaps to be interpreted as (D)iti Smer(trio) Aug(usto), yielding the only evidence thus far for an identification of S. with → Dis Pater.

Lit.: P. M. Duval, 'Le Dieu S. et ses Avatars gallo-romains' (EC 6) 1953/54, 219–238 (= ibid, Travaux sur la Gaule, P. 1989, I 289–302).

smiths. Because of the great importance of → iron for → agriculture, → crafts and → warfare, smiths may be assumed to have played a major role in Celtic society. The requisite specialised knowledge suggests that as early as the Hallstatt period smiths were subdivided into such as concentrated upon weaponry, the blacksmith's craft, and artistic metal-working. In the time of the → oppida, over 200 different iron tools have been identified on the basis of archaeological finds; over 20 different tools were employed in the working of metal in the oppidum of → Manching alone. The worship of the god → Vulcan (Volcanus) in Roman Gaul and the traditions concerning → Gofannon and → Goibniu in Welsh and Irish literature show that smiths also played a role in Celtic → religion and → mythology.

Snettisham. Place c. 40 miles west of Norwich where in 1948 and 1950 a golden bracelet and a richly decorated neck-ring (→ torcs) of electrum were found; these have been dated to the 1stC BC. Both finds are now to be seen in the British Museum.

Lit.: J. Brailsford, Early Celtic Masterpieces from Britain in the British Museum, Lo. 1975.

society. As with regard to the position of → women, few generalisations are possible about the social structure of the Celts. This is particularly true of the political organisation of the Celtic tribes, which developed in very diverse ways. Generally speaking Celtic society was of a markedly rural and agrarian character, its economy relying heavily upon → agriculture and → cattle-breeding, with little development of urban centres (cf. however → oppida).

Celtic society was based less upon the individual than on kinship (Ir. →
fine), with members of the kinship group possessing a large number of common rights and duties. On a higher level there was the communal unit of the
tribe (Ir. → tuath), which frequently constituted the highest form of organisation in political terms, too. Celtic society was, moreover, in no sense
egalitarian, but rather subject to strictly hierarchical organisation. At its head
was a king (Ir. → rí) or the tribal aristocracy, whereas → slaves constituted
the lowest class. The remaining members of society were linked to one
another by various dependant bonds (cf. → ambactus), with priests (→
druids) and warriors occupying prominent positions.

    Lit.: → history, → law.

Souconna. Term denoting the Saône which occurs from the 4thC AD onwards. Prior to that the river was called the Arar (cf. → Ambarri).

    The cult of a goddess named S. is attested by a votive inscription (*ILTG*
314), which came to light in Chalon-sur-Saône in 1912. Another inscription
from the neighbourhood of Sagonne in the Dép. of Cher (CIL XIII 11162)
also bears the name S. However, the considerable distance between the two
sites suggests that the inscriptions refer to two distinct divinities.

souls, transmigration of → reincarnation.

springs / spring sanctuaries → Chamalières, → Glanum, → Hochscheid, →
medicine, → Sequana, → Sirona.

stag. It is apparent from pictorial representations that the stag was of particular significance in the religions of the Stone and Bronze Age, far beyond the
frontiers of Europe. In Celtic → art, the stag appears sometimes on its own,
sometimes as the companion or attribute of a divinity, and there are also
depictions of an anthropomorphic god with a stag's antlers. In recent literature this apparition is frequently referred to as → Cernunnos, even where
there is no record of the name in inscriptions. In insular Celtic tradition the
importance of the stag emerges above all in the → Finn Cycle. A significant
role is played by stags which entice the huntsman away from human habitation into unknown regions, and stags which possess the ability to take on
human form. Many insular Celtic legends of this kind have analogues outside
Celtic lands.

Staré Hradisko. Present-day name of one of the most important eastern Celtic
→ oppida, c. 11 miles east of the town of Prostějov in Moravia. The site covered
an area of almost 40 hectares and was surrounded by a chain of fortifications
some two miles in length. S. has been known of since the 16thC, but only since
1934 has there been methodical archaeological excavation.

    Lit.: J. Meduna, 'Das keltische Oppidum S.H. in Mähren' (*Germania* 48) 1970,

34–59; M. Čižmář, 'Erforschung des keltischen Oppidums S. H. in den Jahren 1983–1988' (*AKorrBl* 19) 1989, 265–268.

Starno. The cunning king of Lochlin (Scandinavia) and adversary of the Scottish king → Fingal in James → Macpherson's "Works of Ossian". His children are → Swaran and → Agandecca, the love of Fingal's youth. In the poem *Cath-Loda* S. tries to kill Fingal, who is stranded on his coast, but is defeated by his enemy in single combat and taken prisoner. Because of his love for Agandecca Fingal grants his arch-enemy life and liberty.

Steinenbronn. Place in Kreis Böblingen (Baden-Württemberg) near which in 1864 two related fragments of a Celtic sandstone stele were found during forestry work. (In the first publication relating to the finds and in some older works the site is erroneously given as the nearby village of Waldenbuch). The surviving part of the four-sided stele is 1.25m high, including the plinth (25cm). The lower part of the stone is decorated with tendrils. Above these on one surface the lower part of a human arm with a hand and fingers is visible; the stone breaks off at elbow point. The stele is thought to have originated in the 5thC BC, and may now be seen in the Württembergisches Landesmuseum in Stuttgart.

Stele from Steinenbronn.

Lit.: K. Bittel, W. Schimmig, S. Schiek (eds.), *Die Kelten in Baden-Württemberg*, St. 1981.

Stephens, James (c. 1880–1950). Anglo-Irish writer, born in Dublin. From 1896 to 1913 he worked in an office, then moved to Paris in 1913, only to return to Dublin two years later. From 1915 to 1924 he worked as an archivist in the National Gallery in Dublin. From 1925 until his death he worked as a freelance author, literary critic and radio reporter in London. In three of his books S. retold works of Old and Middle Irish literature for a modern public. His volume of *Irish Fairy Tales* (1920) was based on the stories → *Scél Tuain meic Chairill,* → *Tochmarc Becfola,* → *Compert Mongáin,* and several stories from the cycle of sagas concerning → Finn mac Cumaill. The novel *Deirdre* (1923) relates to the story → *Longas mac nUislenn* and later reworkings of this legend. In 1924 the last work of this creative phase appeared, *In the Land of Youth,* in which S. combines the tales → *Echtrae Nerai,* → *Aislinge Oenguso,* → *De chophur in da muccida* and → *Tochmarc Étainne* creatively in a single unit.

Lit.: A. Martin, *J. S.,* Du. 1977; P. McFate, *The Writings of J. S.,* Lo. 1979; J. Flynn,

'The Route to the Táin: J. S.' preparation for his unfinished epic' (*PHCC* 1) 1981, 125–143.

Stern, Ludwig Christian (1846–1911). Egyptologist and Celticist, who together with Kuno → Meyer edited the *Zeitschrift für celtische Philologie* from 1896 until his death.

Stokes, Whitley (1830–1909). Linguist and Celticist, born in Dublin. After studying at Trinity College Dublin he worked as a lawyer, first in Dublin, later in Madras and Calcutta. Through his acquaintance with Eugene → O'Curry and John → O'Donovan his interest in the area of Irish philology was aroused. From 1859 right up to his death he published many editions and translations of Irish literary works, as well as grammatical and lexical studies. Together with John → Strachan he published the two-volume *Thesaurus Palaeohibernicus* (1901–1903), an edition of the oldest Irish linguistic documents, with English translations. With Kuno → Meyer he founded the *Archiv für Celtische Lexikographie* (3 vols., 1900–1907), and with Ernst → Windisch the five-volume series *Irische Texte mit Übersetzungen und Wörterbuch* (1880–1905).

Stonehenge ("Hanging Stones"). Neolithic place of worship near Salisbury. Its builders took astronomical observations into consideration, but the original purpose of the site had lapsed into obscurity by the Middle Ages. Thus → Geoffrey of Monmouth in the first half of the 12thC records in his *Historia Regum Britanniae* that the magician Merlin (→ Myrddin) erected S. as a national monument commissioned by the king Aurelius Ambrosius (→ Emrys Wledig). By the 17thC antiquarians were uncertain whether the Britons, the Romans, the Phoenicians, or the Danes built S. The view that S. was a place of worship of the Celtic → druids occurs for the first time in the writings of the antiquarian John → Aubrey and won widespread recognition in the 18thC through the writings of William → Stukeley. There is in reality no indication whatever of a link between the Celts and S. (→ Celtic ideology).
    Lit.: S. Piggott, *Ancient Britons and the Antiquarian Imagination*, Lo. 1989.

Strabo (c. 64 BC -c. 20 AD). Born in Amaseia (Asia Minor). After studying philosophy he undertook extensive travels. He was the author of a work of history which has survived in fragmentary form (*Historika Hypomnemata*) and a geographical work (*Geographika*), most of which has survived. The latter is based less on his own experience than on the works of earlier authors. The description of the Celtic areas north of the Alps (in the fourth book of the *Geographika*) is of great importance, particularly because of its quotations from the lost work of → Poseidonios.
    Lit.: A. Dirkzwager, *S. über Gallia Narbonensis*, Lei. 1975; P. Thollard, *Barbarie et civilisation chez S.: ét. crit. des livres III et IV de la Géographie*, P. 1987.

Strachan, John (1862–1907). Linguist and Celticist, born in the Highland town of Keith. After studying in Cambridge and Jena he taught classical philology and comparative linguistics at the University of Manchester. He played a major role in the development of the → School of Irish Learning, and with Kuno → Meyer was founder and co-editor of its journal *Ériu*. Apart from linguistic aids and practical introductions to the study of Old Irish, he published together with Whitley → Stokes the two-volume *Thesaurus Palaeo-hibernicus* (1901–1903), an edition of the oldest Irish linguistic documents with English translations.

Stukeley, William (1687–1765). Antiquarian, born in Holbeach (Lincoln-shire). After studying in Cambridge and London, he worked as a general practitioner in London and Lincolnshire from 1710 to 1729. From 1730 to his death he served as a clergyman of the Anglican church in Stamford and London. Extensive research in the field had made S. familiar with such prehistoric and early historical monuments of England as were then known. His main interest was in Stone and Bronze Age stone monuments. In his works *Stonehenge* (1740) and *Abury* (= Avebury, 1743) he attributes the circles, like his predecessor John → Aubrey, to the Celtic → druids. This idea soon acquired popularity and had a lasting influence on the modern image of Celtic religion and its priests (→ Celtic ideology, → Stonehenge). In fact, both Stonehenge and Avebury were erected before the advent of the Celts. There is no evidence whatever that they played a role in Celtic religion.
   Lit.: S. Piggott, *W. S.: An Eighteenth-Century Antiquary*, rev. ed., Lo. 1985.

Sualtaim mac Roich (Ir. /'suaLtiv' mak Roiç/). In the tales of the → Ulster Cycle the mortal foster-father of the hero Cú Chulainn. In later manuscripts the name is also rendered as Su(b)altach. The story → *Compert Chon Culainn* reports of how King Conchobar of Ulster betrothes his daughter Deichtine to S., after the latter has been made pregnant by the elf Lug mac Ethnenn. The story of the Cattle-Raid of Cuailnge (→ *Táin Bó Cuailnge*) tells of how S. meets his death, when at the royal residence Emain Macha he seeks to warn the inhabitants of Ulster of the advance of the army of the men of Connacht.

substrate. In linguistics a term denoting the language of the indigenous population of a linguistic area which is suppressed by the language of a stratum of invaders or conquerors, but is still discernible in many words, geographical names or linguistic habits. In the area of Celtic philology atten-tion has focused on the hypothesis that many peculiarities of the insular Celtic languages, such as for example the position of the verb at the begin-ning of the sentence, may be explained by reference to the linguistic traits of the pre-Celtic inhabitants of Western Europe. Investigations intended to establish more precisely the influence of pre-Celtic languages on Celtic have been undertaken by, among others, John → Morris-Jones, Julius → Pokorny, and Heinrich → Wagner. Their research in this area remains, however, contentious, given the fact that scarcely anything is known of the pre-Celtic languages of Western Europe.

Lit.: D. E. Evans, 'The Celts in Britain', in: K. H. Schmidt (ed.), *Geschichte und Kultur der Kelten*, Hei. 1986, 102–115; H. Wagner, 'The Celtic Invasions of Ireland and Great Britain: Facts and Theories' (ZCP 42) 1987, 1–40; K. H. Schmidt, 'The Postulated Pre-Indo-European Substrates in Insular Celtic and Tocharian', in: T. L. Markey & J. A. C. Greppin (eds.), *When Worlds Collide: Indo-Europeans and Pre-Indo-Europeans*, Ann Arbor, Mich. 1990, 179–202.

Sucellus. Celtic god, whose name has been linked etymologically with a root *kel- "to beat, strike" and interpreted as meaning "the Good Striker". The name is attested (together with the variants Sucelus and Sucaelus) in ten votive inscriptions from southern Gaul, Switzerland, Roman Germania, the Province of Gallia Belgica and Roman Brittany (cf. CIL XII 1836; CIL XIII 4542, 5057, 6224 and 6730; Fi 87 and 134; ILTG 497 and 565).

In an altar found at Sarrebourg near Metz in 1895 (CIL XIII 4542) the goddess → Nantosuelta appears as a companion of Sucellus. Beneath the inscription DEO SUCELLO NANTOSVELTE there is a depiction of the pair, showing S. as a standing figure with a beard, clothed in a short, belted tunic and boots. In his raised left hand the god holds a sceptre, the base of which rests on the ground, the top resembling a mallet, and in his right is a round-bellied pot, with no handle.

Other depictions of S. have been sought in well over 100 stone sculptures and bronze statuettes, which have for the most part been found in the valleys of the Saône and the Rhône. Like the Sarrebourg altar they generally show a god holding a staff ending in a hammer in one hand, and a vessel in the other. In some images the god holds a knife, a sword, a club or a purse, rather than a vessel. In a few images he is shown together with a goddess. Quite frequently a dog is depicted next to the god. As the Etruscan death-god Charon was also depicted with a club, S. has been seen as a god of the underworld and identified with → Dis Pater. The mallet also appears however as a symbol in a number of dedications to the wood-god Silvanus, the hair and beard of S. resemble most closely those found in depictions of → Jupiter.

Lit.: E. Linckenheld, 'S. et Nantosuelta' (*RHR* 99) 1929, 40–92; J. de Vries, *Keltische Religion*, St. 1961; P.-M. Duval, *Les Dieux de la Gaule*, P. 1976; S. Boucher, 'L'image et les fonctions du dieu S.' (*Caes* 23) 1988, 77–86; G. Baratta, 'Una divinità gallo-romana: Sucellus. Un "ipotesi interpretiva" ' (*Archeologia Classica* 45) 1993, 233–247.

Suessiones. In classical → ethnography a Celtic tribe in the area between the Marne and the Oise. According to → Caesar (Bell. Gall. 2,3), they were originally close kin to the neighbouring → Remi. In contrast to the latter, however, the S. resisted fiercely the advance of the Romans. In 57 BC they were subjugated, along with other tribes. Their name survives in that of the city of Soissons.

Suibne mac Colmáin (Ir. /'suv'n'e mak 'kolmaːn'/). Eponymous hero of the story → *Buile Suibne*, in which he is said to be a king of the family of the Dál nAraide, living in the first half of the 7thC AD. In reality he is a fictitious invention, not attested historically.

Suleviae. Group of Celtic goddesses. The name, a plural form, is thought to be cognate with the name of the goddess → Sulis and the Irish word suíl "eye". The cult of S. is attested in some 40 votive inscriptions, most of them from Rome, upper and lower Germania and Britain. The comparatively high proportion of inscriptions from urban Rome is to be explained by the fact that in the 2nd/3rdC AD many Celts and Germani did military service in the capital of the Roman Empire. The significance of S. for the individual believer is far from clear from the surviving monuments, but an inscription from Ladenburg (Rhineland/Pfalz: CIL XIII 11740) shows that they were worshipped as a group of sisters. An inscription from the city of Rome (CIL VI 31161) indicates that S. was clearly distinct from the → Matrones/Matres, who were also worshipped as a plural unit. The terms MEISQVE SULEVIS (CIL VI 31161), SVLEIS SVIS (CIL XIII 5027) and SVLEVIS DOMESTICIS SVIS (CIL XIII 12056) suggest that the S. were personal protective deities.

Sulis. Celtic goddess identified with → Minerva on the basis of the → interpretatio romana. The chief centre of her cult was at the healing springs named after her, Aquae Sulis, the city of Bath. There an extensive temple area was dedicated to her. The worship of S. is attested by several altars (*RIB* 143–150) and the gravestone of one of her priests (*RIB* 155). The name of the goddess also apears on some curse tablets (AE 1982, 658a, 660, 661, 666, and AE 1983, 636). Outside Bath the name only occurs in one dedication, from Alzey, near Heidelberg (CIL XIII 6266).
    Lit.: B. Cunliffe & P. Davenport, *The Temple of S. Minerva at Bath*, 2 vols., O. 1985–1988.

sun. The paucity of sources means that one can only speculate about the function of the sun in Celtic religion. It is generally assumed that the sun was worshipped primarily because of its significance for → agriculture. The oldest evidence for this is thought to lie in the depictions of the sun as a swastika, as a spoked wheel or as a round disc. In many cases it is not however clear whether the monuments in question are of Celtic or pre-Celtic origin.
    That the sun played an important part in Bronze Age ritual is certain from numerous archaeological finds. Various allusions in Greek and Roman authors have been adduced as evidence that the Celts worshipped the sun itself as a divinity, but it is possible that this is no more than a cliché of

classical → ethnography, in which the worship of the planets was viewed as an indication of ignorant superstition. A late echo of this view is to be found in the 18thC, in the "Works of Ossian" of James → Macpherson, who provided the Celtic religion with such pantheistic characteristics.

From the 19thC onwards the idea occurs in comparative religion that the myths and legends of ancient peoples were nothing but a constant expression in coded form of the daily course of the sun. It was above all the German scholar of comparative religion, Max Müller (1823–1900), who popularised this view. In the area of Celtic mythology interpretations of Welsh and Irish literary works along these lines were made in particular by John → Rhŷs and Thomas Francis → O'Rahilly. In the more popular accounts of Celtic religion such interpretations still occur today, although comparative religion has long since abandoned them as erroneous.

Sutugius. God worshipped on the evidence of votive inscriptions (CIL XIII 164 and *ILTG* 45–48) in the area around the present-day town of Saint-Placard in the Dép. of Haute-Garonne. He is thought to be of pre-Celtic origin; after the Roman conquest of Gaul he was equated with → Mars.

Lit.: E. Thevenot, *Sur les traces des Mars celtiques*, Bruges 1955; J.-J. Hatt, *Mythes et Dieux de la Gaule*, P. 1989.

Swaran. Son of the king Starno of Lochlin (Scandinavia) in James → Macpherson's "Works of Ossian". His sister is → Agandecca, the beloved of the Scottish king → Fingal in his youth. In the epic *Fingal*, S. invades Ireland with a mighty army and defeats the troops of the Irish general → Cuthullin, but soon afterwards is himself defeated by Fingal's relief force, and compelled by Fingal to make peace and return to his homeland.

symbols → ornamentation.

syncretism. Term denoting the intermingling of philosophical or religious ideas of diverse origin.

In the history of Celtic → religion, it is probable that as early as pre-Roman times the religious concepts of the Celtic conquerors merged with those of the indigenous population of central and western Europe. It is possible by means of a comparison with the religious concepts of other peoples of the Indo-European linguistic group to reconstruct in part the role the Celts played in this process of fusion.

Apart from the pre-Celtic inhabitants of ancient Europe, it is probable that from the middle of the first millennium BC the cultures of the Mediterranean area also influenced Celtic religion. This is evident in marginal areas such as southern France, upper Italy and the Balkans, where an active cultural interchange took place between Greek colonists, Etruscans and Thracians, and their Celtic neighbours. To what extent merchants and travellers spread knowledge of alien religious concepts to areas further north is scarcely to be determined.

One distinct and relatively well-attested example of religious syncretism occurred in the 1stC AD in Roman Gaul, when native, Roman and oriental cults co-existed and influenced one another (cf. → interpretatio romana). After the → christianisation of the Celts syncretisation of pre-Christian and Christian concepts and practices occurred, particularly in rural areas.

Tacitus (Publius Cornelius T.). Roman historian of the 1st/2ndC AD. His most important work is a history of the Roman state from 14 to 96 AD, which survives in incomplete form under the titles *Annales* (14–68 AD) and *Historiae* ("contemporary history": 69–96 AD). Apart from this he wrote a dialogue about the rhetoricians (*Dialogus de oratoribus*), a book concerning the origins and territories of the Germani (*De origine et situ Germanorum*, better known as the *Germania*), and a biography of his father-in-law, the general Gnaeus Iulius Agricola (*De Vita Iulii Agricolae Liber*, better known as the *Agricola*). The last work is an important source for our knowledge of the Roman conquest of Britain.

Lit.: W. S. Hanson, *Agricola and the Conquest of the North*, Lo. 1987; G. Maxwell, *A Battle Lost; Romans and Caledonians at Mons Graupius*, E. 1990; W. S. Hanson, 'Tacitus' "Agricola": An Archaeological and Historical Study' (*ANRW* II.33.3) 1991, 1741–1784.

Tailtiu (Ir. /'tal't'u/). Place in County Meath north-west of Tara (→ Temair), said to have been in pre-Christian times the site of a great annual feast held at the beginning of autumn (→ Lugnasad).

Tradition holds that T. was the spouse of the last king of the → Fir Bolg and the stepmother of → Lug. She is said to be buried in the place named after her.

táin (Ir. /taːn'/). Term denoting the raiding of cattle. In the → Lists of Sagas the word serves to classify narratives whose focal point is the theft of cattle.

Táin Bó Cuailnge (Ir. /taːn' vo: 'gual'n'g'e/ "The Cattle Raid of Cuailnge"). Most important and longest story of the → Ulster Cycle. It describes how the royal couple → Ailill and → Medb make their way, accompanied by the great army they have summoned, from their residence of Cruachain in the Province of Connacht to Cuailnge in the Province of Ulster. The aim of the people of Connacht is to capture the famed bull Donn Cuailnge. As the full-grown males of Ulster are at this point in a periodically recurring state of weakness, it is only the youth → Cú Chulainn who is capable of standing up to the enemy. In innumerable fights he repeatedly delays the advance of the army, but cannot prevent the theft of the bull. However, his fierce resistance has led to the campaign being so protracted that the warriors of Ulster are at last capable of intervening in the battle. As the invaders retreat they inflict upon them such a heavy defeat that only a few survivors return with the stolen bull to Connacht. There Donn Cuailnge meets Findbennach, the most famed bull of Connacht, and in the fierce fight that takes place between them both animals meet their deaths.

The oldest surviving version of this story is preserved in the "Book of the Dun Cow" (→ Lebor na hUidre), in the → "Yellow Book of Lecan", and in two other manuscripts of the 16thC. It reworks older sources of diverse origin and contains many repetitions and contradictions. In a later version preserved in the "Book of Leinster" (→ Lebor Laignech) and in other manuscripts of the 17th/18thC these contradictions are resolveed. A later reworking of this second version is preserved in fragmentary form in two manuscripts of the 15th/16thC.

Ed. and trans.: E. Windisch, T. B. C. nach dem Buch von Leinster, L. 1905 (Ir.-German); J. Strachan & J.-G. O'Keefe, The T. B. C. from the Yellow Book of Lecan, with Variant Readings from the Lebor na hUidre, Du. 1912 (with no trans.); C. O'Rahilly, The Stowe Version of T. B. C., Du. 1961 (Ir.-Engl.); P. Ó Fiannachta, T. B. C., Du. 1966 (with no trans.); C. O'Rahilly, T. B. C. from the Book of Leinster, Du. 1967 (Ir.-Engl.); ead., T. B. C. Recension I., Du. 1976 (Ir.-Engl.).

Lit.: R. Thurneysen, Die irische Helden- und Königsage, Hl. 1921; K. H. Jackson, The Oldest Irish Tradition: A Window on the Iron Age, C. 1964; N. B. Aitchison, 'The Ulster Cycle: heroic image and historical reality' (Journal of Medieval History 13) 1987, 87–116; H. Tristram, 'Aspects of Tradition and innovation in the T. B. C.', in: Papers on language and mediaeval studies presented to A. Schopf, F. 1988, 19–38; J. P. Mallory (ed.), Aspects of the Táin, Belfast 1992; H. L. C. Tristram (ed.), Studien zur Táin Bó Cuailnge, T. 1993.

Táin Bó Froích (Ir. /ta:n' vo: vroiç/ "The Cattle-Raid of Froech"). Title of a prefatory tale (→ remscéla) to the story of the Cattle-Raid of Cuailnge (→ Táin Bó Cuailnge). It is preserved in the "Book of Leinster" (→ Lebor Laignech), in the → "Yellow Book of Lecan" and in two further manuscripts of the 15th/16thC. In its surviving form the story consists of two parts which are only loosely connected. The first part tells of the titular hero Froech's wooing of Findabair, the daughter of the royal couple Ailill and Medb. This episode ends with Froech promising, in return for his betrothal to Findabair, that he will participate in the campaign of the Men of Connacht against the Province of Ulster, on the side of Aillil and Medb. The second part of the story treats of how Froech, with the aid of the warrior Conall Cernach, frees his wife (not in this case Findabair), his three sons and his cattle from the clutches of raiders.

The story of Froech's wooing of Findabair occurs in ballad form in the → Book of the Dean of Lismore. An English translation appeared as early as 1756, and influenced James → Macpherson among others. The story was retold by Lady Augusta → Gregory in the ninth chapter of her book *Cuchulain of Muirthemne*.

Ed. and trans.: W. Meid, *Die Romanze von Froech und Findabair*, I. 1970.
Trans.: J. Gantz, *Early Irish Myths and Sagas*, Harm. 1981.
Lit.: R. Thurneysen, *Die irische Helden- und Königsage*, Hl. 1921; J. Carney, *Studies in Irish Literature and History*, Du. 1955; D. E. Meek, 'T. B. F. and Other "Fraech" Texts' (CMCSt 7), 1984, 1–37 & (8) 1984, 65–85.

Tair Rhamant, Y (Welsh /ə tair 'ʀamant/ "the Three Romances"). Customary Welsh collective term referring to the three narratives → *Iarlles y Ffynnawn*, → *Peredur fab Efrawg* and → *Gereint fab Erbin*. These stories, like → *Culhwch ac Olwen* and → *Breuddwyd Rhonabwy*, belong to the cycle of legends concerning → Arthur. They occupy something of a special position in the Welsh tradition owing to their closeness to French and Anglo-Norman courtly romances. This applies in the first place to the material and intellectual culture depicted or presupposed in the stories. All the descriptions of clothing, weapons and castles, as well as the way in which battle and social intercourse are depicted, are influenced by the courtly ideal of the 12thC. Nor does Arthur appear (as in *Culhwch ac Olwen*) as the leader of a band of warriors with magical abilities, but rather as the highest feudal lord of a community of exemplary knights. In contrast to *Culhwch ac Olwen* and *Breuddwyd Rhonabwy* the action of the T. Rh. is not set in places in Wales and Cornwall, but in a fairy-tale world.

Despite these common factors there are considerable differences between the three narratives with regard to style, structure and plot. It is therefore thought that they are the work of different authors. There are clear correspondences between the T.Rh. and the verse romances of → Chrétien de Troyes, *Yvain*, *Perceval* and *Erec*. Probably the Welsh authors were acquainted with stories which bore a considerable resemblance to these French romances, but they shaped the material to hand in a totally independent way.

Lit.: D. Edel, 'The "Mabinogionfrage": Arthurian Literature between Orality and Literacy', in: H. L. C. Tristram (ed.), *(Re)Oralisierung*, T. 1996, 311–333.

Taliesin. Held to be one of the first poets of the British Celts known to us by name (→ Cynfeirdd). According to the → *Historia Brittonum* he lived in the North of England in the second half of the 6thC AD. His native language was therefore in all probability → Cumbrian, of which very little is known. In medieval Wales T. was regarded as the author of a large number of poems in Middle Welsh which survive in what is called the "Book of Taliesin" (→ Llyfr Taliesin). The content and language suggest that at best twelve of these poems can be attributed to the historical T. The others are of later date, from a period when the poet had already become a figure of legend.

Like the poet → Myrddin, T. was stylised as a great seer and sage. The story → *Branwen ferch Lŷr* names him as one of the survivors of the campaign against the Irish king Matholwch. He appears as a member of the retinue of → Arthur in the tale → *Culhwch ac Olwen*. The oldest complete narrative concerned with T. is as late as the 16thC (→ *Hanes Taliesin*). – T. is also the name of the literary journal of the Welsh writers' association, Yr Academi Gymreig, founded in 1959.

Lit.: I. Williams & J. E. C. Williams, *The Poems of T.*, Du. 1968 (MMWS 3); A. O. H. Jarman, *The Cynfeirdd*, Car. 1981.

Tara → Temair.

Taranis. Celtic god mentioned by → Lucan (Pharsalia 1,444–446). His name derives from the Celtic word for "thunder" (Ir. torann, Welsh taran). According to the Roman poet the Gauls made human sacrifices to T. The → Berne Scholia, commenting on Lucan, add that these victims were burned in a wooden tub. In inscriptions the name occurs not as that of a god, but of a person (CIL III 7437, 6150 and 12346). There are however votive dedications to gods named Taranucus (CIL III 2804: Iovi Taranuco) and Taranucnus (CIL XIII 6094: deo Taranucno). The genitive Taranou, written in Greek letters in a Gaulish inscription (RIG I G–27), points to the reconstruction of a nominative *Taranus. The name Tanarus, attested in an inscription (RIB 452: Iovi Optimo Maximo Tanaro), may possibly be a mis-spelling for *Taranus. The etymology suggests that T. was regarded as a sky-god or thunder-god, which fits in with the equation with the Roman god → Jupiter attested for Taranucus and Tanarus. The Berne Scholia also identify T. with Jupiter.

Lit.: F. Le Roux, 'T.: Dieu celtique du ciel et de l'orage' (*Ogam* 10) 1958, 30–39; D. Gricourt & D. Hollard, 'T.: Le Dieu celtique à la roue' (*Dialogues d'histoire ancienne* 16) 1990, 273–315; id., 'T.: caelestium deorum maximus' (*Dialogues d'histoire ancienne* 17) 1991, 343–400.

tarbfeis (Ir. /'tarveʃ/ "bull-sleep"). Ritual in the stories → *Togail Bruidne Da Derga* and → *Serglige Con Culainn* serving to determine the successor of a king. The tales describe how a man feasts on the meat and broth of a slaughtered white bull and then lies down to sleep, chanted over by druids. He then sees a vision of the future king in his dreams.

Tarvos Trigaranus. Celtic god, whose name is formed from the Celtic word for "bull" (O.Ir. tarb, Welsh tarw) and an adjective with the meaning "who has three cranes" (cf. Welsh tri "three" and garan "crane"). The name and image of T.T. are preserved on the monument of the → Nautae Parisiaci in Paris. The relief shows a bull standing behind a tree, with three cranes perched on his back and head. Behind the bull some twigs are to be seen, which may indicate a second tree, or possibly a whole forest. Otherwise the name T.T. is not attested in inscriptions or literature. Theories linking the adjective trigaranus with the Greek words trikárēnos ("three-headed") or trygéranos (name of an animal in a comedy of the writer Philemon) have failed to find general acceptance (cf. RIG II,1 *L-14). There is however an iconographic parallel in the relief on a stele from Trier, which shows in the thick foliage of a treetop the head of a bull and three birds (to all appearances not cranes). In the lower part of the relief a man in the clothing of an artisan sets about felling the tree with an axe. This is possibly a depiction of the god → Esus, who is portrayed in a similar way on the monument of the Nautae Parisicai right next to T.T., on a separate panel. Perhaps, then, the relief from Trier and the two depictions from Paris derive from a myth lost to us, in which both Esus and T.T. played a role.

Lit.: → Esus; → Nautae Parisiaci.

Taurini. In classical → ethnography a Celtic tribe which settled at the foot of the Alps in the region of present-day Piedmont. The name survives in that of the city of Turin (Lat. Augusta Taurinorum).

Tech Duinn (Ir. /t'ex duN'/ "the House of Donn"). The ancient name of a rock near the island of Dursey, south-west of Ireland (now Bull Rock). Allusions in texts of the 8th-10thCs suggest that in pre-Christian times it was regarded as the seat of a god of the dead named → Donn, and as a meeting-point for the dead.

Tecosca Cormaic (Ir. /'t'egoska 'kormik' "The Instructions of Cormac"). Title of an anonymous collection of aphorisms preserved in the "Book of Leinster" (→ Lebor Laignech) and other, later manuscripts. In its surviving version the work takes the form of a dialogue between King → Cormac mac Airt and his son. According to Irish tradition both lived in the 3rdC AD. On linguistic grounds the work is however dated to the 8th-9thC. It contains an enumeration of the rights and duties of a ruler, as well as numerous aphorisms of a more general kind.

Ed. and trans.: K. Meyer, *The Instructions of King Cormac mac Airt*, Du. 1909.
Lit.: R. M. Smith, 'The Speculum Principum in Early Ir. Lit.' (*Speculum* 2) 1927, 411–445.

Tectosages. In classical → ethnography a sub-tribe of the Celtic → Volcae. One group of the T. settled in the region between Narbonne and Toulouse, were conquered by the Romans in 121–118 BC and integrated into the newly created Province of Gallia Narbonensis. Another group migrated across the Balkans to Asia Minor soon after 278 BC, there to form together with the Tolisto(b)agii and Trocmi the people of the → Galatians.

teinm laeda (Ir. /t'en'm' 'Laiða/). Type of divination attributed to poets (→ fili). According to a comment in the Glossary of Bishop Cormac (→ *Sanas Chormaic*), it was forbidden by Saint → Patrick, on the grounds that it was associated with sacrifices to idols.

Teltown → Tailtiu.

Temair (Ir. /'t'evir'/). In Irish tradition the seat of the Irish High Kings (→ rí). It is identical with the archaeological site of Tara in County Meath; excavations show that the site was settled continuously from the Neolithic Age to the beginning of the christianisation of Ireland. The famed "Feast of Tara" (feis Temro) was a pre-Christian ritual celebration marking the inauguration of a new king, and is thought to have still been held in the 6thC AD (cf. → Diarmait mac Cerbaill). In Irish tradition the remains of T., still visible today, were from the early Middle Ages onwards attributed to the building activities of the legendary king → Cormac mac Airt. The stone → Fál, supposed to have been brought to Ireland by the → Tuatha Dé Danann, is regarded as a symbol of the kingship of Tara.

Temora. Irish royal seat in James → Macpherson's "Works of Ossian". The original Irish form of the name is → Temair.

temple. Term customarily referring in the study of religion to buildings of stone and/or wood, which in contrast to Christian churches, Islamic mosques or Jewish synagogues were not regarded as the places of assembly of a worshipping community, but as the residence of a deity. Temples in this sense were not an indigenous part of Celtic culture, but developed in the areas settled by the Celts under Mediterranean, above all Roman influence. In a few cases it is possible to ascertain the existence of pre-Roman Celtic → places of worship on the sites of Gallo-Roman temples. The temples in their turn were later frequently replaced by Christian churches.

   Lit.: D. R. Wilson, 'Romano-Celtic Temple Architecture' (*Journal of the British Archaeological Association* 38) 1975, 3–27; P. D. Horne & H. C. King, 'Romano-Celtic temples in Continental Europe', in: W. Rodwell (ed.), *Temples, Churches and Religion*, O. 1980, 369–555.

tête coupée (Fr. "cut-off head"). In Celtic → art the (misleading) term referring to any depiction of a human → head without the body belonging to it.

Tethra (Ir. /'t'eθra/). A king of the → Fomoire in the tales of the → Mythological Cycle. He is thought to live in the sea, which is why the ocean is termed his "field" and the fish his "cattle". In the story of the Battle of Mag Tuired (→ *Cath Maige Tuired*) → Ogma finds T.'s sword Orna on the battlefield. When he pulls it out of its scabbard and cleans it, it tells of the deeds executed by it.

Teutates (later form: Toutates). Name of a Celtic god, possibly deriving from an older form *teuto-tatis, meaning perhaps "father of the tribe". This etymology is however uncertain, because it stipulates that the word through haplology was deprived of its second syllable. Moreover it would have to be assumed that the surviving a was originally short, which is by no means certain. T. is mentioned by the Roman authors → Lucan (Pharsalia, 1,444–446) and Lactantius (Divinae Institutiones 1,21,3). According to Lucan the Gauls made human sacrifices to him. The → Berne Scholia, commenting on Lucan, add that the victims were put head-first in a tub full of water and thus drowned. T. is attested in several votive inscriptions from Britain (*RIB* 219 and 1017), Styria (CIL III 5320) and Rome (CIL VI 31182). The last of these equates him with a god named Meduris, while the first three identify him with the Roman god → Mars on the basis of the → interpretatio romana. This may, taken together with the accounts concerning human sacrifices, point to the war-like character of the god. Consequently, some depictions of armed deities have been assumed to portray T., but this is uncertain, given the absence of corroboratory inscriptions.

Lit.: P.-M. Duval, 'Teutates – Esus – Taranis' (*EC* 8) 1958–59, 41–58 (= ibid., *Travaux sur la Gaule*, R. 1989, I 275–287).

textiles. Only rarely have textiles from Celtic antiquity survived. The sites which have yielded most finds thus far are the saltmines of → Hallein and → Hallstatt, and the grave-mounds of → Hochdorf and → Hohmichele. To judge from these finds, the Celts developed weaving of a high degree of sophistication at an early stage. The chief materials were linen and wool, but others were also woven; the grave of Hochdorf, for example, has yielded weavings of bast and badger-hair. The woven materials were assigned patterns in many cases by the wool and linen yarn being spun in two different directions. Yarn of different colours was also used, or the materials were died after weaving. Some examples of materials worked with gold have even been found (Hohmichele → Grafenbühl), as well as silk embroidery (Hohmichele, Hochdorf).

Lit.: H.-J. Hundt, 'Vorgeschichtliches Gewebe aus dem Hallstätter Salzberg' (JRGZM 6) 1959, 66–100; (7) 1960, 126–150 & (14) 1967, 38–67; L. Schwinden, 'Gallo-römisches Textilgewerbe' (*Trierer Zeitschrift* 52) 1989, 279–318; G. Roche-Bernard, *Costumes et textiles en Gaule romaine*, P. 1993.

Teyrnon Twrf Liant (Welsh /'teirnon turv liant/). Member of the retinue of Prince Pwyll of Dyfed in the tale → *Pwyll Pendefig Dyfed*. One night he finds the son of Pwyll, who has been mysteriously abducted, and brings him up.

Thomas, William Jenkyn (1870–1959). Folklorist and collector of oral traditions, born in North Wales. After studying in Cambridge he at first lectured at the University of Bangor, then worked as a headmaster in Aberdare (South Wales) and London. He published his collections of Welsh folk tales in the two volumes *The Welsh Fairy Book* (1907) and *More Welsh Fairy and Folk Tales* (1958).

Three Functions Theory → Dumézil, Georges.

Thurneysen, Rudolf (1857–1940). One of the most important Celticists, born in Basle. After studying with, among others, Jacob Burckhardt and Friedrich Nietzsche, he at first taught at the University of Jena, then in 1887 became Professor of Comparative Philology at the University of Freiburg i. Br. In 1913 he was elected to a chair in Bonn, where he taught for ten years until his retirement. T. was one of the most knowledgeable experts in the field of Old and Middle Irish and the author of many definitive studies. His *Handbuch des Altirischen* (1909) is still the standard work today. Since 1946 it has been reprinted several times in a revised version by D. A. → Binchy and O. → Bergin under the title *A Grammar of Old Irish*. He never completed his magnum opus, *Die irische Helden- und Königsage bis zum siebzehnten Jahrhundert* ("The Sagas of the Irish heroes and kings from the beginnings to the 17thC"). The first volume, which appeared in 1921, concerns itself, after a general introduction, with the tales of the → Ulster Cycle and remains a definitive study today. Also of lasting importance is his work on early Irish → law.

> Coll. works: R. Thurneysen, *Gesammelte Schriften*, ed. P. de Bernardo Stempel & R. Ködderitzsch, 3 vols., T. 1991–1995; P. de Bernardo Stempel, 'Rudolf Thurneysen und sein sprachwissenschaftliches Werk' (ZCP 46) 1994, 216–248.

Tigernmas (Ir. /'t'iɣ'ernvas/). A descendant of King → Éremón in the "Book of the Invasions of Ireland" (→ *Lebor Gabála Érenn*). Under his rule Ireland is supposed to have discovered gold for the first time and worked it into jewellery. He is also said to have been the first to prescribe that his subjects should wear clothes of different colours, depending upon their social status. According to tradition T. met his death during a ceremony held to honour the stone idol Crom Cruach during the feast of → Samain.

time. Through references in classical → ethnography, the tablet known as the calendar of → Coligny, and some data in Irish and Welsh sources it is possible to obtain an approximate picture of the Celtic concept of time. These sources suggest that the Celts were oriented by nights rather than days in the division of t. Thus → Caesar reports of the Gauls: "they calculate birthdays and the beginnings of months and years in such a way that the day follows the night" (Bell. Gall. 6,18). This kind of division of time is still suggested today in the Welsh words wythnos "week" (= "eight nights") and pythefnos "fortnight" (= "15 nights"). The Celts also therefore calculated the year according to the cycles of the moon rather than those of the sun. There is a reference to this by → Pliny the Elder, in his celebrated account of the sanctity of → mistletoe. According to Pliny the new moon constituted for the Celts the beginning of the months and years, as well as – after a period of thirty years – an age (Hist. Nat. 16,249–251).

By "age" Pliny in all probability means the Celtic word *saitlom, cognate with the Latin term saeculum. It survives in the Welsh word hoedl "lifetime"; its original meaning (as that of saeculum) presumably approximated to "generation". Apart from this period of 30 years, a unit of five years also seems to have played an important role, as is indicated by the calendar of Coligny, which spans five years. There two thirty-day leap months after every two and a half lunar years compensate for the deviation from the solar year over the whole period.

The Celts divided the year in the first place into two halves, winter and summer. It is not until medieval Irish sources that a distinction is drawn between four seasons, the beginning of each of which was celebrated by special → feasts. The calendar of Coligny divides the individual months into two equal or approximately equal halves. The seven-day week, on the other hand, was only introduced with christianisation. The Irish word for "week", and the Irish and Welsh terms for the individual days of the week thus derive from Latin.

Lit.: → Coligny, → feasts.

tin. In ancient times tin was employed primarily in the manufacture of → bronze, which generally consisted of a mixture of nine parts copper to one part tin. The most important deposits of the metal were in Cornwall and the West of England; from there it was transported, sometimes by sea, sometimes by land, to the Celts of the European mainland, and on to the peoples of the Mediterranean area. Passage through the Straits of Gibraltar was denied to Greek ships after the victory at sea of the Carthaginians in the battle of Alalia, c. 535 BC, and as a result the land route from the Greek colony of Massalia (Marseille) gained in importance following the battle. It is thought that the early Celtic settlement of → Mont Lassois was a first handling place for the transport of tin from Britain by land. The luxurious goods found in the grave of → Vix are seen as due in part to the trading of tin.

Tírechán (Ir. /'t'i:r'exa:n/). Irish cleric of the 7thC who composed a Latin biography of Saint → Patrick c. 670.

Tír na n-Óg (Ir. /t'i:r' na no:g/ "The Land of the Young"). Term denoting a paradisian world beyond the realms peopled by mankind (cf. → Tír Tairngiri, → Otherworld, conceptions of), whose inhabitants are ignorant of sickness, old age and death.

Lit.: C. Dröge, 'Le pays de la jeunesse dans les littératures celtiques', in: *Les Ages de la vie au Moyen Age*, P. 1992, 23–36.

Tír Tairngiri (Ir. /t'i:r' 'tar'n'γ'ir'i/ "Land of Promise"). Term denoting a paradisian world beyond the realms peopled by mankind. It is thought that the ideas associated with this land are at least in part of pre-Christian origin.

The expression itself is however a literal translation from ecclesiastical Latin: terra repromissionis signifies the Promised Land (Israel) or the (Christian) Paradise.

Tlachtga (Ir. /'tlaxtɣa/). Hill in County Meath, c. 20 miles north-west of Tara (→ Temair). Geoffrey → Keating thought T. was the site of pre-Christian religious ceremonies. The → druids were thought, on the feast of → Samain, to have lit a fire there every year from which all the hearths of the whole of Ireland had to be lit in turn.

According to the → *Dindsenchas*, T. was originally the name of the magically gifted daughter of the druid → Mog Ruith, who is said be buried beneath the hill named after her.

tochmarc (Ir. /'toxmark). Term denoting a wooing expedition, which serves in the → Lists of Sagas to classify stories concerned with such wooing and the concomitant exploits of the hero.

Tochmarc Becfola (Ir. /'toxmark 'b'egola/ "The Wooing of Becfola"). Title of a tale from the → Historical Cycle, the oldest version of which is preserved in the → "Yellow Book of Lecan" and in a 16thC manuscript. The story tells of the love of the Irish king → Diarmait mac Aeda Sláine for the eponymous heroine Becfola, who makes her way from the land of the fairies to the royal seat of Tara (→ Temair) and there becomes Diarmait's wife, but later deserts her husband for another. – The material is reworked by Austin → Clarke in his poem *The Wooing of Becfola* and James → Stephens in his book *Irish Fairy Tales*.
    Ed. and trans.: S. H. O'Grady, *Silva Gadelica*, Lo. 1892; M. Bhreathnach, 'A new ed. of T. B.' (*Ériu* 35) 1984, 59–91.

Tochmarc Emire (Ir. /'toxmark 'ev'ir'e/ "The Wooing of Emer"). One of the prefatory tales (→ remscéla) to the story of the Cattle-Raid of Cuailnge (→ *Táin Bó Cuailnge*). It is preserved fragmentarily in a version dating from the 10thC, and in its entirety in a later, considerably expanded reworking of the 12thC. The story tells of how the youthful → Cú Chulainn wins a bride and learns the use of weapons at the hands of the feared she-warrior → Scáthach (cf. → *Aided Oenfir Aífe* and → *Serglige Con Culainn*). – The story is reworked by Lady → Gregory in the third chapter of her book *Cuchulain of Muirthemne*.
    Ed.: A. G. van Hamel, *Compert Con Culainn and Other Stories*, Du. 1933 (MMIS 3).
    Lit.: D. Edel, *Helden auf Freiersfüßen*, A. 1980.

Tochmarc Étaíne (Ir. /'toxmark 'e:dain'e/ "The Wooing of Étaín"). Title of a story from the → Mythological Cycle. At the centre of the story is Étaín, the daughter of a king of the people of the elves (cf. → síd). At the beginning we learn how the elf-prince Midir wins her as his bride, with the aid of his foster-son → Oengus. Out of jealousy, Midir's former wife Fuamnach transforms her into a fly and brings about by magic a storm which sends Étaín far from Midir's seat Brí Leíth to the house of the warrior Étar. There Étar's wife swallows the fly and becomes pregnant in consequence. In this way Étaín is born for a second time, 1012 years after her first birth. She grows up and ultimately becomes the wife of the king → Eochaid Airem. Midir, in the guise of Eochaid's brother Ailill Anguba, attempts three times, each time in vain, to seduce his former wife. Finally he succeeds in abducting Étaín from Eochaid's castle and deceiving her husband by supplanting her with a woman identical in looks and dress. This is however in truth Eochaid's own daughter, to whom Étaín gave birth after leaving her husband. Eochaid sires by her the mother of the famed king → Conaire Mór. – The tale is reworked by James → Stephens in his book *In the Land of Youth*.

Ed.: O. Bergin & R. I. Best, 'T. É.' (*Ériu* 12) 1938, 137–196 (with Engl. trans.).

Trans.: J. Gantz, *Early Irish Myths and Sagas*, Harm. 1981.

togail (Ir. /ˈtoɣalʹ/). Term denoting the siege or destruction (of a stronghold), which serves in the → Lists of Sagas to classify stories telling of such undertakings.

Togail Bruidne Da Derga (Ir. /ˈtoɣalʹ ˈvruðʹnʹe da ˈdʹerga/ "The Destruction of Da Derga's Hostel"). Title of a tale from the → Ulster Cycle. It is preserved intact in the → "Yellow Book of Lecan" and in one other manuscript of c. 1300, fragmentarily in the "Book of the Dun Cow" (→ Lebor na hUidre) and some later manuscripts. It is thought that in the 11thC two different versions of the 9thC merged.

The hero of the tale is the young Conaire Mór. His mother is Mes Buachalla, wife of King Etarscél; his father is an unknown person who mated with Mes Buachalla in the form of a bird, before her marriage to Etarscél. After the death of Etarscél Conaire is appointed to be the next king on the basis of the custom of the "bull-sleep" (→ tarbfeis). At first his rule is blessed by good fortune, but then his foster-brothers, disregarding his authority, plunder the country. In hesitating to punish them fittingly, Conaire offends against the obligation of the "justice of the ruler" (→ fír flathemon), thereby bringing about his own downfall. Tragic circumstances compel him to deeds which are taboo (→ geis) for him. In the hostel of his friend Da Derga he is attacked by his foster-brothers and despite his fierce resistance, slain. – The story is retold by Lady Augusta → Gregory in the sixth chapter of her book *Cuchulain of Muirthemne*.

Ed.: E. Knott, *T. B. D. D.*, Du. 1936 (MMIS 8).

Trans.: J. Gantz, *Early Ir. Myths and Sagas*, Harm. 1981.

Lit.: R. Thurneysen, *Die irische Helden- und Königsage*, Hl. 1921; T. Ó Concheanainn, 'Notes on T. B. D. D.' (*Celtica* 17) 1985, 73–90; M. West, 'Leabhar na hUidre's Portion in the Manuscript History of T. B. D. D. and Orgain Brudne Uí Dergae' (CMCSt 20) 1990, 61–98.

Tolistobogii, Tolistobagi (Gk. Tolostobogioi, Tolistoagioi). In classical → ethnography one of the three Celtic tribes which in 278 BC migrated to Asia Minor. There they formed, together with the Trocmi and the Tectosages the people of the → Galatians.

Tóraigheacht Dhiarmada agus Ghráinne (Ir. /ˈtoːrijaxt ˈjiarmada ˈagus ˈγraːNʲe/ "The Pursuit of Diarmaid and Gráinne"). One of the best-known tales of the → Finn-Cycle. Allusions and references in various works of early Irish literature suggest that it was already circulating in the 9th/10thC, but the oldest surviving version dates from the 15thC.

The story tells of the tragic love of Gráinne, the young wife of the ageing → Finn mac Cumaill, for the warrior Diarmaid Ua Duibne, famed for his beauty. By magic Gráinne compels Diarmaid to abduct her, thus incurring the anger of Finn. With the help of the elf-prince → Oengus, Diarmaid's foster-father, the two lovers succeed in the course of an adventurous flight in escaping the pursuit of Finn and his warriors. In the end Oengus brings about a reconciliation between Diarmaid, Gráinne and Finn, enabling the lovers to live happily together for many years. Yet Finn in secret ponders vengeance and remembers that it is Diarmaid's fate to die by the wild boar of Beann Ghulban. He therefore one day involves Diarmaid in a hunt for the boar, in the course of which Diarmaid does indeed meet his death.

The story of Diarmaid and Gráinne survived in Ireland and Scotland in many oral versions into the recent past. It inspired the poem *The Vengeance of Finn* (1917) by Austin → Clarke.

Ed. and trans.: N. Ní Shéaghdha, T. D. A. G.: The Pursuit of Diarmaid and Gráinne, Du. 1967 (ITS 48).
Lit.: D. E. Meek, 'The Death of Diarmaid in Scottish and Irish Tradition' (Celtica 21) 1990, 335–361.

torcs (Lat. torques). Spiral neck-rings of coiled metal, worn by various peoples from the Bronze Age onwards as ornaments and to denote rank. Where Celtic culture is concerned, we know of them through archaeological finds, depictions, and from accounts in classical → ethnography.

C. 360 BC the Roman general Titus Manlius was given the byname Torqatus when he slew a Gaulish prince in single combat and took his torc as booty. There is an account of this episode from the Gallic wars by the historian Livy (Ab urbe condita 7,9–11). The historian → Polybios reports that many Celtic warriors wore golden torcs and arm-rings in the battle of Telamon in 222 BC (Hist. 2,29). This description tallies with Celtic depictions such as that of the warrior of → Hirschlanden or Hellenistic images such as that of the "Dying Gaul". As Polybios goes on to state (Hist. 2,31), after the battle the torcs were hung up as trophies in the Capitol, together with the battle-standards of the defeated Gauls. It is thought that these torcs were marks of social status rather than ornaments.

The adorning of images of the gods with torcs is attested by a report of the historian Pompeius Trogus, who was born in Gaul. It survives in the extract of Justinus (3rdC AD) and records how the Gaulish prince Catamandus, after making peace with the city of Massilia (Marseille), dedicates a golden torc to a goddess designated as → Minerva (Epit. 43,4). Among the best-known depictions of Celtic gods with torcs are the images of a horned god on the → Gundestrup cauldron, the depiction of → Cernunnos on the monument of the → Nautae Parisiaci, the bronze sculpture of the god of → Bouray, and the sandstone sculptures from → Euffigneix and → Mšecké Žehrovice.

For the Romans the coiled neck-ring was so characteristically Celtic that the poet Claudian (c. 400 AD), in his poem celebrating the consulate of Stilicho, has the personification of Gaul wear a torc (Laud. Stilich. 2,240).

Lit.: → art.

totemism. In comparative religion a term denoting the belief that a person, or his kin, or his tribe is associated with a 'totem'. This generally takes the form of a certain kind of animal or plant, sometimes however of an inanimate object or a celestial entity. Characteristic features of totemism are the naming of the kin group or the tribe after the totem, and ritual worship of it. Discussion concerning totemism was prominent at the beginning of the 20thC, when scholars such as Émile Dürkheim (1858–1917) and Sigmund Freud (1856–1939) thought they had found in totemism the origin of religion. Later research has shown that quite distinct religious and social phenomena lie behind the term totemism, which should not be confused with one another or traced back to a single common origin. Allusions to totemism in Celtic religion (e.g. animal and plant names used to form → personal names and → tribal names) are few and far between and offer far from convincing evidence.

Totenfolge ("multiple or serial burial"). Term denoting the voluntary or forced suicide of one or more people at the grave of the deceased. It is or was widespread among many peoples, and affected frequently relations, members of the household, or people to whom responsibility for the death of the deceased was attributed. Where Celtic culture is concerned we possess the evidence of → Caesar, according to whom the Gauls, up to a time not long before the arrival of the Romans in the country, buried along with people of distinguished birth not only their possessions and animals, but also slaves and dependants who were dear to the deceased (Bell. Gall. 6,19). Archaeologists have interpreted some double and multiple burials in the vicinity of early Celtic → princely graves along these lines.

Lit.: J. Maringer, 'Menschenopfer im Bestattungsbrauch Alteuropas' (*Anthropos* 37/38) 1942/43, 1–112; K. Spindler, 'Totenfolge bei Skythen, Thrakern und Kelten' (*Abhandlungen der Naturhistorischen Gesellschaft Nürnberg* 39) 1982, 197–214; C. Oeftiger, *Mehrfachbestattungen im Westhallstattkreis: Zum Problem der Totenfolge*, Bo. 1984.

Toutiorix. Celtic god whose name perhaps means "king of the members of the tribe" (cf. Ir. → túath "tribal group" and → rí "king"). The cult of T. is attested by a votive inscription from Wiesbaden (CIL XIII 7564), in which he is identified with → Apollo on the basis of the → interpretatio romana.

trade. Trade and commerce played a significant role in the Celtic economy. Both raw materials and manufactured products were transported over distances amounting to sometimes hundreds of miles. As early as the 6th and 5thCs BC a lively interchange of wares took place between the Celts of the western Hallstatt region on the one hand and on the other the Greek colonies of southern France, the Venetians on the Upper Adriatic and the Etruscans of central and northern Italy. This is attested primarily by archaeological finds in → princely graves and → princely seats, as well as by stylistic influences of Mediterranean art upon Celtic → art. In the course of the Celtic migrations of the 4th-3rdCs BC (cf. → history), trade with the south falls temporarily into a decline, but is revived in the period of the → oppida in the 2nd-1stC BC, when the Celts imported both artistic products such as bronze vessels or pottery, and raw materials such as, for example, coral, or luxuries such as wine. We possess no detailed knowledge of how the Celts paid for these goods, but the main methods of payment were presumably in → gold, → iron, animal skins and → slaves. Within the Celtic regions themselves → salt played an important role as an object of barter, along with iron. Generally products were transported by water. In some cases, Mediterranean wares, as well as traders, must have found their way into the centres of Celtic civilisation north of the Alps.

Lit.: F. Fischer, 'KEIMHΛIA' (*Germania* 51) 1973, 436–459; C. Doherty, 'Exchange and Trade in Early Medieval Ireland' (*JRSAI* 110) 1980, 67–89; S. Macready & F. H. Thompson (eds.), *Cross-Channel Trade between Gaul and Britain in the pre-Roman Iron Age*, Lo. 1984; W. Kimmig, 'Der Handel der Hallstattzeit', in: *Untersuchungen zu Handel und Verkehr der vor- und frühgeschichtlichen Zeit in Mittel- und Nordeuropa I*, Gö. 1985, 214–230; O. H. Frey, 'Zum Handel und Verkehr während der Frühlatènezeit in Mitteleuropa', in: ibidem, 231–257; D. Timpe, 'Der keltische Handel nach historischen Quellen', in: ibidem, 254–284; F. Fischer, 'Der Handel der Mittel- und Spätlatènezeit in Mitteleuropa aufgrund archäologischer Zeugnisse', in: ibidem, 285–298; *Luxusgeschirr keltischer Fürsten: Griechische Keramik nördlich der Alpen*, Wü. 1995.

transmigration of souls → reincarnation.

trees. All the sources suggest that trees played a significant role in Celtic → religion. This is attested above all by the numerous references to sacred groves (→ nemeton). Votive inscriptions to tree gods such as Fagus "beech" (CIL XIII 33 and 223–225) or Robur "oak" (CIL XIII 129) survive from the Gallo-Roman period. Three inscriptions (CIL XIII 129, 132 and 175) refer to six unspecified trees (sex arboribus). Classical authors also stress the religious significance of the → oak. Whether the Celts were familiar, like the Germani, with the concept of the world tree is not clear from ancient sources. The depiction of the god → Esus on the monument of the → Nautae Parisiaci and other sources attest the role played by trees in Celtic myths. In Ireland sacred trees were known as bile (from ancient Celtic *bilios). There are particularly frequent references to the ash of → Uisnech, the ash of Tortu, the yew of Ross, the oak of Mugna and the ash of Dathí. Specific trees were also held sacred by the various confederations of tribes. In the shadow of such trees assemblies were held, and felling them was regarded as a grave sin.

Treveri. In classical → ethnography a Germano-Celtic people on the lower Moselle. Their chief town was Augusta Treverorum, present-day Trier.

tribal names. The oldest and richest source of our knowledge of Celtic tribal names is formed by the works of Greek and Roman → ethnography. However, the interpretation of the nomenclature that survives in these sources causes the Celticist considerable difficulty in many cases. In the first place, it is not clear with regard to many peoples on the margins of the lands settled by the Celts whether they really have a Celtic name. In other cases the etymology is unsatisfactory because, given the lack of exact equivalents, the starting-point has to be a hypothetical root whose basic meaning is imprecisely defined. For example, the name of the → Belgae is derived from a root *belg- "to swell", and the meaning is thought to be something like "those puffed out with pride". The name of the Celts has been compared with the Latin word celsus, "high", and traced back to a root *kel- "to lift, raise", yet the assumption that the name originally meant "the Sublime Ones" remains pure speculation. Other tribal names, on the other hand, have a clear etymology, but because of our deficient knowledge of Celtic culture remain incomprehensible. Thus the names of the Carvetii and Caereni in Britain are in all probability derived from the Celtic words for "stag" (Welsh carw) and "sheep" (Ir. caera), but the meaning behind the nomenclature is obscure. There are only a few tribal names which have such a clear and informative etymology as the Ambidravoi, Ambisontes and Ambilici, whose names show them to be dwelllers near the rivers Drau, Isonzo and Lech.

Celtic tribal names have survived best in France, where towards the end of the classical period many major towns adopted the names of the tribes resident there. Among the best-known examples are Amiens (→ Ambiani), Angers (→ Andecavi), Arras (→ Atrebates), Bayeux (→ Bodiocasses), Beauvais (→ Bellovaci), Bourges (→ Bituriges), Cahors (→ Cadurci), Chartres (→ Carnutes), Chorges (→ Caturiges), Évreux (→ Eburovices), Jublains (→ Diablintes), Langres (→ Lingones), Limoges (→ Lemovices), Lisieux (→ Lexovii), Le Mans (→ Cenomani), Meaux (→ Meldi), Nantes (→ Namneti), Paris (→ Parisii), Périgueux (→ Petrucorii), Poitiers (→ Pictones), Reims (→ Remi), Rennes (→ Redones), Rodez (→ Ruteni), Saintes (→ Santones), Sens (→ Senones), Soissons (→ Suessiones), Tours (→ Turoni), Troyes (→ Tricasses) and Vannes (→ Veneti).

Lit.: A. Holder, *Alt-celtischer Sprachschatz*, 3 vols., L. 1891–1913; K. H. Schmidt, 'Die Komposition in gallischen Personennamen' (ZCP 26) 1957, 33–301.

Trichtingen. Place in the Rottweil district (Baden-Württemberg) close to which in 1928 an oval silver ring, 4cm in diameter, was found during drainage works. The ring has a circumference of 25–29.4cm; its ends take the shape of bulls' heads. As the ring has a core of wrought soft iron, its weight is over 6.7 kilogrammes. This suggests that it is not an ordinary torc, but a votive gift to a deity. The origin and date of the ring are contentious, but appearances suggest that it is not an indigenous product. The ring is now in the Württembergisches Landesmuseum in Stuttgart.

Lit.: F. Fischer et al., 'Studien zum Silberring von T.' (*FBW* 12) 1987, 205–250.

Tricasses. In classical → ethnography a Celtic tribe on the upper Seine and Aube. The name survives in that of the town of Troyes, the Roman name of which was Augustobona, after the Emperor Augustus.

Trioedd Ynys Prydein (Welsh /ˈtrioið ˈənis ˈbrədein/ "The Triads of the Island of Britain"). Title of a collection of mnemonics of historical and legendary content. They survive in varying selections and sequence in over a dozen manuscripts of the 13th-17thC. Each triad groups three famous names under a common heading. Thus one triad, for example, names the "Three Powerful Swineherds of the Island of Britain": → Coll fab Collfrewi, → Drystan fab Tallwch and → Pryderi fab Pwyll Pen Annwfn. In some cases, as in this instance, there follows a brief explanation of the tradition linked with the individual names. The collection as a whole reveals the influence of courtly → Arthurian literature, and must therefore have been reworked at a relatively late date, but the central stock of triads derives from much older, in part oral traditions. Because of the many allusions to lost narratives of the British Celts the T. are of great importance for the study of the Celtic literatures.

Ed. and trans.: R. Bromwich, *T., Y. P.: The Welsh Triads*, Car. ²1978.

Tristan. English, French and German form of the Welsh name → Drystan.

Trocmi (Gk. Trokmoi). In classical → ethnography one of the three Celtic tribes which migrated to Asia Minor in 278 BC. There the T. formed, together with the → Tolisto(b)agii and the → Tectosages, the people of the → Galatians.

Tuan mac Cairill (Ir. /tuan mak 'kar'iL'). Name of one of the first settlers who in the "Book of the Invasions of Ireland" (→ *Lebor Gabála Érenn*) is said to have occupied Ireland after the Flood (→ *Scél Tuain meic Chairill*).

tuath (Ir. /tuaθ/). Tribal group ruled by a king (→ rí). It is thought that there were at least 150 such tribal groups in Ireland in the early and high Middle Ages. The average number of people in a tuath is estimated at c. 3000. The word t. derives from an older form *teutā, which occurs in several western Indo-European languages in the sense of "people". In Gaulish it occurs in the name of the god → Teutates. The Old High German form diot led to the adjective diutisc, which later acquires the sense "deutsch" (German).
  Lit.: F. J. Byrne, 'Tribes and Tribalism in Early Ireland' (*Ériu* 22) 1971, 128–163; F. J. Kelly, *A Guide to Early Ir. Law*, Du. 1988.

Tuatha Dé Danann (Ir. /'tuaθa d'e: 'danaN/). A group of prehistoric beings, possessed of magical powers, in the tales of the → Mythological Cycle. According to the "Book of the Invasions of Ireland" (→ *Lebor Gabála Érenn*), the T. constituted the fourth wave of immigrants who took possession of Ireland after the Flood. Among the objects that they are said to have brought with them were the spear of → Lug, which never missed its mark, the sword of → Nuadu, against which no-one could defend himself, the cauldron of the → Dagda, which proffered inexhaustible supplies of food, and the stone → Fál, which always emitted a cry when the rightful king of Ireland trod upon it. The T. are said to have defeated the → Fir Bolg and then the → Fomoire in the two battles of Mag Tuired (→ *Cath Maige Tuired*), but then they in their turn were defeated by the Sons of → Míl in the Battle of Tailtiu. After this defeat the T., so it was believed, led a phantom existence in subterranean homes (→ síd).
  Lit.: J. Carey, 'The Name "T. D. D." ' (*Éigse* 18) 1980/81, 291–294; J. Carey, 'A Tuath Dé miscellany' (*BBCS* 39) 1992, 24–45.

Tuathal Techtmar (Ir. /'tuaθal 't'extvar/). Grandfather of the king → Conn Cétchathach in the tales of the → Historical Cycle. He is said to have ruled over the whole of Ireland in the 1stC AD and to have been the first to impose the tribute known as the → Bórama on the Province of Leinster. Tradition holds that T. created the fifth province of Mide (Meath) from segments of each of the four provinces of Ulster, Leinster, Connacht and Munster.

Turoni. In classical → ethnography a tribe dwelling by the middle Loire.

Their name survives in that of the city of Tours, whose Roman name was Caesarodunum.

Twrch Trwyth (Welsh /turx truiθ/). In the tale → *Culhwch ac Olwen* a king transformed by God into the shape of a wild boar as a punishment for his sins. The giant Ysbaddaden imposes upon the eponymous hero Culhwch the task of bringing to him the comb and scissors that repose between T.'s ears. After a wild hunt through Ireland, Wales and Cornwall, Culhwch and his companions succeed in gaining possession of these objects. T., however, swims out from the coast of Cornwall into the ocean and vanishes.

twin gods → Dioscures.

Uathach (Ir. /'uaθax/ "the Terrible"). A daughter of the she-warrior → Scáthach in the tale of Cú Chulainn's Courtship of Emer (→ *Tochmarc Emire*). She entertains Cú Chulainn on his arrival in Scáthach's castle and, at her mother's bidding, shares his bed at night.

Ucuetis. Celtic god whose cult is attested by a votive inscription in Gaulish (RIG II L-13), which was found in 1839 on Mont Auxois, on the site of ancient → Alesia. A further inscription in Latin (CIL XIII 11247) was discovered on Mont Auxois in 1908; this names a goddess Bergusia as the companion of U.
   Lit.: R. Martin & P. Varène, *Le monument d'U. à Alésia*, P. 1973.

Üetliberg. Promontory on the north-western tip of Lake Zurich. Since 1980 excavations on the summit have brought to light the ramparts of a site dating from the 5thC BC and remains of imported Greek ceramics. It is thought that around the middle of the first millennium BC there was an early Celtic → princely grave on the summit of the Ü., to which also belonged a small number of graves of the 5thC found in the vicinity.
   Lit.: W. Drack & H. Schneider, *Der Ü.: die archäologischen Denkmäler*, Z. 1979; W. Drack, 'Der frühlatènezeitliche Fürstengrabhügel auf dem Ü.' (*Zeitschrift für schweizerische Archäologie und Kunstgeschichte* 38) 1981, 1–28; W. Kimmig, *Frühe Kelten in der Schweiz im Spiegel der Ausgrabungen auf dem Ü.*, Z. 1983.

Uisnech (Ir. /'uʃn'ex/). Hill in the Province of Mide (Meath). Tradition holds that a stone on the hilltop marks the mid-point of Ireland. According to the → *Dindsenchas*, Mide, the chief druid of → Nemed, lit the first fire of Ireland on the hill of U. Legend has it that it burned for seven years, and all the other fires in the country are said to have been lit from it. The native priests of the island waxed wrath at this, whereupon Mide had their tongues cut out and had them buried beneath the hill. According to various other medieval texts U. was the annual site of a major assembly of the people at the beginning of the summer, known as the mórdáil Uisnig. In → Keating's view this was a kind of annual fair, which in pre-Christian times may also have been of religious significance. The lack of any allusions to these assemblies in the Irish annals renders it unlikely, however, that Keating's description goes back to an ancient source. To what extent U. was indeed a place of assembly and worship cannot be determined with certainty today. In literature, the ash of U. is one of the most important sacred → trees of Ireland.

Ulrich von Zatzikhoven. Middle High German poet writing c. 1200. His only surviving work is the verse romance *Lanzelet*, the first German adaptation of the legend of → Lancelot. U.'s source, by his own testimony, was an Anglo-Norman romance brought to Germany by the English nobleman Hugo of Morville in 1194. The main emphasis in *Lancelot* is on the depiction of courtly culture and the adventures of the eponymous hero. The author evidently attached little value to credible psychological motivation of the characters, or to a clearly defined overall structure. In this respect, his work seems archaic compared with the romances of his contemporaries → Hartmann von Aue and → Wolfram von Eschenbach.

Ulster Cycle. Modern term referring to a group of Old and Middle Irish narratives whose plot is set, according to the Irish tradition, around the time of Christ's birth. The name owes its origin to the protagonists of the stories: the warriors of the "province" (→ coíced) of Ulster, along with their king → Conchobar mac Nesa and their chief hero → Cú Chulainn. The longest and most important tale in the cycle is the story of the Cattle-Raid of Cuailnge (→ Táin Bó Cuailnge). Associated with this are a number of other narratives termed "prefatory tales" (→ remscéla). Other important stories are → Aided Oenfir Aífe, → Fled Bricrenn, → Scéla mucce Meic Dathó and → Togail Bruidne Da Derga.

For a long time it was thought that the stories of this cycle painted a true picture of Irish culture prior to christianisation. More recently it has emerged, however, that the tales combine realistic and mythical elements. Moreover, many of the descriptions of everyday life are not to be understood as historical sources of the pre-Christian period, but are based on the experiences of the medieval monastic culture that wrote down the stories.

Lit.: R. Thurneysen, *Dir irische Helden- und Königsage bis zum 17. Jahrhundert*, Hl. 1921; K. H. Jackson, *The Oldest Irish Tradition: a Window on the Iron Age*, C. 1964; N. B. Aitchison, 'The Ulster Cycle: heroic image and historical reality' (*Journal of Medieval History* 13) 1987, 87–116; K. McCone, *Pagan Past and Christian Present in Early Ir. Lit.*, May. 1990; J. P. Mallory & G. Stockman (eds.), *Ulidia. Proceedings of the First International Conference on the Ulster Cycle of Tales*, Belfast 1994.

Urien (Welsh /'irjen/). Ruler over the Celtic kingdom of Rheged in north-west England in the second half of the 6thC. The → *Historia Brittonum* reports, that U., together with three other kings, fought against the advance of the Angles from the East. He is said to have fallen victim to an attack from a rival called Morgant during the siege of the island of Medgawdd (present-day Lindisfarne).

The "Book of Taliesin" (→ Llyfr Taliesin) contains eight panegyrics concerned with U., which may have been composed during his lifetime by the poet → Taliesin. A few other poems which survive in the "Red Book of Hergest" (→ Llyfr Coch Hergest) and some other manuscripts are thought to date from the 9th/10thC. Conceivably these depict the dramatic climaxes of sagas concerning U., whose actual plots were narrated in prose or presumed to be known by the audience. *Pen U.* ("The Head of U."), with fourteen three-line strophes, is the longest of these poems; the author tells with great sadness and dark presentiments of how he carries the decapitated head of the dead king away from the battlefield. In *Celein U.* ("The Corpse of U.") the poet, who describes himself as the cousin of the dead man, depicts the burial of the king's corpse. Finally *Aelwyd Rheged* ("The Hearth of Rheged") portrays the now disconsolate and decrepit state of the house in which guests were accorded lavish hospitality during the lifetime of the deceased king. Older scholarship regarded these, with a small number of other poems, as parts of the saga concerning → Llywarch Hen. This view has recently been contested, probably justifiably. In the → *Trioedd Ynys Prydein* U. is seen as one of the "Three Battle-Leaders of the Island of Britain". The name of his murderer is there given as Llofan Llaw Ddifo.

Lit.: R. Bromwich, *Trioedd Ynys Prydein*, Car. ²1978; J. Rowland, *Early Welsh Saga Poetry*, C. 1990.

Urnfield culture. The culture of the late European Bronze Age (13th-8thC BC). The name refers to the prevalent custom of burning the dead and interring the ashes in clay urns, in huge cemeteries. It is not possible to identify the people of this civilisation ethnically or linguistically with the Celts, nor with any other people of ancient Europe known by name.

Lit.: L. Pauli, 'Die Herkunft der Kelten', in: *Die Kelten in Mitteleuropa*, Sa. 1980, 16–24; *Beiträge zur Urnenfelderzeit nördlich und südlich der Alpen. Ergebnisse eines Kolloquiums*, Bo. 1995.

Uthyr Bendragon (Welsh /'iθir ben'dragon/). In → Geoffrey of Monmouth the youngest brother of the British King Constantine. After the latter's murder he is taken into exile by friends, but later he returns to Britain, and with the aid of his brother Aurelius Ambrosius deposes the usurper Vortigern (→ Gwrtheyrn). After the death of Aurelius U. becomes king of Britain. With the help of the magician Merlin (→ Myrddin), he takes on the form of the duke of Cornwall and seduces in the duke's absence his wife Ygerna (→

Eigr). Their son is → Arthur, who after the killing of his father succeeds him. "Pendragon", Geoffrey tells us, means "dragon-head". This surname was given to U. because Merlin is said to have greeted him as the future king of Britain when a dragon-headed meteor appeared in the sky. In reality P. must originally have meant "head (= leader) of the warriors (= dragons)", rather than "dragon-head". The mention of U. in the poem → *Pa ŵr yw'r porthor?* is proof that U. played a role in the legends concerning Arthur even before Geoffrey's account, but all earlier stories about him are lost.

Val Camonica. Valley area in the Italian alps north of Brescia, where near the village of Capo di Ponte several hundred rock-carvings of the Stone, Bronze and Iron Age have been found. The image of an erect horned figure (→ Cernunnos), 60 x 90cm in size, is now famous; it is thought to date from the 5thC BC.

Lit.: E. Anati, *I Camuni: alle radici della civiltà europea*, Mi. 1984; id., *Felsbilder: Wiege der Kunst und des Geistes*, Z. 1991.

vates (Gk. pl. Ouáteis). According to the geographer → Strabo the name given by the Celts to the members of that class which, apart from the → bards and the → druids, enjoyed the highest respect; they concerned themselves with the interpretation of natural phenomena and with the carrying out of → sacrifices (Geogr. 4,4,4). A similar description is found in the historian Ammianus Marcellinus (Res Gestae 15,9). The word derives from Old Celtic *wātis (sing.) and presumably originally designated the inspired seer. Cognates are Gothic wods "posessed" and Old Norse óðr "poetry". The Latin word vates "seer, poet" may derive from the same root, but it is also possible that it is a borrowing from the Celtic. The corresponding Irish word is fáith, which in medieval texts designates both the pre-Christian seer and prophet, and the Biblical prophet.

Lit.: T. Köves-Zulauf, 'Les V. des Celtes' (*Acta Ethnographica (Budapest)* 4) 1955, 171–275; H. Wagner, 'Ir. fáith, Welsh gwawd, Old Icelandic óðr "poetry" and the Germanic god Wotan/Óðinn' (ZCP 31) 1970, 46–57.

Vendryes, Joseph (1875–1960). Celticist and linguist, born in Paris. After studying with, among others, → d'Arbois de Jubainville, → Gaidoz and → Thurneysen, he then taught classical philology in Clermont-Ferrand and in Caen. From 1907 he was professor of Celtic philology and comparative Indo-European linguistics in Paris. He was influential as the founder and editor of the journal *Études celtiques* (1936ff.), the successor to the *Revue celtique* founded by Gaidoz. V. also inaugurated the Old Irish Etymological Dictionary (*Lexique étymologique de l'Irlandais Ancien* 1959ff.), and published many studies in the fields of Celtic philology, literature and comparative religion. Some of his work was republished in 1952 by the Société de Linguistique de Paris under the title: *Choix d'études linguistiques et celtiques.*

Veneti. Celtic tribe in south-west Brittany. According to → Caesar (Bell. Gall. 3,8) they enjoyed the greatest reputation of all the inhabitants of the Breton coast because of the large number of their harbours and ships. In 56 BC the V. were subjugated to the Romans after their fleet was destroyed. Their name survives in that of the city of Vannes, whose Roman name was Darioritum.

Verba Scáthaige → Scáthach.

Verbeia. Celtic goddess whose name survives in that of the River Wharfe (Teesdale). Her cult is attested by a sandstone altar (*RIB* 563), found as early as the 16thC in the Roman fort of Ilkley in Yorkshire. The goddess is also thought to be the subject of a relief, again found in Ilkley, which depicts a standing female figure grasping a snake in each hand. The absence of any accompanying inscription does however render the interpretation of the image uncertain.

Vercingetorix. Leader of the last great rebellion of the Gauls against → Caesar. Son of a prince of the tribe of the Arverni, V. successfully opposed that party in his tribe which was cordially disposed towards Rome and was elected king by his followers. An alliance of Gaulish tribes made him supreme commander of the united Gaulish troops, which sought to provoke the occupying Roman power by a scorched earth policy. After the city of Avaricum was conquered by the Romans, V. succeeded in forcing Caesar to retreat from his siege of → Gergovia, his home town. Not long afterwards, however, he and his forces were trapped in → Alesia and had to surrender to the Romans. In 46 BC Caesar led him in triumph through Rome and, it is thought, had him executed soon afterwards.

The interest in V. as a tragic figure and champion of a united Gaul arose in the first half of the 19thC, and received new stimulus particularly from the excavations in Alesia which were instigated by Napoleon III. The sculptor Aimé Millet (1819–1891) was commissioned by Napoleon to create a colossal statue of the Gaulish prince, worked in copper, which was erected on the site of ancient Alesia on Mont Auxois. A bronze statue of a rider representing V. by Frédéric-Auguste Bartholdi (1834–1904) was erected in 1903 in Clermont-Ferrand, the site of ancient Gergovia. Other statues of V. by Emile-François Chatrousse (1829–1896), Eugène-Ernest Chrétien (1840–1909) and Max Claudet (1840–1893) are in the Musée Bargoin in Clermont-Ferrand and the Musée des Beaux-Arts in Besançon. Three bronze statues of V. by Jules Bertin (1826–1892), François Mouly (1846–1886) and Victor-Joseph Ségoffin (1867–1925), in Saint-Denis, Bordeaux and Rodez, were melted down during the German occupation. Two depictions of the capitulation of V. by Henri Motte (1846–1922) and Lionel Royer (1852–1926) are in the Musée Crozatier in Le Puy. The fate of V. also inspired the ballad "Das Geisterroß" ("The Phantom Horse") by Conrad Ferdinand Meyer (1825–1898).

Lit.: F. Graus, 'V. und die Franzosen als Nachkommen der Gallier', in: id., *Lebendige Vergangenheit*, Co./V. 1975, 254–267; J. Harmand, *V.*, P. 1984; *V. et Alesia*, P. 1994.

Vergobretus. In → Caesar (Bell. Gall. 1,16) the highest magistrate (Lat.: magistratus) of the → Aedui. According to Caesar's account he was elected for a year by the nobility and held the power of life and death over his fellow-countrymen for the length of his period of office. The word V. is also attested in an inscription on a vase of the 1stC AD, discovered during excavations in the Gallo-Roman settlement of Argentomagus, in the region of the tribe of the → Bituriges.

Lit.: J. Allain, L. Fleuriot & L. Chaix, 'Le Vergobret des Bituriges à Argentomagus' (*RAE* 32) 1981, 11–32.

Veteris. Celtic deity whose name appears in various spellings in over 50 inscriptions from the North of England. The forms V./Vitiris/Hveteris etc. occur both in the singular and in the plural. In most cases the following word DEO ("to the god") or DIBUS ("to the gods") makes it clear that the god or gods in question were male. Twice, however, the name occurs (*RIB* 1047 and 1048) designating female deities.

Viereckschanzen ("square fortifications"). Term denoting a type of ritual site, separated from the outside world by a rampart and ditch. The term is traditional but misleading, in that the V., contrary to earlier assumptions, were not fortifications.

V. occur in a broad ribbon-shaped zone stretching from the French Atlantic coast to Bohemia. They are particularly frequent in the southern German area between the Rhine, the Main and the Inn. The geographical location of the V. varies greatly, but it is only rarely the case that they are in a particularly exposed place. Whether the recurring proximity of springs or courses of water influenced the choice of terrain is contentious.

The typical appearance of the V. is a roughly square or slightly rectangular form, the length of the sides being irregular. Of the 200 sites that have been surveyed in Baden-Württemberg and Bavaria, the biggest occupy more than 1.7 and the smallest less than 0.2 hectares. Generally, V. have only one gate, which in the case of the south German V.s is frequently to the east, more rarely to the south and west, but never to the north. The study of three sites has yielded the proportions of a total of nine internal buildings, which may have served ritual purposes. Moreover, excavations or aerial photographs have revealed the existence of shafts on the inner margin of several V.s. Whether these were shafts for the disposal of sacrificial remains, or wells, is not always clear.

In many cases the remains of hand-worked pottery dating from the 2nd-1stC BC were found during excavations. Finds of Roman pottery suggest that many V. were still employed in Roman times, perhaps for different purposes.

Lit.: K. Bittel et al., Die keltischen V., St. 1990; O. Buchsenschutz & L. Olivier (eds.), Les V. et les enceintes quadrilaterales en Europe celtique, P. 1990; H. Zürn & F. Fischer, Die keltische Viereckschanze von Tomerdingen, St. 1992; W. Irlinger, 'Viereckschanzen und Siedlungen – Überlegungen zu einem forschungsgeschicht-lichen Problem anhand ausgewählter südbayerischer Fundorte', in: C. Dobiat (ed.), Festschrift für Otto-Hermann Frey zum 65. Geburtstag, Marburg 1994, 385–304.

Vindonnus. Celtic god whose cult is attested by three votive inscriptions from Essarois in the Dép. of Côte-d'Or (CIL XIII 5644–5646). In two of these V. is identified with → Apollo on the basis of the → interpretatio romana.

Visucius. Celtic god whose cult is attested by a total of seven inscriptions. Apart from one dedication from Bordeaux (CIL XIII 577), there are three from the region of the → Treveri and → Mediomatrici in the Roman Prov-ince of Gallia Belgica (CIL XIII 3660, 4257 and 4478), and three from the Province of Germania Superior (CIL XIII 5991, 6347 and 6404). In three of these inscriptions V. is equated with → Mercury on the basis of the → interpretatio romana.

Vita Tripartita. Name given because of its tripartite structure to the oldest Irish biography of Saint → Patrick.

Vix. Site near Châtillon-sur-Seine in the Dép. of Côte-d'Or where in January 1953, in the immediate vicinity of the bank of the Seine, an intact Celtic → princely grave of the 5thC BC was found. It contains the poorly preserved skeleton of a probably female corpse, a few items of jewellery, the remains of a four-wheeled waggon, and a large set of drinking vessels. Among the most impressive finds are a golden neck-ring weighing 480 grams, and a mixing vessel (krater) of bronze, measuring 1.64m in height and weighing 208.6 kilograms. This vessel, imported from the Mediterranean, has a capacity of 1100 litres, the biggest surviving vessel of this kind from ancient times.

In the 19thC four further Celtic princely graves were found in the imme-diate proximity of V. The grave goods found therein are however – as is to be expected of the methods of excavation which were then customary – not fully documented. The consensus holds that all five grave sites belonged to an early Celtic → princely seat, traces of which have been found on nearby

→ Mont Lassois. The finds from the grave of V. may now be seen in the municipal museum of Châtillon-sur-Seine.

Lit.: R. Joffroy, V. et ses trésors, P. 1979; W. H. Gross, 'Zu Problemen des "Fürsten-grabes" von V.' (HBA 7) 1980, 69–76; J. Driehaus, 'Zum Krater von V.' (HBA 8) 1981, 103–113; M. Egg & A. France-Lanord, Le char de V., Bo. 1987.

Vocontii. In classical → ethnography a Celtic tribe in the area between the Rhône, the Isère, the Alps and the Durance. Their most important neigh-bours were the → Allobroges to the north and the → Salluvii to the south. In 125/124 BC the V. were conquered by the Romans. Their chief towns in Roman times were Vasio (now Vaison) and Dea Augusta Vocontiorum (now Die). The goddess (Lat. dea) which gave the town of Die her name was probably → Andarta.

Volcae. In classical → ethnography a Celtic tribe in the area between the Rhône, the Cévennes, the Garonne and the Pyrenees. Latin authors distin-guish between the two sub-tribes of the Arecomici, whose chief town was Nemausus (present-day Nîmes) and the → Tectosages, whose chief town was Tolosa (present-day Toulouse). In 121 BC the V. were conquered by the Romans and incorporated into the newly-created Province of Gallia Nar-bonensis. Their name survives in the German adjective "welsch", which the Germani originally employed to denote the V., thereafter the Romanised Celts of Gaul, and ultimately Romance peoples in general. Thus the walnut, originally indigenous to the Mediterranean area, was designated the "welsche Nuß", because it was particularly frequent in Gaul and came to Germany from there. In English the adjective "Welsh" serves to denote the inhabitants of Wales and their Celtic language, whereas the Welsh themselves call the latter Cymraeg (→ Welsh).

Volcanus → Vulcan.

Vorocius. Celtic god, identified in accordance with the → interpretatio romana with → Mars in a votive inscription from Vichy (CIL XIII 1497). The name is thought to be connected with the place-name Vouroux, a suburb of Varennes-sur-Allier c. 12 miles north of Vichy.

Lit.: R. Thevenot, Sur les traces des Mars celtiques, Bruges 1955; J.-J. Hatt, Mythes et dieux de la Gaule I, P. 1989.

Vortigern → Gwrtheyrn.

Vortimer → Gwerthefyr.

Vosegus or (later) Vosagus. In classical → ethnography an extensive, wooded mountain area in eastern Gaul. It reached from the valleys of the Saône and the Moselle to the Rhine valley, and included Vogesen, named after the tribe, and the Palatinate Forest ("Pfälzer Wald"). In imperial times the V. formed the border between the Roman Provinces of Gallia Belgica and Germania Superior.

The cult of a god V. is attested by several votive inscriptions (CIL XIII 6029, 6059 and 6080, and Ne 73).

votive gifts. Term denoting presents dedicated to the gods which the believer presents at a place of worship in order to fulfil a vow (Lat.: ex voto). The initiative behind this is generally a danger which has been happily averted, such as pestilence, famine or war. Where the healing of illnesses is concerned, votive gifts frequently take the form of sculptured images of the sick person or of the diseased part of the body. Among the most important sites where Celtic v. have been found are a place of worship at the sources of the Seine (→ Sequana) and a sanctuary near → Chamalières. There several thousand unusually well-preserved wooden sculptures were discovered. The majority of them are depictions of human beings, but there are also images of limbs and inner organs.

Lit.: M. & P. Vauthey, 'Les Ex-Voto anatomiques de la Gaule romaine: essai sur les maladies et infirmités de nos ancêtres', in: La Médecine en Gaule, P. 1985, 111–117; A.-M. Romeuf, 'Exvoto en bois de Chamalières (Puy-de-Dôme) et des Sources de la Seine: essai de comparaison' (Gallia 44) 1986, 65–89; G. Kurz, Keltische Hort- und Gewässerfunde in Mitteleuropa, Stuttgart 1995.

Vulcan. In Roman religion the god of fire, lightning and the blacksmith's craft. The name V. occurs to denote a Celtic deity in the Roman historian Jordanes (6thC AD), according to whom the Gaulish king Viridomarus promised the weapons of the Romans to V. if the assault of the Gauls on northern Italy in 222 BC proved victorious (Romana 179). It is worthy of note that → Caesar (Bell. Gall. 6,21) ascribes the worship of Vulcan only to the Germani, not to the Celts. In all probability, however, there was an indigenous god comparable to V. in Gaul. This is assumed from the many votive inscriptions to V., which occur far more frequently in Gaul than in other parts of the Roman Empire. There are also a large number of visual depictions of V. as a → smith which have survived from Roman Gaul. We do not know the Celtic name of the god venerated as V. Perhaps it was derived from *gobann-, the Gaulish word for smith. This is suggested particularly by the names of the mythological figures → Goibniu and → Gofannon in Irish and Welsh tradition. The personal name Gobannitio, derived from *gobann-, is attested in Gaul itself. According to Caesar (Bell. Gall. 7,4), this was the name of an uncle of → Vercingetorix.

Lit.: P.-M. Duval, 'Vulcain et les métiers du métal' (Gallia 10) 1952, 43–57 (= id., Travaux sur la Gaule, R. 1989, I 303–321).

Wace. Anglo-Norman poet of the 12thC. His *Roman de Brut* (completed c. 1155) is one of the first vernacular adaptations of the *Historia Regum Britanniae* of → Geoffrey of Monmouth. The work embraces some 1500 lines and includes the first mention of the Round Table; it influenced the Middle English poet → Layamon, and in particular French → Arthurian literature.

waggons. Archaeological evidence exists of waggons or carts from late Neolithic times. Graves of the early → Urnfield culture have yielded ceremonial carts or chariots with spoked wheels, of the kind characteristic of the early Celtic → princely graves of the late Hallstatt Age. Many of these waggons have a large number of metal fittings, some being completely covered in iron or bronze sheet metal. One well-known example is the waggon from the famous grave at → Hochdorf. From the early La Tène Age onwards, two-wheeled war-chariots occur in graves. Their use in combat is thought to derive from Mediterranean models; they were normally occupied by one charioteer and one warrior. On the European mainland chariots ceased to be employed in warfare in the course of the 1stC BC at the latest, but → Caesar encountered them in his expeditions to Britain (cf. Bell. Gall. 4,13). In Ireland it is possible that the tradition of the war-chariot was still alive in the second half of the 1st millennium AD.

Lit.: D. van Endert, *Die Wagenbestattungen der späten Hallstattzeit u. der Latènezeit im Gebiet westlich des Rheins*, O. 1987; U. Schaaff et al., *Vierrädrige Wagen der Hallstattzeit*, Mz. 1987; C. F. E. Pare, *Wagons and Wagon-Graves of the Early Iron Age in Central Europe*, O. 1992; F. Müller, 'Keltische Wagen mit elastischer Aufhängung: Eine Reise von Castel di Decima nach Clonmacnoise', in: *Trans Europam. Fs für Margarita Primas*, Bo. 1995, 265–275.

Wagner, Heinrich (1923–1988). Linguist and Celticist, born in Zurich. After studying with Julius → Pokorny and other scholars, he taught medieval German, at first in Utrecht, later in Basle. From 1958 to 1979 he was professor of Celtic philology and comparative linguistics at the University of Belfast. He then became a professor of the → School of Celtic Studies in Dublin. His major works are *Das Verbum in den Sprachen der Britischen Inseln* ("The Verb in the Languages of the British Isles", 1956) and the four-volume *Linguistic Atlas and Survey of Irish Dialects* (1958–1969). W. also published numerous essays on the history of Celtic religion and culture, in which he was concerned primarily with the influence of pre-Celtic → substrata and the problem of prehistoric cultural contacts between the Celts and other peoples of ancient Europe.

Waldalgesheim. Site c. 3 miles west of Bingen (North Rhine-Westphalia) where in 1869 a Celtic → princely grave dating from the middle of the 4thC BC was found. Grave goods included a golden neck-ring, two golden arm-rings, a tubular bronze jug and the metal remains of a two-wheeled waggon with the harness belonging to it. It was these finds, now to be seen in the Rheinisches Landesmuseum, which led Paul → Jacobsthal to term the second phase in the history of Celtic art the "W. style".

Lit.: H. E. Joachim et al., *Waldalgesheim: das Grab einer keltischen Fürstin*, Bo. 1995.

Waldenbuch → Steinenbronn.

warfare. Celtic warfare is known to us from the accounts of classical authors, depictions in Greek and Roman art, indigenous Celtic images and archaeological finds. Taken as a whole, these sources suggest that the bulk of Celtic warriors entered battle on foot. Only those of a high social status fought on horseback, or riding in a light two-wheeled chariot, manned by the armed warrior and his charioteer. The employment of the war-chariot is last attested on the European mainland in the battle of Telamon (225 BC). In Gaul it is not attested after the middle of the first century BC, although a description in → Caesar indicates that the British Celts continued to employ chariots (Bell. Gall. 4,33). Moreover, chariots are frequently mentioned in the tales of the → Ulster Cycle.

The most important weapon of the Celtic warrior was the iron sword. It had a straight blade up to a yard in length and was carried in a metal scabbard hung at the right hip. According to → Polybios (2,30), it was suitable not merely for the striking of sideways blows but also for stabbing. Lances and spears with iron points were also employed. The light weapons of the Celts were bows and arrows, and slings made with leather straps, with which balls could be projected made from stone or clay, ranging in size from that of a plum to that of an egg. Shields were made of wood and leather, and in consequence their presence in graves is only to be detected by the survival of the metal shield buckles. It is thought to have been only the nobility who wore helms and armour; these were not always made of metal, but frequently of leather or other organic material. Frequently, classical authors such as Polybios (2,28–29) or → Athenaios (5,29) report that the Celts also went into battle naked.

Depictions confirming these descriptions show the Celtic warrior with his characteristic metal neck-ring (→ torcs).

The accounts of classical authors tell of the Celtic custom of challenging individuals of the enemy camp to single combat before the assembled army by means of insulting speeches. It is also said to have been their custom to cut the heads off the slain. Both these motifs continue to play a significant role in medieval Irish narratives.

Lit.: J. L. Brunaux & B. Lambot, *Guerre et armement chez les Gaulois*, P. 1988; R. Pleiner, *The Celtic sword*, O. 1993.

weapons → warfare.

Weisgerber, Leo (1899–1985). Linguist and Celticist, born in Metz. After studying in Bonn and Munich he was professor of comparative linguistics and Sanskrit in Rostock from 1927 to 1938. He was then elected to the chair in General and Indo-European Linguistics in Marburg. From 1942 to 1967 he taught General Linguistics and Celtic Studies in Bonn. As a Celticist W. was particularly concerned with continental Celtic, concentrating upon the personal names of the Rhineland in Roman times and the study of Germano-Celtic linguistic relationships. A selection of his studies was republished in 1969 under the title *Rhenania Germano-Celtica.*

Weiskirchen. Place in the district of Merzig-Wadern in the Saar, near which in 1851 and 1866 two Celtic → princely graves of the 5th/4thC BC were excavated. The grave goods discovered there are now to be seen in the Rheinisches Landesmuseum in Bonn and in the Rheinisches Landesmuseum in Trier.
Lit.: A. Haffner, *Die westliche Hunsrück-Eifel-Kultur,* B. 1976.

Welsh (Cymric). The Celtic language of Wales; its name derives from a Germanic term for the Celts. The Welsh however call their language Cymraeg and themselves Cymry (< *kombrog-es "compatriots").

Welsh, together with → Breton, → Cornish and → Cumbrian, forms the British branch of the insular Celtic family of languages. Historically, the customary subdivision is between Early, Old, Middle and Modern Welsh. Early Welsh is known only from a few inscriptions and names in Latin texts of the 6th-8thC. Old Welsh is attested primarily by proper names and in → glosses in Latin and Anglo-Saxon sources, dating from the late 8th to the 12thCs. Continuous texts are still rare in this period and generally very short. Middle Welsh, on the other hand, is known through extensive literary documents. The texts are transmitted in manuscripts of the 13th/14thC, but were to some extent written down earlier. The oldest documents of Modern Welsh are dated to the 14th/15thC.

In the 19th and 20thC the ability to speak Welsh has declined considerably because English is the preferred language in education, because rural areas have suffered from depopulation, and because of the growing numbers of English immigrants. Welsh is still spoken as an everyday language, primarily in North and West Wales.
Lit.: D. S. Evans, *A Grammar of Middle Welsh,* Du. 1964; G. Price, *The Languages of Britain,* Lo. 1984; H. Lewis, *Datblygiad yr Iaith Gymraeg,* Cardiff ²1946, rpt. 1983 (= *Die kymrische Sprache: Grundzüge ihrer Entwicklung,* trans. W. Meid, I. 1989); T. A. Watkins, 'Welsh', in: *The Celtic Languages,* ed. M. Ball, Lo. 1993, 289–348.

Williams, Edward (1747–1826). Poet, collector of manuscripts and antiquarian, born in Llancarfan in South Wales. His chief occupation was as a stonemason in England and Wales. Attracted by the Romantic retrospective view of Celtic culture, he sought, under the pseudonym Iolo Morganwg, to adduce evidence of the continuity between the Welsh poetry of his own time and the tradition of the Celtic → bards and → druids. Literary forgeries served his purpose in this respect, which were only recognised as such long after his death. In 1792 W., with a few like-minded spirits in London, founded the Gorsedd Beirdd Ynys Prydein ("Assembly of the Bards of the Island of Britain"), a community of Welsh poets and musicians which still exists today, albeit in changed format.

Lit.: P. Morgan, *Iolo Morganwg*, Car. 1975; C. W. Lewis, *Iolo Morganwg*, Caernarfon 1995 (in Welsh); G. H. Jenkins, 'Iolo Morganwg and the Gorsedd of the Bards of the Isle of Britain' (*Studia Celtica Japonica* N. S. 7) 1995, 45–60.

Williams, Ifor (1881–1965). One of the most important Welsh Celticists, born in Tregarth, near Bethesda in North Wales. After studying with John → Morris-Jones, he was at first lecturer, later professor of Welsh Language and Literature at the University of Bangor, from 1907 to 1947. His editions of the → Pedeir Ceinc y Mabinogi (1930) and of the oldest Welsh poetry (→ Cynfeirdd) were milestones in the history of Welsh philology.

Windisch, Ernst (1844–1918). Linguist and Celticist, born in Dresden. He taught Sanskrit and comparative linguistics at the universities of Heidelberg, Strasbourg and Leipzig. His study of the works of James → Macpherson led to his interest in the area of Celtic languages and literatures. While publishing many studies in the area of Old and Middle Indian, he returned again and again to the literature of medieval Ireland. With Whitley → Stokes he edited the five-volume collection *Irische Texte mit Übersetzungen und Wörterbuch* ("Irish texts with translations and a glossary", 1880–1905). His most important pupil was Kuno → Meyer.

wine → food and drink.

Wolfram von Eschenbach. Middle High German poet, c. 1200. His major work is the romance of *Parzival*, some 25,000 lines in length, with which he introduced the legend of the → Grail to German literature. His chief source was the Old French verse romance *Perceval ou Li contes del graal*, composed by → Chrétien de Troyes c. 1190. The question of what other sources were available to W. for his reworking of the material remains contentious. The Celtic equivalent of *Parzival* is the Middle Welsh prose narrative → *Peredur fab Efrawg*.

women. Few valid generalisations can be made concerning the position of women among the Celts. Their social status presumably varied in the different settlement areas and strata of society, and in the course of time may well have undergone considerable change. Moreover, the sources often bar the way to an objective view.

In pre-Roman times the evidence is limited to grave finds, as archaeological finds from settlements yield little that is useful, and there is a dearth of literary sources. Graves such as those in → Bad Dürkheim, → Reinheim, → Vix and → Waldalgesheim show that it was possible for women to occupy a high social position. We are ignorant, however, concerning the basis of this position and to what extent it was dependant on the status of the family or the husband. The observations of classical authors relate for the most part to isolated cases and may not therefore be taken unreservedly as the basis for generalisations. This applies for example to the classical reports concerning the female rulers → Boudicca and → Cartimandua. Moreover the possibility must be taken into account that objective observations might be distorted in a moralising or propagandistic direction. This applies for example to the remark of Plutarch (Mulierum virtutes 6) concerning the positive role of women as mediators in disputes, or, conversely, the observation made by the historian → Diodoros of Sicily (5,32) concerning female participation in violent quarrels. With regard to the legal status of women we possess the observation of → Caesar (Bell. Gall. 6,19) that men had the power of life and death over their wives and children, but here too the veracity and general applicability of the statement are scarcely susceptible of proof.

Extensive data concerning the position of women are to be found at a later stage, in Irish and Welsh → law, as recorded in the early and high Middle Ages. According to these sources women were legally and politically subordinate to men, initially to their fathers, later to their husbands. They were permitted to own possessions but could not automatically bequeath these; they were not permitted to act as witnesses in court, nor to make contracts on their own behalf. Marriages were therefore arranged by the male relatives of the bride. The texts furthermore discuss questions of divorce and the permissibility of polygamy (a man's conjugal cohabitation with several women). Female → slaves were, it is thought, at least as common as male slaves, if one takes as evidence the employment of the word for "female slave" (Ir. → cumal) as a unit of currency.

The idea of woman occupying a strong position among the Celts or even of a Celtic matriarchy only emerged in the 19thC, and is based in part on the projection of stories about mythical figures such as → Macha, → Medb, → Rhiannon or → Scáthach onto social reality (cf. → Celtic ideology). Indisputably, → goddesses were of great significance in Celtic religion (cf. → Matronae/Matres). It ought not to be forgotten, however, that the stories known to us concerning dominant, self-willed or warlike women were always told by men for men (cf. also → Bansenchas).

Lit.: A. Lehmann, *Le rôle de la femme dans l'histoire de la Gaule*, P. 1944; D. Ó. Corráin, 'Women in Early Irish Society', in: M. MacCurtain & D. Ó Corráin (eds.), *Women in Irish Society*, Du. 1978, 1–13; P. O'Leary, 'The honour of women in early Ir. lit.' (*Ériu* 37) 1986, 27–44; P. K. Ford, 'Celtic Women' (*Viator: Medieval and Renaissance Studies* 19) 1988, 417–438; L. Allason-Jones, *Women in Roman Britain*, Lo. 1989; W. Davies, 'Celtic Women in the Early Middle Ages', in: A. Cameron & A. Kuhrt (eds.), *Images of Women in Antiquity* (rev. ed.), Lo. 1993, 145–166 & 307.

world, creation of → cosmogony.

world, end of → eschatology.

writing → literature.

Yeats, William Butler (1865–1939). Anglo-Irish poet and dramatist, born in Sandymount near Dublin. He spent his childhood in London and in Sligo on the west coast of Ireland. After studying art in Dublin and London he settled permanently in Ireland in 1896, and with Lady Augusta → Gregory sought to establish a national Irish theatre.

In his works Y. adapted a large number of European and non-European literary traditions. With regard to the Celtic material of his Irish homeland, the most persistent influence was that of the tales concerning → Cú Chulainn. He adapted these in the dramas *On Baile's Strand* (1904), *The Green Helmet* (1910), *At the Hawk's Well* (1917), *The Only Jealousy of Emer* (1919) and *The Death of Cuchulain* (1939). He reworked the story → *Longas mac nUislenn* in his play *Deirdre* (1907).

Yeats' poetry turned for inspiration, particularly in the early phase of his output, to the medieval literature of Ireland. In his first significant poem *The Wanderings of Oisin* (1889) he was inspired by the story → *Acallam na Senórach*. The stories → *Aided Oenfir Aífe* and → *Baile Binnbérlach mac Buain* were reworked in *Cuchulain's Fight with the Sea* (1891/92) and *Baile and Ailinn* (1903). The poem *Fergus and the Druid* (1892), by contrast, is only indirectly indebted to Irish sources; its immediate source was the poem *The Abdication of Fergus Mac Roy* by Samuel → Ferguson.

Y. is regarded as one of the most important poets writing in English in the early twentieth century. He was the leading author of the → Irish Renaissance, which earned international recognition mainly on the back of his works.

Lit.: D. M. Hoare, *The Works of Morris and Y. in Relation to Early Saga Literature*, C. 1937; P. L. Marcus, *Y. and the Beginning of the Irish Renaissance*, Ithaca, NY 1970; R. Skene, *The Cuchulain Plays of W. B. Y.*, Lo. 1974; M. H. Thuente, *W. B. Y. and Ir. Folklore*, Du. 1980; J. J. Blake, 'Y., Oisin and Ir. Gaelic Lit.', in: B. Bramsbäck & M. Croghan (eds.), *Anglo-Ir. and Ir. Lit.*, Up. 1988, 39–48; A. F. Macrae, *W. B. Yeats. A Literary Life*, Lo. 1995.

Yellow Book of Lecan. Irish compendium manuscript, the chief parts of which date from the late 14thC. It contains numerous tales from the → Historical, → Mythological and → Ulster Cycles and is now preserved in the library of Trinity College, Dublin. It is not to be confused with the "Book of Lecan", a manuscript of the early 15thC, which is now in the library of the Royal Irish Academy (also in Dublin).

Lit.: R. Atkinson, *The Yellow Book of Lecan*, Du. 1896 (facs.); H. P. A. Oskamp, 'The Yellow Book of Lecan Proper' (*Ériu* 26) 1975, 102–119.

Ygerna. Mother of → Arthur in the *Historia Regum Britanniae* of → Geoffrey of Monmouth. The Welsh form of the name is → Eigr.

Yonne → Icauna.

Ysbaddaden Bencawr (Welsh /əsba'ðaden 'benkaur/ "Y., the Foremost of the Giants"). Father of the eponymous heroine Olwen in the story → *Culhwch ac Olwen*. According to a prophecy he could only live until such time as his daughter married; in consequence he seeks to disrupt Culhwch's wooing of Olwen by making his assent dependent upon the fulfilment of a sequence of seemingly impossible tasks. After Culhwch, with the aid of his cousin → Arthur, has carried out these tasks, Y. is slain by a member of Arthur's retinue, → Goreu fab Custennin.

Yvain. French equivalent of the Welsh name → Owein. The romance of → Chrétien de Troyes concerned with Yvain has its Celtic equivalent in the Middle Welsh prose tale → *Iarlles y Ffynnawn*.

Zangentor ("pincer gate"). Term denoting a type of gate construction characteristic of the late Celtic fortified settlements (→ oppida) particularly on the right of the Rhine. The fortifying walls on both sides of the gate bend inwards almost at right angles, so that, seen from the outside, the gate appears to be at the end of a long alleyway. For defensive purposes this meant that only a small number of warriors could attack the gate, and that these had at the same time to cope with the defenders on the walls on both sides of the gateway.

Závist. Present-day name of a Celtic settlement on a steeply descending hill at the confluence of the Beraun and the Moldau south of Prague. A Celtic sanctuary there and a square fortified by ramparts and pallisades date back to the 6th-5thC BC. In the 2ndC BC Z. developed into one of the most important East Celtic town sites (→ oppida); at the point of its greatest expansion it occupied a surface of c. 170 hectares. In the last decades BC, Z.

was destroyed by fire, and later woods grew over it. Since 1963 the site has been systematically researched by archaeologists.

Lit.: K. Motyková et al., Z.: ein keltischer Burgwall in Mittelböhmen, Prague 1978; K. Motyková et al., 'Die bauliche Gestalt der Akropolis auf dem Burgwall Z. in der Späthallstatt- und Frühlatènezeit' (Germania 66) 1988, 391–436; K. Motyková et al., 'Die Siedlungsstruktur des Oppidums Z.' (AKorrBl 20) 1990, 415–426.

Zeuss, Johann Kaspar (1806–1856). Founder of modern → Celtic studies, born in Vogtendorf (Upper Franconia). After studying in Bamberg and Munich he taught Hebrew at a grammar school in Munich from 1832 to 1839. From 1839 until shortly before his death he was professor of history in Speyer, Munich and Bamberg. His first major work was the historical and ethnographical study Die Deutschen und die Nachbarstämme ("The Germans and their Neighbouring Tribes", 1837), a comprehensive collection and interpretation of the accounts from ancient times of the peoples of central Europe. After prolonged study of manuscripts in libraries in Germany and elsewhere Z. published his second major work in 1853, the Grammatica Celtica. This is the first overall survey of the Celtic languages, based on a scholarly study of the oldest discernible linguistic survivals. It was revised in 1871 by the Indo-European scholar Hermann Ebel (1820–1875) and remained for half a century the definitive study of the ancient Celtic languages.

Lit: F. Shaw, 'The Background to "Grammatica Celtica" ' (Celtica 3) 1956, 1–16; H. Hablitzel, Prof. Dr. J. K. Z., Kronach 1987; B. Forssmann (ed.), Erlanger Gedenkfeier für J. K. Z., Erlangen 1989; E. Poppe, 'Lag es in der Luft? J. K. Z. und die Konstituierung der Keltologie' (Beiträge zur Geschichte der Sprachwissenschaft 2) 1992, 41–56.

Zimmer, Heinrich (1851–1910). Celticist and linguist, born in Kastellaun in the Hunsrück. After studying in Strasbourg, Tübingen and Berlin he first taught linguistics and Sanskrit in Greifswald. In 1901 he was elected to the first German chair in Celtic Philology at the Friedrich-Wilhelms-Universität in Berlin. Z. was concerned with virtually every aspect of his discipline. Not only did he devote himself to the study of historical sources, but he also learned the modern Celtic languages in the course of journeys in Ireland and Wales.

His son, who bore the same Christian name (1890–1943), became well-known primarily because of his studies in the area of the history of Indian religions and his collaboration with the psychologist C. G. Jung (1875–1961). He concerned himself with Celtic sagas and myths in the posthumously published The King and the Corpse (1948).

Zürich-Altstetten → Altstetten.

291

Appendix

MUSEUMS

WITH COLLECTIONS OF CELTIC
AND/OR GALLO-ROMAN FINDS

The following list, arranged alphabetically according to country and town, contains a selection of the most important supra-regional collections, as well as some specialist museums of particular interest for the history and culture of the Celts. There is of course much to be discovered in the smaller regional museums, which for reasons of space could not be included here. All readers are urged to inquire about opening times by telephone in advance of their visit, particularly if they have a long journey ahead of them.

Austria

Hallein: Keltenmuseum, Pflegerplatz 5 (→ Hallein)
Hallstatt: Prähistorisches Museum, Seestr. 56 (→ Hallstatt)
Salzburg: Museum Carolino Augusteum, Museenplatz
Vienna: Naturhistorisches Museum, Prähistorische Abteilung (Prehistoric Section)

Belgium

Brussels: Musées Royaux d'Art et d'Histoire
Tongern: Provinciaal Gallo-Romeins Museum

Bulgaria

Sofia: Narodnija Archeologiceski Muzej

Czech Republic

Brno: Moravské Muzeum (→ Staré Hradisko)
Prague: Národní Muzeum (→ Duchcov, → Mšecké Žehrovice, → Závist)

Denmark

Copenhagen: Nationalmuseet (→ Gundestrup)

France

Aix-en-Provence: Musée Granet (→ Entremont)
Aix-les-Bains: Musée Archéologique et Lapidaire

Alise-Sainte-Reine: Musée Alesia (→ Alesia)
Angoulême: Musée des Beaux-Arts (→ Agris)
Argenton-sur-Creuse: Musée Archéologique d'Argentomagus
Autun: Musée Rolin
Auxerre: Musée Archéologique (Musée d'Art et d'Histoire)
Avignon: Musée Calvet
Bordeaux: Musée d'Aquitaine
Carnac: Musée de Préhistoire
Châlons-sur-Marne: Musée Municipal
Chalon-sur-Saône: Musée Denon
Châtillon-sur-Seine: Musée Archéologique (→ Mont Lassois, → Vix)
Clermont-Ferrand: Musée Bargoin (→ Chamalières)
Compiègne: Musée Vivenel (→ Gournay-sur-Aronde)
Dijon: Musée Archéologique (→ Sequana)
Épernay: Musée Municipal
Guiry-en-Vexin: Musée Archéologique Départemental du Val d'Oise
Lyon: Musée de la Civilisation Gallo-Romaine (→ Coligny)
Marseilles: Musée d'Archéologie Méditerranéenne (→ Roquepertuse)
Morlaix: Musée Municipal
Nancy: Musée Historique Lorrain
Nantes: Musée Vivenel (→ Gournay-sur-Aronde)
Nîmes: Musée Archéologique
Orléans: Musée Historique et Archéologique (→ Neuvy-en-Sullias)
Paris: Bibliothèque Nationale, Cabinet des Médailles; Musée de Cluny (→ Nautae
    Parisiaci)
Quimper: Musée Départemental Breton
Reims: Musée Saint-Rémi
Rennes: Musée de Bretagne
Roanne: Musée Déchelette
Rouen: Musée des Antiquités de la Seine-Maritime
Saint-Germain-en-Laye: Musée des Antiquités Nationales (→ Amfreville, → Bouray,
    → Euffigneix)
Saint-Rémy-de-Provence: Hôtel de Sade (→ Glanum)
Strasbourg: Musée Archéologique
Toulouse: Musée Saint-Raymond
Tours: Musée Archéologique de Touraine
Troyes: Musée des Beaux-Arts et d'Archéologie
Vienne: Musée des Beaux-Arts et d'Archéologie

Germany

Berlin: Museum für Vor- und Frühgeschichte, Schloß Charlottenburg (→
    Matzhausen)
Bonn: Rheinisches Landesmuseum, Colmantstr. 16 (→ Niederzier, → Pfalzfeld, →
    Waldalgesheim)
Eberdingen-Hochdorf: Keltenmuseum Hochdorf/Enz, Keltenstr. 2 (→ Hochdorf)
Freiburg i. Br.: Museum für Ur- und Frühgeschichte, Colombischlößle, Rotteckring 5

Herbertingen-Hundersingen: Heuneburgmuseum in der ehemaligen Zehntscheuer, Binzwanger Straße (→ Heuneburg)

Ingolstadt: Stadtmuseum, Auf der Schanz 45 (→ Manching)

Karlsruhe: Badisches Landesmuseum, formerly Großherzogliches Schloß (→ Heidelberg)

Mainz: Landesmuseum, Große Bleiche 49–51; Römisch-Germanisches Zentralmuseum, Ernst-Ludwig-Platz 2

Manching: Museum Manching, Rathaus (→ Manching)

Mannheim: Städtisches Reiss-Museum, Zeughaus

Munich: Prähistorische Staatssammlung, Lerchenfeldstr. 2 (→ Manching)

Saarbrücken: Landesmuseum für Vor- und Frühgeschichte, Am Ludwigsplatz 15 (→ Reinheim)

Speyer: Historisches Museum der Pfalz, Große Pfaffengasse 7 (→ Rodenbach)

Stuttgart: Württembergisches Landesmuseum, Schillerplatz 6, im Alten Schloß (→ Fellbach-Schmieden, → Grafenbühl, → Heuneburg, → Hirschlanden, → Hochdorf, → Hohmichele, → Kleinaspergle, → Steinenbronn, → Trichtingen)

Trier: Rheinisches Landesmuseum, Ostallee 44 (→ Hochscheid, → Weiskirchen)

Villingen-Schwemmingen: Franziskaner-Museum, Rietstr. 39, Villingen (→ Magdalenenberg)

Great Britain and Northern Ireland

Belfast: Ulster Museum

Cardiff: National Museum of Wales (→ Llyn Cerrig Bach)

Edinburgh: National Museum of Antiquities

London: British Museum (→ Aylesford, → Basse-Yutz, → Battersea, → Ipswich, → Lindow Moss, → Snettisham)

Hungary

Budapest: Magyar Nemzeti Múzeum

Ireland

Dublin: National Museum of Ireland (→ Broighter)

Italy

Ancona: Museo Nazionale Archeologico delle Marche

Bologna: Museo Civico Archeologico

Brescia: Museo Civico Romano

Como: Museo Civico Archeologico

Milan: Civiche Raccolte Archeologiche del Castello Sforzesco

Padua: Museo Civico Archeologico

Rome: Musei Capitolini

Turin: Museo di Antichità

Roumania

Bucharest: Muzeul National de Istorie (→ Ciumeşti)

Slovakian Republic

Bratislava: Slovenské Národné Muzeum

Spain

Madrid: Museo Arqueológico Nacional
Soria: Museo Numantino (→ Numantia)

Switzerland

Basle: Historisches Museum, Barfüßerplatz
Berne: Historisches Museum, Helvetiaplatz 5
Biel/Bienne: Museum Schwab, Seevorstadt 50
Geneva: Musée d'Art et d'Histoire, Rue Charles-Galland 2
Lausanne: Musée Cantonal d'Archéologie, Avenue du Peyrou (→ La Tène)
Zurich: Schweizerisches Landesmuseum, Museumstr. 2 (→ Altstetten, → Erstfeld)

Countries formerly constituting Yugoslavia

Belgrade: Narodni Muzej
Ljubljana: Narodni Muzej
Sarajevo: Zemaljski Muzej
Zagreb: Arheološki Muzej

SELECT BIBLIOGRAPHY

1. Bibliographies

(a) Ancient History, Archaeology

L'Année philologique, Paris 1924ff.
Archäologische Bibliographie, Berlin 1913ff.

(b) Language, Literature, Folklore

Baumgarten, R., *Bibliography of Irish Linguistics and Literature 1942–1971*, Dublin 1986.
Best, R. I., *Bibliography of Irish Philology and Manuscript Literature. Publications 1913–1941*, Dublin 1942.
———, *Bibliography of Irish Philology and of Printed Irish Literature*, Dublin 1913 (repr. with augm. indexes Dublin 1992).
Bibliotheca Celtica: A Register of Publications relating to Wales and the Celtic Peoples and Languages, Aberystwyth 1912ff.
Bromwich, R., *Medieval Celtic Literature: A Select Bibliography*, Toronto 1974.
Broudic, F., *Langue et littérature bretonnes: bibliographie*, 3 vols, Rennes 1984–1992.
Lapidge, M. & R. Sharpe, *A Bibliography of Celtic-Latin Literature 400–1200*, Dublin 1985.
Parry, T. & M. Morgan, *Llyfryddiaeth Llenyddiaeth Gymraeg: Bibliography of Welsh Literature*, Cardiff 1976.
Schneiders, M. & K. Veelenturf, *Celtic Studies in the Netherlands: a bibliography*, Dublin 1992.
Smith, P., *Oidhreacht Oirghiall. A bibliography of Irish literature and philology realting to the south-east Ulster – north Leinster region: printed sources*, Belfast 1995.
Watts, G. O., *Llyfryddiaeth Llenyddiaeth Gymraeg, Cyfrol 2 (1976–1986)*, Cardiff 1993.
Williams, J. E. C. & M. B. Hughes, *Llyfryddiaeth yr Iaith Gymraeg: Bibliography of the Welsh Language*, Cardiff 1988.

(c) Reception (Arthurian literature, Ossian)

Black, G. F., 'Macpherson's Ossian and the Ossianic Controversy. A Contribution towards a Bibliography' (*Bulletin of the New York Public Library* 30) 1926, 424–439 & 508–524.
Bulletin bibliographique de la Société internationale arthurienne, Paris 1949ff.
Dunn, J. J., 'Macpherson's Ossian and the Ossianic Controversy: A Supplementary Bibliography' (*Bulletin of the New York Public Library* 75) 1971, 465–473.
Palmer, C., *Arthurian bibliography III: 1978–1992*, Cambridge 1997.

Pickford, C. E. & R. Last, *The Arthurian Bibliography*, 2 vols., Cambridge 1981–1983.
Reiss, E. et al., *Arthurian Legend and Literature. Annotated Bibliography, I: The Middle Ages*, New York 1984.

2. Works of Reference

(a) General works of reference

Dictionary of the Middle Ages, 13 vols., New York 1982–1989.
Kindlers Neues Literaturlexikon, 20 vols., Munich 1988–1992.
Lexikon Iconographicum Mythologiae Classicae, Munich 1981ff.
Lexikon des Mittelalters, Munich 1977ff.
Realencyclopädie der classischen Altertumswissenschaft, Stuttgart/Munich 1894–1980.
Reallexikon der germanischen Altertumskunde, Berlin 1973ff.
Sachwörterbuch der Mediävistik (KTA 477), Stuttgart 1992.

(b) Specialised works of reference

Bartrum, P. C., *A Welsh Classical Dictionary. People in History and Legend up to about AD 1000*, Aberystwyth 1993.
Green, M. J., *Dictionary of Celtic Myth and Legend*, London 1992.
Lacy, N. J. (ed.), *The New Arthurian Encyclopedia*, London 1991.
Ó hÓgáin, D., *Myth, Legend and Romance: An Encyclopedia of the Irish Folk Tradition*, London 1990.
Pelletier, A., *La civilisation gallo-romaine de A à Z*, Lyon 1993.
Stephens, M. (ed.), *The Oxford Companion to the Literature of Wales*, Oxford 1986.
Thomson, D. (ed.), *The Companion to Gaelic Scotland*, Oxford 1983.
Welch, R. (ed.), *The Oxford Companion to Irish Literature*, Oxford 1996.

3. Editions and Translations of Texts

(a) Classical authors

Duval, P.-M., *Les sources de l'histoire de France*, T. 1, 2 vols., Paris 1971.
Herrmann, J. (ed.), *Griechische und lateinische Quellen zur Frühgeschichte Mitteleuropas*, 4 vols., Berlin 1988–1992.
Tierney, J. J., 'The Celtic Ethnography of Posidonius' (PRIA 60) 1960, 189–275.
Zwicker, J., *Fontes historiae religionis Celticae*, Berlin 1934–1936.

(b) Irish, Welsh and Medieval Latin texts

Ahlqvist, A., *The Early Irish Linguist. An Edition of the Canonical Part of the Auraicept na nÉces*, Helsinki 1983.
————, 'Le Testament de Morann' (EC 21) 1984, 151–170 & (EC 24) 1987, 325.
Anderson, M. O., *Adomnán's Life of Columba*, rev. ed., Oxford 1991.
d'Arbois de Jubainville, H., *Cours de littérature celtique*, 12 vols., Paris 1883–1902.
Atkinson, R., *The Book of Leinster*, Dublin 1880.
————, *The Book of Ballymote*, Dublin 1887.
————, *The Yellow Book of Lecan*, Dublin 1896.
Bergin, O. & R. I. Best, 'Tochmarc Étaíne' (Ériu 12) 1938, 137–196.
Best, R. I. & O. Bergin, *Lebor na hUidre: The Book of the Dun Cow*, Dublin 1929.
Best, R. I., O. Bergin, M. A. O'Brien & A. O'Sullivan, *The Book of Leinster, formerly Lebar na Núachongbála*, 6 vols., Dublin 1954–1983.
Bhreathnach, M., 'A new edition of Tochmarc Becfhola' (Ériu 35) 1984, 59–91.
Binchy, D. A., *Críth Gablach*, Dublin 1941 (MMIS 11).
————, *Scéla Cano meic Gartnáin*, Dublin 1963 (MMIS 18).
————, *Corpus iuris hibernici*, 6 vols., Dublin 1978.
Birkhan, H., *Keltische Erzählungen vom Kaiser Arthur*, 2 vols., Kettwig 1989.
Bromwich, R., *Trioedd Ynys Prydein: The Welsh Triads*, Cardiff ²1978.
————, 'The "Tristan" Poems in the Black Book of Carmarthen' (StC 14/15) 1979/80, 54–65.
Bromwich, R. & D. S. Evans, *Culhwch ac Olwen: an edition and study of the oldest Arthurian tale*, Cardiff 1992.
Byrne, F. J. & P. Francis, 'Two Lives of Saint Patrick: Vita Secunda and Vita Quarta' (JRSAI 124) 1994, 5–117.
Calder, G., *Auraicept na n-Éces: The Scholar's Primer*, Edinburgh 1917.
Carey, J., 'Scél Túain meic Chairill' (Ériu 35) 1984, 93–111.
Carney, J., *The Poems of Blathmac, Son of Cú Brettan, together with The Irish Gospel of Thomas and A Poem on the Virgin Mary*, Dublin 1964 (ITS 47).
Clarke, B., *Geoffrey of Monmouth: Vita Merlini*, Cardiff 1973.
Comyn, D. S. & P. S. Dinneen, *Foras Feas ar Éirinn: Elements of the History of Ireland*, 4 vols., London 1902–1914 (ITS 4,8,9,15).
Connolly, S. & J.-M. Picard, 'Cogitosus: Life of Saint Brigit' (JRSAI 117) 1987, 5–27.
Cross, T. P. & A. C. L. Brown, 'Fingen's Night-Watch' (*Romanic Review* 9) 1918, 29–47.
Cross, T. P. & C. H. Slover, *Ancient Irish Tales*, London 1936.
Dillon, M. 'The Trinity College Text of Serglige Con Culainn' (SGS 6) 1949, 139–175.
————, 'The Wasting Sickness of Cú Chulainn' (SGS 7) 1953, 47–88.
————, *Serglige Con Culainn*, Dublin 1953 (MMIS 14).
————, *Stories from the Acallam*, Dublin 1970 (MMIS 23).
Dobbs, M, 'The Ban-Shenchas' (RC 47) 1930, 283–339, (RC 48) 1931, 163–234 & (RC 49) 1932, 437–489.
Evans, J. G. & J. Rhŷs, *The Text of the Mabinogion from the Red Book of Hergest*, Oxford 1887.
————, *The Text of the Bruts from the Red Book of Hergest*, Oxford 1890.
Evans, J. G., *The Black Book of Carmarthen*, Pwllheli 1906.

————, *The White Book Mabinogion*, Pwllheli 1907.

————, *Facsimile and Text of the Book of Aneirin*, 2 vols., Pwllheli 1908.

————, *Facsimile of the Black Book of Carmarthen*, Oxford 1908.

————, *Facsimile and Text of the Book of Taliesin*, Llanbedrog 1910.

————, *The Poetry in the Red Book of Hergest*, Llanbedrog 1911.

Ford, P. K., *The Mabinogi and other Medieval Welsh Tales*, Berkeley (Calif.) 1977.

————, *Ystoria Taliesin*, Cardiff 1992.

Gantz, J., *The Mabinogion*, Harmondsworth 1976.

————, *Early Irish Myths and Sagas*, Harmondsworth 1981.

Gray, E. A., *Cath Maige Tuired: The Second Battle of Mag Tuired*, Dublin 1982 (ITS 52).

Greene, D. *Fingal Rónáin and other stories*, Dublin 1955 (MMIS 16).

Guyonvarc'h, Ch.-J., 'La Mort du fils unique d'Aife' (*Ogam* 9) 1957, 115–121.

————, 'Le Meurtre de Conchobar' (*Ogam* 10) 1958, 129–138.

————, 'La Maladie de Cuchulainn et l'unique jalousie d'Emer' (*Ogam* 10) 1958, 285–310.

————, 'La mort violente de Celtchar fils d'Uthecar' (*Ogam* 10) 1958, 371–380.

————, 'La mort violente de Loegaire Victorieux' (*Ogam* 11) 1959, 423–424.

————, 'La Naissance de Conchobar' (*Ogam* 11) 1959, 56–65 & 335–336, (*Ogam* 12) 1960, 235–240.

————, 'La Conception des deux porchers' (*Ogam* 12) 1960, 73–90.

————, 'L'ivresse des Ulates' (*Ogam* 12) 1960, 487–506 & (*Ogam* 13) 1961, 343–360.

————, 'La Mort tragique des enfants de Tuireann' (*Ogam* 16) 1964, 231–256 & (*Ogam* 17) 1965, 189–192.

Guyonvarc'h, Ch.-J. & F. Le Roux, 'La Conception de Cúchulainn' (*Ogam* 17) 1965, 363–410.

————, 'Le Rêve d'Óengus' (*Ogam* 18) 1966, 117–150.

————, 'La Courtise d'Étain' (*Celticum* 15) 1966, 283ff.

————, 'La Mort de Cúchulainn. Version A' (*Ogam* 18) 1966, 343–399.

Gwynn, E. H., *The metrical Dindsenchas*, 5 vols., Dublin 1903–1935.

Gwynn, J., *Liber Ardmachanus: The Book of Armagh*, Dublin 1913.

Hamel, A. G. van, *Compert Con Culainn and other stories*, Dublin 1933 (MMIS 3).

Haycock, M., 'Preiddeu Annwn and the figure of Taliesin' (*StC* 18/19) 1983/84, 52–78.

Henderson, G., *Fled Bricrenn: The Feast of Briciu*, London 1899 (ITS 2).

Henry, P. L., 'Verba Scáthaige' (*Celtica* 21) 1990, 191–207.

Hollo, K., 'The Feast of Bricriu and the Exile of the Sons of Dóel Dermait' (*Emania* 10) 1992, 18–24.

Hull, V., *Longes mac nUislenn: The Exile of the Sons of Uisliu*, London 1949.

————, 'Noinden Ulad: The Debility of the Ulidians' (*Céltica* 8) 1968, 1–42.

Jackson, K. H., *The Gododdin: The Oldest Scottish Poem*, Edinburgh 1970.

————, *A Celtic Miscellany: Translations from the Celtic Literatures*, Harmondsworth 1971.

————, *Aislinge Meic Con Glinne*, Dublin 1990.

Jarman, A. O. H. & E. O. Jones, *Llyfr Du Caerfyrddin gyda rhagymadrodd, nodiadau testunol a geirfa*, Cardiff 1982.

Jarman, A. O. H., *Aneirin: Y Gododdin*, Llandysul 1988.

Jones, B., *Y Tair Rhamant*, Aberystwyth 1960.

Jones, G. & T. Jones, *The Mabinogion*, rev. ed., London 1974.

Jones, T., 'The Black Book of Carmarthen "Stanzas of the Graves" ' (PBA 53) 1967, 97–137.

Kelly, F., *Audacht Morainn*, Dublin 1976.

Knott, E., *Togail Bruidne Da Derga*, Dublin 1936 (MMIS 8).

Lautenbach, F., *Der keltische Kessel. Wandlung und Wiedergeburt in der Mythologie der Kelten. Irische, walisische und arthurianische Texte*, Stuttgart 1991.

Lehmann, R., *Fled Dúin na nGéd*, Dublin 1964 (MMIS 21).

———, 'The Banquet of the Fort of the Geese' (*Lochlann* 4) 1969, 131–159.

Macalister, R. A. S., *Lebor Gabála Érenn: The Book of the Taking of Ireland*, Dublin 1938–1956 (ITS 34, 35, 39, 41, 44).

MacGerailt, U., 'The Edinburgh Text of Mesca Ulad' (*Ériu* 37) 1986, 133–180.

MacMathúna, S., *Immram Brain: Bran's Journey to the Land of the Women*, Tübingen 1985.

MacNeill, E. & G. Murphy, *Duanaire Finn: The Book of the Lays of Fionn*, London/Dublin 1908–1953 (ITS 7, 28 & 43).

MacNeill, E., 'Ancient Irish Law: The Law of Status or Franchise' (PRIA 36) 1923, 265–316.

MacQueen, W. & J. MacQueen, 'Vita Merlini Silvestris' (*Scottish Studies* 29) 1989, 77–93.

Marstrander, C., 'A new version of the Battle of Mag Rath' (*Ériu* 6) 1911, 226–247.

Meid, W., *Die Romanze von Froech und Findabair: Táin Bó Froích*, Innsbruck 1970.

Meyer, K., 'Compert Conchobuir, "The Conception of Conchobar" ' (RC 6) 1884, 173–182.

———, *The "Cath Finntrága" or Battle of Ventry*, Oxford 1885.

———, 'The Adventures of Nera' (RC 10) 1889, 212–228.

———, 'Scél Baili Binnbérlaig' (RC 13) 1892, 220–228.

Meyer, K. & A. Nutt, *The Voyage of Bran, Son of Febal, to the Land of the Living*, 2 vols., London 1895–1897.

Meyer, K. 'Baile in Scáil' (ZCP 3) 1901, 457–466, (ZCP 12) 1918, 232–238, (ZCP 13) 1921, 371–382.

———, *The Death-Tales of the Ulster Heroes*, Dublin 1906 (RIA Todd Lecture Series 14).

———, *The Instructions of King Cormac mac Airt*, Dublin 1909 (RIA Todd Lecture Series 15).

Mulchrone, K., *Caithréim Cellaig*, Dublin 1971 (MMIS 24).

Nic Dhonnchadha, L., *Aided Muirchertaig meic Erca*, Dublin 1964 (MMIS 19).

Ní Shéaghda, N., *Agallamh na Seanórach*, 3 vols., Dublin 1942–1945.

———, *Tóruigheacht Dhiarmada agus Ghráinne: The Pursuit of Diarmaid and Gráinne*, Dublin 1967 (ITS 48).

O'Curry, E., 'The Fate of the Children of Tuireann' (*Atlantis* 4) London 1863, 157–227.

Ó Cuív, B., *Cath Muighe Tuireadh: The Second Battle of Magh Tuireadh*, Dublin 1945.

O'Daly, M., *Cath Maige Mucraime: The Battle of Mag Mucraime*, Dublin 1975 (ITS 50).

Ó Donovan, J. & W. Stokes, *Cormac's Glossary (Sanas Chormaic)*, Calcutta 1868.

O'Duffy, R., 'Oidhe Chloinne Tuireann' (*Society for the Preservation of the Irish Language*, vol. 8), Dublin 1901, 1–64.

Ó Fiannachta, P., *Táin Bó Cuailnge*, Dublin 1966.

O'Grady, S. H., *Silva Gadelica: A Collection of Tales in Irish*, 2 vols., London 1892.

Ó hAodha, D., *Bethu Brigte*, Dublin 1978.

———, 'The Lament of the Old Woman of Beare', in: D. Ó Corráin et al. (eds.), *Sages, Saints, and Storytellers: Celtic Studies in Honour of Prof. J. Carney*, Maynooth 1989, 308–331.

O'Keeffe, J. G., *Buile Shuibhne*, Dublin 1932 (MMIS 1).

O'Mara, R., *König der Bäume: Das altirische Epos von der "Ekstase des Suibhne"*, Munich 1985.

O'Rahilly, C., *The Stowe Version of Táin Bó Cuailnge*, Dublin 1961.

———, *Cath Finntrágha*, Dublin 1962 (MMIS 1962).

———, *Táin Bó Cuailnge from the Book of Leinster*, Dublin 1967.

———, *Táin Bó Cuailnge: Recension I*, Dublin 1976.

Ó Riain, P. & M. Herbert, *Betha Adamnáin: the Irish Life of Adamnán*, London 1988 (ITS 54).

Oskamp, H. P. A., *The Voyage of Máel Dúin*, Groningen 1970.

———, 'Echtra Condla' (EC 14) 1974, 207–228.

Pokorny, J., 'Conle's abenteuerliche Fahrt' (ZCP 17) 1927, 193–205.

———, *Altkeltische Dichtungen*, Berne 1944.

Quiggin, E. C., *Poems from the Book of the Dean of Lismore*, Cambridge 1937.

Richards, M., *Breudwyt Ronabwy allan o'r Llyfr Coch o Hergest*, Cardiff 1948.

Roberts, B. F., *Cyfranc Lludd a Llefelys*, Dublin 1976 (MMWS 7).

———, 'Rhai o Gerddi Ymddiddan Llyfr Du Caerfyrddin', in: R. Bromwich & R. B. Jones (eds.), *Astudiaethau ar yr Hengerdd*, Cardiff 1978, 281–325.

Roider, U., *Wie die beiden Schweinehirten den Kreislauf der Existenzen durchwanderten: De chophur in da muccida*, Innsbruck 1979.

Ross, N., *Heroic Poetry from the Book of the Dean of Lismore*, Edinburgh 1939.

Rowland, J., *Early Welsh Saga Poetry: A Study and Edition of the 'Englynion'*, Cambridge 1990.

Shaw, F., *The Dream of Oengus (Aislinge Óenguso)*, Dublin 1934.

Stern, L. C., 'Fled Bricrenn nach dem Codex Vossianus' (ZCP 4) 1903, 143–177.

Stokes, W. & E. Windisch, *Irische Texte mit Übersetzungen und Wörterbuch*, 5 vols., Leipzig 1880–1905.

Stokes, W., 'The Bórama' (RC 13) 1892, 32–124.

———, 'The Bodleian Dindshenchas' (*Folk-Lore* 3) 1892, 467–516.

———, 'The Edinburgh Dindshenchas' (*Folk-Lore* 4) 1893, 471–497.

———, 'The Prose Tales of the Rennes Dindshenchas' (RC 15) 1894, 272–336 & 418–484, (RC 16) 1895, 31–83, 135–167 & 269–313.

———, 'The Bodleian Amra Choluim Chille' (RC 20) 1899, 30–55, 132–183, 248–289, 400–437 & (RC 21) 1900, 133–136.

Stokes, W. & J. Strachan, *Thesaurus palaeohibernicus: a collection of Old Irish glosses, scholia, prose, and verse*, Cambridge 1901–1903.

Stokes, W., 'The Colloquy of the Two Sages' (RC 26) 1905, 4–64.

Strachan, J. & J. G. O'Keeffe, *The Táin Bó Cuailnge from the Yellow Book of Lecan, with Variant Readings from the Lebor na hUidre*, Dublin 1912.

Thomson, D. S., *Branwen uerch Lyr*, Dublin 1961 (MMWS 2).

Thomson, R. L., *Pwyll Pendeuic Dyuet*, Dublin 1957 (MMWS 1).

———, *Owein, or Chwedyl Iarlles y Ffynnawn*, Dublin 1968 (MMWS 4).

Thorpe, L., *Geoffrey of Monmouth: The History of the Kings of Britain*, Harmondsworth 1966.

Thurneysen, R., *Sagen aus dem alten Irland*, Berlin 1901.

———, 'Eine irische Parallele zur Tristan-Sage' (*Zeitschrift für romanische Philologie* 43) 1924, 385–402.

———, *Scéla Mucce Meic Dathó*, Dublin 1935 (MMIS 6).

———, 'Baile in Scáil' (*ZCP* 20) 1936, 213–227.

Vendryes, J., *Airne Fíngein*, Dublin 1953 (MMIS 15).

———, 'La Destruction de Dind Rig' (*EC* 8) 1958/59, 7–40.

Vielhauer, I., *Geoffrey of Monmouth: Vita Merlini. Das Leben des Zauberers Merlin*, Amsterdam 1964.

Watson, J. C., *Mesca Ulad*, Dublin 1941 (MMIS 13).

———, 'Mesca Ulad' (*SGS* 5) 1942, 1–34.

Watson, W. J., *Scottish Verse from the Book of the Dean of Lismore*, Edinburgh 1937.

Williams, I., *Pedeir Keinc y Mabinogi*, Cardiff 1930.

———, *Canu Aneirin*, Cardiff 1938.

Williams, I. & J. E. C. Williams, *The Poems of Taliesin*, Dublin 1968 (MMWS 3).

Williams, I. & R. Bromwich, *Armes Prydein*, Dublin 1972 (MMWS 6).

Windisch, E., *Táin Bó Cualnge nach dem Buch von Leinster*, Leipzig 1905.

Winterbottom, M., *Gildas: The Ruin of Britain and other works*, London 1978.

Wright, N., *The Historia Regum Britanniae of Geoffrey of Monmouth I: Bern, Burgerbibliothek MS. 568*, Cambridge 1985.

———, *The Historia Regum Britanniae of Geoffrey of Monmouth II: The First Variant Version*, Cambridge 1988.

4. Archaeology, Religious and Cultural History until Late Antiquity

Alcock, L., *Arthur's Britain*, Harmondsworth 1971.

———, 'Cadbury-Camelot: A fifteen-year perspective' (*PBA* 68) 1982, 354ff.

Allain, J., L. Fleuriot & L. Chaix, 'Le Vergobret des Bituriges à Argentomagus. Essai d'interpretation d'une fosse cultuelle' (*RAE* 32) 1981, 11–32.

Allason-Jones, L. & B. McKay, *Coventina's Well*, Chesters 1985.

Allason-Jones, L., *Women in Roman Britain*, London 1989.

Allen, D. F., *The Coins of the Ancient Celts*, Edinburgh 1980.

Almagro-Gorbea, M. et al., 'Les fouilles du Mont-Beuvray, Nièvre, Saône-et-Loire. Rapport biennal 1988–1989' (*RAE* 42) 1991, 271–298.

Almagro-Gorbea, M. & G. Ruiz Zapatero (eds.), *Los Celtas: Hispania y Europa*, Madrid 1993.

Anati, E., *I Camuni: alle radici della civiltà europea*, Milan 1984.

———, *Felsbilder: Wiege der Kunst und des Geistes*, Zurich 1991.

Archéologie d'Entremont au Musée Granet, Aix-en-Provence 1987.

Arsdell, R. D. van, *Celtic Coinage of Britain*, London 1989.

Aspects de la religion celtique et gallo-romaine dans le nord-est de la Gaule à la lumière des découvertes récentes, Saint-Dié-des-Vosges 1989.

Audin, P., 'Césaire d'Arles et le maintien de pratiques païennes dans la Provence du 6e siècle', in: *La patrie gauloise d'Agrippa au 6e siècle*, Lyon 1983, 327–338.

————, 'Les Eaux chez les Arvernes et les Bituriges', in: *La Médecine en Gaule*, Paris 1985, 121–144.

Audouze, F. & O. Buchsenschutz, *Villes, villages et campagnes de l'Europe celtique. Du début du IIe millénaire à la fin du Ier siècle avant JC*, Paris 1989.

Bammesberger, A. & A. Wollmann (eds.), *Britain 400–600: Language and History*, Heidelberg 1990.

Baratta, G., 'Una divinità gallo-romana: Sucellus. Un "ipotesi interpretiva" (*Archeologia Classica* 45) 1993, 233–247.

Barker, G., *Prehistoric Farming in Europe*, Cambridge 1985.

Barruol, G., 'Mars Nabelcus et Mars Albiorix' (*Ogam* 15) 1963, 345–368.

Bauchhenss, G., *Jupitergigantensäulen*, Stuttgart 1976.

Bauchhenss, G. & P. Noelke, *Die Iupitersäulen in den germanischen Provinzen*, Cologne 1981.

Bauchhenss, G. & G. Neumann (eds.), *Matronen und verwandte Gottheiten*, Bonn 1987.

Beck, A., 'Der hallstattzeitliche Grabhügel von Tübingen-Kilchberg' (*FBW* 1) 1974, 251–281.

Beck, C. & S. Shennan, *Amber in Prehistoric Britain*, Oxford 1991.

Beeser, J., 'Der Kouro-Keltos von Hirschlanden' (*FBW* 8) 1983, 21–46.

Beiträge zur Urnenfelderzeit nördlich und südlich der Alpen. Ergebnisse eines Kolloquiums, Bonn 1995.

Bémont, C., 'Rosmerta' (*EC* 9) 1960, 29–43.

————, 'A propos d'un nouveau monument de Rosmerta' (*Gallia* 27) 1969, 23–44.

————, 'A propos des couples mixtes gallo-romains', in: L. Kahil et al. (eds.), *Iconographie classique et identité régionales*, Paris 1986, 131–153.

Benoit, F., *Les Mythes de l'Outre-Tombe. Le Cavalier à l'anguipède et l'écuyère Epona*, Brussels 1950 (Coll. Latomus 3).

————, 'L'Ogmius de Lucien et Hercule Psychopompe', in: *Beiträge zur älteren europäischen Kulturgeschichte. FS für Rudolf Egger I*, Klagenfurt 1952, 144–158.

————, *Mars et Mercure. Nouvelles recherches sur l'interprétation gauloise des divinités romaines*, Aix-en-Provence 1959.

————, *Art et dieux de la Gaule*, Paris 1969.

————, *Entremont: capitale celto-ligure des Salyens de Provence*, Paris 1969.

————, *Le Symbolisme dans les sanctuaires de la Gaule*, Brussels 1970 (Coll. Latomus 105).

Berchem, D. van, *Les Routes et l'Histoire. Études sur les Hélvètes et leurs voisins*, Geneva 1982.

Bergquist, A. & T. Taylor, 'The Origin of the Gundestrup Cauldron' (*Antiquity* 61) 1987, 10–24.

Bertin, D. & J.-P. Guillaumont, *Bibracte (Saône-et-Loire): une ville gauloise sur le Mont Beuvray*, Paris 1987 (Guides archéologiques de la France 13).

Biel, J., *Der Keltenfürst von Hochdorf*, Stuttgart 1985.

Bieńkowski, P., *Die Darstellung der Gallier in der hellenistischen Kunst*, Vienna 1908.

————, *Les Celtes dans les arts mineurs gréco-romains*, Kracow 1928.

Billy, P.-H., *Thesaurus Linguae Gallicae*, Hildesheim 1993.

———, *Atlas Linguae Gallicae*, Hildesheim 1995.

Birkhan, H., *Germanen und Kelten bis zum Ausgang der Römerzeit*, Vienna 1970.

Birley, E. 'The Deities of Roman Britain' (*ANRW II* 18.1) 1986, 3–112.

Bittel, K., W. Kimmig & S. Schiek (eds.), *Die Kelten in Baden-Württemberg*, Stuttgart 1981.

Bittel, K., S. Schiek & D. Müller, *Die keltischen Viereckschanzen*, Stuttgart 1990.

Bober, Ph. P., 'Cernunnos: Origin and Transformation of a Celtic Divinity' (*American Journal of Archaeology* 55) 1951, 13–51.

Les Bois sacrés. Actes du colloque international Naples, 23–25 nov. 1989, Naples 1993.

Botheroyd, P. & S. Botheroyd, *Deutschland – Auf den Spuren der Kelten*, Munich 1989.

Boucher, S., *Recherches sur les bronzes figurés de Gaule préromaine et romaine*, Rome 1976.

———, 'L'image de Mercure en Gaule', in: *La patrie gauloise d'Agrippa au 6e siècle*, Lyon 1983, 57–69.

———, 'L'image et les fonctions du dieu Sucellus' (*Caes* 23) 1988, 77–86.

Bourgeois, C., *Divona. 1. Divinités et ex-voto du culte gallo-romain de l'eau. 2. Monuments et sanctuaires gallo-romains de l'eau*, Paris 1991–1992.

Brailsford, J. W. & J. E. Stapley, 'The Ipswich Torcs' (*Proceedings of the Prehistoric Society* 38) 1972, 219–234.

Brailsford, J., *Early Celtic Masterpieces from Britain in the British Museum*, London 1978.

Brun, P., *Princes et princesses de la Celtique. Le premier âge du fer en Europe 850–450 av. J.-C.*, Paris 1987.

Brunaux, J. L. & P. Meniel, 'Das Oppidum von Gournay-sur-Aronde' (*Antike Welt* 14,1) 1983, 41–45.

Brunaux, J. L. et al., *Gournay I. Les fouilles sur le sanctuaire et l'oppidum (1975–1984)*, Amiens 1985.

Brunaux, J. L., *Les Gaulois: sanctuaires et rites*, Paris 1986.

Brunaux, J. L. & A. Rapin, *Gournay II. Boucliers et lances; dépôts et trophées*, Paris 1988.

Brunaux, J. L. & B. Lambot, *Guerre et armement chez les Gaulois 450–52 av. J.-C.*, Paris 1988.

Büchsenschütz, O., 'Neue Ausgrabungen im Oppidum Bibracte' (*Germania* 67) 1989, 541–550.

Büchsenschütz, O. & L. Olivier (eds.), *Les Viereckschanzen et les enceintes quadrilatérales en Europe celtique*, Paris 1990.

Cahen-Delhaye, A. et al. (eds.), *Les Celtes en Belgique et dans le Nord de la France*, Lille 1984.

Campanile, E. (ed.), *I Celti d'Italia*, Pisa 1981.

Capelle, T., 'Eisenzeitliche Bauopfer' (*Frühmittelalterliche Studien* 21) 1987, 182–205.

Le Carnyx et la Lyre. Archéologie musicale en Gaule celtique et romaine, Besançon 1993.

Les Celtes dans le Jura, Yverdon 1991.

Les Celtes en Champagne. Cinq siècles d'histoire, Epernay 1991.

Celtíberos, Saragossa 1988.

Celtic Coinage: Britain and beyond. The 11th Oxford Symposium on Coinage and Monetary History, Oxford 1992.

The Celts, Milan 1991.

Chadwick, N. K., *The Druids*, Cardiff 1966.

Champion, T. C., 'Written sources and the study of the European Iron Age', in: T. C. Champion & J. V. S. Megaw (eds.), *Settlement and Society*, Leicester 1985, 9–22.

Charles-Edwards, T. M., 'Native Political Organization in Roman Britain and the Origin of MW brenin', in: M. Mayrhofer et al. (eds.), *Anitquitates Indogermanicae: Gedenkschrift für H. Güntert*, Innsbruck 1974, 35–45.

Chevallier, R., 'Des dieux gaulois et gallo-romains aux saints du christianisme. Recherches sur la christianisation des cultes de la Gaule', in: *La patrie gauloise d'Agrippa au 6e siècle*, Lyon 1983, 283–326.

———, *La Romanisation de la Celtique du Pô*. Essai d'histoire provinciale, Rome 1983.

La Civilisation de Hallstatt. Bilan d'une rencontre, Liège 1989.

Čižmář, M., 'Erforschung des keltischen Oppidums Staré Hradisko in den Jahren 1983–1988' (AKorrBl 19) 1989, 265–268.

Collis, J., *Oppida: Earliest Towns north of the Alps*, Sheffield 1984.

Coulon, G., *Les Gallo-Romains. Au carrefour de deux civilisations*, 2 vols, Paris 1990.

———, *L'enfant en Gaule romaine*, Paris 1994.

Cunliffe, B. (ed.), *Coinage and Society in Britain and Gaul*, London 1981.

Cunliffe, B. & P. Davenport, *The Temple of Sulis Minerva at Bath*, 2 vols., Oxford 1985–1988.

Cunliffe, B., *Die Kelten und ihre Geschichte*, Bergisch Gladbach 1988.

———, *Iron Age Communities in Britain*, London [3]1991.

Cunliffe, B. (ed.), *The Oxford Illustrated Prehistory of Europe*, Oxford 1994.

Dannheimer, H. & R. Gebhard (eds.), *Das keltische Jahrtausend*, Mainz 1993.

Dauzat, A. & C. Rostaing, *Dictionnaire étymologique des noms de lieux en France*, Paris [2]1979.

Dayet, M., 'Recherches archéologiques au "Camp du Château" (1955–1959)' (*RAE* 18) 1967, 52–106.

Deonna, W., 'Télesphore et le "genius cucullatus" celtique' (*Latomus* 14) 1959, 43–74.

Deyts, S., *Divinités indigènes en Bourgogne à l'époque gallo-romaine*, Dijon 1967.

———, *Les Bois sculptés des Sources de la Seine*, Paris 1983.

———, *Les Sanctuaires des Sources de la Seine*, Dijon 1985.

———, *Images des dieux de la Gaule*, Paris 1992.

Dillon, M. & N. K. Chadwick, *The Celtic Realms*, London 1973 (History of civilisation).

Dirkzwager, A., *Strabo über Gallia Narbonensis*, Leiden 1975.

Dobesch, G., *Die Kelten in Österreich nach den ältesten Berichten der Antike*, Vienna 1980.

———, 'Caesar als Ethnograph' (*Wiener humanistische Blätter* 31) 1989, 18–51.

———, 'Ancient Literary Sources', in: *The Celts*, Milan 1991, 35–41.

———, *Das europäische "Barbaricum" und die Zone der Mediterrankultur*, Vienna 1995.

Dottin, G., *La langue gauloise*, Paris 1920.

Drack, W. & H. Schneider, *Der Üetliberg – die archäologischen Denkmäler*, Zurich 1979 (Archäologische Führer der Schweiz 10).

Drack, W. 'Der frühlatènezeitliche Fürstengrabhügel auf dem Üetliberg' (*Zeitschrift für Schweizerische Archäologie und Kunstgeschichte* 38) 1981, 1–28.

Drda, P. & A. Rybová, *Les Celtes de Bohême*, Paris 1994.

Dressler, W., 'Galatisches', in: W. Meid (ed.), *Beiträge zur Indogermanistik und Keltologie*, *Julius Pokorny zum 80. Geburtstag gewidmet*, Innsbruck 1967, 147–154.

Driehaus, J., 'Zum Krater von Vix. Fragen an die klassische Archäologie' (*HBA* 8) 1981, 103–113.

Drinkwater, J. F., *Roman Gaul*, Ithaca (New York) 1983.

Drioux, G., *Cultes indigènes des Lingons*, Paris 1934.

Duval, A., *L'art celtique de la Gaule au Musée des antiquités nationales*, Paris 1989.

Duval, P.-M., 'Vulcan et les métiers du métal' (*Gallia* 10) 1952, 43–57.

———, 'Le dieu Smertrios et ses avatars gallo-romains' (*EC* 6) 1953/54, 219–238.

———, 'Le groupe de bas-reliefs des "Nautae Parisiaci" ' (*Monuments et mémoires de la Fondation Eugène Piot* 48,2) 1956, 64–90.

———, 'Teutates – Esus – Taranis' (*EC* 8) 1958/59, 41–58.

———, 'Esus und seine Werkzeuge auf Denkmälern in Trier und Paris' (*Trierer Zeitschrift* 36) 1973, 81–88.

———, *Les Dieux de la Gaule*, Paris 1976.

———, *Die Kelten*, Munich 1978 (Universum der Kunst).

———, 'Problèmes des rapports entre la religion gauloise et la religion romaine', in: P. MacCana & M. Meslin (eds.), *Rencontres de religions*, Paris 1986, 39–56.

———, *Monnaies gauloises et mythes celtiques*, Paris 1987.

———, *La vie quotidienne en Gaule pendant la paix romaine (Ier-IIIe siècle ap. J. C.)*, Paris ³1988.

———, *Travaux sur la Gaule*. Textes revus et mis à jour, 2 vols., Rome 1989.

Ebel, C., *Transalpine Gaul: the emergence of a Roman province*, Leiden 1976.

Echt, R., 'Technologische Untersuchungen an frühlatènezeitlichem Goldschmuck aus Bad-Dürkheim (Rheinland-Pfalz)' (*AKorrBl* 18) 1988, 183–195.

Egg, M. & A. France-Lanord, *Le char de Vix*, Bonn 1987.

Egger, R., 'Genius cucullatus' (*Wiener Prähistorische Zeitschrift* 19) 1932, 311–323.

Eggert, M. K. H., 'Die "Fürstensitze" der Späthallstattzeit: Bemerkungen zu einem archäologischen Konstrukt' (*Hammaburg N. F.* 9) 1989, 53–66.

Eluère, C., J. Gomez de Soto & A. Duval, 'Un chef-d'œuvre de l'orfèvrerie celtique, le casque d'Agris' (*Bulletin de la Société Préhistorique Française* 84) 1987, 8–21.

Eluère, C., *Das Gold der Kelten*, Munich 1987.

Endert, D. van, *Die Wagenbestattungen der späten Hallstattzeit und der Latènezeit im Gebiet westlich des Rheins*, Oxford 1987.

———, *Die Bronzefunde aus dem Oppidum von Manching*, Stuttgart 1991 (Die Ausgrabungen in Manching 13).

Engels, H.-J., 'Der Fürstengrabhügel von Rodenbach' (*Bonner Hefte zur Vorgeschichte* 3) 1972, 25–52.

Eska, J. F., *Towards an Interpretation of the Hispano-Celtic Inscription of Botorrita*, Innsbruck 1989.

———, 'Syntactic notes on the great inscription of Peñalba de Villastar' (*BBCS* 37) 1990, 104–107.

Euskirchen, M., 'Epona' (*BRGK* 74) 1993, 607–850.

Evans, D. E., *Gaulish Personal Names*, Oxford 1967.

———, 'Celts and Germans' (*BBCS* 29) 1980/82, 230–255.

———, 'The Celts in Britain (up to the formation of the Brittonic languages): history, culture, linguistic remains, substrata', in: K. H. Schmidt (ed.), *Geschichte und Kultur der Kelten*, Heidelberg 1986, 102–115.

————, 'The identification of Continental Celtic with special reference to Hispano-Celtic', in: J. Untermann & F. Villar (eds.), *Lengua y cultura en la Hispania pre-romana*, Salamanca 1993, 563–608.

Fasce, S., 'Le guerre galliche di Livio e l'epopea mitologica celtica' (*Maia* 37) 1985, 27–43.

Fauduet, I., *Les temples de tradition celtique en Gaule romaine*, Paris 1993.

————, *Atlas des sanctuaires romano-celtiques de Gaule romaine*, Paris 1993.

Fellendorf-Boerner, G., 'Die bildlichen Darstellungen der Epona auf den Denkmälern Baden-Württembergs' (*FBW* 10) 1985, 77–141.

Feugère, M. (ed.), *Le verre préromain en Europe occidentale*, Montagnac 1989.

Fichtl, S., *Les Gaulois du Nord de la Gaule (150–20 av. J.-C.)*, Paris 1994.

Filip, J., 'Keltische Kultplätze und Heiligtümer in Böhmen', in: H. Jankuhn (ed.), *Vorgeschichtliche Heiligtümer und Opferplätze in Mittel- und Nordeuropa*, Göttingen 1970, 55–77.

————, *Celtic Civilization and its Heritage*, rev. ed., Prague 1976.

Filtzinger, P et al. (eds.), *Die Römer in Baden-Württemberg*, Stuttgart [3]1986.

Finlay, I., *Celtic Art: An Introduction*, London 1973.

Fischer, F., 'Die Kelten bei Herodot: Bemerkungen zu einigen geographischen und ethnographischen Problemen' (*Madrider Mitteilungen* 13) 1972, 109–124.

————, KEIMHΛIA. Bemerkungen zur kulturgeschichtlichen Interpretation des so-genannten Südimports in der späten Hallstatt- und frühen Latène-Kultur des westlichen Mitteleuropa' (*Germania* 51) 1973, 436–459.

————, *Der Heidengraben bei Grabenstetten. Ein keltisches Oppidum auf der Schwäb-ischen Alb bei Urach*, Stuttgart [3]1982.

Fischer, F., D. Müller & H. Schäfer, 'Neue Beobachtungen am Heidengraben bei Grabenstetten, Kreis Reutlingen' (*FBW* 6) 1981, 333–349.

Fischer, F. & J. Biel, 'Frühkeltische Fürstengräber in Mitteleuropa' (*Antike Welt* 13, Sondernummer) 1982.

Fischer, F., 'Das Handwerk bei den Kelten zur Zeit der Oppida', in: *Das Handwerk in vor- und frühgeschichtlicher Zeit II*, Göttingen 1983, 39–49.

————, 'Der Handel der Mittel- und Spätlatènezeit in Mitteleuropa aufgrund ar-chäologischer Zeugnisse', in: *Untersuchungen zu Handel und Verkehr der vor- und frühgeschichtlichen Zeit in Mittel- und Nordeuropa I*, Göttingen 1985, 285–298.

————, 'Caesar und die Helvetier. Neue Überlegungen zu einem alten Thema' (*BJb* 185) 1985, 1–26.

Fischer, F. et al., 'Studien zum Silberring von Trichtingen' (*FBW* 12) 1987, 205–250.

Fleuriot, L., 'Le vocabulaire de l'inscription gauloise de Chamalières' (*EC* 15) 1976/77, 173–190.

Focke, F., 'Das Dreigötterrelief von der Brigachquelle' (*Badische Fundberichte* 20) 1956, 123–126.

Forrer, R., *Keltische Numismatik der Rhein- und Donaulande*, rev. ed., 2 vols., Graz 1968.

Foster, J., *Bronze Boar Figurines in Iron Age and Roman Britain*, Oxford 1977.

Fox, C., *A Find of the Early Iron Age from Llyn Cerrig Bach, Anglesey*, Cardiff 1947.

————, *Pattern and Purpose. A Survey of Early Celtic Art in Britain*, Cardiff 1958.

Freeman, P., 'Elements of the Ulster Cycle in Pre-Posidonian Literature', in: J. P. Mallory & G. Stockman (eds.), *Ulidia*, Belfast 1994, 207–216.

Frei-Stolba, R., 'Götterkulte in der Schweiz zur römischen Zeit unter besonderer

Berücksichtigung der epigraphischen Zeugnisse' (*Bulletin des antiquités luxembourgoises* 15) 1984, 75–126.

Frey, O.-H., 'Die Goldschale von Schwarzenbach' (*HBA* 1) 1971, 85–100.

Frey, O.-H. & H. Roth (eds.), *Studien zu Siedlungsfragen der Latènezeit*, Marburg 1984.

Frey, O.-H., 'Zum Handel und Verkehr während der Frühlatènezeit in Mitteleuropa', in: *Untersuchungen zu Handel und Verkehr der vor- und frühgeschichtlichen Zeit in Mittel- und Nordeuropa I*, Göttingen 1985, 231–257.

————, 'Einige Überlegungen zu den Beziehungen zwischen Kelten und Germanen in der Spätlatènezeit', in: *Gedenkschrift für G. v. Merhart*, Marburg 1986, 45–79.

Friell, J. G. P. & W. G. Watson, *Pictish Studies. Settlement, Burial and Art in Dark Age Northern Britain*, Oxford 1984.

Furger-Gunti, A., *Die Helvetier. Kulturgeschichte eines Keltenvolkes*, Zurich 1984.

Gager, J. G., *Curse Tablets and Binding Spells from the Ancient World*, New York 1992.

Gauthier, N., *L'évangelisation des pays de la Moselle. La province romaine de Première Belgique entre antiquité et moyen âge (IIIe–VIIIe siècle)*, Paris 1980.

Gebhard, R., *Der Glasschmuck aus dem Oppidum von Manching*, Stuttgart 1989 (Die Ausgrabungen in Manching 11).

————, *Die Fibeln aus dem Oppidum von Manching*, Stuttgart 1991 (Die Ausgrabungen in Manching 14).

Göbel, J. et al., 'Der spätkeltische Goldschatz von Niederzier' (*BJb* 191) 1991, 27–84.

Gold der Helvetier, Zurich 1991.

Gorrochategui Churruca, J., *Estudio sobre la onomástica indígena de Aquitania*, Bilbao 1982.

Gose, E., *Der Tempelbezirk des Lenus Mars in Trier*, Berlin 1955.

Goudineau, C., *César et la Gaule*, Paris 1990.

Goudineau, C. & C. Peyre, *Bibracte et les Eduens*, Paris 1993.

Gräber – Spiegel des Lebens: zum Totenbrauchtum der Kelten und Römer am Beispiel des Treverer-Gräberfeldes Wederath-Belginum, Mainz 1989.

Graf, F., 'Menschenopfer in der Burgerbibliothek. Anmerkungen zum Götterkatalog der "Commenta Bernensia" zu Lucan 1,445' (*ASchw* 14) 1991, 136–143.

Grassi, M. T., *I Celti in Italia*, Milan 1991.

Green, M., 'The Iconography and Archaeology of Romano-British Religion' (*ANRW* II 18.1) 1986, 113–162.

————, *The Gods of the Celts*, Gloucester 1986.

————, *Symbol and Image in Celtic Religious Art*, London 1989.

————, *Animals in Celtic Life and Myth*, London 1992.

————, *Celtic Myths*, London 1993.

Green, M. (ed.), *The Celtic World*, London 1995.

Gricourt, D. & D. Hollard, 'Taranis, le dieu celtique à la roue' (*Dialogues d'histoire ancienne* 16) 1990, 275–315.

————, 'Taranis, caelestium deorum maximus' (*Dialogues d'histoire ancienne* 17) 1991, 343–400.

Grilli, A., 'La migrazione dei Galli in Livio', in: *Studi in onore di F. R. Vonwiller II*, Como 1980, 183–192.

Gross, W. H., 'Zu Problemen des "Fürstengrabes" von Vix' (*HBA* 7) 1980, 69–76.

Gruel, K., *La Monnaie chez les Gaulois*, Paris 1989.

Gutenbrunner, S., 'Mars Cnabetius' (*ZCP* 20) 1936, 278–283.

————, 'Mercurius Gebrinius' (*ZCP* 20) 1936, 391–394.

Guyonvarc'h, Ch.-J., '*nemos, nemetos, nemeton; les noms celtiques du "ciel" et du "sanctuaire" ' (*Ogam* 12) 1960, 185–197.

———, 'Le théonyme gaulois (Mars) Mullo "aux tas (de butin)", irlandais mul, mullach "sommet arrondi, colline" ' (*Ogam* 12) 1960, 452–458.

———, 'Le théonyme gaulois BELISAMA "la très brillante" ' (*Ogam* 14) 1962, 161–173.

Hachmann, R., 'Gundestrup-Studien' (*BRGK* 71) 1990, 565–904.

Härke, H., *Settlement Types and Settlement Patterns in the West Hallstatt Province*, Oxford 1979.

Haffner, A., *Die westliche Hunsrück-Eifel-Kultur*, Berlin 1976.

Hafner, G., 'Herakles – Geras – Ogmios' (*JRGZM* 5) 1958, 139–153.

Die Hallstattkultur. Bericht über das Symposium in Steyr 1980 aus Anlaß der Internationalen Ausstellung des Landes Oberösterreich, Linz 1981.

Hanoteau, M. T., 'Epona, déesse des chevaux. Figurations découvertes en Suisse' (*Helvetia archaeologica* 11) 1980, 2–20.

Hanson, W. S., *Agricola and the Conquest of the North*, London 1987.

———, 'Tacitus' "Agricola": An Archaeological and Historical Study' (*ANRW* II 33.3) 1991, 1741–1784.

Harmand, J., 'Le portrait de Gaule dans le "De Bellico Gallico" I–VII' (*ANRW* I 3) 1973, 523–595.

———, *Vercingétorix*, Paris 1984.

Harrison, F., 'Celtic musics: characteristics and chronology', in: K. H. Schmidt (ed.), *Geschichte und Kultur der Kelten*, Heidelberg 1986, 252–263.

Hatt, J.-J., 'Les croyances funéraires des Gallo-Romains d'après les tombes' (*RAE* 21) 1970, 7–97.

———, 'Les dieux gaulois en Alsace' (*RAE* 22) 1971, 187–276.

———, 'La divinité féminine souveraine chez les Celtes continentaux, d'après l'épigraphie gallo-romaine et l'art celtique' (*CRAI*) 1981, 12–20.

———, 'Apollon Guérisseur en Gaule', in: C. Pelletier (ed.), *La Médecine en Gaule*, Paris 1985, 205–238.

———, *La Tombe gallo-romaine*, Paris ²1986.

———, *Mythes et dieux de la Gaule. I. Les grandes divinités masculines*, Paris 1989.

Hawkes, C. F. C., 'Britain and Julius Caesar' (*PBA* 63) 1977, 125–192.

Heichelheim, F. M., 'Genii cucullati' (*Archaeologia Aeliana* (4) 12) 1935, 187–194.

Heinz, W., 'Der Diana Abnoba-Altar in Badenweiler' (*Antike Welt* 13,4) 1982, 37–41.

Henderson, I., *The Picts*, London 1967.

Henig, M., *Religion in Roman Britain*, London 1984.

Henry, P. L., 'Interpreting the Gaulish Inscription of Chamalières' (*EC* 21) 1984, 141–150.

Heuneburg-Studien, Berlin 1962ff.

Höckmann, U., 'Gallierdarstellungen in der etruskischen Grabkunst des 2. Jhs. v. Chr.' (*Jahrbuch des Deutschen Archäologischen Instituts* 106) 1991, 199–230.

Holder, A., *Alt-celtischer Sprachschatz*, 3 vols., Leipzig 1891–1913.

Homeyer, H., 'Zum Keltenexkurs in Livius' 5. Buch (33,4–35,3)' (*Historia* 9) 1960, 345–361.

Horne, P. D. & H. C. King, 'Romano-Celtic Temples in Continental Europe: a gazeteer of those with known plans' in: W. Rodwell (ed.), *Temples, Churches and Religion: recent research in Roman Britain*, Oxford 1980, 369–555.

Hoz, J. de, 'La epigrafia celtibérica', in: *Reunión sobre epigrafía hispánica de época romana-republicana*, Saragossa 1986, 43–102.

———, 'Hispano-Celtic and Celtiberian', in: G. W. MacLennan (ed.), *Proceedings of the First North American Congress of Celtic Studies*, Ottawa 1988, 191–207.

———, 'The Celts of the Iberian Peninsula' (ZCP 45) 1990, 1–37.

Hundert Meisterwerke keltischer Kunst, Trier 1992.

Hundt, H.-J., 'Vorgeschichtliche Gewebe aus dem Hallstätter Salzberg' (JRGZM 6) 1959, 66–100, (7) 1960, 126–150 & (14) 1967, 38–67.

———, 'Neunzehn Textilreste aus dem Dürrnberg bei Hallein' (JRGZM 8) 1961, 7–25.

Hutton, R., *The Pagan Religions of the Ancient British Isles. Their Nature and Legacy*, London 1991.

Irlinger, W., *Der Dürrnberg bei Hallein IV: Die Siedlung auf dem Ramsaukopf*, Munich 1994.

———, 'Viereckschanzen und Siedlungen – Überlegungen zu einem forschungsgeschichtlichen Problem anhand ausgewählter südbayerischer Fundorte', in: C. Dobiat (ed.), *Festschrift für Otto-Hermann Frey zum 65. Geburtstag*, Marburg 1994, 285–304.

Jackson, K. H., *Language and History in Early Britain*, Edinburgh 1953.

Jacobi, G., *Werkzeug und Gerät aus dem Oppidum von Manching*, Stuttgart 1974 (Die Ausgrabungen in Manching 5).

Jacobsthal, P., *Early Celtic Art*, 2 vols., Oxford 1944.

James, S., *Exploring the World of the Celts*, London 1993.

Joachim, H.-E., 'Die Verzierung auf der keltischen Röhrenkanne von Waldalgesheim' (AKorrBl 8) 1978, 119–125.

———, 'Eine Rekonstruktion der keltischen "Säule" von Pfalzfeld' (BJb 189) 1989, 1–14.

Joachim, H.-E. et al., *Waldalgesheim: das Grab einer keltischen Fürstin*, Bonn 1995.

Joffroy, R., *L'Oppidum de Vix et la civilisation hallstattiène finale*, Paris 1960.

———, *Vix et ses trésors*, Paris 1979.

Jolliffe, N., 'Dea Brigantia' (Archaeological Journal 98) 1942, 36–61.

Jud, P. (ed.), *Die spätkeltische Zeit am Oberrhein – Le Rhin supérieur à la fin de l'époque celtique*, Basle 1993.

Kappel, I., *Die Graphittonkeramik von Manching*, Wiesbaden 1969 (Die Ausgrabungen in Manching 2).

Kaul, F. et al., *Thracian Tales on the Gundestrup Cauldron*, Amsterdam 1991.

Keller, F. J., *Das keltische Fürstengrab von Reinheim I*, Mainz 1965.

Die Kelten in Mitteleuropa: Kultur, Kunst, Wirtschaft, Hallein 1980.

Der Keltenfürst von Hochdorf. Methoden und Ergebnisse der Landesarchäologie, Stuttgart 1985.

Kenner, H., 'Zu namenlosen Göttern der Austria Romana II: Genius cucullatus' (Römisches Österreich 4) 1976, 147–161.

———, 'Die Götterwelt der Austria Romana' (ANRW II 18,2) 1989, 875–974 & 1652–1655.

Kimmig, W., *Die Heuneburg an der oberen Donau*, Stuttgart ²1983.

———, 'Die Goldschale von Zürich-Altstetten', in: *Homenaje a Martin Almagro*, Madrid 1983, 101–118.

————, *Frühe Kelten in der Schweiz im Spiegel der Ausgrabungen auf dem Üetliberg*, Zurich 1983.

————, 'Der Handel in der Hallstattzeit', in: *Untersuchungen zu Handel und Verkehr der vor- und frühgeschichtlichen Zeit in Mittel- und Nordeuropa I*, Göttingen 1985, 214–230.

————, 'Eisenzeitliche Grabstelen in Mitteleuropa. Versuch eines Überblicks' (*FBW* 12) 1987, 251–297.

Kimmig, W. et al., *Das Kleinaspergle. Studien zu einem Fürstengrabhügel der frühen Latènezeit bei Stuttgart*, Stuttgart 1988.

King, A., *Roman Gaul and Germany*, London 1990.

Klingshirn, W. E., *Caesarius of Arles. The Making of a Christian Community in Late Antique Gaul*, Cambridge 1993.

Ködderitzsch, R., 'Die große Felsinschrift von Peñalba de Villastar', in: H. Ölberg & G. Schmidt (eds.), *Sprachwissenschaftliche Forschungen: FS für J. Knobloch*, Innsbruck 1985, 211–222.

Köves-Zulauf, T.: 'Les Vates des Celtes' (*Acta Ethnographica*, Budapest 4) 1955, 171–275.

————, 'Helico, Führer der gallischen Wanderung' (*Latomus* 36) 1977, 40–92.

Kremer, B., *Das Bild der Kelten bis in augusteische Zeit: Studien zur Instrumentalisierung eines antiken Feindbildes bei griechischen und römischen Autoren*, Stuttgart 1994.

Kromer, R., *Das Gräberfeld von Hallstatt*, Florence 1959.

Krüger, E., 'Die gallischen und die germanischen Dioskuren' (*Trierer Zeitschrift*) 1940, 8–27 & 1941/42, 1–66.

Kruta, V., 'Remarques sur les fibules de la trouvaille de Duchcov (Dux), Bohème', in: P.-M. Duval et al. (eds.), *Recherches d'archéologie celtique et gallo-romaine*, Paris 1973, 1–33.

————, 'Le casque d'Amfreville-sous-les-Monts (Eure) et quelques problèmes de l'art celtique du IVe siècle avant notre ère' (*EC* 15) 1978, 405–424.

————, *Les Celtes*, Paris ²1979 (Coll. Que sais-je?).

————, *Die Kelten*, Lucerne 1986.

Künzl, E., *Die Kelten des Epigonos von Pergamon*, Würzburg 1971.

Kurz, G., *Keltische Hort- und Gewässerfunde in Mitteleuropa*, Stuttgart 1995.

Kurz, S., 'Figürliche Fibeln der Frühlatènezeit in Mitteleuropa' (*FBW* 9) 1984, 249–278.

Kyll, N., 'Zum Fortleben der vorchristlichen Quellenverehrung in der Trierer Landschaft', in: *Festschrift Matthias Zender*, Bonn 1972, 497–510.

Laet, S. de, *La Belgique d'avant les Romains*, Wetteren 1982.

Laing, Ll. & J. Laing, *Celtic Britain and Ireland, AD 200–800*, Dublin 1990.

————, *The Picts and the Scots*, London 1993.

Lambert, P.-Y., 'La tablette gauloise de Chamalières' (*EC* 16) 1979, 141–169.

————, 'A restatement on the Gaulish tablet from Chamalières' (*BBCS* 34) 1987, 10–17.

————, *La langue gauloise*, Paris 1994.

————, 'Sur la bronze celtibère de Botorrita', in: R. Bielmeier et al. (eds.), *Indogermanica et Caucasica. FS Karl Horst Schmidt*, Berlin 1994, 363–374.

P. Lambrechts, *Contributions à l'étude des divinités celtiques*, Bruges 1942.

————, *L'exaltation de la tête dans la pensée et dans l'art des Celtes*, Bruges 1954.

Landes, C. (ed.), *Dieux Guérisseurs en Gaule Romaine*, Lattes 1992.

Lantier, R., 'Le dieu celtique de Bouray' (*Monuments et mémoires de la Fondation Eugène Piot* 34) 1934, 35–58.

Lavagne, H., 'Les dieux de la Gaule Narbonnaise: "romanité" et romanisation' (*Journal des Savants*) 1979, 155–197.

Le Gall, J., *Alésia*, Paris 1985 (Guides arch. de la France).

———, *Fouilles d'Alise-Sainte-Reine 1861–1865*, 2 vols., Paris 1989.

———, *Alesia. Archéologie et Histoire*. rev. ed., Paris 1990.

Lehmann, A., *Le rôle de la femme dans l'histoire de la Gaule*, Paris 1944.

Lejars, Th., *Gournay III. Les fourreaux d'épées*, Paris 1994.

Lejeune, M., 'Lepontica' (*EC* 12) 1968/71, 337–500.

Lejeune, M. & R. Marichal, 'Textes gaulois et gallo-romains en cursive latine I Lezoux' (*EC* 15) 1976/77, 151–156.

———, 'Textes gaulois et gallo-romains en cursive latine II Chamalières' (*EC* 15) 1976/77, 156–168.

Lejeune, M. et al., 'Textes gaulois et gallo-romains en cursive latine III Le plomb du Larzac' (*EC* 22) 1985, 95–177.

Lejeune, M., 'Les premiers pas de la déesse Bibracte' (*Journal des savants*) 1990, 69–96.

Lenerz-de Wilde, M., *Iberia Celtica: Archäologische Zeugnisse keltischer Kultur auf der Pyrenäenhalbinsel*, 2 vols., Wiesbaden 1991.

Le Roux, F., 'Des chaudrons celtiques à l'arbre d'Esus. Lucain et les Scholies Bernoises' (*Ogam* 7) 1955, 33–58.

———, 'Le cheval divin et le zoomorphisme chez les Celtes' (*Ogam* 7) 1955, 101–122.

———, 'Taranis: dieu celtique du ciel et de l'orage' (*Ogam* 10) 1958, 30–39.

———, 'Le dieu celtique aux liens: De l'Ogmios de Lucain à l'Ogmios de Dürer' (*Ogam* 12) 1960, 209–234.

———, 'La Divination chez les Celtes', in: A. Caquot & M. Leibovici (eds.), *La Divination*, Paris 1968, 233–256.

———, 'La Religion des Celtes', in: H. C. Puech (ed.), *Histoire des Religions*, Paris 1970, I 781–840.

Le Roux, F. & Ch.-J. Guyonvarc'h, *Les Druides*, Rennes 1986.

Lessing, E., *Die Kelten. Entwicklung und Geschichte einer europäischen Kultur*. Mit Texten von V. Kruta, Freiburg 1979.

———, *Hallstatt: Bilder aus der Frühzeit Europas*, Vienna 1980.

Leunissen, P. M. M., 'Römische Götternamen und einheimische Religion in der Provinz Germania Superior' (*FBW* 10) 1985, 155–195.

Linckenheld, E., 'Sucellos et Nantosuelta' (*RHR* 99) 1929, 40–92.

Linduff, K. M., 'Epona. A Celt among the Romans' (*Latomus* 38) 1979, 817–837.

Loicq, J., 'Ogmios-Varuṇa et l'organisation de la fonction de souveraineté dans le panthéon celtique', in: *Orientalia Jacques Duchesne-Guillemin emerito oblata*, Leiden 1984, 341–382.

Lorenz, H., 'Totenbrauchtum und Tracht. Untersuchungen zur regionalen Gliederung in der frühen Latènezeit' (*BRGK* 59) 1978, 1ff.

Luxusgeschirr keltischer Fürsten: Griechische Keramik nördlich der Alpen, Würzburg 1995.

Lynch, F., *Prehistoric Anglesey*, Llangefni 1970.

McManus, D., *A Guide to Ogam*, Maynooth 1991.

MacReady, S. & F. H. Thompson (eds.), *Cross-Channel Trade between Gaul and Britain in the pre-Roman Iron Age*, London 1984.

Magnen, R. & E. Thevenot, *Epona. Déesse gauloise des chevaux, protrectrice des cavaliers*, Bordeaux 1953.

Maier, B., 'Of Celts and Cyclopes: notes on Ath. IV 36 p. 152' (*StC* 30; in press).

———, 'Is Lug to be identified with Mercury (Bell. Gall. VI 17,1)? New suggestions on an old problem' (*Ériu* 147; in press).

Maier, F., *Die bemalte Spätlatène-Keramik von Manching*, Stuttgart 1970 (Die Ausgrabungen in Manching 3).

Malitz, J., *Die Historien des Poseidonios*, Munich 1983.

Mansfeld, G., *Die Fibeln der Heuneburg 1950–1970: Ein Beitrag zur Geschichte der Späthallstattfibel*, Berlin 1973 (Heuneburgstudien 2).

Marco Simón, F., 'El dios céltico Lug y el santuario de Peñalba de Villastar', in: *Estudios en homenaje a A. Beltrán Martínez*, Saragossa 1986, 731–753.

Marek, J., 'Das helvetisch-gallische Pferd und seine Beziehung zu den prähistorischen und zu den rezenten Pferden' (*Abhandlungen der Schweizerischen Paläontologischen Gesellschaft* 25) 1988, 1–62.

Marichal, R., *Les graffites de La Graufesenque*, Paris 1988.

Maringer, J., 'Menschenopfer im Bestattungsbrauch Alteuropas' (*Anthropos* 37/38) 1942/43, 1–112.

Marinis, R. C. de, 'Golasecca Culture and its Links with Celts beyond the Alps', in: *The Celts*, Milan 1991, 93–102.

Martin, R. & P. Varène, *Le monument d'Ucuetis à Alésia*, Paris 1973.

Maxwell, G., *A Battle Lost. Romans and Caledonians at Mons Graupius*, Edinburgh 1990.

Meduna, J., 'Das keltische Oppidum Staré Hradisko in Mähren' (*Germania* 48) 1970, 34–59.

Megaw, R. & V. Megaw, 'The Stone head from Mšecké Žehrovice: a reappraisal' (*Antiquity* 62) 1988, 630–641.

———, *Early Celtic Art*, London 1989.

———, *The Basse-Yutz find*, London 1990.

Megaw, J. V. S., 'Music Archaeology and the Ancient Celts', in: *The Celts*, Milan 1991, 643–648.

Meid, W., 'Remarks on the Celtic Ethnography of Posidonius in the Light of Insular Celtic Traditions' (*Abhandlungen der Österreichischen Akademie der Wissenschaften* 123,4) 1986, 60–74.

———, *Zur Lesung und Deutung gallischer Inschriften*, Innsbruck 1989.

———, *Gaulish Inscriptions*, Budapest 1992.

———, *Die erste Botorrita-Inschrift*, Innsbruck 1993.

———, 'Die "große" Felsinschrift von Peñalba de Villastar', in: R. Bielmeier et al. (eds.), *Indogermanica et Caucasica. FS Karl Horst Schmidt*, Berlin 1994, 385–394.

———, *Celtiberian Inscriptions*, Budapest 1994.

———, *Kleinere keltiberische Sprachdenkmäler*, Innsbruck 1996.

Meid, W. & P. Anreiter (eds.), *Die größeren altkeltischen Sprachdenkmäler. Akten des Kolloquiums Innsbruck 1993*, Innsbruck 1995.

Méniel, P., *Chasse et élevage chez les Gaulois (450–52 av. J.-C.)*, Paris 1987.

———, *Les sacrifices d'animaux chez les Gaulois*, Paris 1992.

Merten, H., 'Der Kult des Mars im Trevererraum' (*Trierer Zeitschrift* 48) 1985, 7–113.

Mitchell, S., *Anatolia: Land, Men and Gods in Asia Minor. I. The Celts in Anatolia and the Impact of Roman Rule*, Oxford 1993.

Moosleitner, F., *Die Schnabelkanne vom Dürrnberg*, Salzburg 1985.

Moreau, J. *Die Welt der Kelten*, Stuttgart 1958.

Motyková, K. et al., *Závist: ein keltischer Burgwall in Mittelböhmen*, Prague 1978.

———, 'Die bauliche Gestalt der Akropolis auf dem Burgwall Závist in der Späthall-statt- und Frühlatènezeit' (*Germania* 66) 1988, 391–436.

———, 'Die Siedlungsstruktur des Oppidums Závist' (*AKorrBl* 20) 1990, 415–426.

Müller, F., 'Der zwanzigste Brief des Gregor von Nyssa' (*Hermes* 74) 1939, 66–91.

Müller, F., 'Zur Datierung des Goldschatzes von Erstfeld UR' (*Jahrbuch der Schweizeri-schen Gesellschaft für Ur- und Frühgeschichte* 73) 1990, 83–94.

Müller, K. E., *Geschichte der antiken Ethnographie und ethnologischen Theoriebildung*, 2 vols., Wiesbaden 1972–1980.

Müller, U. A., 'Das Pferd in der griechisch-keltischen Frühgeschichte' (*Helvetia ar-chaeologica* 21) 1990, 153–166.

———, 'Keltische Wagen mit elastischer Aufhängung: Eine Reise von Castel di Decima nach Clonmacnoise', in: *Trans Europam. FS für Margarita Primas*, Bonn 1995, 265–275.

Nagy, P., 'Technologische Aspekte der Goldschale von Zürich-Altstetten' (*Jahrbuch der Schweizerischen Gesellschaft für Ur- und Frühgeschichte* 75) 1992, 101–116.

Nash, D., 'Reconstructing Posidonius' Celtic Ethnography: some considerations' (*Bri-tannia* 7) 1976, 111–126.

———, *Coinage in the Celtic World*, London 1987.

Navarro, J. M. de, 'A Doctor's Grave of the Middle La Tène Period from Bavaria' (*Proceedings of the Prehistoric Society* 21) 1955, 231–248.

Nerzic, C., *La Sculpture en Gaule Romaine*, Paris 1989.

Nicolaisen, W. F. H., *Scottish Place-Names. Their Study and Significance*, London 1976.

Nicoll, E. H. (ed.), *A Pictish Panorama*, Forfar 1995.

Nierhaus, R., 'Zu den ethnographischen Angaben in Lukans Gallienexkurs' (*BJb* 153) 1953, 46–62.

Nortmann, H., *Die Altburg bei Bundenbach: ein Führer zur keltischen Burg*, Bundenbach 1990.

Oeftiger, C., *Mehrfachbestattungen im Westhallstattkreis: Zum Problem der Totenfolge*, Bonn 1984.

Olmsted, G., *The Gundestrup Cauldron*, Brussels 1979 (Coll. Latomus 162).

———, *The Gaulish Calendar. A Reconstruction from the Bronze Fragments from Coligny*, Bonn 1992.

Overbeck, B., *Die Welt der Kelten im Spiegel der Münzen*, Munich 1980.

Padel, O. J., *Cornish Place-Name Elements*, Cambridge 1985.

———, *A Popular Dictionary of Cornish Place-Names*, Newmill, Penzance 1988.

Pare, C. F. E., 'Fürstensitze: Celts and the Mediterranean World. Developments in the West Hallstatt Culture in the 6th and 5th Centuries BC' (*Proceedings of the Prehistoric Society* 57) 1991, 183–202.

———, *Wagons and Wagon-Graves of the Early Iron Age in Central Europe*, Oxford 1992.

Parzinger, H., 'Zur Belegungsabfolge auf dem Magdalenenberg bei Villingen' (*Germa-nia* 64) 1986, 391–407.

Pascal, C. B., *The Cults of Cisalpine Gaul*, Brussels 1964 (Coll. Latomus 75).

Pauli, L., *Die Gräber vom Salzberg zu Hallstatt*, Mainz 1975.

————, *Keltischer Volksglaube. Amulette und Sonderbestattungen am Dürrnberg bei Hallein und im eisenzeitlichen Mitteleuropa*, Munich 1976.

————, 'Die Herkunft der Kelten: Sinn und Unsinn einer alten Frage', in: *Die Kelten in Mitteleuropa*, Hallein 1980, 16–24.

————, 'Heilige Plätze und Opferbräuche bei den Helvetiern und ihren Nachbarn' (*ASchw* 14) 1991, 124–135.

Pelletier, C. (ed.), *La Médecine en Gaule*, Paris 1985.

Peschel, K., 'Kelten und nordwestalpine Hallstattkultur. Ethnographische Bemerkungen zu einer archäologischen Karte' (*Ethnographisch-archäologische Zeitschrift* 29) 1988, 259–300.

Petres, E. F., 'On Celtic Animal and Human Sacrifices' (*Acta Archaeologica Academiae Scientiarum Hungaricae* 24) 1972, 365–383.

Piboule, A. & M., 'Le Culte des sources rurales en Bourbonnais', in: *La Médecine en Gaule*, Paris 1985, 145–156.

Piggott, S., 'The Carnyx in Early Iron Age Britain' (*The Antiquaries Journal* 39) 1959, 19–32.

————, 'Nemeton, Temenos, Bothros. Sanctuaries of the Ancient Celts', in: *I Celti e la loro cultura nell'epoca preromana e romana nella Britannia*, Rome 1978, 37–54.

————, *The Druids*, London 1985.

Pingel, V., *Die glatte Drehscheiben-Keramik von Manching*, Stuttgart 1971 (Die Ausgrabungen in Manching 4).

Pink, K., *Einführung in die keltische Münzkunde mit besonderer Berücksichtigung des österreichischen Raumes*, Vienna 1974.

Planck, D. et al., 'Eine neuentdeckte keltische Viereckschanze in Fellbach-Schmieden, Rems-Murr-Kreis. Vorbericht der Grabungen 1977–1980' (*Germania* 60) 1982, 105–172.

Planck, D., 'Die Viereckschanze von Fellbach-Schmieden', in: *Der Keltenfürst von Hochdorf. Methoden und Ergebnisse der Landesarchäologie*, Stuttgart 1985, 341–354.

Pleiner, R., *The Celtic sword*, Oxford 1993.

Plonéis, J.-M., *La toponymie celtique. L'origine des noms de lieux en Bretagne*, Paris 1989.

Powell, T. G. E., *The Celts*, London 1958.

Prosdocimi, A. L., 'Note sul celtico in Italia' (*Studi etruschi* 57) 1991, 139–177.

Py, M., *Les Gaulois du Midi. De la fin de l'Age de Bronze à la conquête romaine*, Paris 1993.

Raftery, B. (ed.), *L'art celtique*, Paris 1990.

Raftery, B., *Pagan Celtic Ireland*, London 1994.

Rambaud, M., *L'Art de la déformation historique dans les Commentaires de César*, Paris [2]1966.

Ramseyer, D., 'Châtillon-sur-Glâne (FR) – Un habitat de hauteur du Hallstatt final. Synthèse de huit années de fouilles (1974–1981)' (*Jahrbuch der Schweizerischen Gesellschaft für Ur- und Frühgeschichte* 66) 1983, 161–188.

Rankin, H. D., *Celts and the Classical World*, London 1987.

Reddé, M., 'Les scènes de métier dans la sculpture funéraire gallo-romaine' (*Gallia* 36) 1978, 43–63.

Reichenberger, A., 'Temenos – Templum – Nemeton – Viereckschanze: Bemerkungen zu Namen und Bedeutung' (*JRGZM* 35) 1988, 285–298.

Rémy, B., 'Les inscriptions de médecins en Gaule' (*Gallia* 42) 1984, 115–152.

Reynolds, P., 'The Food of the Prehistoric Celts', in: J. Wilkins et al. (eds.), *Food in Antiquity*, Exeter 1995, 303–315.

Riek, G. & H.-J. Hundt, *Der Hohmichele: Ein Fürstengrabhügel der späten Hallstattzeit bei der Heuneburg*, Berlin 1962 (Heuneburg-Studien 1).

Rivet, A. L. F. & C. Smith, *The Place-Names of Roman Britain*, London 1979.

Rivet, A. L. F., *Gallia Narbonensis. Southern Gaul in Roman Times*, London 1988.

Roche-Bernard, G., *Costumes et textiles en Gaule romaine*, Paris 1993.

Romeuf, A.-M., 'Ex-voto en bois de Chamalières (Puy-de-Dôme) et des Sources de la Seine: essai de comparaison' (*Gallia* 44) 1986, 65–89.

Roquepertuse et les Celto-Ligures, Marseille 1992.

Ross, A., 'Esus et les trois "grues" ' (EC 9) 1960, 405–438.

———, *Pagan Celtic Britain*, London 1967.

———, *The Pagan Celts*, London 1986.

Rozoy, J. G. et al. (eds.), *Les Celtes en Champagne. Les Ardennes au second âge du fer*, Charleville-Mézières 1987.

Rusu, M., 'Das keltische Fürstengrab von Ciumeşti in Rumänien' (BRGK 50) 1969, 267–300.

Salviat, F., *Entremont antique*, Aix-en-Provence 1973.

———, *Glanum*, Paris 1979.

Les sanctuaires celtiques et leurs rapports avec le monde méditerranéen, Paris 1991.

Les sanctuaires de tradition indigène en Gaule romaine, Paris 1994.

Sanquer, R., 'La grande statuette de bronze de Kerguilly en Dineault (Finistère)' (*Gallia* 31) 1973, 61–80.

Schaaff, U. et al., *Vierrädrige Wagen der Hallstattzeit. Untersuchungen zu Geschichte und Technik*, Mainz 1987.

Schiering, W., 'Zeitstellung und Herkunft der Bronzesitula von Waldalgesheim' (HBA 5) 1975, 77–97.

Schindler, R., *Die Altburg bei Bundenbach. Eine befestigte Höhensiedlung des 2./1. Jhs. v. Chr. im Hunsrück*, Mainz 1977.

Schlette, F., *Kelten zwischen Alesia und Pergamon*, Leipzig 1976.

Schmidt, K. H., 'Die Komposition in gallischen Personennamen' (ZCP 26) 1957, 33–301.

———, 'Gallisch nemeton und Verwandtes' (*Münchener Studien zur Sprachwissenschaft* 12) 1958, 49–60.

———, 'The Gaulish Inscription of Chamalières' (BBCS 29) 1980/82, 256–268.

———, 'Handwerk und Handwerker in altkeltischen Sprachdenkmälern', in: *Das Handwerk in vor- und frühgeschichtlicher Zeit II*, Göttingen 1983, 751–763.

———, 'Keltisch-germanische Isoglossen und ihre sprachgeschichtlichen Implikationen', in: H. Beck (ed.), *Germanenprobleme in heutiger Sicht*, Berlin 1986, 231–247.

Schmidt, K. H. (ed.), *Geschichte und Kultur der Kelten*, Heidelberg 1986.

Schmidt, K. H., 'The Postulated Pre-Indo-European Substrates in Insular Celtic and Tocharian', in: T. L. Markey & J. A. C. Greppin (eds.), *When Worlds Collide: Indo-Europeans and Pre-Indo-Europeans*, Ann Arbor 1990, 179–202.

———, 'Zum plomb du Larzac', in: A. T. E. Matonis & F. Melia (eds.), *Celtic Languages, Celtic Culture: A FS for E. P. Hamp*, Van Nuys, Calif. 1990, 16–25.

———, 'The Celts and the ethnogenesis of the Germanic people' (*Historische Sprachforschung* 104) 1991, 129–152.

————, 'Celtic Movements in the First Millennium B.C.' (*Journal of Indo-European Studies* 20) 1992, 145–178.

————, 'The Celtic Problem: Ethnogenesis (Location, Date?)' (*ZCP* 45) 1992, 38–65.

————, 'Galatische Sprachreste', in: E. Schwertheim (ed.), *Forschungen in Galatien*, Bonn 1994, 15–28.

Schwerteck, H., 'Zur Deutung der großen Felsinschrift von Peñalba de Villastar', in: *Actas del II colloquio sobre lenguas y culturas prerromanas de la Península Ibérica*, Salamanca 1979, 185–196.

Schwinden, L., 'Gallo-römisches Textilgewerbe nach Denkmälern aus Trier und dem Trevererland' (*Trierer Zeitschrift* 52) 1989, 279–318.

Seewald, P., 'Die Lyrendarstellung der ostalpinen Hallstattkultur', in: *Festschrift A. Orel*, Vienna 1960, 159–171.

Simone, C. de, 'Gallisch *Nemetios – etruskisch Nemetie' (*Zeitschrift für vergleichende Sprachforschung* 94) 1980, 198–202.

————, 'Celtico nemeto- "bosco sacro" ed i suoi derivati onomastici', in: *Navicula Tubingensis: studia in honorem A. Tovar*, Tübingen 1984, 349–351.

Sjoestedt, M.-L., *Dieux et Héros des Celtes*, Paris 1940.

Small, A. (ed.), *The Picts. A new look at old problems*, Dundee 1987.

Spindler, K., *Magdalenenberg I–VI*, Villingen-Schwenningen 1971–1980.

————, *Der Magdalenenberg bei Villingen*, Stuttgart 1976.

————, 'Totenfolge bei Skythen, Thrakern und Kelten' (*Abhandlungen der naturhistorischen Gesellschaft Nürnberg* 39) 1982, 197–214.

————, *Die frühen Kelten*, Stuttgart ²1991.

Stähelin, F., *Geschichte der kleinasiatischen Galater*, Basle 1907.

Stead, I. M., *Celtic Art*, London 1985.

————, *The Battersea Shield*, London 1985.

Stead, I. M. et al., *Lindow Man: the Body in the Bog*, London 1986.

Sterckx, C., *Elements de cosmogonie celtique*, Brussels 1986.

Stöckli, W., *Die Grob- und Importkeramik von Manching*, Stuttgart 1979 (Die Ausgrabungen in Manching 8).

Stöllner, T., 'Neue Grabungen in der latènezeitlichen Gewerbesiedlung im Ramsautal am Dürrnberg bei Hallein. Ein Vorbericht' (*AKorrBl* 21) 1991, 255–269.

Strobel, K., 'Die Galater im hellenistischen Kleinasien. Historische Aspekte einer keltischen Staatenbildung', in: *Hellenistische Studien. Gedenkschrift für H. Bengtson*, Munich 1991, 101–134.

Sutherland, E., *In Search of the Picts*, London 1994.

Szabó, M., *Auf den Spuren der Kelten in Ungarn*, Budapest 1971.

Szabó, M. et al., *Les Celtes en Pannonie. Contributions à l'histoire de la civilisation celtique dans la cuvette des Karpates*, Paris 1988.

Szabó, M., *Les Celtes de l'est. Le second âge du fer dans la cuvette des Karpates*, Paris 1992.

Taylor, J. J., 'Lunulae reconsidered' (*Proceedings of the Prehistoric Society* 36) 1970, 38–81.

————, *Bronze Age Goldwork of the British Isles*, Cambridge 1980.

Thevenot, E., 'Le monument de Mavilly' (*Latomus* 14) 1955, 75–99.

————, *Sur les traces des Mars celtiques*, Bruges 1955.

————, *Divinités et sanctuaires de la Gaule*, Paris 1968.

————, *Les Gallo-Romains*, Paris [6]1983 (Coll. Que sais-je?).

————, *Histoire des Gaulois*, Paris [8]1987 (Coll. Que sais-je?).

Thollard, P., *Barbarie et civilisation chez Strabon. Étude critique des livres III et IV de la Géographie*, Paris 1987.

Thomas, C., *Christianity in Roman Britain to AD 500*, London 1981.

————, *Celtic Britain*, London 1986.

Tibiletti Bruno, M. G., 'Ligure, leponzio e gallico', in: A. L. Prosdocimi (ed.), *Ligure e dialetti dell'Italia antica*, Rome 1978, 129–208.

Timpe, D., 'Der keltische Handel nach historischen Quellen', in: *Untersuchungen zu Handel und Verkehr der vor- und frühgeschichtlichen Zeit in Mittel- und Nordeuropa I*, Göttingen 1985, 258–284.

Tovar, A., 'The god Lugus in Spain' (*BBCS* 29) 1982, 591–599.

————, 'The Celts in the Iberian Peninsula: archaeology, history, language', in: K. H. Schmidt (ed.), *Geschichte und Kultur der Kelten*, Heidelberg 1986, 68–101.

Toynbee, J. M. C., 'Genii cucullati in Roman Britain', in: *Hommages à Waldemar Deonna*, Brussels 1957, 456–469.

Trésors des princes celtes, Paris 1987.

Troisgros, H., *Borvo et Damona. Divinités gallo-romaines des eaux thermales*, Bourbonne-les-Bains 1975.

Truscelli, M., 'I "Keltika" di Posidonio e loro influsso sulla posteriore etnografia' (*Rendiconti della Reale Accademia Nazionale dei Lincei* 11) 1935, 609–730.

Tuffreau-Libre, M., *La ceramique en Gaule romaine*, Paris 1992.

Turner, R. C. & R. G. Scaife, *Bog Bodies. New Discoveries and New Perspectives*, London 1995.

Urban, R., 'Die Kelten in Italien und in Gallien bei Polybios', in: *Hellenistische Studien. Gedenkschrift für H. Bengtson*, Munich 1991, 135–157.

Vauthey, M. & P. Vauthey, 'Les Ex-voto anatomiques de la Gaule romaine (Essai sur les maladies et infirmités de nos ancêtres)', in: C. Pelletier (ed.), *La Médecine en Gaule*, Paris 1985, 111–117.

Vendryes, J., 'La religion des Celtes', in: A. Grenier (ed.), *Mana: Introduction à l'histoire des religions III: Les religions de l'Europe ancienne*, Paris 1948, 239–320.

Verger, S., 'De Vix à Weiskirchen. La transformation des rites funéraires aristo-cratiques en Gaule du Nord et de l'Est au Ve siècle avant J.-C.' (*Mélanges de l'École Française de Rome* 107) 1995, 335–458.

Vertet, H., 'Observations sur le dieu Cernunnos de l'autel de Paris' (*Bulletin des Antiquaires de France*) 1985, 163–175.

Villar Liébana, F., 'La linea inicial del bronze de Botorrita', in: F. Villar (ed.), *Studia indogermanica et palaeohispanica in honorem A. Tovar et L. Michelena*, Salamanca 1990, 375–392.

Vitali, D. (ed.), *Celti ed Etruschi nell'Italia centrosettentrionale dal V secolo a. C. alle romanizzazione*, Bologna 1987.

Vollkommer, R., 'Vater Rhein und seine römischen Darstellungen' (*BJb* 194) 1994, 1–42.

Voyage en Massalie: 100 ans d'archéologie en Gaule du Sud, Marseille 1990.

Vries, J. de, 'Die Interpretatio Romana der gallischen Götter', in: *Indogermanica. FS W. Krause*, Heidelberg 1960, 204–213.

————, *Keltische Religion*, Stuttgart 1961.

Wagner, H., 'Irish fáith, Welsh gwawd, Old Icelandic óðr "poetry", and the Germanic god Wotan/Óðinn' (ZCP 31) 1970, 46–57.

———, 'The Celtic Invasions of Ireland and Great Britain: Facts and Theories' (ZCP 42) 1987, 1–40.

Wailes, B., 'The Irish Royal Sites in History and Achaeology' (CMCSt 3) 1982, 1–29.

Wainwright, F. T. (ed.), The Problem of the Picts, Edinburgh 1956.

Wait, G. A., Ritual and Religion in Iron Age Britain, London 1985.

Warner, R. B., 'The Broighter Hoard', in: B. G. Scott (ed.), Studies on Early Ireland: Essays in Honour of M. V. Duignan, Belfast 1982, 29–38.

Watts, D., Christians and Pagans in Roman Britain, London 1991.

Webster, G., Boudicca. The British revolt against Rome AD 60, London 1978.

———, The British Celts and their Gods under Rome, London 1986.

Webster, J., 'Translation and Subjection: Interpretatio and the Celtic Gods', in: J. D. Hill & G. C. Cumberpatch (eds.), Different Iron Ages, Oxford 1995, 175–181.

Weisgerber, G., Das Pilgerheiligtum des Apollo und der Sirona von Hochscheid im Hunsrück, Bonn 1975.

Weisgerber, L., 'Die Sprache der Festlandkelten' (BRGK 20) 1930, 147–226.

———, 'Galatische Sprachreste', in: Natalicium. Johannes Geffcken zum 70. Geburtstag, Heidelberg 1931, 151–175.

Wernicke, I., Die Kelten in Italien, Stuttgart 1991.

Whatmough, J., The Dialects of Ancient Gaul, Cambridge (Mass.) 1970.

Wiegels, R., 'Die Inschrift auf dem Diana Abnobna-Altar aus Badenweiler' (Antike Welt 13,4) 1982, 41–43.

Wightman, E. M., Gallia Belgica, London 1985.

———, 'Pagan Cults in the Province of Belgica' (ANRW II 18.1) 1986, 542–589.

Williams, J. E. C., 'Posidonius's Celtic Parasites' (StC 14/15) 1979/80, 313–342.

Wilson, D. R., 'Romano-Celtic temple architecture' (The Journal of the British Archaeological Association 38) 1975, 3–27.

Wissowa, G., 'Interpretatio Romana: Römische Götter im Barbarenlande' (Archiv für Religionswissenschaft 19) 1918, 1–49.

Wyss, R., Der Schatzfund von Erstfeld. Frühkeltischer Goldschmuck aus den Zentralalpen, Zurich 1975.

Zachar, L., Keltische Kunst in der Slowakei, Bratislava 1987.

Zahlhaas, G., 'Der Bronzeeimer von Waldalgesheim' (HBA 1) 1971, 115–129.

Zecchini, G., I Druidi e l'opposizione dei Celti a Roma, Milan 1984.

Zürn, H. 'Eine hallstattzeitliche Stele von Hirschlanden, Kr. Leonberg' (Germania 42) 1964, 27–36.

Zürn, H. & F. Fischer, Die keltische Viereckschanze von Tomerdingen, Stuttgart 1992.

5. Linguistic, Literary and Cultural History from the Early Middle Ages to the Beginning of the Modern Period

Aguirre, M., 'The Hero's Voyage in Immram Curaig Mailduin' (EC 27) 1990, 203–220.

Ahlqvist, A., 'Two notes on Audacht Morainn' (Celtica 21) 1990, 1–2.

Aitchison, N. B., 'The Ulster Cycle: heroic image and historical reality' (Journal of Medieval History 13) 1987, 87–116.

Almqvist, B. et al. (eds.), The Heroic Process, Dun Laoghaire 1987.

Alphandéry, P., 'L'Evhémérisme et les débuts de l'histoire des religions au moyen âge' (RHR 109) 1934, 5–27.

Anton, H. H., 'Pseudo-Cyprian De duodecim abusivis saeculi und sein Einfluß auf den Kontinent, insbesondere auf die karolingischen Fürstenspiegel', in: H. Löwe (ed.), Die Iren und Europa im früheren Mittelalter, Stuttgart 1982, 568–617.

Backhaus, N., 'The Structure of the List of Remscéla Tána Bó Cualngi in the Book of Leinster' (CMCSt 19) 1990, 19–26.

Ball, M. J. with J. Fife (eds.), Celtic Languages, London 1993.

Bartlett, R., Gerald of Wales, 1146–1223, Oxford 1982.

Bellingham, D., An Introduction to Celtic Mythology, London 1990.

Beneš, B., 'Spuren von Schamanismus in der Sage Buile Suibhne' (ZCP 28) 1960/61, 309–334.

Binchy, D. A., 'Patrick and his Biographers Ancient and Modern' (StHib 2) 1962, 7–173.

——, Celtic and Anglo-Saxon Kingship, Oxford 1970.

——, 'Varia Hibernica I. The so-called "rhetorics" of Irish saga', in: H. Pilch & J. Thurow (eds.), Indo-Celtica. Gedächtnisschrift für Alf Sommerfelt, Munich 1972, 29–38.

Boivin, J.-M., L'Irlande au moyen âge. Giraud de Barri et la Topographia Hibernica (1188), Paris 1993.

Bollard, J. K., 'The Role of Myth and Tradition in the Four Branches of the Mabinogi' (CMCSt 6) 1983, 67–86.

——, 'Sovereignty and the Loathly Lady in English, Welsh and Irish' (Leeds Studies in English 17) 1986, 41–59.

Bolle, K. W., 'In Defense of Euhemerism', in: J. Puhvel (ed.), Myth and Law among the Indo-Europeans, Berkeley, Calif., 1970, 19–38.

Bowen, C., 'A Historical Inventory of the Dindshenchas' (StC 10/11) 1975/76, 113–137.

Bradshaw, B., 'Geoffrey Keating: Apologist of Irish Ireland', in: B. Bradshaw et al. (eds.), Representing Ireland. Literature and the origins of conflict, 1534–1660, Cambridge 1993, 166–190.

Breatnach, L., 'Canon Law and Secular Law in Early Ireland: The Significance of Bretha Nemed' (Peritia 3) 1984, 439–459.

——, 'Zur Frage der roscada im Irischen', in: H. L. C. Tristram (ed.), Metrik und Medienwechsel, Tübingen 1991, 197–205.

Breatnach, P. A., 'The Chief's Poet' (PRIA 83) 1983, 37–79.

Breatnach, R. A., 'The Lady and the King: A Theme of Irish Literature' (*Studies* 42) 1953, 321–336.

Breen, A., 'The Evidence of Antique Irish Exegesis in Pseudo-Cyprian "De Duodecim Abusivis Saeculi" ' (*PRIA* 87) 1987, 71–101.

Broderick, G., *A Handbook of Late Spoken Manx*, 3 vols., Tübingen 1984–1986.

———, *Placenames of the Isle of Man*, 2 vols, Tübingen 1994–1995.

Bromwich, R., 'Celtic Dynastic Themes and the Breton Lays' (*EC* 9) 1961, 439–474.

———, 'Concepts of Arthur' (*StC* 10/11) 1975/76, 163–181.

———, 'Cynon fab Clydno', in: R. Bromwich & R. B. Jones (eds.), *Astudiaethau ar yr Hengerdd*, Cardiff 1978, 150–64.

Bromwich, R. & R. B. Jones (eds.), *Astudiaethau ar yr Hengerdd: Studies in Old Welsh Poetry*, Cardiff 1978.

Bromwich, R., 'The Tristan of the Welsh', in: R. Bromwich et al. (eds.), *The Arthur of the Welsh*, Cardiff 1991, 209–228.

Bromwich, R. et al. (eds.), *The Arthur of the Welsh. The Arthurian legend in Medieval Welsh Literature*, Cardiff 1991.

Broudic, F., *La pratique du breton de l'Ancien Régime à nos jours*, Rennes 1995.

Bruford, A., 'Song and recitation in early Ireland' (*Celtica* 21) 1990, 61–74.

———, 'Oral and Literary Fenian Tales', in: B. Almqvist et al. (eds.), *The Heroic Process*, Dún Laoghaire 1987, 25–56.

———, 'Cú Chulainn – An Ill-Made Hero?', in: H. L. C. Tristram (ed.), *Text und Zeittiefe*, Tübingen 1994, 185–215.

Budgey, A., ' "Preiddeu Annwn" and the Welsh Tradition of Arthur', in: C. J. Byrne et al. (eds.), *Celtic Languages and Celtic Peoples*, Halifax 1992, 391–404.

Buttimer, C. G., 'Scéla Muicce Meic Dathó: a reappraisal' (*PHCC* 2) 1982, 61–73.

Byrne, F. J., 'Tribes and Tribalism in Early Ireland' (*Ériu* 22) 1971, 128–168.

———, *Irish Kings and High-Kings*, London 1973.

Carey, J., 'The Name "Tuatha Dé Danann" ' (*Éigse* 18) 1980/81, 291–294.

———, 'Coll son of Collfrewi' (*StC* 16/17) 1981/82, 168–174.

———, 'Notes on the Irish War-Goddess' (*Éigse* 19) 1982/83, 263–275.

———, 'Nodons in Britain and Ireland' (*ZCP* 40) 1984, 1–22.

———, 'Suibne Geilt and Túan mac Cairill' (*Éigse* 20) 1984, 93–105.

———, 'Origin and development of the Cesair Legend' (*Éigse* 22) 1987, 37–48.

———, 'Sequence and Causation in Echtra Nerai' (*Ériu* 39) 1988, 67–74.

———, 'Fir Bolg: A Native Etymology Revisited' (*CMCSt* 16) 1988, 77–83.

———, 'Myth and Mythography in Cath Maige Tuired' (*StC* 24/25) 1989/90, 53–69.

———, 'A Tuath Dé miscellany' (*BBCS* 39) 1992, 24–45.

Carney, J., *Studies in Irish Literature and History*, Dublin 1955.

Carson, J. A., 'The Structure and Meaning of "The Dream of Rhonabwy" ' (*Philological Quarterly* 53) 1974, 289–303.

Celtic Law Papers, Aberystwyth 1971.

Chadwick, N. K., 'Imbas forosnai' (*SGS* 4) 1935, 97–135.

———, 'The Story of Mac Dathó's Pig' (*SGS* 8) 1958, 130–145.

Charles-Edwards, G., 'The Scribes of the Red Book of Hergest' (*Journal of the National Library of Wales* 21) 1980, 246–256.

Charles-Edwards, T. M., 'The Authenticity of the Gododdin: An Historian's View', in: R. Bromwich & R. B. Jones (eds.), *Astudiaethau ar yr Hengerdd*, Cardiff 1978, 44–71.

————, 'Críth Gablach and the Law of Status' (*Peritia* 5) 1986, 53–73.

————, *The Welsh Laws*, Cardiff 1989.

————, 'The Arthur of History', in: R. Bromwich et al. (eds.), *The Arthur of the Welsh*, Cardiff 1991, 15–32.

————, *Early Irish and Welsh Kinship*, Oxford 1993.

Chotzen, Th. M. Th., 'Emain Ablach – Ynys Afallach – Insula Avallonis – Ile d'Avalon' (*EC* 4) 1948, 255-274.

Clancy, T. O. & G. Márkus, *Iona: The Earliest Poetry of a Celtic Monastery*, Edinburgh 1995.

Clark, R., 'Aspects of the Morrígan in Early Irish Poetry' (*Irish University Review* 17) 1987, 223–236.

Cohen, D. J., 'Suibhne Geilt' (*Celtica* 12) 1977, 113–124.

Cooke, J. D., 'Euhemerism: A Mediaeval Interpretation of Classical Paganism' (*Speculum* 2) 1927, 396–410.

Cormier, R. J., 'Remarks on "The Tale of Deirdriu and Noisiu" and the Tristan Legend' (*EC* 15) 1976/77, 303–315.

Corthals, J., 'The Retoiric in Aided Conchobuir' (*Ériu* 40) 1989, 41–59.

Cronin, A., 'Sources of Keating's Forus Feasa ar Érinn' (*Celtica* 4) 1943/44, 235–279 & (*Celtica* 5) 1945/47, 122–135.

Cunningham, B., 'Seventeenth-century interpretations of the past: the case of Geoffrey Keating' (*Irish Historical Studies* 25) 1986, 116–128.

Davidson, H. E., *Myths and symbols in pagan Europe. Early Scandinavian and Celtic religions*, Manchester 1988.

Davies, C., *Welsh Literature and the Classical Tradition*, Cardiff 1995.

Davies, S., *Crefft y Cyfarwydd. Astudiaeth o dechnegau naratif yn y Mabinogion*, Cardiff 1995.

Davies, W., 'The place of healing in early Irish society', in: D. Ó Corráin et al. (eds.), *Sages, Saints, and Storytellers. Celtic Studies in Honour of Prof. J. Carney*, Maynooth 1989, 43–55.

————, 'Celtic Women in the Early Middle Ages', in: A. Cameron & A. Kuhrt (eds.), *Images of Women in Antiquity*, rev. ed., London 1993, 145–166 & 307.

Dillon, M., *The Cycles of the Kings*, London 1946.

————, *Early Irish Literature*, Chicago 1948.

Dillon, M. (ed.), *Irish Sagas*, Dublin 1959.

Diverres, A. H., 'Iarlles y Ffynnawn and Le chevalier au lion: Adaptation or Common Source?' (*StC* 16/17) 1981/82, 144–162.

Doherty, C., 'Exchange and Trade in Early Medieval Ireland' (*JRSAI* 110) 1980, 67–89.

Dröge, C. Ein irischer saṃsāra? Betrachtungen zur Frage der "keltischen Seelenwanderungslehre" ' (*ZCP* 39) 1982, 261–268.

————, 'Le pays de la jeunesse dans les littératures celtiques', in: *Les Ages de la vie au Moyen age*, Paris 1992, 23–36.

Dumézil, G., 'La quatrième branche du Mabinogi et la théologie des trois fonctions', in: P. MacCana & M. Meslin (eds.), *Rencontres de religions*, Paris 1986, 25–38.

Dumville, D. N., 'Echtrae and Immram: some problems of definition' (*Ériu* 27) 1976, 73–94.

————, 'Brittany and "Armes Prydein Vawr" ' (*EC* 20) 1983, 145–159.

————, 'The Historical Value of the Historia Brittonum' (*AL* 6) 1986, 1–26.

————, 'Historia Brittonum: an Insular History from the Carolingian Age', in: A. Scharer & G. Scheibelreiter (eds.), *Historiographie im frühen Mittelalter*, Vienna 1994, 406–434.

Edel, D., *Helden auf Freiersfüßen. "Tochmarc Emire" und "Mal y Kavas Kulhwch Olwen". Studien zur inselkeltischen Erzähltradition*, Amsterdam 1980.

————, 'The Arthur of Culhwch ac Olwen as a Figure of Epic-Heroic Tradition' (*Reading Medieval Studies* 9) 1983, 3–15.

————, 'The "Mabinogionfrage": Arthurian Literature between Orality and Literacy', in: H. L. C. Tristram (ed.), *(Re)Oralisierung*, Tübingen 1996, 311–333.

Evans, D. S., *A Grammar of Middle Welsh*, Dublin 1964.

Falaky Nagy, J., *The Wisdom of the Outlaw. The Boyhood Deeds of Finn in Gaelic Narrative Tradition*, Berkeley (Calif.) 1985.

————, 'Compositional Concerns in the Acallam na Senórach', in: D. Ó Corráin et al. (eds.), *Sages, Saints, and Storytellers: Celtic Studies in Honour of Prof. J. Carney*, Maynooth 1989, 149–158.

Fife, J., 'Legal aspects of the hunting scene in "Pwyll" ' (*BBCS* 39) 1992, 71–79.

Ford, P. K., 'Prolegomena to a Reading of the Mabinogi: "Pwyll" and "Manawydan" ' (*StC* 16/17) 1981/82, 110–125.

————, 'Aspects of the Patrician Legend', in: P. K. Ford (ed.), *Celtic Folklore and Christianity. Studies in Memory of W. W. Heist*, Los Angeles, Calif. 1983, 29–49.

————, 'The Death of Aneirin' (*BBCS* 34) 1987, 41–50.

————, 'Branwen: A Study of the Celtic Affinities' (*StC* 22/23) 1987/88, 29–41.

————, 'Celtic Women: The Opposing Sex' (*Viator* 19) 1988, 417–438.

Gerriets, M., 'Kingship and exchange in pre-Viking Ireland' (*CMCSt* 13) 1987, 39–72.

————, 'The King as Judge in Early Ireland' (*Celtica* 20) 1988, 1–24.

Gillies, W., 'The craftsman in early Celtic literature' (*Scottish Archaeological Forum* 11) 1981, 70–85.

Gillies, W. (ed.), *Gaelic and Scotland: Alba agus a'Ghaidhlig*, Edinburgh 1989.

Goetinck, G., *Peredur: A Study of Welsh Tradition in the Grail Legends*, Cardiff 1975.

————, 'Peredur . . . upon reflection' (*EC* 25) 1988, 221–232.

Gourvil, F., *Langue et littérature bretonnes*, Paris 1952.

Gray, E. A., 'Cath Maige Tuired: Myth and Structure' (*Éigse* 18) 1981, 183–209 & (*Éigse* 19) 1982/83, 1–35, 230–262.

Greene, D., 'Tabu in early Irish narrative', in: H. Bekker-Nielsen et al. (eds.), *Medieval Narrative: A Symposium*, Odense 1979, 9–19.

Griffiths, J. G., 'Giraldus Cambrensis Descriptio Kambriae' (*BBCS* 31) 1984, 1–16.

Gruffydd, R. G., 'Canu Cadwallawn ap Cadfan', in: R. Bromwich & R. B. Jones (eds.), *Astudiaethau ar yr Hengerdd*, Cardiff 1978, 25–43.

————, 'From Gododdin to Gwynedd: reflections on the story of Cunedda' (*StC* 24/25) 1989/90, 1–14.

Gruffydd, W. J., *Math fab Mathonwy: An Enquiry into the Origins and Development of the Fourth Branch of the Mabinogi*, Cardiff 1928.

Guyonvarc'h, Ch.-J., 'Irlandais síd, gaulois *sedos "siège, demeure des dieux" ' (*Ogam* 14) 1962, 329–340.

Gwara, S., 'Gluttony, lust and penance in the B-text of Aislinge Meic Conglinne' (*Celtica* 20) 1988, 53–72.

Hamp, E., 'imbolc, óimelc' (*StC* 14/15) 1979/80, 106–113.

Hanson, R. P. C., *The Life and Writings of the Historical St. Patrick*, New York 1983.

Hanson-Smith, E., 'Pwyll Prince of Dyfed: The Narrative Structure' (StC 16/17) 1981/82, 126–134.

Harbison, P., *The High Crosses of Ireland. An iconographic and photographic survey*, 3 vols, Bonn 1992 (Monographien des Römisch-Germanischen Zentralmuseums Mainz 17).

Harrison, F. L., *Music in Medieval Britain*, London 1968.

Hemon, R., *A Historical Morphology and Syntax of Breton*, Dublin 1975.

Henderson, G., *From Durrow to Kells: the insular Gospel-Books 650–800*, London 1987.

Henken, E. R., *Traditions of the Welsh Saints*, Cambridge 1987.

Henry, F., *Irish High Crosses*, Dublin 1964.

——, *The Book of Kells*, London 1974.

Henry, P. L., 'Interpreting Críth Gablach' (ZCP 36) 1978, 54–62.

——, *Saoithiúlacht na Sean-Ghaeilge*, Dublin 1978.

——, 'The Cruces of Audacht Morainn' (ZCP 39) 1982, 33–53.

Herbert, M., *Iona, Kells and Derry. The History and Hagiography of the Monastic Family of Columba*, Oxford 1988.

——, 'The preface to Amra Coluim Cille', in: D. Ó. Corráin et al. (eds.), *Sages, Saints, and Storytellers: Celtic Studies in Honour of Prof. J. Carney*, Maynooth 1989, 67–75.

——, 'Fled Dúin na nGéd: a reappraisal' (CMCSt 18) 1989, 75–87.

——, 'Goddess and king: The sacred marriage in early Ireland', in: L. O. Fradenburg (ed.), *Women and Sovereignty*, Edinburgh 1992, 264–295.

——, 'Celtic Heroine? The archaeology of the Deirdre story', in: T. O'Brien Johnson & D. Cairnes (eds.), *Gender in Irish Writing*, Philadelphia 1991, 13–29.

Higham, N. J., *The English conquest. Gildas and Britain in the fifth century*, Manchester 1994.

Hull, V., 'On Amra Choluim Chille' (ZCP 28) 1961, 242–252.

Hunt, T., 'The Art of Iarlles y Ffynnawn and the European Volksmärchen' (StC 8/9) 1973/74, 107–120.

——, 'Some Observations on the Textual Relationship of Li Chevaliers au Lion and Iarlles y Ffynnawn' (ZCP 33) 1974, 93–113.

Huws, D., 'Llyfr Gwyn Rhydderch' (CMCSt 21) 1991, 1–37.

Isaac, G. R., *The verb in the Book of Aneirin*, Tübingen 1996.

Jackson, K. H., 'Common Gaelic. The Evolution of the Goedelic Languages' (PBA 37) 1951, 71–97.

——, *The International Popular Tale and Early Welsh Tradition*, Cardiff 1961.

——, *The Oldest Irish Tradition: A Window on the Iron Age*, Cambridge 1964.

——, *A Historical Phonology of Breton*, Dublin 1967.

——, *The Gaelic Notes in the Book of Deer*, Cambridge 1972.

Jarman, A. O. H. & G. Hughes, *A Guide to Welsh Literature*, 2 vols., Swansea 1976–1979.

Jarman, A. O. H., 'Early stages in the development of the Myrddin legend', in: R. Bromwich & R. B. Jones (eds.), *Astudiaethau ar yr Hengerdd*, Cardiff 1978, 326–349.

——, 'The Delineation of Arthur in early Welsh Verse', in: K. Varty (ed.), *An Arthurian Tapestry: Essays in Memory of Lewis Thorpe*, Glasgow 1981, 1–21.

————, *The Cynfeirdd*, Cardiff 1981.

————, 'Llyfr Du Caerfyrddin, The Black Book of Carmarthen' (*PBA* 71) 1985, 333–356.

————, 'The Merlin Legend and the Welsh tradition of prophecy', in: R. Bromwich et al. (eds.), *The Arthur of the Welsh*, Cardiff 1991, 117–145.

Jenkins, D. & M. E. Owen (eds.), *The Welsh Law of Women*, Cardiff 1980.

Johnston, D., *The Literature of Wales*, Cardiff 1994.

Jones, T., 'The Early Evolution of the Legend of Arthur' (*Nottingham Medieval Studies* 8) 1964, 3–21.

Keefer, S. L., 'The Lost Tale of Dylan in the Fourth Branch of the Mabinogi' (*StC* 24/25) 1989/90, 26–37.

Kelly, F., *A Guide to Early Irish Law*, Dublin 1988.

Kerlouégan, F., *Le De Excidio Britanniae de Gildas. Les destinées de la culture latine dans l'île de Bretagne au VIe siècle*, Paris 1987.

Klar, K. et al., 'Welsh poetics in the Indo-European tradition. The case of the Book of Aneirin' (*StC* 18/19) 1983/84, 30–51.

Koch, J. T., 'Ériu, Alba and Letha: When was a language ancestral to Gaelic first spoken in Ireland?' (*Emania* 9) 1991, 17–27.

Lambert, P.-Y., *Les Littératures celtiques*, Paris 1981.

Lambkin, B., 'The Structure of the Blathmac Poems' (*StC* 20/21) 1985/86, 67–77.

Lapidge, M. & D. Dumville (eds.), *Gildas: New Approaches*, Woodbridge 1984.

Lehmann, R. P., 'A study of the Buile Shuibhne' (*EC* 6) 1953/54, 289–311 & (*EC* 7) 1955/56, 115–138.

Le Roux, F., 'Etudes sur le festiaire celtique' (*Ogam* 13) 1961, 481–506, (*Ogam* 14) 1962, 174–184 and 343–372.

————, 'Le dieu-roi Nodons/Nuadu' (*Celticum* 6) 1963, 424–454.

Le Roux, F. & Ch.-J. Guyonvarc'h, *Mórrígan-Bodb-Macha: La Souveraineté guerrière de l'Irlande*, Rennes 1983.

Lewis, H. & H. Pedersen, *A Concise Comparative Celtic Grammar*, Göttingen [2]1961.

Lewis, H., *Die kymrische Sprache. Grundzüge ihrer Entwicklung* (German trans. by W. Meid), Innsbruck 1990.

————, *Handbuch des Mittelkornischen* (German trans. by S. Zimmer), Innsbruck 1990.

Lewis, H. & J. R. F. Piette, *Handbuch des Mittelbretonischen*, Innsbruck 1990.

Lloyd-Morgan, C., 'Narrative Structure in Peredur' (*ZCP* 38) 1981, 187–231.

————, 'Breuddwyd Rhonabwy and later Arthurian Literature', in: R. Bromwich et al. (eds.), *The Arthur of the Welsh*, Cardiff 1991, 183–208.

Loth, J., 'Le Mabinogi de Math vab Mathonwy d'après W. J. Gruffydd et la méthode en celto-mythologie' (*RC* 46) 1929, 272–300.

Lovecy, I., 'Historia Peredur ab Efrawg', in: R. Bromwich et al. (eds.), *The Arthur of the Welsh*, Cardiff 1991, 171–182.

Low, M., *Celtic Christianity and Nature. The Early Irish and Hebridean Traditions*, Edinburgh 1995.

Lucas, A. T., *Cattle in Ancient Ireland*, Kilkenny 1989.

MacAulay, D. (ed.), *The Celtic Languages*, Cambridge 1992.

MacCana, P., 'Aspects of the Theme of King and Goddess in Irish Literature' (*EC* 7) 1955, 76–114, 356–413 & (*EC* 8) 1959, 59–65.

————, *Branwen Daughter of Llŷr: A Study of the Irish Affinities and of the Composition of the Second Branch of the Mabinogi*, Cardiff 1958.

————, 'On the use of the term retoiric' (*Celtica* 7) 1966, 65–90.

————, 'The Sinless Otherworld of Immram Brain' (*Ériu* 27) 1976, 95–115.

————, *The Mabinogi*, Cardiff 1977 (^{2}1992).

————, *The Learned Tales of Medieval Ireland*, Dublin 1980.

————, *Celtic Mythology*, London 1983.

————, 'Early Irish Ideology and the Concept of Unity', in: R. Kearney (ed.), *The Irish Mind*, Dublin 1985, 56–78.

————, 'The Voyage of St Brendan: Literary and historical origins', in: J. de Courcy Ireland & D. C. Sheehy (eds.), *Atlantic Visions*, Dun Loaghaire 1989, 3–16.

————, 'On the early development of written narrative prose in Irish and Welsh' (*EC* 29) 1992, 51–67.

McCone, K., 'Brigit in the seventh century: a saint with three lives?' (*Peritia* 1) 1982, 107–145.

————, 'Aided Cheltchair Maic Uthechair: Hounds, Heroes and Hospitallers in Early Irish Myth and Story' (*Ériu* 35) 1984, 1–30.

————, 'The Würzburg and Milan Glosses: Our Earliest Sources of "Middle Irish" ' (*Ériu* 36) 1985, 85–106.

————, 'A tale of two ditties: poet and satirist in Cath Maige Tuired', in: D. Ó Corráin et al. (eds.), *Sages, Saints, and Storytellers: Celtic Studies in Honour of Prof. J. Carney*, Maynooth 1989, 122–143.

————, *Pagan Past and Christian Present in Early Irish Literature*, Maynooth 1990.

McKenna, C. M., 'The Theme of Sovereignty in Pwyll' (*BBCS* 29) 1980/82, 35–52.

McKenna, M., 'The Breton Literary Tradition' (*Celtica* 16) 1984, 35–51.

Mackey, J. P. (ed.), *An Introduction to Celtic Christianity*, Edinburgh 1989.

MacKinnon, K., *Gaelic: a past and future prospect*, Edinburgh 1991.

McLeod, N., *Early Irish contract law*, Sydney 1992.

MacMathúna, S., 'The Structure and Transmission of Early Irish Voyage Literature', in: H. L. C. Tristram (ed.), *Text und Zeittiefe*, Tübingen 1994, 313–357.

————, 'Motif and Episodic Clustering in Early Irish Voyage Literature', in: H. L. C. Tristram (ed.), *(Re)Oralisierung*, Tübingen 1996, 247–262.

MacQueen, J., 'Maponus in Mediaeval Tradition' (*Transactions of the Dumfriesshire and Galloway Natural History and Antiquarian Society* 31) 1954, 43–57.

Maier, B., 'Die keltische Auffassung des Königtums und ihre orientalischen Parallelen', Diss. Bonn 1991.

Mallory, J. P. (ed.), *Aspects of the Táin*, Belfast 1992.

Mallory, J. P. & G. Stockman (eds.), *Ulidia. Proceedings of the First International Conference on the Ulster Cycle of Tales*, Belfast 1992.

Martin, B. K., 'The Old Woman of Beare: A Critical Evaluation' (*Medium Aevum* 38) 1969, 245–261.

————, 'Medieval Irish aitheda and Todorov's "Narratologie" ' (*StC* 10/11) 1975/76, 138–151.

————, ' "Truth" and "modesty": a reading of the Irish Noínden Ulad' (*Leeds Studies in English* 20) 1989, 99–117.

Meek, D. E., 'Táin Bó Fraích and other "Fraech" Texts: A Study in Thematic Relationships' (*CMCSt* 7) 1984, 1–37, (*CMCSt* 8) 1984, 65–85.

————, 'The Gaelic Ballads of Mediaeval Scotland' (*Transactions of the Gaelic Society of Inverness* 55) 1989, 47–72.

————, 'The death of Diarmaid in Scottish and Irish Tradition' (*Celtica* 21) 1990, 335–361.

Meid, W., 'Dichtkunst, Rechtspflege und Medizin im alten Irland. Zur Struktur der altirischen Gesellschaft', in: M. Mayrhofer et al. (eds.), *Antiquitates Indogermanicae: Gedenkschrift für H. Güntert*, Innsbruck 1974, 21–34.

————, *Aspekte der germanischen und keltischen Religion im Zeugnis der Sprache*, Innsbruck 1991.

Melia, D. F., 'Remarks on the structure and composition of the Ulster death tales' (*StHib* 17/18) 1978, 36–57.

Meyer, K., 'Der irische Totengott und die Toteninsel' (*Sitzungsberichte der Königlich Preußischen Akademie der Wissenschaften*, Phil.-hist. Klasse) 1919, 537–546.

Middleton, R., *Chwedl Gereint ap Erbin*, in: R. Bromwich et al. (eds.), *The Arthur of the Welsh*, Cardiff 1991, 147–157.

Morgan, T. J. & P. Morgan, *Welsh Surnames*, Cardiff 1985.

Müller-Lisowski, K., 'Texte zur Mog Ruith Sage' (*ZCP* 14) 1923, 145–163.

Murdoch, B., 'In pursuit of the Cailleach Bérre: an early Irish poem and the medievalist at large' (*ZCP* 44) 1991, 80–127.

————, *Cornish Literature*, Cambridge 1993.

Murphy, G., *Saga and Myth in Ancient Ireland*, Dublin 1955.

————, *The Ossianic Lore and Romantic Tales of Medieval Ireland*, Dublin 1955.

Mytum, H., *The Origins of Early Christian Ireland*, London 1992.

Ní Chatháin, P. & M. Richter (eds.), *Irland und Europa. Die Kirche im Frühmittelalter*, Stuttgart 1984.

————, *Irland und die Christenheit. Bibelstudien und Mission*, Stuttgart 1987.

Ní Chonghaile, N. & H. L. C. Tristram, 'Die mittelirischen Sagenlisten zwischen Mündlichkeit und Schriftlichkeit', in: H. L. C. Tristram (ed.), *Deutsche, Kelten und Iren*, Hamburg 1990, 249–268.

Ó Briain, M., 'Oisín's Biography: Conception and Birth', in: H. L. C. Tristram (ed.), *Text und Zeittiefe*, Tübingen 1994, 455–486.

Ó Broin, T., 'Lia Fáil: fact and fiction in the tradition' (*Celtica* 21) 1990, 393–401.

Ó Catháin, S., *The Festival of Brigit. Celtic Goddess and Holy Woman*, Blackrock 1995.

Ó Cathasaigh, T., *The Heroic Biography of Cormac Mac Airt*, Dublin 1977.

————, 'The Semantics of síd' (*Éigse* 17) 1978, 137–155.

————, 'The Theme of Lommrad in Cath Maige Mucrama' (*Éigse* 18) 1980/81, 211–224.

————, 'The Theme of Ainmne in Scéla Cano Meic Gartnáin' (*Celtica* 15) 1983, 78–87.

————, 'Cath Maige Tuired as Exemplary Myth', in: P. de Brún et al. (eds.), *Folia Gadelica*, Cork 1983, 1–19.

————, 'The Rhetoric of Fingal Rónáin' (*Celtica* 17) 1985, 123–144.

————, 'The Rhetoric of Scéla Cano Meic Gartnáin', in: D. Ó Corráin et al. (eds.), *Sages, Saints, and Storytellers: Celtic Studies in Honour of Prof. J. Carney*, Maynooth 1989, 233–250.

Ó Coileáin, S., 'Echtrae Nerai and its analogues' (*Celtica* 21) 1990, 427–440.

Ó Concheanainn, T., 'Notes on Togail Bruidne Da Derga' (*Celtica* 17) 1985, 73–90.

————, 'The Manuscript Tradition of Mesca Ulad' (*Celtica* 19) 1987, 13–30.

————, 'A Connacht Medieval Literary Heritage: Texts Derived from Cín Dromma Snechtai through Leabhar na hUidre' (CMCSt 16) 1988, 1–40.

————, 'The textual tradition of Compert Con Culainn' (Celtica 21) 1990, 441–455.

Ó Corráin, D., 'Nationality and Kingship in pre-Norman Ireland', in: T. W. Moody (ed.), Nationality and the Pursuit of National Independence, Belfast 1978, 1–35.

————, 'Women in Early Irish Society', in: M. MacCurtain & D. Ó Corráin (eds.), Women in Irish Society – the historical dimension, Dublin 1978, 1–13.

Ó Corráin, D. & F. Maguire, Gaelic Personal Names, Dublin 1981.

Ó Corráin, D., 'Irish origin legends and genealogy: recurring genealogies', in: T. Nyberg et al. (eds.), History and Heroic Tale, Odense 1985, 51–96.

Ó Crualaoich, G., 'Continuity and Adaptation in Legends of Cailleach Bhéarra' (Béaloideas 56) 1988, 153–178.

Ó Cuív, B. (ed.), A View of the Irish Language, Dublin 1969.

Ó Cuív, B., 'Is tre fír flathemon: An Addendum' (Celtica 13) 1980, 146–149.

————, 'Dindshenchas: the literary exploitation of Irish placenames' (Ainm 4) 1989/90, 90–106.

O'Dwyer, P., Céli Dé: Spiritual Reform in Ireland, 750–900, Dublin 1981.

Ó Flaithearta, M., 'Echtra Nerai, Táin Bó Regamna und ihr Verhältnis zu Táin Bó Cuailnge', in: H. L. C. Tristram (ed.), Deutsche, Kelten und Iren, Hamburg 1990, 155–176.

Ó hÓgáin, D., Fionn mac Cumhaill. Images of the Celtic Hero, Dublin 1988.

Ó hUiginn, R., 'Fergus, Russ, and Rudraige: A Brief Biography of Fergus mac Róich' (Emania 11) 1993, 31–40.

————, 'Cú Chulainn and Connla', in: H. L. C. Tristram (ed.), (Re)Oralisierung, Tübingen 1996, 223–246.

O'Leary, P., 'Contention at Feasts in Early Irish Literature' (Éigse 20) 1984, 115–127.

————, 'Honour-bound: the social context of early Irish heroic geis' (Celtica 20) 1988, 85–107.

————, 'The honour of women in early Irish literature' (Ériu 37) 1986, 27–44.

Ó Madagáin, B., 'Echoes of Magic in the Gaelic Song Tradition', in: C. J. Byrne et al. (eds.), Celtic Languages and Celtic Peoples, Halifax 1992, 125–140.

O'Mahoney, F. (ed.), The Book of Kells. Proceedings of a conference at Trinity College Dublin 6–9 September 1992, Dublin 1994.

O'Rahilly, T. F., Early Irish History and Mythology, Dublin 1946.

Orel, V. E., 'OIr. áer' (BBCS 32) 1985, 164–166.

Ó Riain, P., 'A Study of the Irish Legend of the Wild Man' (Éigse 14) 1971/72, 179–206.

Oskamp, H. P. A., 'The Yellow Book of Lecan proper' (Ériu 26) 1975, 102–119.

Owen, M. E., 'Hwn yw e Gododin. Aneirin ae Cant', in: R. Bromwich & R. B. Jones (eds.), Astudiaethau ar yr Hengerdd, Cardiff 1978, 123–150.

Padel, O. J., 'The Cornish background of the Tristan stories' (CMCSt 1) 1981, 53–81.

————, 'Geoffrey of Monmouth and Cornwall' (CMCSt 8) 1984, 1–27.

————, 'The Nature of Arthur' (CMCSt 27) 1994, 1–31.

Parry, T. A., A History of Welsh Literature. Translated from the Welsh by H. Idris Bell, Oxford 1955.

Patterson, N. W., 'Gaelic Law and the Tudor Conquest of Ireland: the social background to the last recensions of the Prologue to the Senchas Már' (Irish Historical Studies 27) 1991, 1–23.

————, *Cattle-Lords and Clansmen: Kingship and Rank in Early Ireland*, London 1991.

Pilch, H., 'The Earliest Arthurian Tradition: The Preiddiau Annwfn of the Book of Taliesin', in: id. (ed.), *Orality and Literacy in Early Middle English*, Tübingen 1996, 147–166.

Power, R., 'Geasa and Álög: Magic Formulae and Perilous Quests in Gaelic and Norse' (*Scottish Studies* 28) 1987, 69–89.

Price, G., *The Languages of Britain*, London 1984.

Price, G. (ed.), *The Celtic Connection*, Gerrards Cross 1992.

Pryce, H., *Native Law and the Church in Medieval Wales*, Oxford 1993.

Quin, E. G., 'The Irish glosses', in: P. Ní Chatháin & M. Richter (eds.), *Irland und Europa*, Stuttgart 1984, 210–217.

Radner, J. N., 'Interpreting Irony in Medieval Celtic Narrative: the case of Culhwch ac Olwen' (*CMCSt* 16) 1988, 41–59.

Rees, A. D. & B. Rees, *Celtic Heritage: Ancient Tradition in Ireland and Wales*, London 1961.

Richter, M., *The Formation of the Medieval West. Studies in the Oral Culture of the Barbarians*, Blackrock 1994.

Roberts, B. F., *Gerald of Wales*, Cardiff 1982.

————, 'The Welsh Romance of the Lady of the Fountain (Owein)', in: P. B. Grout et al. (eds.), *The Legend of Arthur in the Middle Ages*, Cambridge 1983, 170–182.

————, *Early Welsh Poetry: Studies in the Book of Aneirin*, Aberystwyth 1988.

————, 'Geoffrey of Monmouth, Historia Regum Britanniae and Brut y Brenhinedd', in: R. Bromwich et al. (eds.), *The Arthur of the Welsh*, Cardiff 1991, 97–116.

————, *Studies on Middle Welsh Literature*, Lewiston/New York 1992.

Robinson, N. F., 'Satirists and Enchanters in Early Irish Literature', in: D. G. Lyon & G. F. Moore (eds.), *Studies in the History of Religions presented to C. H. Toy*, New York 1912, 95–130.

Rockel, M., 'Fiktion und Wirklichkeit im Breuddwyd Macsen', in: H. L. C. Tristram (ed.), *Medialität und mittelalterliche insulare Literatur*, Tübingen 1992, 170–182.

Russell, P., 'The Sounds of a Silence: The Growth of Cormac's Glossary' (*CMCSt* 15) 1988, 1–30.

Ryan, M. (ed.), *Ireland and Insular Art A. D. 500–1200*, Dublin 1987.

Saint Patrick, A. D. 493–1993, Woodbridge 1993.

Sayers, W., ' "Mani maidi an nem . . .": Ringing changes on a cosmic motif' (*Ériu* 37) 1986, 99–116.

————, 'Bargaining for the life of Bres in "Cath Maige Tuired" ' (*BBCS* 34) 1987, 26–40.

Schmidt, K. H., 'Die Würzburger Glossen' (*ZCP* 39) 1982, 54–77.

————, 'The Celtic Languages in their European Context', in: *Proceedings of the Seventh International Congress of Celtic Studies*, Oxford 1986, 199–221.

Schrijver, P., *Studies in British Celtic Historical Phonology*, Amsterdam 1995.

Scowcroft, R. M., 'Leabhar Gabhála' (*Ériu* 38) 1987, 80–142, (*Ériu* 39) 1988, 1–66.

Sellar, W. D. H., 'Celtic law and Scots law: survival and integration' (*Scottish Studies* 29) 1989, 1–27.

Sharpe, R., 'Vitae S. Brigitae: the oldest texts' (*Peritia* 1) 1982, 81–106.

————, *Medieval Irish Saints' Lives. An Introduction to Vitae Sanctorum Hiberniae*, Oxford 1991.

Sigurðsson, G., *Gaelic Influence in Iceland*, Reykjavik 1988 (Studia Islandica 46).

Simms, K., 'Guesting and Feasting in Gaelic Ireland' (JRSAI 108) 1978, 67–100.

Sims-Williams, P., 'The Significance of the Irish Personal Names in Culhwch ac Olwen' (BBCS 29) 1980/82, 600–620.

———, 'Gildas and the Anglo-Saxons' (CMCSt 6) 1983, 1–30.

———, 'Some Functions of Origin Stories in Early Medieval Wales', in: T. Nyberg et al. (eds.), History and Heroic Tale, Odense 1985, 97–131.

———, 'Some Celtic Otherworld Terms', in: A. T. E. Matonis & F. Melia (eds.), Celtic Languages, Celtic Culture: A FS for E. P. Hamp, Van Nuys (Calif.) 1990, 57–81.

———, 'The early Welsh Arthurian poems', in: R. Bromwich et al. (eds.), The Arthur of the Welsh, Cardiff 1991, 33–71.

Slotkin, E. M., 'The Structure of Fled Bricrenn before and after the Lebor na hUidre Interpolations' (Ériu 29) 1978, 64–77.

———, 'The Fabula, Story, and Text of Breuddwyd Rhonabwy' (CMCSt 18) 1989, 89–111.

———, 'Noínden: Its Semantic Range', in: A. T. E. Matonis & F. Melia (eds.), Celtic Languages, Celtic Culture: A FS for E. P. Hamp, Van Nuys (Calif.) 1990, 137–150.

Smith, R. M., 'The Speculum Principum in Early Irish Literature' (Speculum 2) 1927, 411–445.

Spaan, D. B., 'The Place of Mannanán mac Lir in Irish Mythology' (Folklore 76) 1965, 176–195.

Stacey, R. C., The Road to Judgment: From custom to court in medieval Ireland and Wales, Philadelphia 1994.

Stewart, J., 'Topographia Hiberniae' (Celtica 21) 1990, 642–657.

Thomas, N., ' "Geraint" and "Erec": a Welsh Heroic Text and its Continental Successors' (Trivium 22) 1987, 37–48.

Thomson, D., An Introduction to Gaelic Poetry, Edinburgh ²1989.

Thomson, D. S. (ed.), Gaelic and Scots in Harmony, Glasgow 1990.

Thomson, R. L., 'The Manx traditional ballad' (EC 9) 1960/61, 521–548 & (EC 10) 1962/63, 60–87.

———, 'The Study of Manx Gaelic' (PBA 55) 1969, 177–210.

———, 'Owain: Chwedl Iarlles y Ffynnon', in: R. Bromwich et al. (eds.), The Arthur of the Welsh, Cardiff 1991, 159–169.

Thurneysen, R., 'Zu Cormacs Glossar', in: Festschrift Ernst Windisch, Leipzig 1914, 8–37.

———, Die irische Helden- und Königsage bis zum siebzehnten Jahrhundert, Halle 1921.

———, A Grammar of Old Irish, rev. ed., Dublin 1975.

———, Gesammelte Schriften, ed. P. de Bernardo Stempel & R. Ködderitzsch, 3 vols, Tübingen 1991–1995.

Tranter, S. N. & H. L. C. Tristram (eds.), Early Irish Literature – Media and Communication. Mündlichkeit und Schriftlichkeit in der frühen irischen Literatur, Tübingen 1989.

Trindade, W. A., 'The Celtic Connections of the Tristan Story' (Reading Mediaeval Studies 12) 1986, 93–107 & (13) 1987, 71–80.

Tristram, H. L. C., 'Aspects of tradition and innovation in the Táin Bó Cuailnge', in: Papers on language and medieval studies presented to A. Schopf, Frankfurt 1988, 19–38.

Tristram, H. L. C. (ed.), *Deutsche, Kelten und Iren. 150 Jahre deutsche Keltologie. Gearóid MacEoin zum 60. Geburtstag gewidmet*, Hamburg 1990.

Tristram, H. L. C., 'Feis und fled: Wirklichkeit und Darstellung in mittelalterlichen irischen Gastmahlerzählungen', in: H. L. C. Tristram (ed.), *Medialität und mittelalterliche insulare Literatur*, Tübingen 1992, 183–220.

Tristram, H. L. C. (ed.), *Medialität und mittelalterliche insulare Literatur*, Tübingen 1992.

Tristram, H. L. C. (ed.), *Studien zur Táin Bó Cuailnge*, Tübingen 1993.

Tymoczko, M., 'Animal Imagery in Loinges mac nUislenn' (*StC* 20/21) 1985/86, 145–166.

Uhlich, J., *Die komponierten Personennamen des Altirischen*, Tübingen (forthcoming).

Vendryes, J., 'Manannán mac Lir' (*EC* 6) 1952, 239–254.

Vries, J. de, 'Le conte irlandais Aided oenfír Aífe et le thème du combat du père et du fils dans quelques traditions indo-européennes' (*Ogam* 9) 1957, 122–138.

Wagner, H., 'Old Irish fír "truth, oath" ' (*ZCP* 31) 1970, 1–45, 57–58 & 146.

———, 'Zur Etymologie von keltisch Nodons, Ir. Nuadu, Kymr. Nudd/Lludd' (*ZCP* 41) 1986, 180–188.

Wakelin, M. F., *Language and History in Cornwall*, Leicester 1975.

Watkins, C., 'Is tre fír flathemon. Marginalia to Audacht Morainn' (*Ériu* 30) 1979, 181–198.

Watson, A., 'A structural analysis of Echta Nerai' (*EC* 23) 1986, 129–142.

Watson, J. C., ' "Mesca Ulad": the redactor's contribution to the later version' (*Ériu* 13) 1942, 95–112.

Weisweiler, J., *Heimat und Herrschaft. Wirkung und Ursprung eines irischen Mythos*, Halle 1943.

Welsh, A., 'The traditional narrative motifs of The Four Branches of the Mabinogi' (*CMCSt* 15) 1988, 51–62.

———, 'Traditional tales and the harmonizing of story in Pwyll Pendeuic Dyuet' (*CMCSt* 17) 1989, 15–41.

West, M., 'Leabhar na hUidhre's Portion in the Manuscript History of Togail Bruidne Da Derga and Orgain Brudne Uí Dergae' (*CMCSt* 20) 1990, 61–98.

Williams, G., *An Introduction to Welsh Literature*, Cardiff ²1992.

Williams, J. E. C., 'The Court Poet in Medieval Ireland' (*PBA* 57) 1971, 1–51.

———, *The Irish Literary Tradition*. Transl. P. K. Ford, Cardiff 1992.

Withers, C. W. J., *Gaelic in Scotland 1698–1981*, Edinburgh 1984.

Wood, J., 'The Folklore Background of the Gwion Bach Section of Hanes Taliesin' (*BBCS* 29) 1980/82, 621–634.

———, 'The Elphin Section of Hanes Taliesin' (*EC* 18) 1981, 229–244.

———, 'Maelgwn Gwynedd: A Forgotten Welsh Hero' (*Trivium* 19) 1984, 103–117.

Wormald, P., 'Celtic and Anglo-Saxon kingship: some further thoughts', in: Paul E. Szarmach (ed.), *Sources of Anglo-Saxon Culture*, Kalamazoo (Mich.) 1986, 151–183.

Wright, N., 'Geoffrey of Monmouth and Gildas' (*AL* 2) 1982, 1–40.

———, 'Gildas's Reading: a survey' (*Sacris Erudiri* 32) 1991, 121–162.

6. Reception, History of Scholarship, Celtic Ideology

(a) Modern folk belief and folk customs, folk-tales

Aitken, H. & R. Michaelis-Jena, *Märchen aus Schottland*, Cologne 1965.

Batany, P., *Luzel, poète et folkloriste breton, 1821–1895*, Rennes 1941.

Breathnach, B., *Folk music and dances of Ireland*, Dublin 1971.

Bruford, A., *Gaelic Folktales and Mediaeval Romances*, Dublin 1969.

———, ' "Deirdire" and Alexander Carmichael's Treatment of Oral Sources' (*SGS* 14) 1983, 1–24.

Campbell, J. L., 'Notes on H. Robertson's "Studies in Carmichael's Carmina Gadelica" ' (*SGS* 13) 1978, 1–17.

———, 'Carmina Gadelica: G. Henderson's Corrections and Suggestions' (*SGS* 13) 1978, 183–218.

Clemen, U. (ed.), *Irische Märchen*, Munich 1971.

Collinson, F., *The traditional and national music of Ireland*, London 1966.

Cross, T. P., *Motif Index of Early Irish Literature*, Bloomington (Indiana) 1952.

Danaher, K., *The Year in Ireland*, Dublin 1972.

Delargy, J., 'The Gaelic Story-Teller' (*PBA* 31) 1967, 177–221.

Dunleavy, J. & G. Dunleavy, 'Jeremiah Curtin's Working Methods: The Evidence from the Manuscripts' (*Éigse* 18) 1981/82, 67–86.

Ellis, O., *The Story of the Harp in Wales*, Cardiff 1980.

Guilcher, J.-M., *La tradition de la danse populaire en Basse-Bretagne*, Paris 1963.

Hennig, J., 'The Brothers Grimm and Th. C. Croker' (*Modern Language Review* 41) 1946, 44–54.

Irische Elfenmärchen, Frankfurt 1987.

Irische Land- und Seemärchen, Frankfurt 1988.

Karlinger, F., *Der Graal im Spiegel romanischer Volkserzählungen*, Vienna 1996.

Lysaght, P., *The Banshee*, Dublin 1986.

MacCarthy, B. G., 'Thomas Crofton Croker 1798–1854' (*Studies* 32) 1943, 539–556.

MacNéill, M., *The Festival of Lughnasa. A Study of the Survival of the Celtic Festival of the Beginning of the Harvest*, Dublin 2·1982.

Moritz, W. et al. (eds.), *Irische Land- und Seemärchen*, Marburg 1986.

Mühlhausen, L., *Diarmuid mit dem roten Bart: Irische Zaubermärchen*, Kassel 1956.

Müller-Lisowski, K., 'Contributions to a study in Irish folklore: traditions about Donn' (*Béaloideas* 18) 1948, 142–199.

———, *Irische Volksmärchen*, Cologne 1962.

Ó Briain, M., 'Cluasa Capaill ar an Rí – AT 782 i d'Traidisiún na hÉireann' (*Béaloideas* 53) 1985, 11–74.

Ó Giolláin, D., 'The Leipreachán and Fairies, Dwarfs and the Household Familiar' (*Béaloideas* 52) 1984, 75–150.

Ó Súillebháin, S. & R. T. Christiansen, *The Types of the Irish Folktale*, Helsinki 1963.

Patton, L., 'Alexander Carmichael, Carmina Gadelica, and the Nature of Ethnographic Representation' (*PHCC* 8) 1988, 58–84.

Robertson, H., 'Studies in Carmichael's Carmina Gadelica' (*SGS* 12) 1976, 220–265.

333

Sanger, K. & A. Kinnaird, *Tree of Strings – A history of the harp in Scotland*, Shillinghill Temple 1992.

Sorlin, É., *Cris de vie, cris de mort: Les fées du destin dans les pays celtiques*, Helsinki 1991 (FFC 248).

Soupault, R., *Bretonische Märchen*, Cologne 1959.

Thompson, F. G., 'The Folklore Elements in Carmina Gadelica' (*Transactions of the Gaelic Society of Inverness* 44) 1966, 226–255.

(b) Celtic material and motifs in non-Celtic literature

Barber, R., *King Arthur: Hero and Legend*, Woodbridge 1986.

Baumstark, R. & M. Koch, *Der Gral. Artusromantik in der Kunst des 19. Jahrhunderts*, Cologne 1995.

Blake, J. J., 'Yeats, Oisín and Irish Gaelic Literature', in: B. Bramsbäck & M. Crogham (eds.), *Anglo-Irish and Irish Literature*, Uppsala 1988, 39–48.

Bromwich, R., 'Celtic Elements in Arthurian Romance: A General Survey', in: *The Legend of Arthur in the Middle Ages*, Cambridge 1983, 41–55 and 230–233.

Brown, M., *Sir Samuel Ferguson*, Lewisburg (Penn.) 1973.

Brown, T. & B. Hayley, *Samuel Ferguson: a centenary tribute*, Dublin 1987.

Brugger-Hackett, S., *Merlin in der europäischen Literatur des Mittelalters*, Stuttgart 1991.

Busse, W. G., 'Brutus in Albion: Englands Gründungssage', in: P. Wunderli (ed.), *Herkunft und Ursprung*, Sigmaringen 1994, 207–223.

Bysveen, J., *Epic Tradition and Innovation in James Macpherson's 'Fingal'*, Uppsala 1982.

Crick, J. C., *The 'Historia Regum Britanniae' of Geoffrey of Monmouth III. A Summary Catalogue of the Manuscripts*, Cambridge 1989.

———, *The 'Historia Regum Britanniae' of Geoffrey of Monmouth IV. Dissemination and Reception in the later Middle Ages*, Cambridge 1991.

Denman, P., *Samuel Ferguson: the literary achievement*, Gerrards Cross 1990.

Eisner, S., *The Tristan Legend. A Study in Sources*, Evanston (Ill.) 1969.

Fackler, H. V., *That Tragic Queen: The Deirdre Legend in Anglo-Irish Literature*, Salzburg 1978.

Fallis, R., *The Irish Renaissance*, Syracuse (New York) 1977.

Flynn, J., 'The Route to the Táin: James Stephens' preparation for his unfinished epic' (PHCC 1) 1981, 125–143.

Foster, J. W., *Fictions of the Irish Literary Revival: A Changeling Art*, Dublin 1987.

Frappier, J., 'La matière de Bretagne: ses origines et son développement', in: *Grundriß der romanischen Literaturen des Mittelalters* 4, Heidelberg 1978, 183–211.

Gaskill, H., ' "Ossian" Macpherson: towards a rehabilitation' (*Comparative Criticism* 8) 1986, 113–146.

———, 'What did James Macpherson really leave on display at his publisher's shop in 1762?' (SGS 16) 1990, 67–89.

Gaskill, H. (ed.), *Ossian revisited*, Edinburgh 1991.

Gategno, P. J. de, *James Macpherson*, Boston 1989.

Gilardino, S. M., *La scuola romantica: la tradizione ossianica nella poesia dell'Alfieri, del Foscolo e del Leopardi*, Ravenna 1982.

Göller, K. H. (ed.), *The Alliterative Morte Arthure: a reassessment of the poem*, Cambridge 1981.

Goodrich, P. (ed.), *The Romance of Merlin: an Anthology*, London 1990.

Gottzmann, C. L., *Artus-Dichtung*, Stuttgart 1989.

Gowans, L., *Cei and the Arthurian Legend*, Cambridge 1988.

Grewe, A., 'Ossian und seine europäische Wirkung', in: K. Heitmann (ed.), *Europäische Romantik II* (Neues Handbuch der Literaturwissenschaft 15), Wiesbaden 1982, 171–188.

Harmon, M., *Austin Clarke 1894–1974: A Critical Introduction*, Dublin 1989.

Hill, J. (ed.), *The Tristan Legend*, Leeds 1977.

Hoare, D. M., *The Works of Morris and Yeats in Relation to Early Saga Literature*, Cambridge 1937.

Jackson, K. H., 'Les sources celtiques du Roman du Graal', in: *Les Romans du Graal au XIIe et XIIIe siècles*, Paris 1956, 213–227.

Jahrmärker, M., *Ossian: eine Figur und eine Idee des europäischen Musiktheaters um 1800*, Cologne 1993.

Kelly, D. (ed.), *The Romances of Chrétien de Troyes: A Symposium*, Lexington (Kentucky) 1985.

Kohlfeldt, M. L., *Lady Gregory. The Woman behind the Irish Renaissance*, New York 1985.

Korrel, P., *An Arthurian Triangle: A Study of the Origin, Development and Characterization of Arthur, Guinevere and Modred*, Leiden 1984.

Kosok, H., *Geschichte der anglo-irischen Literatur*, Berlin 1990.

Lacy, N. J., *The Craft of Chrétien de Troyes*, Leiden 1980.

Lange, W.-D., 'Keltisch-romanische Literaturbeziehungen im Mittelalter', in: *Grundriß der romanischen Literaturen des Mittelalters I*, Heidelberg 1972, 163–205.

Levin, I. D., *Ossian v russkoy literature*, Leningrad 1980.

Loomis, R. S. (ed.), *Arthurian Literature in the Middle Ages*, Oxford 1959.

Macdonald, A. A., *The Figure of Merlin in Thirteenth Century French Romance*, New York 1990.

McFate, P., *The Writings of James Stephens*, London 1979.

McKillop, J., *Fionn mac Cumhaill: Celtic Myth in English Literature*, Syracuse (New York) 1986.

Macpherson, J., *The Poems of Ossian and Related Works*, ed. H. Gaskill with an introduction by F. Stafford, Edinburgh 1995.

Macrae, A. F., *W. B. Yeats. A Literary Life*, London 1995.

Maddox, D., *The Arthurian Romances of Chrétien de Troyes: Once and Future Fictions*, Cambridge 1991.

Manning, S., 'Ossian, Scott, and Nineteenth-century Scottish Literary Nationalism' (*Studies in Scottish Literature* 17) 1982, 39–54.

Marcus, P. L., *Yeats and the Beginning of the Irish Renaissance*, Ithaca (New York) 1970.

——, *Standish James O'Grady*, Lewisburg (Penn.) 1971.

Martin, A., *James Stephens*, Dublin 1977.

Merriman, J. D., *The Flower of Kings: A Study of the Arthurian Legend in England between 1485 and 1835*, Lawrence 1973.

Noble, P., 'The heroic tradition of Kei' (*Reading Medieval Studies* 14) 1988, 125–137.

Okun, H., 'Ossian in Painting' (*Journal of the Warburg and Courtauld Institute* 30) 1967, 327–356.

O'Leary, P., *The prose literature of the Gaelic revival, 1881–1921: ideology and innovation*, Univ. Park/ Penna 1994.

Ossian und die Kunst um 1800, Hamburg 1974.

Pilch, H., *Layamon's 'Brut'*, Heidelberg 1960.

Riddy, F., *Sir Thomas Malory*, Leiden 1987.

Rubel, M. M., *Savage and Barbarian: Historical Attitudes in the Criticism of Homer and Ossian in Britain, 1760–1800*, Amsterdam 1978.

Saddlemyer, A. & C. Smythe (eds.), *Lady Gregory: Fifty Years After*, Gerrards Cross 1987.

Saux, F. H. M., *Layamon's Brut. The Poem and its Sources*, Cambridge 1989.

Schirmer, W., *Die frühen Darstellungen des Arthurstoffes*, Cologne 1958.

Sheehy, J., *The Rediscovery of Ireland's Past: The Celtic Revival 1830–1930*, London 1980.

Skene, R., *The Cuchulain Plays of W. B. Yeats: A Study*, London 1974.

Spisak, J. W. (ed.), *Studies in Malory*, Kalamazoo (Mich.) 1985.

Stafford, F., *The Sublime Savage: James Macpherson and the Poems of Ossian*, Edinburgh 1988.

Stern, L. C., 'Die ossianischen Heldenlieder' (*Zeitschrift für vergleichende Literaturgeschichte* 8) 1895, 51–86, 143–174.

Strijbosch, C., *De bronnen van De reis van Sint Brandaan*, Hilversum 1995.

Takayima, T. & D. Brewer (eds.), *Aspects of Malory*, Cambridge 1981.

Taylor, B. & E. Brewer, *The Return of King Arthur: British and American Arthurian Literature since 1800*, Cambridge 1983.

Thompson, R. H., *The Return from Avalon: A Study of the Arthurian Legend in Modern Fiction*, Westport (Conn.) 1985.

Thomson, D. S., *The Gaelic Sources of Macpherson's 'Ossian'*, Edinburgh 1952.

———, 'Macpherson's Ossian: ballads to epics' (*Béaloideas* 54/55) 1986/87, 243–264.

Thuente, M. H., *W. B. Yeats and Irish Folklore*, Dublin 1980.

Tieghem, P. van, *Ossian en France*, 2 vols., Paris 1917.

———, *Ossian et l'Ossianisme dans la littérature européenne au XVIIIe siècle*, Groningen 1920.

Tombo, R., *Ossian in Germany*, New York 1901.

Topsfield, L. T., *Chrétien de Troyes: A Study of the Arthurian Romances*, Cambridge 1981.

Webster, K. G. T., *Guinevere: A Study of Her Abductions*, Milton (Mass.) 1951.

Weisweiler, J., 'Hintergrund und Herkunft der ossianischen Dichtung' (*Literaturwissenschaftliches Jahrbuch der Görres-Gesellschaft* 4) 1963, 21–42.

Whitaker, M., *The Legends of King Arthur in Art*, Cambridge 1990.

Zaenker, K. A., *Sankt Brandans Meerfahrt. Ein lateinischer Text und seine drei deutschen Übertragungen aus dem 15. Jh.*, Stuttgart 1987.

(c) History of scholarship and Celtic ideology

Belier, W. W., *Decayed Gods: Origin and Development of George Dumézil's 'Idéologie tripartite'*, Leiden 1991.

de Bernardo Stempel, P., 'Rudolf Thurneysen und sein sprachwissenschaftliches Werk' (*ZVP* 46) 1994, 584–605.

Bonfante, G., 'Some Renaissance Texts on the Celtic Languages and their Kinship' (*EC* 7) 1955/56, 414–427.

————, 'A Contribution to the History of Celtology' (*Celtica* 3) 1956, 17–34.

Boyne, P., *John O'Donovan (1806–1861): a biography*, Kilkenny 1987.

Bromwich, R., *Matthew Arnold and Celtic Literature: a Retrospect 1865–1965*, Oxford 1965.

————, 'The Mabinogion and Lady Charlotte Guest' (*Transactions of the Honourable Society of Cymmrodorion*) 1986, 127–141.

Brown, T. (ed.), *Celticism*, Amsterdam 1996.

Camille Jullien, l'histoire de la Gaule et le nationalisme français. Colloque organisé à Lyon, 6. déc. 1988, Lyon 1991.

Chapman, M., *The Gaelic Vision in Scottish Culture*, London 1978.

————, *The Celts: the construction of a myth*, London 1992.

Daly, D., *The Young Douglas Hyde*, Dublin 1974.

Dietler, M., 'Our Ancestors the Gauls' (*American Anthropologist* 94) 1994, 584–605.

Dubois, C.-G., *Celtes et Gaulois au XVIe siècle. Le développement littéraire d'un mythe nationaliste*, Paris 1972.

Dunleavy, J. E. & G. W Dunleavy, *Douglas Hyde: A Maker of Modern Ireland*, Berkeley (Calif.) 1991.

Emery, F., *Edward Lhuyd F. R. S. 1660–1709*, Cardiff 1971.

Faverty, F. E., *Matthew Arnold the Ethnologist*, Evanston (Ill.) 1951.

Forssmann, B. (ed.), *Erlanger Gedenkfeier für Johann Kaspar Zeuss*, Erlangen 1989.

Freitag, B., *Keltische Identität als Fiktion. Eine Untersuchung zu den sozio-kulturellen Bedingungen der anglo-irischen Literatur*, Heidelberg 1989.

Galand, R. M., *L'Ame celtique de Renan*, Paris 1959.

Graus, F., 'Vercingetorix und die Franzosen als Nachkommen der Gallier', in: F. Graus, *Lebendige Vergangenheit*, Cologne 1975, 254–267.

Grote, G., *Torn between politics and culture: the Gaelic League 1893–1993*, New York 1994.

Hablitzel, H., *Prof. Dr. Johann Kaspar Zeuss. Begründer der Keltologie und Historiker aus Vogtendorf/Oberfranken 1806–1856*, Kronach 1987.

Hadfield, A. D. & J. McVeagh, *'Strangers to that Land': British Perceptions of Ireland from the Reformation to the Famine*, Gerrards Cross 1993.

Hunter, M., *John Aubrey and the Realm of Learning*, London 1975.

James, A., *John Morris-Jones*, Cardiff 1987.

Jenkins, G. H., 'Iolo Morganwg and the Gorsedd of the Bards of the Isle of Britain' (*Studia Celtica Japonica N. S.* 7) 1995, 45–60.

Leerssen, J. T., *Mere Irish and Fíor-Ghael. Studies in the idea of Irish nationality, its development and literary expression prior to the 19th century*, Amsterdam 1986.

Lewis, C. W., *Iolo Morganwg*, Carnarfon 1995.

Littleton, C. S., *The New Comparative Mythology. An Anthropological Assessment of the Theories of Georges Dumézil*, Berkeley (Calif.) ³1982.

Morgan, P., *Iolo Morganwg*, Cardiff 1975.

Motte, O., *Camille Julian: Les années de formation*, Rome 1990.

Ó Glaisne, R., *Dúbhglas de h-Íde (1860–1949): Ceannródaí Cultúrtha, 1860–1910*, Dublin 1991.

Ó Lúing, S., *Kuno Meyer 1858–1919*, Dublin 1991.

Orr, L., 'The mid-nineteenth-century Irish context of Arnold's Essay on Celtic Literature', in: C. Machann & F. D. Burt (eds.), *Matthew Arnold in His Time and Ours*, Charlottesville 1988, 135–155.

Ó Tuama, S. (ed.), *The Gaelic League Idea*, Cork 1972.

Owen, A. L., *The Famous Druids. A survey of three centuries of English literature on the Druids*, Oxford 1962.

Parry-Williams, J., *John Rhŷs, 1840–1915*, Cardiff 1954.

Phillips, D. Rh., *Lady Charlotte Guest and the Mabinogion*, Swansea 1921.

Piggott, S., *William Stukeley: An Eighteenth-Century Antiquary*, London 1985.

——, *Ancient Britons and the Antiquarian Imagination*, London 1989.

Pokorny, J., 'Keltologie', in: K. Hönn (ed.), *Wissenschaftliche Forschungsberichte, Geisteswissenschaftliche Reihe*, Bd. 2, Berne 1953, 95–186.

Poppe, E., 'Lag es in der Luft? J. K. Zeuß und die Konstituierung der Keltologie' (*Beiträge zur Geschichte der Sprachwissenschaft 2*) 1992, 41–56.

Roberts, B. F., *Edward Lhuyd: The Making of a Scientist*, Cardiff 1980.

——, 'Edward Lhuyd and Celtic Linguistics', in: *Proceedings of the seventh international congress of Celtic Studies*, Oxford 1986, 1–9.

Schmidt, K. H., 'Stand und Aufgaben der deutschsprachigen Keltologie', in: M. Rockel & S. Zimmer (eds.), *Akten des ersten Symposiums deutschsprachiger Keltologen*, Tübingen 1993, 1–35.

School of Celtic Studies: Fiftieth Anniversary Report 1940–1990, Dublin 1990.

Shaw, F., 'The Background to Grammatica Celtica' (*Celtica 3*) 1956, 1–16.

Sims-Williams, P., 'The Visionary Celt: The Construction of an Ethnic Preconception' (CMCSt 11) 1986, 71–96.

Sommerfelt, A., 'Edward Lhuyd and the comparative method in linguistics' (*Norsk Tidsskrift for Sprogvidenskap* 16) 1952, 370–374.

Stoll, A., *Asterix: das Trivialepos Frankreichs*, Cologne 1974.

Tierney, M., 'Eugene O'Curry and the Irish tradition' (*Studies 51*) 1962, 449–462.

Tourneur, V., *Esquisse d'une histoire des études celtiques*, Liège 1905.

Vercingetorix et Alesia, Paris 1994.

Viallaneix, P. & J. Ehrard (eds.), *Nos ancêtres les Gaulois*, Clermont-Ferrand 1982.

Williams, G. J., 'The History of Welsh Scholarship' (StC 8/9) 1973/74, 195–219.